ANDALUCÍA

ANTHONY HAM
STUART BUTLER, VESNA MARIC, JOHN NOBLE, ZORA O'NEILL

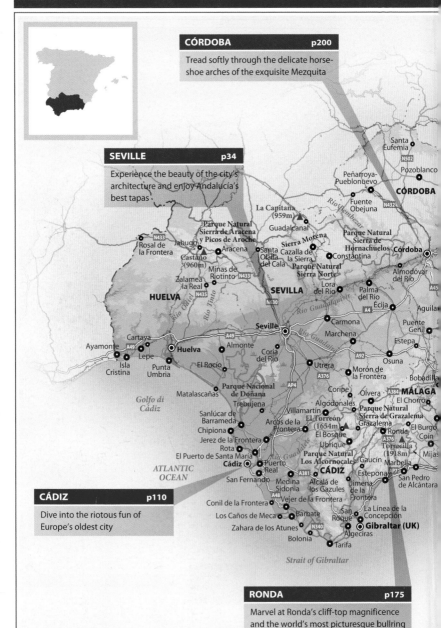

CÓRDOBA   p200

Tread softly through the delicate horse-shoe arches of the exquisite Mezquita

SEVILLE   p34

Experience the beauty of the city's architecture and enjoy Andalucía's best tapas

CÁDIZ   p110

Dive into the riotous fun of Europe's oldest city

RONDA   p175

Marvel at Ronda's cliff-top magnificence and the world's most picturesque bullring

0 ———— 100 km
0 ———— 50 miles

LEGEND

- ═══ Freeway
- ─── Primary Road
- ─── Secondary Road
- ─── Tertiary Road
- +—+—+ Railway line

ELEVATION

- 2000m
- 1500m
- 1000m
- 500m
- 200m
- 100m
- 0

BAEZA & ÚBEDA   p230 & p234

Discover the extraordinary Renaissance legacy in the heart of Jaén province

PARQUE NATURAL DE CABO DE GATA-NÍJAR   p301

Lose yourself in the sandy coves of Andalucía's most unusual wilderness area

LAS ALPUJARRAS   p272

Linger in valleys and beautiful white villages in the Sierra Nevada foothills

GRANADA   p247

Explore the Alhambra – one of the world's premier architectural and cultural masterpieces

---

Map labels:

Sierra Morena · Parque Natural Despeñaperros · Santa Elena · La Carolina · JAÉN · Segura de la Sierra · Río Guadalimar · El Yelmo (1809m) · Hornos · Parque Natural Sierra de Andújar · Bailén · Linares · Villacarrillo · Torreperogil · Parque Natural Sierras de Cazorla, Segura y Las Villas · Empanadas (2107m) · Puebla de Don Fadrique · N420 · Andújar · A4 · Montoro · Mengíbar · Baeza · Úbeda · A4 · A306 · Torre del Campo · Jódar · A315 · Cazorla · Huéscar · Río Guadiana Menor · Cabañas (2028m) · Orce · Magina (2167m) · Jaén · Espejo · Baena · A316 · Martos · A44 · Vélez Rubio · Montilla · Zuheros · Alcaudete · Alcalá la Real · Zújar · A92N · Priego de Córdoba · La Tiñosa (1570m) · Baza · Huércal-Overa · Moreda · GRANADA · Santa Bárbara (2271m) · A334 · Lucena · Benamejí · Parque Natural Sierras Subbéticas · Río Genil · ALMERÍA · Loja · Granada · A92 · Guadix · Sierra de los Filabres · Sorbas · A7 · Mojácar · Antequera · Alhama de Granada · San Juan (2786m) · Chullo (2612m) · Tabernas · Maroma (2069m) · El Lucero (1779m) · Parque Nacional Sierra Nevada · Nijar · Carboneras · El Torcal (1336m) · Mulhacén (3479m) · Cádiar · Morrón (2236m) · Alhama de Almería · Parque Natural de Cabo de Gata-Níjar · Competa · Orgiva · Almería · Lora · A45 · Vélez · Nerja · Salobreña · El Ejido · A7 · El Cabo de Gata · San José · Málaga · Torre del Mar · Almuñécar · Motril · Adra · Cabo de Gata · Torremolinos · Parque Natural Sierras de Tejeda, Almijara y Alhama · MEDITERRANEAN SEA · Fuengirola · Parque Natural Sierra de las Nieves

---

DISTANCE CHART (KM)

	Seville	Cádiz	Málaga	Córdoba	Jaén	Granada
Cádiz	126					
Málaga	209	240				
Córdoba	143	261	165			
Jaén	246	330	203	108		
Granada	252	296	125	160	93	
Almería	410	463	207	316	220	162

Note: Distances between destinations are approximate

INTRODUCING
ANDALUCÍA

ANDALUCÍA IS THE HEART AND SOUL OF SPAIN, ITS WILD BEAUTY, ITS EPIC ARCHITECTURAL STORY AND ITS GRAND PASSIONS WRIT LARGE.

Monument-strewn cities filled with life. A spectacular coastline that spans two oceans. Mountain wilderness areas of rare beauty. A culinary scene that encompasses the best of Spanish cooking, old and new. Welcome to Andalucía, Spain's deep south and its most intoxicating region.

Seville, Granada and Córdoba: visit any of these cities and you'll quickly fall in love with Andalucía's astonishing architectural heritage from a glorious past and its wonderful tapas culture. Elsewhere, there's Úbeda, a little-known centre of Renaissance splendour, and Cádiz, the infectiously cheerful oldest city in Europe.

Andalucía's villages, whitewashed and set against mountain backdrops, are at their best in Las Alpujarras. But such landscapes do more than frame Andalucía's evocative human landmarks. Their diversity is summed up in a simple statistic: mainland Spain's highest peak, Mulhacén (3479m) in the Sierra Nevada, lies less than 100km from the country's most dramatic coastline, the Parque Natural de Cabo de Gata-Níjar.

GRANADA

CÓRDOBA

TOP The Palacios Nazaríes at the Alhambra, Granada
BOTTOM LEFT The minaret soars above the Mezquita in Córdoba BOTTOM RIGHT The whitewashed village of Válor in Las Alpujarras, Granada province

LAS ALPUJARRAS

RONDA

CABO DE GATA

CÁDIZ

SEVILLE

TOP LEFT The town of Ronda perches above El Tajo gorge TOP RIGHT Take in the simple beauty of the rooftops of Cádiz BOTTOM LEFT Hike to the coastal coves of Cabo de Gata BOTTOM CENTRE Head up the Giralda for a bird's-eye view over Seville BOTTOM RIGHT Explore the architectural gems of Úbeda, Jaén province

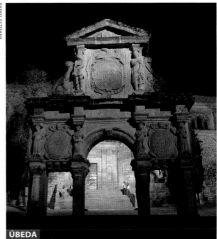

ÚBEDA

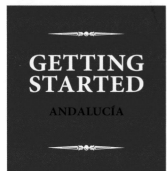

PATRICK SYDER

GETTING STARTED

ANDALUCÍA

WHAT'S NEW?

* Seville's Museo del Baile Flamenco with flamenco performances (p50)
- -
* Swish new tram service around Seville (p62)
- -
* La Moraga, Daní García's innovative Málaga tapas bar (p170)
- -
* Sabores (p132) and Hotel Chancilleria (p386) in Jerez de la Frontera
- -
* Hotel V, a stunning boutique conversion in Vejer de la Frontera (p387)

CLIMATE: SEVILLE

Average Max/Min

Temp/Humidity

Rainfall

PRICE GUIDE

	BUDGET	MIDRANGE	TOP END
SLEEPING	< €65	€65-120	> €120
MEALS	< €10	€10-25	> €25
PARKING	€10/day	€10-20/day	€20/day

RICHARD ROSS

KARL BLACKWELL

TOP Whitewashed walls and terracotta rooftops in Cádiz province BOTTOM LEFT Semana Santa celebrations, Seville BOTTOM RIGHT *Vino dulce* in Ronda FAR RIGHT Take to the waves in Tarifa

ACCOMMODATION

One of the highlights of visiting Andalucía is its architecture, and many of the region's hotels are architectural gems in their own right. Centuries-old mansions and palaces have been converted into stunning places to stay, sometimes re-creating old-world decor or the aesthetics of Islamic Al-Andalus, but just as often revelling in ultramodern yet affordable luxury. A touch more modest perhaps, but the cool, whitewashed walls of Andalusian towns and villages conceal hotels of more rustic charm, often with high levels of comfort. For more on Andalucía's accommodation, turn to p378.

MAIN POINTS OF ENTRY

MÁLAGA AIRPORT (AGP; ☎ 952 04 88 38; www.aena.es) Andalucía's busiest airport attracts both international and domestic flights by more than 60 regular and charter airlines.

SEVILLE AIRPORT (SVQ; ☎ 954 44 90 00; www.aena.es) International and domestic departures, but few charter airlines.

GRANADA AIRPORT (GRX; ☎ 958 24 52 07; www.aena.es) Fewer flights.

THINGS TO TAKE

* Michelin's No 578 *Andalucía* map (see p406)

* Warning triangles and a reflective jacket if you're going by car (see p420)

* Lonely Planet's *Spanish Phrasebook*

* A compact pair of binoculars for wildlife-watching

* Clothes to cope with cold snaps between October and May

DIEGO LEZAMA

WEBLINKS

ANDALUCÍA TE QUIERE (www.andalucia.org) Encyclopedic official tourism site

OK SPAIN (www.okspain.org) Another useful official site

ANDALUCIA.COM (www.andalucia.com) Excellent privately run site

LONELY PLANET (www.lonelyplanet.com/spain/andalucia) Build your own itinerary

IBERIA NATURE (www.iberianature.com) Devoted to Spain's natural world

BRUCE BI

FESTIVALS & EVENTS
ANDALUCÍA

FEBRUARY/MARCH

CARNAVAL

CÁDIZ

Cádiz celebrates Carnaval with riotous abandon as costumed street performers party for 10 days before the Tuesday 47 days before Easter Sunday. (www.carnavaldecadiz.com)

FESTIVAL DE JEREZ

JEREZ DE LA FRONTERA

Jerez's two-week festival has flamenco as the centrepiece of a music-and-dance-dominated program, drawing many of the biggest stars. (www.festivaldejerez.es)

FESTIVAL INTERNACIONAL DE TANGO

GRANADA

International tango performances and dancing in the streets from 21 to 26 March makes this one of Andalucía's best music festivals. (www.eltango.com)

APRIL

SEMANA SANTA (HOLY WEEK)

Semana Santa is dominated by daily processions of hooded *nazarenos* (penitents).

Seville's celebrations are the most intense, followed by Granada, Córdoba, Arcos de la Frontera, Baeza and Úbeda. Sometimes held in March.

FERIA DE ABRIL

SEVILLE

Seville's April Fair in the second half of April (sometimes into May) is the doyen of Andalucía's *ferias* (fairs) with bullfighting, horse parades and general merriment.

MAY/JUNE

FERIA DEL CABALLO

JEREZ DE LA FRONTERA

Jerez's weeklong horse fair, held in early May, is one of Andalucía's biggest festivals, combining the usual Andalusian merrymaking with bullfights and horse competitions.

ROMERÍA DEL ROCÍO

EL ROCÍO

This stirring pilgrimage, which takes place seven weeks after Easter, draws hundreds of thousands who arrive dressed in their Andalusian finest and on horseback or in festively decorated covered wagons.

TOP *Hermandad* (brotherhood) penitent with candle in hand as part of Semana Santa proceedings in Seville
RIGHT Riding a horse as part of the family-friendly celebrations at the Feria de Abril

HOGUERAS DE SAN JUAN

Bonfires and fireworks, especially on beaches, are the heart of this midsummer celebration held 23 June; many thousands of people camp overnight along Andalucía's beaches.

FESTIVAL INTERNACIONAL DE LA GUITARRA

CÓRDOBA
Flamenco is the focus of this two-week guitar festival in late June or early July, but you'll also hear live classical, rock and blues performances. (www.guitarracordoba.com)

AUGUST

FERIA DE MÁLAGA

MÁLAGA
The pick of Andalucía's summer *ferias,* Málaga's nine-day version has it all: fireworks, rock and flamenco concerts, and round-the-clock music and dancing.

SEPTEMBER

BIENAL DE FLAMENCO

SEVILLE
Spain's flamenco stars enliven this major flamenco festival in September of even-numbered years. The Alcázar provides the wonderful backdrop for many of the performances.

FERIA DE PEDRO ROMERO

RONDA
Ronda comes alive during the first two weeks of September with the flamenco Festival de Cante Grande and the Corridas Goyescas (bullfights in antique finery).

FIESTAS DE OTOÑO

JEREZ DE LA FRONTERA
Jerez's autumn fiestas coincide with the grape harvest for two weeks in September, with flamenco, horse events and the traditional treading of the first grapes.

CULTURE

ANDALUCÍA

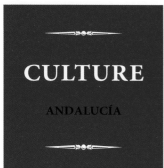

BOOKS

THE ORNAMENT OF THE WORLD (Maria Rosa Menocal) A fascinating look at the tolerance and sophistication of the region during Andalucía's Islamic centuries.

SOUTH FROM GRANADA (Gerald Brenan) An acutely perceptive account of village life in Las Alpujarras during the 1920s.

DRIVING OVER LEMONS (Chris Stewart) The entertaining, anecdotal, bestselling tale of life on a small Andalusian farm in Las Alpujarras.

TALES OF THE ALHAMBRA (Washington Irving) Enchanting stories from inside Granada's abandoned Alhambra in the 1820s.

GETTING TO MAÑANA (Miranda Innes) One of the best books about starting a new life in an Andalusian farmhouse.

FLAMENCO

Flamenco is the sound of Andalucía. Sometimes melancholy, sometimes joyful, but always soulful, flamenco has become a byword for the passions of Andalusian life. You'll hear it across the region, from beautifully tiled Seville patios to renovated Arab-era water cisterns in Almería. But its true home is around Seville, Jerez de la Frontera and Cádiz: it's in their working-class barrios – Jerez's Barrio de Santiago or Cádiz's Barrio de Santa María – where flamenco stays true to its roots. That's not to say that flamenco is stuck in the past. The flamenco stars of the 1980s pioneered some wonderful flamenco fusion and *nuevo flamenco* that continue to breathe new life into the flamenco world. But it's in the smoky *peñas* – as much meeting places for flamenco aficionados as for live performances – that you'll most likely catch its spirit. See p354 for more.

TOP Semana Santa procession, Seville **BOTTOM** An evening of flamenco in Cádiz **RIGHT** The bullring at Ronda is considered the region's finest **FAR RIGHT** The grandeur of typical bullfighting posters

TOP ARCHITECTURAL LANDMARKS

ALHAMBRA, GRANADA Andalucía's high point of Islamic architecture with gardens, palaces and exquisite decorative detail (p254).

MEZQUITA, CÓRDOBA One of the world's most beautiful mosques (p201).

ALCÁZAR, SEVILLE The tranquil splendour of Islamic Al-Andalus (p44).

CAPILLA REAL, GRANADA A flight of Isabelline Gothic fancy and Christian Andalucía's most beautiful landmark (p258).

LAS ALPUJARRAS Whitewashed villages set against a mountain backdrop (p275).

KARL BLACKWELL

WITOLD SKRYPCZAK

DON'T MISS EXPERIENCES

- ★ Horses in Jerez – The supreme elegance of world-famous Andalusian horses (p130)

- ★ Flamenco in Seville – Uplifting flamenco song, guitar and dance (p60)

- ★ Semana Santa in Seville – Weird and wonderful Easter processions (p55)

- ★ Music festivals – Andalucía's year-round flamenco, classical and other musical events (see the boxed text, p359)

- ★ Carnaval in Cádiz – Andalucía's most riotous festival fun (p111)

- ★ Corridas Goyescas – Spain's most picturesque and theatrical bullfights in the magnificent bullring in Ronda (see the boxed text, p178)

FINE ARTS

MUSEO PICASSO More than 200 works by Málaga's favourite son, on show in a restored 16th-century palace (p164).

MUSEO ANTONIO MANUEL CAMPOY Picasso and Miró on show in a castle (p309).

MUSEO DE BELLAS ARTES Check out works from Spain's Siglo de Oro on display in Seville (p50).

CENTRO DE ARTE CONTEMPORÁNEO Málaga's temple to modern art (p167).

CULTURE

ANDALUCÍA

HP CANADA / ALAMY

FILMS

THE WAY OF THE ENGLISH (2006) Directed by Antonio Banderas.

CAMARÓN (2005) A biopic of flamenco's greatest legend.

TUNA AND CHOCOLATE (2004) Black comedy set on Cádiz's coast.

SOUTH FROM GRANADA (2003) Andalusian life in the 1920s.

THE GOOD, THE BAD AND THE UGLY (1966) Spaghetti Western starring Clint Eastwood and shot on location in Almería province.

FLAMENCO PLAYLIST

Any flamenco journey has to begin with the biggest names.

EL CAMARÓN DE LA ISLA Flamenco's late, all-time singing legend.

PACO DE LUCÍA (www.pacodelucia.org) The most celebrated flamenco guitarist.

TOMATITO (www.tomatito.com) Another guitar legend forever associated with El Camarón.

ENRIQUE MORENTE (www.enriquemorente.com) Pleases both purists and *nuevo flamenco* fans.

CARMEN LINARES (www.carmenlinares.org) Flamenco's most enduring voice.

JOAQUÍN CORTÉS (www.joaquincortes.eu) Dance star fusing flamenco with jazz and ballet.

BULLFIGHTING

Love it or loathe it, bullfighting runs deep through Andalusian culture. Like flamenco – that other internationally renowned Spanish pastime – bullfighting was born in Andalucía with its heartland around Ronda, which is still home to Spain's most striking *plaza de toros* (bullring). As cruel as it may seem to outsiders, bullfighting continues to be embraced by many Andalusians who see it as an important cultural patrimony, a form of art and theatre and an important industry that spans bull breeders to the restaurants serving *rabo de toro* (bull's tail stew). *Corridas* (bullfights) run from Easter to October. For more, see p363.

TOP The interior of a cave dwelling in Guadix, Granada province RIGHT Riders on parade at the Feria del Caballo in Jerez de la Frontera

THE RENAISSANCE IN ANDALUCÍA

The magnificent Al-Andalus landmarks may have cast into shadow everything that came after, but Andalucía also has some of Spain's finest Renaissance architecture. Much of it was the work of Andrés de Vandelvira, who transformed the town of Úbeda into a Renaissance gem. With colonnaded patios adorning the lavish private residences of the region's nobility, Vandelvira's legacy is unusual in the annals of Andalusian architecture: he left his most enduring mark on private urban spaces rather than grand public monuments. His clean-lined approach nonetheless provided inspiration for architects who would bring a Renaissance aesthetic to public buildings in Granada, Seville, Málaga and Guadix. For more on Andalucía's Renaissance architecture, see p340.

RURAL CASTLES

* Almodóvar del Río – Eight-towered castle, just west of Córdoba (p217)
---
* Castillo de los Guzmán – Falcons nest in this 15th-century fortress (p83)
---
* Castillo de Miramonte – Islamic-era ruin with sweeping views over northern Córdoba province (p219)
---
* Castillo de La Calahorra – Formidable yet with a graceful courtyard (p271)
---
* Antequera's Alcazaba – A favourite of Granada's rulers and still splendid (p185)
---
* Castillo de Vélez Blanco – Sixteenth-century castle clinging to the summit (p309)

FOOD & DRINK

ANDALUCÍA

RAFAEL ESTEFANIA

CULINARY STAPLES

JAMÓN Some of Spain's most sought-after cured ham comes from the acorn-fed pigs of Jabugo in Huelva province (p370).

OLIVE OIL Andalucía's extra virgin olive oil, especially from prolific Jaén province, sets the standard as the elite of world olive oils (p371).

GAZPACHO A cold tomato-based soup, whether *gazpacho andaluz* or *salmorejo cordobés,* that is the taste of the Andalusian summer (p371).

PESCAITO FRITO Lightly fried fish and seafood sum up Andalucía's passion for seafood, especially in Cádiz province (p369).

SHERRY The world's most famous sherries come from the aptly named Sherry Triangle in the eastern part of Cádiz province (p373).

TAPAS

Legend has it that tapas were invented by a small beachside bar in Cádiz province. Whether true or not, tapas have become an Andalusian culinary institution and it's one that's perfectly suited to the local way of life – casual eating and a means of sampling the region's diverse tastes in just one meal. Andalusian tapas can be incredibly varied, but the region's purveyors of tapas pride themselves on taking the finest and freshest local ingredients and interfering with them as little as possible, allowing the unadulterated flavours of *jamón,* seafood or any other Andalusian produce to shine through. Wash it down with a glass of sherry from El Puerto de Santa María or Jerez de la Frontera, or a manzanilla from Sanlúcar de Barrameda, and you're halfway towards becoming an honorary Andalusian. For more on tapas, see p367.

KARL BLACKWELL

TOP Freshly caught sardines BOTTOM Andalucía's prized *jamón* (ham) RIGHT Breakfast Andalucía-style FAR RIGHT Gazpacho, a local soup served cold, is the perfect antidote to the hot weather

TOP RESTAURANTS

CAFÉ DE PARÍS Michelin-starred chef José Carlos García creates breathtaking nouvelle cuisine (p169).

RESTAURANTE TRAGABUCHES Daniel García not only has a Michelin star, but a weird-and-wonderful way with food (p181).

LA CASA DEL ÁNGEL Astonishing fusion of Andalusian and Arab flavours (p170).

LOS COLONIALES Seville's best tapas bar, bar none (p58).

SABORES Local staples with creative twists and standing ovations for the chef (p132).

RAFAEL ESTEFANÍA

BON APPÉTIT / ALAMY

DON'T MISS EXPERIENCES

★ Bodega tours – History, production processes and subtle tastes (p120 and p130)

★ Tapas crawl – Bars clustered close, each with its own specialities (p367)

★ Fried fish – The local art of eating seafood (p116 and p123)

★ Taking hours over lunch – Food as the day's main event (p367)

★ Arab-inspired flavours – Dishes steeped in the history of Al-Andalus (see the boxed text, p267)

★ Olive oil – Visit Andalucía's standout working olive-oil mill (p213)

★ Pedro Ximénez – Learn the secrets of one of Andalucía's most unusual and best-loved wines (see the boxed text, p218)

TAPAS CITIES

GRANADA Some of Andalucía's best tapas for free (p265).

SEVILLE Andalucía's tapas obsession, heart-and-soul (p55).

ALMERÍA Delicious free tapas to enjoy with your drinks (p294).

CÓRDOBA Numerous bars to choose from all across the city centre (p210).

MÁLAGA A wide selection served up with a sea breeze (p172).

DIANA MAYFIELD

FOOD & DRINK

ANDALUCÍA

TOP BOOKS

THE FLAVOUR OF ANDALUSIA (Pepita Aris) Recipes and anecdotes.

A LATE DINNER (Paul Richardson) A fascinating Spanish culinary journey.

MORO: THE COOKBOOK (Samuel & Samantha Clark) Andalusian and North African cuisine.

DINING SECRETS OF ANDALUCÍA (Jon Clarke) A Santana Books guide.

WORLD FOOD SPAIN (Richard Sterling) Definitive guide to Spanish food.

COOKING COURSES

Learn how to cook and appreciate food Andalusian-style.

ALL WAYS SPAIN (www.allwaysspain.com) Cookery and food-appreciation courses near Granada.

FINCA BUEN VINO (www.fincabuenvino.com) Cookery classes in Huelva province.

ON THE MENU (www.holidayonthemenu.com) Week-long or weekend courses.

L'ATELIER (www.ivu.org/atelier) Vegetarian cooking courses in Las Alpujarras.

COOKING HOLIDAY SPAIN (www.cooking holidayspain.com) Fun, weeklong, Ronda-based cooking classes.

JAMÓN

It's often said that in Andalucía they eat every part of the pig except the walk. But special devotion is reserved for *jamón* (cured ham) from the Jabugo region (Huelva province). A bar where the ceiling is obscured by dozens, even hundreds of hanging hams is one of the most recognisable images of Andalucía, although not all hams are created equal. At a minimum go for a *jamón ibérico,* and at least once order the *jamón ibérico de bellota,* the king of Iberian hams, to see just what all the fuss is about. For more on *jamón,* see p370.

TOP Barrels of sherry await sampling at the bodegas of Jerez de la Frontera RIGHT Groves of olives surround the pretty *pueblo blanco* (white village) of La Iruela in the Sierra de Cazorla

SHERRY

One of Spain's most celebrated gastronomic exports, sherry is a way of life in the three towns in Cádiz province – El Puerto de Santa María, Sanlúcar de Barrameda and Jerez de la Frontera – which make up the Sherry Triangle. Even Jerez's name is intricately tied to the drop: The Muslims originally called the town 'Scheris', from which the words 'Jerez' and 'sherry' are both derived. Today, many families in the three towns are descendants of British wine traders who intermarried with locals after the wineries began producing their iconic brands – Tio Pepe, Sandeman, Osborne, Terry and Harveys, to name a select few – in the 1830s. The secrets lie in the region's chalky soils and a complicated maturing process. To learn more about sherry, see p373.

EAT LIKE A LOCAL

Andalucía's culinary culture is Spain's most casual, but there are a few tricks to ensuring that you fully experience the local gastronomic scene.

* Eat to a new rhythm: lunch rarely begins before 1.30pm, dinner seldom before 9pm
* Have your main meal at lunchtime and graze on tapas in the evening
* Be prepared to elbow your way to the bar and shout your order
* Always ask for the house speciality
* Don't discard your tapas toothpicks – they're often used to calculate your bill

DAVID TOMLINSON

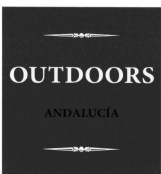

OUTDOORS

ANDALUCÍA

ROBIN CHAPMAN

PROTECTED AREAS

PARQUE NACIONAL DE DOÑANA Stirring wildlife and a range of habitats, from wetlands to coastal dunes (p84).

PARQUE NACIONAL SIERRA NEVADA The roof of Andalucía with ibexes, high-altitude vistas and great hiking (p272).

PARQUE NATURAL SIERRA DE GRAZALEMA Heavily wooded hillsides, *pueblos blancos* and terrific hiking (p139).

PARQUE NATURAL DE CABO DE GATA-NÍJAR Deserts and volcanic cliffs, flamingos and sandy beaches (p301).

PARQUE NATURAL SIERRA DE LAS NIEVES Glorious mountain panoramas, fir forests and ibexes (p183).

PARQUE NATURAL SIERRAS DE CAZORLA, SEGURA Y LAS VILLAS Spain's largest park with diverse wildlife and plenty of activities (p241).

WILDLIFE

Nowhere else in Spain matches Andalucía for the diversity of its wildlife. Endangered species – Iberian lynx, wolf, black vulture and Spanish imperial eagle – have retreated here to the southernmost tip of Europe, drawn by the most extensive wilderness stretches in the country. But Andalucía is more than a haven for mammals and birds that long ago disappeared elsewhere in Europe. More common (and more easily observed) species abound from the high-altitude ibex to the great marine mammals of the deep in the waters off Tarifa, such as dolphins (striped, bottlenose and common) and long-finned pilot whales, orcas (killer whales), sperm whales and fin whales. And then there are Europe's only wild primates, the Barbary apes that occupy the heights of Gibraltar, looking out across the water towards their ancestral home of North Africa. For more on Andalucía's wildlife, see p345.

ALBERTO PAREDES / ALAMY

TOP The wide expanse of the Costa de la Luz **BOTTOM** Cooling off at the beach in Cabo de Gata **RIGHT** Scaling the heights at El Chorro gorge **FAR RIGHT** The endangered Iberian lynx, Parque Nacional de Doñana

TOP SECRET WALKS

* ★ Río Borosa, Parque Natural Sierras de Cazorla, Segura y Las Villas (p243)
* ★ Round the headland of Cabo de Gata in three days (p303)
* ★ Climb El Lucero in La Axarquía region for cross-continent views (p190)
* ★ The villages of the Sierra de Aracena (p101)
* ★ Pinsapar trail from Grazalema to Benamahoma, Parque Natural Sierra de Grazalema (p139)

DON'T MISS EXPERIENCES

* ★ Whale-watching – Giants of the deep in the Strait of Gibraltar (p143)
* ★ Flamingos – Epic colonies up to 40,000-strong (p346)
* ★ Horse riding – In the high country of Sierra Nevada (p275)
* ★ Windsurfing – Tarifa is Spain's windsurfing capital (p145)
* ★ Sierra de Aracena – Lose yourself in stone villages time forgot (p101)
* ★ Sierra Norte – Wildflowers in spring bring colour to the rolling hills (p72)
* ★ Parque Nacional de Doñana – Explore some of Andalucía's most interesting coastal scenery and great wildlife country (p84)

DRIVES

* ★ Sierra de Grazalema – White villages, Arcos to Vejer (p137)
* ★ North of Córdoba – Wild landscapes and castles (p219)
* ★ Sierra de Cazorla – Quiet backroads through the wilderness (p242)
* ★ Road to Ohanes – A short, dramatic climb (p300)
* ★ Carretera del Suspiro del Moro – Granada to the coast (p283)

KARL BLACKWELL

OUTDOORS

ANDALUCÍA

TOP BEACHES

EL PALMAR Almost 5km of white sand (p142).

ZAHARA DE LOS ATUNES A 12km-long beach unspoiled by tourism (p142).

ISLA CRISTINA Huelva's finest beach and a Spanish crowd (p83).

PARQUE NATURAL DE CABO DE GATA-NÍJAR Deserted, sandy inlets (p301).

PLAYA DE LOS LANCES, TARIFA A 10km stretch of sand and one of Europe's windsurfing hot spots (p145).

WEBLINKS

Before heading outdoors, get online to learn about the Andalusian wilds.

IBERIANATURE (www.iberianature.com) The premier website for information about Andalusian flora and fauna.

BLUE FLAG (www.blueflag.org) Beaches with a clean bill of health.

ECOLOGISTAS EN ACCIÓN (www.ecologistasenaccion.org, in Spanish) Beaches awarded black flags.

EX-SITU (www.lynxexsitu.es, in Spanish) Best website on the Iberian lynx.

SPANISH ORNITHOLOGICAL SOCIETY (www.seo.org, in Spanish) Birdwatchers' best Andalusian friend.

BIRDWATCHING

Andalucía lies along the main route for migrating bird species between Europe and Africa and hundreds of thousands of species, including 80% of Europe's wild ducks, pass the winter in the region's wetlands. Andalucía also has its share of endemic species and is particularly known for its raptors: the black vulture (Europe's largest bird), golden eagle, griffon vulture, Egyptian vulture and the Spanish imperial eagle, while the bearded vulture or lammergeier is making a human-assisted comeback. Storks and flamingos are easier to find, but they nonetheless rank among birdwatching's most rewarding sights. For more on Andalucía's birds, see p346.

TOP Take advantage of the perfect kitesurfing conditions at Tarifa, Cádiz province **RIGHT** The iconic limestone form of the Rock of Gibraltar looms large over visitors to the Bay of Algeciras

ENVIRONMENTAL PROTECTION

Andalucía leads the way when it comes to environmental protection in Spain – almost one-fifth of its territory is protected in some way. But Andalucía's regional government has favoured a pragmatic approach to wilderness areas, with a sliding scale of public access. Only two areas – Parque Nacional de Doñana and Parque Nacional Sierra Nevada – have full-on national park status with strictly controlled access, while most protected areas are *parques naturales* (natural parks): there are 24 of these and there are often villages and public walking trails within their boundaries. Permits are sometimes required to visit the natural parks, but the emphasis is on recognising that wilderness areas are to be enjoyed as much as protected. For more information, see p345.

LANDFORMS

Andalucía's rugged coastline and equally rugged, mountain-spined interior contain some extraordinary natural landforms that invite either awe or up-close exploring.

* Rock of Gibraltar: one of the soaring Pillars of Hercules (p150)

* Mulhacén: at 3479m, mainland Spain's highest peak (p275)

* Cabo de Gata: wild and semi-desert coast unspoiled by the human hand (p301)

* Paraje Natural Torcal de Antequera: weird, wonderful limestone formations (p187)

* Garganta del Chorro: sheer rock walls and a gorge half-a-kilometre deep (p182)

WITOLD SKRYPCZAK

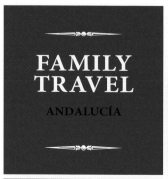

FAMILY TRAVEL

ANDALUCÍA

JON DAVISON

TOP RESOURCES

TRAVEL WITH CHILDREN (Brigitte Barta et al) Lonely Planet's comprehensive lowdown on travelling with kids.

TRAVEL FOR KIDS (www .travelforkids.com) The Spain section of this website offers a child-friendly perspective on Andalucía's signature sights.

COLOURS OF SPAIN (www .coloursofspain.com) The Andalucía page has a helpful list of theme parks, water parks, zoos and other ideas.

SANDI TOKSVIG'S TRAVEL GUIDE TO SPAIN Beginner's guide to Spain with games and a travel journal.

DON'T MISS EXPERIENCES

Many of the most enjoyable Andalusian experiences are fun (and accessible) for all the family.

★ Royal Equestrian School – Watch horses dance (p130)

★ Western film sets – Explore the Wild West (p297)

★ Cave Hotels – Sleep in a cave in Guadix (p396)

★ Horse riding – Ride off into the Andalusian sunset (p349)

★ Whale camp – Whale- and dolphin-watching, snorkelling and games (p143)

★ Windsurfing – Catch the wind on a kid-sized board (p145)

★ Gibraltar – Apes, caves and a cable-car ride (p150)

TRAVEL WITH CHILDREN

Andalucía is as much a playground for kids as for adults, not least because locals too love to do things in family groups. Eating out is a pleasure – most kids love the local staples and are welcomed in tapas bars and restaurants. Many activities are similarly child-friendly – the possible exception is hiking. Local tourist offices can also point you in the direction of the nearest pool or child-centred activity; the Costa del Sol (p174) and Seville (p62) in particular have a host of child-friendly attractions. Car-hire companies and hotels are used to accommodating family needs, while children get free or discounted admission into most sights. For more on travelling with children, see p400.

TOP See how the west was won, Almería-style, at one of Andalucía's movie sets

CONTENTS

INTRODUCING ANDALUCÍA   **4**

GETTING STARTED   **8**
FESTIVALS & EVENTS   **10**
CULTURE   **12**
FOOD & DRINK   **16**
OUTDOORS   **20**
FAMILY TRAVEL   **24**
THE AUTHORS   28

ITINERARIES   30

SEVILLE   34

Introducing Seville   35
Essential Information   35
GETTING STARTED   **38**
Orientation   40
Exploring Seville   40
Festivals & Events   55
Gastronomic Highlights   55
Nightlife   59
Recommended Shops   60
Transport   61
AROUND SEVILLE   **62**
Santiponce   63
Carmona   63
Osuna   69
Écija   70
Cazalla de la Sierra   71
Parque Natural Sierra Norte   72
HUELVA PROVINCE   74

HUELVA   **75**
Essential Information   75
Orientation   75
Exploring Huelva   75
GETTING STARTED   **78**
Festivals & Events   80
Gastronomic Highlights   80
Transport   81
AROUND HUELVA   **82**
Lugares Colombinos   82
Costa de la Luz   82
EAST OF HUELVA   **84**

Parque Nacional de Doñana   84
El Rocío   88

THE BEST OF ANDALUCÍA   **89**

NORTH OF HUELVA   **97**
Minas de Riotinto   98
Aracena   99
Sierra de Aracena   101
CÁDIZ PROVINCE & GIBRALTAR   105

GETTING STARTED   **108**
CÁDIZ   **110**
Essential Information   110
Orientation   110
Exploring Cádiz   111
Gastronomic Highlights   116
Nightlife   118
Transport   119
THE SHERRY TRIANGLE   **119**
El Puerto de Santa María   119
Sanlúcar de Barrameda   124
Jerez de la Frontera   126
Around Jerez de la Frontera   133
**ARCOS & THE SIERRA DE
GRAZALEMA**   **133**
Arcos de la Frontera   133
Driving Tour: Sierra de Grazalema   137
Parque Natural Sierra de Grazalema   139
**COSTA DE LA LUZ & THE
SOUTHEAST**   **140**
Vejer de la Frontera   140
The Vejer Coast   142
Tarifa   142
Around Tarifa   147
Parque Natural Los Alcornocales   147
GIBRALTAR   **148**
Essential Information   149
Orientation   149
Exploring Gibraltar   149
Gastronomic Highlights   153
Transport   154
MÁLAGA PROVINCE   156

MÁLAGA   **157**
Essential Information   157

Orientation	157
Exploring Málaga	157
GETTING STARTED	**160**
Festivals & Events	169
Gastronomic Highlights	169
Nightlife	171
Recommended Shops	171
Transport	172
COSTA DEL SOL	**173**
Mijas	173
THE INTERIOR	**175**
Ronda	175
Around Ronda	182
Ardales & El Chorro	182
Antequera	184
Around Antequera	187
EAST OF MÁLAGA	**188**
La Axarquía	188
Nerja	191
CÓRDOBA PROVINCE	**195**

GETTING STARTED	**198**
CÓRDOBA	**200**
Essential Information	201
Orientation	201
Exploring Córdoba	201
Festivals & Events	210
Gastronomic Highlights	210
Nightlife	212
Transport	212
SOUTH OF CÓRDOBA	**213**
Baena	213
Zuheros & Around	213
Priego de Córdoba	215
Montilla	217
WEST OF CÓRDOBA	**217**
NORTH OF CÓRDOBA	**219**
JAÉN PROVINCE	**220**

JAÉN	**221**
Essential Information	221
Orientation	221
Exploring Jaén	221
GETTING STARTED	**224**
Festivals & Events	228
Gastronomic Highlights	228
Transport	229
NORTH OF JAÉN	**229**

Parque Natural Despeñaperros & Santa Elena	229
EAST OF JAÉN	**230**
Baeza	230
Úbeda	234
Cazorla	239
Parque Natural Sierras de Cazorla, Segura y Las Villas	241
GRANADA PROVINCE	**246**

GRANADA	**247**
GETTING STARTED	**250**
Essential Information	253
Orientation	254
Exploring Granada	254
Festivals & Events	264
Gastronomic Highlights	265
Nightlife	268
Transport	269
LA VEGA & EL ALTIPLANO	**269**
Guadix	270
La Calahorra	271
Baza	271
SIERRA NEVADA & LAS ALPUJARRAS	**272**
Essential Information	273
Orientation	273
Exploring the Sierra Nevada	273
Exploring Las Alpujarras	275
COSTA TROPICAL	**281**
Salobreña	281
Almuñécar & La Herradura	282
ALMERÍA PROVINCE	**285**

GETTING STARTED	**288**
ALMERÍA	**290**
Essential Information	290
Orientation	290
Exploring Almería	290
Festivals & Events	295
Gastronomic Highlights	295
Transport	296
AROUND ALMERÍA	**297**
NORTH OF ALMERÍA	**297**
LAS ALPUJARRAS DE ALMERÍA	**299**
COSTA DE ALMERÍA	**301**
Parque Natural de Cabo de Gata-Níjar	301
Mojácar	305
LOS VÉLEZ	**308**

BACKGROUND 312

HISTORY 313
ANDALUSIAN ARCHITECTURE 332
EXPLORING NATURAL
ANDALUCÍA 343
FLAMENCO & BEYOND 354
ANDALUSIAN ARTS
(& BULLFIGHTING) 360
THE ANDALUSIAN KITCHEN 367
FOOD & DRINK GLOSSARY 375
ACCOMMODATION 378

Sevilla Province 379
Huelva Province 383
Cádiz Province 385
Málaga Province 388
Córdoba Province 391
Jaén Province 392
Granada Province 394
Almería Province 398
DIRECTORY 400

Business Hours 400
Children 400
Customs Regulations 401
Dangers & Annoyances 402
Discounts 402
Food & Drink 402
Gay & Lesbian Travellers 403
Health 404
Holidays 404
Insurance 404
Internet Access 405
Legal Matters 405
Maps 406
Money 407
Post 408
Telephone 408
Time 409
Toilets 409
Tourist Information 409
Travellers with Disabilities 410
Visas 410
Women Travellers 411
TRANSPORT 412

Arrival & Departure 412
Getting Around 416

LANGUAGE 422

GLOSSARY 430

BEHIND THE SCENES 434

INDEX 440

MAP LEGEND 448

THE AUTHORS

ANTHONY HAM

Coordinating Author, Cádiz & Gibraltar
Anthony lives in Madrid but spends almost two months of every year in and around El Puerto de Santa María. Whenever he can, he heads across the water to Cádiz, one of his favourite cities in Spain, and can be found frequenting the wonderful seafood restaurants of El Puerto.

STUART BUTLER

Seville, Huelva
Stuart's first taste of Andalucía was many years ago during a school trip to Parque Nacional de Doñana, which he decided was the very definition of the word 'exotic'. The only change now is that he applies this definition to the whole region and he considers Seville his favourite European city. Despite this, home for Stuart is the Basque Country on the opposite side of the peninsula, though he returns to Andalucía as much as possible.

LONELY PLANET AUTHORS

Why is our travel information the best in the world? It's simple: our authors are passionate, dedicated travellers. They don't take freebies in exchange for positive coverage so you can be sure the advice you're given is impartial. They travel widely to all the popular spots, and off the beaten track. They don't research using just the internet or phone. They discover new places not included in any other guidebook. They personally visit thousands of hotels, restaurants, palaces, trails, galleries, temples and more. They speak with dozens of locals every day to make sure you get the kind of insider knowledge only a local could tell you. They take pride in getting all the details right, and in telling it how it is. Think you can do it? Find out how at lonelyplanet.com.

VESNA MARIC

Málaga, Córdoba, Jaén

Vesna's love for Andalucía grows with every visit. She travels to the region at least four times a year, continuing to discover new places, recipes and beaches, and family and close friends in Málaga, Cádiz, Granada and Seville make sure that Andalucía now feels like a second home.

ZORA O'NEILL

Granada, Almería

Zora studied 11th-century Andalusian Arabic poetry in graduate school, but finds the cultural mix of modern-day southern Spain much more intriguing – mostly because it involves eating. Usually a city mouse, she developed a fresh appreciation for the outdoors – and for the nourishing power of ham – while hiking in the Alpujarras for this guide. Zora has written guidebooks since 2003; this is her third title for Lonely Planet. She lives in Queens, New York City.

JOHN NOBLE

History

John, originally from England's Ribble Valley, has lived in the provinces of Málaga and Cádiz since the mid-1990s and explored Andalucía from end to end but still finds its nooks and crannies endlessly intriguing to investigate. Every little village and valley reveals more about Andalucía's story, which becomes more fascinating the more one delves into it. John and his wife Susan Forsyth, who died in 2008, wrote the first two editions of this guide together, and were authors on all subsequent editions.

ITINERARIES

AL-ANDALUS HEARTLAND

10 DAYS // SEVILLE, CÓRDOBA & GRANADA // 300KM

Seven centuries of Islamic rule in Andalucía bequeathed to the region some of Europe's most exotic architecture. Begin in Seville (p34), with jewels such as the Alcázar (p44),

and the monumental Gothic cathedral and Giralda (p40), the city's great mosque and minaret in Islamic times. Northeast of Seville, Córdoba's Mezquita (p201) is one of the world's most beautiful mosques. The nearby Judería (p207) and the caliphs' palace Medina Azahara (p209), to the west just outside the city, are also significant landmarks to Al-Andalus. Granada (p247), southeast of Córdoba, is watched over by the peerless magnificence of the Alhambra (p254) and its exquisite Generalife gardens. Just across the valley, the Albayzín (p260) is Andalucía's best-preserved old Islamic quarter.

SEVILLE

EL CENTRO

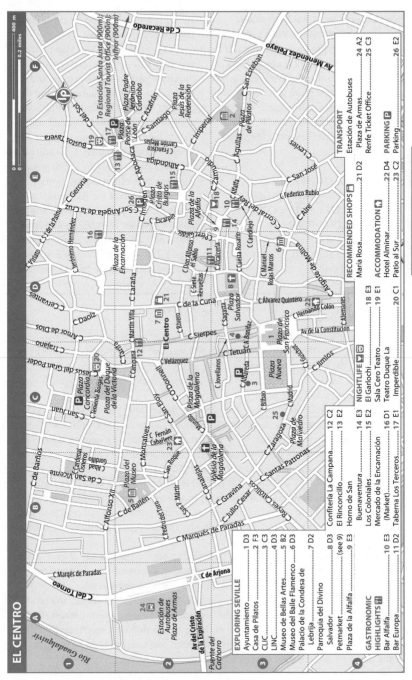

EXPLORING SEVILLE

Ayuntamiento	1 D3
Casa de Pilatos	2 F3
CLIC	3 C3
LINC	4 D3
Museo de Bellas Artes	5 B2
Museo del Baile Flamenco	6 D3
Palacio de la Condesa de Lebrija	7 D2
Parroquia del Divino Salvador	8 D3
Petmarket	(see 9)
Plaza de la Alfalfa	9 E3

GASTRONOMIC HIGHLIGHTS

Bar Alfalfa	10 E3
Bar Europa	11 D2
Confitería La Campana	12 C2
El Rinconcillo	13 E2
Horno de San Buenaventura	14 E3
Los Coloniales	15 E2
Mercado de la Encarnación (Market)	16 D1
Taberna Los Terceros	17 E1

NIGHTLIFE

El Garlochi	18 E3
Sala Cero Teatro	19 E1
Teatro Duque La Imperdible	20 C1

RECOMMENDED SHOPS

María Rosa	21 D2

ACCOMMODATION

Hotel Alminar	22 D4
Patio al Sur	23 C2

TRANSPORT

Estación de Autobuses Plaza de Armas	24 A2
Renfe Ticket Office	25 C3

PARKING

Parking	26 E2

Museum; Map p51; ☎ 954 34 03 11; www.museo
flamenco.com; Calle Manuel Rojas Marcos 3; adult/child
€10/6; ☼ 9am-7pm), but though it contains
all kinds of flashing and beeping displays,
it has a rather confusing layout and lacks
any real substance. More worthwhile are
the daily flamenco performances (performance only €12, performance & museum €20; ☼ 7pm)
and the 20-minute flamenco classes (€10;
☼ 6.30pm Mon-Thu).

♥ ALAMEDA DE HÉRCULES &
AROUND // HIPPIES, VIRGINS
AND PAINTED LADIES: IT'S
'ALTERNATIVE' SEVILLE
While the Barrio de Santa Cruz and
Cathedral area are where things once
happened in Seville it's the Alameda de

Hércules area where the young are making things happen today.

Alameda de Hércules (Map p54)
was once a no-go area reserved only for
the city's 'painted ladies', pimps and a
wide range of shady characters, but the
parklike strip has undergone the 'Soho
makeover' and is now crammed with
trendy bars, chic shops and the popular
Teatro Alameda (Map p54; ☎ 954 90 01 64; Calle
Crédito 11; admission around €8), which is one of
the city's best experimental theatres.

Further north of the Alameda the
1940s Basílica de La Macarena (Map p54;
☎ 954 90 18 00; Calle Bécquer 1; ☼ 9.30am-2pm &
5-9pm), off Calle San Luis, is the home of
Seville's most revered Virgin and will
give you a whiff of the fervour inspired

∼ WORTH A TRIP ∼

If you're heading towards **El Rocío** (p88) or the **Parque Nacional de Doñana** (p84),
rather than follow the crowds down the fast A49 road why not follow the crowds of birds
heading to the ponds, marshes and rice fields around the northeast fringes of the Doñana
area? You'll see plenty of large birds – flamingos, storks, eagles, hawks and herons – even
before you get out of your car.

Leave Seville southwestward by Avenida de la República Argentina and the A3122
to Coria del Río and La Puebla del Río. Twenty-two kilometres from central Seville is
La Cañada de los Pájaros (☎ 955 77 21 84; www.canadadelospajaros.com; Carretera Puebla del Río-
Isla Mayor Km8; adult/child €9/5; ☼ 10am-dusk), a private wetland that is part zoo, part nature
reserve with thousands of easy-to-see birds of 150-plus species.

Time for lunch? **Venta El Cruce** (☎ 955 77 21 96; Carretera Puebla del Río-Isla Mayor Km9.5;
raciones €8), 1.75km beyond La Cañada de los Pájaros at the turn-off for Isla Mayor, is
a typical road-junction restaurant but it drags in more punters at lunchtime than any
other restaurant for miles around. Try the house speciality: *pato con arroz* (duck with
rice).

After lunch follow the road 3km to **Dehesa de Abajo**, a small nature reserve with
walkways to observation points over Europe's largest woodland nesting colony of
white storks (400 pairs) and hides overlooking a lake filled with exotics such as the
crested coot. A variety of raptors also nest here. To continue to El Rocío, carry on
southwest from Dehesa de Abajo to the Vado de Don Simón causeway across the
shallow Río Guadiamar. At the far end of the causeway turn right (northward) to
Villamanrique de la Condesa, from where it's 20km southwest to El Rocío by a small
and narrow road where encounters with wildlife are common.

by Semana Santa. The *Virgen de la Esperanza Macarena* (Macarena Virgin of Hope), a magnificent statue adorned with a golden crown, lavish vestments, and five diamond-and-emerald brooches donated by a famous 20th-century matador, Joselito El Gallo, stands in splendour behind the main altarpiece. La Macarena, as she is commonly known, is the patron of bullfighters and Seville's supreme representation of the grieving, yet hopeful, mother of Christ. The power of this fragile, beautiful statue is most evident in the wee hours of the *madrugá* (Good Friday) Semana Santa procession. Where she passes, a rain of rose petals falls, and crazed *sevillanos* shout: '*Macarena, guapa*' (Beautiful Macarena). To top it all off a *saeta* (sacred Andalusian song) is sung, praising the Virgin's beauty. The church's **museum** was closed for renovations at the time of research, but promises to reopen sometime in 2010. Across the street is the longest surviving stretch of Seville's 12th-century **Almohad walls**.

One of Seville's most impressive churches, **Iglesia de San Luis** (Map p54; ☎ 954 55 02 07; Calle San Luis s/n; admission free; 9am-2pm Tue-Thu, 9am-2pm & 6-9pm Fri & Sat, closed Aug) stands 500m south of the Basílica de La Macarena. Designed for the Jesuits by Leonardo de Figueroa in 1731, the baroque San Luis has an unusual equal-armed cross plan, 16 twisting stone pillars and a superb soaring dome. Look out for the human skulls with crowns of flowers.

For a different kind of religious experience – shopping! – check out **El Jueves Market** (Map p54; Calle de la Feria; Thu), east of Alameda de Hércules, where you can find everything from hatstands to antiquated household appliances. It's as interesting for those who like people-watching as it is for those with an eye for a bargain.

❦ CONJUNTO MONUMENTAL DE LA CARTUJA // BE DAZZLED BY THE VISION OF MODERN SEVILLE

Founded in 1399, the **Conjunto Monumental de la Cartuja** (Cartuja Monastery; Map p54; ☎ 955 03 70 70; www.caac.es; admission complete visit/monument or temporary exhibitions €3.01/1.80, EU citizen free Tue; 10am-9pm Tue-Fri, 11am-9pm Sat, 10am-3pm Sun, to 8pm Tue-Fri Oct-Mar, last admission half an hr before closing time) became the favourite *sevillano* lodging place for Columbus, King Felipe II and other luminaries. In 1839 the complex was bought by a Liverpudlian, Charles Pickman, who turned it into a porcelain factory, building the tall bottle-shaped kilns that stand incongruously beside the monastery buildings.

The porcelain factory ceased functioning in 1982 and today the complex is the home of the superb **Centro Andaluz de Arte Contemporáneo** (Andalusian Contemporary Art Centre), which has a collection of modern Andalusian art and frequent temporary exhibitions. When we last cruised past these included a fascinating photographic history of flamenco and another entitled 'Identity' which was full of top-notch photographic portraits.

❦ BAÑOS ÁRABES // YOU'RE ON HOLIDAY. PAMPER YOURSELF!

Rest your weary, sightseeing muscles by taking a soak, a massage and even a chocolate treatment (apparently it's good for you!) at the Arabic-style baths at **Aire de Sevilla** (Map p42; ☎ 955 01 00 25; www.airedesevilla.com; Calle Aire 15; from €20; on the hr every 2hr from 10am-midnight).

❦ LANGUAGE COURSES // YOU'RE ON HOLIDAY. IMPROVE YOURSELF!

Seville is a great city in which to hang around for a while and learn a new

SEVILLE

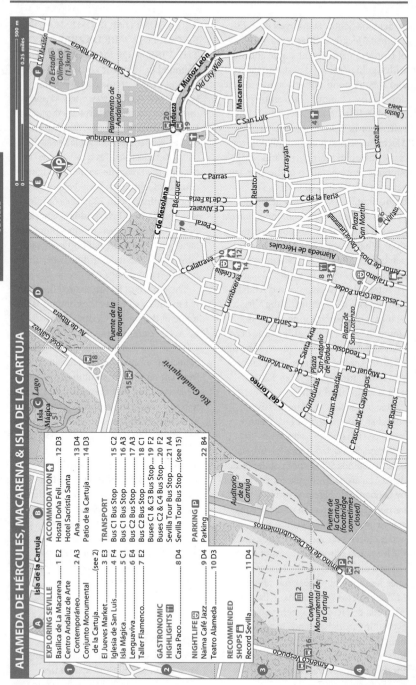

ALAMEDA DE HÉRCULES, MACARENA & ISLA DE LA CARTUJA

EXPLORING SEVILLE
Basílica de La Macarena........1 E2
Centro Andaluz de Arte
Contemporáneo...................2 A3
Conjunto Monumental
de la Cartuja......................(see 2)
El Jueves Market.....................3 E3
Iglesia de San Luis..................4 F4
Isla Mágica.............................5 C1
Lenguaviva.............................6 E4
Taller Flamenco......................7 E2

GASTRONOMIC
HIGHLIGHTS 🍴
Casa Paco..............................8 D4

NIGHTLIFE 🍸
Naima Café Jazz......................9 D4
Teatro Alameda....................10 D3

RECOMMENDED
SHOPS 🛍
Record Sevilla......................11 D4

ACCOMMODATION 🛏
Hostal Doña Feli...................12 D3
Hotel Sacristía Santa
Ana......................................13 D4
Patio de la Cartuja................14 D3

TRANSPORT
Bus C1 Bus Stop....................15 C2
Bus C1 Bus Stop....................16 A3
Bus C2 Bus Stop....................17 A3
Bus C2 Bus Stop....................18 C1
Buses C1 & C3 Bus Stop........19 F2
Buses C2 & C4 Bus Stop........20 F2
Sevilla Tour Bus Stop............21 A4
Sevilla Tour Bus Stop.........(see 15)

PARKING 🅿
Parking.................................22 B4

skill. Many visitors from overseas join a Spanish language course and there are dozens of schools offering courses. The following list is by no means exhaustive, but it highlights the best known schools. CLIC (Map p51; ☎ 954 50 21 31; www.clic.es; Calle Albareda 19) is a well-established language centre with a good social scene; courses in business Spanish and Hispanic studies available. The Giralda Center (Map p42; ☎ 954 22 13 46; www.giraldacenter.com; Calle Mateos Gago 17) has a friendly atmosphere, plenty of excursions and a reputation for good teaching. Lenguaviva (Map p54; ☎ 915 94 37 76; www.lenguaviva.net; Calle Viriato 24) is good on spare-time activities like tapas tours and social drinks; courses in business Spanish available. Finally there is LINC (Map p51; ☎ 954 50 04 59; www.linc.tv; Calle General Polavieja 13), a small, popular school, which is good on cultural activities and excursions.

♥ DANCE COURSES // YOU'RE ON HOLIDAY. LET YOURSELF GO!

If learning a language is just too scholarly then how about learning how to shimmy with the best of them? Seville has many dance and flamenco schools open to visitors staying a while. The Fundación Cristina Heeren de Arte Flamenco (off Map pp36-7; ☎ 954 21 70 58; www.flamencoheeren.com; Av de Jerez 2) is by far the best known school and offers long-term courses in all flamenco arts; also one-month intensive summer courses. Taller Flamenco (Map p54; ☎ 954 56 42 34; www.tallerflamenco.com; Calle Peral 49) offers flamenco dance and guitar courses.

FESTIVALS & EVENTS

Semana Santa (Holy Week) The passion and theatre of life in Seville reaches its pinnacle with the spectacular Semana Santa celebrations. Every day from Palm Sunday to Easter Sunday, large, richly bedecked images and life-sized tableaux of scenes from the Easter story are carried from Seville's churches through the streets to the cathedral. They're accompanied by long processions, which may take more than an hour to pass, and are watched by vast crowds. Programs showing each procession's schedule and route are widely available. *El País* newspaper publishes a daily route leaflet and *ABC* newspaper prints maps showing the churches, recommended viewing spots and other details; also see www.semana-santa.org, in Spanish.

Feria de Abril The April Fair, held in the second half of the month (sometimes edging into May), is the jolly counterpart to the sombre Semana Santa. The biggest and most colourful of all Andalucía's *ferias* is less invasive (and also less inclusive) than the Easter celebration – it takes place on El Real de la Feria, in the Los Remedios area west of the Guadalquivir. The ceremonial lighting-up of the fairgrounds on the opening Monday night is the starting gun for six nights of *sevillanos'* favourite activities: eating, drinking, dressing up and dancing till dawn.

Corpus Christi An important early-morning procession of the Custodia de Juan de Arfe, along with accompanying images from the cathedral. Held 3 June 2010, 23 June 2011 and 7 June 2012.

Bienal de Flamenco Most of the big names of the flamenco world participate in this major flamenco festival. Held in the September of even-numbered years; www.bienal-flamenco.org.

GASTRONOMIC HIGHLIGHTS

Seville's hundreds of tapas bars are the city's culinary pride, and food is a highlight for nearly every visitor to Seville. To decode your tapas menu, see p375.

Mercado del Arenal (Map p48; Calle Pastor y Landero) and the Mercado de la Encarnación (Map p51; Plaza de la Encarnación) are central Seville's two food markets. The Encarnación, which mainly sells fruit, vegies and fish, has been in its current 'temporary' quarters, awaiting construction of a new permanent building, since 1973!

BARRIO DE SANTA CRUZ, ALCÁZAR & CATHEDRAL

🍴 ALVARO PEREGIL €

Map p42; 20 Calle Mateos Gago; tapas €2-2.50

This tiny bar has not much more in terms of decoration than garlic bunches hanging overhead and a couple of tall tables outside to rest your tapas on. But the food is so good you'll need nothing more. The *salmorejo* (a thicker version of gazpacho) is particularly good and is served with strips of *jamón* sprinkled over the top; try the orange wine, made from Seville's famous (and ubiquitous) oranges.

🍴 CAFÉ ALIANZA €

Map p42; Plaza de la Alianza; tapas €2-3

Old-fashioned street lights, a trickling fountain and colourful wall plants make this small plaza a charming place to relax with a coffee, and Café Alianza is positioned perfectly for just that. Its tapas nibbles are also good.

🍴 CAFÉ BAR LAS TERESAS €

Map p42; ☎ 954 21 30 69; Calle Santa Teresa 2; tapas €2-4, media-raciones €8

This atmospheric bar has *jamones* dangling from the ceiling in tidy rows, lovely Andalusian tiles lining the walls and a red wooden bar propping up the chatting crowd. A great place to stop and have some good, traditional tapas.

🍴 CASA TOMATE €€

Map p42; ☎ 954 22 04 21; Calle Mateos Gago 24; media-raciones €8-9, raciones €12

This new place is unusual in such a tourist hot spot in that it cares more about satisfying the palates of locals than making a fast buck off tourists. The waiters recommend the garlic prawns and the pork sirloin in a white-wine-and-pine-nut sauce. The waiters are right.

🍴 CATALINA €

Map p42; ☎ 954 41 24 12; Paseo Catalina de Ribera 4; raciones €10

INSIDE SEMANA SANTA

Visit Seville at Easter and you'll be up all week, getting excited about men carrying crosses, following Virgin Marys and Jesuses, alongside all the *sevillanos* who are dressed up to the nines.

There are more than 50 *hermandades* or *cofradías* (brotherhoods). Each brotherhood normally carries two lavishly decorated *pasos* (platforms) and you can work out which *hermandad* is passing by the emblems and the colours of their capes.

The climax of the week is the *madrugá* (night/dawn) of Good Friday, when the most respected and popular *hermandades* file through the city, starting with the oldest, El Silencio, which goes in complete silence. Next comes Jesús del Gran Poder followed by La Macarena. Then come El Calvario from the Iglesia de la Magdalena, Esperanza de Triana, and lastly, at dawn, Los Gitanos, the *gitano* (Roma) brotherhood. On the Saturday evening just four *hermandades* make their way to the cathedral, and finally, on Easter Sunday morning, the Hermandad de la Resurrección.

City-centre brotherhoods, such as El Silencio, are traditionally linked with the bourgeoisie. They are austere and wear black tunics, usually without capes. *Hermandades* from the working-class districts outside the centre (such as La Macarena) have bands and more brightly decorated *pasos*. Their *nazarenos* wear coloured, caped tunics, often of satin, velvet or wool. They also have to come from further away, and some are on the streets for more than 12 hours.

This is one of the least touristy restaurants in the neighbourhood and the local community appreciates its excellent, innovative dishes, which include a delectable pile of aubergine, goats cheese and potato topped with paprika. You can sit outside gazing at the palms in the Jardines de Murillo opposite or eat inside surrounded by walls covered in comic strips.

☘ CORRAL DEL AGUA €€
Map p42; ☎ 954 22 07 14; Callejón del Agua 6; mains €18-20; ◷ noon-4pm & 8pm-midnight Mon-Sat

If you're hankering for inventive food on a hot day, then book a table at Corral del Agua. Its leafy courtyard makes a pleasant spot to sample traditional stews and Arabic-inspired desserts.

☘ RESTAURANTE EGAÑA ORIZA €€€
Map p42; ☎ 954 22 72 11; Calle San Fernando 41; mains €29, menú €60; ◷ closed Sat lunch & Sun

One of the better, and certainly more up-market restaurants in Seville, the Basque-by-name, Basque-by-nature Egaña Oriza cooks up a superb mix of Andalusian-Basque cuisine. While the restaurant is undeniably good, it's a shame about the fume-choked location.

☘ RESTAURANTE LA ALBAHACA €€€
Map p42; ☎ 954 22 07 14; Plaza de Santa Cruz 12; mains €20-25; menú €19

Gastronomic inventions are the mainstay of this swish restaurant. Housed inside an imposing building with massive studded doors it looks as if a trip here may break the bank, but in fact the lunchtime *menú del día* is a really great deal. Try the pork trotter with mushroom, young garlic and pea mousse (essentially just a posh version of mushy peas), or the rabbit stew.

☘ VINERÍA SAN TELMO €€
Map p42; ☎ 954 41 06 00; Paseo Catalina de Ribera 4; tapas €3.50, media-raciones €10

If the thought of the Andalusian-Basque dishes on offer here – such as foie gras with quails eggs and lychees or exquisitely cooked bricks of tuna or maybe the *rascacielos de tomate, berenjena, queso de cabra y salmón* (which roughly translates into a pyramid of tomato, aubergine, goats cheese and salmon) – don't make you drool with expectation then you're probably dead. In our opinion this is the best place to eat in Barrio de Santa Cruz.

EL CENTRO

Plaza de la Alfalfa is the hub of the tapas scene, and has some excellent bars.

☘ BAR ALFALFA €
Map p51; ☎ 954 22 23 44; cnr Calles Alfalfa & Candilejo; tapas €2-3

This tiny 'you and the barman are a crowd' kind of place is one of the most charming tapas bars in the city. The Italian chef fuses the culinary highlights of Rome and Seville. The *bruschetta con salmorejo* is spot on. Fear not if it's too busy to fit through the door – you can stand on the street and order through the window!

☘ BAR EUROPA €
Map p51; ☎ 954 22 13 54; Calle Siete Revueltas 35; tapas €3, media-raciones €6-8

Up there with the best of the best, this neighbourhood institution has tapas so exciting they've won awards for several years in a row. The highly unusual, and rather tasty, *quesadilla los balanchares gratinada sobre manzana* was voted the most innovative tapa in 2006. This beauty involves turning a boring old Granny Smith into a taste sensation by covering it in goats cheese and laying it on a bed of strawberries.

♥ CONFITERÍA LA CAMPANA €
Map p51; cnr Calles Sierpes & Martín Villa

La Campana has been heaving with sugar addicts since 1885, and workers and the elite alike storm Seville's most popular bakery for a *yema* (a soft, crumbly biscuit cake wrapped like a toffee), or a delicious *nata* (custard cake) that quivers under the glass. It's about the only business left on this road that hasn't been gobbled up by a multinational – hopefully its maturity and quality will keep it safe for a while longer.

♥ EL RINCONCILLO €
Map p51; ☎ 954 22 31 83; Calle Gerona 40; tapas €3, raciones €12

Seville's oldest bar first opened in 1670 and has been dishing out the goods since before many countries were even a twinkle in someone's eye. Time has allowed it to build up an impressive range of little morsels; though to be fair you do probably come here more for the sense of history than for the food. However, the *ortiguillas fritas* (fried sea anemones) are memorable for all the right reasons and it serves the biggest olives we've ever seen.

♥ HORNO DE SAN BUENAVENTURA €
Map p51; Plaza de la Alfalfa 10

The Buenaventura chain is much loved in this city, and the cakes are pretty good. No, sorry, that's a lie. The cakes are stupendous and they're treated like precious jewels, showcased in shiny glass cabinets and wrapped up like Christmas presents if you take them away. There's another branch in El Arenal on the corner of Avenida de la Constitución and Calle García de Vinuesa.

♥ LOS COLONIALES €
Map p51; cnr Calle Dormitorio & Plaza Cristo de Burgos; tapas €2.50, raciones €10

It might not look like much from the outside but trust us; this is something very special. It's hard to pick a favourite dish as everything is outstanding, but we'd never turn down a plate of *chorizo a la Asturiana,* a divine spicy sausage in an onion sauce served on a bed of lightly fried potato. To follow up try the aubergines in honey. There is another, inferior and more touristy branch, Taberna Los Coloniales (Map p48), on Calle Jimios near the cathedral.

♥ TABERNA LOS TERCEROS €
Map p51; Calle del Sol; tapas €3, media-raciones €7-8

It might lack the visual 'stop dead in your tracks' look of the nearby El Rinconcillo, but more than a few people say it tops its neighbour for taste. Plus it has a younger, more bohemian clientele. Snails *(caracoles)* are the house special.

EL ARENAL & TRIANA

♥ CASA CUESTA €
Map p48; ☎ 954 33 33 37; Calle de Castilla 3-5; mains €9-10

Something about the carefully buffed wooden bar and gleaming beer pumps gives a sense that the owners are proud of Casa Cuesta. Indeed they should be; it's a real find for food and wine lovers alike.

♥ ENRIQUE BECERRA €€
Map p48; ☎ 954 21 30 49; Calle Gamazo 2; mains €17-22; ☺ closed Sun

Squeeze in with the locals at lunchtime and enjoy some hearty Andalusian dishes. The lamb drenched in honey sauce and stuffed with spinach and pine nuts (€22) is just one of many delectable offerings, but be warned that it charges a whopping €2.50 for bread and olives!

❦ MESÓN CINCO JOTAS €

Map p48; ☎ 954 21 05 21; Calle Castelar 1; tapas €3,
media-raciones €7-8

In the world of *jamón*-making, if you are
awarded 'Cinco Jotas' (Five Js) for your
jamón, it's like getting an Oscar. The
owner of this place, Sánchez Romero
Carvajal, is the biggest producer of
Jabugo ham, and has a great selection on
offer. It's best to try a range of different
things here, but note that the top-pig
jamones can cost just under €40!

❦ MESÓN DE LA INFANTA €

Map p48; ☎ 954 56 15 54; Calle Dos de Mayo 26;
tapas €2-3

If you like your tapas with a touch of
class and a glass of cool sherry, indulge
in innovative, well-presented dishes
at this *sevillano* favourite. While eating you can ponder the purpose of the
tins of peas and jars of jam lined up on
the shelves – see if you can solve the
mystery!

❦ MESÓN SERRANITO €

Map p48; ☎ 954 21 12 43; Calle Antonia Díaz 11;
media-raciones €7

Specialising in the *serranito,* a Spanish
gastronomic institution consisting of a
slice of toasted bread heaped with a pork
fillet, roasted pepper, a nice bit of *jamón*
and garlic, this place is tops for trying
this simple but scrumptious bite. It's also
has tasty bull's tail on the menu to go
with the less tasty bulls' heads hanging
on the wall – next to pictures of the final
few seconds of their lives.

ALAMEDA DE HÉRCULES

❦ CASA PACO €

Map p54; ☎ 954 90 01 48; Alameda de Hércules 23;
raciones €8-10, menú €12

This small bar is very popular with students on account of its well-priced meals
and laid-back vibe. If there isn't room
inside then spread your wings on the
sunny outdoor terrace.

NIGHTLIFE

Bars usually open from 6pm to 2am on
weekdays and 8pm to 4am on the weekend. Drinking and partying get going as
late as midnight on Friday and Saturday
(daily when it's hot), upping the tempo
as the night goes on.

In summer, dozens of *terrazas de verano* (summer terraces; temporary, open-
air, late-night bars), many of them with
live music and plenty of room to dance,
spring up along both banks of the river.
They change names and ambience from
year to year.

For a real treat, prop yourself up with
a drink by the banks of the Río Guadalquivir in Triana (Map p48); the wall
along Calle del Betis forms a fantastic
makeshift bar. Carry your drink out from
one of the nearby watering holes.

For information on flamenco in Seville, see the boxed text, p60.

EL CENTRO

❦ EL GARLOCHI

Map p51; Calle Boteros 4

Dedicated entirely to the iconography,
smells and sounds of Semana Santa, the
ubercamp El Garlochi is a true marvel.
A cloud of church incense hits you as
you go up the stairs, and the faces of
baby Jesus and the Virgin welcome you
into the velvet-walled bar, decked out
with more Virgins and Jesuses. Taste the
rather revolting cocktails Sangre de Cristo (Blood of Christ) or Agua de Sevilla,
both heavily laced with vodka, whisky
and grenadine, and pray they open more
bars like this.

♥ SALA CERO TEATRO
Map p51; ☎ 954 22 51 65; Calle del Sol 5; admission
around €10
This former flamenco haunt has had a
change of name and a change of heart
and now stages art-house plays as well as
a few moments of flamenco.

♥ TEATRO DUQUE LA IMPERDIBLE
Map p51; ☎ 954 90 54 58; www.imperdible.org; Plaza
del Duque de la Victoria s/n; admission €12
This is Seville's epicentre of experimental
arts. Its small theatre stages lots of contemporary dance and a bit of drama and
music, usually at 9pm. Wednesday night
is flamenco night.

ALAMEDA DE HÉRCULES

In terms of hipness and trendy places to
go out, La Alameda is where it's at. The
slightly rundown feeling of the area adds
to the exclusivity and discourages some
sevillanos, so the boho lot get to keep the
place more or less to themselves.

♥ NAIMA CAFÉ JAZZ
Map pp54-5; ☎ 954 38 24 85; Calle Trajano 47;
admission free; ⊙ live performances from 11pm
If you're getting tired of the flamenco then
you can jazz out at this intimate place,
which sways to the sound of mellow jazz
(live at weekends). Ask the bar staff for
details of who's playing and when.

RECOMMENDED SHOPS

Shopping in Seville is a major pastime,
and shopping for clothes is at the top of
the list for any *sevillano*.

Calles Sierpes, Velázquez/Tetuán and
de la Cuna (all on Map p51) have retained
their charm with a host of small shops
selling everything from polka-dot *trajes de
flamenca* (flamenco dresses) and trendy
Camper shoes to diamond rings and antique fans. Most shops open between 9am
and 9pm, but expect ghostly quiet between
2pm and 5pm when they close for siesta.

For a more alternative choice of shops,
such as independent and rare-recordings
music shops or vintage clothes, head for
Calle Amor de Dios and Calle Doctor
Letamendi, close to Alameda de Hércules (Map p54).

Tourist-oriented craft shops are dotted
all around the Barrio de Santa Cruz (Map
p42), east of the Alcázar. Many sell local
tiles and ceramics with colourful Al-Andalus designs, scenes of old rural life etc,
as well as a lot of gaudy T-shirts.

♥ BACO
Map p48 ; Calle Arfe 20
If you've enjoyed sampling the food that
much (and who hasn't?) then you can
take some of it home with you from this
wonderful deli stocked with quality local

SEVILLE'S TOP FLAMENCO SPOTS

Casa de la Memoria de Al-Andalus (Map p42; ☎ 954 56 06 70; Calle Ximénez de Enciso 28; adult/con-
cession/child €15/13/9; ⊙ 9pm daily) Highly recommended show in a great patio setting.
La Carbonería (Map p42; ⊙ 954 21 44 60; Calle Levíes 18; admission free; ⊙ around 8pm-4am) A converted
coal yard in the Barrio de Santa Cruz with two large rooms, each with a bar, that has flamenco shows of varying
quality.
Los Gallos (Map p42; ☎ 954 21 69 81; www.tablaolosgallos.com; Plaza de Santa Cruz 11) A *tablao* above average. Some top-notch flamenco artists have trodden Los Gallos' boards in the early stages of their careers. There are
two-hour shows at 8pm and 10.30pm nightly for €30, including one drink.
Also see **Teatro Duque La Imperdible** (above) and **Museo del Baile Flamenco** (p50).

food products such as olives and olive oil, *jamón*, cheeses and *bacalao* (salted cod).

❦ EL POSTIGO
Map p48; cnr Calles Arfe & Dos de Mayo
A covered arts and crafts market housing a few shops selling everything from pottery and textiles to silverware.

❦ MARÍA ROSA
Map p51 ; Calle de la Cuna 13
Full of flamenco flounces, polka dots and frills this is the place to get dressed up like a flamenco queen. Blokes, and children, needn't feel left out as they also stock a men's and children's range in addition to all the shiny accessories you might want.

❦ RECORD SEVILLA
Map p54; Calle Amor de Dios 27
Fancy mixing flamenco with house? Then grab your vinyl here. Staff are knowledgeable about the local music scene too.

TRANSPORT

TO/FROM THE AIRPORT

AIR // Seville's **Aeropuerto San Pablo** (off Map pp36-7; ☎ 902 40 47 04), 7km east of the city, has a fair range of international and domestic flights (see p412).

BUS // Buses (€2.40) make the trip between the airport and the city centre roughly every 15 minutes throughout the day. The service is reduced to every 30 minutes on Sundays as well very early in the morning and late in the evening. The first bus from the airport to the city is at 5.45am and the last at 12.15am. From the city to the airport the first bus is at 5.15am and the last at 12.45am. It picks up and drops off in the city centre near the Puerta de Jerez (Map p42), and also makes stops along Avenida del Cíd, Avenida de Carlos V and a number of other places.

TAXI // A taxi costs a set €21 with a charge of €1 per bag from the airport to the centre, but going the other way you'll be lucky to pay less than €25. There's a surcharge late at night, and on weekends and holidays.

CITY DRIVING

If you like getting hot, sweaty, frustrated, angry and sometimes frightened then you'll enjoy driving in Seville. If you don't then avoid picking up your hire car until after you leave the city. Car crime is rampant – never leave anything in your car. There are numerous underground car parks (many marked on the relevant maps), which cost around €18 per 24 hours. Street parking (€0.60 per hour) is metered and often limited to three hours.

GETTING AROUND

CAR // For car hire there's **Avis** (☎ 902 48 03 21; Avenida de Italia 107) or **National/Atesa** (☎ 959 28 17 12) in the Santa Justa train station concourse and all the normal brands at the airport.

PARKING // Take our advice and head for an underground car park. Most street parking is metered and virtually the same price as an underground car park, minus the security. The most convenient car park in Barrio de Santa Cruz is on the corner of Avenida Menéndez Pelayo and the northern edge of the Jardines de Murillo; see Map p42. Some top-end hotels have private parking.

BUS // Seville has two bus stations. Buses to/from the north of Sevilla province, Huelva province, Portugal, Madrid, Extremadura and northwest Spain use the **Estación de Autobuses Plaza de Armas** (Map p51; ☎ 954 90 65 93) Other buses use the **Estación de Autobuses Prado de San Sebastián** (Map p42; ☎ 954 41 71 18; Plaza San Sebastián). Buses run roughly hourly to Huelva, Cádiz, Córdoba, Granada, Málaga and Madrid.

TRAIN // Seville's **Estación Santa Justa** (Map pp36-7; ☎ 902 43 23 43; Avenida Kansas City) is 1.5km northeast of the centre. There's also a city-centre Renfe information and ticket office (Map p51; Calle Zaragoza 29). Fourteen or more superfast AVEs whizz daily to/from Madrid in just 2½ hours. Every couple of hours throughout the day trains rattle off to Cádiz and Córdoba while several a day chug down to Huelva, Granada and Málaga.

SEVILLE

SEVILLE FOR KIDS

Seville's myriad cultural diversions might be interesting for adults, but the little 'uns will quickly get bored of the procession of monuments and galleries. In no particular order here are our top picks to keep the children as enamoured with Seville as you are.

Isla Mágica (Map p54; ☎ 902 16 17 16; www.islamagica.es; adult/child €28/20; ☼ high season around 11am-10pm) A huge theme park that gives kids of all ages a great (but expensive) day of fun, though those aged over about 10 will get the most out of the rides. Hours of operation change monthly; see website for details.

City Tours Take the kids on a terrific tour of the town in an open-topped double-decker bus, up the river by boat, or around town in a horse-drawn carriage (p44).

Pet Market On Sunday morning visit the pet market in **Plaza de la Alfalfa** (Map p51), but remember a dog's not just for Christmas in Seville.

Aquópolis Sevilla (off Map pp36-7; ☎ 902 34 50 10; www.aquopolis.es, in Spanish; Avenida del Deporte s/n; adult/child €18.95/13.95; ☼ 11am-7 or 8pm approx late May-early Sep) On a hot summer day kids will want to do nothing more than dive in a pool. The waterslides and wave pools here will keep them happy for hours. It's located in Barrio Las Delicias in the east of the city (off the A92 towards Málaga).

La Reserva del Castillo de las Guardas (Map pp64-5; ☎ 955 95 25 68; www.lareservadel castillodelasguardas.es; Finca Herrerías Bajas s/n, Carretera A476 Km6.82; adult/child under 13yr €20/15; ☼ 10.30am-5.30pm) About 1000 animals from around the planet roam in semi-liberty and can be viewed from your own vehicle or the park's road-train. It's 58km northwest of Seville in the village of El Castillo de las Guardas, off the N433 towards Aracena. The dog you bought at the pet market is not allowed in.

BIKE // By far one of the nicest ways to cruise the streets of central Seville is by bicycle. SeVici (☎ 902 01 10 32; www.sevici.es) is a city-wide bike-hire scheme whereby you pick up your bright green bike from one of around 200 automated pick-up/drop-off points found throughout the city. A one-week sub-scription costs €10 after which your first half-hour of bike hire is free, up to 1½ hours is €0.50 and every hour beyond that is €1. There is a €150 deposit (payable on credit card).

LOCAL BUS // Buses C1, C2, C3 and C4 do useful circular routes linking the main transport terminals and the city centre. The standard ticket is €1.20 but a range of passes are available (from stations and kiosks next to stops) if you're likely to use it a lot.

TAXI // Taxis are common and a journey across the city centre during normal daylight hours is unlikely to cost more than €5-7.

METRO // First mooted some 30 years ago Seville's metro system has finally emerged from the darkness and

seen the light of day (so to speak). The first line opened in April 2009 and connects Ciudad Expo with Olivar de Quinto (this line isn't that useful for visitors). The stand-ard ticket is €1.20 but a range of passes are available if you're likely to use it a lot.

TRAM // Tranvia (www.tussam.es, in Spanish) is the city's sleek new tram service. Currently only two lines are operational, which whizz in pollution-free bliss between Plaza Nueva, Avenida de la Constitucíon to the Archivo de Indias and Puerta de Jerez and San Sebastián. The standard ticket is €1.20 but a range of passes are available if you're likely to use it a lot.

AROUND SEVILLE

· · · · · ·

For many visitors a journey through Sevilla province begins, ends and goes no further than the city of Seville itself. But Seville the province also offers an enormous wealth of sights and experiences and well rewards any time spent bumbling around its back lanes. Just northwest of the city you'll find the Roman ruins of Itálica, at Santiponce. To the east you'll find La Campiña, the flat and fertile farmland stretching into the fiery distance, a land of huge agricultural estates belonging to a few landowners, dotted with scattered towns and villages. History goes back a long way here: you'll find traces of Tartessians, Iberians, Carthaginians, Romans, early Christians, Visigoths, Muslims and many others.

Head north and you'll find the Parque Natural Sierra Norte, a 1648-sq-km natural park, stretching across Sevilla province, in the beautiful, rolling, often wild Sierra Morena country. It's an ever-changing landscape of green valleys and hills, woodlands, rivers and atmospheric old towns and villages with Islamic-era forts or castles, part-Mudéjar churches and narrow, zigzagging white streets.

SANTIPONCE

The small town of Santiponce, about 8km northwest of Seville, is the location of Itálica (☎ 955 99 65 83; Avenida de Extremadura 2; non-EU/EU citizen €1.50/ free; ☯ 8.30am-8.30pm Tue-Sat, 9am-3pm Sun & holidays Apr-Sep, 9am-5.30pm Tue-Sat, 10am-4pm Sun & holidays Oct-Mar, closed 1 & 6 Jan, 28 Feb, Good Friday, 1 May, 15 Aug, 1 Nov, 25 Dec), the most impressive Roman site in Andalucía. It makes for a superb day trip from Seville.

Itálica was the first Roman town in Spain, founded in 206 BC, and was the birthplace of the 2nd-century-AD Roman emperor Trajan, and prob-

ably of his adopted son and successor Hadrian (he of the wall across northern England).

Although emperors are fairly rare at Itálica today what is left of those times is the incredible remains of the town that once stood here. The site includes broad paved streets and ruins of houses built around patios with beautiful mosaics. The most notable houses are the Casa del Planetario (House of the Planetarium), with a mosaic depicting the gods of the seven days of the week, and the Casa de los Pájaros (House of the Birds). Itálica also contains one of the biggest of all Roman amphitheatres (able to hold 20,000 spectators), and for the layperson this is probably the most impressive site. You enter the amphitheatre through what was once the main gates and the excited crowd in the stands roar in appreciation as you prepare for gladiatorial battle – or something like that anyway.

To the south, in the old town, you can also visit a restored Roman theatre.

CARMONA

pop 27,000 / elevation 250m
Charming Carmona, dotted with old palaces and impressive monuments and perched on a low hill overlooking a wonderful *vega* (valley) that sizzles in the summer heat, is one of the most exquisite towns in western Andalucía.

This strategic site was important as long ago as Carthaginian times. The Romans laid out a street plan that survives to this day: the Via Augusta, running from Rome to Cádiz, entered Carmona by the eastern Puerta de Córdoba and left by the western Puerta de Sevilla. The Muslims built a strong defensive wall around Carmona but the town fell in

SEVILLE

SEVILLA PROVINCE

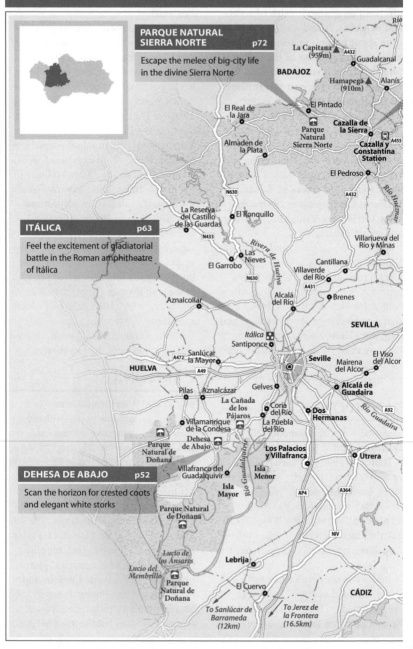

SEVILLE

PARQUE NATURAL SIERRA NORTE p72

Escape the melee of big-city life in the divine Sierra Norte

ITÁLICA p63

Feel the excitement of gladiatorial battle in the Roman amphitheatre of Itálica

DEHESA DE ABAJO p52

Scan the horizon for crested coots and elegant white storks

Río

La Capitana (959m)   A432

Guadalcanal

BADAJOZ

Hamapega (910m)   Alanís

El Pintado

El Real de la Jara

Parque Natural Sierra Norte

Cazalla de la Sierra

Almadén de la Plata

Cazalla y Constantina Station   A455

El Pedroso

A432

Río Huéznar

N630

La Reserva del Castillo de las Guardas

El Ronquillo

Rivera de Huelva

Villanueva del Río y Minas

N433

Las Nieves

El Garrobo

Cantillana

Villaverde del Río

N630

Alcalá del Río   A431

Brenes

Aznalcóllar

SEVILLA

Itálica

Santiponce

A472   Sanlúcar la Mayor

Seville   Mairena del Alcor

El Viso del Alcor

HUELVA   A49

Gelves

Alcalá de Guadaira

A92

Pilas   Aznalcázar

La Cañada de los Pájaros

Coria del Río

Dos Hermanas

Río Guadaira

Villamanrique de la Condesa

La Puebla del Río

Dehesa de Abajo

Río Guadalquivir

Parque Natural de Doñana

Villafranco del Guadalquivir

Isla Menor

Los Palacios y Villafranca

Utrera

Isla Mayor

AP4   A364

Parque Natural de Doñana

NIV

Lucio de los Ánsares

Lebrija

Lucio del Membrillo

Parque Natural de Doñana

El Cuervo

CÁDIZ

To Sanlúcar de Barrameda (12km)

To Jerez de la Frontera (16.5km)

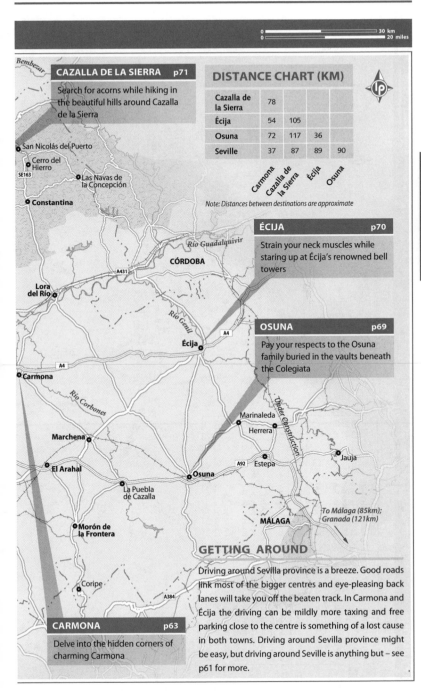

CAZALLA DE LA SIERRA   p71

Search for acorns while hiking in the beautiful hills around Cazalla de la Sierra

DISTANCE CHART (KM)

	Carmona	Cazalla de la Sierra	Écija	Osuna
Cazalla de la Sierra	78			
Écija	54	105		
Osuna	72	117	36	
Seville	37	87	89	90

Note: Distances between destinations are approximate

ÉCIJA   p70

Strain your neck muscles while staring up at Écija's renowned bell towers

OSUNA   p69

Pay your respects to the Osuna family buried in the vaults beneath the Colegiata

CARMONA   p63

Delve into the hidden corners of charming Carmona

GETTING AROUND

Driving around Sevilla province is a breeze. Good roads link most of the bigger centres and eye-pleasing back lanes will take you off the beaten track. In Carmona and Écija the driving can be mildly more taxing and free parking close to the centre is something of a lost cause in both towns. Driving around Sevilla province might be easy, but driving around Seville is anything but – see p61 for more.

SEVILLE

SEVILLE

CARMONA

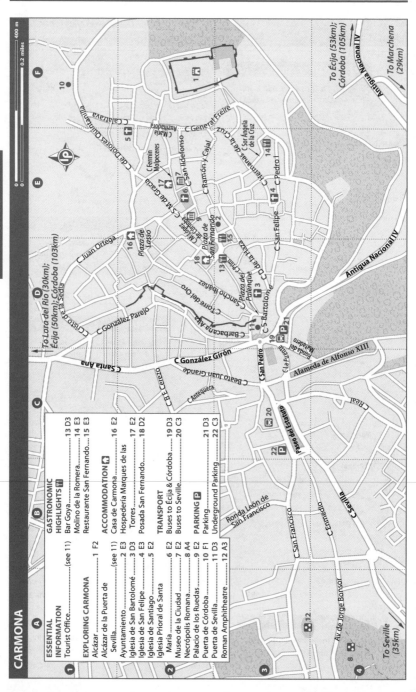

ESSENTIAL
INFORMATION
Tourist Office..........................(see 11)

EXPLORING CARMONA
Alcázar...................................... 1 F2
Alcázar de la Puerta de
  Sevilla.................................(see 11)
Ayuntamiento......................... 2 E3
Iglesia de San Bartolomé....... 3 D3
Iglesia de San Felipe.............. 4 E3
Iglesia de Santiago................. 5 E2
Iglesia Prioral de Santa
  María.................................... 6 E2
Museo de la Ciudad................ 7 E2
Necrópolis Romana................. 8 A4
Palacio de los Ruedas............. 9 E2
Puerta de Córdoba................ 10 F1
Puerta de Sevilla................... 11 D3
Roman Amphitheatre........... 12 A3

GASTRONOMIC
HIGHLIGHTS
Bar Goya................................ 13 D3
Molino de la Romera.............. 14 E3
Restaurante San Fernando.... 15 E3

ACCOMMODATION
Casa de Carmona.................. 16 E2
Hospedería Marqués de las
  Torres................................. 17 E2
Posada San Fernando............ 18 D2

TRANSPORT
Buses to Écija & Córdoba...... 19 D3
Buses to Seville.................... 20 C3

PARKING
Parking................................. 21 D3
Underground Parking............ 22 C3

1247 to Fernando III. The town was later adorned with fine churches, convents and mansions by Mudéjar and Christian artisans.

Carmona stands just off the A4, 38km east of Seville.

ESSENTIAL INFORMATION

TOURIST OFFICE // The helpful **tourist office** (☎ 954 19 09 55; www.turismo.carmona.org; ☉ 10am-6pm Mon-Sat, 10am-3pm Sun & holidays) is inside the Puerta de Sevilla.

WALKING TOUR

Distance: 2.3km
Duration: two to three hours
You can walk through the best of old Carmona in an easy stroll, starting from the **Puerta de Sevilla (1)**, the impressive main gate of the old town, which has been fortified for well over 2000 years. Today it houses the tourist office and the **Alcázar de la Puerta de Sevilla** (adult/child €2/1, Mon free; ☉ 10am-6pm Mon-Sat, 10am-3pm Sun & holidays), which has hawklike views from its Almohad patio.

From the Puerta de Sevilla walk up the central Calle Prim to Plaza de San Fernando (or Plaza Mayor), whose 16th-century buildings are painted a pretty variety of colours. Just off this square, the patio of the 17th-century **ayuntamiento** (2; ☎ 954 14 00 11; Calle El Salvador; admission free; ☉ 8am-3pm Mon-Fri, 4-6pm Tue & Thu) contains a large, very fine Roman mosaic showing the Gorgon Medusa.

Calle Martín López de Córdoba leads northeast off Plaza de San Fernando past the noble **Palacio de los Ruedas (3)** to the splendid **Iglesia Prioral de Santa María (4;** ☎ 954 19 14 82; admission €3; ☉ 9am-2pm & 5.30-7.30pm Mon-Fri, 9am-2pm Sat). Santa María was built mainly in the 15th and 16th centuries, on the site of the former main mosque. The Patio de los Naranjos by which you enter (formerly the mosque's ablutions courtyard) has a 6th-century Visigothic calendar carved into one of its pillars. Note that the above opening hours are very flexible!

An interesting background of the town can be explored at the **Museo de la Ciudad (5;** City History Museum; ☎ 954 14 01 28; www.museociudad.carmona.org; Calle San Ildefonso 1; adult/child €3/free, Tue free; ☉ 10am-2pm & 6.30-8.30pm Mon-Fri, 9.30am-2pm Sat & Sun 16 Jun-31 Aug, 11am-7pm Tue-Sun, 11am-2pm Mon rest of year), behind the church of Santa María. The Roman and Tartessos sections, the latter including a unique collection of large earthenware vessels with Middle Eastern decorative motifs, are the highlights. Labels are in Spanish only.

From the Iglesia de Santa María, Calle Santa María de Gracia and Calle de Dolores Quintanilla continue to the mightily impressive **Puerta de Córdoba (6)**, which was originally one of the Roman gates protecting access to the city.

Retracing your steps, head back uphill and turn southwest down Calle Calatrava, to reach the **Iglesia de Santiago (7)**, with a pretty Mudéjar tower. South

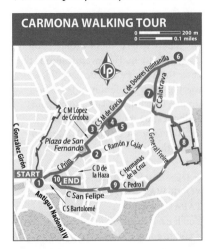

CARMONA WALKING TOUR

of here are the ruins of the **Alcázar (8)** fortress, with the luxury parador (state-owned hotel) built within its precinct.

Start back along Puerta de Marchena, on the southern rim of the town, then head into the tangle of streets to see the 14th-century **Iglesia de San Felipe (9)**, notable for its pretty brick Mudéjar tower and Renaissance facade, and the 15th- to 18th-century **Iglesia de San Bartolomé (10)**.

EXPLORING CARMONA

❦ NECRÓPOLIS ROMANA // DESCEND INTO THE UNDERWORLD

Are you scared of ghosts? If so, keep well away from the **Necrópolis Romana** (Map p66; Roman cemetery; ☎ 955 64 95 53; Avenida de Jorge Bonsor s/n; admission free; ⏲ 9am-6pm Tue-Fri, 9am-3.30pm Sat & Sun, 8.30am-3.30pm holidays) on the southwestern edge of town. In the 1st and 2nd centuries AD a dozen or more family tombs were hewn into the rock here, some of them elaborate and many-chambered. Most of the dead were cremated, and in the tombs are wall niches for the boxlike stone urns containing the ashes.

It used to be possible to clamber down into many of these tombs but nowadays you'll have to be content with peering down into them. However, you can still enter the huge **Tumba de Servilia**, which was the tomb of a family of Hispano-Roman bigwigs. The site also contains an interesting museum and across the street is a 1st-century-BC **Roman amphitheatre**.

❦ DES TAPA CARMONA // GORGE YOUR WAY AROUND CARMONA'S TAPAS TRAIL

You'll need to have had a small breakfast if you're going to survive Carmona's very own tapas trail. The tourist office has produced a map and route description, **Des Tapa Carmona**, that takes you through the 20 best tapas bars in town – an impressive number for so small a place! See how many you can squeeze in by closing time.

GASTRONOMIC HIGHLIGHTS

❦ BAR GOYA €

☎ 954 14 30 60; Calle Prim 2; tapas €2, raciones €8
From the kitchens of this ever-crammed bar come forth the finest tapas that lips in Carmona can wrap themselves around. As well as all the meaty and fishy standards vegetarians will be delighted to know that it produces an excellent spinach and chickpea vegie special.

❦ MOLINO DE LA ROMERA €€

☎ 954 14 20 00; Calle Sor Ángela de la Cruz 8; mains €12-20; ⏲ lunch only Sun, Tue-Fri, lunch & dinner Sat, closed Mon & second half Jul
Serving hearty, well-prepared, very traditional Andalusian meals in a lovely 15th-century oil mill with views to the valley below. This is one of the nicest places to eat in Carmona and, if you fancy something lighter, there's a bar and cafe as well.

❦ RESTAURANTE SAN FERNANDO €€

☎ 954 14 35 56; Calle Sacramento 3; mains €14-20; ⏲ 1.30-4pm Tue-Sun, 9pm-midnight Tue-Sat, closed Aug
This classy restaurant, overlooking Plaza de San Fernando, uses the freshest market produce to create exciting dishes. How exciting? How does a meal of cream of green apple soup followed by stuffed salmon pastries, then pears in red wine to finish sound? It's also renowned for its *bacalao* (salted cod).

TRANSPORT

PARKING // There's around-the-clock underground parking on Paseo del Estatuto (24 hr €11). Parking in the old town is very limited.

BUS // Casal runs buses to Seville roughly every half-hour from the bus stop on Paseo del Estatuto. Two buses a day go to Córdoba via Écija from the car park next to the Puerta de Sevilla.

OSUNA

pop 17,430 / elevation 330m

Osuna could make a song and a dance about its stash of beautifully preserved baroque mansions, but instead it chooses to lay low and is a sleepy and unassuming kind of place. It is also a fairly pious town, thanks to an impressive Spanish Renaissance monastery and a large community of nuns, but it's one that is well worth a bit of your time.

It is 91km southeast of Seville, along the Granada–Seville A92.

ESSENTIAL INFORMATION

TOURIST OFFICE // The **Municipal Tourist Office** (☎ 954 81 57 32; Calle Carnera 82; ⏰ 9.30am-1.30pm & 4-6pm Tue-Sat, 9.30am-1.30pm Sun).

EXPLORING OSUNA

🌿 BAROQUE MANSIONS // GAZE AT THE ARTISTIC BEAUTY OF OSUNA'S MANSIONS

You can't go inside most of Osuna's mansions, but their facades are still mesmerising. One is the **Palacio de los Cepeda** (Calle de la Huerta), behind the town hall, with rows of Churrigueresque columns topped by stone halberdiers holding the Cepeda family coat of arms. The 1737 portal of the **Palacio de Puente Hermoso** (Palacio de Govantes y Herdara; Calle Sevilla 44), a couple of blocks west of Plaza Mayor, has twisted pillars encrusted with grapes and vine leaves.

The **Cilla del Cabildo Colegial** (Calle San Pedro 16) bears a sculpted representation of Seville's Giralda. Further down, the **Palacio del Marqués de La Gomera** (Calle San Pedro 20) has elaborate pillars, with the family shield at the top of the facade. This is now a hotel – step inside for a drink.

🌿 COLEGIATA & AROUND // DELVE INTO A RICH RELIGIOUS HERITAGE

The **Colegiata de Santa María de la Asunción** (☎ 954 81 04 44; Plaza de la Encarnación; admission by guided tour only €2.50; ⏰ 10am-1.30pm & 4-7pm Mon-Sat Oct-Apr, 10am-1.30pm & 4-7pm Tue-Sun May-Sep, closed Sun afternoon Jul & Aug) is a large 16th-century former collegiate church containing a wealth of fine art and treasure collected by the Duques de Osuna.

The guided tour (in Spanish only) also includes the lugubrious underground Sepulcro Ducal, created in 1548 with its own chapel as the family vault of the Osunas, who are entombed in wall niches.

Opposite the Colegiata is the **Monasterio de la Encarnación** (☎ 954 81 11 21; Plaza de la Encarnación; admission €2; ⏰ 10am-1.30pm & 4-7pm Mon-Sat Oct-Apr, 10am-1.30pm & 4-7pm Tue-Sun May-Sep, closed Sun afternoon Jul & Aug), now Osuna's museum of religious art and well worth a visit. The 18th-century tiles in the cloister are among the most beautiful of all *sevillano* tilework, and the monastery church is richly decked with baroque sculpture and art. Entry is by guided tour only (in Spanish) which is led by one of the resident nuns.

GASTRONOMIC HIGHLIGHTS

🌿 RESTAURANTE DOÑA GUADALUPE €€

☎ 954 81 05 58; Plaza Guadalupe 6; 4-course menú €15, mains €17-19; ⏰ closed Tue & 1-15 Aug; 🞖
To the contented murmurings of its numerous patrons the Doña Guadalupe, on

a small square between Calles Quijada and Gordillo (both off Calle Carrera), serves up quality Andalusian fare from partridge with rice to wild asparagus casserole. There's a good list of Spanish wines too.

ÉCIJA

pop 38,900 / elevation 110m

Of all the towns of the La Campiña region Écija (*ess*-i-ha) is currently the one least likely to receive visitors. At first glance this is fairly understandable; the town lacks any dramatic 'must see' sights, the outskirts are fairly grim and there's a chronic lack of decent (or even poor) accommodation. But this very lack of visitors means that *la ciudad de las torres* (the city of towers) offers a genuine insight into small-town Andalusian life. And the city of towers label? Well, OK, the town does have one worthwhile calling card – a stack of Gothic-Mudéjar palaces and churches, the towers of which glitter in the sun.

Talking of the sun, you might want to avoid visiting Écija during high summer because it's then that the town's other nickname, *la sartén de Andalucía* (the frying pan of Andalucía), comes to the fore with temperatures frequently approaching a sweaty 45°C.

Écija lies 53km east along the A4 from Carmona.

ESSENTIAL INFORMATION

TOURIST OFFICE // The helpful **tourist office** (☎ 955 90 00 00; www.turismoecija.com; Plaza de España 1; ☼ 10am-6pm Mon-Fri, 10am-2pm Sat, Sun & holidays) is in the front of the *ayuntamiento* (town hall) on the central plaza.

EXPLORING ÉCIJA

The centre of life in Écija is the cafe-lined Plaza de España; before you dive into the old quarter which surrounds this square

you'd be wise to drop by **Casa Emilio** (☎ 954 83 15 30; Plaza de España 24) for a drink and a spot of people-watching.

☙ CHURCHES & BELL TOWERS // CRANE YOUR NECK UP, UP AND UP

The famed **Iglesia de Santa María** (Plaza Santa María), just off Plaza de España, has one of Écija's finest church towers. Further startling towers an be found on the **Iglesia de San Juan** (Plaza San Juan) and the **Convento de San Pablo y Santo Domingo** (Plazuela de Santo Domingo) – the latter hung with a gigantic set of rosary beads. The **Parroquia Mayor de Santa Cruz** (Plazuela de Nuestra Señora del Valle; admission free; ☼ 9am-1pm & 5-8pm Mon-Sat, 10am-1pm & 5-8pm Sun May-Sep, 9am-1pm & 6-8pm Mon-Sat, 10am-1pm & 6-9pm Sun Oct-Apr) is Écija's parish church but was once the town's principal mosque and still has traces of Islamic features and some Arabic inscriptions.

☙ PALACES // PRACTISE LIVING LIKE ROYALTY

The huge 18th-century **Palacio de Peñaflor** (Calle Emilio Castelar 26) or 'the palace of the long balconies' is Écija's most iconic image. Its attractive curved facade is lined with frescoes, but the interior was closed to visitors at time of research due to renovations. The impressive 16th- to 18th-century **Palacio de los Palma** (☎ 955 90 20 82; Calle Espíritu Santo 10; admission €3; ☼ 10am-2pm) has a porticoed patio and richly decorated halls with Mudéjar *artesonados*.

☙ MUSEO HISTÓRICO MUNICIPAL // LESSON 101: ROMAN HISTORY

The handsome 18th-century Palacio de Benamejís houses the fascinating **Museo Histórico Municipal** (☎ 954 83 04 31; Plaza de la Constitución 1; admission free; ☼ 10am-2.30pm Tue-Fri, 10am-2pm & 8-10pm Sat, 10am-3pm Sun & holidays Jun-Sep, 10am-1.30pm & 4.30-6.30pm Tue-Fri, 10am-2pm

& 5.30-8pm Sat, 10am-3pm Sun & holidays Oct-May).
Pride of place goes to the best Roman finds from the area, including a full-sized sculpture of an Amazon (legendary female warrior), an athlete's torso and a white marble male head (possibly the god Mars).

GASTRONOMIC HIGHLIGHTS

🐦 BODEGÓN DEL GALLEGO €€
☎ 954 83 26 18; Calle Arcipreste Juan Aparicio 3; mains €10-15

Pass through the wooden doors here and you enter the watery and green world of Galician cuisine. It's all about seafood in Galicia so what better thing to munch than octopus Galician style (€12.95) – it's a style that suits most people. The speciality though is the goose barnacles *(percebes gallegos).*

CAZALLA DE LA SIERRA

pop 5242 / elevation 600m
This attractive little white town sits on a hilltop 85km northeast of Seville, and is the gateway for exploring the Parque Natural Sierra Norte, which stretches out to the west. Cazalla has a great little selection of places to stay and pleasant local walks through the surrounding woods.

ESSENTIAL INFORMATION

TOURIST OFFICE // The tourist office (☎ 954 88 35 62; ⏰ 10am-2pm Tue & Wed, 10am-2pm & 6-8pm Thu-Sat, 10am-1pm Sun) is on Plaza Mayor, next to the Iglesia de la Consolación.

EXPLORING CAZALLA DE LA SIERRA

🐦 LA CARTUJA DE CAZALLA // LEARN A NEW CRAFT IN THE SHADOW OF HISTORY
This large 15th-century monastery, La Cartuja de Cazalla (☎ 954 88 45 16; www

.cartujadecazalla.com; adult/child €5/1; ⏰ 9am-2pm & 4-8pm), is situated in a beautiful, secluded nook of the Sierra Morena, 4km from Cazalla (take the signposted turn-off from the A455 Constantina road, 2.5km from Cazalla). Built on the site of an Islamic mill and mosque (which in turn is said to have been built on a Roman religious site), the monastery fell into ruin in the 19th century. In 1977 it was bought by art lover Carmen Ladrón de Guevara, who is devotedly restoring it, in part as an arts centre and the restored church functions as a concert hall. As well as making a quick tour of the monastery you could also join a course in ceramics, painting and horse riding. A good guest house is part of the project (see p382).

🐦 HIKING // PUT YOUR BEST FOOT FORWARD
Two tracks lead from Cazalla down to the Huéznar Valley and by combining them you can enjoy a round trip of 9km. They pass through typical Sierra Norte evergreen oak woodlands, olive groves and small cultivated plots, plus the odd chestnut wood and vineyard.

One track is the Sendero de las Laderas, which starts at El Chorrillo fountain on the eastern edge of Cazalla at the foot of Calle Parras. A 'Sendero de las Laderas 900m' sign on Paseo El Moro, just down from the Posada del Moro, directs you to this starting point. The path leads down to the Puente de los Tres Ojos bridge on the Río Huéznar, from where you go up the western bank of the river a short way, then head west under the Puente del Castillejo railway bridge (first take a break at the picnic area on the far bank, if you like) and return to Cazalla by the Camino Viejo de la Estación (Old Station Track).

GASTRONOMIC HIGHLIGHTS

♣ AGUSTINA RESTAURANTE €

☎ 954 88 32 55; www.agustinarestaurante.com; Plaza del Concejo s/n; tapas €2, raciones €10

This discreet, truly excellent restaurant is a breath of fresh, young air compared with all the olde-worlde places that fill these hills. The youthful owners create traditional sierra dishes with a nod to the wider world. The *magret de pato con miel y vinagre de módena* (duck with honey and vinegar) is sensational. If you just want a tapas snack then try the speciality *queso de cabra con miel* (goats cheese with honey).

♣ LAS NAVEZUELAS €€

☎ 954 88 47 64; www.lasnavezuelas.com; 2km south of town along the A432; menú €19

Several nights a week this *finca* (farm) hotel (see p382) prepares superb meals the old-fashioned way. In other words, they try to use only produce that's sprouted out of the farm's very own soil. The difference reveals itself in the wonderful tastes and a perfect ambience; with soft classical music playing in the background and the managers' real attention to service. It all helps to make this one of the nicest places to eat in the sierra. It's open to nonguests if you reserve in advance.

♣ PALACIO DE SAN BENITO €€

☎ 954 88 33 36; www.palaciodesanbenito.com; Paseo El Moro; menú €25, mains €12-15

Dine like a medieval lord or lady under the gaze of stag heads in the banquet hall of this magnificent hotel restaurant (open to all but reservations are recommended) where the emphasis is on country specialities such as venison, partridge and salmon. The daily *menú* is very good value.

PARQUE NATURAL SIERRA NORTE

You could spend days drifting around the lazy back roads of the sierra enjoying

~ WORTH A TRIP ~

If you're heading north into Extremadura, or just fancy a day out from Cazalla de la Sierra, don't miss the magnificent vistas from the highest point in Sevilla province, **La Capitana** (Map pp64-5), which soars 959m.

Head north on the A432 from Cazalla, pass Alanís and continue 11km along the A432 to Guadalcanal. At a junction as you enter this village, follow the 'Sendero de la Capitana' sign pointing to the right up a bypass road. After 1.5km, above the village, turn left down a minor road, then almost immediately right up an unpaved road with another 'Sendero de la Capitana' sign. Though signposted as a *sendero* (footpath) this is perfectly driveable, with a little care, in a car of normal clearance. Follow the track as it climbs in a general northwest direction along the Sierra del Viento (Windy Range), taking the major track at all forks. Expansive views open out as you pass an observatory on the left after 1.6km and TV towers up on the right after 2.1km and 4.3km. Keep your eyes open for vultures and birds of prey roaming the updrafts. Some 500m after passing below the second TV tower, you pass through a gate: just beyond it, park and follow the 'Mirador de la Sierra del Viento 300m' sign to the hilltop, and the summit, ahead of you.

Return the way you came.

the gentle vibes, numerous walking trails and shining white villages. Having your own wheels is a huge advantage.

At least 14 walks of a few hours each are signposted in various areas. The routes are shown on the IGN/Junta de Andalucía 1:100,000 map *Parque Natural Sierra Norte,* and described in Spanish in the booklet *Rutas Comarcales: Sierra Norte de Sevilla.*

EXPLORING PARQUE NATURAL SIERRA NORTE

❦ VILLAGES & MOUNTAIN TRAILS // BACK LANES THROUGH THE SIERRA

A pleasant village of broad cobbled streets, **El Pedroso** lies 16km south of Cazalla de la Sierra on the A432 from Seville. The **Sendero del Arroyo de las Cañas**, a 10km marked walking route around the flattish country west of El Pedroso, beginning opposite Bar Triana on the western side of town, is one of the prettiest walks in the park. It goes through a landscape strewn with boulders and, in spring, gorgeous wild flowers.

Constantina is the largest town in the Sierra Norte and home of the Parque Natural Sierra Norte's visitor centre, the **Centro de Interpretación El Robledo** (☎ 955 88 15 97; Carretera Constantina-El Pedroso Km1). It has interesting displays on the park's flora, fauna and history, and a clearly labelled botanical garden of Andalusian plants that is a picture in spring. The opening hours are somewhat random, so it's worth calling ahead for details. The western side of Constantina is topped by a ruined Almoravid-era **Islamic fort** – worth the climb for the views alone. Below are the medieval streets and 18th-century mansions of the **Barrio de la Morería.**

The **Sendero Los Castañares**, a 7km marked walk, starts from the north end of Paseo de la Alameda in the north of town. It takes you up through thick chestnut woods to a hilltop viewpoint, then back into Constantina below the fort (about two hours in total).

TRANSPORT

CAR // It's a definite advantage to have your own set of wheels in order to explore the sierra in any depth.

BUS // Buses wind along the mountain roads between Cazalla de la Sierra and Seville five to six times a day during the week, twice on Saturdays and three times on Sundays.

SEVILLE

HUELVA PROVINCE

3 PERFECT DAYS

DAY 1 // DOÑANA DAYS

Most visitors to Huelva province have only one word on their mind – Doñana. The perfect Doñana day will involve a half-day park tour (p86). Cross your fingers and hope to spot that lynx! Cat sightings or not, head back to El Rocío after your safari and dine at the Aires de Doñana (p97). In the late afternoon grab some binoculars and take a hike around the Charco de la Boca (p86), a 3.5km walk where close encounters of the furry and feathered kind are a given.

DAY 2 // OVERGROUND, UNDERGROUND

This day will give you a brief glimpse of the delights of the Sierra de Aracena – both above and below the ground! Skip through the flower meadows on the walk from Alájar to Castaño del Robledo (p102), but instead of following this route on to Galaroza turn around in Castaño del Robledo and loop back to Alájar so making a pleasant three-hour hike. From Alájar drive to Aracena for lunch at the Mesón Rural las Tinajas (p101), and then see the sierra (and some rock-shaped bottoms) from underneath at the Gruta de las Maravillas (p100).

DAY 3 // TO AMERICA!

Don your sea legs, because today you're off to discover America! The Monasterio de la Rábida (p82) is where Columbus drummed up support for his idea to discover new worlds. Pop round to the Casa Museo Martín Alonso Pinzón, in nearby Palos de la Frontera (p82), where one of Columbus' captains lived. Finish up in the pleasant town of Moguer (p82), where you'll find several Columbus-related sites.

HUELVA

· · · · · ·

pop 145,763

Unassuming Huelva is a modern, unsentimental, industrial port city that knows that you have to work hard for a living. Perhaps it's this attitude that has meant it has never really felt the need to tart itself up for the tourist industry and, consequently, tourists have generally kept away. While it's true that there isn't a lot to see or do here, central Huelva is a likeable, lively place and the city's people are noted for their warmth.

Though there's little evidence of it today, Huelva's history dates back an impressive 3000 years to the Phoenician town of Onuba, one of several locations postulated for the legendary Tartessos. Today Huelva has a sizeable fishing fleet, a dose of petrochemical industry and, it's one nod to tourism, an excellent museum filled with ancient Roman and modern Andalusian art.

ESSENTIAL INFORMATION

TOURIST INFORMATION // Municipal Tourist Information Kiosk (☎ 959 25 12 18; Plaza de las Monjas; ◷ 10am-2pm & 3.30-8.30pm Mon-Fri, 10am-2pm & 4.30-6.30pm Sat) Regional Tourist Office (☎ 959 25 74 03; othuelva@ andalucia.org; Plaza Alcalde Coto Mora 2; ◷ 9am-7.30pm Mon-Fri, 10am-2pm Sat & Sun) Well informed and helpful.

ORIENTATION

Huelva's central area is about 1sq km, with the main bus station on Calle Doctor Rubio at its western edge, and the train station on Avenida de Italia at its southern edge. The main street is Avenida Martín Alonso Pinzón (also called Gran Vía). Parallel to Avenida Pinzón, one block south, is a long, narrow, pedestrianised shopping street that runs through several names west to east, from Calle Concepción to Calle Berdigón.

EXPLORING HUELVA

Despite a history that heads way back to sometime just before the year dot, modern Huelva contains very little to waylay the expectant visitor.

🌹 MUSEO PROVINCIAL // DISCOVER ROMAN RELICS AND DARING ART

A short walk to the east of the city centre, the Museo Provincial (☎ 959 65 04 24; Alameda Sundheim 13; non-EU/EU citizens €1.50/free; ◷ 2.30-8.30pm Tue, 9am-8.30pm Wed-Sat, 9am-2.30pm Sun) is stuffed to the gills with art and history. The museum's permanent exhibitions concentrate on the province's archaeological pedigree, especially its Roman and mining history (see p98). Perhaps of greater interest are the constantly changing temporary exhibitions which showcase some fantastic work by pioneering young Spanish artists. When we last visited there was an incredible exhibition of sculptures created out of all kinds of scrap. Labelling is in Spanish only.

🌹 PARAJE NATURAL MARISMAS DEL ODIEL // SING ALONG WITH THE BIRDS OF ODIEL

This 72-sq-km wetland reserve, across the Odiel estuary from Huelva, harbours a large, varied bird population, including up to 1000 blushing-pink greater flamingos in winter. There are also about 4000 pairs of spoonbills, plus ospreys, grey and purple herons and many other waterfowl.

(Continued on page 80)

HUELVA PROVINCE

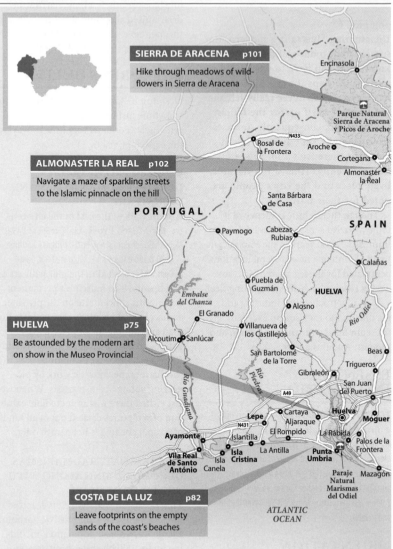

SIERRA DE ARACENA   p101

Hike through meadows of wild-flowers in Sierra de Aracena

ALMONASTER LA REAL   p102

Navigate a maze of sparkling streets to the Islamic pinnacle on the hill

HUELVA   p75

Be astounded by the modern art on show in the Museo Provincial

COSTA DE LA LUZ   p82

Leave footprints on the empty sands of the coast's beaches

GETTING AROUND

Travelling around Huelva province by private vehicle is a breeze with fast, toll-free roads linking the main towns and beautiful bendy back roads linking the smaller settlements. Parking is only ever a problem in Huelva itself and the beach resorts in summer; these are also the only places with paid parking and any car crime issues. Public transport to the smaller centres can be quite limited.

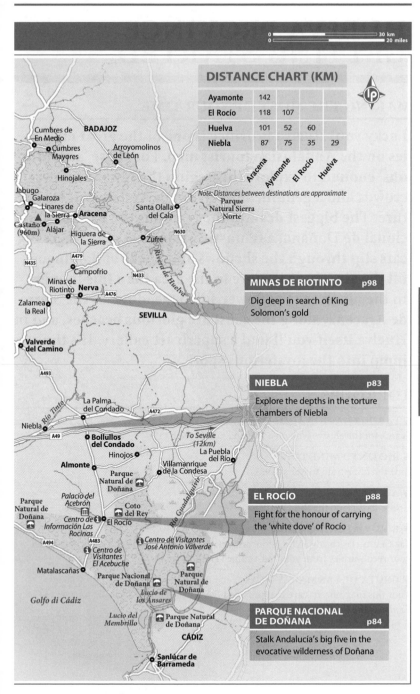

DISTANCE CHART (KM)				
Ayamonte	142			
El Rocío	118	107		
Huelva	101	52	60	
Niebla	87	75	35	29
	Aracena	Ayamonte	El Rocío	Huelva

Note: Distances between destinations are approximate

MINAS DE RIOTINTO   p98

Dig deep in search of King Solomon's gold

NIEBLA   p83

Explore the depths in the torture chambers of Niebla

EL ROCÍO   p88

Fight for the honour of carrying the 'white dove' of Rocío

PARQUE NACIONAL DE DOÑANA   p84

Stalk Andalucía's big five in the evocative wilderness of Doñana

HUELVA PROVINCE

HUELVA PROVINCE
GETTING STARTED

MAKING THE MOST OF YOUR TIME

Lucky you! Huelva province is one of the great mysteries on the Andalusian tourist map. For those 'adventurous' enough to explore this region the reward is fewer crowds and a genuine immersion in Andalusian culture. The biggest draw of the region is the Parque Nacional de Doñana, a fantastic wilderness area where big cats slip through the shadows and flocks of flamingos fill the air. There is more to the area than this though: to the north are the flower-filled meadows of the Sierra de Aracena, along the coast are glorious beaches, and in Huelva itself you'll find a superb art gallery. It's time to jump into the mysterious spot!

TOP TOURS

PARQUE NACIONAL DE DOÑANA
Search for the elusive lynx on a Doñana safari (p86).

RIOTINTO MINE TOUR
Ride the mine train to Mars (p98).

AYAMONTE BOAT TRIP
Cruise in style up the Río Guadiana (p84).

BIRDWATCHING TOUR
Take a top-class birdwatching tour with an expert expat guide and learn how to tell your reed warbler from your red-rumped swallow (p86).

GRUTA DE LAS MARAVILLAS
Tour this magnificent cave that provided the location for sci-fi classic *Journey to the Centre of the Earth* (p100).

GETTING AWAY FROM IT ALL

Huelva province *is* getting away from it all. In fact, the only places you might feel as if you're drowning in crowds are Huelva city itself and the beach resorts in high summer.

★ **Parque Nacional de Doñana** Doñana offers the largest road-free tract of wilderness in Western Europe (p84)

★ **Sierra de Aracena** Indulge in a sleepy picnic in the beautiful wildflower meadows of the Sierra de Aracena (p101)

★ **The beaches** As crowded as a can of sardines in the summer; come winter and you can walk for miles down stormy beaches with only gulls for company (p82)

ADVANCE PLANNING

As quiet and easy as travel is here, at times a little advance planning goes a long way.

★ **Doñana tours** Whether run by the park authorities or a private operator, demand far outstretches supply during the busy holiday periods so book ahead (p86)

★ **Romería del Rocío** If you're planning on galloping into El Rocío during the legendary pilgrimage you'll need to book a room in advance – two years in advance! (p88)

★ **Gruta de las Maravillas** If you want to journey to the centre of the earth then it's a good idea to book your tour in advance during the school holidays (p100)

★ **Binoculars** This is world-class twitching territory, so don't forget to bring your binoculars if you want to be able to tell your flamingo from your sparrow

TOP BIRDWATCHING SPOTS

❦ **PARAJE NATURAL MARISMAS DEL ODIEL**
Thousands of herons, spoonbills and other waterfowl (p75)

❦ **MATALASCAÑAS**
The beach east of the town is a hot spot for gulls, terns and waders (p83)

❦ **CHARCO DE LA BOCA**
Egrets, storks, bitterns and purple gallinules (p86)

❦ **PARQUE NACIONAL DE DOÑANA**
Spanish imperial eagles, glossy ibises and flocks of flamingos (p84)

❦ **CASTILLO DE LOS GUZMÁN**
Hundreds of hawks, kites and falcons (p83)

❦ **SIERRA DE ARACENA**
Walk through the wildflowers and spot birds in the woodlands (p101)

RESOURCES

★ **Turismo de Huelva** (www.turismohuelva
.org) Official website of the Huelva province tourist board

★ **Sierra de Aracena** (www.sierradearacena
.net, in Spanish) Everything you ever wanted to know – and much that you didn't know – about the mountainous north

★ **Doñana** (http://reddeparquesnacionales.mma
.es, in Spanish) Spanish government website for national parks; click on the link for the Parque Nacional de Doñana

HUELVA PROVINCE

(Continued from page 75)

The marshes can be reached by car along the A497 Punta Umbría road west from Huelva. Cross either of the parallel bridges over Río Odiel, then follow 'PN Marismas del Odiel' signs to reach the **Centro de Visitantes Anastasio Senra** (Visitor Centre Anastasio Senra; ☎ 959 50 90 11; ☾ 10am-2pm & 6-8pm Tue-Sun Apr-Sep, 10am-2pm & 4-6pm Tue-Sun Oct-Mar). South of here, several paths to good birdwatching spots strike off the road through the reserve, but some are only opened to guided groups (€8); check at the visitor centre.

FESTIVALS & EVENTS

Fiestas Colombinas From 29 July to 3 August each year, Huelva celebrates Columbus' departure for the Americas (3 August 1492) with this six-day festival of music, dancing, funfairs, cultural events and bullfighting.

GASTRONOMIC HIGHLIGHTS

It might come as something of a surprise to discover that Huelva is nothing to sing about when it comes to food.

♥ LAS CANDELAS €€
☎ 959 31 83 01; Avenida Huelva s/n, Aljaraque; mains €12-18; ☾ closed Sun

Huelva's most renowned restaurant is 7km west of the city in the town of Aljaraque. This old inn, with its wood-panelled bar and toasty open fireplace, specialises in delicious fresh fish for hot summer nights and *carnes a la brasa* (chargrilled meats) for cooler winter evenings. To get to there turn off the A497 Punta Umbría road at the Aljaraque sign and you'll see the restaurant as you enter the town.

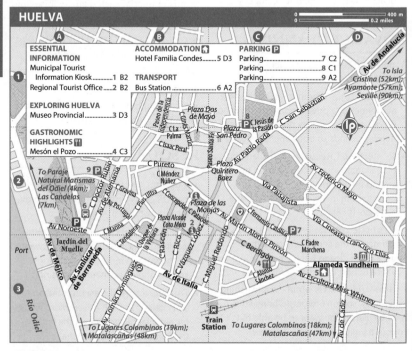

HUELVA PROVINCE

HUELVA
0 _____ 400 m
0 _____ 0.2 miles

ESSENTIAL INFORMATION	ACCOMMODATION 🏠	PARKING 🅿
Municipal Tourist Information Kiosk 1 B2	Hotel Familia Condes........5 D3	Parking...............7 C2
Regional Tourist Office 2 B2	**TRANSPORT**	Parking...............8 C1
	Bus Station 6 A2	Parking...............9 A2

EXPLORING HUELVA
Museo Provincial 3 D3

GASTRONOMIC HIGHLIGHTS 🍴
Mesón el Pozo 4 C3

To Isla Cristina (52km); Ayamonte (57km); Seville (90km);

Av de Andalucía

Plaza Dos de Mayo
Paseo de la Independencia
C/nes Martín
C/ta Palma
C/Isaac Peral
Plaza San Pedro
Jesús de la Pasión
C San Sebastián
Av Pablo Rada

Paseo Santa Fe

C Pureto
C Méndez Núñez
Plaza Quintero Baez
Av Federico Mayo
Via Paisajista

To Paraje Natural Marismas del Odiel (4km); Las Candelas (7km)
C/us Ultra
C Gravina
Av de Alemania
C Doctor Rubio
Av Portugal
Plaza Alcade Coto Mora
C Concepción
C Palacios
Plaza de las Monjas
Av Martín Alonso Pinzón
C Fernando Católico
Via Cineasta Francisco Elías

Av Noroeste
Marina
C/endaleras
Oduque de la Victoria
C Rascón
C Rico
C Vázquez López
C Miguel Redondo
C Berdigón
C Padre Marchena
3 🏛

Av de Méjico
Jardín del Muelle
Port
Av Sanlúcar de Barrameda
C Tomás Domínguez
Av de Italia
C Alonso Sánchez
Av Escultora Miss Whitney
Alameda Sundheim

Río Odiel
To Lugares Colombinos (19km); Matalascañas (48km)
Train Station
To Lugares Colombinos (18km); Matalascañas (47km)
Av de Cádiz

THE FOUR VOYAGES OF CHRISTOPHER COLUMBUS

In April 1492 Christopher Columbus (Cristóbal Colón to Spaniards) finally won Spanish royal support for his proposed westward voyage of exploration to the spice-rich Orient, a proposal that was to result in no fewer than four voyages by the great navigator and a fabulous golden age for Spain.

On 3 August 1492 Columbus embarked from Palos de la Frontera with 100 men and three ships. After a near mutiny as the crew despaired of finding land, they finally made landfall on the Bahamian island of Guanahaní on 12 October, naming it San Salvador. The expedition went on to discover Cuba and Hispaniola, where the *Santa María* sank. Its timbers were used to build a fort, Fuerte Navidad, which 33 Spaniards were left to hold. The *Niña* and the *Pinta* got back to Palos on 15 March 1493.

Columbus – with animals, plants, gold ornaments and six Caribbean Indians – received a hero's welcome on his return, as all were convinced that he had reached the fabled East Indies (in fact, his calculations were some 16,000km out).

Columbus made further voyages in 1493 and 1498, discovering Jamaica, Trinidad and the mouth of the Orinoco River. But he proved a disastrous colonial administrator, enslaving the indigenous people and alienating the Spanish settlers. Eventually his mishandling led to a revolt by settlers on Hispaniola and before he could suppress the uprising he was arrested by a royal emissary from Spain and sent home in chains. In a final attempt to redeem himself and find a strait to Asia, Columbus embarked on his fourth and final voyage in April 1502. This time he reached Honduras and Panama, but then became stranded for a year in Jamaica, having lost his ships to sea worms.

Columbus died in 1506 in Valladolid, northern Spain – impoverished and apparently still believing he had reached Asia. His remains were eventually returned to the Caribbean, as he had wished, before being brought back to Seville. Or were they? The story of Columbus' posthumous voyages has recently become quite a saga itself – see p41.

♣ MESÓN EL POZO €

☎ 959 25 42 40; Calle Alonso Sánchez 14; tapas €2-2.50, raciones €12; ⊗ closed Sun & Aug

This atmospheric back-street restaurant is always jam-packed with locals in search of a lunch with class. In a salty city like Huelva we probably don't need to tell you that it's the fruits of the sea that are the stars of the menu.

TRANSPORT

PARKING // There's street-side parking around the bus station and on Avenida Escultora Miss Whitney (parallel to Alameda Sundheim), and multistorey or underground car parks on Calle Doctor Rubio near the bus station, Calle Padre Marchena off Avenida Martín Alonso Pinzón, and Calle Jesús de la Pasión. These charge around €11 per 24 hours.

CAR // Poor signage and a user-unfriendly one-way system can make driving in Huelva a frustrating experience.

BUS // Most buses from the bus station (Calle Doctor Rubio s/n) are operated by Damas (☎ 959 25 69 00; www.damas-sa.es). Frequency to most destinations in Huelva province is reduced on Saturday, Sunday and public holidays. Destinations include daily buses to Aracena, Ayamonte, Lagos (Portugal) and Seville.

TRAIN // Three services daily run to Seville and once a day to Córdoba and Madrid from the train station (☎ 902 43 23 43; www.renfe.com; Avenida de Italia).

AROUND HUELVA

······

LUGARES COLOMBINOS

The Lugares Colombinos (Columbus Sites) are the three townships of La Rábida, Palos de la Frontera and Moguer, along the eastern bank of the Tinto estuary. All three played a key role in Columbus' preparation for his journey of discovery and can be visited in an enjoyable 40km return trip from Huelva.

❦ LA RÁBIDA // SEE WHERE COLUMBUS SULKED

In tiny La Rábida you'll find the not-so-tiny Monasterio de la Rábida (☎ 959 35 04 11; admission €3, audioguide €1.50; ◷ 10am-1pm & 4-7pm Tue-Sat Apr-Jul & Sep, 10am-1pm & 4-6.15pm Tue-Sat Oct-Mar, 10am-1pm & 4.45-8pm Tue-Sat Aug, 10.45am-1pm Sun year-round) where Columbus retreated after his grand plans to discover the sea route to the East Indies had been rejected by Portugal's King João II. Here Columbus met Abbot Juan Pérez, who took up his cause and drummed up support for his far-fetched plans to discover new lands and in the process make Spain very rich. Highlights of the 14th-century Mudéjar monastery include the church where Martín Alonso Pinzón, captain of the *Pinta*, is buried; a chapel with a 13th-century alabaster Virgin before which Columbus prayed; and the peaceful 15th-century cloister.

❦ PALOS DE LA FRONTERA // FIND A WORTHY CREW FOR YOUR SHIP

The small town of Palos de la Frontera is the next stop on your magical mystery voyage. The town provided Columbus with two of his ships, two captains (Martín Alonso Pinzón and Vicente Yañez Pinzón) and more than half his crew. It was from the port of Palos that the whole merry band set sail into the unknown.

In town the Casa Museo Martín Alonso Pinzón (☎ 959 10 00 41; Calle Cristóbal Colón 24; admission free; ◷ 10am-2pm & 5-9pm Tue-Sat) is the former home of the captain of the *Pinta*. Inside are changing exhibitions on themes related to Columbus and Palos.

❦ MOGUER // PRAY FOR A SAFE VOYAGE

From Palos de la Frontera it's a 7km drive along the A494 to the pretty icy-white town of Moguer. It was here that Columbus' ship, the *Niña*, was built. Simply taking a stroll round Moguer's pleasing-to-the-eye streets is a delight. There are fine buildings everywhere. The main Columbus site in town is the 14th-century Monasterio de Santa Clara (☎ 959 37 01 07; Plaza de las Monjas; guided tour €3; ◷ 11am-1pm & 5-7pm Tue-Fri, 11am-1pm Sat) where Columbus spent a night of vigil and prayer after returning from his first voyage. You'll see a lovely Mudéjar cloister and an impressive collection of Renaissance religious art. We can imagine that all this sightseeing has made you rather peckish. In which case Mesón El Lobito (☎ 959 37 06 60; Calle Rábida 31, Moguer; raciones €10; ◷ closed Wed), which occupies an old winery a couple of blocks west of Plaza del Cabildo, is an atmospheric restaurant that should be able to silence most rumbling tummies. Stacks of wine barrels and curious artefacts adorn the walls and locals occasionally sell home-grown fruit and vegetables. The fish and meat *a la brasa* (chargrilled) are tasty and the house wine is cheap.

COSTA DE LA LUZ

Sprawling along the coast is the Huelva province stretch of the Costa de la Luz –

a wild, soft-sand beach a world away from the 'Costa del Chaos' of Andalucía's Mediterranean coast. The main resort east of Huelva is Matalascañas, while to the west the biggest beaches of note are Isla Cristina and Ayamonte. All are unpretentious places, more popular with Spanish holidaymakers than visitors from overseas. Splashing about in the waves is the main event at any of these resorts, but a couple of low-key attractions add to the seaside fun.

♥ MATALASCAÑAS // LEARN ABOUT DOÑANA'S UNDERWATER ENVIRONMENT

Abutting the Doñana national and natural parks (p84) Matalascañas is a typical slap-it-up-quick, wham-bam-thank-you-ma'am tourist resort and the result is none too pretty. Fortunately, as is so often the case, Mother Nature is a lot more appealing than human nature and the beach here is simply gorgeous. The Parque Dunar (☎ 959 44 80 86; www.parque dunar.com; Avenida de las Adelfas; ☀ 9am-8pm) is a 1.3-sq-km expanse of high, pine-covered dunes at the west end of town laced with cycling routes and a maze of sandy pathways. Within this dune park is the interesting Museo del Mundo Marítimo (Museum of the Maritime World; ☎ 959 44 84 09; adult/child under 15yr €5.50/3.50; ☀ 11am-2.30pm & 6-9.30pm Tue-Sat, 11am-2.30pm Sun mid-Jun–mid-Sep, 10am-2pm & 3.30-6pm Tue-Sat, 10am-2pm Sun mid-Sep–mid-Jun) with five themed rooms devoted to the coasts and seas of the Doñana area and people's interaction with them.

♥ ISLA CRISTINA // MUNCH SEAFOOD BY THE SEASHORE

Isla Cristina is a developing beach resort and bustling fishing port with a 250-strong fleet. Birdwatchers will find some feathered friends among the waterways at the western end of the beach. For a succulent seafood lunch overlooking the waves the Restaurante Sol y Mar (☎ 959 33 20 50; Playa Central; mains €8-12; ☀ lunch & dinner Apr-Oct), which is part of the hotel of the same name, is easily the best value in town. It offers everything from hefty portions of crispy-fried sardines to delicious cockles in rice and swordfish steaks.

HUELVA PROVINCE

∼ WORTH A TRIP ∼

Twenty-five kilometres east of Huelva on the old A472 to Seville, and 4km north of the modern A49, stands the ancient town of Niebla, population 4000, encircled by 2km-long, red-ochre, Muslim-era walls. Complete with 50 towers and five gates, it has some of the most perfectly preserved medieval remains in Andalucía.

Inside the walls the major monument is the enormous 15th-century Castillo de los Guzmán (☎ 959 36 22 70; www.castillodeniebla.com; admission €4; ☀ 10am-10pm Sun-Fri Jun-Sep, 10am-3pm Sat Jul-Aug, 10am-2pm & 3-6pm Oct-May), built around two large patios. The upper floors of the castle contain displays recalling the town's history. Down in the dark and dank dungeons is a grisly and comprehensive torture museum that most people find fascinating, but then wonder if they should find it so fascinating! Niebla used to be famous for its falconry and come spring you won't fail to notice the reason for this fame; dozens of pale red kestrels and hawks nesting in the gaps of the castle walls. For a romantic evening take in one of the dance or drama productions staged here on Saturday nights in July and August.

☘ **AYAMONTE // ROW, ROW, ROW YOUR BOAT GENTLY OVER TO PORTUGAL**

Staring across the Río Guadiana to Portugal, **Ayamonte** has a cheerful border-town buzz. The old town is dotted with attractive plazas and old churches and riddled with cafes, shops and restaurants.

The town's **Parque Municipal** is noteworthy for its tinkling fountains, shady trees, a flock or two of macaws and the odd herd of zebras!

If you'd like to get to know more of the Río Guadiana, one of Spain's longest rivers, **Cruceros del Guadiana** (☎ 959 64 10 02) and **Transporte Fluvial del Guadiana** (☎ 959 47 06 11; www.rioguadiana.net) run daily cruises that head 35km upstream to the Portuguese village of Alcoutim (€50 including lunch, 7½ hours). Purchase tickets and check departure times from the kiosks on the ferry dock. If you're hungry then the **Casa Luciano** (Calle Palma del Condado 1; mains €14-18; ☒ closed Sun) is a great seafood restaurant. Everything on your plate is freshly cooked and only minutes out of the water. There's lamb or wild asparagus *revuelto* (scrambled-egg dish) if you fancy something more land-based.

For Portuguese-bound romantics it's possible to skip the fast modern road and enjoy a slower pace on the half-hourly **ferry** (adult/child/car €1.50/0.90/5; ☒ 9.30am-9pm Jul–mid Sep, 9.30am-8pm May-Jun & mid-Sep–Oct, 9.30am-7.30pm Nov-Apr) across the Guadiana to Portugal's Vila Real de Santo António.

EAST OF HUELVA

· · · · · ·

PARQUE NACIONAL DE DOÑANA

The Parque Nacional de Doñana is a place of haunting natural beauty and exotic horizons. It's a place where flocks of flamingos tinge the evening skies pink, huge herds of deer and boar flit between the trees and the beautiful Iberian lynx slinks ever closer to extinction. Here, in the largest roadless region in Western Europe, and Spain's most celebrated national park, you can literally taste the scent of nature at her most raw and powerful. It's as close as Europe gets to the wild majesty of Africa.

The 542-sq-km national park extends 32km along or close to the Atlantic coast and up to 25km inland. El Rocío (p88) and the town of Matalascañas (p83) are the most convenient locations for visiting the park. Much of the national park's perimeter is bordered by the separate Parque Natural de Doñana (Doñana Natural Park), under less strict protection, which comprises four distinct zones totalling 540 sq km and forming a buffer for the national park. The two *parques* together provide a refuge for 419 bird species and 39 types of mammal, including endangered species such as the Iberian lynx (with an estimated population of 50) and Spanish imperial eagle (about eight breeding pairs). It's also a crucial habitat for millions of migrating birds. About six million birds spend at least part of each year in the national park.

Since its inception in 1969 the national park has been under pressure from tourism, agriculture, hunters, developers and constructors. Many locals believe the park's interests take unfair priority over their own concerns about much-needed jobs. Meanwhile, ecologists argue that Doñana is increasingly hemmed in by tourism and agricultural schemes, roads and other infrastructure that threaten to deplete its water supplies and cut it off from other undeveloped areas. A great number of resident lynx are killed on the roads around Doñana. Recently a pregnant female was found dead next to the road; an autopsy on her body indicated that in the past she had also been shot, thus illustrating the numerous threats to Doñana's lynx population. It's not all bad news though, as for the past few years the lynx population has been steady at around 50 individuals. There's also an increasingly successful captive breeding program and the Sierra Morena in northern Andalucía is now thought to be a home to around 150 lynx. All this leads to hopes that there may be light ahead for the Iberian lynx.

ESSENTIAL INFORMATION

TOURIST OFFICES // The park's **Centro de Visitantes El Acebuche** (El Acebuche Visitor Centre; ☎ 959 44 87 39; Carretera A483 Km12; ◷ 8am-3pm & 4-9pm May-Sep, 8am-3pm & 4-7pm Oct-Apr) is just off the A483 Matalascañas–El Rocío road. The centre has an interactive exhibit on the park, a cafe and a shop with a large screen showing live video feeds of the Iberian lynxes in El Acebuche captive-breeding program. (The program itself is not open to visitors – see p347 for more information.) Here you'll also find good walking paths (1.5km and 3.5km round-trip) leading to birdwatching hides overlooking nearby lagoons. The national park has two other visitor centres on its western fringes, both also with paths to nearby lagoons: the **Centro de Información Las Rocinas** (☎ 959 44 23 40; ◷ 9am-3pm & 4-7pm Sep-Mar, to 8 or 9pm Apr-Aug), beside the A483 1km south of El Rocío, which has an exhibition on the history of the El Rocío pilgrimage; and the **Palacio del Acebrón** (◷ 9am-3pm & 4-7pm Sep-Mar, to 8 or 9pm Apr-Aug), 6km along a paved road west from Las Rocinas, housing an ethnographic exhibition of the park.

HUELVA PROVINCE

DOÑANA LIFE CYCLES

The many interwoven ecosystems that make up Parque Nacional de Doñana give rise to fantastic diversity. Nearly half the park is occupied by marshes. These are almost dry from July to October but in autumn they start to fill with water, eventually leaving only a few islets of dry land. Hundreds of thousands of waterbirds arrive from the north to winter here, including an estimated 80% of Western Europe's wild ducks. As the waters sink in spring, greater flamingos, spoonbills, storks, herons, avocets, hoopoes, bee-eaters, stilts and other birds arrive for the summer, many of them to nest. Fledglings flock around the ponds known as *lucios* and as these dry up in July, herons, storks and kites move in to feast on trapped perch.

Between the marshlands and the park's 28km-long beach is a band of sand dunes, pushed inland by the wind at a rate of up to 6m per year. The shallow valleys between the dunes, called *corrales*, host pines and other trees favoured as nesting sites by raptors. When dune sand eventually reaches the marshlands, rivers carry it back down to the sea, which washes it up on the beach – and the cycle begins all over again.

Elsewhere in the park, stable sands support 144 sq km of *coto*, the name given here to areas of woodland and scrub. *Coto* is the favoured habitat of many nesting birds and the park's abundant mammal population – 39 species including red and fallow deer, wild boars, mongooses and genets.

The park is also a haven for much smaller creatures, but ones that are no less spectacular. Reptiles and amphibians are abundant and include the charming spur-thighed tortoise, the less charming Lataste's viper, and the warty midwife toad.

EXPLORING PARQUE NACIONAL DE DOÑANA

To get the most out of the Doñana region you need to think carefully about your main interests – are you a birdwatcher who wants to focus on ticking off a rare type of moorhen or are you after a general-interest tour of the park? Do you want to explore on foot or are you happiest in a jeep?

For the general-interest explorer it'll be Doñana's Big Five (Iberian lynx, fallow deer, wild boar, Spanish imperial eagle and flamingo) that really light up the imagination, and though the chances of seeing either lynx or imperial eagle are somewhat limited, you do stand a very good chance of seeing the other three, as well as much more, on a general tour of the park.

❦ SAFARI // SAFARI IN SEARCH OF THE WORLD'S RAREST BIG CAT

Access to the interior of the national park is restricted, although anyone may walk along the 28km Atlantic beach between Matalascañas and the mouth of the Río Guadalquivir (which can be crossed by boats from Sanlúcar de Barrameda in Cádiz province), as long as they do not stray inland. To visit the interior of the national park, you must book a guided tour leaving either from El Acebuche visitor centre or from Sanlúcar de Barrameda (see p124). The tours from El Acebuche, in all-terrain vehicles each holding 20 people, are run by **Cooperativa Marismas del Rocío** (☎ 959 43 04 32/51; www.donanavisitas.es; per person €26; ☼ 8.30am & 3pm Tue-Sun mid-Sep–Apr, 8.30am & 5pm Mon-Sat May–mid-Sep). You need to book ahead by telephone – the tours can be full more than a month before in spring, summer and all holiday times.

Bring binoculars, if you can, plus mosquito repellent (except in winter) and drinking water (in summer). The tours last four hours.

These tours are perfect for the interested amateur who just wants an overview of the park, but for the dedicated nature-lover the tours organised by private operators, which have much more flexibility, are the way to go. These trips normally spend part of their time in the national park and part in the natural park, and range through pine and oak forests and across marshlands, with a great diversity of birds and high chances of seeing deer and boar. The following operators use smallish vehicles carrying a maximum of eight or nine people:

Discovering Doñana (☎ 959 44 24 66, 620 96 43 69; www.discoveringdonana.com; Calle Águila Imperial 150, El Rocío; 6hr trip 1-4 people €120, each extra person €30, 12hr trip 1-3 people €180, each extra person €45) Expert English-speaking guides; most trips are of broad interest but personalised tours also available; binoculars, telescopes, reference books available at no extra cost.

Doñana Bird Tours (☎ 955 75 53 99, 662 03 59 19; www.donanabirdtours.com; 9hr trip 1-3 people €150, each extra person €30) Top-class birdwatching tours led by resident British bird expert and author John Butler; also offers longer birdwatching holidays.

Doñana Nature (☎ 959 44 21 60, 630 97 82 16; www.donana-nature.com; Calle Las Carretas 10, El Rocío; 3½hr trip per person €25) Half-day trips, at 8am and 3.30pm daily, are general interest and may not go as far as the Valverde centre, but specialised ornithological and photographic trips are also offered; English- and French-speaking guides available.

❦ WALKS // WANDER THE WILDERNESS

The walking trails near the park's three visitor centres are an unmissable highlight, and are easy enough to be undertaken by most. The superb **Charco de la**

Boca path at the Las Rocinas centre is a 3.5km round-trip with four birdwatching hides and takes you through a range of habitats.

The more remote **Centro de Visitantes José Antonio Valverde** (⏰ 10am-7pm Sep-Mar, to 8pm or 9pm Apr-Aug), on the eastern edge of the park, is generally an excellent birdwatching spot as it overlooks a year-round *lucio* (pond). The Caño de Rosalimán waterway, just west of here, is also a fine site. The easiest way to reach the Valverde centre is by taking an authorised tour from El Rocío (see p88); the alternative is to drive yourself on rough roads from Villamanrique de la Condesa or La Puebla del Río to the northeast.

The March–May and September–November migration seasons are overall the most exciting for birdwatchers.

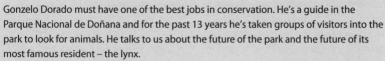

INTERVIEW: GONZELO DORADO

Gonzelo Dorado must have one of the best jobs in conservation. He's a guide in the Parque Nacional de Doñana and for the past 13 years he's taken groups of visitors into the park to look for animals. He talks to us about the future of the park and the future of its most famous resident – the lynx.

'I love my job because I am working in my hobby, I'm a birdwatcher and I get paid to go birdwatching! If you can manage to make your hobby your job then you will be happy.

'When I first started working in the park I used to see lots of lynx, maybe one a week, but now things are different and I haven't seen one for two years. Even so, the lynx breeding program has been successful. Three years ago they bred for the first time. It's hoped that in a few years time we can start to release them back into the park. Before this happens though we must save the rabbit population, which has crashed thanks to disease and other problems. Rabbits are the main food of the lynx so without a healthy rabbit population we cannot have a healthy lynx population.

'Today the park continues to grow. In 1969 it covered 35,000 hectares, but today it's more than three times that size. We buy land from the surrounding farmers and then let it return to its natural state. Even so the park faces many problems, mainly from agriculture and development. In the winter the beach resort of Matalascañas has a population of around 1000, but in summer it grows to around 200,000. This uses a huge amount of water which comes from the marshes and rivers around the park. In addition many people from Seville live here for the summer and commute every day to Seville. This traffic is a big problem as the road runs along the edge of the park and it's common for lynx and other animals to be killed on the road. There are only around 45 lynx so if just one dies it's a disaster.

'The local people have different attitudes to the park. Some like it, but others wish it would burn. This is normal because when you protect a place and tell locals they cannot do certain things they do not like it. It's mainly the people in the construction industry who dislike the park as they want to build all along the coast. We try to educate people about the park. We bring local school groups here and show them around. They are the important ones to educate, because they will be the ones who decide the future of Doñana.'

HUELVA PROVINCE

HUELVA PROVINCE

TRANSPORT

CAR & BUS // You cannot enter the park in your own vehicle. Buses between El Rocío and Matalascañas (see p82) will stop at the El Acebuche turn-off on the A483. Otherwise all tour companies, as well as the tours run by the national park, will pick you up from Matalascañas if you give advance notice.

EL ROCÍO

pop 1200

On first arriving in El Rocío many people simply shake their head in disbelief. With its sandy streets, bejewelled church, hoof prints, hitching posts and hat-clad honchos it's hard not to think of this extraordinary village as a Wild West film set come to life. But El Rocío has been around for a lot longer than either Hollywood or Clint Eastwood and there's nothing remotely fake about this important pilgrimage town. The quiet houses, with their sweeping verandahs, aren't merely show homes but are the well-tended properties of over 90 *hermandades* (brotherhoods) whose pilgrims converge on the town every Pentecost (Whitsuntide) for the Romería del Rocío, Spain's largest religious festival.

If the bizarre guns-at-noon atmosphere wasn't enough then El Rocío also impresses with its striking setting in front of luminous *marismas* (wetlands) where herds of deer drink at dawn and, at certain times of year, pink flocks of flamingos gather in massive numbers. Whatever way you look at it El Rocío is one of the most exotic villages in Europe.

ESSENTIAL INFORMATION

TOURIST OFFICE // The tourist office (☎ 959 44 38 08; Avenida de la Canaliega s/n; ☽ 9.30am-2pm & 4-6pm Tue-Fri, 9.30am-2pm Mon & Sat) is beside the main road (A483) at the western end of the village.

EXPLORING EL ROCÍO

Whether it's the play of the light on the marshes in front of the town, an old woman praying to the Virgin in the church or a girl passing by in a sultry flamenco dress there is always something of interest to catch the eye on the dusky, sand-blown streets.

❦ **ERMITA DEL ROCÍO // WITNESS THE RELIGIOUS DEVOTION OF ANDALUCÍA**
In the heart of the village stands the Ermita del Rocío (☎ 959 44 24 25; admission free; ☽ 8am-10pm), built in its present form in 1964. This is the home of the celebrated **Nuestra Señora del Rocío** (Our Lady of El Rocío), a small wooden image of the Virgin dressed in long, jewelled robes, which normally stands above the main altar. People arrive to see the Virgin every day of the year and especially on weekends, when the brotherhoods of El Rocío often gather here for colourful celebrations.

❦ **ROMERÍA DEL ROCÍO // BE CONSUMED BY THE PASSION OF THE VIRGIN**
Seven weeks after Easter El Rocío turns from a quiet backwater into an explosive mess of noise, colour and passion. This is the culmination of the Romería del Rocío, Spain's biggest religious pilgrimage, which draws hundreds of thousands of festive pilgrims, most of whom belong to one of the 90 *hermandades*. These *hermandades* travel to El Rocío on foot, horseback and in gaily decorated covered wagons from towns all across southern Spain.

Solemn is the last word you'd apply to this quintessentially Andalusian event. In an atmosphere similar to Seville's Feria de Abril (p55), participants dress in fine Andalusian costume and sing, dance,

(Continued on page 97)

THE BEST OF
ANDALUCÍA

An exotic history has bequeathed to Andalucía extraordinary architectural and cultural signposts to the past which, in many cases, are experiences to immerse yourself in and satisfy all the senses – and all are set against the backdrop of stunning mountain scenery that amply rewards those who set out on foot.

ABOVE The Puente Nuevo stone bridge over El Tajo gorge in Ronda, Málaga province

THE BEST OF ARAB CULTURE

1 HAMMAM ANDALUSI // JEREZ DE LA FRONTERA

Sophistication lay at the heart of life in Arab Al-Andalus and this spirit lives on in these traditional Arab baths (p128). From the soothing architecture to the sensory indulgence of classical Arab music, you'll leave transported to the Andalucía of another age.

2 TETERÍAS OF THE ALBAYZÍN // GRANADA

The rulers of Andalucía left their mark with the grand monuments of Islam, but it's in the *teterías* (teahouses) of Granada's Albayzín (p260) that the heartbeat of public life still beats.

JOHN ELK III

3 WHITE VILLAGES // LAS ALPUJARRAS

If you've travelled throughout North Africa, it's hard not to do a double-take in Las Alpujarras (p275). Like an echo of the past, these whitewashed villages, many of which are Berber in origin, betray an unmistakeably Arab influence.

4 MEZQUITA // CÓRDOBA

Nowhere is the complexity of Andalucía's history more stunningly told than in Córdoba's Mezquita (p201). One of the world's most beautiful landmarks of Islamic architecture, this former mosque also marks the transition to the dominance of Catholic Spain.

5 GENERALIFE // GRANADA

Islam was born in the deserts of Arabia, which partly explains the privileged position occupied by paradiselike gardens in Islamic architecture. The Generalife (p258), inside Granada's Alhambra, is perhaps the pinnacle of this obsession – an exquisite, near-perfect space.

4

TOP LEFT The fountains of the Generalife, Alhambra, Granada BOTTOM LEFT Taking tea in the *teterías* (teahouses) of the Albayzín, Granada BOTTOM RIGHT The horseshoe arches of the Mezquita, Córdoba

THE BEST
JOURNEYS INTO THE PAST

1 BAELO CLAUDIA // BOLONIA
There are no more beautiful signposts to
the powerful presence of ancient Rome in
Andalucía than Baelo Claudia (p147). The
views across the water to Africa are no
accident: the city connected Europe with
Rome's North African colonies.

2 MEDINA AZAHARA // CÓRDOBA
The sophistication of 10th-century Córdoba was all well and good, but the rulers
longed to escape the rigours of city life,
even as they conducted essential government business. Thus was born Medina
Azahara (p209). Exquisite decorative detail, harmonious horseshoe arches and the
ghosts of caliphs past are all that remain.

KARL BLACKWELL

3 ALCÁZAR // SEVILLE

Patios, palaces and perfectly formed gardens: such are the masterpieces of Seville's Alcázar (p44). But so important was the Alcázar as a symbol of power and prestige that centuries of rulers scrambled to leave their mark upon the building. The result is an extraordinary palace-fortress complex that is Andalucía's story writ large.

4 JAÉN CATHEDRAL // JAÉN

When Jaén's Christians decided to build a cathedral they did so on a grand scale, after having worshipped in a mosque for 100 years. Opulent and cavernous, Renaissance with hints of baroque, Jaén's cathedral (p221) is one of Christian Andalucía's most astonishing structures.

5 ALMODÓVAR DEL RÍO // WEST OF CÓRDOBA

Rising from plains west of Córdoba, this forbidding castle (p217), with eight monumental towers and impregnable walls, was first built in the 8th century, then rebuilt after the Christian Reconquista.

2

TOP LEFT Encounter Andalucía's ancient Roman ruins at Baelo Claudia, Cádiz province **BOTTOM LEFT** The splendid architecture of the Alcázar, Seville **BOTTOM RIGHT** The remains of Medina Azahara, Córdoba

THE BEST WALKS

1 PARQUE NATURAL SIERRA DE
GRAZALEMA // **CÁDIZ PROVINCE**
One of Andalucía's greenest mountain
areas, the Sierra de Grazalema (p139)
combines high-altitude trekking up to El
Torreón with steep descents into the vertiginous depths of the Garganta Verde. The
whitewashed villages of the sierra perfectly
complement the drama of the landscapes.

2 PARQUE NATURAL SIERRA DE
ARACENA // **HUELVA PROVINCE**
A world away from the clamour of the
region's cities and coast, the Sierra de
Aracena (p101), in far northwestern
Andalucía, is like a time capsule of the
region's past.

TONY WEST / ALAMY

3 PARQUE NATURAL SIERRAS DE CAZORLA, SEGURA Y LAS VILLAS // JAÉN PROVINCE

The Parque Natural Sierras de Cazorla, Segura y Las Villas (p241) is a wonderful world of jagged summits and impossibly deep valleys. Its trails are quiet, enabling abundant wildlife (ibex, deer and wild boar) to thrive.

4 PARQUE NATURAL DE CABO DE GATA-NÍJAR // ALMERÍA PROVINCE

Unlike anywhere else in Andalucía, the Parque Natural de Cabo de Gata-Níjar (p301) combines cliffs plunging down into secluded coves with desertlike landscapes in the hinterland.

5 SIERRA NEVADA // GRANADA PROVINCE

Mainland Spain's two highest peaks – Mulhacén (3479m) and Veleta (3395m) – set the scene for Andalucía's highest altitude trekking in the Sierra Nevada (p272). Climbing these and other summits is possible, and summer is best for a visit.

TOP LEFT Hiking the trails of the Sierra Nevada **BOTTOM LEFT** Walking through the Parque Natural Sierra de Grazalema **BOTTOM RIGHT** The approach to Cala de San Pedro in Cabo de Gata, Almería province

1

TOP The sumptuous interior of the Palacio de San Benito **RIGHT** Dine in style at the Hotel Duques de Medinaceli

2

THE BEST CONVERTED PALACE HOTELS

**1 PALACIO DE SAN BENITO //
CAZALLA DE LA SIERRA**

The Palacio de San Benito (p382) is an extraordinary place. Built in the 15th century as a hermitage, this habitable museum overflows with period detail that spans the centuries. There's also an on-site Mudéjar church.

**2 HOTEL DUQUES DE MEDINACELI //
EL PUERTO DE SANTA MARÍA**

The best hotels tell a story and this hotel (p385) is El Puerto de Santa María in microcosm. Inhabiting the palatial, 300-year-old mansion of the Terry Irish sherry family, the public areas are wedded to seigneurial, sumptuous details in the rooms.

**3 AC PALACIO DE SANTA PAULA //
GRANADA**

This hotel (p395) spans six centuries of history, occupying aristocratic homes and a former convent. Wood-beamed ceilings look down on the state-of-the-art fittings that grace the warm-coloured rooms.

**4 HOSPEDERÍA DUQUES DE
MEDINA SIDONIA // SANLÚCAR DE
BARRAMEDA**

This rambling stately home (p385) dates back to Guzmán El Bueno, the 13th-century ancestor of a powerful aristocratic family who once owned more of Spain than anyone else. The lavishly restored house is bursting with wonderful decorations.

(Continued from page 88)

THE WHITE DOVE

Like most of Spain's holiest images, Nuestra Señora del Rocío – also known as La Blanca Paloma (The White Dove) – has legendary origins. Back in the 13th century, a hunter from Almonte village found the effigy in a marshland tree and started to carry her home. But when he stopped for a rest, the Virgin magically returned to the tree. Before long, a chapel was built on the site of the tree (El Rocío) and it became a place of pilgrimage.

drink, laugh and romance their way to their goal. The total number of people in the village on this special weekend can reach about a million.

The weekend reaches an ecstatic climax in the very early hours of Monday. Members of the Almonte *hermandad,* which claims the Virgin as its own, barge into the church and bear her out on a float. Violent struggles ensue as others battle for the honour of carrying La Blanca Paloma (see above). The crush and chaos are immense, but somehow the Virgin is carried round to each of the *hermandad* buildings before finally being returned to the church in the afternoon.

❦ **SWAMPS & TRAILS // PLAY SPOT THE GREBE, SPOONBILL AND BOAR**
The marshlands in front of El Rocío, which have water all year round, offer some of the best bird- and beast-watching in the entire Doñana region. Deer and horses graze in the shallows and you may be lucky enough to see a flock of flamingos wheeling through the sky in a big pink cloud. The bridge over the river 1km south of the village on the A483 is a great viewing spot, and just past the bridge is the

Centro de Información Las Rocinas (see p85), with paths to birdwatching hides.

For a longer walk from El Rocío, cross the Puente del Ajolí, at the northeastern edge of the village, and follow the track into the woodland. This is the Raya Real, one of the most important routes used by Romería pilgrims on their journeys to and from El Rocío. The track crosses the Coto del Rey, a large woodland zone where you may spot deer or boar in early morning or late evening.

GASTRONOMIC HIGHLIGHTS

❦ **AIRES DE DOÑANA** €€
☎ 959 44 27 19; Avenida de la Canaliega 1; mains €12-18; ✆ Sat & Sun
Many El Rocío eateries focus more on feeding hungry pilgrims than on culinary delights. Aires de Doñana, set inside a thatch-roofed cottage, makes a great alternative with its picture-view windows overlooking the *marismas,* polished service and successfully imaginative menu.

❦ **RESTAURANTE TORUÑO** €€
☎ 959 44 24 22; Plaza Acebuchal; mains €12-18
Although you may find you pay over the odds for food (as with a number of places in El Rocío), the traditional Andalusian atmosphere, complete with numerous signed photos of bullfighters and horse riders adorning the walls, and the solid old-fashioned food makes this place better than most.

NORTH OF HUELVA

· · · · · ·

As you travel north from Huelva's southern plains, straight highways are replaced by winding byways and you enter a more temperate zone, up

HUELVA PROVINCE

to 960m higher than the coast. The rolling hills of Huelva's portion of the Sierra Morena are covered with a thick pelt of cork oak, and pines and punctuated by winding river valleys, enchanting villages of stone and tile, and bustling market towns such as the area's 'capital', Aracena.

This is a still little-discovered rural world, threaded with beautiful walking and riding trails and blessed with a rich hill-country cuisine that abounds in game, local cheeses and fresh vegetables, but is most well known for the best *jamón serrano* in Spain. Most of the area lies within the 1840-sq-km Parque Natural Sierra de Aracena y Picos de Aroche, Andalucía's second-largest protected area.

MINAS DE RIOTINTO

pop 4500 / elevation 420m
Tucked away on the southern fringe of the sierra is one of the world's oldest mining districts, so old that even King Solomon of faraway Jerusalem is said to have mined gold here for his famous temple. Though the miners clocked off for the last time in 2001 it's still a fascinating place to explore, with its superb museum and the opportunity to visit the old mines and ride the mine railway.

ESSENTIAL INFORMATION

TOURIST OFFICE // The **Parque Minero de Riotinto Ticket Office** (☎ 959 59 00 25; www.parquemineroderiotinto.com; Plaza Ernest Lluch; ☺ 10.30am-3pm & 4-8pm mid-Jul–Sep, to 7pm Oct–mid-Jul) is at the well-signposted Museo Minero.

EXPLORING MINAS DE RIOTINTO

❦ MUSEO MINERO // DIG DEEP INTO THE HISTORY OF MINING
The fascinating **Museo Minero** (Plaza Ernest Lluch; adult/child under 13yr €4/3; ☺ 10.30am-3pm &

4-7pm) is a figurative goldmine for devotees of industrial archaeology, taking you right through the Riotinto area's unique history from the megalithic tombs of the 3rd millennium BC to the Roman and British colonial eras and finally the closure of the mines in 2001, with some information in English as well as Spanish.

❦ FERROCARRIL TURÍSTICO-MINERO // PLATFORM FOUR FOR THE UNDERGROUND TRAIN
A fun way to see the mining area (especially with children) is to ride the **Ferrocarril Turístico-Minero** (adult/child €10/9; ☺ 1.30pm 1 Jun-15 Jul, 1.30 & 5.30pm 16 Jul-30 Sep, 4pm Sat, Sun & holidays Oct-Feb, 1pm Mon-Fri, 4pm Sat, Sun & holidays Mar-May), taking visitors 22km (round-trip) through the surreal landscape in restored early-20th-century railway carriages. It's essential to book ahead for the train, and schedules may change, especially in winter.

THE MARTE PROJECT

Since 2003, scientists from NASA and Spain's Centro de Astrobiología in Madrid have been conducting a research program around the Minas de Riotinto known as Marte (Mars Analog Research and Technology Experiment) in preparation for seeking life on Mars. It's thought that the high acid levels that give the Río Tinto its colour (by the action of acid on iron) are a product of underground micro-organisms comparable with those that scientists believe may exist below the surface of Mars. Experiments in locating these microbes up to 150m below ground level are being used to help develop techniques and instruments for looking for similar subterranean life on the red planet.

TRANSPORT

BUS // Buses run several times daily between Minas de Riotinto and Huelva and a couple of times a day to Seville.

ARACENA

pop 7000 / elevation 730m

Sparkling white in its mountain bowl, the thriving, old market town of Aracena is an appealingly lively place that's wrapped like a ribbon around a medieval church and ruined castle. With a stash of good places to stay and eat it makes an ideal base from which to explore this lovely area.

ESSENTIAL INFORMATION

TOURIST OFFICE // Municipal tourist office (☎ 959 12 82 06; Calle Pozo de la Nieve; ☸ 10am-2pm & 4-6pm) Facing the entrance to the

Gruta de las Maravillas; also sells some maps of the area.

EXPLORING ARACENA

❤ **THE OLD TOWN //** **GET LOST IN A HAZE OF WHITEWASH**

Dramatically dominating the town are the tumbling, hilltop ruins of the castillo, an atmospheric fort built by the Portuguese in the 13th century. Today it's as popular with grazing sheep as it is with camera-toting tourists. Next door is the Iglesia Prioral de Nuestra Señora del Mayor Dolor (admission free; ☸ 9.30am-7pm), built around the same time, and a Gothic-Mudéjar hybrid that combines an interior of ribbed vaults with attractive brick tracery on the tower. Its bell tower is notable for its distinctive Islamic influence. The castle is reached up a steep road from Plaza Alta, a handsome,

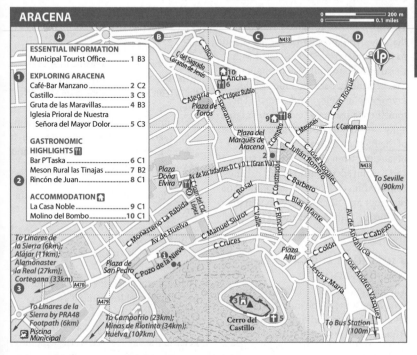

ARACENA

ESSENTIAL INFORMATION
Municipal Tourist Office 1 B3

EXPLORING ARACENA
Café-Bar Manzano 2 C2
Castillo 3 C3
Gruta de las Maravillas 4 B3
Iglesia Prioral de Nuestra
   Señora del Mayor Dolor 5 C3

GASTRONOMIC HIGHLIGHTS
Bar P'Taska 6 C1
Meson Rural las Tinajas 7 B2
Rincón de Juan 8 C1

ACCOMMODATION
La Casa Noble 9 C1
Molino del Bombo 10 C1

HUELVA PROVINCE

cobbled square that was originally the centre of the town. Today more life is to be found on and around the **Plaza del Marqués de Aracena**, a lively square fronted by handsome buildings and a couple of decent pavement cafes including the **Café-Bar Manzano** (☎ 959 12 63 37; tapas €2-3.50, raciones €9-18; ☻ 8am-8pm or later Mon & Wed-Sat, 10am-8pm Sun), whose outdoor tables are a fine spot from which to watch the world go by while enjoying the varied tapas and *raciones*, including many types of wild mushroom.

☙ GRUTA DE LAS MARAVILLAS // JOURNEY TO THE CENTRE OF THE EARTH

Beneath the castle hill is a web of caves and tunnels full of stalagmites and stalactites. The **Gruta de las Maravillas** (Cave of Marvels; ☎ 959 12 83 55; Calle Pozo de la Nieve; tour adult/child under 19yr €8/5.50; ☻ 10.30am-1.30pm & 3-6pm, tours every hr Mon-Fri, every half-hr Sat, Sun & holidays) is an extraordinary 1km route that takes you through 12 chambers and past six underground lakes, filled with weird and wonderful rock formations that provided a backdrop for the film *Journey to the Centre of the Earth*. The tour (in Spanish only) culminates at the aptly named **Sala de los Culos** (Chamber of the Bottoms), usually met with roars of laughter from elderly Spanish ladies and bashful silence from their husbands. A maximum of 35 people are allowed on each tour and tickets can sell out in the afternoons and on weekends when busloads of visitors arrive.

☙ HIKING // LACE UP YOUR WALKING BOOTS

The hills and mountains around Aracena offer some of the most beautiful, and least known, walking country in Andalucía. Any time of year is a good time to hike here but spring, when the meadows are awash in wildflowers and carnival-coloured butterflies, is by far the best time to strike out on the trail. The tourist office can recommend a number of simple day walks. A sublime and fairly gentle round trip of about 12km can be made by leaving Aracena between the Piscina Municipal (municipal swimming pool) and the A470 road at the western end of town. It should take around four hours, excluding stops. This path (see Map p102), the PRA48, rollercoasters down a verdant valley to Linares de la Sierra (opposite). To return by a different (and less steep) route, the PRA39, find a small stone bridge over the river below Linares, beyond which the path goes round Cerro de la Molinilla, passing old iron mines for a stony ascent to Aracena, coming out on the A479 in the southwest of town.

GASTRONOMIC HIGHLIGHTS

The hills around Aracena have given rise to some of the finest cuisine in Andalucía. Big tummy-filling delights include the region's mushrooms; dozens of different varieties pop up out of the ground every autumn. And then there's the ham. *Jamón serrano* of nearby Jubugo is considered the best in the entire country and as you explore these hills you won't fail to notice the secret to this *jamón* – contented-looking black pigs foraging in the forests for acorns.

☙ BAR P'TASKA €

☎ 625 47 21 38; Calle Esperanza 48; tapas €1.50-2, raciones €7-9

There's a real local vibe to this small bar at the top of town and it's a great place to come for a traditional breakfast of toast smeared in garlic and tomato. Later in the day it's well worth wrapping your lips around some of its fungi-filled meals that go with the fungi-flavoured decorations.

♥ MESÓN RURAL LAS TINAJAS €€
☎ 959 12 78 82; Calle Juan del Cíd López; mains €8-10
Most of the ingredients at this rustic, yet slightly upmarket restaurant are locally sourced, fully bio and almost impossible to go wrong with. In such a pig-popular town it would be rude not to tackle the superb *solomillo ibérico relleno con salsa oloroso* (bacon and cheese wrapped in pork). The homemade pâté is also worthy of appreciation.

♥ RINCÓN DE JUAN €
☎ 627 33 47 66; Calle Jose Nogales; tapas €1.60-1.80, raciones €7-10; ⏲ 7am-4pm & 6.30pm-midnight Mon-Fri, 8am-midnight Sat
Indisputably the best tapas bar in town. It's standing room only at this tapa-sized bar with – you guessed it – ham and mushroom specialities. Other good bets are the octopus or the house special, *chorizo serrano dulce*.

TRANSPORT

CAR // Driving around Aracena is easy enough, though the lack of decent signposting means it's easy to get lost.
PARKING // Aracena has plenty of free street-side parking.
BUS // Casal (☎ 954 99 92 90 in Seville) runs two buses daily to/from Seville. Buses to Huelva include two a day during the week and one daily at weekends.

SIERRA DE ARACENA

Stretching west of Aracena is one of Andalucía's most unexpectedly picturesque landscapes, a lumpy, flower-sprinkled hill-country dotted with old stone villages where time seems to tick-tock forward at a very lazy pace. Many of the valleys are full of wood-

lands, while elsewhere are expanses of *dehesa* – evergreen oak pastures where the region's famed black pigs forage for acorns. The area is threaded by an extensive network of well-maintained walking trails, with ever-changing vistas and mostly gentle ascents and descents, making for some of the most delightful rambling in Andalucía.

Great routes for walking extend over all parts of the **Parque Natural Sierra de Aracena y Picos de Aroche**, but they're particularly thick in the area between Aracena and Cortegana, making attractive villages such as Alájar, Castaño del Robledo, Galaroza and Almonaster la Real good bases from which to set forth.

EXPLORING THE SIERRA DE ARACENA

♥ LINARES DE LA SIERRA & ALÁJAR // DISCOVER THE SIERRA'S MAN-MADE BEAUTY
Almost as beautiful as nature's undulating mountain art, the villages of the Sierra de Aracena are an idyllic place to bumble slowly about poking your nose into hidden corners and taking regular refreshment breaks. Head west of Aracena 7km along the A470 and you'll bump into one of the cutest, **Linares de la Sierra**, with its cobbled streets, a minute unpaved bullring plaza and thick silence pervading the tiny streets.

Five kilometres west of Linares de la Sierra is the region's most picturesque village, **Alájar**. Bigger than Linares, it still retains its tiny cobbled streets and cubist stone houses, as well as a fine baroque church. Above the village a rocky spur, the **Peña de Arias Montano**, provides magical views over the village and is reached 1km up the road towards Fuenteheridos. The *peña*'s 16th-century

HUELVA PROVINCE

SIERRA DE ARACENA

chapel, the **Ermita de Nuestra Señora Reina de los Ángeles** (⏰ 11am-sunset), contains a small 13th-century carving of the Virgin, which is considered the patron of the whole Sierra de Aracena. The chapel is the focus of the area's biggest annual religious event, the **Romería de la Reina de los Ángeles** (8 September), when people from all around the sierra and beyond converge here to honour their Virgin. Outside the chapel are stalls selling local cheeses, and also the 6th- or 7th-century **Arco de los Novios**: by legend any couple who walk together through this 'Arch of the Fiancés' will marry. So think carefully about who you visit with!

♥ CASTAÑO DEL ROBLEDO // VILLAGES DON'T COME MORE IDYLLIC THAN THIS

North of Alájar on a minor road between Fuenteheridos and Jabugo, the small village of **Castaño del Robledo** is easily one of the most idyllic spots in the sierra. Surrounded by hazy green olive and cork forests, barely a single modern building pollutes the beauty of this village. Its jigsaw of tiled terracotta roofs is overlooked by two large churches, either of which could easily accommodate the entire village population.

♥ ALMONASTER LA REAL // MARVEL AT THE ISLAMIC PERFECTION

Tiny **Almonaster la Real**, on the western side of the N435, feels as if it's been lifted straight out of a fairy tale. The highlight of a visit here is the picturesque little 10th-century **mezquita** (mosque; admission free; ⏰ approx 8.30am-7pm) standing atop the hill five minutes' walk from the main square. Despite being Christianised in the 13th century, the building retains nearly all its original Islamic features: the horseshoe arches, the semicircular mihrab, an ablutions fountain and various Arabic inscriptions. Even older are the capitals of the columns nearest the mihrab, which are Roman.

♥ EXPLORING SIERRA DE ARACENA ON FOOT // SAUNTER THROUGH THE HIGHLIGHTS OF THE SIERRA DE ARACENA

The **Alájar–Castaño del Robledo– Galaroza Figure of Eight** is a beautiful day hike and a superb introduction to walking in the Sierra de Aracena. It connects three of the area's most attractive villages in a figure of eight, allowing you to vary the route by starting from any of the three or walking only part of it. Most of the way is through varied woodlands but you'll also enjoy long-distance panoramas, wonderful wildflowers in spring, and the spectacular Peña de Arias Montano. The whole route takes about six hours at an average walking pace, not counting stops. The steeper bits are done downhill and there's nothing any modestly fit walker couldn't cope with.

If you want to make this walk shorter (three hours) follow the first part of the walk from Alájar to Castaño del Robledo and, after some lunch there, return to Alájar following the route description in the final section.

Alájar to Castaño del Robledo

Leave Alájar by the track to El Calabacino, signposted from the A470 at the western end of the village. El Calabacino is an international artist/hippie colony and a few creative signs from its inhabitants help you along your way. The route crosses a stream on a wooden bridge,

and passes a small, square, stone-and-brick church on your right, then ascends through a cork-oak forest. Ten minutes past the small church, fork directly right at an 'El Castaño' sign. Another 10 minutes and you will cross a small stream bed to follow a path marked by a yellow paint dot. Within a further 10 minutes the path becomes a vehicle track. Fifteen minutes along this, carry straight on at a crossroads, and in three minutes more you crest a rise and Castaño del Robledo comes into view. Some 200m past the crest, take the shadier path diverging to the left, indicated again by dots of yellow paint. After 10 to 15 minutes this track starts to veer down to the left, passing between tall cork oaks and gradually wending into Castaño del Robledo.

Castaño del Robledo to Galaroza to Castaño del Robledo

After lunch at one of Castaño's basic bar-restaurants, leave via the path through the shady Área Recreativa Capilla del Cristo, on the north side of the HV5211 road passing along the north of the village. To the left you'll soon be able to see Cortegana and Jabugo, before you fork right at a tree with yellow and white paint stripes, 15 minutes along the track. Your path starts winding downhill. Go straight on at a crossing of tracks after 10 minutes, and right at a fork one minute after that (a ruined stone building is up the left-hand path here). In 10 minutes Galaroza comes into view as you pass between its outlying *fincas* (rural properties). Cross a small river on a footbridge and emerge on the N433 road three minutes later. Walk left towards Galaroza, skirting the town along the unpleasant N433 for around 800m, then leave by the track on the left marked by a 'Sendero Ribera del Jabugo' route sign.

HUELVA PROVINCE

ACCOMMODATION

Huelva province is all about the great outdoors and as such all the best places to stay are found hidden in the backwoods. You'll also find rates to be among the lowest in Andalucía. Read all about the options in our dedicated accommodation chapter (p378). Standout choices include the following:

★ **El Cortijo de los Mimbrales** (p383)

★ **Hotel Toruño** (p384)

★ **La Casa Noble** (p384)

Fork right one minute out from the mentioned sign, then turn left four or five minutes later down to a footbridge that stretches over a stream. The path soon starts winding up the valley of the Río Jabugo, a particularly lovely stretch. Half an hour from the footbridge you will reach a vehicle track marked 'Camino de Jabugo a Galaroza'. Head right, passing a couple of *cortijos* (country properties), to cross the river on a low bridge. Turn left 50m past the bridge, then left at a fork 30m further on. You re-cross the river, then gradually wind up and away from it. Ten minutes from the river, turn left at a red-tile-roofed house (Monte Blanco) and in 15 minutes (mostly upward) you're re-entering Castaño del Robledo, this time from the west.

Castaño del Robledo to Alájar

To leave again, start by retracing the route by which you arrived from Alájar earlier – up Calle Arias Montano from Plaza del Álamo, right along the first cobbled lane, up through the cork oaks to the crest then down to the crossing of tracks (30 minutes out of Castaño del Robledo). From here turn left, across the southwestern flank of Castaño (960m, the highest hill in the Sierra de Aracena). The track curves sharply to the left after 12 to 15 minutes. Some 300m further, turn right along a path beside a stone wall, which is marked by yellow paint. At a fork, 10 minutes' walk down from here, take the lesser path down to the right, and within another 20 minutes you will reach the Peña de Arias Montano. Leaving here, start along the paved road down the hill, but after 50m diverge right down on to a cobbled track. Within 10 minutes this track re-emerges on the road: follow the road down for 25m then turn right down a track through a gap

in the wall. Cross the A470 a minute or two later to carry on down into the middle of Alájar. Find a chair in a bar, slump down, drink.

GASTRONOMIC HIGHLIGHTS

♥ CASA PADRINO €€
☎ 959 12 56 01; Plaza Miguel Moya 2, Alájar; mains €10-15; ☯ lunch Sat & Sun, dinner Fri & Sat

Situated in what was once a chapel, Casa Padrino serves scrumptious country fare loosely based on old village recipes. The *revuelto de hiervas del campo* (scrambled eggs with wild herbs) is memorable and a good range of tapas are available in the front bar.

♥ RESTAURANT LOS ARRIEROS €€
☎ 959 46 37 17; Calle Arrieros 2, Linares de la Sierra; mains €9-15; ☯ lunch, closed Mon & first week of Jan, mid-Jun–mid-Jul & last Sat in May

The art of slow food is taken to the extreme here with meals normally spinning out over several lazy hours. Its innovative approach to the area's pork products and wild mushrooms, such as the latter caramelised in sweet sherry, means that this is considered the best place to eat in the entire sierra.

TRANSPORT

CAR // You really need your own set of wheels in order to explore the sierra in any depth.

BUS // Almost all the villages are linked to Aracena by one or two buses a day (though at weekends the service is usually reduced). Most of these buses are making the school runs and leave the villages for Aracena early in the morning and returning when school's over.

TRAIN // There are two daily trains running each way between Huelva and the stations of Almonaster-Cortegana and Jabugo-Galaroza. Almonaster-Cortegana station is 1km off the Almonaster-Cortegana road, about halfway between the two villages. Jabugo-Galaroza station is in El Repilado, on the N433, 4km west of Jabugo.

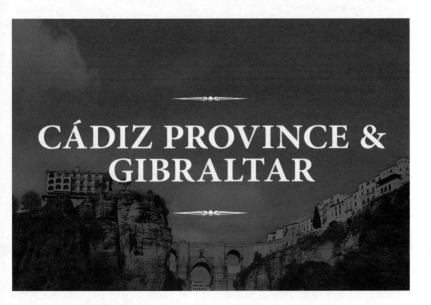

CÁDIZ PROVINCE & GIBRALTAR

3 PERFECT DAYS

❦ DAY 1 // CÁDIZ IMMERSION
Cádiz is a city that rewards those who linger. With extraordinary monuments, high-above-it-all vantage points, fantastic places to eat, beaches and a fun-loving spirit renowned throughout Spain, a day is an absolute minimum for soaking up its charms. Stay at Hotel Argantonio (p385) for a sophisticated retreat and don't miss the views from the Torre Tavira (p115) and the cathedral's Torre de Poniente (p114). At ground level, the gorgeous Plaza de la Catedral and the Barrio de la Viña (p114) are both focal points for much of the city's life.

❦ DAY 2 // HEAD FOR THE HILLS
The coastal hinterland of Cádiz province is a world away from the clamour of city life. A drive from Arcos de la Frontera (p133) to Vejer de la Frontera (p140) via the Sierra de Grazalema takes in some of Andalucía's most picturesque mountain scenery and prettiest whitewashed villages. At either end of the drive, Arcos and Vejer are hill towns par excellence, while the high country en route is like a stereotype brought to life of Andalucía's rural beauty.

❦ DAY 3 // SOAK UP THE COAST
The Costa de la Luz (p140) is one of Spain's most unspoiled coastlines with a range of sights and activities. Gibraltar (p148) and Tarifa (p142) provide the urban charms and stunning views across the Strait of Gibraltar to Africa, but there are also Roman ruins and kilometre upon kilometre of white sandy beaches, especially at Zahara de los Atunes (p142), Los Caños de Meca (p142) and El Palmar (p142).

CÁDIZ PROVINCE & GIBRALTAR

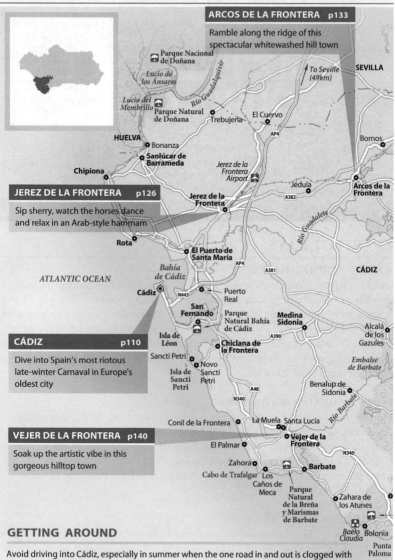

ARCOS DE LA FRONTERA p133

Ramble along the ridge of this spectacular whitewashed hill town

JEREZ DE LA FRONTERA p126

Sip sherry, watch the horses dance and relax in an Arab-style hammam

CÁDIZ p110

Dive into Spain's most riotous late-winter Carnaval in Europe's oldest city

VEJER DE LA FRONTERA p140

Soak up the artistic vibe in this gorgeous hilltop town

GETTING AROUND

Avoid driving into Cádiz, especially in summer when the one road in and out is clogged with slow-moving traffic. Instead leave the car in El Puerto de Santa María's ridiculously cheap waterfront parking station and catch the ferry. If you really must drive in any of the coastal towns in summer, do so between 2pm and 5pm when sun-loving locals are either eating or having a siesta. The route through the Sierra de Grazalema (see the Driving Tour, p137) is one of Andalucía's loveliest drives.

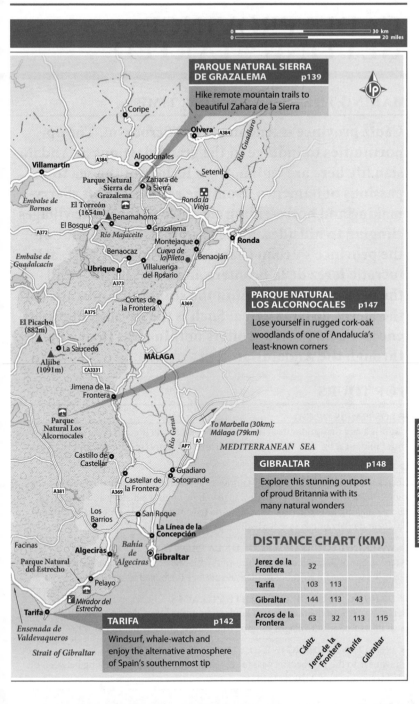

PARQUE NATURAL SIERRA DE GRAZALEMA p139

Hike remote mountain trails to beautiful Zahara de la Sierra

PARQUE NATURAL LOS ALCORNOCALES p147

Lose yourself in rugged cork-oak woodlands of one of Andalucía's least-known corners

GIBRALTAR p148

Explore this stunning outpost of proud Britannia with its many natural wonders

TARIFA p142

Windsurf, whale-watch and enjoy the alternative atmosphere of Spain's southernmost tip

To Marbella (30km);
Málaga (79km)

MEDITERRANEAN SEA

Strait of Gibraltar

DISTANCE CHART (KM)

	Cádiz	Jerez de la Frontera	Tarifa	Gibraltar
Jerez de la Frontera	32			
Tarifa	103	113		
Gibraltar	144	113	43	
Arcos de la Frontera	63	32	113	115

CÁDIZ PROVINCE & GIBRALTAR

CÁDIZ PROVINCE GETTING STARTED

MAKING THE MOST OF YOUR TIME

Cádiz province is Andalucía in microcosm. The opportunities to indulge in the grand passions of Andalusian life here are legion, from its love of the sea to the passions of flamenco, from the serious arts of sherry-making and horse-riding elegance to the white villages clinging to hillsides. More than that, the clamour of the province's urban charms – fun-loving Cádiz, aristocratic Jerez de la Frontera and artsy Tarifa – finds the perfect complement in the stunning landscapes of the Sierra de Grazalema. Such is the breadth of experiences, Cádiz province offers nothing less than a journey through the Andalusian soul.

TOP TOURS

❦ **LOS PIMPIS DE CAI**
Cádiz is a city that prides itself on its casual approach to life and there's no better way to get under Cádiz' skin than with these irreverent tours (see the boxed text, p111).

❦ **BODEGA TOURS**
Sherry is one of Andalucía's most famous exports and it's a fascinating world to explore. Numerous bodegas (wineries) take you through the history and process of sherry-making in El Puerto de Santa María (p120), Jerez de la Frontera (p130) or Sanlúcar de Barrameda (see Barbadillo, p126).

❦ **WALKING TOURS OF ARCOS DE LA FRONTERA**
Arcos is one of Andalucía's most beautiful whitewashed hill towns and behind its high walls is a wonderful world of hidden secrets (see the boxed text, p136).

❦ **DRIVING TOUR OF THE WHITE VILLAGES**
Set off by car into the magnificent landscapes of the Sierra de Grazalema high country, with its whitewashed villages clinging to the most unlikely places (p137).

❦ **WHALE-WATCHING IN THE STRAIT OF GIBRALTAR**
Draw near to the Moroccan coast to see whales and dolphins travelling between the Mediterranean and Atlantic (p143).

GETTING AWAY FROM IT ALL

Cádiz province can be sensory overload, but there are some places to escape the crowds.

★ **Climb above the clamour** Survey Cádiz from above with extraordinary views from the Torre de Poniente and Torre Tavira (p114)

★ **Jerez' Hammam** Indulge the senses at these baths that evoke the sophistication of Arab Al-Andalus (p128)

★ **Hike the Sierra de Grazalema** Leave the well-travelled roads behind and strike out into the wilderness of these gorgeous mountains (p139)

★ **La Casa Grande** Retreat to this calming mansion atop Arcos de la Frontera's cliff, with massages, yoga and views (p386)

ADVANCE PLANNING

If you want to go hiking in the Sierra de Grazalema, you'll need to arrange a permit up to two weeks in advance from the Centro de Visitantes El Bosque (p139). Cádiz' calendar is filled to overflowing with festivals for which advance booking of accommodation is essential. For accommodation options, see p385. Popular festivals include the following:

★ **Carnaval, Cádiz** (p111)

★ **Feria de Primavera y Fiestas del Vino Fino, El Puerto de Santa María** (p123)

★ **Feria de la Manzanilla, Sanlúcar de Barrameda** (p126)

★ **Carreras de Caballos, Sanlúcar de Barrameda** (p126)

★ **Semana Santa, Arcos de la Frontera** (p134)

TOP RESTAURANTS

❦ **EL ALJIBE**
Cádiz' most creative tapas (p117)

❦ **ROMERIJO**
El Puerto's casual and wildly popular seafood haunt (p123)

❦ **CASA BALBINO**
One of Andalucía's best bars for seafood tapas (p126)

❦ **SABORES**
Traditional Andalusian specialities with a twist in intimate surrounds (p132)

❦ **LA TABERNA DE BOABDIL**
Cave location and tapas that tell the history of Arcos de la Frontera (p134)

❦ **EL JARDÍN DE LA CALIFA**
Vejer's Islamic culinary tradition in all its glory (p141)

❦ **THYME**
Gibraltar's best restaurant with some stunning innovations (p154)

RESOURCES

★ **Cádiz Net** (www.cadiznet.com, in Spanish) Expansive guide to Cádiz province

★ **Cádiz Turismo** (www.cadizturismo.com) Official government overview of tourism in Cádiz province

★ **Centro Andaluz de Flamenco** (www.centroandaluzdeflamenco.es, in Spanish) Terrific links to all things flamenco

★ **Sherry, by Julian Jeffs** A classic book on Jerez and sherry's development into one of Andalucía's highest art forms

CÁDIZ PROVINCE & GIBRALTAR

CÁDIZ

· · · · · ·

pop 128,600

Crammed onto a long promontory like some huge, crowded, ocean-going ship, Cádiz (pronounced *ca*-i in the local accent) really gets under your skin. Cádiz has a long and fascinating history, plenty of absorbing monuments and museums, a near limitless supply of great bars, some memorable restaurants and lively nightlife.Yet it's the *gaditanos* (people of Cádiz) themselves who make their city truly special. Warm, open, cultured and independently minded, most *gaditanos* are above all concerned with making the most of life – whether simply enjoying good company over a drink, staying out late, or indulging in Spain's most riotous carnival in late winter.

Cádiz could be the oldest city in Europe. It was founded under the name Gadir, in the 8th century BC, by the Phoenicians. Later, it became Gades, a naval base for the Romans, who heaped praise on its culinary, sexual and musical delights. Cádiz boomed again with the discovery of the Americas in 1492: Columbus sailed from here on his second and fourth voyages of exploration, returning with vast quantities of precious metals and treasure. Cádiz attracted Spain's enemies too: in 1587, for example, England's Sir Francis Drake 'singed the king of Spain's beard' with a raid on the harbour, delaying the imminent Spanish Armada.

Cádiz' golden age was the 18th century, when it enjoyed 75% of Spanish trade with the Americas. It grew into the richest and most cosmopolitan city in Spain and gave birth to the country's first progressive, liberal middle class. In 1780, it was home to 70,000 people (12% of whom were foreigners). During the Spanish War of Independence (part of the Napoleonic Wars), Cádiz underwent a two-year French siege during which the Cortes de Cádiz (the Spanish national parliament) convened here. In 1812 this decidedly liberal gathering adopted Spain's first constitution (known as La Pepa), proclaiming sovereignty of the people. Massive celebrations are planned for La Pepa's 200-year anniversary in 2012.

ESSENTIAL INFORMATION

EMERGENCIES // Hospital Puerta del Mar (☎ 956 00 21 00; Avenida Ana de Viya 21) Two-and-a-quarter kilometres southeast of the Puerta de Tierra. Medical Emergency (☎ 061) Policía Nacional (National Police; ☎ 091, 956 28 61 11; Avenida de Andalucía 28) Five-hundred metres southeast of the Puerta de Tierra.

TOURIST OFFICES // Municipal tourist office (☎ 956 24 10 01; Paseo de Canalejas s/n Dios 11; ⏲ 8.30am-6.30pm Mon-Fri, 9am-5pm Sat & Sun) Regional tourist office (☎ 956 20 31 91; Avenida Ramón de Carranza s/n; ⏲ 9am-7.30pm Mon-Fri, 9.30am-3pm Sat, Sun & holidays)

ORIENTATION

The four key squares for initial orientation are Plaza San Juan de Dios, Plaza de la Catedral and Plaza de Topete in an arc in the southeast, and Plaza de Mina in the north. Pedestrianised Calle San Francisco runs most of the way between Plaza San Juan de Dios and Plaza de Mina.

The train station is just east of the old city, off Plaza de Sevilla. The main harbour lies between the two, with the Terminal Marítima Metropolitana on the east side of the harbour.

The 18th-century Puerta de Tierra (Land Gate) marks the eastern boundary

CÁDIZ TOURS & DISCOUNTS

The municipal tourist office has a handy *Walks Through Cádiz* brochure outlining four themed routes through the old city. Bicycles can be rented from **Urban Bike Cádiz** (☎ 664 08 13 81; www.urbanbikecadiz.com; Calle Magistral Cabrera 7; half-day/full-day/24hr/weekend €7/10/14/20). Other options include the following:

★ **Cádiz Card** (☎ 956 25 17 88; www.cadizcard.com; 7 days €22) Discounted access to city sights, tours and some shops and restaurants.

★ **City Sightseeing Cádiz** (adult/child €11/5.50; ☎ 10am-9pm mid-Jun–mid-Sep, shorter hours rest of year) Hop-on, hop-off bus tours that circle Old Cádiz and head east along the beach.

★ **Cádiz Virtual Siglo XVIII** (Virtual Cádiz 18th Century; ☎ 956 25 26 81; www.cadiz-virtual.com; admission €4; ☼ 10am-6pm Mon-Fri, to 5pm Sat, to 3pm Sun) Don a '3D stereoscopic' helmet to take interactive tours of 18th-century Cádiz.

★ **Hip Segway Cádiz** (☎ 663 80 07 93; jdd@segwaycadiz.es; Calle Valverde 4) Guided routes through Cádiz aboard a Segway.

★ **Los Pimpis de Cai** (☎ 646 15 99 94; www.lospimpisdecai.es.gd) These fun and irreverent tours take you into the *gaditano* world. They set out from Plaza San Juan de Dios at noon and 6pm Friday to Sunday, or at other times by appointment.

of the old city. Modern Cádiz extends back along the peninsula.

EXPLORING CÁDIZ

With such a distinguished history to call upon, Cádiz' smorgasbord of sights spans the full spectrum of 3000 years of history, with some outstanding vantage points from which to put the city in its stunning geographical perspective.

♥ CARNAVAL // DIVE INTO ONE OF SPAIN'S HAPPIEST FIESTAS

No other Spanish city celebrates **Carnaval** (www.carnavaldecadiz.com, in Spanish) with the verve, dedication and humour of Cádiz, where it turns into a 10-day singing, dancing and drinking fancy-dress party spanning two weekends in February. The fun, abetted by huge quantities of alcohol, is irresistible. Costumed groups called *murgas* tour the city on foot or on floats, dancing, singing satirical ditties or performing sketches (most

of their famed verbal wit will be lost on all but fluent Spanish speakers). In addition to the 300-or-so officially recognised *murgas,* who are judged by a panel in the Gran Teatro Falla, there are also the *ilegales* – any group that fancies taking to the streets and trying to play or sing.

Some of the liveliest and most drunken scenes are in the working-class Barrio de la Viña, between the Mercado Central and Playa de la Caleta, and along Calle Ancha and around Plaza de Topete, where *ilegales* tend to congregate.

If you plan to be here during Carnaval, book accommodation months in advance.

♥ TRADITIONAL BARRIOS // IMMERSE YOURSELF IN THESE HUBS OF GADITANO LIFE

Plaza San Juan de Dios is a picturesque introduction to Old Cádiz, surrounded as it is by cafes and dominated by the imposing neoclassical **ayuntamiento** (city hall), built in the early days of the 19th century. South of the plaza, behind

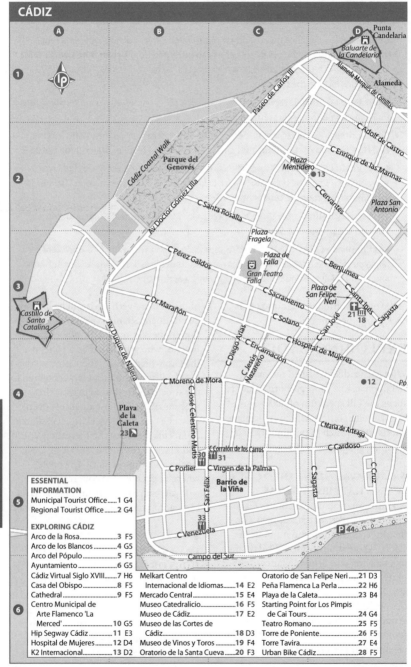

CÁDIZ

ESSENTIAL INFORMATION

Municipal Tourist Office 1 G4
Regional Tourist Office 2 G4

EXPLORING CÁDIZ

Arco de la Rosa 3 F5
Arco de los Blancos 4 G5
Arco del Pópulo 5 F5
Ayuntamiento 6 G5
Cádiz Virtual Siglo XVIII 7 H6
Casa del Obispo 8 F5
Cathedral 9 F5
Centro Municipal de
  Arte Flamenco 'La
  Merced' 10 G5
Hip Segway Cádiz 11 E3
Hospital de Mujeres 12 D4
K2 Internacional 13 D2

Melkart Centro
  Internacional de Idiomas 14 E2
Mercado Central 15 E4
Museo Catedralicio 16 F5
Museo de Cádiz 17 E2
Museo de las Cortes de
  Cádiz 18 D3
Museo de Vinos y Toros 19 F4
Oratorio de la Santa Cueva 20 F3

Oratorio de San Felipe Neri 21 D3
Peña Flamenca La Perla 22 H6
Playa de la Caleta 23 B4
Starting Point for Los Pimpis
  de Cai Tours 24 G4
Teatro Romano 25 F5
Torre de Poniente 26 F5
Torre Tavira 27 E4
Urban Bike Cádiz 28 F5

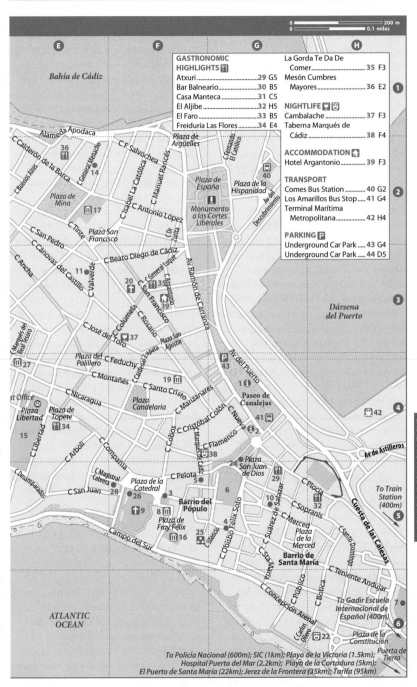

**GASTRONOMIC
HIGHLIGHTS** 🍴
Atxuri.................................29 G5
Bar Balneario....................30 B5
Casa Manteca 31 C5
El Aljibe............................32 H5
El Faro..............................33 B5
Freiduría Las Flores 34 E4

La Gorda Te Da De
   Comer............................35 F3
Mesón Cumbres
   Mayores.........................36 E2

NIGHTLIFE 🍷 🍸
Cambalache.......................37 F3
Taberna Marqués de
   Cádiz 38 F4

ACCOMMODATION 🏠
Hotel Argantonio...............39 F3

TRANSPORT
Comes Bus Station 40 G2
Los Amarillos Bus Stop.....41 G4
Terminal Marítima
   Metropolitana.................42 H4

PARKING 🅿
Underground Car Park 43 G4
Underground Car Park 44 D5

the *ayuntamiento*, the **Barrio del Pópulo** neighbourhood was once the kernel of medieval Cádiz, a fortified enclosure wrecked by Anglo-Dutch raiders in 1596. Its boundaries are still marked by three 13th-century gate arches: the **Arco de los Blancos**, **Arco de la Rosa** and **Arco del Pópulo**.

The adjacent **Barrio de Santa María** was, in the 19th century, one of Cádiz' poorest barrios. From its lanes emerged one of Andalucía's strongest flamenco traditions, a legacy that lives on at the **Centro Municipal de Arte Flamenco 'La Merced'** (☎ 956 28 51 89; Plaza de la Merced s/n; ☾ 10am-2pm & 6-9pm Mon-Sat), which has regular flamenco performances and occasional courses. For something a little more earthy and spontaneous, the waterfront **Peña Flamenca La Perla** (☎ 956 25 91 01; Calle Carlos Ollero s/n; admission free), a cavernlike den of a club, hosts flamenco at 10pm on many Fridays in spring and summer.

Many visitors' favourite Cádiz barrio is the old fishers' quarter of **Barrio de la Viña**, close to the western end of the old city. The outdoor tables lining Calle Virgen de la Palma are the year-round hub of barrio life and the surrounding streets are *the* place to be during Carnaval.

☙ TEATRO ROMANO // SURVEY THE LAST VESTIGE OF ROMAN GADES

On the seaward edge of the Barrio del Pópulo, drop into the excavated **Teatro Romano** (Roman Theatre; ☎ 956 26 47 34; Campo del Sur s/n; admission free; ☾ 10am-2.30pm Wed-Mon), Cádiz' most easily accessible Roman site. It's a small seaside theatre and its ancient stage lies buried beneath the surrounding buildings, but you can walk along the gallery beneath the tiers of seating.

☙ SACRED CÁDIZ // SAVOUR CÁDIZ' CATHOLIC CHARACTER THEN JOURNEY BACK IN TIME

Cádiz' yellow-domed **cathedral** (☎ 956 28 61 54; Plaza de la Catedral; adult/child €5/3, 7-8pm & 11am-1pm Sun free; ☾ 10am-6.30pm Mon-Sat, 1-6.30pm Sun) fronts a handsome, broad, palm-lined plaza. Begun in 1716, the cathedral wasn't actually finished until 1838. The exterior, especially when flood-lit at night, and the large, circular underground crypt, built of stone excavated from the sea bed, are the highlights.

Outside the cathedral's eastern exterior wall is the fascinating **Casa del Obispo** (☎ 956 26 47 34; Plaza de Fray Félix 5; adult/child/senior €4/3.30/3.30, combined ticket with Torre de Poniente €6, audioguides €1; ☾ 10am-6pm mid-Sep–mid-Jun, to 8pm mid-Jun–mid-Sep). This expansive museum of glass walkways over 1500 sq metres of excavated ruins takes you through every conceivable period of Cádiz' history, from the 8th century BC to the 18th century. It served as a Phoenician funerary complex, Roman temple and the city's mosque, before becoming the city's Episcopal Palace in the 16th century. There are four free guided tours in Spanish daily.

A stone's throw to the east, the **Museo Catedralicio** (Cathedral Museum; ☎ 956 28 66 20; Plaza de Fray Félix; ☾ 10am-6.30pm Mon-Sat, 1-6.30pm Sun) has an excavated medieval street alongside cathedral treasures and assorted art.

☙ TOWERS OF CÁDIZ // CÁDIZ IN ALL ITS 360-DEGREE GLORY

Next to the main cathedral entrance on Plaza de la Catedral you can climb up inside the **Torre de Poniente** (Western Tower; ☎ 956 25 17 88; adult/child/senior €4/3.30/3.30, combined ticket with Casa del Obispo €6; ☾ 10am-6pm mid-Sep–mid-Jun, to 8pm mid-Jun–mid-Sep) for marvellous views over the old city with its many 18th-century

48 HOURS IN CÁDIZ

DIVE INTO THE BARRIOS

Cádiz is all about enjoying life and the best way to do this is wandering the streets of the old city's barrios (districts). **Barrio del Pópulo** (p111), **Barrio de Santa María** (p111), with its flamenco soundtrack, and **Barrio de la Viña** (p111), with its abundant outdoor tables, have the clearest identities, but the long narrow streets between the first two and the Barrio de la Viña take you through the heart of *gaditano* life.

THREE THOUSAND YEARS OF HISTORY

Cádiz is rich in signposts to the great civilisations that have called the Mediterranean home. Traces of Phoenician, Roman, Islamic and Christian Cádiz are on display at the **Museo de Cádiz** (below) and the **Casa del Obispo** (opposite). The **Teatro Romano** (opposite) is Cádiz' most impressive survivor from the Roman era, while the soaring aspirations of Catholic Spain are nowhere more glorious than in its **cathedral** (opposite).

CLIMB TO THE SUMMIT, RECOVER ON THE BEACH

There's no better way to appreciate Cádiz' crush of white buildings surrounded by a splendid arc of the Atlantic than from above. The **Torre de Poniente** (opposite) and **Torre Tavira** (below) provide panoramic views that you'll never forget. After the exertions of the climb, while away an afternoon on the **Playa de la Caleta** (p116) or the expansive beaches further east.

watchtowers (built so citizens could keep an eye on shipping movements without stepping outside their front doors). Back then, Cádiz had no less than 160 of these watchtowers: 127 still stand.

Northwest of Plaza de Topete, the **Torre Tavira** (☎ 956 21 29 10; www.torretavira .com; Calle Marqués del Real Tesoro 10; adult/child/senior €4/3.30/3.30; ☯ 10am-6pm mid-Sep–mid-Jun, to 8pm mid-Jun–mid-Sep) has another dramatic panorama of Cádiz and a camera obscura that projects live, moving images of the city onto a screen (sessions start every half-hour).

♥ PLAZA DE TOPETE // WANDER AMID FLOWERS AND FISH

A short walk northwest from the cathedral, this triangular plaza is one of Cádiz' most intimate, bright with flower stalls and still widely known by its old name, Plaza de las Flores (Square of the Flowers). It adjoins the large, animated **Mercado Central** (Central Market; ☯ 9.30am-2pm Mon-Sat), built in 1837 and the oldest covered market in Spain, but undergoing major renovations when we were there.

♥ MUSEUMS OF CÁDIZ // RAMBLE THROUGH HISTORY FROM GADIR TO CÁDIZ

The **Museo de Cádiz** (☎ 956 21 22 81; Plaza de Mina s/n; non-EU/EU citizen €1.50/free; ☯ 2.30-8.30pm Tue, 9am-8.30pm Wed-Sat, 9.30am-2.30pm Sun), on one of Cádiz' leafiest squares, is excellent. The ground-floor archaeology section includes two Phoenician marble sarcophagi carved in human likeness, lots of headless Roman statues, plus Emperor Trajan, with head, from the ruins of Baelo Claudia (see p147). The fine arts collection, upstairs, features a group of 18 superb canvases of saints, angels and monks by Francisco de Zurbarán. Also here is the painting that cost Murillo his life, the beautifully composed altarpiece from the chapel of Cádiz' Convento de Capuchinas (the artist died in 1682 after falling from the scaffolding).

The **Museo de las Cortes de Cádiz** (☎ 956 22 17 88; Calle Santa Inés s/n; admission free; ☿ 9am-6pm Tue-Fri, to 2pm Sat & Sun) is full of memorabilia of the 1812 Cádiz parliament. Pride of place goes to a large, marvellously detailed model of 18th-century Cádiz, made in mahogany and ivory.

For a complete change of pace, the engaging **Museo de Vinos y Toros** (Museum of Wine & Bulls; ☎ 956 28 97 16; www.vinosytoros.com, in Spanish; Calle Feduchy 17; admission €5; ☿ 10am-8pm) is like a window on the Andalusian soul. Displays include over 1000 (mostly antique) wine bottles from Cádiz province and a host of bullfighting photos, posters and lithographs, and the entry ticket includes a glass of wine.

❦ BEACHES // **ENJOY SOME OF SPAIN'S BEST CITY BEACHES**
Old Cádiz has one short curve of beach, **Playa de la Caleta**, while the newer part of the city is fronted by a superb, wide ocean beach of fine Atlantic sand, **Playa de la Victoria**; it begins about 1.5km beyond the Puerta de Tierra and stretches 4km back along the penin-

sula. On summer weekends almost the whole city seems to be here. Where the city ends, the beach continues under the name **Playa de la Cortadura**. Bus 1 ('Plaza España–Cortadura') from Plaza de España will get you to both beaches (€0.90).

❦ SPANISH COURSES // **LEARN SPANISH BY THE BEACH**
Cádiz is a terrific place to study Spanish language and culture. **Gadir Escuela Internacional de Español** (☎ /fax 956 26 05 57; www.gadir.net; Calle Pérgolas 5) is a recommended, long-established school southeast of the Puerta de Tierra. Other good language schools include: **Melkart Centro Internacional de Idiomas** (☎ /fax 956 22 22 13; www.centromelkart.com; Calle General Menacho 7); **K2 Internacional** (☎ 956 21 26 46; www.k2internacional.com; Plaza Mentidero 19); and **SIC** (☎ 956 25 27 24; www.spanishincadiz.com; Calle Condesa Villafuente Bermeja 7), about 1km southeast of the Puerta de Tierra. These schools also organise flamenco, salsa and even surf courses and a range of other activities, as well as accommodation.

GASTRONOMIC HIGHLIGHTS

Cádiz spans the full spectrum of earthy tapas bars and refined fine-dining restau-

FINE ARTS IN CÁDIZ

Hospital de Mujeres (Women's Hospital; ☎ 956 80 70 18; Calle Hospital de Mujeres 26; admission free; ☿ 10am-1.30pm & 6-8pm Mon-Thu, 10am-1.30pm Fri & Sat) El Greco's *Extasis de San Francisco* (Ecstasy of St Francis) adorns the extravagantly decorated church.
Museo de Cádiz (p115) Works by Zurbarán, Miró and Murillo.
Oratorio de la Santa Cueva (☎ 956 22 22 62; Calle Rosario 10; admission €2.50; ☿ 10am-1pm & 4.30-7.30pm Tue-Fri mid-Sep–mid-Jun, 10am-1pm & 5-8pm Tue-Fri mid-Jun–mid-Sep, 10am-1pm Sat & Sun year-round) Three impressive paintings by Goya in its richly decorated Capilla Alta.
Oratorio de San Felipe Neri (☎ 956 21 16 12; Plaza de San Felipe Neri; admission €2; ☿ 10am-1.30pm Mon-Sat) A masterly Murillo *Inmaculada* of 1680 in its main retable.

rants. The unifying theme is quality with an emphasis on seafood and hearty meat dishes from the Andalusian interior.

❦ ATXURI €€

☎ 956 25 36 13; www.atxuri.es, in Spanish; Calle Plocia 7; mains from €12; ⏰ 1-4.30pm daily & 9-11pm Thu-Sat
One of Cádiz' most decorated and long-standing restaurants, Atxuri fuses Basque and Andalusian influences and the result is a sophisticated range of flavours. *Bacalao* (cod) and high-quality steaks are recurring themes, as you'd expect in a place with Basque roots, but fish and meat tastes are such staples of Andalusian cooking that the boundary between Andalucía and the Basque Country is often deliciously blurred.

❦ BAR BALNEARIO €€

☎ 636 94 65 66; cnr Calle Virgen de la Palma & Calle San Félix; mains €10-18; ⏰ closed Sun evening & Mon
Most of the eateries in the Barrio de la Viña are pretty informal places in keeping with its working-class roots, but Bar Balneario has a touch of class. Perhaps that's why it's almost always full, but it could also be the *arroz señorito* (rice with peeled seafood) or *arroz negro* (black rice, cooked in squid ink), which requires a minimum of two people. Service is fast and friendly.

❦ CASA MANTECA €

☎ 956 21 36 03; Calle Corralón de los Carros 66; tapas €1.50-2; ⏰ closed Sun evening & Mon
The hub of La Viña's Carnaval fun, and with almost every inch of wall covered in colourful flamenco, bullfighting and Carnaval memorabilia, Casa Manteca is inevitably one of the barrio's liveliest and best tapas bars. They don't stand on ceremony here. Ask the amiable bar staff for a tapa of *chicharrones* – pressed pork dressed with a squeeze of lemon, served on a paper napkin and amazingly delicious.

❦ EL ALJIBE €€

☎ 956 26 66 56; www.pablogrosso.com; Calle Plocia 25; tapas €2-4, mains €11-15
Refined restaurant upstairs and super-cool tapas bar downstairs, El Aljibe on its own is almost reason enough to come to Cádiz. The cuisine developed by *gaditano* chef Pablo Grosso is a delicious combination of the traditional and the adventurous – *solomillo ibérico* (Iberian pork sirloin) stuffed with emmental cheese, ham and piquant peppers; seafood-stuffed halibut in puff pastry… There is no end to the surprises that may end up on your plate here.

❦ EL FARO €€

☎ 956 22 99 16; Calle San Félix 15; raciones & mains €6.50-24
Ask many *gaditanos* for their favourite Cádiz restaurant and there's a fair chance they'll choose El Faro. Close to the Playa de la Caleta, this place is at once crammed-to-the-rafters tapas bar and upmarket restaurant decorated with pretty ceramics. Seafood is why people come here, although the *rabo de toro* (bull's tail stew) has its devotees. If any place in this casual city has a dress code, it's El Faro, although even here it extends only to a prohibition on swimsuits…

❦ FREIDURÍA LAS FLORES €

☎ 956 22 61 12; Plaza de Topete 4; seafood per 250g €3-8
Cádiz' addiction to fried fish finds wonderful expression here. If it comes from the sea, chances are that it's been fried and served in Las Flores as either a tapa, *ración* (meal-sized serving of tapas) or *media-ración* (half a *ración*), or served in an improvised paper cup, fish-and-chips style. You order by weight (250g is the usual order). If you're finding it hard to choose, order a *surtido* (a mixed fry-up).

Tables can be hard to come by, especially at lunchtime.

🍴 LA GORDA TE DA DE COMER €

☎ 956 28 94 93; Calle General Luque 1; tapas €1.75, raciones €6; ⏱ 9-11.30pm Mon, 1.30-4pm & 9-11.30pm Tue-Thu, 1.30-4pm & 9pm-midnight Fri & Sat

Incredibly tasty food at incredibly low prices amid cool pop-art design. The tastes are fresh and innovative but it's almost always done with a discernibly local twist. No wonder competition for the half-dozen tables is fierce: get there at least 10 minutes before opening to avoid a long wait. Try the curried chicken strips with Marie-Rose sauce, the deep-fried aubergines with honey or a dozen other mouth-watering concoctions.

🍴 MESÓN CUMBRES MAYORES €€

☎ 956 21 32 70; Calle Zorrilla 4; tapas from €2, mains €9-19.50

This ever-busy place, dangling with hams and garlic, has, like so many of the best places in Cádiz, an excellent tapas bar in the front and a small restaurant in the back, both serving delicious fare at reasonable prices. In the bar it's hard to beat the *montaditos* (open sandwiches). In the restaurant, there are great salads, seafood, barbecued meats and the *guisos* (stews) that this part of Andalucía is famous for.

NIGHTLIFE

Cádiz has intriguing bars around every corner. They range from old tile-walled joints with a few locals chinwagging over a *vino tinto* (red wine) to chic music bars with a cool young clientele. The area around Plazas San Francisco, España and Mina is the hub of the old city's late-night bar scene. Things get going around 11pm or midnight at these places but can be quiet in the first half of the week.

🍴 CAMBALACHE

Calle José del Toro 20; ⏱ closed Sun

This long, dim, jazz and blues bar often hosts live music on Thursdays around

---

CÁDIZ PROVINCE ACCOMMODATION

Cádiz has numerous outstanding accommodation choices – read about them in detail in our dedicated accommodation chapter (p378). We recommend that you book somewhere in advance, and base yourself there for a week or two while you make day trips around the region. Gibraltar's accommodation is fairly unexciting, which may be why many travellers visit the area just for a day trip. Some of our favourites in Cádiz province include the following:

★ In the heart of Andalucía's sherry country, **Casa No 6** (p385) occupies a converted mansion in El Puerto de Santa María

★ **La Casa Grande** (p386) is a gorgeous cliff-side mansion in Arcos de la Frontera with massage, yoga and a roof terrace

★ A short walk from the beach in Los Caños de Meca, **Casas Karen** (p387) is a stylish, laid-back rural retreat with apartments and traditional huts

★ Tumbling down the steep hillside in Vejer de la Frontera, **Hotel La Casa del Califa** (p386) has Islamic-style decor and a terrific location

★ Tarifa's **Posada La Sacristía** (p387) is a charming boutique hotel close to Spain's southernmost tip

10.30pm, but it's the sort of place that has a great atmosphere most nights of the week.

♥ TABERNA MARQUÉS DE CÁDIZ

☎ 956 25 42 88; Calle Marqués de Cádiz 3; admission free

In addition to the flamenco options listed on p114, this stone-walled grotto not far from Plaza San Juan de Dios offers flamenco nights starting at 10pm every Friday.

TRANSPORT

BOAT // The catamaran (www.cmtbc.es, in Spanish) leaves from the Terminal Marítima Metropolitana with 18 daily departures for El Puerto de Santa María (€1.95) Monday to Friday, but just six/five on Saturdays/Sundays.

CAR & MOTORCYCLE // The AP4 motorway from Seville to Puerto Real, on the eastern side of the Bahía de Cádiz, carries a toll of €5.64. From Puerto Real, a bridge crosses the neck of the bay to join the A48 entering Cádiz from the south.

PARKING // Twenty-four-hour car parks in the old city include the following:

Underground car park (Campo del Sur; per 24hr €17)

Underground car park (Paseo de Canalejas; per 24hr €9)

TRAIN // From the train station (☎ 956 25 43 01; Plaza de Sevilla), plenty of trains run daily to/from El Puerto de Santa María, Jerez de la Frontera, Seville and Madrid. The high-speed AVE service from Madrid should reach Cádiz by 2012.

BUS // Comes (☎ 956 80 70 59; www.tgcomes .es; Plaza de la Hispanidad) has regular departures to Arcos de la Frontera, El Puerto de Santa María, Granada, Jerez de la Frontera, Los Caños de Meca (via El Palmar), Málaga, Ronda, Seville, Tarifa, Vejer de la Frontera and Zahara de los Atunes. In addition to some of the above destinations, Los Amarillos (www.losamarillos .es) also runs buses to El Bosque, Sanlúcar de Barrameda and Ubrique from the southern end of Avenida Ramón

de Carranza. Buses M050 and M051, run by the Consorcio de Transportes Bahía de Cádiz (☎ 956 01 21 00; www.cmtbc.com), travel from Jerez de la Frontera airport to Cádiz' Comes bus station, via Jerez city and El Puerto de Santa María.

THE SHERRY TRIANGLE

· · · · · ·

North of Cádiz, the towns of Jerez de la Frontera, Sanlúcar de Barrameda and El Puerto de Santa María are best known as the homes of that unique, smooth Andalusian wine, sherry. But the 'sherry triangle' also offers a rich mixture of additional attractions: beaches, music, horses, trips into the Parque Nacional de Doñana, and a fascinating history.

EL PUERTO DE SANTA MARÍA

pop 85,100

El Puerto, 10km northeast of Cádiz across the Bahía de Cádiz (22km by road), is easily and enjoyably reached by ferry – a fitting way to arrive at a town with such a rich seagoing history. Christopher Columbus was a guest of the knights of El Puerto from 1483 to 1486: it was here that he met Juan de la Cosa, the owner of his 1492 flagship, the *Santa María*. El Puerto's heyday came in the 18th century, when it flourished on American trade and earned the name Ciudad de los Cien Palacios (City of the Hundred Palaces). A lingering sense of this era is what gives the town its charm, with its high-walled white facades suggesting more than they reveal, only for the whole town to emerge from their patios onto the streets during summer

THE SECRET OF SHERRY

How you get your bottle of sherry is intriguing. Once sherry grapes have been harvested, they are pressed and the resulting must is left to ferment. Within a few months a frothy veil of *flor* (yeast) appears on the surface. The wine is then transferred to the bodegas (wineries) in big barrels of American oak.

Wine enters the *solera* (from *suelo,* meaning floor) process when it's a year old. The barrels, about five-sixths full, are lined up in rows at least three barrels high. The barrels on the bottom layer, called the *solera,* contain the oldest wine. From these, around three times a year, 10% of the wine is drawn off. This is replaced with the same amount from the barrels in the layer above, which is in turn replaced from the next layer. The wines age for between three and seven years. A small amount of brandy is added to stabilise the wine before bottling, bringing the alcohol content to 16% to 18%, which stops fermentation.

See p373 for an explanation of the various types of sherry. Jerez *coñac* (brandy), widely drunk in Spain, is also a profitable, locally made product – around 65 million bottles are produced annually.

evenings. The town also has a fine array of restaurants, beaches and world-renowned sherry bodegas.

ESSENTIAL INFORMATION

TOURIST OFFICE // Tourist office (☎ 956 54 24 13; www.turismoelpuerto.com; Calle Luna 22; ☾ 10am-2pm & 6-8pm May-Sep, 10am-2pm & 5.30-7.30pm Oct-Apr)

EXPLORING EL PUERTO DE SANTA MARÍA

El Puerto can seem like southern Andalucía in microcosm, offering an abundance of good beaches, sherry bodegas and a smattering of architectural gems.

♥ SHERRY BODEGAS // LEARN ABOUT EL PUERTO'S MOST FAMOUS EXPORT

Much of the world's best-loved sherry comes from this region and visiting one of the local bodegas affords a fascinating insight into what makes El Puerto tick. Most of El Puerto's sherry producers open their doors to the public, their

guided tours taking you through the various stages of production and the bottling process, and you can visit their on-site museums and sample the final product. The bodegas customarily boast extensive gardens fringed with tall palm trees. Tours are in Spanish with English translations as required (or all in English if only English-speakers are present).

Phone ahead to visit **Bodegas Osborne** (☎ 956 86 91 00; www.osborne.es/rrpp; Calle los Moros 7; admission €7.50; ☾ tours English 10.30am, Spanish noon & German 12.30pm Mon-Fri, English 11am & Spanish noon Sat), which was founded in 1772, making it one of Andalucía's oldest. You'll also need to book ahead at **Bodegas 501** (☎ 956 85 55 11; Calle Valdés 9; admission €6; ☾ 9am-1pm Mon-Fri), but bookings aren't necessary at **Bodegas Gutiérrez Colosía** (☎ 956 85 28 52; www.gutierrez-colosia .com; Avenida de la Bajamar 40; admission €4-5; ☾ tours 1pm Mon-Thu, 1pm & 7.30pm Fri, 12.30pm & 1.30pm Sat). At **Bodegas Terry** (☎ 956 15 15 00; www .bodegasterry.com; Calle Toneleros 1; tour €8, tour & horse show €15; ☾ 10.30am & 12.30pm Mon-Fri, noon Sat), famous for its brandy, prior bookings are necessary only for the Saturday tour;

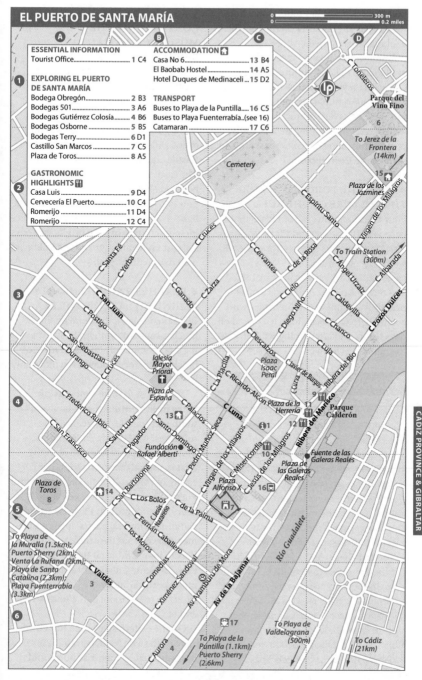

EL PUERTO DE SANTA MARÍA

0 _____ 300 m
0 _____ 0.2 miles

ESSENTIAL INFORMATION
Tourist Office.................................. 1 C4

**EXPLORING EL PUERTO
DE SANTA MARÍA**
Bodega Obregón............................ 2 B3
Bodegas 501.................................... 3 A6
Bodegas Gutiérrez Colosía.......... 4 B6
Bodegas Osborne 5 B5
Bodegas Terry................................. 6 D1
Castillo San Marcos 7 C5
Plaza de Toros................................ 8 A5

**GASTRONOMIC
HIGHLIGHTS**
Casa Luis 9 D4
Cervecería El Puerto.....................10 C4
Romerijo 11 D4
Romerijo 12 C4

ACCOMMODATION
Casa No 6.. 13 B4
El Baobab Hostel 14 A5
Hotel Duques de Medinaceli ... 15 D2

TRANSPORT
Buses to Playa de la Puntilla..... 16 C5
Buses to Playa Fuenterrabía..(see 16)
Catamaran 17 C6

Parque del
Vino Fino

To Jerez de la
Frontera
(14km)

Plaza de los
Jazmines

Cemetery

To Train Station
(300m)

Iglesia
Mayor
Prioral

Plaza de
España

Plaza
Isaac
Peral

Parque
Calderón

Plaza de la
Herrería

Fundación
Rafael Alberti

Fuente de las
Galeras Reales

Plaza de
las Galeras
Reales

Plaza
Alfonso X

Plaza de
Toros

To Playa de
la Muralla (1.5km);
Puerto Sherry (2km);
Venta La Rufana (2km);
Playa de Santa
Catalina (2.3km);
Playa Fuenterrabía
(3.3km)

Río Guadalete

To Playa de
Valdelagrana
(500m)

To Cádiz
(21km)

To Playa de la
Puntilla (1.1km);
Puerto Sherry
(2.6km)

CÁDIZ PROVINCE & GIBRALTAR

Bodegas Terry also has tours with a horse spectacular at 11am on Fridays, for which bookings are required.

Less a winery than an essential part of El Puerto's sherry culture, **Bodega Obregón** (☎ 956 85 63 29; Calle Zarza 51; ☺ 9am-2pm & 6-9pm Mon-Fri, 10am-3pm Sat) claims to be the oldest tavern in town. It overflows with barrels, bullfighting memorabilia, posters from Semana Santas past and old men taking their tipple.

♠ PLAZA DE TOROS // EXPLORE THE CULTURE OF THE BULL

Four blocks southwest from Plaza de España is El Puerto's grand **Plaza de Toros** (Plaza Elías Ahuja; admission free; ☺ 11am-1.30pm & 6-7.30pm Tue-Sun May-Sep, 11am-1.30pm & 5.30-7pm Tue-Sun Oct-Apr), which was built in 1880 and remains one of Andalucía's most beautiful and important bullrings, with room for 15,000 spectators. It's closed on days before and after bullfights. Entry to the bullring is from Calle Valdés.

ROADSIDE BULLS

From time to time along the highways of Spain, the silhouette of a truly gigantic black bull looms on the horizon. When you get closer, you'll realise it's made of metal and held up by scaffolding. These are the *toros de Osborne,* silent and unlettered advertisements for the Osborne sherry and brandy company of El Puerto de Santa María. In the 1990s, the bulls were set to disappear after a law was enacted banning roadside advertising in the interests of road safety. But such was the public outcry that the authorities relented and the bulls were allowed to remain as a recognised national symbol. At last count there were 92 Osborne bulls, each weighing up to four tonnes, looming beside roads all over Spain.

♠ CASTILLO SAN MARCOS // CONTEMPLATE THE MUSLIM-CHRISTIAN PAST BENEATH THE TURRETS

Heavily restored in the 20th century, the fine **Castillo San Marcos** (☎ 956 85 17 51; Plaza Alfonso X; admission Tue/Thu & Sat free/€5; ☺ tours 11.30am, 12.30pm & 1.30pm Tue, 10.30am, 11.30am, 12.30pm & 1.30pm Thu & Sat) was built over a Muslim mosque by Alfonso X of Castile after he took the town in 1260. The castle's decorated battlements are beautiful, but the old mosque inside, now converted into a church, is the highlight. The Thursday and Saturday tours include a tasting of local products. Tours last just under an hour and the last ones each day are in English.

♠ BEACHES // LEAVE THE CITY BEHIND TO LAZE ON THE BEACH

El Puerto is one of the more popular beach escapes in southern Spain, drawing a predominantly Spanish crowd of beach-lovers for its fabulous white sandy beaches.

The closest to town is pine-flanked **Playa de la Puntilla**, a half-hour walk southwest (or take bus 26, heading southwest on Avenida Aramburu de Mora). A couple of kilometres further west is a swish marina development called, of course, **Puerto Sherry**. Beyond Puerto Sherry is picturesque **Playa de la Muralla**, and the 3km **Playa de Santa Catalina**, with beach bars open in summer. Bus 35 from the centre runs out to **Playa Fuenterrabía**, at the far end of Playa de Santa Catalina. If you're driving, take the 'Rota' and 'Playas' road west from the roundabout at the northwest end of Calle Valdés.

On the eastern side of the Río Guadalete is **Playa de Valdelagrana**, a fine beach backed by high-rise hotels and apartments and a strip of bars and restaurants. Bus 35 also runs there.

❦ FERIA DE PRIMAVERA Y FIESTAS DEL VINO FINO // CELEBRATE THE DRINK THAT MADE EL PUERTO GREAT

This four-day fiesta (the Spring Fair) confirms that El Puerto's *fino* (sherry) is not just produced for export. During the fiesta, in late April or early May, around 200,000 half-bottles are drunk.

FESTIVALS & EVENTS

In addition to the Feria de Primavera y Fiestas del Vino Fino (above), El Puerto also hosts the following:

Campeonato del Mundo de Motociclismo de Jerez An unofficial motorbike fiesta takes over El Puerto for the weekend in early May of the Jerez Grand Prix event of the World Motorcycle Championship (see p131).

Festividad Virgen del Carmen Fisherfolk Andalucía-wide pay homage to their patron on the evening of 16 July; in El Puerto the virgin's image is paraded along the Río Guadalete followed by a flotilla.

GASTRONOMIC HIGHLIGHTS

El Puerto is rightly famed for its outstanding seafood, fine restaurants and terrific tapas bars. Try the local speciality *urta roteña* (sea bream cooked in white wine, tomatoes, peppers and thyme), and it would be sacrilege to wash it down with anything other than a local wine.

❦ CASA LUIS €€

☎ 956 87 20 09; Ribera del Marisco s/n; ☽ 1.30-4pm & 9-11pm Tue-Sat, 1.30-4pm Sun

This is a tightly packed little den with just a few tables inside and out, and a bar you can only elbow towards. Come for amiable Luis' innovative tapas, such as *paté de cabracho* (red scorpion fish pâté)

or *hojaldres* (puff pastries) with prawn, or cheese and anchovy filling.

❦ CERVECERÍA EL PUERTO €€

☎ 956 85 89 39; Calle Misericordia 15; tapas/raciones €3/8; ☽ 11.30am-4.30pm & 8-11.30pm Wed-Mon, closed Dec

In its own words this place specialises in seafood and beer here, which is clearly a winning combination if the lack of room at the bar is any indication. The restaurant offers a full range of Mediterranean fish and seafood specialities, as well as plenty of dishes from Galicia, a world away to the northwest; the *navajas* (razor clams) are unrivalled along this stretch of coast.

❦ ROMERIJO €€

☎ 956 54 12 54; www.romerijo.com; Ribera del Marisco s/n; seafood per 250g from €4

Arguably one of the most famous purveyors of seafood in Andalucía, this El Puerto institution occupies two facing buildings. One building boils the seafood, the other fries it, and you buy portions in paper cones to take away or eat at the many tables. Everything's on display (boggle at the nearly 20 types of fresh seafood) and you just take your pick and buy by the quarter-kilo. You haven't been to El Puerto if you haven't eaten here.

❦ VENTA LA RUFANA €€

☎ 956 85 66 16; Carretera Fuentebravía Km2; raciones from €6, mains from €9; ☽ Fri-Wed

Around 2km west of the bullring on the road to Fuentebravía, Venta La Rufana is wildly popular for its fantastic fish and seafood with a few meat dishes thrown in. It's hard to know where to start, but the *salmonetes fritos* (fried red mullet) and *urta roteña* are recurring favourites, as is the *tarta de queso* (cheesecake) for dessert. Be prepared to wait for a table, especially in summer.

TRANSPORT

BOAT // The catamaran (www.cmtbc.es, in Spanish) leaves from in front of the Hotel Santa María bound for Cádiz' Terminal Marítima Metropolitana (€1.95) with 18 daily departures Monday to Friday and six/five on Saturdays/Sundays.

PARKING // You shouldn't pay more than €1 per day in most supervised parking areas, including at the train station, around the Plaza de Toros and along the riverfront. The partly covered parking next to the catamaran departure costs €10 per day.

TRAIN // Dozens of trains travel daily to/from Jerez de la Frontera, Cádiz and Seville.

BUS // Regular bus services connect El Puerto de Santa María's Plaza de Toros to Cádiz, Jerez de la Frontera and Sanlúcar de Barrameda. Buses to Seville go daily from the train station.

SANLÚCAR DE BARRAMEDA

pop 67,000

The northern tip of the sherry triangle and a thriving summer resort, Sanlúcar has a likeable, mellow atmosphere just across the Guadalquivir estuary from the Parque Nacional de Doñana. The Atlantic waters here provide the freshest of succulent seafood (Sanlúcar prawns carry a high price tag) and the town's bodegas produce a perfect complement, the distinctive sherrylike wine, manzanilla. Sanlúcar also lays on the fabulous spectacle of its unique August horse races when sleek horses thunder along the sands beside the estuary.

This is a town with a distinguished history. Columbus sailed from Sanlúcar in 1498 on his third voyage to the Caribbean, as did the Portuguese Ferdinand Magellan in 1519, seeking – like Columbus – a westerly route to the Asian Spice Islands. His Basque pilot Juan Sebastián Elcano completed the first circumnavigation of the globe by returning to Sanlúcar

with just one of the expedition's five ships, the *Victoria*.

ESSENTIAL INFORMATION

TOURIST OFFICE // Tourist office (☎ 956 36 61 10; Calzada del Ejército s/n; ◷ 10am-2pm & 4-6pm Mon-Fri Nov-Mar, 10am-2pm & 5-7pm Mon-Fri Apr, May & Oct, 10am-2pm & 6-8pm Mon-Fri, 10am-12.45pm Sat, 10am-2pm Sun Jun-Sep)

ORIENTATION

Sanlúcar stretches along the southeast side of the Guadalquivir estuary. Calzada del Ejército (often just called La Calzada), running 600m inland from the seafront Paseo Marítimo, is the main avenue and has underground parking (€8 to €16 per day). A block beyond its inland end is Plaza del Cabildo, the central square. The old town spreads around and uphill from here. The old fishing quarter, Bajo de Guía, site of Sanlúcar's best restaurants and boat departures to Doñana, is 750m northeast along the riverfront from La Calzada.

EXPLORING SANLÚCAR DE BARRAMEDA

Sanlúcar has a number of calling cards, from its monument-strewn old town and numerous bodegas, to wonderful seafood restaurants by the water. It's also a good base for visits to the Parque Nacional de Doñana.

♥ **OLD TOWN // DISCOVER ORNATE MONUMENTS ALONG QUIET WHITEWASHED STREETS**
Although Sanlúcar draws massive summer crowds, the old town atop the hill is another world altogether. As you climb up the Cuesta de Belén, watch out for the elaborate Gothic facade of **Las Covachas** (Cuesta de Belén), all that remains of a set of

15th-century wine cellars. The brightly painted **Palacio de Orleans y Borbon** (cnr Cuesta de Belén & Calle Caballero; admission free; 10am-1.30pm Mon-Fri) is a beautiful neo-Mudéjar palace. Built in the 19th century as an aristocratic summer home, today it's Sanlúcar's *ayuntamiento* (town hall). It has a ritzy restored patio with glass roof.

Southwest along Calle Caballero, the 15th-century **Iglesia de Nuestra Señora de la O** (Plaza de la Paz; mass 7.30pm Mon-Fri, 9am, noon & 7.30pm Sun) has a Mudéjar facade and ceiling. Next door is the **Palacio de los Duques de Medina Sidonia** (956 36 01 61; www.fcmedinasidonia.com; Plaza Condes de Niebla 1; admission €3; tours 11am & noon Mon-Sat, by appointment Sun), a rambling stately home that dates all the way back to Guzmán El Bueno, the 13th-century Reconquista hero. The house is bursting with antique furniture and paintings by famous Spanish artists, even Goya and Zurbarán. To soak up the old-world vibe, treat yourself to afternoon tea at the beautiful patio **cafe** (8am-9.30pm Sun-Fri, 9.30am-2am Sat), or, better still, enjoy a night of luxury (see p385).

Further along Calle Caballero is the 15th-century **Castillo de Santiago** (956 08 83 29; www.castillodesantiago.com, in Spanish; Plaza del Castillo de Santiago s/n; guided tours 11am, noon & 1pm Thu-Sun). There are fine views over the town from the towers if you take the tour, or there's the **Restaurante El Castillo de Santiago** (650 48 17 01; www.restaurantecastillo santiago.com; starters €8.50-14.50, mains €9.50-24.50; 11.30am-4pm & 7.30-11.30pm Tue-Sun), in the Patio de Armas, with exposed stone walls and high wooden beams.

PARQUE NACIONAL DE DOÑANA // LEARN ABOUT DOÑANA THEN JOIN A TOUR

The Parque Nacional de Doñana (p84) is visible just across the Guadalquivir from Sanlúcar, which serves as an excel-lent base for forays into the park. Before setting out, stop by the **Centro de Visitantes Fábrica de Hielo** (956 38 16 35; Bajo de Guía s/n; 9am-7pm or 8pm), an original visitor centre run by the national parks folk. This is also where you buy tickets for the **Real Fernando** (956 36 38 13; www.visitasdonana.com; adult/student/senior/child €17/12/12/9; 10am Nov-Feb, 10am & 4pm Mar-May & Oct, 10am & 5pm Jun-Sep), a leisurely 3½-hour boat trip around the park's fringes; it's more for day trippers than serious nature enthusiasts. Book up to a week in advance.

To delve a little deeper, **Viajes Doñana** (956 36 25 40; viajesdonana@hotmail.com; Calle San Juan 20; 8.30am & 4.30pm Tue & Fri May–mid-Sep, 8.30am & 2.30pm Tue & Fri mid-Sep–Apr) and **Viajes Recorrecaminos** (956 38 20 40; correcaminosvipvip@sarenet.es; Calle Ramón y Cajal 4) run fun tours in 4WD vehicles holding about 20 people, going deep into the national park through the dunes, marsh-lands and pine forests. Expect to pay around €40 per person.

SEAFOOD BY THE SEA // SAVOUR THE SEAFOOD AND MANZANILLA BY THE GUADALQUIVIR

Strung out along the Bajo de Guía is one of Andalucía's most famous restaurant strips, which is reason enough for visit-ing Sanlúcar. Most restaurants have outdoor tables and an upstairs dining area, and the undisputed speciality is *arroz caldoso a la marinera* (seafood rice), which usually costs around €9 per person and requires at least two for an order. And, of course, don't think about washing it down with anything other than a fresh local manzanilla. The most renowned of these restaurants is **Casa Bigote** (956 36 26 96; www.restaurantecasa bigote.com; Bajo de Guía; fish mains €8-15; Mon-Sat), which has a classier air than most places and serves only fish and seafood. Its tapas bar across the small lane is always packed. Other recommended options among many include **Casa Juan** (☎ 956 36 11 44; Bajo de Guía; ☺ lunch & dinner daily mid-Jul–mid-Sep, lunch daily & dinner Fri & Sat mid-Sep–mid-Jul) and the more informal **Bar Joselito Huertas** (☎ 956 36 26 94; Bajo de Guía; fried fish from €10).

♥ CASA BALBINO // SIDLE UP FOR SANLÚCAR'S MOST POPULAR TAPAS

It doesn't seem to matter when you're here, but **Casa Balbino** (☎ 956 36 05 13; Plaza del Cabildo 11; tapas/raciones from €2/10) is always overflowing with people, drawn here by the fantastic seafood tapas on offer. Whether you're standing at the bar or lucky enough to have snaffled one of the outdoor tables on the plaza, you'll need to elbow your way to the bar, shout your order to a waiter who'll shout back and then you carry your plate to your chosen corner. The list of possibilities is endless, but the *tortillas de camarones* (crisp shrimp fritters) and *langostinos a la plancha* (grilled king prawns; per kg €100) are the best we've tasted.

♥ BARBADILLO // DISCOVER THE SECRETS OF MANZANILLA

Sanlúcar is famous for its unique manzanilla wine and Barbadillo is easily its most famous export, not to mention the producers of one of Spain's most popular wines. The **Barbadillo bodega** (☎ 956 38 55 00; www.museobarbadillo.com; Calle Luis de Eguilaz 11; tour €3, museum free; ☺ tours noon & 1pm Mon-Sat, in English 11am Tue-Sat, Museo de Manzanilla 10am-3pm Mon-Sat) has a museum in a 19th-century building that traces the 200-year history of manzanilla wine and the history of the Barbadillo family, the first to bottle manzanilla. The tourist office has a list of the other six or so bodegas scattered around Sanlúcar, some of which offer tours.

FESTIVALS & EVENTS

Feria de la Manzanilla The Sanlúcar summer begins with a big fair devoted to Sanlúcar's unique wine, manzanilla; held late May/early June.

Romería del Rocío (Pentecost) Many pilgrims and covered wagons set out for El Rocío (see p88) from here; seventh weekend after Easter.

Music Festivals Summer revs up in July and August with jazz, flamenco and classical music festivals, and one-off concerts by top Spanish bands.

Carreras de Caballos (www.carrerassanlucar .com) Two horse-race meetings of three or four days every August; exciting thoroughbred races on the sands beside the Guadalquivir estuary, held almost every year since 1845.

TRANSPORT

BUS // **Los Amarillos** (☎ 956 38 50 60) runs buses to/from El Puerto de Santa María, Cádiz and Seville from the bus station on Avenida de la Estación. **Linesur** (☎ 956 34 10 63) has buses to/from Jerez de la Frontera.

JEREZ DE LA FRONTERA

pop 202,700

Few cities capture the Andalusian spirit quite like Jerez (heh-*reth* or, in the Andalusian accent, just heh-*reh*). Jerez has it all: sherry bodegas in abundance, a world-renowned centre of Andalusian horse culture, a tangled old town topped by an Islamic-era *alcázar* (Muslim-era fortress) and plenty of places to hear authentic flamenco. But that's only part of Jerez' story. This is an affluent city where the locals dress up to go out and buy bread, yet it's also home to a *gitano* (Roma) community that is a hotbed of flamenco. It's the smell of fragrant lavender on the whitewashed streets that empty on summer afternoons as the city sleeps the siesta en masse. And it's a city whose historical legacy owes as much to Islam as it does to the British families who played such a prominent role in the development of Jerez' sherry culture.

ESSENTIAL INFORMATION

TOURIST OFFICE // Municipal tourist office (☎ 956 33 88 74; www.turismojerez.com; Alameda Cristina; ☺ 9am-3pm & 5-7pm Mon-Fri, 9.30am-2.30pm Sat & Sun mid-Jun–mid-Sep, 9am-3pm & 4.30-6.30pm Mon-Fri, 9.30am-2.30pm Sat & Sun mid-Sep–mid-Jun)

ORIENTATION

The centre of Jerez is between the Alameda Cristina and the revamped Plaza del Arenal, which are connected by the north–south Calle Larga and Calle Lancería (both pedestrianised). The old quarter extends west and southeast of Calle Larga.

EXPLORING JEREZ DE LA FRONTERA

The main architectural sights in Jerez are clustered around the old town. But this is a city that's as much about experiencing as seeing, from the subtle tastes in the sherry bodegas to the soul-stirring strains of flamenco, from the sensory overload in Jerez' hammam to the uplifting elegance of Andalusian horses on show.

❧ OLD QUARTER // FOLLOW THE SIGNPOSTS TO JEREZ' ISLAMIC AND CHRISTIAN PAST

The centrepiece of Old Jerez is the impressive 11th- and 12th-century Islamic fortress southwest of Plaza del Arenal, the **Alcázar** (☎ 956 14 99 55; www.webjerez

.com; Alameda Vieja; admission incl/excl camera obscura €5.40/3; ☺ 10am-7.30pm Mon-Sat, to 2.30pm Sun May–mid-Sep, 10am-5.30pm Mon-Sat, to 2.30pm Sun mid-Sep–Apr). Soon after entering the Alcázar, you enter the beautiful mezquita (mosque), which was converted to a chapel by Alfonso X in 1264. Beyond the Patio de Armas, the lovely gardens recreate the ambience of Islamic times with their geometrical plant beds and tinkling fountains, while the domed Baños Árabes (Arab Baths) with their shafts of light are another highlight. Back on the Patio de Armas, the 18th-century Palacio Villavicencio, built over the ruins of the old Islamic palace, contains works of art, but is best known for its bird's-eye view of Jerez from the summit; the palace's tower also contains a camera obscura, which provides a picturesque live panorama of Jerez.

Immediately northwest of the Alcázar, Jerez' mainly 18th-century **Catedral de San Salvador** (Plaza de la Encarnación; admission free; ☺ 11am-1pm Mon-Fri, mass 8am Tue-Sat, 5.30pm Sun & Mon), which has Gothic, baroque and neoclassical features, was built on the site of the Islamic town's main mosque.

A couple of blocks northeast of the cathedral is Plaza de la Asunción and the handsome 16th-century **Antiguo Cabildo** (Old Town Hall), with a Renaissance facade and an entrance flanked by statues of Hercules and Julius Caesar.

Southeast of Plaza del Arenal is one of Jerez' loveliest churches, the 16th-century **Iglesia de San Miguel** (Plaza San Miguel; ☺ mass 8pm Mon-Sat, 9am, noon & 8pm Sun), built in Isabelline Gothic style but with a baroque main facade. It features superb stone carving, beautiful stained-glass windows, an elaborate retable by Juan Martínez Montañés, and a distinctive blue-and-white-tiled steeple.

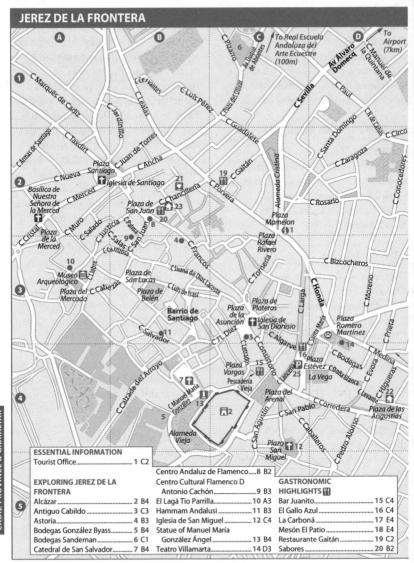

JEREZ DE LA FRONTERA

ESSENTIAL INFORMATION
Tourist Office...................................... 1 C2

EXPLORING JEREZ DE LA FRONTERA
Alcázar... 2 B4
Antiguo Cabildo 3 C3
Astoria... 4 B3
Bodegas González Byass.................. 5 B4
Bodegas Sandeman........................... 6 C1
Catedral de San Salvador................. 7 B4

Centro Andaluz de Flamenco.....8 B2
Centro Cultural Flamenco D
   Antonio Cachón...........................9 B3
El Lagá Tio Parrilla......................... 10 A3
Hammam Andalusi 11 B3
Iglesia de San Miguel 12 C4
Statue of Manuel María
   González Ángel......................... 13 B4
Teatro Villamarta.......................... 14 D3

GASTRONOMIC HIGHLIGHTS
Bar Juanito.. 15 C4
El Gallo Azul..................................... 16 C4
La Carboná.. 17 E4
Mesón El Patio................................. 18 E4
Restaurante Gaitán........................ 19 C2
Sabores... 20 B2

♥ HAMMAM ANDALUSI // PAMPER YOURSELF IN A RE-CREATION OF ISLAMIC-ERA BATHS

Jerez is replete with echoes of the city's Islamic past, but there is none more evocative than the **Hammam Andalusi** (Arabic baths; ☎ 956 34 90 66; www.hammam andalusi.com; Calle Salvador 6; baths €18, with 15min massage €28, full Andalusian bath €85; ☾ 10am-midnight). As soon as you enter, you're greeted by the wafting scent of incense and essential oils, and the soothing sound of tinkling water and Arab music. Once inside, you pass, depending on the

NIGHTLIFE
Tetería La Jaima 21 B2

ACCOMMODATION
Hotel Casa Grande 22 D4
Hotel Chancillería 23 B2

TRANSPORT
Bus Station 24 F4

PARKING
Parking Doña Blanca 25 C4

package you choose, through the three pools (hot, tepid or cold) as well as add a massage and/or a variety of beauty treatments. There's even a chocolate bath (€85). Numbers per session are limited to 15 people, so be sure to reserve beforehand.

🌸 FLAMENCO // IMMERSE YOURSELF IN FLAMENCO IN THE GENRE'S HOMELAND

Jerez is at the heart of the Seville–Cádiz axis where flamenco began and where its heartland remains today, and the **Barrio de Santiago**, north and west of the old town and with a sizeable *gitano* population, is Jerez' true home of flamenco. The barrio is littered with *peñas flamencas,* flamenco 'clubs', where flamenco is taken seriously by their members and where performances generally capture the flamenco spirit better than the pricier *tablaos*, with their tourist-oriented dinner-and-floor-show nights.

Your first stop should be the **Centro Andaluz de Flamenco** (Andalusian Flamenco Centre; ☎ 856 81 41 32; www.centroandaluz deflamenco.es, in Spanish; Plaza de San Juan 1; ⏰ 9am-2pm Mon-Fri). At once architecturally interesting (note the original 15th-century Mudéjar *artesonado* ceiling in the entrance and the 18th-century Andalusian baroque courtyard) and a fantastic flamenco resource, the centre has print and music libraries holding thousands of works. Flamenco videos are screened at 10am, 11am, noon and 1pm, and staff can provide you with a list of 17 local *peñas,* as well as flamenco dance and singing classes in Jerez. Its website also lists upcoming performances under the 'Festivales' tab.

One of the better *peñas* in the area is the **Centro Cultural Flamenco D Antonio Cachón** (☎ 956 34 74 72; Calle Salas 2; ⏰ noon-3.30pm & 8pm-midnight), which often hosts top-notch flamenco performers on Saturdays at 10pm. At other times, wander inside to catch a glimpse of the dark and smoky *peña* atmosphere and you may occasionally be rewarded with some impromptu flamenco in the evenings.

If the *peñas* are quiet when you're in town and you're still keen to get a flavour for flamenco, one reputable *tablao* worth trying is **El Lagá Tio Parrilla** (☎ 956 33 83 34; Plaza del Mercado; admission around €25; ☺ shows 10.30pm Mon-Sat).

In late February and/or early March there's the two-week **Festival de Jerez** (www.festivaldejerez.com), which draws some of the biggest names in flamenco. The **Teatro Villamarta** (☎ 956 32 71 00; www .villamarta.com; Plaza Romero Martínez) is the main venue. There are also flamenco performances in September during the Fiestas de Otoño (opposite). Finally, the Viernes Flamencos season sees open-air flamenco performances on August Friday nights at the **Astoria** (Calle Francos); the season culminates in the Fiesta de la Bulería, a festival of flamenco song and dance held in the Plaza de Toros, one Saturday in September.

♥ SHERRY BODEGAS // UNLOCK THE SECRETS OF SHERRY IN JEREZ'S BODEGAS

Jerez has at least 20 sherry producers, including famous names such as González Byass, Williams & Humbert, Sandeman,

WHAT'S IN A NAME?

Tio Pepe, the famous dry sherry produced by Jerez' Bodegas González Byass, is one of the best-known popular icons in Spain, but very few people know where its name comes from. Mystery solved. Between Jerez' Alcázar and the Catedral de San Salvador stands a large **statue of Manuel María González Ángel** (1812–87), the founder of Bodegas González Byass. It was this man's uncle, José Ángel, who was the original Tio Pepe (*tío* meaning uncle and Pepe being a nickname for José).

Pedro Domecq, Garvey and Harveys. Most bodegas require you to book your visit, though a few offer tours where you can just turn up. Confirm arrangements and hours with the wineries or with the tourist office, which has the contact and tour details for 14 bodegas. Tours are in Spanish, and sometimes English, German and French. Most include sherry tasting.

Wineries where you can turn up without booking include the following: **Bodegas González Byass** (Bodegas Tio Pepe; ☎ 956 35 70 70; www.bodegastiopepe.com; Calle Manuel María González 12; tour €10, with tapas €15; ☺ tours in English & Spanish hourly 11am-6pm Mon-Sat, to 2pm Sun Oct-Apr)
Bodegas Sandeman (☎ 956 15 17 11; www .sandeman.com; Calle Pizarro 10; tour in English €6, tapas €5.50; ☺ tours hourly 11.30am-2.30pm Mon, Wed & Fri, 10.30am & hourly noon-3pm Tue & Thu, 11am, 1pm & 2pm Sat)

♥ JEREZ & ITS HORSES // WATCH THE FAMOUSLY ELEGANT ANDALUSIAN HORSES

Jerez is where Andalusian horse culture is really taken seriously and it's in the area around Jerez that the world-famous Spanish thoroughbred horse, also known as the Cartujano or Andaluz, is bred and trained. As a result, the **Real Escuela Andaluza del Arte Ecuestre** (Royal Andalusian School of Equestrian Art; ☎ 956 31 80 08; www.realescuela.org; Avenida Duque de Abrantes), in the north of town, is a top Jerez attraction. This respected school trains horses and riders in dressage and you can watch them being put through their paces in **training sessions** (adult/child €10/7.50; ☺ 10am-2pm Mon, Wed & Fri Sep-Jul, 10am-2pm Mon & Wed Aug). There's an official **espectáculo** (show; adult/child €25/18; ☺ noon Tue & Thu Sep-Jul, noon Tue, Thu & Fri Aug), where the handsome white horses show off their tricks to classical music; there are additional performances on some public holidays. Tickets entitle you to tour the beautiful grounds and visit the museums.

If horses are your thing, you really must try to be in town in early May for the weeklong **Feria del Caballo** (Horse Fair), one of Andalucía's biggest festivals. The feria includes bullfights and music, but these are sideshows to all kinds of horse competitions, while colourful parades of horses pass through the Parque González Hontoria fairgrounds in the north of town. The aristocratic-looking male riders are traditionally decked out in flat-topped hats, frilly white shirts, black trousers and leather chaps, their female *crupera* (sideways pillion) partners in long, frilly spotted dresses. The September Fiestas de Otoño (below) also culminate in a massive parade of horses, riders and horse-drawn carriages.

The final pieces of Jerez' equestrian puzzle are found southeast of Jerez, with La Cartuja Monastery (p133) and the Yeguada de la Cartuja (p133) having long played an important role in breeding the Cartujano horses.

FESTIVALS & EVENTS

In addition to the Festival de Jerez (opposite) and Feria del Caballo (above), Jerez also hosts the following:

Campeonato del Mundo de Motociclismo de Jerez (World Motorcycle Championship) Held in April or May at Jerez' Circuito Permanente de Velocidad (www.circuitodejerez.com), on the A382 10km east of town, this is one of Spain's biggest sporting events, with around 150,000 spectators.
Fiestas de Otoño The 'Autumn Fiestas' celebrate the grape harvest for two weeks or so in September, with flamenco, horse events and the traditional treading of the first grapes on Plaza de la Asunción.

GASTRONOMIC HIGHLIGHTS

Jerez food combines an Islamic heritage and maritime influences with English and French touches. Not surprisingly, sherry flavours many local dishes such as *riñones al jerez* (kidneys braised in sherry) and *rabo de toro*.

In addition to the following, some fine tapas bars surround quiet little Plaza Rafael Rivero, about 500m north of Plaza del Arenal, with tables out under the sky.

♥ BAR JUANITO €
☎ 956 33 48 38; www.bar-juanito.com; Pescadería Vieja 8-10; tapas from €2.20, media-raciones €5-7
One of the best tapas bars in Jerez, 60-year-old Bar Juanito, with its outdoor tables and checked tablecloths, is like a slice of village Andalucía in the heart of the city. Its *alcachofas* (artichokes) are a past winner of the National Tapa Competition, but there's so much local cuisine to choose from here and it's all served up with the best local wines. Pescadería Vieja, which runs off Plaza del Arenal, catches a refreshing breeze on a hot day.

♥ EL GALLO AZUL €€
☎ 956 32 61 48; www.casajuancarlos.com; Calle Larga 2; tapas from €2.40, raciones from €11.50
Another top place for tapas, El Gallo Azul ('The Blue Cockerel') occupies a beautiful, circular, historic building with a tapas bar downstairs and restaurant upstairs. The terrific tapas are served in a range of sizes to suit all appetites. Good choices include the *huevas aliñadas* (fish roe) and *puntas de solomillo al brandy* (sirloin pieces in brandy). The *timbal de huevo relleno con langostino* (eggs stuffed with prawns in a mould) is a work of art.

♥ LA CARBONÁ €€

☎ 956 34 74 75; www.lacarbona.com; Calle San Francisco de Paula 2; mains €12.50-16.50; ☺ closed Tue; Ⓥ

This popular, cavernous restaurant with an eccentric menu occupies an old bodega with a hanging fireplace that's oh-so-cosy in winter. Specialities include grilled meats and fresh fish and the quirky quail with foie gras and rose petals, while we also enjoyed the *presa ibérica macerada en frambuesas con castañas y tirabeques* (Iberian pork cooked with raspberries, chestnuts and snow peas). If you can't decide, there is a set menu with Jerez wines (€30).

♥ MESÓN EL PATIO €€

☎ 956 34 07 36; Calle San Francisco de Paula 7; mains €7-18; ☺ closed Sun evening & Mon

This place combines a touch of refinement with local conviviality. It occupies a restored sherry warehouse, which means lofty ceilings, warm tones and carved wooden chairs, but there are echoes of other eras of the city's history with Islamic-style tile work and a collection of old radios. Above all, the food (a snapshot of Andalucía's obsession with fish and meat dishes) is terrific.

♥ RESTAURANTE GAITÁN €€

☎ 956 16 80 21; www.restaurantegaitan.es; Calle Gaitán 3; starters from €8.50, mains from €12; ☺ closed Sun

There's an intimacy to the eating experience here with a cosy dining area and walls adorned with antlers and photos of past clients. Alongside the staples of Andalusian meat and fish, there are some surprising local twists – the *cordero confitado con miel al brandy de Jerez* (lamb in a honey and Jerez brandy sauce), for example. A stroll down nearby Calle Porvera, with its breath of lavender from the honour guard of trees, is the perfect encore to the meal.

♥ SABORES €€

☎ 956 32 98 35; www.hotelchancilleria.com; Calle Chancilleria 21; mains from €12; ☺ closed lunch Sun

New to Jerez' culinary scene but already with a devoted local following, Sabores is outstanding. There's African art on the walls and the small but carefully selected menu has some of the best local Jerez staples (such as oxtail and *salmorejo cordobés* – a cold tomato-based soup served with *jamón* and crumbled egg) you'll find in town. There are also some delicious surprises, among them the carpaccio of venison stuffed with prawns and cooked with dry wine and a cheese reduction. It's part of the equally excellent Hotel Chancilleria (p386).

NIGHTLIFE

To find out what's on in Jerez, check www.turismojerez.com, watch for posters and look in the newspapers *Diario de Jerez* and *Jerez Información*.

♥ TETERÍA LA JAIMA

Calle Chancillería 10; ☺ 4pm-midnight Mon-Thu, to 2am Fri & Sat, to 10.30pm Sun

This tea-drinkers' haven adds depth to your experience of Jerez' Islamic roots with Moroccan-style decor, including carpets and cushions on the floor and tiled tables of various heights. Sip from an extensive list of teas.

TRANSPORT

AIR // Jerez airport (☎ 956 15 00 00; www.aena.es), the only one serving Cádiz province, is 7km northeast of town on the NIV. Over a dozen airlines fly into Jerez from elsewhere in Europe including: **Ryanair** (www.ryanair.com); **Thomas Cook Airlines Belgium** (www.thomascookairlines.com); and **Air-Berlin** (www.airberlin.com). For more details see p412. **Iberia** (www.iberia.com) flies daily to/from Madrid and Barcelona. Taxis from the airport start at €14. The local airport buses

M050 and M051 (€1, 30 minutes) run 12 times daily Monday to Friday and six times daily on weekends. From Jerez this service continues to El Puerto de Santa María and Cádiz.

TRAIN // There are regular trains to/from Seville, El Puerto de Santa María and Cádiz from the **train station** (Plaza de la Estación).

PARKING // Parking Doña Blanca (cnr Plaza Estévez & Calle Doña Blanca; per 24hr €15)

BUS // The bus station (☎ 956 33 96 66; Plaza de la Estación) is 1.3km southeast of the centre. Comes (☎ 956 34 21 74) runs buses to/from Arcos de la Frontera, Cádiz, El Puerto de Santa María, Los Caños de Meca, Ronda, Seville and Tarifa. Linesur (☎ 956 34 10 63) has services to/from Seville, Sanlúcar de Barrameda and Málaga, while Los Amarillos (☎ 956 32 93 47) has more frequent buses to Arcos and to El Bosque and Ubrique.

AROUND JEREZ DE LA FRONTERA

❦ LA CARTUJA MONASTERY // A STUNNING ARCHITECTURAL LANDMARK WHERE ANDALUSIAN HORSES WERE SAVED

This **monastery** (Cartuja de Santa María de la Defensión; ☎ 956 15 64 65; Carretera Jerez-Algeciras; ☽ gardens 9.30-11.15am & 12.45-6.30pm Mon-Sat, mass 8am Tue-Sat, 5.30pm Mon & Sun) is an architectural gem founded in the 15th century, set amid lovely gardens beside the A381, 9km from central Jerez. The early Carthusian monks here are credited with breeding the Cartujano at a time when the horse's popularity had declined. You can look around the gardens and admire the church's impressive baroque facade, but you can only peep inside during mass.

❦ YEGUADA DE LA CARTUJA – HIERRO DEL BOCADO // LEARN THE FINE ART OF BREEDING ANDALUSIAN HORSES

This **stud farm** (☎ 956 16 28 09; www.yeguada cartuja.com; Finca Fuente del Suero; adult/child €18/13; ☽ 11am-1pm Sat) is dedicated to improving the Cartujano stock, on land that once belonged to La Cartuja Monastery. You're allowed to take a look around, followed by a spectacular show consisting of free-running colts, demonstrations by a string of mares, and dressage. Book ahead. To get here, turn off the A381 at the 'La Yeguada' sign 5km after La Cartuja, and follow the side road for 1.6km to the entrance.

ARCOS & THE SIERRA DE GRAZALEMA

· · · · · ·

The Sierra de Grazalema in northeastern Cádiz province is one of Andalucía's most beautiful mountain areas, populated with stunning white villages and ideal for hiking. En route to the sierra from the coast stands the spectacular cliff-top town, Arcos de la Frontera.

ARCOS DE LA FRONTERA

pop 29,900 / elevation 185m
From a distance, Arcos de la Frontera unfolds along a narrow ridge, a stunning collection of white houses and church spires and topped by a castle, all seeming to cling to the sheer cliff-face. From within, Arcos possesses a more intimate charm, its quiet, narrow streets snaking along the hilltop, tumbling down steep inclines and opening out onto lookouts offering panoramic views over the rolling country that rises eventually to the distant peaks of the Sierra de Grazalema. Arcos' strategic location has been prized since time immemorial: during the 11th

CÁDIZ PROVINCE & GIBRALTAR

century it was an independent Berber-ruled kingdom before being absorbed by Seville, then taken over by Christian Alfonso X in 1255. In short, Arcos de la Frontera is one of Andalucía's largest, most important and most spectacular *pueblos blancos* (white villages).

ESSENTIAL INFORMATION

TOURIST OFFICES // Tourist information kiosk (Paseo de Andalucía; ☺ 10.30am-1.30pm Mon-Fri) Tourist office (☎ 956 70 22 64; www .arcosdelafrontera.es; Plaza del Cabildo; ☺ 10am-2.30pm & 5-8pm Mon-Fri, 10.30am-1.30pm & 5-7pm Sat mid-Mar–mid-Oct, 10am-2.30pm & 4-7pm Mon-Fri, 10.30am-1.30pm & 4-6pm Sat mid-Oct–mid-Mar, 10.30am-1pm Sun year-round)

EXPLORING ARCOS DE LA FRONTERA

Arcos' charm today lies in exploring the old, mazelike upper town with its Renaissance palaces, beautiful Gothic churches, whitewashed houses and uniquely spectacular setting.

❦ UPPER ARCOS // LOSE YOURSELF IN MAZELIKE STREETS ATOP THE CLIFF
More than Arcos' specific sights, it's the experience of rambling along its ridge-line that will live longest in the memory. The focal point of Arcos' summit is the pleasing Plaza del Cabildo, which is dominated on the northern side by the distinctive Basílica Menor de Santa María de la Asunción, which was be-gun on the site of a mosque in the 13th century but not completed until the 18th century. The beautiful baroque tower and the intricate Gothic western facade are the basilica's most beautiful features. Inside (if the renovations have finished), watch for the beautiful 1731 choir stalls

carved in stone and exotic woods, and lovely Isabelline ceiling tracery. On the southern side of the plaza, don't miss the vertiginous mirador. There are more fine views from the Parador Casa del Corregidor (see p386).

Dropping down the hill to the east, watch for the early-16th-century Convento de la Encarnación (Calle Marqués de Torresoto), with its Gothic facade, and the Iglesia de San Pedro (Calle Núñez de Prado; admission €1; ☺ 10.30am-2pm & 5-7pm Mon-Fri, 11am-2pm Sat), in 15th-century Gothic style but with an impressive 18th-century baroque facade and bell tower. Nearby, the 17th-century Palacio Mayorazgo (Calle Núñez de Prado; admission free; ☺ 10am-1.30pm & 5-8pm Mon-Sat, 11am-2pm Sun) has a Renaissance facade. Its rear patio, entered independently, has a small Islamic-style garden, the Jardín Andalusí (Calle Tallista Morales; admission free; ☺ 11am-2pm & 5-7pm Mon-Fri mid-Sep–mid-Jun, 11am-2pm & 7-10pm Mon-Fri mid-Jun–mid-Sep, 11am-2pm Sat year-round).

❦ SEMANA SANTA // IMMERSE YOURSELF IN ARCOS' UNIQUE TAKE ON EASTER
Arcos' Semana Santa (Holy Week) pro-cessions are among the most famous in the region and there's no finer Easter spectacle than the hooded penitents inching through the town's pretty nar-row streets. The solemnity of Good Fri-day has its slightly manic counterpoint on Easter Sunday, when a running of the bulls takes over the streets.

❦ LA TABERNA DE BOABDIL // ARCOS' BEST TAPAS IN AN ENCHANTED ALADDIN'S CAVE
Occupying caves whose origins are lost in legend, and extravagantly decorated in an eclectic style that spans the polyglot sweep of Arcos' history, La Taberna de

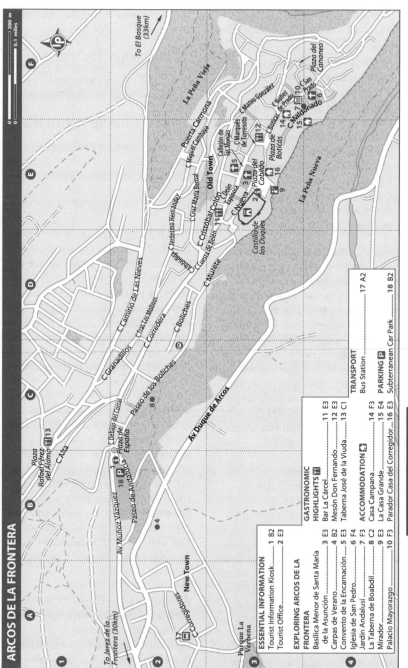

ARCOS DE LA FRONTERA

ESSENTIAL INFORMATION
Tourist Information Kiosk......1 B2
Tourist Office......2 E3

EXPLORING ARCOS DE LA
FRONTERA
Basílica Menor de Santa María
de la Asunción......3 E3
Carpas de Verano......4 B2
Convento de la Encarnación......5 E3
Iglesia de San Pedro......6 F4
Jardín Andalusí......7 F3
La Taberna de Boabdil......8 C2
Mirador......9 E3
Palacio Mayorazgo......10 F3

GASTRONOMIC
HIGHLIGHTS
Bar La Cárcel......11 E3
Mesón Don Fernando......12 E3
Taberna José de la Viuda......13 C1

ACCOMMODATION
Casa Campana......14 F3
La Casa Grande......15 E4
Parador Casa del Corregidor...16 E3

TRANSPORT
Bus Station......17 A2

PARKING
Subterranean Car Park......18 B2

CÁDIZ PROVINCE & GIBRALTAR

ARCOS TOURS

Guided walking tours (€7, one hour) of the old town's monuments set out from Arcos' tourist office on Plaza del Cabildo at 11am Monday to Friday. The tours offer a rare (and otherwise impossible) glimpse of Arcos' pretty patios. Early evening and Saturday morning tours also happen but you need to book ahead for these. The tours are in Spanish and English.

For an excellent self-guided walking tour of Arcos, pick up the *Walking Tour* brochure from Casa Campana (p386).

Boabdil (☎ 956 70 51 91; latabernadeboabdil@ hotmail.com; off Paseo de los Boliches 35; tasting menu €18; ⏰ 10am-midnight) serves up imaginative tapas with Sephardic, Muslim and other historical inflections. Best of all, Francisco, the ebullient owner, brings much personality to the place and is happy to regale guests with the caves' history. Although the kitchen closes at midnight, the doors don't close until you've had time to enjoy your tea or something a little stronger. It's signposted down the steps off Paseo de los Boliches, not far southeast of Plaza de España.

♥ MUSICAL SUMMERS // EXPERIENCE THE PASSION OF SOULFUL FLAMENCO

Arcos bursts into song in July and August. The **Jueves Flamenco** are a series of weekly flamenco nights on Thursday at 10.30pm throughout the two months, at various old-town locations including the small, atmospheric Plaza del Cananeo. Also in July and August, free world music and jazz gigs are staged in Parque La Verbena, west of the bus station, and live pop, salsa, rock and the like can be heard on Friday nights at the Carpas de Verano, an open-air entertainment area on Avenida Duque de Arcos.

FESTIVALS & EVENTS

Feria de San Miguel Arcos celebrates its patron saint with a four-day fair; held around 29 September.

GASTRONOMIC HIGHLIGHTS

Arcos won't win any prizes for gastronomic excellence, but we have no hesitation recommending the following places. For our favourite place to eat, see La Taberna de Boabdil, p134.

♥ BAR LA CÁRCEL €€

☎ 956 70 04 10; Calle Deán Espinosa 18; tapas & montaditos €2.50, raciones €8-12; ⏰ 8am-noon Mon, to late Tue-Sun

Easily the pick of the numerous tapas bars in the old town, Bar La Cárcel has a loyal local following. Its tapas include the usual Spanish staples, plus a few creative twists, including the sensational *pinchitos de langostino con béicon* (prawns wrapped in bacon).

♥ MESÓN DON FERNANDO €€

☎ 956 71 73 26; Calle Boticas 5; raciones €7-15, mains €10-20; ⏰ closed Mon

Probably the best of several bars-cumeateries along the old town's Calle Boticas, Don Fernando has a lively Spanish atmosphere and flamenco soundtrack. Good *montaditos* and *raciones* are served in the vaulted bar or at the outdoor tables, while the small restaurant focuses on meaty main dishes and tempting desserts.

♥ TABERNA JOSÉ DE LA VIUDA €€

☎ 956 70 12 09; Plaza Rafael Pérez del Álamo 13; tapas/raciones €2.50/9; ⏰ 11.30am-late

There may not be many reasons to leave behind the old town, but this temple of all that's *típico andaluz* is one of them. Hung with hams and sausages, stacked with wines and cheeses and swaying to flamenco rhythms, Taberna José de la Viuda is presided over by the amiable Alfonso. Whatever you select from the lengthy tapas menu, he'll probably suggest you choose something else. Take his advice.

TRANSPORT

BUS // From the bus station (☎ 956 70 49 77), Los Amarillos and/or Comes have regular daily buses (fewer on weekends) to Cádiz, El Bosque and Jerez de la Frontera, with less frequent departures to Málaga, Ronda and Seville.

PARKING // Park in the underground parking on Paseo de Andalucía, then catch the half-hourly minibus (€0.95) to the top of the old town from the adjacent Plaza de España.

DRIVING TOUR: SIERRA DE GRAZALEMA

Distance: 207km
Duration: one to two days

This driving tour (Map p138) cuts a swathe through some of Andalucía's prettiest mountain scenery in the Parque Natural Sierra de Grazalema, which provides a backdrop for the beautiful whitewashed villages dotted throughout Cádiz province.

From Arcos de la Frontera (p133), one of the region's prettiest hill towns, drive east along the A372 to El Bosque, gateway to the Sierra de Grazalema. Stop long enough to pick up information on the park at the Centro de Visitantes El Bosque (p139).

From El Bosque, the A372 continues up through wooded hillsides, passing the turn-off to the white but largely modern village of Benamahoma, before continuing up to the Puerta de El Boyar (1103m) which has sweeping views to the east.

The road then drops steeply before a turn-off to the north marks the start of the CA531, one of the most beautiful roads in the region. It climbs up steeply to the Puerta de las Palomas (1357m); Doves' Pass (but with more vultures than doves) sits on a saddle between two high ridges and can be quite otherworldly if there's heavy mist.

After the pass, the road plunges via a succession of hairpin bends to Zahara de la Sierra. Zahara is the most dramatically sited of the Grazalema villages and is impossibly picturesque when seen from the north across the Embalse de Zahara reservoir. The town itself has steep, winding streets with vistas framed by tall palms, hot-pink bougainvillea or fruited orange trees. You can climb on foot up to the 13th-century Muslim-built castle; the castle fell to the Christians in 1407 and its brief recapture by Abu al-Hasan of Granada in a daring night raid in 1481 provoked the Catholic Monarchs to launch the last phase of the Reconquista of Andalucía, leading to the fall of Granada in 1492. In town, hearty mountain meals are on offer at Restaurante Los Naranjos (☎ 956 12 33 14; Calle San Juan 15; mains €9-18). There are also a couple of hotels.

Return to the Puerta de las Palomas (this is one road that's worth doing twice), then rejoin the A372 for the last few kilometres into Grazalema. The most popular travellers' base in the sierra, Grazalema is a picture-postcard, red-tile-roofed village tucked into a pretty corner of the sierra.

Leaving town, follow the signs to Ubrique and the A374, which runs along the southern wall of the sierra with the bare, rocky landscapes standing in stark contrast to the greener terrain on the other side of the ridge. Huddling at the foot of the cliffs of the Sierra del Caillo,

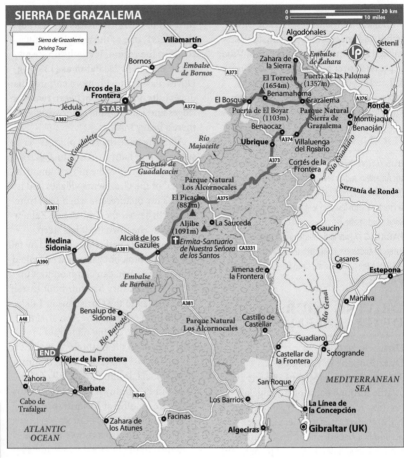

SIERRA DE GRAZALEMA

Sierra de Grazalema
Driving Tour

Villamartín

Algodonales

Setenil

Bornos

*Embalse
de Bornos*

Zahara de
la Sierra

*Embalse
de Zahara*

El Torreón
(1654m)

Puerta de las Palomas
(1357m)

Arcos de la
Frontera

Jédula

START

El Bosque

Benamahoma

Grazalema

Ronda

Montejaque

Parque Natural
Sierra de
Grazalema

Benaoján

Puerta de El Boyar
(1103m)

Benaocaz

*Río
Majaceite*

Ubrique

Villaluenga
del Rosario

Río Guadalete

*Embalse de
Guadalcacín*

Cortés de la
Frontera

Serranía de Ronda

Parque Natural
Los Alcornocales

El Picacho
(882m)

Aljibe
(1091m)

La Sauceda

Gaucín

Casares

Estepona

Medina
Sidonia

Alcalá de los
Gazules

Ermita-Santuario
de Nuestra Señora
de los Santos

Jimena de
la Frontera

Manilva

*Embalse
de Barbate*

Benalup de
Sidonia

Río Barbate

Parque Natural
Los Alcornocales

Castillo de
Castellar

Guadiaro

Sotogrande

END

Vejer de la Frontera

Castellar de
la Frontera

San Roque

*MEDITERRANEAN
SEA*

Zahora

Barbate

Facinas

Los Barrios

La Línea de
la Concepción

Cabo de
Trafalgar

Zahara de
los Atunes

Algeciras

Gibraltar (UK)

*ATLANTIC
OCEAN*

the quiet villages of **Villaluenga del
Rosario** and **Benaocaz** line the roadside
before it descends to **Ubrique**, one of
the largest white villages in the area and
spread out against the backdrop of the
Sierra de Grazalema.

The A373 leads south, then southwest
as the A375, through the beautiful northern woodlands of the **Parque Natural
Los Alcornocales** (p147), the Grazalema
park's southern neighbour. In early
summer the roadside wildflowers are
unbelievable and, en route, you'll pass
Los Alcornocales' most prominent peaks,

El Picacho (882m) and Aljibe (1091m).
Watch for the turn-off to the **Ermita-
Santuario de Nuestra Señora de los
Santos** (admission free; 10am-6pm Jul-Sep, 10am-
2pm & 5-9pm Oct-Jun), a remote hermitage and
pilgrimage site with a pretty courtyard
and a reputation for healing powers.

Around 5km after the hermitage turn-
off, you'll pass through the attractive
white town of **Alcalá de los Gazules**,
before a brief spell on the A381 *autopista*
(tollway), bound for **Medina Sidonia**, a
dramatic white hill town rising up from
the plains. Medina Sidonia's turbulent

history goes at least as far back as Phoenician times; at the top of the hill, the helpful **tourist office** (☎ 956 41 24 04; Plaza de la Iglesia Mayor; ☽ 10am-2pm & 5-6pm Sep-Jun, 10am-2pm & 5-9pm Jul & Aug) can point you in the direction of the town's numerous historical sights.

From Medina Sidonia, it's a 26km drive south to one of Andalucía's most charming white hill villages, **Vejer de la Frontera** (p140).

PARQUE NATURAL SIERRA DE GRAZALEMA

The Cordillera Bética – the band of rugged mountain ranges that stretches across Andalucía – has beautiful beginnings in the Sierra de Grazalema in northeastern Cádiz province. This is one of the greenest parts of Andalucía (Grazalema village has the highest rainfall in Spain at an average 2153mm a year) and yields some of its most stunning landscapes, from pastoral river valleys and white villages to precipitous gorges and rocky summits; the prettiest villages are Grazalema and Zahara de la Sierra (see the Driving Tour, p137). Much of the area is covered in beautiful Mediterranean woodland, and snow is common on the mountains in late winter. This is also prime hiking country.

EXPLORING PARQUE NATURAL SIERRA DE GRAZALEMA

❦ **WALK THE HIGH COUNTRY //**
FOLLOW SOME OF ANDALUCÍA'S BEST HIKING TRAILS
The Sierra de Grazalema is criss-crossed by beautiful trails, many of which require a free permit from the **Centro de Visitantes El Bosque** (☎ 956 72 70 29; Calle Federico García Lorca 1, El Bosque; ☽ 10am-2pm & 5-7pm Mon-Sat, 9am-

2pm Sun); you'll usually have to contact the centre two weeks in advance of your hike.

El Torreón (1654m) is the highest peak in Cádiz province and from the summit on a clear day you can see Gibraltar, the Sierra Nevada and the Rif Mountains of Morocco. The usual route starts 100m east of the Km40 marker on the Grazalema–Benamahoma road, about 8km from Grazalema. It takes about 2½ hours of walking to reach the summit and 1½ hours back down.

The 14km **Pinsapar** walk runs between Grazalema and Benamahoma and takes around six hours. Apart from the beautiful scenery, watch out for the *pinsapo,* a dark-green Spanish fir that's a rare and beautiful relic of the great Mediterranean fir forests of the Tertiary period, and survives in significant numbers only in pockets of southwest Andalucía and northern Morocco. The trailhead is signposted off the CA531 (the road to Zahara de la Sierra), a 40-minute uphill walk from Grazalema.

The path into the **Garganta Verde** (literally 'Green Throat'), a lushly vegetated ravine more than 100m deep, starts 3.5km from Zahara de la Sierra on the Grazalema road. It passes a large colony of enormous griffon vultures before the 300m descent to the bottom of the gorge. Allow three to four hours' walking if you drive to the start.

Other walks are signposted off the CA531 and the Centro de Visitantes El Bosque has general maps outlining the main possibilities. Far better, equip yourself with a good walking guide such as *Walking in Andalucía* by Guy Hunter-Watts or *Eight Walks from Grazalema* by RE Bradshaw. The best map is Editorial Alpina's *Sierra de Grazalema* (1:25,000), with a walking-guide booklet in English and Spanish. Some of these are sold locally, but don't count on it.

CÁDIZ PROVINCE & GIBRALTAR

For the Pinsapar walk in July, August and September, when fire risk is high, it's obligatory to go with a guide from an authorised local company such as **Horizon Grazalema** (☎ 956 13 23 63; www.horizon aventura.com; Calle Corrales Terceros 29, Grazalema), **Al-Qutun** (☎ 956 13 78 82; www.al-qutun.com; Calle Zahara de la Sierra 13, Algodonales) or **Zahara Catur** (☎ 956 12 31 14; www.zaharacatur.com; Plaza del Rey 3, Zahara de la Sierra); all three can arrange the permits. The Torreón route is sometimes closed from July to September. The best months for walking are May, June, September and October.

TRANSPORT

BUS // **Los Amarillos** (☎ 902 21 03 17; www .losamarillos.es) runs buses to El Bosque, in the west of the park, from Jerez, Cádiz, Arcos de la Frontera and Seville. Daily buses (except Sunday) run between El Bosque and Grazalema. Los Amarillos also runs twice daily from Málaga to Ronda, Grazalema, Villaluenga del Rosario, Benaocaz and Ubrique, and vice versa. **Comes** (☎ 902 19 92 08; www.tgcomes.es) operates two buses each way Monday to Friday between Ronda and Zahara de la Sierra, via Algodonales.

COSTA DE LA LUZ & THE SOUTHEAST

. . . . . .

The 90km coast between Cádiz and Tarifa is an unspoiled, wild and windy shore with some of the longest white-sand beaches in Andalucía. In a refreshing change from much of Spain's Mediterranean coastline, tourism developments have been kept to a minimum with relatively few villages strung out along the shoreline. Andalusians are, however, well aware of the area's attractions and they

flock here in their thousands during July and August, bringing a fiesta atmosphere to otherwise quiet coastal settlements.

Apart from hip Tarifa on Spain's southernmost tip, the main attraction here lies just inland from the coast – the charming hill town of Vejer de la Frontera.

VEJER DE LA FRONTERA

pop 12,800 / elevation 190m
A whitewashed hill town par excellence, Vejer looms mysteriously atop a rocky hill above the busy A48, 50km southeast from Cádiz. In the oldest part of town, labyrinthine lanes climb the hillside to its summit, passing quirky boutiques and gorgeous hotels en route. In recent years, Vejer has become home to plenty of foreign artists and others who simply couldn't bear to leave. It's that sort of place, where you'll end up staying longer than you planned.

ESSENTIAL INFORMATION

TOURIST OFFICE // **Municipal tourist office** (☎ 956 45 17 36; www.turismovejer.com; Avenida de los Remedios; ⏰ 10am-2pm Mon-Fri, 11am-1pm Sat mid-Oct–mid-Jun, 10am-2pm & 5-9pm daily mid-Jun–mid-Oct).

ORIENTATION

The oldest area of town, which is quite compact, sits atop the easternmost hill. The easiest way to get your bearings if you're coming by car is to follow the signs to the tourist office, pick up a map, park nearby and walk up the hill following the remnants of the old city wall. The old town effectively begins at the small Plazuela. You can either climb to the top from here, or continue along the wall for around 800m to the lovely Plaza de España, a beautiful introduction to what lies ahead.

CÁDIZ PROVINCE & GIBRALTAR

EXPLORING VEJER DE LA FRONTERA

Vejer has some beautiful places to see, but losing yourself in cobblestone lanes running off in all directions is when you'll really succumb to its charms.

❦ OLD TOWN // WANDER WITHOUT HASTE THROUGH TIMELESS LANES

Vejer's imposing **walls** date from the 15th century and enclose the 40,000-sq-metre old quarter; the ramparts peep out from the old town's perimeter all across Vejer. One of the most accessible stretches is between the **Arco de la Puerta Cerrada** and the **Arco de la Segur**, two of the four original gateways to survive; the area around the Arco de la Segur was, in the 15th century, the **Judería** (the Jewish Quarter). The much-reworked **castillo** (castle; ☺ 10am-2pm & 5.30-8.30pm Jul & Aug) has great views from its battlements, but it's closed most of the year. Not far from the Arco de la Puerta Cerrada, the interior of the **Iglesia del Divino Salvador** (☎ 956 45 00 56; Plaza Padre Ángel; ☺ 11am-1pm & 5-7pm Mon, Wed, Fri & Sat, 11am-1pm Tue, Thu & Sun) is Mudéjar at the altar end and Gothic at the other.

Down the hill to the east, the gorgeous palm-filled **Plaza de España** is many visitors' favourite Vejer corner. Its elaborate Seville-tiled fountain provides the centrepiece, while the white town hall rises up on the south side. For good views down onto the plaza, there's a small **mirador** above the plaza's western side (and accessible from Calle de Sancho IV). If the door's open, as it often is, the 15th-century **Casa del Mayorazgo** (Callejón de La Villa; admission by donation) has a pretty patio and one of just three original towers that kept watch over the city – the views from here, including down onto Plaza de España, are worth the short climb.

FESTIVALS & EVENTS

Easter Sunday *Toro embolao* (running of the bulls, with bandaged horns) at noon and 4pm.
Feria Music and dancing nightly in Plaza de España, with one night devoted entirely to flamenco, from 10 to 24 August.

GASTRONOMIC HIGHLIGHTS

You're spoilt for choice when it comes to eating out in Vejer.

❦ EL JARDÍN DE LA CALIFA €€

☎ 956 44 77 30; Plaza de España 16; starters €6-9, mains €8.30-15; Ⓥ

Tucked away down in a private patio in the hotel of the same name, the Caliph's Garden could just be our favourite place to eat in Vejer. Moroccan-tiled tables under tall trees, the scent of jasmine, and walls with ancient brickwork set the mood. But everything here speaks of Vejer's Islamic past, especially the food with flavours from all across the Arab world, which you enjoy to a quiet soundtrack of Middle Eastern music. The choice is endless: salads, soups, *mezze* (a collection of Arab-style appetisers or small plates of food), tagine, couscous and barbecued meats, often with subtle hints of cinnamon, saffron and almonds.

❦ FELAFEL €

Calle de Juan Relinque 14; ☺ 9am-12.30am

Just down the hill southwest of La Plazuela, this inviting place does more than just serve up delicious felafel (€4), *mezze* (€6.50) and fresh juices (€3). It also offers live music from local musicians at 10pm on Thursdays, hosts art exhibitions and generally provides a quiet but very cool place to rest your legs after a day of exploring Vejer's hilly streets.

CÁDIZ PROVINCE & GIBRALTAR

☙ RESTAURANTE TRAFALGAR €€

☎ 956 44 76 38; Plaza de España 31; mains €10-19

If you can snaffle one of the outdoor tables on Plaza de España, you've won the lottery here – there are few more beautiful vantage points in which to eat in Vejer. The food is excellent, with the full range of produce from Cádiz province: fish, seafood and meat, all prepared with a flourish. It also does some terrific rice dishes and has a more formal indoor dining area.

TRANSPORT

BUS // Comes (☎ 902 19 92 08; www.tgcomes.es) buses leave from Avenida de los Remedios, the road up from the A48, about 500m below the Plazuela; tickets can be purchased on board. There are buses to/from Cádiz and towns around Cádiz province and beyond.
PARKING // There's free parking alongside Parque Los Remedios, immediately north of the tourist office. In the old town, it's hard-to-find street parking only.

THE VEJER COAST

The villages along the coast close to Vejer are some of the least pretentious *pueblos* anywhere along Spain's shoreline. Sleepy El Palmar, 10km southwest of Vejer, has a lovely 4.8km sweep of white sandy beach that draws surfers from October to May, while Los Caños de Meca, for decades a hippie hideaway, straggles along a series of gorgeous sandy coves beneath a pine-clad hill about 7km southeast of El Palmar. Further down the coast to the southeast, past the fishing port of Barbate, Zahara de los Atunes fronts onto a broad, 12km-long, west-facing sandy beach.

EXPLORING THE VEJER COAST

A laid-back beachy atmosphere is the most appealing aspect of this stretch of coast, but a few sites provide good reasons to drag yourself off the beach towel.

☙ CABO DE TRAFALGAR // SEE WHERE THE SPANISH ARMADA MET ITS END

At the western end of Los Caños de Meca, a side road leads out to a lighthouse on a low spit of land, the famous Cabo de Trafalgar. It was off this cape that Spanish naval power was terminated in a few hours one day in 1805 by a British fleet under Admiral Nelson. A plaque commemorating those who died in the battle was erected at Trafalgar on the bicentennial in October 2005.

Wonderful beaches stretch either side of Cabo de Trafalgar. The main beach is straight in front of Avenida Trafalgar's junction with the Barbate road. Nudist beachgoers head to the small headland at its eastern end where there are more secluded beaches, including Playa de las Cortinas.

☙ FUNDACIÓN NMAC // CONTEMPORARY ART INSTALLATIONS OVERLOOKING THE SEA

The innovative set-up at Fundación NMAC (☎ 956 45 51 34; www.fundacionnmac.org; Dehesa de Montenmedio, Km42.5 N340; adult/child €5/free, 1st Sun of month free; ☺ 10am-2pm & 5-8.30pm mid-Jun–mid-Sep, 10am-2.30pm & 4.30-6pm mid-Sep–mid-Jun), 6km east of Vejer, combines stunning works of contemporary art in harmony with their natural surrounds. There's a sculpture park spread throughout the trees and the internal project rooms include DVD presentations that will appeal to kids.

TARIFA

pop 17,200

Laid-back Tarifa, on Spain's southernmost tip, may be best known as Spain's windsurfing and kitesurfing capital, but it's so much more than this. The compact old town is as pretty as a postcard – its narrow lanes are lined with boutique hotels and artsy shops, not to mention a striking castle, whitewashed houses and flowers cascading from balconies with fancy ironwork and window boxes. The beaches along the Tarifa coast have clean, white sand and good waves. And from just about wherever you are, the African coast, just 14km across the strait, seems almost close enough to touch.

Tarifa may be as old as Phoenician Cádiz and was definitely a Roman settlement, but it takes its name from Tarif ibn Malik, who led a Muslim raid in AD 710, the year before the main Islamic invasion of the peninsula.

ESSENTIAL INFORMATION

TOURIST OFFICE // Municipal tourist office (☎ 956 68 09 93; www.aytotarifa.com, in Spanish; Paseo de la Alameda; ❍ 10am-2pm & 4-6pm Oct-Jun, 10am-2pm & 6-8pm Jul-Sep)

ORIENTATION

Two roads lead into Tarifa from the N340. The one from the northwest becomes Calle Batalla del Salado, which runs into the Puerta de Jerez, the main entry point to the old town. The one from the east becomes Calle Amador de los Ríos, which also runs right to the Puerta de Jerez.

EXPLORING TARIFA

Tarifa is easy to enjoy: stroll through the tangled streets of the old town to the castle walls, check out the castle, stop in at the busy port and sample the beaches.

❦ OLD TARIFA // DISCOVER THE INTIMATE CHARM OF TARIFA'S OLDEST QUARTER

After entering through the Mudéjar **Puerta de Jerez**, which was built after the Reconquista, wind your way down into the heart of the old town, taking any one of the enticing little lanes that lead down the hill. In the centre, the streets south of the mainly 15th-century **Iglesia de San Mateo** are little-changed since Islamic times. Climb the stairs at the end of Calle Coronel Moscardó and go left on Calle Aljaranda to reach the **Mirador El Estrecho** atop part of the castle walls, with spectacular views across to Africa.

The **Castillo de Guzmán** (Calle Guzmán el Bueno) extends west from here. The castle was originally built in AD 960 under the orders of the Cordoban caliph, Abd ar-Rahman III, as fortification against Norse and African raids. The castle's formidable battlements notwithstanding, Christian forces took Tarifa in 1292 and the castle is named after the Reconquista hero Guzmán El Bueno. Until the rest of the castle reopens after renovations, you can walk along the castle's parapets and stand atop the 13th-century **Torre de Guzmán El Bueno** (which houses the town museum) for 360-degree views.

❦ WATCH WHALES // SPOT WHALES IN THE STRAIT OF GIBRALTAR

The waters off Tarifa are one of the best places in Europe to see whales and dolphins as they swim between the Atlantic and the Mediterranean between April and October; sightings of some description are almost guaranteed between these months. In addition to striped and bottlenose dolphins, and long-finned pilot whales, orcas (killer whales) and sperm whales, you may also, if you're lucky, see endangered fin whales and the misleadingly named common dolphin. The best months for orcas are July and August, while sperm whales are present in the Strait of Gibraltar from April to July.

CÁDIZ PROVINCE & GIBRALTAR

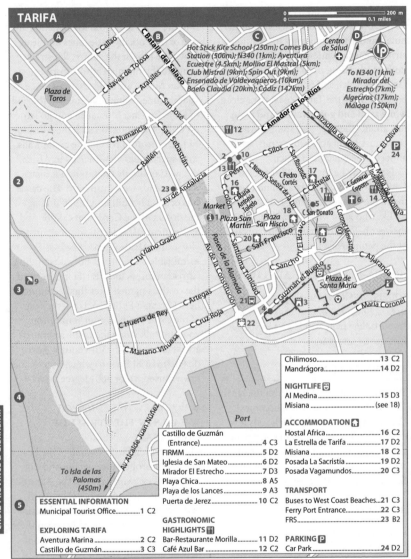

Chilimoso	13 C2
Mandrágora	14 D2
NIGHTLIFE	
Al Medina	15 D3
Misiana	(see 18)
ACCOMMODATION	
Hostal Africa	16 C2
La Estrella de Tarifa	17 D2
Misiana	18 C2
Posada La Sacristía	19 D2
Posada Vagamundos	20 C3
TRANSPORT	
Buses to West Coast Beaches	21 C3
Ferry Port Entrance	22 C3
FRS	23 B2
PARKING	
Car Park	24 D2

Castillo de Guzmán	
(Entrance)	4 C3
FIRMM	5 D2
Iglesia de San Mateo	6 D2
Mirador El Estrecho	7 D3
Playa Chica	8 A5
Playa de los Lances	9 A3
Puerta de Jerez	10 C2

ESSENTIAL INFORMATION	
Municipal Tourist Office	1 C2
EXPLORING TARIFA	
Aventura Marina	2 C2
Castillo de Guzmán	3 C3

GASTRONOMIC	
HIGHLIGHTS	
Bar-Restaurante Morilla	11 D2
Café Azul Bar	12 C2

Dozens of places offer whale-watching trips, but we recommend the not-for-profit **FIRMM** (Foundation for Information & Research on Marine Mammals; ☎ 956 62 70 08, 619 45 94 41; www.firmm.org; Calle Pedro Cortés 4; 2hr trip adult/child under 14/child under 6 €30/20/10; ☼ Apr-Oct), not least because its primary purpose is to study the whales, record data and encourage environmentally sensitive tours; unlike other operators, its trips (between one and eight daily) are preceded by a 45-minute introductory lecture. It also organises camps for children in July and runs one-/two-week courses

(€310/540) designed for children and families, which include daily boat trips, lectures about oceanography and dune science, multimedia shows and snorkelling with a marine biologist.

❤ TAKE TO THE WATER // WINDSURF, KITESURF, DIVE OR JUST LIE ON THE BEACH

Occupying the spot where the Atlantic meets the Mediterranean, Tarifa's legendary winds have turned the city into one of Europe's premier windsurfing and kitesurfing destinations. The most popular strip is along the coast between Tarifa and Punta Paloma, 10km to the northwest. Dozens of places offer equipment rental and classes (from beginners to experts, young and old), but two places we recommend are **Club Mistral** (☎ 956 68 90 90; www.hotelhurricane.com/en/mistral.html; Hostal Valdevaqueros) and **Spin Out** (☎ 956 23 63 52; www.tarifaspinout.com; Valdevaqueros; board, sail & wetsuit rental per hr/day €36/78, adult/child beginners' class €55/42; ☺ Apr–Oct), both of which are signposted off the N340 northwest of town. Kitesurfing rental and classes are available from the same places as for windsurfing, or from **Hot Stick Kite School** (☎ 647 15 55 16; www.hotsticktarifa.com; Calle Batalla del Salado 41; 1-/2-day courses €70/135).

Diving is another possibility and it's generally done from boats around the Isla de las Palomas where shipwrecks, corals, dolphins and octopuses await. Of the handful of dive companies in Tarifa, try **Aventura Marina** (☎ 956 05 46 26; www.aventuramarina.org; Avenida de Andalucía 1), which offers 'Discover Scuba Diving' courses (€75, three hours). One-tank dives with equipment rental and guide cost €50.

If, on the other hand, you just want to lie on the beach, the popular town beach is the sheltered but small **Playa Chica**, on the isthmus leading out to the

Isla de las Palomas. From here **Playa de los Lances** stretches 10km northwest to the huge sand dune at **Ensenada de Valdevaqueros**.

In summer, buses run every 90 minutes to the beaches along the coast northwest of Tarifa.

❤ HORSE RIDING // TROT ALONG THE BEACH OR CANTER THROUGH HILLY HINTERLAND

Contemplating Tarifa's stunning coastline (or heading off into the hilly hinterland) on horseback is a terrific way to pass an afternoon or even longer. A one-hour beach ride along Playa de los Lances costs €30, a two-hour beach-and-mountain ride costs €50, while three-/five-hour rides start at €70/80. One recommended place, with excellent English-speaking guides, is **Aventura Ecuestre** (☎ 956 23 66 32; www.aventuraecuestre.com; Hotel Dos Mares), which also has private lessons (one hour €30), pony rides for kids (half-/one hour €15/30) and five-hour rides into the Parque Natural Los Alcornocales (p147). **Molino El Mastral** (☎ 956 10 63 10; www.mastral.com; Carretera Sanctuario de la Luz), 5km northwest of Tarifa, is also excellent.

FESTIVALS & EVENTS

Reggae Festival International and Spanish reggae acts delight the crowds in Tarifa's humble bullring, one night in August.

Feria de la Virgen de la Luz The town fair in honour of its patron, in the first week in September, mixes religious processions, featuring the area's beautiful horses, and your typical Spanish fiesta.

GASTRONOMIC HIGHLIGHTS

Tarifa brims with eateries with an especially good selection along Paseo de la Alameda, at the western end of the old town, and on Calle Sancho IV El Bravo, in its centre. You could also try the recommended restaurant at the Posada La Sacristía (p387).

☙ BAR-RESTAURANTE MORILLA €€
☎ 956 68 17 57; Calle Sancho IV El Bravo 2; mains from €10

One of numerous places lying in wait along Calle Sancho IV El Bravo in the heart of the old town, Morilla attracts more locals than other places. They come here for the high-quality tapas and lamb dishes, and an outstanding *cazuela de pescados y mariscos* (fish-and-seafood stew). Servings are huge and one traveller described it as 'worth going to Tarifa just to eat there'.

☙ CAFÉ AZUL BAR €
Calle Batalla del Salado 8; breakfast €3.50-8; ☺ 9am-3pm, closed Wed winter

This eccentric place with eye-catching decor has been energised by its new Italian owners who prepare the best breakfasts in town. Don't miss the large muesli, fruit salad and yoghurt. There's good coffee, milkshakes, juices, *bocadillos* (filled rolls), crêpes and healthy cakes. In summer, they sometimes open into the early evening and serve light meals with a Thai or Italian twist.

☙ CHILIMOSO €
☎ 956 68 50 92; Calle Peso 6; mains €4.60-7.50; Ⓥ

A tiny place in the old town just inside the Puerta de Jerez, Chilimoso is an intimate, well-priced gem for vegetarians and others fleeing Andalucía's meat-heavy diet. The dining area is cosy, the staff friendly and to get the full range of tastes we recommend the *plato de degustación,* a platter of hummus, felafel, Indian dumplings and salad. It also does takeaway for a little cheaper.

☙ MANDRÁGORA €€
☎ 956 68 12 91; Calle Independencia 3; mains €12-18; ☺ dinner Mon-Sat, closed 2 weeks in Feb; Ⓥ

Behind Iglesia de San Mateo, this intimate place serves Andalusian-Arabic food and does so terrifically well. It's hard to know where to start, but the options for mains include lamb with plums and almonds, prawns with *ñora* (Andalusian sweet pepper) sauce, or monkfish in a wild mushroom and sea urchin sauce. Sitting as it does just away from the main eating hub of Tarifa, it attracts a quieter and generally more discerning crowd.

NIGHTLIFE

With a mixed crowd of surfies, locals and artsy expats, Tarifa's nights are a whole lot of fun, especially in summer. Most of the best places are in the old town.

☙ AL MEDINA
☎ 669 63 97 51; www.almedinacafe.net; off Plaza de Santa María; ☺ 10.30pm-2am Wed, 9pm-2am Thu, 10.30pm-3am Fri & Sat

On the steps just down from the Plaza de Santa María at the southern end of the old town, this cosy place stands out for many reasons, but it's the only place in town where you can consistently hear live flamenco (free); this happens on Thursday nights when people spill out onto the steps to catch a cooling evening breeze. At other times, it's good for mojitos and other *copas* (drinks), and a generally easygoing vibe.

☙ MISIANA
☎ 956 62 70 83; www.misiana.com; Calle Sancho IV El Bravo; ☺ 9am-3am

Very cool. You could come here for breakfast or lunch, but this place is one of *the* places to be seen on a Tarifa evening. With exposed brick walls, mosaic-tiled floors and vivid lime-green or lilac sofas, this lounge bar does shakes and cocktails. There's also either live music or a DJ on Friday and Saturday nights, with free 90-minute tango classes from 9.30pm Wednesdays.

TRANSPORT

BOAT // FRS (☎ 956 68 18 30; www.frs.es; Avenida de Andalucía) runs a fast (35-minute) ferry between Tarifa and Tangier in Morocco (one-way per adult/child/car/motorcycle €37/20/93/31) up to eight times daily. All passengers need a passport.

PARKING // There's free parking (with a guard) east of the old town off Calle El Olivar.

BUS // Comes (☎ 956 68 40 38; Calle Batalla del Salado) operates from the small open lot near the petrol station at the north end of Calle Batalla del Salado. It has regular departures to Cádiz, Jerez de la Frontera, La Línea de La Concepción (for Gibraltar), Málaga, Seville and Zahara de los Atunes.

AROUND TARIFA

♣ BAELO CLAUDIA // STEP BACK INTO THE DAYS OF ROMAN HISPANIA

In the tiny village of Bolonia, signposted off the N340 20km northwest of Tarifa, you'll find the impressive ruins of Roman **Baelo Claudia** (☎ 956 10 67 97; non-EU/EU citizen €1.50/free; ⊙ 9am-7pm Tue-Sat Mar-May & Oct, to 8pm Tue-Sat Jun-Sep, to 6pm Tue-Sat Nov-Feb, to 2pm Sun year-round). The ruins' highlights include fine views across the water to Africa, the substantial remains of a theatre (purists won't appreciate the modern seating used for concerts), a paved forum, the market, the marble statue and columns of the basilica, and the workshops that turned out the products – salted fish and *garum* (a spicy seasoning derived from fish) – that made Baelo Claudia famous in the Roman world. The place particularly flourished in the

time of Emperor Claudius (AD 41 to 54) but declined after an earthquake in the 2nd century. There are live musical performances on some July and August evenings.

PARQUE NATURAL LOS ALCORNOCALES

This large (1700 sq km) and beautiful natural park stretches 75km north almost from the Strait of Gibraltar to the border of the Parque Natural Sierra de Grazalema. It's a spectacular jumble of sometimes rolling, sometimes rugged hills of medium height, much of it covered in Spain's most extensive *alcornocales* (cork-oak woodlands).

Los Alcornocales is rich in archaeological, historical and natural interest, but it's well off the beaten track and sparsely populated. There are plenty of walks and opportunities for other activities in the park, but you need your own wheels to make the most of it.

ESSENTIAL INFORMATION

TOURIST OFFICES // Centro de Visitantes Cortes de la Frontera (☎ 952 15 45 99; Avenida de la Democracia s/n, Cortes de la Frontera; ⊙ 10am-2pm Thu year-round, 10am-2pm & 6-8pm Fri-Sun Apr-Sep, 10am-2pm & 4-6pm Fri-Sun Oct-Mar) Centro de Visitantes Huerta Grande (☎ 956 67 91 61; Km96 N340, Pelayo; ⊙ 10am-2pm Thu year-round, 10am-2pm & 6-8pm Fri-Sun Apr-Sep, 10am-2pm & 4-6pm Fri-Sun Oct-Mar) On the Tarifa–Algeciras road. Punto de Información Castillo de Castellar (☎ 956 23 66 24; Taraguilla, Castellar de la Frontera; ⊙ 11.30am-2pm & 5-7.30pm Wed-Sun May-Sep, 10am-2pm & 3-5pm Wed-Sun Oct-Apr) Punto de Información Jimena de la Frontera (☎ 956 23 68 82; Calle Misericordia s/n, Jimena de la Frontera; ⊙ 10am-2pm & 4-8pm Mon-Fri, 10am-2pm Sat & Sun)

MIGRATING BIRDS

The Strait of Gibraltar is a key point of passage for migrating birds between Africa and Europe. Soaring birds such as raptors, black-and-white storks and vultures rely on thermals and updraughts, and there are just two places where the seas are narrow enough for the stork to get into Europe by this method. One is the Bosphorus (the strait between the Black Sea and the Sea of Marmara); the other is right here at the Strait of Gibraltar. White storks sometimes congregate in flocks of up to 5000 to cross the strait (January and February northbound, July and August southbound). In general, northward migrations occur between mid-February and early June, and southbound flights between late July and early November. When a westerly wind is blowing, Gibraltar is usually a good spot for seeing the birds. When the wind is calm or easterly, the Tarifa area (including the Mirador del Estrecho lookout 7km east of the town) is usually better.

GIBRALTAR

······

pop 29,000

An astonishing rocky outcrop and a curious outpost of British culture grafted onto the Spanish coast, Gibraltar is a fascinating place. Gibraltar's vast limestone ridge – 5km long, up to 1.6km wide and 426m high – is one of the two Pillars of Hercules, split from the other, Jebel Musa in Morocco, that marked the edge of the ancient world of the Greeks and Romans. The ridge (or 'the Rock' in local parlance) is where you'll find Gibraltar's most worthwhile sights: Europe's only wild primates, the Barbary apes; stirring lookouts across the straits to Africa and along Spain's coast; and fortifications and gun emplacements that serve as a reminder of Gibraltar's tumultuous history.

The town itself, with red post boxes, and British-style pubs and phone booths, is home to an interesting cultural melange, and dolphins play in the waters off the Rock.

Both the Phoenicians and the ancient Greeks left traces here, but Gibraltar really entered the history books in AD 711 when Tariq ibn Ziyad, the Muslim governor of Tangier, made it the initial bridgehead for the Islamic invasion of the Iberian Peninsula, landing with an army of some 10,000 men. The name Gibraltar is derived from Jebel Tariq (Tariq's Mountain).

The Almohad Muslims founded a town here in 1159 and were usurped by the Castilians in 1462. Then in 1704 an Anglo-Dutch fleet captured Gibraltar during the War of the Spanish Succession. Spain ceded the Rock of Gibraltar to Britain by the Treaty of Utrecht in 1713, but didn't give up military attempts to regain it until the failure of the Great Siege of 1779–83.

In 1969 Francisco Franco (infuriated by a referendum in which the Gibraltarians voted by 12,138 to 44 to remain under British sovereignty) closed the Spain–Gibraltar border. The same year a new constitution committed Britain to respecting Gibraltarians' wishes over sovereignty, and gave Gibraltar domestic self-government and its own parliament, the House of Assembly. In 1985, just prior to Spain joining the European Community (now the EU) in 1986, the border was opened after 16 long years.

Gibraltarians speak English, Spanish and a curiously accented, singsong mix of the two, slipping back and forth from one to the other, often in mid-sentence. Signs are in English.

ESSENTIAL INFORMATION

EMERGENCIES // Emergency (☎ 199) Summons the police or an ambulance. **Police Headquarters** (Map p150; ☎ 20072500; Rosia Rd) In the south of the town at New Mole House. **Police station** (Map p152; ☎ 20072500; 120 Irish Town) Just off Main St. **Primary Care Centre** (Map p152; ☎ 20072355; ICI Bldg, Grand Casemates Sq) For medical care. **St Bernard's Hospital** (Map p150; ☎ 20079700; Europort) Offers 24-hour emergency facilities.

TOURIST OFFICE // Tourist office (Map p152; ☎ 20074982; www.visitgibraltar.gi; Grand Casemates Sq; ◷ 9am-5.30pm Mon-Fri, 10am-3pm Sat, 10am-1pm Sun & public holidays)

ORIENTATION

To reach Gibraltar by land you pass through the Spanish frontier town of La Línea de La Concepción. After passing through immigration and customs, the road into Gibraltar crosses the runway of Gibraltar airport. The town and harbours of Gibraltar lie along the Rock's western side, facing the Bahía de Algeciras. From Grand Casemates Sq, just inside Grand Casemates Gate, Main St with all the shops runs south for about 1km.

EXPLORING GIBRALTAR

You could easily spend a day on the Rock, taking the cable car up then meandering back down through its numerous sights. In addition to the attractions listed following, the tourist office has a list of diving, sailing and fishing tours.

GIBRALTAR'S FUTURE

To cut a very long story short, Spain wants the Rock, Britain won't hand it back, while Gibraltarians would be perfectly happy if everyone just left them alone.

In December 2005, the governments of the UK, Spain and Gibraltar set up a new, trilateral process of dialogue where all decisions must be agreed by all three participants – a departure from previous agreements where Gibraltarians were often left out in the cold. Valuable decisions reached include Spain's removal of restrictions on cruise ships sailing directly between Gibraltar and Spanish ports, and also the removal of the ban on Gibraltar-bound civilian air flights diverting, if at all necessary, to nearby Spanish airports.

However, the big-picture issues remain unresolved. On 7 November 2002, the Gibraltar government held a referendum asking its people whether Britain should share sovereignty with Spain over Gibraltar. Gibraltarians rejected the idea resoundingly. Both Britain and Spain said they would not recognise the referendum, but the British government reiterated its position that it would not relinquish Gibraltar's status against local wishes. Spain's official long-term goal is a period of joint British-Spanish sovereignty leading to Gibraltar eventually becoming the 18th Spanish region, with greater autonomy than any of the others. For their part, Gibraltarians want self-determination and to retain British citizenship. In such a climate, Spanish (or even joint) sovereignty seems highly unlikely.

Numerous operators (including one that resembles a tourist office right on the Spanish side of the frontier, and the cable car operators) offer deals that combine a number of sights for an all-inclusive price. We recommend buying tickets as you go, which adds up to the same and allows more flexibility to make up your mind as you go along.

❧ UPPER ROCK // A BIRD'S-EYE VIEW OF TWO CONTINENTS

The Rock, Gibraltar's huge pinnacle of limestone, is one of the most dramatic landforms in southern Europe. Unless you decide to drive, the best way to explore the Rock is to take the **cable car** (Lower Cable-Car Station; Map p152; ☎ 20077826; Red Sands Rd; adult one-way/return £6.50/8, child one-way/return £4/4.50; ☺ 9.30am-7.15pm Apr-Oct, 9.30am-5.15pm Nov-Mar) then walk back down, perhaps catching the cable car at the middle station (if you already have a return ticket) for the final descent if the legs are weary.

At the top station there are breathtaking views over the Bahía de Algeciras and across the Strait of Gibraltar to Morocco

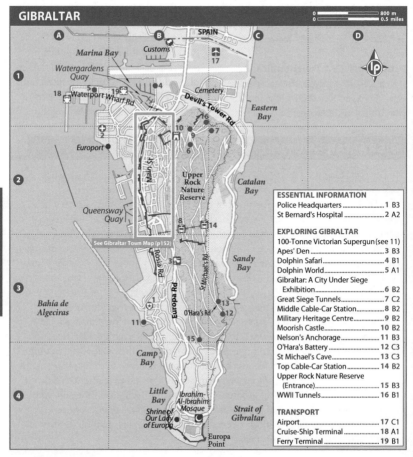

GIBRALTAR

0 ——— 800 m
0 ——— 0.5 miles

ESSENTIAL INFORMATION
Police Headquarters	1 B3
St Bernard's Hospital	2 A2

EXPLORING GIBRALTAR
100-Tonne Victorian Supergun	(see 11)
Apes' Den	3 B3
Dolphin Safari	4 B1
Dolphin World	5 A1
Gibraltar: A City Under Siege Exhibition	6 B2
Great Siege Tunnels	7 C2
Middle Cable-Car Station	8 B2
Military Heritage Centre	9 B2
Moorish Castle	10 B2
Nelson's Anchorage	11 B3
O'Hara's Battery	12 C3
St Michael's Cave	13 C3
Top Cable-Car Station	14 B2
Upper Rock Nature Reserve (Entrance)	15 B3
WWII Tunnels	16 B1

TRANSPORT
Airport	17 C1
Cruise-Ship Terminal	18 A1
Ferry Terminal	19 B1

GIBRALTAR PRACTICALITIES

VISAS & DOCUMENTS

To enter Gibraltar you need a passport or, for those EU nationalities that possess them, an identity card. Passport holders from Australia, Canada, the EU, Israel, New Zealand, Singapore, South Africa and the USA are among those who don't need visas for Gibraltar. For further information contact Gibraltar's **Immigration Department** (Map p152; ☎ 20072500; Joshua Hassan House, Secretary's Lane; ⏰ 9am-12.45pm Mon-Fri). For those intending to return or travel to Spain after visiting Gibraltar, a valid Schengen visa is essential to ensure re-entry to Spain.

MONEY

The currencies in Gibraltar are the Gibraltar pound and the pound sterling, which are interchangeable. You can use euros (except in payphones and post offices) but you'll get better value if you convert them into pounds or pay by credit card. You can't use Gibraltar money outside Gibraltar.

TELEPHONE

To phone Gibraltar from Spain, precede the eight-digit local number with the code ☎ 9567; from other countries dial the international access code, then ☎ 350 (Gibraltar's country code) and the local number. To make a call to Spain, just dial the nine-digit number. To make a call to any other country, dial the international access code (☎ 00), followed by the country code, area code and number.

if the weather is clear. You can also look down the sheer precipices of the Rock's eastern side. Most of the upper parts of the Rock (but not the main lookouts) come within the **Upper Rock Nature Reserve** (Map p150; adult/child/vehicle £8/4/1.50, pedestrians excl attractions £0.50; ⏰ 9.30am-7.15pm, last entry 6.45pm); entry tickets include admission to St Michael's Cave, the Apes' Den, the Great Siege Tunnels, the Moorish castle, Military Heritage Centre, the 100-tonne supergun and the 'Gibraltar: A City Under Siege' exhibition. The upper Rock is home to 600 plant species and is the perfect vantage point for observing the migrations of birds between Europe and Africa.

The Rock's most famous inhabitants are the tailless Barbary macaques. Some of the 240 apes hang around the top cable-car station (Map p150), while others are found at the **Apes' Den** (Map p150; near the middle cable-car station) and the Great Siege Tunnels. Legend has it that when the apes (which may have been introduced from North Africa in the 18th century) disappear from Gibraltar, so will the British. Summer is the ideal time to see newborn apes, but keep a safe distance to avoid their sharp teeth and short tempers for which they're well known.

About 15 minutes' walk south down St Michael's Rd from the top cable-car station, O'Hara's Rd leads up to the left to **O'Hara's Battery** (Map p150), an emplacement of big guns on the Rock's summit. A few minutes further down is the extraordinary **St Michael's Cave** (Map p150; St Michael's Rd; ⏰ 9.30am-7.15pm), a spectacular natural grotto full of stalagmites and stalactites. In the past, people thought the cave was a possible subterranean link with Africa. Today, apart from attracting

CÁDIZ PROVINCE & GIBRALTAR

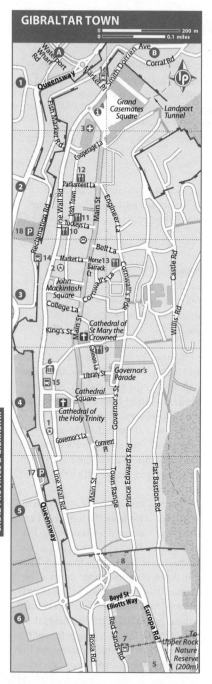

GIBRALTAR TOWN

ESSENTIAL INFORMATION

Immigration Department	1	A4
Police Station	2	A3
Primary Care Centre	3	A1
Tourist Office	4	A1

EXPLORING GIBRALTAR TOWN

Alameda Botanical Gardens	5	B6
Gibraltar Museum	6	A4
Lower Cable-Car Station	7	B6
Trafalgar Cemetery	8	B5

GASTRONOMIC HIGHLIGHTS

Cannon Bar	9	A4
Clipper	10	A2
House of Sacarello	11	A2
Star Bar	12	A2
Thyme	13	B3

TRANSPORT

Bus 10	14	A3
Bus 3	15	A4
Bus 9	16	A1

PARKING

Parking	17	A5
Parking	18	A2

tourists in droves, it's used for concerts, plays and even fashion shows. For a more extensive look at the cave system, the **Lower St Michael's Cave Tour** (tickets £8; 6pm Wed, 2.30pm Sat) is a three-hour guided adventure into the lower cave area, which ends at an underground lake. This tour involves scrambling and minor climbing with ropes, so a reasonable degree of physical fitness and appropriate footwear are essential. Children must be over 10 years old. Contact the tourist office (p149) to arrange your guide.

About 30 minutes' walk north (downhill) from the top cable-car station is Princess Caroline's Battery, housing the **Military Heritage Centre** (Map p150). From here one road leads down to the Princess Royal Battery – more gun emplacements – while another leads up to the **Great Siege Tunnels** (Map p150), a complex defence system hewn out of the Rock by the British during the siege of 1779–83 to provide gun emplacements. The **WWII tunnels** (Map p150; adult/child £6/free; 10am-4pm Mon-Fri), where the Allied invasion of North Africa

CÁDIZ PROVINCE & GIBRALTAR

was planned, can also be visited. Even combined, these tunnels constitute only a tiny proportion of more than 70km of tunnels and galleries in the Rock, most of which are off limits to the public.

On Willis's Rd, the way down to the town from Princess Caroline's Battery, you'll find the 'Gibraltar: A City Under Siege' exhibition (Map p150), in the first British building on the Rock, and the Moorish Castle (Tower of Homage; Map p150), the remains of Gibraltar's Islamic castle built in 1333.

❤ DOLPHIN WATCHING // WATCH DOLPHINS AT PLAY BETWEEN EUROPE AND AFRICA

The Bahía de Algeciras has a sizeable year-round population of dolphins and at least three companies run excellent dolphin-watching trips. From about April to September most outfits make two or more daily trips; at other times of the year they make at least one trip daily, depending on the weather and numbers. Most of the boats go from Watergardens Quay or the adjacent Marina Bay, northwest of the town centre. Trips last from 1½ to 2½ hours. You'll be unlucky if you don't get plenty of close-up dolphin contact, and you may even encounter whales. The tourist office has a list of operators, which include Dolphin World (Map p150; ☎ 54481000; Ferry Terminal, Waterport; adult/child £20/10) and Dolphin Safari (Map p150; ☎ 20071914; Marina Bay; adult/child £25/15). Advance bookings are essential.

❤ GIBRALTAR TOWN // CATCH MEDITERRANEAN LIFE WITH AN ENGLISH ACCENT

Begin your exploration in Grand Casemates Square, which once hosted public executions and is accessible through Landport Tunnel (once the only land entry through Gibraltar's walls), then stroll along Main Street, a slice of British high street with a Mediterranean lilt. History buffs will enjoy the Gibraltar Museum (Map p152; ☎ 20074289; Bomb House Lane; adult/child £2/1; ☼ 10am-6pm Mon-Fri, to 2pm Sat), with an engaging assortment of historical, architectural and military displays dating back to prehistoric times.

Near Southport Gate, the atmospherically overgrown Trafalgar Cemetery (Map p152; Prince Edward's Rd; ☼ 9am-7pm) contains the graves of British sailors who died at Gibraltar after the Battle of Trafalgar (1805). Further south again, Nelson's Anchorage (Map p150; Rosia Rd; admission £1; ☼ 9.30am-6.15pm) pinpoints the site where Nelson's body was brought ashore from HMS Victory – preserved in a rum barrel, so legend says. A 100-tonne Victorian supergun, made in Britain in 1870, commemorates the spot.

History aside, don't miss the Alameda Botanical Gardens (Map p152; Europa Rd; admission free; ☼ 8am-sunset), the lushly overgrown scene of Molly Bloom's famous deflowering in James Joyce's Ulysses.

GASTRONOMIC HIGHLIGHTS

Most of the many pubs in Gibraltar do typical British pub meals, but other cuisines also appear pretty regularly along or just off Main St or on Grand Casemates Sq. Out of town, you'll find a few places doing seafood by the water on Catalan Bay, on the east side of the Rock.

❤ CANNON BAR €
Map p152; ☎ 20077288; 27 Cannon Lane; mains from £6.25, fish & chips £5.75
You can get good fish and chips all over Gibraltar, but a sizeable proportion of

PUBLIC HOLIDAYS

Gibraltar's public holidays follow many of those of the UK.

New Year's Day 1 January
Commonwealth Day March (second Monday)
Good Friday 2 April 2010, 22 April 2011
Easter Monday 5 April 2010, 25 April 2011
May Day 1 May
Spring Bank Holiday May (last Monday)
Queen's Birthday June (Monday after the second Saturday)
Late Summer Bank Holiday August (last Monday)
Gibraltar National Day 10 September
Christmas Day 25 December
Boxing Day 26 December

Gibraltar's residents claim that Cannon Bar is the pick of the crop. There's nothing flash about the surrounds, but you'll love what comes out of the kitchen. It also does roast chicken, steak-and-kidney pie and salads, and everything is served in large portions.

❤ CLIPPER €€

Map p152; ☎ 20079791; 78B Irish Town; mains from £5.95

One of the busiest pubs, this place has the best in British pub atmosphere (varnished wood, full-on football and a cracking Sunday roast), but we love it because of the Mediterranean breeze that blows in when the doors onto the street are open. You never have to wait long for a table or for your meal to arrive and there's a range of tastes on offer, from the tasty Greek salad to bangers and mash.

❤ HOUSE OF SACARELLO €€

Map p152; ☎ 20070625; 57 Irish Town; mains £6.20-14.25; ☺ closed Sun; Ⓥ

A chic place in a converted coffee warehouse right in the centre of town, House of Sacarello is a slightly more sophisticated choice. It serves a good range of vegetarian options and some tasty homemade soups, alongside pastas, salads and a few pub-style dishes; check out its daily specials. You can linger over afternoon tea (£3.50) between 3pm and 7.30pm. It also hosts regular art exhibitions.

❤ STAR BAR €€

Map p152; ☎ 20075924; 12 Parliament Lane; breakfast £3.50-5, mains £5-11; ☺ 24hr

Gibraltar's oldest bar, if the house advertising is to be believed, the Star Bar is still one of its best having won the Golden Egg Award (a local culinary award) on numerous occasions in recent years. Hearty main dishes include lamb chops, Irish fillet, and hake in a Spanish-style green sauce. With typical pub decor and outdoor tables, it's where *East Enders* meets the Med.

❤ THYME €€€

Map p152; ☎ 20049199; www.dineatthyme.com; 5 Cornwall's Lane; mains £10-18; ☺ closed Sun

Middle Eastern, Italian, Spanish or Thai – Thyme's menu reflects Gibraltar's joyful muddle of ethnicities, and does it with class. Its 'Seafood Slammer' – seven large shot glasses filled with seafood masterpieces in miniature – wins our vote for Gibraltar's most original dish. Add chilled jazz, smart decor and a warm welcome and you'll quickly understand why we love this place.

TRANSPORT

BORDER CROSSINGS // The border is open 24 hours daily. Bag searches at Spanish customs are *usually* perfunctory.

CAR & MOTORCYCLE // Gibraltar's streets are congested and vehicle queues at the border often make it less time-consuming to park in La Línea de La Concepción (on the Spanish side of the frontier), then walk across the border (1.5km from the border to Grand

Casemates Sq). You do not have to pay any fee (ignore opportunists who say otherwise) to take a car into Gibraltar. In Gibraltar, driving is on the right, as in Spain.

PARKING // There are car parks on Line Wall Rd and Reclamation Rd (Map p152), and at the Airport Car Park on Winston Churchill Ave; the hourly charge at these car parks is 80p. Street parking meters in La Línea cost €1 for one hour or €5 for six hours and are free from 8pm until 9am Monday to Friday and from 2pm Saturday until 9am Monday. Meters are plentiful on Avenida Príncipe Felipe opposite the frontier.

AIR // Easyjet (www.easyjet.com) flies daily to/from London Gatwick, while Monarch Airlines (www.flymonarch.com) flies daily to/from London Luton and Manchester. Gibraltar's airport (Map p150; ☎ 20073026) is right next to the border.

BUS // There are no cross-border bus services. Buses 3, 9 and 10 (Map p152) go from the border into town (and back) every 15 minutes on weekdays, and every 30 minutes on weekends. Bus 3 goes to Cathedral Sq and the lower cable-car station, then on to Europa Point. Bus trips cost per adult/child/senior 60/40/30p. From La Línea de La Concepción, Comes (☎ 956 17 00 93) runs regular buses to/from Algeciras, Cádiz, Granada, Seville and Tarifa.

BOAT // One ferry (www.frs.es) a week sails between Gibraltar and Tangier in Morocco (adult/child/car/motorcycle one-way £32/21/83/30, 70 minutes). Ferries to/from Tangier are more frequent from Algeciras.

MÁLAGA PROVINCE

3 PERFECT DAYS

❦ DAY 1 // PICASSO'S MÁLAGA

One of Málaga's claims to fame (apart from the wonderful weather, beaches and food) is its most celebrated son – and father of modern art – Pablo Picasso. Born in the city, Picasso grew up here and you can visit his house, Casa Natal de Picasso (p164), and spend a good few hours in the Museo Picasso (p164), appreciating the permanent collection and changing exhibitions. Afterwards, take a stroll around Málaga's old town and imagine how the artist was inspired by its aesthetic.

❦ DAY 2 // EXPLORE RONDA

Take at least a day to explore Málaga province's most spectacular town, Ronda (p175). Perched dramatically on a mountain fissure and overlooking a vertiginous gorge, Ronda's monuments, streets, restaurants and the famous Puente Nuevo (p177) are a treat. Easily seen in a day (but happily enjoyed over a few), Ronda is Málaga's unmissable destination.

❦ DAY 3 // MOUNTAIN VILLAGE TOUR

Take the dizzying roads up for a rustic day in the villages of La Axarquía (p188), Comares (p189) and Cómpeta (p189), or opt for an architectural feast in Antequera (p184). Comares and Cómpeta are pretty white villages, with plenty of local culture, tasty food and quiet life, especially Comares, while Antequera is rich with cultural heritage, with Roman, Islamic and Spanish structures and remains. From La Axarquía, you could pop down to Nerja (p191), on the coast, before heading back to Málaga.

MÁLAGA

· · · · · ·

pop 558,000

Málaga is a world apart from the adjoining Costa del Sol; a briskly modern yet historic city, it still has the atmosphere and swagger of a Mediterranean port. The charming, historic centre is vibrant and exciting, its backdrop the blue Mediterranean, and all around are wide, leafy boulevards dotted by impressive monuments. Climbing up to Gibralfaro hill to appreciate the soaring cityscape can't fail to impress.

Málaga has been sprucing itself up for tourists for a few years now, and vying for the 2016 European City of Culture title means that its cultural appeal is ever increasing: there's the great Picasso museum, the modernistic contemporary arts centre, a fine arts museum that's still a work in progress, plus the ongoing modernisation of the port that's looking to become a leisure zone.

ESSENTIAL INFORMATION

EMERGENCIES // **Policía Local** (Local Police; Map p162; ☎ 952 12 65 00; Avenida de la Rosaleda 19) **Policía Nacional** (National Police; off Map p162; ☎ 952 04 62 00; Plaza de Manuel Azaña) The main police station is 3km west of the centre.

TOURIST OFFICES // **Municipal tourist office** (Map p165; ☎ 952 12 20 20; www.malaga turismo.com, in Spanish; Plaza de la Marina; ☺ 9am-7pm Mon-Fri Apr-Oct, to 6pm Mon-Fri Nov-Mar, 10am-6pm Sat & Sun year-round) Offers a range of city maps and booklets, including the monthly *¿Qué Hacer?*, which gives day-by-day upcoming events in the province. It operates another office in the **Casita del Jardinero** (Map p165; ☎ 952 13 47 31; Avenida de Cervantes 1; ☺ 9am-7pm Mon-Fri Apr-Oct, to 6pm Mon-Fri Nov-

Mar, 10am-6pm Sat & Sun year-round) and information kiosks on Plaza de la Aduana, at the main bus station, on Plaza de la Merced, in front of the main post office and on the eastern beaches. **Regional tourist office** (Map p165; ☎ 951 30 89 11; www.andalucia.org; Pasaje de Chinitas 4; ☺ 9am-7.30pm Mon-Fri, 10am-7pm Sat, 10am-2pm Sun) On an alley off Plaza de la Constitución. Provides a range of information including maps of the regional cities. The staff speak numerous languages. It operates a second office at the airport.

ORIENTATION

The eastern and western halves of the city are neatly separated from each other by the Río Guadalmedina. Málaga's central axis, running from west to east, comprises Avenida de Andalucía, the Alameda Principal and finally the landscaped Paseo del Parque (ending in the upmarket district of La Malagueta). From La Malagueta, Avenida de Príes takes you, with several changes to its name, out to the eastern beaches of El Pedregalejo and El Palo.

Rising up above the eastern half of Paseo del Parque, the Alcazaba and Castillo de Gibralfaro dominate the city and overlook the *casco antiguo* (old town) with its narrow winding streets. The main streets leading north into the old town are Calle Marqués de Larios, ending at Plaza de la Constitución, and Calle Molina Lario.

The modern central shopping district stretches between Calles Marqués de Larios and Puerta del Mar.

The airport is 9km from the city centre – for details on getting to/from the airport, see p172.

EXPLORING MÁLAGA

Essentially a Renaissance city with its wide boulevards and decorative facades,

(Continued on page 163)

MÁLAGA PROVINCE

MÁLAGA PROVINCE

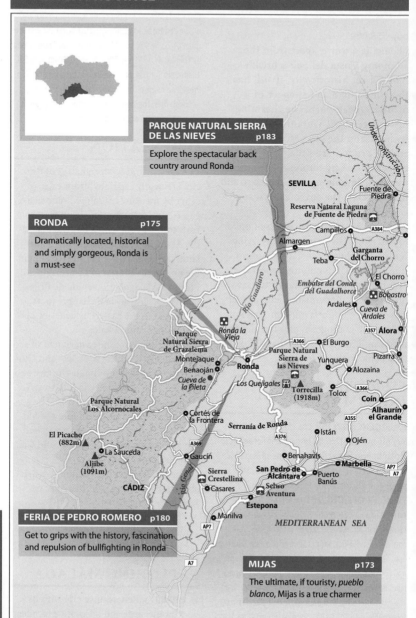

PARQUE NATURAL SIERRA DE LAS NIEVES p183

Explore the spectacular back country around Ronda

RONDA p175

Dramatically located, historical and simply gorgeous, Ronda is a must-see

FERIA DE PEDRO ROMERO p180

Get to grips with the history, fascination and repulsion of bullfighting in Ronda

MIJAS p173

The ultimate, if touristy, *pueblo blanco*, Mijas is a true charmer

SEVILLA

Fuente de Piedra

Reserva Natural Laguna de Fuente de Piedra

Campillos
A384

Almargen

Garganta del Chorro

Teba

El Chorro

Embalse del Conde del Guadalhorce

Bobastro

Ardales

Cueva de Ardales

A357 Álora

Parque Natural Sierra de Grazalema

Ronda la Vieja

A366 El Burgo

Parque Natural Sierra de las Nieves

Pizarra

Montejaque

Yunquera

Benaoján

Ronda

Alozaina

Cueva de la Pileta

Los Quejigales

A366

Torrecilla (1918m)

Tolox

Coín

Parque Natural Los Alcornocales

Alhaurín el Grande

A355

Cortés de la Frontera

Serranía de Ronda

A376

Istán

Ojén

El Picacho (882m)

La Sauceda

A369

Gaucín

Benahavís

Marbella AP7

Aljibe (1091m)

Sierra Crestellina

San Pedro de Alcántara

Puerto Banús

A7

CÁDIZ

Casares

Selwo Aventura

Estepona

Manilva

MEDITERRANEAN SEA

AP7

A7

Under Construction

Río Guadiaro

Río Genal

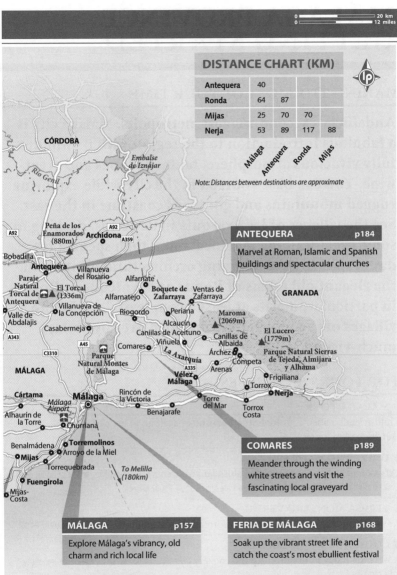

DISTANCE CHART (KM)

	Málaga	Antequera	Ronda	Mijas
Antequera	40			
Ronda	64	87		
Mijas	25	70	70	
Nerja	53	89	117	88

Note: Distances between destinations are approximate

ANTEQUERA p184

Marvel at Roman, Islamic and Spanish buildings and spectacular churches

COMARES p189

Meander through the winding white streets and visit the fascinating local graveyard

MÁLAGA p157

Explore Málaga's vibrancy, old charm and rich local life

FERIA DE MÁLAGA p168

Soak up the vibrant street life and catch the coast's most ebullient festival

GETTING AROUND

Parking in any of the towns is, frankly, a nightmare, so you may want to opt for buses or trains from Málaga. Be sure to remember where you parked your car in places such as Mijas or Ronda, which can seem easier to navigate than they actually are. The white village streets can seem identical, causing quite a headache. Countryside drives are charming with plenty of scenic routes. Try the road to Comares for the soaring views from the top.

MÁLAGA PROVINCE

MÁLAGA PROVINCE
GETTING STARTED

MAKING THE MOST OF YOUR TIME

Andalucía's second-biggest metropolis, Málaga city is a fabulous introduction to the region with its wonderfully vivacious atmosphere, fantastic tapas and great wine. You can base yourself in the city while exploring rugged mountains and gorgeous coastline in the east. See the villages of La Axarquía in day trips, packing in some great walking and local food, then spend a few days exploring the stunning architectural heritage in the elegant old towns of Ronda and Antequera. Ronda, in particular, merits at least a couple of days. White villages of the interior are presided over by pretty, much-visited Mijas.

TOP TOURS & COURSES

❧ MÁLAGA TOUR
Child-friendly, open-topped, hop-on-and-off bus circuit of the city. (Map p162; ☎ 902 10 10 81; www.malaga-tour.com)

❧ UNIVERSIDAD DE MÁLAGA
Very popular and easy-to-grasp Spanish language courses. (Map p162; ☎ 952 27 82 11; www.uma.es/estudios/extranj/extranjeros.htm; Avenida de Andalucía 24, 29007 Málaga)

❧ TERESA MONTERO VERDÚ
An engaging tour of Ronda with an informative local guide. (☎ 952 87 21 02, 609 87 94 06)

❧ COOKING HOLIDAY SPAIN
A week's holiday in Ronda and a fun cookery course. (☎ 637 80 27 43; www.cookingholidayspain.com)

❧ LET'S TREK SPAIN
Four-day trek around the wilds of the gorgeous El Chorro. (☎ 654 65 76 03; www.letstrekspain.com)

GETTING AWAY FROM IT ALL

* Get some shut-eye at Malagueta beach Escape the city buzz with a couple of hours of lounging on the sandy Malagueta (p167)

* Take a coffee break at the Parador Málaga Gibralfaro Gorgeous views of the city of Málaga are best taken in from the terrace of this lovely cliff-top cafe (p171)

* Go wild in El Chorro Go trekking or take a light explorative walk in El Chorro, one of Málaga's rare slices of wilderness (p182)

ADVANCE PLANNING

* Plaza de Toros, Ronda (p179) Catch a fight during bullfighting season or book an early ticket for the annual July concerts

* Castillo de Gibralfaro (p164) Though you can go up at any time of the day, it's best to plan the castle visit as a morning walk, followed by a nice breakfast somewhere

* Feria de Málaga (p168) Get your accommodation organised early if you want to take part in the city's biggest party

TOP RESTAURANTS

LA MORAGA
A modern tapas bar that serves traditional food with a stylish twist (p170)

BAR ORELLANA
Historic tapas bar much-loved by loyal locals (p169)

RESTAURANTE TRAGABUCHES
Ronda's best restaurant and one of the province's favourites (p181)

RESTAURANTE PLAZA DE TOROS
Eat inside a bullring, and perhaps catch a fight (p187)

EL PAPAGAYO
Summertime dining and entertainment under the stars, on Nerja's beach (p193)

RESOURCES

* Málaga City (www.malaga.com) Málaga city information

* Ronda Tourism (www.turismoenronda.es) All about Ronda

* Sur in English (www.surinenglish.com) A free weekly English-language digest

* English-language radio Between 97MHz and 105MHz on FM

* Twitter Ronda (http://twitter.com/ronda spain) Follow Ronda's events on Twitter

MÁLAGA PROVINCE

MÁLAGA

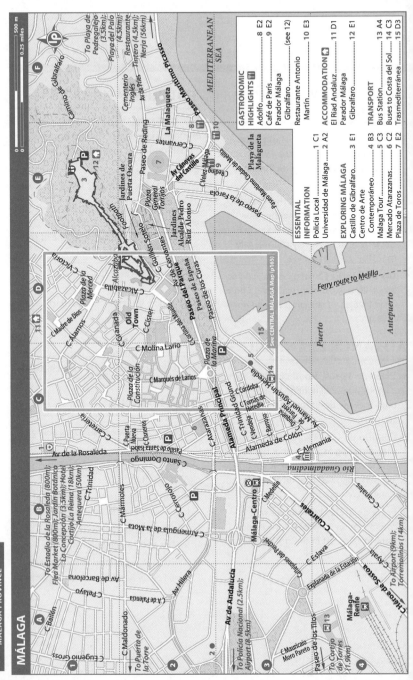

ESSENTIAL INFORMATION
Policía Local 1 C1
Universidad de Málaga 2 A2

EXPLORING MÁLAGA
Castillo de Gibralfaro 3 E1
Centro de Arte
Contemporáneo 4 B3
Malaga Tour 5 C3
Mercado Atarazanas 6 C2
Plaza de Toros 7 E2

GASTRONOMIC HIGHLIGHTS
Adolfo 8 E2
Café de París 9 E2
Parador Málaga
Gibralfaro .... (see 12)
Restaurante Antonio
Martín 10 E3

ACCOMMODATION
El Riad Andaluz 11 D1
Parador Málaga
Gibralfaro 12 E1

TRANSPORT
Bus Station 13 A4
Buses to Costa del Sol 14 C3
Trasmediterránea 15 D3

(Continued from page 157)

Málaga bears the stamp of Fernando and Isabel's ambitious transformation of Islamic Andalucía as they united Spain under a single rule in the 15th century.

Málaga's major cultural sights are clustered in or near the charming old town, which is situated beneath the Alcazaba and the Castillo de Gibralfaro. However, many visitors take an additional day or two to head out to the beaches on the eastern edge of the city.

❤ CATHEDRAL // TWO HUNDRED YEARS OF HISTORY IN THE MAKING

Málaga's **cathedral** (Map p165; ☎ 952 21 59 17; Calle Molina Lario; cathedral & museum admission €3.50; ☽ 10am-6pm Mon-Sat, closed holidays) was started in the 16th century and building continued for some 200 years. From the start, the project was plagued by over-ambition, and the original proposal for a new cathedral had to be shelved. Instead, a series of architects (five in total) set about transforming the original mosque – of this, only the **Patio de los Naranjos** survives, a small courtyard of fragrant orange trees where the ablutions fountain used to be.

Inside, it is easy to see why the epic project took so long. The fabulous domed ceiling soars 40m into the air, while the vast colonnaded nave houses an enormous cedar-wood choir. Aisles give access to 15 chapels with gorgeous retables and a stash of 18th-century religious art. Such was the project's cost that by 1782 it was decided that work would stop. One of the two bell towers was left incomplete, hence the cathedral's well-worn nickname, *La Manquita* (the one-armed lady). The cathedral entrance is on Calle Císter. The cathedral's **museum** displays a collection of

48 HOURS IN MÁLAGA

HAVE AN ARTY DAY

One of the city's main draws is the fact that it is the birthplace of modern art's most influential and important artist, Pablo Picasso. Málaga has put a lot of effort into its **Museo Picasso** (p164), investing vast amounts into the restoration of a historic palace and displaying a canon of art by its most famous son. Picasso's early childhood can be glimpsed at **Casa Natal de Picasso** (p164), where the artist grew up and started painting alongside his father. Once you're done with Picasso, head over to the **Centro de Arte Contemporáneo** (p167) for great contemporary exhibitions.

BE A BEACH BODY

OK, perhaps *this* is the city's main draw – the lovely weather and kilometres of beaches. Start the day at **Malagueta beach** (p167), where you can relax on the sand and dip into the Mediterranean. Walk down the Malagueta and discover less crowded beaches, mostly perused by exercising *malagueños*.

CLIMB TO THE CASTLE, FOLLOWED BY A GOOD LUNCH

Get an early start and go on an energising walk up to the **Castillo de Gibralfaro** (p164), descending via the lovely gardens of the **Alcazaba** (p166). Go for a wander around Málaga centre's tiny streets and have a long lunch in one of its **restaurants** (p169). In the afternoon, take a lazy stroll through **Paseo del Parque** (p166) and **Paseo de España** (p167).

religious items covering a period of 500 years. These include sacred paintings and sculptures, liturgical ornaments, and valuable pieces made of gold, silver and ivory.

🐾 PALACIO EPISCOPAL // SEE ART EXHIBITIONS IN AN OPULENT PALACE

In front of the cathedral spreads the sumptuous Plaza del Obispo, where the blood-red Bishop's Palace, the Palacio Episcopal (Map p165; admission free; ⏰ 10am-2pm & 6-9pm Tue-Sun), forms an exhibition space. The square provided an atmospheric set for Inquisition burnings in the filming of *The Bridge of San Luis Rey,* starring Robert de Niro.

🐾 MUSEO PICASSO // MÁLAGA'S HOMAGE TO ITS MOST CELEBRATED SON

From the cathedral, a short walk up Calle San Agustín brings you to the holy grail of Málaga's tourist scene, the Museo Picasso (Map p165; ☎ 902 44 33 77; www.museo picassomalaga.org; Calle San Agustín 8; permanent/temporary exhibition €6/4, combined ticket €8, 11-16yr with adult; ⏰ 10am-8pm Tue-Thu & Sun, to 9pm Fri & Sat). It has an enviable collection of 204 works, 155 donated and 49 loaned to the museum by Christine Ruiz-Picasso (wife of Paul, Picasso's eldest son) and Bernard Ruiz-Picasso (his grandson). Good temporary exhibitions of Picasso's work and themes fill out the collection.

The regional government of Andalucía invested €66 million in the restoration of the 16th-century Palacio de los Condes de Buenavista to house the museum, with fabulous results. Be sure not to miss the atmospherically preserved Phoenician, Roman, Islamic and Renaissance archaeological remains in the museum's basement, or the fantastic Café Museo

Picasso (p170). Students under 26 years and seniors get half-price admission.

🐾 CASA NATAL DE PICASSO // SEE THE ROOTS OF PICASSO'S TALENT

For a more intimate insight into the painter's childhood, head to the Casa Natal de Picasso (Map p165; ☎ 952 06 02 15; Plaza de la Merced 15; admission €1; ⏰ 10am-8pm Mon-Sat, to 2pm Sun, closed holidays), the house where Picasso was born in 1881, which now acts as a study foundation. The house has a replica 19th-century artist's studio and small quarterly exhibitions of Picasso's work. Personal memorabilia of Picasso and his family make up part of the display. Ironically, the Picasso family had to move from this house, which was too expensive, to the cheaper number 17.

🐾 CASTILLO DE GIBRALFARO // ENJOY SOARING VIEWS AND DIZZYING HISTORY

One remnant of Málaga's Islamic past is the craggy ramparts of the Castillo de Gibralfaro (Map p162; ☎ 952 22 72 30; admission €2.10, Alcazaba & Castillo de Gibralfaro €3.40; ⏰ 9am-8pm Apr-Sep, to 6pm Oct-Mar), spectacularly located high on the hill overlooking the city. Built by Abd ar-Rahman I, the 8th-century Cordoban emir, and later rebuilt in the 14th century when Málaga was the main port for the emirate of Granada, the castle originally acted as a lighthouse (its name means 'beacon hill') and a military barracks.

Nothing much remains of the interior of the castle, but the airy walkway around the ramparts affords the best views over Málaga. There is also a military museum, which includes a small-scale model of the entire castle complex and the lower residence, the Alcazaba. The model clearly shows the 14th-century curtain wall that connected the

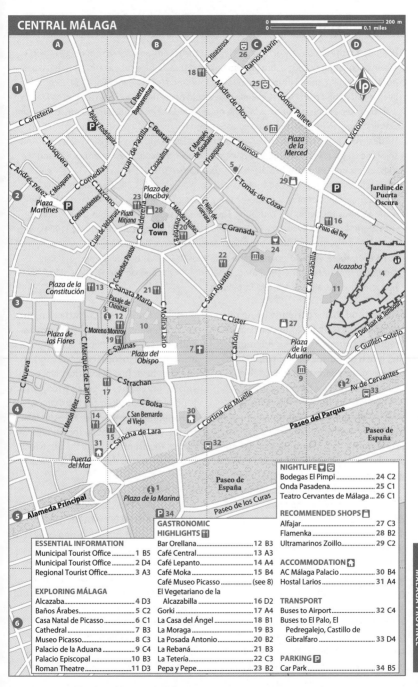

CENTRAL MÁLAGA

ESSENTIAL INFORMATION
Municipal Tourist Office 1 B5
Municipal Tourist Office 2 D4
Regional Tourist Office................ 3 A3

EXPLORING MÁLAGA
Alcazaba.. 4 D3
Baños Árabes................................. 5 C2
Casa Natal de Picasso................. 6 C1
Cathedral.. 7 B3
Museo Picasso............................... 8 C3
Palacio de la Aduana................... 9 C4
Palacio Episcopal......................... 10 B3
Roman Theatre............................. 11 D3

GASTRONOMIC
HIGHLIGHTS 🍴
Bar Orellana................................... 12 B3
Café Central................................... 13 A3
Café Lepanto................................. 14 A4
Café Moka...................................... 15 B4
Café Museo Picasso .... (see 8)
El Vegetariano de la
    Alcazabilla............................... 16 D2
Gorki.. 17 A4
La Casa del Ángel 18 B1
La Moraga 19 B3
La Posada Antonio....................... 20 B2
La Rebaná....................................... 21 B3
La Tetería....................................... 22 C3
Pepa y Pepe................................... 23 B2

NIGHTLIFE 🍷 🎭
Bodegas El Pimpi 24 C2
Onda Pasadena............................. 25 C1
Teatro Cervantes de Málaga ... 26 C1

RECOMMENDED SHOPS 🛍
Alfajar.. 27 C3
Flamenka 28 B2
Ultramarinos Zoillo...................... 29 C2

ACCOMMODATION 🏠
AC Málaga Palacio 30 B4
Hostal Larios 31 A4

TRANSPORT
Buses to Airport............................ 32 C4
Buses to El Palo, El
    Pedregalejo, Castillo de
    Gibralfaro 33 D4

PARKING 🅿
Car Park.. 34 B5

PICASSO: MÁLAGA'S NATIVE SON

Perhaps it is the luminosity of Málaga's light or the severe, angular shapes of the region's dozens of pueblos (villages), but Picasso believed that 'to be a cubist one has to have been born in Málaga'. Banned from Spain by General Franco for his 'degenerate' art, Picasso lived much of his life in France, claiming he would never return to Spain as long as Franco was in power. But his passion for Málaga never faded. When the idea for a Picasso museum was first mooted in 1954, the town council asked him to send a few paintings from Paris. He declared: 'I will not send one or two examples. I will send lorry-loads of paintings.' And so, some 50 years later, around 200 paintings, drawings, sculptures, ceramics and engravings are proudly exhibited in Málaga's Museo Picasso (p164).

Picasso was surrounded and influenced by women all his life, from his mother, sisters, grandmother and aunts to a string of beautiful muses, and women form the most obvious theme in the museum. There are famous works such as *Olga Kokhlova with Mantilla* (1917), *Woman with Raised Arms* (1939) and *Jacqueline Sitting* (1954), with each woman evoking a different stylistic response from the artist.

As ever, there are also doves in the paintings. It is said that doves and pigeons reminded him of his early childhood, when they scratched on the window sill of his house in the Plaza de la Merced in Málaga.

two sites and that is currently being restored. As the walk up to the castle and around the ramparts takes a full morning, lunch or a drink on the panoramic terrace of the nearby Parador Málaga Gibralfaro (p171) is recommended.

The best way to reach the castle is walking via the scenic Paseo Don Juan de Temboury, to the south of the Alcazaba. From there a path winds pleasantly (and steeply) through lushly gardened terraces with viewpoints over the city. Alternatively you can drive up the Camino de Gibralfaro or take bus 35 from Avenida de Cervantes.

🌱 ALCAZABA // GAZE AT THE MUSLIM GOVERNORS' SUMPTUOUS PALACE

In the shadow of the Gibralfaro, the 11th-century Alcazaba (Map p165; ☎ 952 22 51 06; Calle Alcazabilla; admission €2.10, Alcazaba & Castillo de Gibralfaro €3.40; ⏰ 9.30am-8pm Tue-Sun Apr-Sep, 8.30am-7pm Tue-Sun Oct-Mar; ♿) was the lush palace-fortress of the Muslim gover-

nors. Its multifaceted construction, meandering waterways and leafy terraces, with their rising sequence of viewpoints, are a pleasure to visit, especially in the summer heat. Just below the palace is a small Roman theatre (Map p165), which is perfect for outdoor performances.

For immediate access to the Alcazaba from Calle Guillén Sotelo (behind the municipal tourist office), take the lift, which brings you out in the heart of the palace.

🌱 ALAMEDA PRINCIPAL & AROUND // DISCOVER QUIET OASES AND BUSY MARKETS

The Alameda Principal, now a busy thoroughfare, was created in the late 18th century as a boulevard on what were then the sands of the Guadalmedina estuary. It's adorned with old trees from the Americas and lined with 18th- and 19th-century buildings.

The Paseo del Parque, a palm-lined extension of the Alameda, was created in the 1890s on land reclaimed from the sea. The garden along its southern side, Paseo de España, is full of exotic tropical plants, making a pleasant refuge from the bustle of the city. Elderly and young *malagueños* stroll around and take refuge in the deep shade of the tall palms. On the northern side, the grand Palacio de la Aduana (Map p165; Paseo del Parque) was in the midst of being refurbished at the time of research (works to be completed around 2012), after which it will be the permanent home of the Museo de Málaga (originally housed in the Picasso Museum). The collection includes fine works by great artists such as Francisco de Zurbarán, Bartolomé Esteban Murillo, José de Ribera and Pedro de Mena.

North of the Alameda, in what's now the commercial district, you'll find the neo-Moorish Mercado Atarazanas (Map p162; Calle Atarazanas), entered through its huge horseshoe-shaped arch. The daily market in here is pleasantly noisy and animated and there is a whole host of food on sale. You can choose from swaying legs of ham and rolls of sausages or cheese, fruit, fish and sweets. Nearby are plenty of cafes on pedestrianised Calle Herredería del Rey.

♥ **CENTRO DE ARTE CONTEMPORÁNEO** // **MARVEL AT MODERN ART INSIDE A STUNNING BUILDING**

If you strike out south of the Alameda you will find the funky Centro de Arte Contemporáneo (Map p162; ☎ 952 12 00 55; www.cacmalaga.org; Calle Alemania; admission free; ☼ 10am-8pm Tue-Sun 25 Sep-19 Jun, 10am-2pm & 5-9pm Tue-Sun 20 Jun-24 Sep), which is housed in a skilfully converted 1930s wholesale market on the river estuary. The bizarre triangular floor plan of the building has been retained, with its cubist lines and shapes displaying the modern art brilliantly. Painted entirely white, windows and all, the museum exhibits works from well-known 20th-century artists and collectors such as Roy Lichtenstein, Gerhard Richter and Miquel Barceló. For a good introduction to the museum, ask about the free half-hour guided tours.

♥ **LA MALAGUETA & THE BEACHES** // **REVEL IN THE SUN AND PESCAITO FRITO**

At the end of the Paseo del Parque lies the exclusive residential district of La Malagueta. Situated on a spit of land

MÁLAGA PROVINCE ACCOMMODATION

Take advantage of fantastically positioned hotels that boast sweeping views or relax in luxurious farmhouses in the mountains. Read all about the options in our dedicated accommodation chapter (p378). Here are our five top choices for Málaga province:

★ A lush old country house, Hotel Cortijo La Reina (p388) sits high up on the mountain 30 minutes from Málaga city.

★ Jardín de la Muralla (p389) is an old mansion house with antiques and elegance in a quiet Ronda street.

★ Hotel Fuente de la Higuera (p390), outside Ronda, offers a chic colonial countryside villa experience.

★ Providing bird's-eye views of Málaga city, Parador Málaga Gibralfaro (p388) is a beautiful parador (luxurious state-run hotel).

★ Hotel San Gabriel (p389) is a charming hotel that relishes Ronda's history.

protruding into the sea, apartments here have frontline sea views, and some of Málaga's best restaurants are found near the local Playa de la Malagueta (the beach closest to the city centre; Map p162). Take a walk along the beach before settling down to a fish lunch at Adolfo (opposite).

East of Playa de la Malagueta, sandy beaches continue to line most of the waterfront for several kilometres. Next along are two human-made beaches, Playa de Pedregalejo (off Map p162) and Playa del Palo (off Map p162), El Palo being the city's original, salt-of-the-earth fishing neighbourhood. This is a great place to bring children and an even better place to while away an afternoon with a cold beer and a plate of fantastic sizzling seafood. To reach either beach, take bus 11 from Paseo del Parque.

♥ PLAZA DE TOROS // CATCH A BULLFIGHT OR TOUR THE MUSEUM

See a fight during the bullfighting season, or if that's not up your street, simply visit the museum of the Plaza de Toros (bullring; Map p162; Paseo de Reding; admission €2; ☉ 10am-1pm & 5-8pm Mon-Fri), the busiest bullring on the coast. The museum is fine if you want to see some stuff on bullfighting, but Ronda's Museo Taurino (p179) is much better.

♥ JARDÍN BOTÁNICO LA CONCEPCIÓN // RELAX IN A MEDITERRANEAN TROPICAL OASIS

Four kilometres north of the city centre is the large, tropical Jardín Botánico La Concepción (off Map p162; ☎ 952 25 21 48; http://laconcepcion.malaga.eu; adult/child €4.20/2.10; ☉ 9.30am-8.30pm Tue-Sun Apr-Sep, to 5.30pm Tue-Sun Oct-Mar, closed 25 Dec & 1 Jan). Dating from the mid-19th century, the gardens

are the brainchild of a local aristocratic couple, Amalia Heredia Livermore and Jorge Loring Oyarzabal. They decided to re-create a tropical forest near the shores of the Mediterranean. It is famous for its purple wisteria blooms in spring.

You can visit by 90-minute guided tour or solo, wending your way through some of the 5000 tropical plants, ponds, waterfalls and lakes.

By car, take the A45 Antequera road north from the Málaga ring road (A7) to Km166 and follow the signs for the 'Jardín Botánico'. Alternatively, the Málaga Tour bus (p160) makes a stop here.

♥ BAÑOS ÁRABES // DETOX TRADITIONALLY: SWEAT AND GET PUMMELLED

A most welcome spot in Málaga is the Baños Árabes (Arab Baths; Map p165; ☎ 952 21 23 27; www.elhammam.com; Calle Tomás de Cózar 13; bath €21, massages €16-64; ☉ 10am-10pm), a perfect place to sit back and sweat it out amid the steamy semidarkness to the sound of soothing music. Unlike some Arabic baths in Andalucía, there are no pools to bathe in here, only the steam rooms. Book your visit in advance. Specialist massages, including ayurvedic and aromatherapy treatments, are by appointment only.

♥ FERIA DE MÁLAGA // TAKE PART IN ONE OF ANDALUCÍA'S WILDEST PARTIES

Málaga's nine-day *feria* (fair), launched by a huge fireworks display on the opening Friday in mid-August, is the most ebullient of Andalucía's summer *ferias*. During the day the city jumps with music and dancing: head for Plaza de Uncibay, Plaza de la Constitución, Plaza Mitjana or Calle Marqués de Larios to be in the thick of it. At night the fun switches to large fairgrounds and nightly rock and flamenco shows at Cortijo de Torres, 3km southwest of the city centre; special buses run from all over the city.

FESTIVALS & EVENTS

There's a whole host of festivals throughout the year in Málaga province, and the booklet *¿Qué Hacer?*, available each month from the municipal tourist office, will give you a blow-by-blow account. Besides the Feria de Málaga (p168), the following are the city's main events:

Semana Santa (Holy Week) Each night from Palm Sunday to Good Friday, six or seven *cofradías* (brotherhoods) bear their holy images for several hours through the city, watched by big crowds. A good place to watch is the Alameda Principal.

Fiesta Mayor de Verdiales Thousands congregate for a grand gathering of *verdiales* folk groups at Puerto de la Torre on 28 December. The groups perform an exhilarating brand of music and dance unique to the Málaga area. Bus 21 from the Alameda Principal goes to Puerto de la Torre.

GASTRONOMIC HIGHLIGHTS

A Málaga speciality is fish fried quickly in olive oil. *Fritura malagueña* consists of fried fish, anchovies and squid. Cold soups are popular in summer: as well as gazpacho (a chilled soup of blended tomatoes, peppers, cucumber, garlic, breadcrumbs, lemon and oil) and *sopa de ajo* (garlic soup), try *sopa de almendra con uvas* (almond soup with grapes). *Jamón* (ham) is a requisite in most tapas combinations. Málaga's restaurants are well priced and maintain a good standard due to the largely local clientele.

❦ ADOLFO €€
Map p162; ☎ 952 60 19 14; Paseo Marítimo Picasso 12; starters €7-8, seafood extra, mains €12-22; ☺ 1.30-5pm & 8.30pm-1am Mon-Sat

A classy place for an elegant night out, in the well-heeled La Malagueta area. Adolfo does a range of imaginative Mediterranean dishes: try his goats cheese starters or lobster salad, and for the main opt for kid with rosemary honey, accompanied with some good local wine.

❦ BAR ORELLANA €€
Map p165; ☎ 952 22 30 12; www.barorellana.es; Calle Moreno Monroy 5; tapas €4-5

A Málaga institution, Bar Orellana is a traditional tapas bar famed for its fresh anchovies, gorgeous chickpeas in a tomato sauce, juicy seafood and fried fish. The bar is almost always crowded, but it's all the more fun for that – you can have a real local tapas dinner experience. Just prop yourself up on the bar and shout your order above the crowd's noisy chatter.

❦ CAFÉ CENTRAL €
Map p165; Plaza de la Constitución; mains €5-11.50

This extremely popular cafe is located on the main pedestrianised square. A cold beer and plate of *rosada frita* (fried hake) is a lunchtime must. Choose your table carefully (somewhere in the middle) or you may well be plagued by various musical impresarios determined to serenade you, a feature of outdoor eating in the centre.

❦ CAFÉ DE PARÍS €€€
Map p162; ☎ 952 22 50 43; www.rcafedeparis.com; Calle Velez-Málaga 8; mains €12-36; ☺ 1.30-5pm & 8.30pm-12.30am Tue-Sat

An excellent, long-standing favourite in upmarket La Malagueta, presided over by Michelin-starred José Carlos García. The heavy fin de siècle Parisian decor encourages long somnolent lunches. Flavours are sophisticated Andalusian. Creative concoctions include sardines marinated in angel-hair marmalade (made from quinces) and fried lobster with a creamy lettuce-and-garlic sauce. Reservations are required.

❧ CAFÉ LEPANTO €

Map p165; Calle Marqués de Larios 7; ice creams €3.70-4.20

A delicious local favourite right on pedestrianised Calle Marqués de Larios. As Málaga's poshest *confitería* (sweet shop), Lepanto serves up a whole host of delicious *pasteles* (pastries and cakes), good (some even sugar-free) ice creams, sweets, chocolates, coffees, teas and other drinks.

❧ CAFÉ MOKA €

Map p165; ☎ 952 21 40 02; Calle San Bernardo el Viejo 2; breakfasts €3.50

Just off the main drag, tucked behind Hotel Don Curro, this busy little retro cafe caters to a mainly Spanish crowd. It is a great place for breakfast, but fills up quickly both for breakfast (around 10am) and late lunch (3pm).

❧ CAFÉ MUSEO PICASSO €€

Map p165; ☎ 952 22 50 43; Calle San Agustín 8; coffees €1.50, cakes €6, glasses of wine €3-5, light meals €12

Simply excellent, serving the best rich, dark coffee in town. It was established by Málaga's most dynamic young chef, José Carlos García (of Café de París), though he no longer runs it. The beautiful, secluded little patio at the back of the museum is alone worth a trip here.

❧ EL VEGETARIANO DE LA ALCAZABILLA €

Map p165; ☎ 952 21 48 58; Calle Pozo del Rey 5; mains €9-10.50; 1.30-4pm & 9-11pm Mon-Sat; Ⓥ

Manages to juggle friendly service and good food, while keeping a laid-back vibe. Lacto-vegetarian and vegan meals

are served in good-sized portions. Leave your mark: add to the graffiti on the yellow walls.

❧ LA CASA DEL ÁNGEL €€

Map p165; ☎ 952 60 87 50; Calle Madre de Dios 29; starters €9-10, mains €14-23; 1.30-4pm & 8pm-late Tue-Sun

An extraordinary restaurant filled with the owners' considerable art collection. The brainchild of Ángel Garó, the interior is a series of unusual features: Renaissance arches, beamed and frescoed ceilings, antique tiled floors and heart-warming orange and ochre paint washes. The cuisine is equally sumptuous, a combination of Andalusian, Arab and international tastes. The restaurant's intimate Salón Cervantes, with its heavy red curtains and double French windows overlooking the Teatro Cervantes, is the place to eat. Reservations necessary.

❧ LA MORAGA €€

Map p165; ☎ 952 22 68 51; Calle Fresca 12; tapas €4-5

A relatively new addition to Málaga's food scene, this is a chic tapas bar, opened by Daní García, one of Spain's top chefs. The tapas are presented in fun innovative ways, so the *lasagna de boquerones* (anchovy lasagna) has anchovies served in a tin, layered with *piquillo* peppers and aubergines. The menu has a 'spreads' section, where you get things such as *morcilla* (blood sausage) mashed and topped with pureed apple and served in a small jar, with Melba toast. Also try the cherry gazpacho. The wine is good and the service excellent.

❧ LA TETERÍA €

Map p165; Calle San Agustín 9; speciality teas €2.50, breakfasts €2.30-5; 9am-midnight

This place serves heaps of aromatic and classic teas, herbal infusions, coffees and juices, with teas ranging from peppermint to 'antidepresivo'. You can breakfast on fresh juices and *bocadillos* (filled rolls); there are only crêpes from around 2pm. Sit outside and marvel at the beautiful church opposite or stay inside to enjoy the wafting incense and background music.

♥ PARADOR MÁLAGA GIBRALFARO €€€

Map p162; ☎ 952 22 19 02; www.parador.es; menú €28

Nestled among pine trees and overlooking the Alcazaba and port, the terrace restaurant of the Parador is a fantastic dining experience and very romantic in the evenings. The menu is a tour de force of Andalusian gastronomy, specialising in the popular *fritura de pescaítos a la malagueña* (small fried fish of Málaga). The inside dining room is a formal affair of beamed ceilings, high-backed chairs and heavy tablecloths.

♥ RESTAURANTE ANTONIO MARTÍN €€

Map p162; ☎ 952 22 73 98; Playa de la Malagueta; mains €13-24; ☽ 1-5pm & 9pm-12.30am, closed Sun Nov-Apr

Right on the beach with a large sea-view terrace, this place is one of Málaga's oldest restaurants. Antonio Martín rustles up some of the best fish in town and also does excellent desserts. Celebrities and matadors are rumoured to hang out here. Reservations are recommended.

♥ RESTAURANTE TINTERO €

off Map p162; ☎ 607 60 75 86; Carretera Almería 99, El Palo; plates €7; ☽ 12.30pm-1am

A longstanding, fun seafront eatery where plates of seafood are brought out by the waiters and you call out for what you want. Shout if you want it sizzling hot.

NIGHTLIFE

The best areas to look for bars are from Plaza de la Merced in the northeast to Calle Carretería in the northwest, plus Plaza Mitjana (officially called Plaza del Marqués Vado Maestre) and Plaza de Uncibay. Plaza Mitjana heaves after midnight on Friday and Saturday.

♥ BODEGAS EL PIMPI

Map p165; ☎ 952 22 89 90; Calle Granada 62; ☽ 7pm-2am

A Málaga institution with a warren of rooms and mini patios. The huge wine casks are signed by stars (even Tony Blair!) and walls are lined with celebrity pictures and bullfighting posters. It attracts a fun-loving crowd with its sweet wine.

♥ ONDA PASADENA

Map p165; Calle Gómez Pallete 5

Smoky older and younger audiences mingle on Tuesdays to listen to jazz, while handclapping is all the rage on Thursdays when flamenco gigs take over.

♥ TEATRO CERVANTES DE MÁLAGA

Map p165; ☎ 952 22 41 00; www.teatrocervantes.com; Calle Ramos Marín s/n;

An excellent live music and performance venue featuring Spain's best artists in flamenco, classical and modern music, as well as theatre and, for Spanish speakers, lyrical and literary events. The theatre also stages children's plays.

RECOMMENDED SHOPS

Central Calle Marqués de Larios and nearby streets have glitzy boutiques and shoe shops in handsomely restored old buildings.

MÁLAGA PROVINCE

TAPAS TRAIL

The pleasures of Málaga are essentially undemanding, easy to arrange and cheap. One of the best is a slow crawl around the city's numerous tapas bars and old bodegas (wine bars).

Gorki (Map p165; ☎ 952 22 14 66; Calle Strachan 6; dishes €6-16) A popular upmarket tapas bar with pavement tables and an interior full of wine-barrel tables and stools. It serves an extensive list of Spanish wines, and tangy cheeses. Try the belly-warming *alubias con cordoniz* (white-bean stew with partridge).

La Posada Antonio (Map p165; Calle Granada 33; tapas €1.80, mains €10-17) A very popular place with locals where you will be hard pressed to find a table after 11pm, despite its barnlike proportions. Great for greasy meat in tremendous portions; the filling *paletilla cordero* (shoulder of lamb) will set you back €17.

La Rebaná (Map p165; Calle Molina Lario 5; tapas €3, raciones €5-8.50) A great, noisy and central tapas bar. The dark wooden interior (with its wrought-iron gallery) creates an inviting ambience. Goats cheese with cherries, foie gras and cured meats are among the offerings.

Pepa y Pepe (Map p165; Calle Calderería; tapas €1.30-1.50, raciones €3.60-5.50) A snug tapas bar that brims with young diners chomping their way through *calamares fritos* (battered squid) and fried green peppers.

🌿 ALFAJAR
Map p165; Calle Císter 3

Perfect for hand-crafted Andalusian ceramics produced by local artisans. You can find traditional designs and glazes, to more modern, arty and individualistic pieces. A good place for presents to self and others.

🌿 FLAMENKA
p165; ☎ 952 22 59 65; www.flamenka.com; Galerías Goya, Calle Calderería 6

This is a one-stop shop for flamenco-related goods and music.

🌿 FLEA MARKET
Map p162; Paseo de los Martiricos

On Sunday mornings, near the Estadio de la Rosaleda, this place is perfect for picking up kooky bargains and old English pieces, and hunting for a vintage find.

🌿 ULTRAMARINOS ZOILLO
Map p165; Calle Granada 65

For some tasty *malagueño* treats, look no further than this lovely deli.

TRANSPORT

TO/FROM THE AIRPORT

AIRPORT // Málaga's busy airport (off Map p162; ☎ 952 04 88 38), the main international gateway to Andalucía, is 9km southwest of the city centre and host to a rash of budget airlines. Most airline offices are at the airport. See p412 for information on flights.

CAR // Numerous local and international agencies (including Avis and Hertz) have desks at the airport. You'll find them down a ramp in the luggage-carousel hall, and beside the arrivals hall.

TAXI // A taxi from the airport to the city centre costs €15 to €16.

BUS // Bus 19 to the city centre (€1.20, 20 minutes) leaves from the 'City Bus' stop outside the airport's arrivals hall every 20 or 30 minutes from 6.35am to 11.45pm, stopping at Málaga's main train and bus stations en route. Going out to the airport, you can catch the bus at the western end of Paseo del Parque (Map p165), and from outside the stations, about every half-hour from 6.30am to 11.30pm.

TRAIN // The Aeropuerto train station, located on the Málaga–Fuengirola line, is a five-minute walk from the airport terminal: follow signs from the departures hall. Trains run about every half-hour from 7am to 11.45pm to the Málaga-Renfe station (€1.20, 11 minutes) and the Málaga-Centro station beside the Río Guadalmedina. Departures from the city to the airport and beyond are about every half-hour from 5.45am to 10.30pm.

GETTING AROUND

LOCAL BUS // Useful buses around town (€1.20 for all trips around the centre) include bus 11 to El Palo, bus 34 to El Pedregalejo and El Palo, and bus 35 to Castillo de Gibralfaro, all departing from Avenida de Cervantes (Map p165).

PARKING // Street-side parking, off the south side of Alameda Principal, for example, is metered (€1.60 per 90 minutes). Vacant lots are much cheaper (pay €1 to the attendant). A convenient car park is at Plaza de la Marina (Map p165; per 24hr €25).

TAXI // Taxi fares typically cost around €4 per 2km to 3km. Fares within the city centre, including to the train and bus stations and Castillo de Gibralfaro, are around €6.

BUS // The bus station (Map p162; ☎ 952 35 00 61; www.estabus.emtsam.es; Paseo de los Tilos) is 1km southwest of the city centre, with links to all major cities in Spain. The local destinations include Antequera, Cádiz, Córdoba, Granada, Ronda and Seville. The station has a rather spartan cafe and an internet cabin.

TRAIN // The Málaga-Renfe train station (Map p162; ☎ 952 36 02 02; www.renfe.es; Explanada de la Estación) is around the corner from the bus station. Regular trains run daily to/from Córdoba (including a one-hour AVE train), Madrid, Valencia and Barcelona. There are no direct trains to Granada, but you can get there with a change at Bobadilla. For Ronda, too, you usually change at Bobadilla.

BOAT // Ferries are operated by Trasmediterránea (Map p162; ☎ 952 06 12 18, 902 45 46 45; www.trasmediterranea.com; Estación Marítima, Local E1), which runs a fast ferry (€55, four hours) and a slower ferry (€36, 7½ hours) daily year-round to/from Melilla (€139 per car on both boats).

COSTA DEL SOL

· · · · · ·

The Costa del Sol stretches along the Málaga seaboard like a wall of wedding cakes several kilometres thick – think tacky resort towns like Fuengirola, Torremolinos, Benalmádena and Marbella – all the way down the southwestern coast, to the border of Cádiz province. Until the 1950s the resorts were fishing villages, but there's little to show for that now. Launched as a Francoist development drive for impoverished Andalucía, the Costa del Sol is an eye-stinging example of how to fill all open spaces with concrete buildings and paying customers. One exception is Mijas, however. Far from being an authentic example of Andalusian life, the pretty white village has managed to balance traditional beauty with bustling tourism.

MIJAS

pop 57,000 / elevation 428m
The story of Mijas encapsulates the story of the Costa del Sol. Originally a humble

▶ TOP **FIVE**

MÁLAGA WALKS

★ Castillo de Gibralfaro (p164) A light morning walk with great views of Málaga city

★ Málaga's Beaches (p167) Stroll for several kilometres by the sea

★ Serranía de Ronda (p182) The region's prettiest mountain walk

★ Torrecilla (p183) Climb the highest peak in western Andalucía

★ El Lucero (p190) Enjoy stupendous views of Granada and Morocco from the summit

MÁLAGA PROVINCE

KIDS' COSTA

A growing number of attractions along the coast cater for children of all ages. The oldest and biggest amusement park is **Tivoli World** (☎ 952 57 70 16; www.tivolicostadelsol.com; Avenida de Tivoli, Arroyo de la Miel; admission €7; ☉ 6pm-1am May-Oct, noon-7pm Sat & Sun Nov-Apr). As well as various rides and slides (for which you pay in addition to the admission price), it stages daily dance, musical and children's events. It's five minutes' walk from Benalmádena–Arroyo de la Miel train station. For children, consider the good-value 'Supertivolino' ticket for €12, which covers admission and unlimited use on more than 30 rides.

Alternatively, **Parque Acuático Mijas** (☎ 952 46 04 04; www.aquamijas.com; adult/child €17/12; ☉ 10.30am-5.30pm May, 10am-6pm Jun & Sep, 10am-7pm Jul & Aug), beside the A7 Fuengirola bypass, has pools with chutes and slides, and a separate minipark for toddlers.

Selwo Marina (☎ 902 19 04 82; www.selwomarina.com; Parque de la Paloma, Benalmádena; adult/child €17/13) is a relative of Selwo Aventura in Estepona. It has a dolphinarium and ice-penguinarium, an Amazonian aviary and the awesome option of swimming with sea lions. Selwo offers discounted packages for visits to the two Selwos and the Benalmádena cable car. Note that it has somewhat erratic opening hours – it's open from 10am to 6pm, 8pm or 9pm daily – though sometimes even later, depending on its own peculiar timetable. Selwo is closed for most of the winter, between November and February.

A good cloudy-day option is the **Crocodile Park** (☎ 952 05 17 82; www.crocodile-park.com; Calle Cuba 14, Torremolinos; adult/child €11/8.50; ☉ 10am-6pm), where experienced guides handle and give details about various types of crocodile.

pueblo (village), it is now the richest town in the province. Since finding favour with discerning bohemian artists and writers in the 1950s and '60s, Mijas has sprawled across the surrounding hills and down to the coast yet managed to retain the original pueblo's picturesque charm.

Much like Capri, the effect is somewhat spoiled by the hordes of day-tripping package tourists that pile into the town in summer, but in winter it is blissfully quiet. Actually, wander the back streets at any time and you'll appreciate its charm. Mijas has a foreign population of at least 40% and the municipality includes Mijas-Costa, on the coast southwest of Fuengirola. Golf courses abound, and Mijas is a noted area for rock climbing (particularly in winter), with around 100 grade V-7 climbs.

ESSENTIAL INFORMATION

TOURIST OFFICE // Mijas Tourist Office
(☎ 958 58 90 34; www.mijas.es; Plaza Virgen de la Peña s/n; ☉ 9am-7pm Mon-Fri Oct-Mar, to 8pm Mon-Fri Apr-Sep, 10am-3pm Sat year-round)

EXPLORING MIJAS

☘ **OLD TOWN //** WANDER THROUGH WHITE STREETS AND DISCOVER HOLY SIGHTS
Mijas has an unusual square-shaped bullring, the **Plaza de Toros** (☎ 952 48 52 48; bullfights €50-90; ☉ 10am-8pm). It also has an interesting grotto of the **Virgen de la Peña**, where the Virgin is said to have appeared to two shepherds in 1586. On the cliff edge in an ornamental garden, the spot has wonderful views and is the start of a **panoramic pathway** that wends its

way around the vertical edges of the town. During the annual village procession on 8 September, the effigy of the Virgin is carried 2km up to the **Ermita del Calvario**, a tiny chapel built by Carmelite brothers. Black-iron crosses mark a short walking trail that leads up to the hermitage. Alternatively, you can take one of the donkey taxis from the town centre for €8.

Mijas is also home to the most interesting 'folk' museum on the *costa* (coast), the **Casa Museo de Mijas** (☎ 952 59 03 80; Calle Málaga; admission free; ☑ 10am-2pm & 4-7pm Sep-Mar, 10am-2pm & 5-8pm Apr-Jun, 10am-2pm & 6-9pm Jul & Aug). It was created and is still run by Carmen Escalona, who specialises in crafting folk-themed models. The small models are dotted around the museum, and in light of the explanations and artefacts, show perfectly the style and mode of living of some 40 years ago. There are no explanations in English. It is a great place for children, who will particularly like the donkey made from esparto grass. The museum is just uphill from Plaza de la Constitución, Mijas' second main plaza.

GASTRONOMIC HIGHLIGHTS

It's not the most exciting of places to eat, but Mijas has a couple of decent restaurants.

☙ EL MIRLO BLANCO €€€

☎ 952 48 57 00; Paseo Marítimo 29, Mijas-Costa; mains €16-35; ☑ closed Tue Sep-Jun
The Basque-style El Mirlo Blanco is one of Mijas' best restaurants. The menu varies seasonally but roast lamb and hake in a green sauce are good choices. Finish with a Grand Marnier soufflé.

☙ EL PADRASTRO €€

☎ 952 48 50 00; Paseo del Compás; mains €12-27
The haute-Med Padrastro is perched on a cliff above the Plaza Virgen de la Peña,

with suitably spectacular views. You don't have to climb the stairs as there is a lift, so it's good for mobility-impaired people. Delicious fare includes a leek-filled pastry, rice with seafood, and plenty of fish dishes.

TRANSPORT

BUS // Frequent buses run from Fuengirola (€1.50, 25 minutes).

THE INTERIOR

· · · · · ·

The mountainous interior of Málaga province is an area of raw beauty and romantic *pueblos blancos* (white villages) sprinkled across craggy landscapes. Beyond the mountains, the verdant countryside opens out into a wide chequer-board of floodplains. It's a wonderfully far cry from the tourist-clogged coast.

RONDA

pop 36,000 / elevation 744m
Perched on an inland plateau riven by the 100m fissure of El Tajo gorge, Ronda is Málaga province's most spectacular town. It has a superbly dramatic location, and is the most impressive of all the *pueblos blancos*. It owes its name ('surrounded' by mountains), to the encircling Serranía de Ronda. Established in the 9th century BC, Ronda is also one of Spain's oldest towns. Its existing old town, La Ciudad (the City), largely dates back to Islamic times, when it was an important cultural centre filled with mosques and palaces. Its wealth as a trading depot made it an attractive prospect for bandits and profiteers and the town has a colourful and romantic past in Spanish folklore.

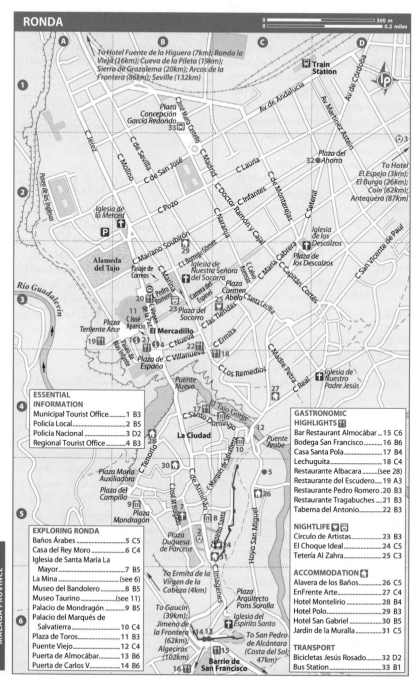

RONDA

To Hotel Fuente de la Higuera (7km); Ronda la
Vieja (16km); Cueva de la Pileta (19km);
Sierra de Grazalema (20km); Arcos de la
Frontera (86km); Seville (132km)

Train
Station

Plaza
Concepción
García Redondo
33

To Hotel
El Espejo (3km);
El Burgo (26km);
Coín (62km);
Antequera (87km)

Plaza del
Ahorro
32

Iglesia de
la Merced

Iglesia
de los
Descalzos

Plaza de
los Descalzos

Alameda
del Tajo

Pasaje de
Correos

Iglesia de
Nuestra Señora
del Socorro

Plaza
Carmen
Abela

Plaza del
Socorro

El Mercadillo

Plaza
Teniente Arce

19

Plaza de
España

Puente
Nuevo

Iglesia de
Nuestro
Padre Jesús

ESSENTIAL
INFORMATION

Municipal Tourist Office............1 B3
Policía Local 2 B5
Policía Nacional 3 D2
Regional Tourist Office...........4 B3

El Tajo Gorge

La Ciudad

Puente
Árabe

Plaza María
Auxiliadora

Plaza del
Campillo

Plaza
Mondragón

EXPLORING RONDA

Baños Árabes 5 C5
Casa del Rey Moro 6 C4
Iglesia de Santa María La
   Mayor................................7 B5
La Mina ....(see 6)
Museo del Bandolero 8 B5
Museo Taurino ....(see 11)
Palacio de Mondragón 9 B5
Palacio del Marqués de
   Salvatierra......................10 C4
Plaza de Toros 11 B3
Puente Viejo 12 C4
Puerta de Almocábar 13 B6
Puerta de Carlos V...............14 B6

Plaza
Duquesa
de Parcent

To Ermita de la
Virgen de la
Cabeza (4km)

To Gaucín
(39km);
Jimena de
la Frontera
(62km);
Algeciras
(102km)

Plaza
Arquitecto
Pons Sorolla

Iglesia del
Espíritu Santo

Barrio de
San Francisco

To San Pedro
de Alcántara
(Costa del Sol;
47km)

GASTRONOMIC
HIGHLIGHTS

Bar Restaurant Almocábar ...15 C6
Bodega San Francisco...........16 B6
Casa Santa Pola....................17 B4
Lechuguita 18 C4
Restaurante Albacara ......(see 28)
Restaurante del Escudero.....19 A3
Restaurante Pedro Romero.20 B3
Restaurante Tragabuches 21 B3
Taberna del Antonio............22 B3

NIGHTLIFE

Círculo de Artistas...............23 B3
El Choque Ideal 24 C5
Tetería Al Zahra..................25 C3

ACCOMMODATION

Alavera de los Baños 26 C5
EnFrente Arte......................27 C4
Hotel Montelirio 28 B4
Hotel Polo...........................29 B3
Hotel San Gabriel.................30 B5
Jardín de la Muralla.............31 C5

TRANSPORT

Bicicletas Jesús Rosado........32 D2
Bus Station...........................33 B1

Ronda was a favourite with the Romantics of the late 19th century, and has attracted an array of international artists and writers, such as David Wilkie, Alexandre Dumas, Rainer Maria Rilke, Ernest Hemingway and Orson Welles, who flocked to admire it. Nowadays, Ronda has a lot to live up to, and at just an hour inland from the Costa del Sol it attracts a weight of day-trippers, who nearly double its population in summer. The best time to enjoy the town with some ease is in the honeyed light of evening, or in early spring and late autumn when the tourist season has lost its sting.

ESSENTIAL INFORMATION

EMERGENCIES // Policía Local (☎ 952 87 13 69; Plaza Duquesa de Parcent s/n) In the *ayuntamiento* (town hall). Policía Nacional (☎ 952 87 10 01; Avenida de Madrid s/n)

TOURIST OFFICES // Municipal tourist office (☎ 952 18 71 19; www.turismoderonda .es; Paseo de Blas Infante; 10am-7.30pm Mon-Fri, 10.15am-2pm & 3.30-6.30pm Sat, Sun & holidays) Helpful and friendly staff with a wealth of information on the town and region. Regional tourist office (☎ 952 87 12 72; www.andalucia.org; Plaza de España 1; 9am-7.30pm Mon-Fri, 10am-2pm Sat)

ORIENTATION

La Ciudad stands on the southern side of El Tajo gorge. Following the Reconquista (Christian reconquest) in 1485, new taxes imposed on La Ciudad forced the residents to set up the newer town, El Mercadillo (the Market), to the north. Three bridges cross the gorge, the main one being the Puente Nuevo linking Plaza de España with Calle de Armiñán. Both parts of town come to an abrupt end on their western sides with cliffs plunging away to the valley of the Río Guadalevín far below. Places of interest are mainly concentrated in La Ciudad, while most places to stay and eat, along with the bus and train stations, are in El Mercadillo.

EXPLORING RONDA

Ronda has traditionally been a haven for artists and that is no less true today than it was in the past. Check out www.art gaucin.com for information about the local art scene.

❤ LA CIUDAD // **GET DIZZY WITH SPECTACULAR VIEWS AND AWESOME ARCHITECTURE**
Straddling the dramatic gorge and the Río Guadalevín (Deep River) is Ronda's most recognisable sight, the towering Puente Nuevo, best viewed from the Camino de los Molinos, which runs along the bottom of the gorge. The bridge separates the old and new towns. The former is surrounded by massive fortress walls pierced by two ancient gates: the Islamic Puerta de Almocábar, which in the 13th century was the main gateway to the castle; and the 16th-century Puerta de Carlos V. Inside, the Islamic layout remains intact, and its maze of narrow streets now takes its character from the Renaissance mansions of powerful families whose predecessors accompanied Fernando el Católico in the taking of the city in 1485.

Nearly all of the mansions still bear the crest of each family, including the Palacio de Mondragón (☎ 952 87 84 50; Plaza Mondragón; adult/concession €2/1; 10am-6pm Mon-Fri, to 3pm Sat, Sun & holidays). Built for Abomelic, ruler of Ronda in 1314, the palace retains its internal courtyards and fountains, the most impressive of these being the Patio Mudéjar, from which a horseshoe arch leads into a cliff-top garden with splendid views. It houses the city museum, which has artefacts and

MÁLAGA PROVINCE

information especially related to both Roman and Islamic funerary systems.

A minute's walk southeast from the Palacio de Mondragón is the city's original mosque, now the ornate **Iglesia de Santa María La Mayor** (☎ 952 87 22 46; Plaza Duquesa de Parcent; admission €3; ◷ 10am-6pm Nov-Mar, to 7pm Apr-Oct). Just inside the church entrance is an arch covered with Arabic inscriptions, which was part of the mosque's mihrab (prayer niche indicating the direction of Mecca). The church has been declared a national monument, and its interior is an orgy of decorative styles and ornamentation. A huge, central, cedar choir stall divides the church into two sections: aristocrats to the front, everyone else at the back.

Just opposite the church, the amusing **Museo del Bandolero** (☎ 952 87 77 85; www.museobandolero.com; Calle de Armiñán 65; admission €3; ◷ 10.30am-6pm Oct-Mar, to 7pm Apr-Sep) is dedicated to the banditry for which central Andalucía was once renowned. Old prints reflect that when the youthful *bandoleros* (bandits) were not being shot, hanged or garrotted by the authorities they were stabbing each other in the back, literally as much as figuratively.

RONDA'S FIGHTING ROMEROS

Ronda can bullishly claim to be the home of bullfighting – and it does. It proudly boasts the Real Maestranza de Ronda equestrian school, founded in 1572 for the Spanish aristocracy to learn to ride and fight. They did this by challenging bulls in an arena, and thus was born the first bullfight.

Legend has it that one of these fights went awry when a nobleman fell from his horse and risked being gored to death. Without hesitation local hero Francisco Romero (b 1698) leapt into the ring and distracted the bull by waving his hat. By the next generation Francisco's son, Juan, had added the *cuadrilla* (the matador's supporting team), consisting of two to three *banderilleros* (who work on foot) and two to three picadors (men on horseback with pike poles). This married both the habits of the aristocracy (who previously conducted fights on horseback) and the common, dangerous bullfights that took place during fiestas in the main square of each town.

Juan's son Pedro Romero (1754–1839), whose distinguished career saw the death of over 5000 bulls, invented the rules and graceful ballet-like movements of the modern bullfight, introducing the *muleta* (a variation on his grandfather's hat), a red cape used to attract the bull's attention.

In 1932 Ronda also gave birth to one of Spain's greatest 20th-century bullfighters, the charismatic Antonio Ordóñez, who was immortalised by Hemingway in *The Dangerous Summer*.

It was the Ordóñez family that inaugurated Ronda's Corridas Goyescas, held each year in early September in honour of Pedro Romero, and which attracts Spain's best matadors. During the bullfights the matadors wear the stiff, ornate 19th-century costume that Goya depicted in his paintings of Romero. Out of the three days of fights the most popular is on Saturday, for which you will need to book tickets at least two months in advance. Tickets cost from around €65 in the *sol* (sun) to €110 in *sombra* (shadow). Buy tickets at the bullring in Ronda from 1 July, or phone **Tazdevil** (☎ 954 50 37 94, 607 90 93 45).

Taking the narrow Calle Marqués de Salvatierra will bring you to the small **Puente Viejo** (Old Bridge), with views down onto the river as it rushes into the gorge. Just before you reach it you will pass the **Palacio del Marqués de Salvatierra**, a huge mansion that required the demolition of 42 houses for it to be built. Owned by the descendants of the Marqués de Moctezuma, the Governor of South America, the palace is decorated on its portal with carvings of Native Americans. The palace and all its antiques are sometimes open to the public.

For a more dramatic view of the river and gorge, leave Puente Viejo and head back along Calle Marqués de Salvatierra, turning right up Calle Santo Domingo to the **Casa del Rey Moro** (☎ 952 18 72 00; Calle Santo Domingo 17; adult/child €4/2; ☺ 10am-7pm). Here, terraced gardens give access to **La Mina**, an Islamic stairway of over 300 steps that are cut into the rock all the way down to the river at the bottom of the gorge. These steps enabled Ronda to maintain water supplies when it was under attack. It was also the point where Christian troops forced entry in 1485. The steps are not well lit and are steep and wet in places. Care should be taken, even by the fit and able. Also backing on to the river are the almost intact, atmospheric 13th- and 14th-century **Baños Árabes** (Arab Baths; ☎ 656 95 09 37; Hoyo San Miguel; admission €2, Sun free; ☺ 10am-7pm Mon-Fri, to 3pm Sat & Sun).

To walk down into the gorge (a good morning's walk), take the path from Plaza María Auxiliadora. It is steep and long but is well worth the effort, and in springtime the valley below is carpeted in flowers. Further afield is the lovely chapel **Ermita de la Virgen de la Cabeza**.

ॐ EL MERCADILLO // SEE HEMINGWAY'S SQUARE AND SPAIN'S TOP BULLRING

Directly across the Puente Nuevo is the main square, **Plaza de España**, made famous by Hemingway in his novel *For Whom the Bell Tolls*. Chapter 10 tells how early in the civil war the 'fascists' of a small town were rounded up in the *ayuntamiento*, clubbed and made to walk the gauntlet between two lines of townspeople before being thrown off the cliff. The episode is based on events that took place here in Plaza de España. What was the *ayuntamiento* is now Ronda's parador.

Nearby, Ronda's elegant **Plaza de Toros** (☎ 952 87 41 32; Calle Virgen de la Paz s/n; admission €5; ☺ 10am-6pm Oct-Mar, to 8pm Apr-Sep) is a mecca for bullfighting aficionados. In existence for more than 200 years, it is one of the oldest and most revered bullrings in Spain. It has also been the site of some of the most important events in bullfighting history (see the boxed text, opposite). Built by Martín Aldehuela, the bullring is universally admired for its soft sandstone hues and galleried arches. At 66m in diameter it is also the largest and, therefore, most dangerous bullring, yet it only seats 5000 spectators – a tiny number compared with the huge 50,000-seater bullring in Mexico City. In July the ring is used for a series of fabulous concerts, and opera.

The on-site **Museo Taurino** is crammed with memorabilia such as blood-spattered costumes worn by Pedro Romero and 1990s star Jesulín de Ubrique. It also includes photos of famous fans such as Orson Welles and Ernest Hemingway, whose novel *Death in the Afternoon* provides in-depth insight into the fear and tension of the bullring.

MÁLAGA PROVINCE

Behind the Plaza de Toros, spectacular cliff-top views open out from **Paseo de Blas Infante** and the leafy **Alameda del Tajo** park nearby. The park has a good play area for younger children.

♨ BARRIO DE SAN FRANCISCO //
A HISTORICAL AREA THAT HIDES
EXCELLENT TAPAS BARS

Outside La Ciudad's city walls is the Barrio de San Francisco, the original Muslim cemetery of the city. A small market was established here in the 15th century, when traders refused to enter the city in order to avoid paying hefty taxes. Some inns and taverns were built and thus began a new quarter. The barrio still has a reputation for down-to-earth tapas bars.

♨ HORSE TREKKING // GET ONTO
GUIDED HORSE TREKS FOR ALL
GENERATIONS

For guided horse treks contact **Hotel El Espejo** (☎ 952 11 40 11; www.serraniaderonda.org, in Spanish; Camino del Cuco), located off the Arriate road, about 3km from Ronda. Cost is €15 per hour with a minimum price of €60, ie one person for four hours or two people for two hours.

FESTIVALS & EVENTS

Corpus Cristi On the Thursday after Trinity (usually falling somewhere between May and June) there are bullfights and festivities after the 900kg Station of the Cross is carried 6km through the town.

Feria de Pedro Romero An orgy of partying during the first two weeks of September, including the important flamenco event, Festival de Cante Grande. Culminates in the Corridas Goyesca (bullfights in honour of legendary bullfighter Pedro Romero – see p178).

GASTRONOMIC HIGHLIGHTS

Typical Ronda food is hearty mountain fare, with an emphasis on stews (called

cocido, estofado or *cazuela*), *trucha* (trout), *toro de rabo* (bull's tail stew) and game such as *conejo* (rabbit), *perdiz* (partridge) and *codorniz* (quail). But, as elsewhere, inspired chefs are trying out new ideas.

♨ BAR RESTAURANT
ALMOCÁBAR €€

☎ 952 87 59 77; Calle Ruedo Alameda 5; tapas €1.50, mains €10-14; ☺ 1.30-5pm & 8pm-1am Wed-Mon
In the Barrio de San Francisco, Almocábar is an excellent authentic tapas bar, little touched by the tourist hordes at the top of town. In fact, the tapas are so good that this spot is normally super packed and finding a place at the bar can be a challenge. If that's the case, try reserving the restaurant section *(comedor)*.

♨ CASA SANTA POLA €€€

☎ 952 87 92 08; Calle Santo Domingo 3; starters €10-12, mains €17-22
This is an atmospheric restaurant spread over three floors of an old aristocratic house. At night each of the small dining rooms is intimate and candlelit and during the day there are good views over El Tajo. The roast lamb cutlets or the roast pork are a must.

♨ RESTAURANTE ALBACARA €€

☎ 952 16 11 84; Calle Tenorio 8; mains €14.50-19
One of Ronda's best restaurants, the Albacara is in the old stables of the Montelirio palace and teeters on the edge of the gorge. It serves up creative meals – try the codfish with a spicy leek sauce. Don't miss the extensive wine list.

♨ RESTAURANTE DEL
ESCUDERO €€

☎ 952 87 13 67; Paseo de Blas Infante 1; menú €17, mains €17-21; ☺ 1.30-3.30pm Tue-Sun, 8-10.30pm Tue-Sat
If you can't afford to dine at Tragabuches (opposite), but want some of the repu-

table cuisine, try its sister restaurant. Situated in an attractive garden near the Plaza de Toros, Escudero has a decent set menu and more reasonable prices than fancy Tragabuches, as well as the good food. The garden makes it popular in the summer.

♥ RESTAURANTE PEDRO ROMERO €€

☎ 952 87 11 10; Calle Virgen de la Paz 18; menú €16, mains €15-18

Opposite the bullring, this celebrated eatery dedicated to bullfighting turns out classic *rondeño* dishes (dishes from Ronda). This is a good place to try the *rabo de toro*, a tender meat dish made from bull's tail. Vegetarians will enjoy the fried goats cheese starter served with apple sauce.

♥ RESTAURANTE TRAGABUCHES €€€

☎ 952 19 02 91; Calle José Aparicio 1; mains €26-29; ☽ 1.30-3.30pm & 8-10.30pm Tue-Sat

Ronda's best and most famous restaurant is a 180-degree turn away from the ubiquitous 'rustic' look and cuisine. Michelin-starred in 1998, Tragabuches is modern and sleek with an innovative menu to match. People flock here from miles away to taste the food, prepared by its creative chef, Daniel García.

TAPAS TIPS

Ronda's ever-popular tapas bars are the **Taberna del Antonio** (Calle Los Remedios 22; ☽ 11am-midnight), serving more than 60 kinds of tapas, and **Lechuguita** (Calle Los Remedios 25; ☽ 11am-midnight). Down in the Barrio de San Francisco, try the heaving **Bodega San Francisco** (Calle Ruedo Alameda; ☽ 11am-midnight) – if you can squeeze in the door.

NIGHTLIFE

♥ CÍRCULO DE ARTISTAS

Plaza del Socorro; admission €25; ☽ Mon-Wed

Stages flamenco shows from 10pm, as well as other song and dance performances.

♥ EL CHOQUE IDEAL

☎ 952 16 19 18; www.elchoqueideal.com; Espíritu Santo 9; ☽ 9.30am-3am Feb-Oct, 1pm-1am Nov-Jan

Hosts a range of events from films out on the terrace to live bands. There are fantastic views and lots of mosaic work on display.

♥ TETERÍA AL ZAHRA

Calle Las Tiendas 17; teas from €3; ☽ 4.30pm-midnight

Come here and try a pot of herbal, Moroccan, Pakistani or a host of other teas, all served in pretty Moroccan ceramic teapots and cups and saucers. There are hookahs for smoking, too, and you can settle in for a few hours of sipping, puffing and gossiping.

TRANSPORT

BUS // The bus station is at Plaza Concepción García Redondo 2. **Comes** (☎ 952 87 19 92) has buses to Arcos de la Frontera, Jerez de la Frontera and Cádiz up to four times daily. **Los Amarillos** (☎ 952 18 70 61) goes to Seville via Algodonales, Grazalema, and Málaga via Ardales. **Portillo** (☎ 952 87 22 62) runs to Málaga via San Pedro de Alcántara.

TRAIN // Ronda's **train station** (☎ 952 87 16 73; www.renfe.es; Avenida de Andalucía) is on the line between Bobadilla and Algeciras. Trains run to Algeciras via Gaucín and Jimena de la Frontera. This train ride is incredibly scenic and worth taking just for the views. Other trains depart for Málaga, Córdoba, Madrid, and Granada via Antequera. For Seville change at Bobadilla or Antequera. It's less than 1km from the train station to most accommodation. Supposedly every 30 minutes, town minibuses run to Plaza de España from Avenida Martínez Astein (across the road from the train station), but they're not very reliable. It's not too far to walk to the town centre but, with luggage, you'll need a taxi (€5).

PARKING // Parking in Ronda is, inevitably, difficult. There are a number of underground car parks and some hotels have parking deals for guests. Parking charges are about €3 per hour, or €15 to €20 for 14 to 24 hours.

BICYCLE // Bicicletas Jesús Rosado (☎ /fax 952 87 02 21, 637 45 77 56; www.bicicletasjesusrosado .com; 87 Plaza del Ahorro 1; one day €15) Rents out well-equipped mountain bikes.

AROUND RONDA

❦ SERRANÍA DE RONDA // HIKE ONE OF THE REGION'S PRETTIEST MOUNTAINS

Curving around the south and southeast of the town, the Serranía de Ronda may not be the highest or most dramatic mountain range in Andalucía, but it's certainly among the prettiest. Any of the roads through it between Ronda and southern Cádiz province, Gibraltar or the Costa del Sol, makes a picturesque route. Cortés de la Frontera, overlooking the Guadiaro Valley, and Gaucín, looking across the Genal Valley to the Sierra Crestellina, are among the most beautiful spots to stop.

To the west and southwest of Ronda stretch the wilder Sierra de Grazalema (p139) and Los Alcornocales (p147) natural parks. There are plenty of walking and cycling possibilities and Ronda's tourist office can provide details of these as well as maps.

❦ RONDA LA VIEJA // WANDER AROUND A RUINED BUT DREAMY ROMAN SITE

To the north of Ronda, off the A376, is the relatively undisturbed Roman site of Acinipo at Ronda la Vieja (☎ 630 42 99 49; admission free; ⊕ 9am-3pm Tue-Sat, 8am-2pm Sun), with its partially reconstructed theatre.

Although completely ruinous, with the exception of the theatre, it is a wonderfully wild site with fantastic views of the surrounding countryside and you can happily while away a few hours wandering through the fallen stones trying to guess the location of various baths and forums.

❦ CUEVA DE LA PILETA // SEE AN ANCIENT CAVE BY CANDLELIGHT

Twenty kilometres southwest of Ronda la Vieja are some of Andalucía's most ancient caves, the Cueva de la Pileta (☎ 952 16 73 43; www.cuevadelapileta.org; adult/child/student €8/5/5; ⊕ hourly tours 10am-1pm & 4-6pm). The guided tour (call for details) by candlelight into the dark belly of the cave reveals Palaeolithic paintings of horses, goats and fish from 20,000 to 25,000 years ago. Beautiful stalactites and stalagmites add to the effect. The guided tours are given by members of the Bullón family, who discovered the paintings in 1905 and who speak some English. The maximum group size is 25, so if you come on a busy day you may have to wait for a place.

Benaoján village is the nearest that you can get to the Cueva de la Pileta by public transport. The caves are 4km south of Benaoján, about 250m off the Benaoján–Cortés de la Frontera road – there is no transport to the caves, so you will need your own car to get here. The turn-off is signposted. Benaoján is served by two Los Amarillos buses (from Monday to Friday) and up to four daily trains to/from Ronda. Walking trails link Benaoján with Ronda and villages in the Guadiaro Valley.

ARDALES & EL CHORRO

Fifty kilometres northwest of Málaga, the Río Guadalhorce carves its way through the awesome Garganta del Chorro (El Chorro gorge). Also called the Desfiladero de los Gaitanes, the gorge is about 4km long, as much as 400m deep, and sometimes just 10m wide. Its sometimes sheer walls, and other rock faces nearby, are the biggest magnet for rock climbers in Andalucía, with hundreds of bolted climbs snaking their way up the limestone cliffs.

Along the gorge runs the main railway into Málaga (with the aid of 12 tunnels and six bridges) and a path called the Camino (or Caminito) del Rey (King's Path), so named because Alfonso XIII walked on it when he opened the Guadalhorce hydroelectric dam in 1921. For long stretches the path becomes a concrete catwalk 100m above the river, clinging to the gorge walls. It has been officially closed since 1992 and has gaping holes in its concrete floor, making it impassable for all but skilled rock climbers. However, you can view much of the gorge and the path by walking along the railway.

The pleasant, quiet town of Ardales (population 2700) is the main centre of the area and is a good base for exploring further afield. However, most people aim for the climbing mecca of El Chorro, a tiny settlement in the midst of a spectacular and surreal landscape of soaring limestone crags.

🐾 ARDALES & AROUND // ANCIENT ARTEFACTS AND PALEOLITHIC PAINTINGS

At the entrance to Ardales is the **Museo de Ardales** (☎ 952 45 80 46; Avenida de Málaga 1; adult/child €1/0.50; ☼ 10am-2pm & 4-6pm Mon-Sat, 10am-2pm Sun mid-Jun–mid-Sep, 9am-2pm & 4-6pm Tue-Sat, 9am-2pm Sun mid-Sep–mid-Jun), an ethnographic and archaeological

---

∼ WORTH A TRIP ∼

Southeast of Ronda lies the 180-sq-km **Parque Natural Sierra de las Nieves** (Map pp158-9), noted for its rare Spanish fir, the *pinsapo*, and fauna including some 1000 ibex and various species of eagle. The *nieve* (snow) after which the mountains are named usually falls between January and March. **El Burgo**, a remote but attractive village 10km north of Yunquera on the A366, makes a good base for visiting the east and northeast of the park. Information is available from Yunquera's **tourist office** (☎ 952 48 28 01; Calle del Pozo 17; ☼ 8am-3pm Tue-Fri), or the **ayuntamiento** (☎ 952 16 00 02) in El Burgo. For a charming accommodation option in this area, see p390.

The most rewarding walk in the Sierra de las Nieves is the ascent of the highest peak in western Andalucía, **Torrecilla** (1918m). Start at the Área Recreativa Los Quejigales, which is 10km east by unpaved road from the A376 Ronda–San Pedro de Alcántara road. The turn-off, 12km from Ronda, is marked by 'Parque Natural Sierra de las Nieves' signs. From Los Quejigales you have a steepish 470m ascent by the **Cañada de los Cuernos gully**, with its tranquil Spanish-fir woods, to the high pass of **Puerto de los Pilones**. After a fairly level section, the final steep 230m to the summit rewards you with marvellous views. The walk takes five to six hours round-trip, and is easy to moderate in difficulty. The IGN/Junta de Andalucía *Parque Natural Sierra de las Nieves* map (1:50,000) shows the relevant path and other hikes.

Buses between Málaga and Ronda (€10, 2½ hours, two daily) through Yunquera and El Burgo are run by **Sierra de las Nieves** (☎ 952 87 54 35).

MÁLAGA PROVINCE

museum largely concerned with the Cueva de Ardales (admission €5; ◷ Tue, Thu, Sat & Sun), a Palaeolithic cave complex similar to the Cueva de la Pileta (p182). For two-hour guided visits to the Cueva de Ardales itself (4km from the museum), contact the museum two to three weeks in advance. The caves contain 60 Palaeolithic paintings and carvings of animals, done between about 18,000 BC and 14,000 BC, and traces of later occupation and burials from about 8000 BC to after 3000 BC. The museum has copies of the prehistoric rock paintings and carvings, an exhibit of Roman and Islamic artefacts and more.

Six kilometres from Ardales is the picturesque Embalse del Conde del Guadalhorce – a huge reservoir that dominates the landscape and is noted for its carp fishing.

Most of the activity in the area centres on the thriving hamlet of El Chorro, amid spectacular scenery. Tienda Aventura El Chorro (☎ 649 24 94 44), near the train station, can organise guided activities – hiking, climbing, cycling (bring your own bike) – at all levels of difficulty.

The best place for organised activities, and great company, is the Finca La Campana (☎ 626 96 39 42; www.el-chorro.com). See the website for full details.

ANTEQUERA

pop 43,000 / elevation 577m

Antequera is a sleepy provincial town with one of the richest historical legacies in Andalucía. Its strategic location – on top of a pair of hills surrounded by craggy mountain tops – ensured its long and illustrious history. The three major influences in the region – Roman, Islamic and Spanish – have left scattered remains that dot the town in a rich tapestry of architectural gems. The highlight is the opulent Spanish baroque style that gives the town its character.

The area also hides Neolithic and Bronze Age gems – some of Europe's largest and oldest dolmens (burial chambers built with huge slabs of rock), from around 2500 BC to 1800 BC, can be found just outside the town's centre. The civic authorities work hard to restore and maintain the town's unique historic character, preserving Antequera's fas-

---

∼ WORTH A TRIP ∼

Back in the 9th century, the rugged El Chorro area was the redoubt of a kind of Andalusian Robin Hood, Omar ibn Hafsun, who resisted the armies of Córdoba for nearly 40 years from the hill fortress of Bobastro. At one stage he controlled territory all the way from Cartagena to the Strait of Gibraltar.

Legend has it that Ibn Hafsun converted to Christianity (thus becoming a Mozarab) and built Bobastro's Iglesia Mozárabe, where he was then buried in AD 917. When Bobastro was finally conquered by Córdoba in 927, Ibn Hafsun's remains were taken away for posthumous crucifixion outside Córdoba's mezquita (mosque).

Although the small church is now only a ruin, the drive and walk to get to it are delightful. From El Chorro follow the road up the valley from the western side of the dam, and after 3km take the signposted Bobastro turn-off. Nearly 3km up, an 'Iglesia Mozárabe' sign indicates the 500m footpath to the remains of the church. The views are magnificent.

cinating architecture, which includes a mass of red-tiled roofs, punctuated by some 30 church spires.

ESSENTIAL INFORMATION

EMERGENCIES // Policía Local (☎ 952 70 81 04; Avenida la Legión s/n) Policía Nacional (☎ 952 84 34 94; Calle Carrera 14)

TOURIST OFFICE // Municipal tourist office (☎ 952 70 25 05; www.antequera.es; Plaza de San Sebastián 7; ⏰ 11am-2pm & 5-8pm Mon-Sat Jun–mid-Oct, 10.30am-1.30pm & 4-7pm Mon-Sat mid-Oct–May, 11am-2pm Sun year-round) Friendly staff with plenty of information.

ORIENTATION

The substantial remains of the Alcazaba, a Muslim-built hilltop castle, dominate Antequera's centre. Down to the north-west is Plaza de San Sebastián, from which the main street, Calle Infante Don Fernando, runs northwest.

EXPLORING ANTEQUERA

❧ ANTEQUERA'S OLD TOWN //
SPECTACULAR CHURCHES AND BREATHTAKING VIEWS
Favoured by the Granada emirs of Islamic times, Antequera's hilltop Alcazaba gives the best views of the town. The main approach to the hilltop is from Plaza de San Sebastián, up the stepped Cuesta de San Judas and then through an impressive archway, the Arco de los Gigantes, built in 1585 and incorporating stones with Roman inscriptions. Not a huge amount remains of the Alcazaba's interior, but it has been turned into a pine-scented, terraced garden. You can visit its Torre del Homenaje (admission free) and there are great views from this high ground, especially towards the northeast and the Peña de los Enamorados (Rock of the Lovers), about which there are

many legends. There were plans to introduce a small admission charge in 2010, so don't be surprised if you have to pay a nominal fee.

Just below the Alcazaba is the large 16th-century Colegiata de Santa María la Mayor (Plaza Santa María; admission free; ⏰ 10am-2pm & 4.30-8pm Tue-Fri, 10.30am-2pm Sat, 11.30am-2pm & 4.30-6.30pm Sun Sep–mid-Jun, 10.30am-2pm Tue & Sat, 10.30am-2pm & 8-10.30pm Wed & Fri, 11.30am-2pm Sun mid-Jun–Sep). This church-cum-college played an important part in Andalucía's 16th-century humanist movement, and boasts a beautiful Renaissance facade, lovely fluted stone columns inside, and a Mudéjar *artesonado* (a ceiling of interlaced beams with decorative insertions). It also plays host to some excellent musical events and exhibitions.

In the town below, the pride of the Museo Municipal (Plaza del Coso Viejo; tours €3; ⏰ 10am-1.30pm & 4.30-6.30pm Tue-Fri, 10am-1.30pm Sat, 11am-1.30pm Sun Oct–mid-Jun, 8-10.30pm Wed & Fri mid-Jun–Sep) is the elegant and athletic 1.4m bronze statue of a boy, *Efebo*. Discovered on a local farm in the 1950s, it is possibly the finest example of Roman sculpture found in Spain. The museum also displays some pieces from a Roman villa in Antequera, where a superb group of mosaics was discovered in 1998. There's also a treasure trove of religious items, containing so much silver that you can only visit by guided tour on the half-hour.

The Museo Conventual de las Descalzas (Plaza de las Descalzas; compulsory guided tour €3.30; ⏰ 10.30am-1.30pm & 5-6.30pm Tue-Fri, 10am-noon & 5-6.30pm Sat, 10am-noon Sun), in the 17th-century convent of the Carmelitas Descalzas (Barefoot Carmelites), approximately 150m east of the Museo Municipal, displays highlights of Antequera's rich religious-art heritage.

Outstanding works include a painting by Lucas Giordano of St Teresa of Ávila (the 16th-century founder of the Carmelitas Descalzas), a bust of the Dolorosa by Pedro de Mena and a *Virgen de Belén* sculpture by La Roldana.

Only the most jaded would fail to be impressed by the Iglesia del Carmen (Plaza del Convento del Carmen; admission €1.50; ☽ 10am-2pm) and its marvellous 18th-century Churrigueresque retable. Carved in red pine (unpainted) by Antequera's own Antonio Primo, it's spangled with statues of angels by Diego Márquez y Vega, and saints, popes and bishops by José de Medina.

☙ DOLMENS // DISCOVER PREHISTORIC BURIAL CHAMBERS

The Dolmen de Menga and Dolmen de Viera (Avenida Málaga 1; admission free; ☽ 9am-6pm Tue-Sat, 9.30am-2.30pm Sun), both dating from around 2500 BC, are 1km from the town centre in a small, wooded park beside the road that leads northeast to the A45. Head down Calle Encarnación from the central Plaza de San Sebastián and follow the signs. Prehistoric people of the Copper Age transported dozens of huge slabs from the nearby hills to construct these burial chambers. The stone frames were covered with mounds of earth. The engineering implications for the time are astonishing. Menga, the larger, is 25m long, 4m high and composed of 32 slabs, the largest of which weighs 180 tonnes. In midsummer the sun rising behind the Peña de los Enamorados hill to the northeast shines directly into the chamber mouth.

A third chamber, the Dolmen del Romeral (Cerro Romeral; admission free; ☽ 9am-6pm Tue-Sat, 9.30am-2.30pm Sun), is further out of town. It is of later construction (around 1800 BC) and features much use of small stones for its walls. To get there, continue 2.5km past Menga and Viera through an industrial estate, then turn left following 'Córdoba, Seville' signs. After 500m, turn left at a roundabout and follow 'Dolmen del Romeral' signs for 200m.

FESTIVALS & EVENTS

Semana Santa (Holy Week) One of the most traditional celebrations in Andalucía; items from the town's treasure trove are actually used in the religious processions. Real Feria de Agosto This festival celebrates the harvest with bullfights, dancing and street parades; held in mid-August.

GASTRONOMIC HIGHLIGHTS

Local specialities you'll encounter on almost every Antequera menu include *porra antequerana,* a cold dip that's similar to gazpacho (before the water is added); *bienmesabe* (literally 'tastes good to me'), a sponge dessert; and *angelorum,* a dessert incorporating meringue, sponge and egg yolk. Antequera also does a fine breakfast *mollete* (soft bread roll).

☙ RESTAURANTE COSO SAN FRANCISCO €€

☎ 952 84 00 14; Calle Calzada 27-29; mains €7-13 The *simpática* (friendly) owner of this *hostal* (budget hotel) restaurant has her own vegetable plot that provides fresh ingredients for her dishes. Meat, fish, Antequeran specialities, traditional Spanish egg dishes and crisp salads await you. On Thursday and Friday evenings classical musicians provide entertainment.

☙ RESTAURANTE LA ESPUELA €€

☎ 952 70 30 31; Calle San Agustín 1; mains €12-18; ☽ 1-4pm & 8-11pm Tue-Sun Found in a gorgeous cul-de-sac off Calle Infante Don Fernando, elegant La Espuela plays background jazz, and offers a fine selection of Antequeran specialities along with some international fare including pasta dishes. Good smells emanate from the kitchen.

❦ RESTAURANTE PLAZA DE TOROS €€

☎ 952 84 46 62; Paseo María Cristina s/n; mains €12-22; ☽ closed Sun evening

A long-established Antequera favourite in the bullring at the northwestern end of Calle Infante Don Fernando. It offers traditional Andalusian food with some modern twists, and quirky local dishes.

TRANSPORT

BUS // The **bus station** (Paseo Garcí de Olmo s/n) is found 1km north of the centre. **Automóviles Casado** (☎ 952 84 19 57) runs frequent buses to Málaga. **Alsina Graells** (☎ 952 84 13 65) runs buses to Seville, Granada, Córdoba, Almería and Málaga. Buses run between Antequera and Fuente de Piedra village (€1, three to six daily).

PARKING // Antequera can be a traffic nightmare and a team of formidable traffic wardens keeps a tight grip on things; buy tickets from them at street-side parking spots (per hour €1). There is underground parking on Calle Diego Ponce north of Plaza de San Sebastián (per hour €1, 12 to 24 hours €12).

TAXI // Taxis (€3 to €4 per 2km to 3km) wait halfway along Calle Infante Don Fernando, or you can call ☎ 952 84 55 30.

TRAIN // The **train station** (☎ 952 84 32 26; www.renfe.es; Avenida de la Estación) is 1.5km north of the centre. Six trains a day run to/from Granada, and there are four daily to Seville and three to Ronda. Another three run to Málaga or Córdoba, but you'll need to change at Bobadilla.

AROUND ANTEQUERA

❦ PARAJE NATURAL TORCAL DE ANTEQUERA // TAKE A WALK AROUND MESMERISING ROCK FORMATIONS

South of Antequera are the weird and wonderful rock formations of the Paraje Natural Torcal de Antequera. A 12-sq-km area of gnarled, serrated and pillared limestone, it formed as a sea bed 150 million years ago and now rises to 1336m (El Torcal). It's otherworldly out here and the air is pure and fresh. There is an **information centre** (☽ 10am-5pm) here that has information about walks, and flora and fauna. Two marked walking trails, the 1.5km 'Ruta Verde' (green route) and the 3km 'Ruta Amarilla' (yellow route) start and end near the information centre. More-dramatic views are along the restricted 'Ruta Rojo' (red route), for which guided tours are organised; contact the Antequera tourist office for details. Wear shoes with good tread as the trails are rocky.

To get to El Torcal, you will need your own car or a taxi. By car, leave central Antequera along Calle Picadero, which soon joins the Zalea road. After 1km or so you'll see signs on the left to Villanueva de la Concepción. Take this road and, after about 11km, a turn uphill to the right leads 4km to the information centre. A return taxi costs €30, with one hour at El Torcal. The tourist office in Antequera will arrange a taxi for you.

❦ LAGUNA DE FUENTE DE PIEDRA // A BIRDWATCHER'S PARADISE AND NATURAL RETREAT

About 20km northwest of Antequera, just off the A92 *autovía* (toll-free dual carriageway), is the Laguna de Fuente de Piedra. When it's not dried up by drought, this is Andalucía's biggest natural lake and one of Europe's two main breeding grounds for the greater flamingo (the other is in the Camargue region of southwest France). After a wet winter as many as 20,000 pairs of flamingos will breed at the lake. The birds arrive in

MÁLAGA PROVINCE

January or February, with the chicks hatching in April and May. The flamingos stay till about August, when the lake, which is rarely more than 1m deep, no longer contains enough water to support them. They share the lake with thousands of other birds of some 170 species.

The **Centro de Información Fuente de Piedra** (☎ 952 11 17 15; ⏰ 10am-2pm & 4-6pm) is at the lakeside. It gives advice on the best spots for birdwatching. It also sells a range of good maps and rents out binoculars (an essential).

Nearby, the well-regarded **Caserío de San Benito** (☎ 952 11 11 03; Km108 Carretera Córdoba-Málaga; menú €15; ⏰ noon-5pm & 8pm-midnight Tue-Sun) is a good place to stop for a quality lunch. A beautifully converted farmhouse, San Benito is stuffed with antiques and serves up exquisitely prepared traditional dishes.

EAST OF MÁLAGA

· · · · · ·

The coast east of Málaga, sometimes described as the Costa del Sol Oriental, is less developed than the coast to the west. The suburban sprawl of Málaga extends east into a series of unmemorable and unremarkable seaside towns – Rincón de la Victoria, Torre del Mar, Torrox Costa – which pass in a blur amid huge plastic greenhouses before culminating in more attractive Nerja, which has a large population of Brits and Scandinavians.

The area's main redeeming feature is the rugged region of La Axarquía, an interior of mountain villages on the slopes leading up to the border of Granada province. The area is full of great walks, which are less 'discovered' than those in the northwest of the province around Ronda. A 406-sq-km area of these mountains was declared the Parque Natural Sierras de Tejeda, Almijara y Alhama in 1999.

LA AXARQUÍA

The Axarquía region is riven by deep valleys lined with terraces and irrigation channels that date back to Islamic times – nearly all the villages dotted around the olive-, almond- and vine-planted hillsides date from this era. The wild inaccessible landscapes, especially around the Sierra de Tejeda, made it a stronghold of *bandoleros* who roamed the mountains without fear or favour. Nowadays, its chief attractions include fantastic scenery; pretty white villages; strong, sweet, local wine made from sun-dried grapes; and good walking in spring and autumn.

The 'capital' of La Axarquía, **Vélez Málaga**, 4km north of Torre del Mar, is a busy but unspectacular town, although its restored hilltop castle is worth a look. From Vélez the A335 heads north past the turquoise Embalse de la Viñuela reservoir and up through the **Boquete de Zafarraya** (a dramatic cleft in the mountains) towards Granada. One bus a day makes its way over this road between Torre del Mar and Granada. The highest mountains in Málaga province stretch east from the Boquete de Zafarraya. Around the Embalse de la Viñuela you'll see white houses all over the place. Most are occupied by foreigners, especially Brits. One outcome of this foreign concentration has been the creation of a good Tuesday **farmers market**, where organic food and handicrafts are sold, at Puente de Don Manuel on the Vélez–Boquete de Zafarraya road.

Some of the most dramatic La Axarquía scenery is up around the highest villages of Alfarnate (925m) and Alfarnatejo (858m), with towering, rugged crags such as Tajo de Gomer and Tajo de Doña Ana rising to their south.

To sample one of Andalucía's oldest inns, dating from 1690, head north from Alfarnate along the Loja road. Just outside town you will find Venta de Alfarnate (☎ 952 75 93 88; Antigua Carretera de Málaga-Granada; mains €8-16; ☷ 11am-7pm Tue-Thu & Sun, to midnight Fri & Sat). It displays mementoes of past visitors including some of the bandits who used to roam these hills. Foodwise, it's renowned for *huevos a la bestia*, a kind of hill-country mixed grill of fried eggs and assorted pork products (€11).

You can pick up information on La Axarquía at the tourist offices in Málaga, Nerja, Torre del Mar or Cómpeta. Prospective walkers should ask for the leaflet on walks in the Parque Natural Sierras de Tejeda, Almijara y Alhama. Good maps for walkers are *Mapa Topográfico de Sierra Tejeda* and *Mapa Topográfico de Sierra Almijara* by Miguel Ángel Torres Delgado, both at 1:25,000. Useful guides include *Walk! Axarquía* published by Discovery Walking Guides (www.walking.demon.co.uk).

❦ COMARES // A PRETTY MOUNTAINTOP VILLAGE AT THE END OF AN EXCITING ROAD ADVENTURE

Comares sits like a snowdrift atop its lofty hill. The adventure really is in getting there. You see it for kilometre after kilometre before a final twist in an endlessly winding road lands you below the hanging garden of its cliff. From a little car park you can climb steep, winding steps to the village. Look for ceramic footprints underfoot and simply follow them through a web of narrow, twisting lanes past the Iglesia de la Encarnación and eventually to the ruins of Comares' castle and a remarkable summit cemetery. The village has a history of rebellion, having been a stronghold of Omar ibn Hafsun (see the boxed text, p184), but today there is a tangible sense of contented isolation, enjoyed by locals and many newcomers. The views across the Axarquía are stunning.

Have lunch and stupendous views at El Molino de los Abuelos (☎ 952 50 93 09; mains €6-14, menú €8), a converted olive mill on the main plaza beside the lookout – the accommodation here is fantastic. There are a couple of friendly bars at the heart of the village.

On weekdays only, a bus leaves Málaga for Comares at 6pm and starts back at 7am the next morning (€2.20, one hour).

❦ CÓMPETA // A BUZZING VILLAGE WITH A LARGE INTERNATIONAL POPULATION

Cómpeta has some of the area's best local wine, and the popular Noche del Vino (Night of the Wine) on 15 August features a program of flamenco and *sevillana* music and dance in the central and pretty Plaza Almijara, and limitless free wine. It has a large mixed foreign population that contributes to an active cultural scene.

By the bus stop at the foot of the village is a tourist office (☎ 952 55 36 85; turismo@competa.es; Avenida de la Constitución; ☷ 10am-2pm & 3-6pm Wed-Sun mid-Sep–Jun, 10am-2pm & 3-6pm Tue-Sat Jul–mid-Sep). There's a car park up the hill from the tourist office. Marco Polo (Calle José Antonio 3), just off Plaza Almijara, sells books in English and several other languages as well as a good selection of maps and Spanish walking guides. Todo Papel (Avenida de la Constitución 31) sells newspapers and books in English, including guidebooks.

The tourist office has varied information on activities in the area, including horse riding at **Los Caballos del Mosquín** (☎ 608 65 81 08; www.horseriding-andalucia.com), which is 2km from Cómpeta, just above the nearby village of Canillas de Albaida. There are also Spanish classes to be had at **Santa Clara Academia de Idiomas** (☎ 952 55 36 66; www.santa-clara-idiomas.com; Calle Andalucía 6). For good art courses, run by the warm Christa Hillekamp, consult www.artworkshop.eu.

For tasty international lunches (weekends only) and dinners, don't miss **El Pilón** (☎ 952 55 35 12; Calle Laberinto; mains €10-15) or the **Museo del Vino** (Avenida Constitución; raciones €8-15), which serves excellent ham, cheese and sausage *raciones* (large tapas servings) and wine from the barrel. It's also something of an Aladdin's cave of regional crafts and produce and Moroccan bits and pieces. Another excellent restaurant, with views to the distant sea, is **Cortijo Paco** (☎ 952 55 36 47; Avenida Canillas 6; mains €10-15; ⊙ closed Mon). Funky **Taberna de Oscar** (☎ 952 51 66 31; Plaza Pantaleón Romero 1; media-raciones €3.50-5.50; Ⓥ) turns out unusual and delicious food. There's something for everyone, but vegetarians will appreciate the spinach dish.

Cómpeta has a thriving music scene; live-music fans will find something on most Saturday nights at **Bar La Roca** (Avenida de la Constitución) and Sunday afternoons at Taberna de Oscar.

Three buses travel daily from Málaga to Cómpeta (€3.20, 1½ hours), via Torre del Mar.

☙ FRIGILIANA // SEE ONE OF THE REGION'S PRETTIEST WHITE VILLAGES

Considered by many as the prettiest village in La Axarquía, Frigiliana is 7km north of Nerja and linked to it by several buses daily (except Sunday). The **tourist office** (☎ 952 53 42 61; Plaza del Ingenio; ⊙ 9am-8pm Mon-Fri, 10am-1.30pm & 4-8pm Sat & Sun) is helpful. El Fuerte, the hill that climbs above the village, was the scene of the final bloody defeat of the *moriscos* (converted Muslims) of La Axarquía in their 1569 re-

---

∼ WORTH A TRIP ∼

Perhaps the most exhilarating walk in La Axarquía region is up the dramatically peaked **El Lucero** (1779m). From its summit on a clear day there are stupendous views as far as Granada in one direction and Morocco in the other. This is a full, demanding day's walking, with an ascent of 1150m from Cómpeta: start by climbing left along the track above Cómpeta's football pitch. About 1½ hours from Cómpeta you pass below and west of a fire observation hut on La Mina hill. Four hundred metres past the turning to the hut, turn right through a gap in the rock (not signed, but fairly obvious). This path leads in about one hour to **Puerto Blanquillo** (1200m), from where a path climbs 200m to **Puerto de Cómpeta**.

One kilometre down from the latter pass, past a quarry, the summit path (1½ hours) diverges to the right across a stream bed, marked by a sign board and map. El Lucero is topped by the ruins of a Guardia Civil post that was built after the civil war to watch for anti-Franco rebels.

It's possible to drive as far up as Puerto Blanquillo on a rough mountain track from Canillas de Albaida, a village 2km northwest of Cómpeta.

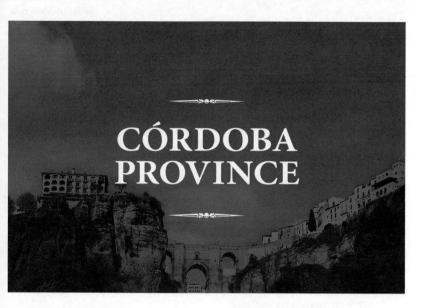

CÓRDOBA PROVINCE

3 PERFECT DAYS

🌱 DAY 1 // EXPLORE THE MEZQUITA AND JUDERÍA

It's indubitable that you'll want to spend your first day in Córdoba diving into the mysteries of the Mezquita (p201), but to make the experience even more special make sure you get up extra early and visit this gorgeous place before the crowds hit it – the first two hours after opening are free, and groups are not allowed in. After that, wander the adjoining streets of the Judería (p207), seeking out the quiet residential areas and peeking inside Córdoba's patios (p208).

🌱 DAY 2 // GASTRONOMIC TOUR

Since food is one of Córdoba's greatest appeals, don't leave without dedicating a day (or two!) to the joys of flexing the taste buds. Take a look at our selection of gastronomic highlights (p210) and sample the tapas, as well as *raciones* (meal-sized tapas) and full-on modern cuisine, all the while sipping local wines. Be sure to take yourself on an exploratory jaunt, popping in to any tapas bar that take your fancy – sometimes great surprises await.

🌱 DAY 3 // RURAL DELIGHTS

Córdoba province has some gorgeous nature – wild and unpopulated mountains and mysterious areas scattered among hard-working villages. Get your hiking boots on and discover the province's beauties, and taste some quality olive oil on the way. Endless groves of olive trees mean that many of the villages make fantastic olive oil – Baena (p213) being the region's foremost producer.

CÓRDOBA PROVINCE

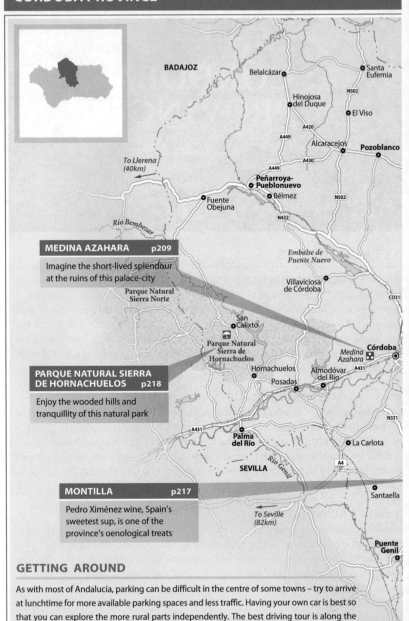

BADAJOZ

Belalcázar

Santa Eufemia

Hinojosa del Duque

N502

El Viso

A420

A449

Alcaracejos

Pozoblanco

To Llerena (40km)

A449

A430

Peñarroya-Pueblonuevo

Bélmez

N502

Fuente Obejuna

N432

Río Bembezar

Embalse de Puente Nuevo

MEDINA AZAHARA   p209

Imagine the short-lived splendour at the ruins of this palace-city

Villaviciosa de Córdoba

C031

Parque Natural Sierra Norte

San Calixto

Parque Natural Sierra de Hornachuelos

Medina Azahara

Córdoba

Hornachuelos

Almodóvar del Río

A431

PARQUE NATURAL SIERRA DE HORNACHUELOS   p218

Enjoy the wooded hills and tranquillity of this natural park

Posadas

N331

A431

Palma del Río

La Carlota

SEVILLA

Río Genil

A4

MONTILLA   p217

Pedro Ximénez wine, Spain's sweetest sup, is one of the province's oenological treats

Santaella

To Seville (82km)

Puente Genil

GETTING AROUND

As with most of Andalucía, parking can be difficult in the centre of some towns – try to arrive at lunchtime for more available parking spaces and less traffic. Having your own car is best so that you can explore the more rural parts independently. The best driving tour is along the N502, from which you can explore Córdoba's northern region.

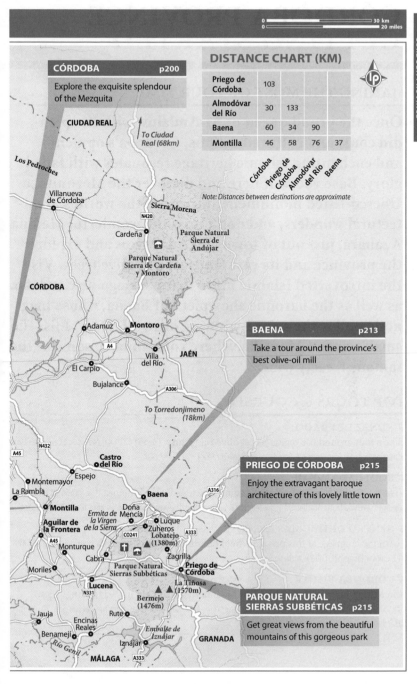

0 ——————————— 30 km
0 ——————————— 20 miles

CÓRDOBA p200

Explore the exquisite splendour of the Mezquita

DISTANCE CHART (KM)

	Córdoba	Priego de Córdoba	Almodóvar del Río	Baena
Priego de Córdoba	103			
Almodóvar del Río	30	133		
Baena	60	34	90	
Montilla	46	58	76	37

Note: Distances between destinations are approximate

CIUDAD REAL

To Ciudad Real (68km)

Los Pedroches

Villanueva de Córdoba

Sierra Morena

N420

Cardeña

Parque Natural Sierra de Andújar

Parque Natural Sierra de Cardeña y Montoro

CÓRDOBA

Adamuz

Montoro

A4

Villa del Río

JAÉN

El Carpio

Bujalance

A306

To Torredonjimeno (18km)

BAENA p213

Take a tour around the province's best olive-oil mill

N432

A45

Castro del Río

Montemayor Espejo

La Rambla

Montilla

Doña Mencía

Baena

A316

PRIEGO DE CÓRDOBA p215

Enjoy the extravagant baroque architecture of this lovely little town

Aguilar de la Frontera

Ermita de la Virgen de la Sierra

Luque

Zuheros

CO241

Lobatejo (1380m)

A333

A45

Monturque

Cabra

Zagrilla

Moriles

Parque Natural Sierras Subbéticas

Priego de Córdoba

Lucena

N331

La Tiñosa (1570m)

Bermejo (1476m)

PARQUE NATURAL SIERRAS SUBBÉTICAS p215

Get great views from the beautiful mountains of this gorgeous park

Jauja

Rute

Encinas Reales

Benamejí

Embalse de Iznájar

GRANADA

Iznájar

Río Genil

MÁLAGA A333

CÓRDOBA PROVINCE
GETTING STARTED

MAKING THE MOST OF YOUR TIME

Once the proud queen of Al-Andalus, with its splendid court and cultured caliphs, Córdoba's opulent and enchanting Islamic heritage resonates with faded glory. Base yourself here and discover the Mezquita, a Unesco-listed monument and one of the world's architectural wonders, and don't miss the wonderful Medina Azahara, just out of town. Take day trips and explore the province and its vast landscape of olive trees. Visit the introverted Islamic maze that is Priego de Córdoba, as well as the baroque showpiece of Baena, whose magnetic pull is the award-winning olive oil. Don't miss the small town of Montilla, where you can taste some of the famous treacly wine.

TOP TOURS & COURSES

❧ NÚÑEZ DE PRADO
Take a tour around the region's best olive-oil factory. (☎ 957 67 01 41; Avenida de Cervantes s/n; admission free; ⊗ 9am-2pm & 4-6pm Mon-Fri, 9am-1pm Sat)

❧ BODEGAS ALVEAR
Visit the Montilla winery and taste some delicious Pedro Ximénez. (☎ 957 66 40 14; www.alvear.es; Avenida María Auxiliadora 1; guided tour & tasting weekday/weekend €5/4; ⊗ shop 10am-2pm Mon-Sat)

❧ CENTRO DE IDIOMAS LARCOS
Learn the language at this private school offering a range of Spanish courses. (☎ 957 47 11 03; www.larcos.net; Calle Manchado 9)

❧ CÓRDOBA VISION
Join a three-hour guided bus tour to Medina Azahara, held in various languages. (☎ 957 23 17 34; Calle Doctor Marañón 1; tour €10; ⊗ tours 4pm Tue-Sat Oct-May, 6pm Tue-Sat Jun-Sep, 10.30am Sat & Sun year-round)

GETTING AWAY FROM IT ALL

* **Mezquita in the morning** Get up early and take advantage of the free early entry and lack of crowds to appreciate the silence and simplicity of one of Spain's greatest structures (p201)

* **Head to Córdoba's mysterious north** Drive and walk across wild landscapes of dark-green hills and visit tiny, scarcely populated villages (p219)

* **Get away to Iznájar** Get your walking shoes on to explore this little-populated area that brims with wild nature and gorgeous landscapes (p217)

ADVANCE PLANNING

You might do well to plan the time of your visit to the following three destinations:

* **Mezquita** (p201) The top Córdoba sight is best seen in the early hours of the morning, so set your alarm for sunrise and head out to enjoy the silence of this amazing structure

* **Medina Azahara** (p209) Travel out of town for this beautiful Arabic palace and try to go at lunchtime when there might be fewer visitors

* **Bodegas Alvear** (p217) Book your tour in advance and taste some of Spain's best sweet wine in this impressive bodega (winery)

TOP RESTAURANTS

TABERNA SALINAS
Córdoba's favourite old-timer, with a charming interior, sumptuous food and excellent wine (p211)

TABERNA SAN MIGUEL/EL PISTO
Come here for local characters, *torero* (bullfighter) cred, great tapas and house wine (p211)

BODEGA CAMPOS
Atmospheric and ancient, with fantastic house-made wine and great food (p211)

EL ASTRONAUTA
A down-to-earth, modern restaurant with fabulous traditional food (p211)

BAR SANTOS
Bar Santos' huge, juicy tortillas are its simple recipe for success (p211)

RESOURCES

* **Info Cordoba** (www.infocordoba.com) A useful site with general information on Córdoba

* **Córdoba 24** (www.cordoba24.info) An international site with great, thorough information about what's on in Córdoba

* **Tourism of Cordoba** (http://english .turismodecordoba.org) Find themed walking tours and info on events in Córdoba on this useful website

* **The Death of Manolete** (Barnaby Conrad) Learn about Córdoba's most famous son, the bullfighter Manolete

CÓRDOBA

· · · · · ·

pop 319,000 / elevation 110m

Córdoba is ideal for those who like to eat well, explore sights on foot, dive into old bodegas (wineries) and relish architectural wonders. The magnificent Mezquita, a symbol of a worldly and sophisticated Islamic culture, lords it over the town centre and pulls thousands of tourists into its arched interior every day. It's no wonder the city is stiff competition for Europe's Culture Capital in 2016. The tiny streets of the Judería (Jewish quarter) stretch out from the Mezquita like capillaries, and while many are peaceful and bare, some, especially those close to the Mezquita, are clogged with kitsch tourist shops. The Islamic ruins of Medina Azahara, outside Córdoba, make the imagination tingle with past glory and grandeur.

The compact town centre has some excellent bars and restaurants. Córdoba has found its niche with gastronomic delights, affordable accommodation, a relaxed feeling and pretty patios alongside the Mezquita. The city is quiet and withdrawn during the winter months, but bursts into life from mid-April to mid-June. At this time of year the skies are blue, the heat is tolerable, the city's many trees and patios drip with foliage and blooms, and Córdoba stages most of its major fiestas.

The Roman colony of Corduba, founded in 152 BC, became the capital of the province of Baetica, covering most of what is today Andalucía, and bringing the writers Seneca and Lucan to the world.

Córdoba fell to Islamic invaders in AD 711 and soon took the role as Islamic capital on the Iberian Peninsula. It was here in 756 that Abd ar-Rahman I set himself up as the independent emir of the Al-Andalus region, founding the Omayyad dynasty, but the town's and region's heyday came under Abd ar-Rahman III (r AD 912–61). He named himself caliph (the title of the Muslim successors of Mohammed) in 929, sealing Al-Andalus' long-standing de facto independence from Baghdad.

Córdoba was by now the biggest city in Western Europe, with a flourishing economy based on agriculture and skilled artisan products, and a population somewhere between 100,000 and 500,000. The city shone with hundreds of dazzling mosques, public baths, patios, gardens and fountains. Abd ar-Rahman III's court was frequented by Jewish, Arab and Christian scholars, and Córdoba's university, library and observatories made it a centre of learning whose influence was still being felt in Christian Europe many centuries later. Córdoba also became a place of pilgrimage for Muslims who could not get to Mecca or Jerusalem.

Towards the end of the 10th century, Al-Mansur (Almanzor), a ruthless general whose northward raids terrified Christian Spain, took the reins of power from the caliphs. But after the death of Al-Mansur's son Abd al-Malik in 1008, the caliphate descended into anarchy. Rival claimants to the title, Berber troops and Christian armies from Castile and Catalonia all fought over the spoils. The Berbers terrorised and looted the city and, in 1031, Omayyad rule ended. Córdoba became a minor part of the Seville *taifa* (small kingdom) in 1069, and has been overshadowed by Seville ever since.

Córdoba was home to two important 11th-century philosopher-poets, Ibn Hazm (who wrote in Arabic) and Judah Ha-Levi (who wrote in Hebrew). Twelfth-century Córdoba produced the two most celebrated scholars of Al-Andalus – the Muslim philosopher Averroës (1126–98; p319) and the Jewish philosopher Moses ben Maimon (known as Maimónides; 1135–1204). Their philosophical efforts to harmonise religion with Aristotelian reason were met with ignorance and intolerance: the Almohads put Averroës in high office, and persecuted Maimon until he fled to Egypt.

When Córdoba was taken by Castile's Fernando III in 1236, much of its population fled. Córdoba became a provincial city and its decline was only reversed through the arrival of industry in the late 19th century. But something of Córdoba's former splendour remained – one of the greatest Spanish poets, Luis de Góngora (1561–1627) was from the city.

ESSENTIAL INFORMATION

EMERGENCIES // Ambulance (☎ 957 21 79 03, 957 29 55 70); Policía Nacional (☎ 95 747 75 00; Avenida Doctor Fleming 2) The main police station.
TOURIST OFFICES // Municipal tourist office (☎ 957 20 05 22; Plaza de Judá Leví; ☟ 8.30am-2.30pm Mon-Fri) A block northwest of the regional tourist office, with information and maps of Córdoba city Regional tourist office (☎ 957 47 12 35; Calle de Torrijos 10; ☟ 9.30am-8pm Mon-Sat, 10am-2pm Sun Apr-Jul, 9.30am-7pm Mon-Sat, 10am-2pm Sun Aug-Mar) A good source of information about Córdoba province.

ORIENTATION

The medieval city is immediately north of the Río Guadalquivir. It's a warren of narrow streets surrounding the Mezquita, which is just a block from the river. Within the medieval city, the area northwest of the Mezquita was known as the Judería, the Muslim quarter was north and east of the Mezquita, and the Mozarabic (Christian) quarter was further to the northeast.

The main square of Córdoba is Plaza de las Tendillas, 500m north of the Mezquita, with the main shopping streets to the plaza's north and west. The train and bus stations are 1km northwest of Plaza de las Tendillas.

EXPLORING CÓRDOBA

☙ MEZQUITA // DISCOVER ANDALUCÍA'S MOST SPECTACULAR STRUCTURE

It's impossible to overestimate the beauty of Córdoba's Mezquita (Mosque; ☎ 957 47 05 12; www.mezquitadecordoba.org; adult/child €8/4, admission free 8.30-10am; ☟ 10am-7pm Mon-Sat Apr-Oct, 10am-6pm Mon-Sat Nov-Mar, 9-10.45am & 1.30-6.30pm Sun year-round). The Church of St Vincent was the original building located on the site of the Mezquita, and Arab chronicles recount how Abd ar-Rahman I purchased half of the church for the use of the Muslim community's Friday prayers. However, the rapid growth of that community soon rendered the space too small and in AD 784 he bought the other half of the church in order to erect a new mosque. Material from Roman and Visigothic ruins was incorporated into the structure and it is often speculated that Abd ar-Rahman I designed the mosque himself with the help of Syrian architects. In 785 the mosque was opened for prayer, although it was subsequently extended southwards by both Abd ar-Rahman II (r 821–852) and Al-Hakim II in the 960s, in order to cater

CÓRDOBA

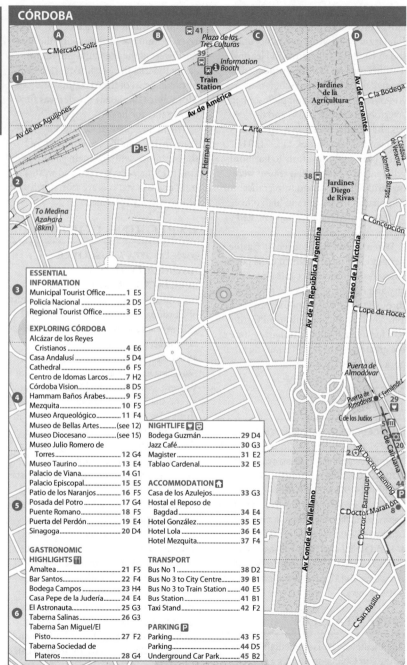

C Mercado Solís

Plaza de las
Tres Culturas

Information
Booth

Train
Station

Av de América

C Arte

C Hernán R

Av de los Agujones

To Medina
Azahara
(8km)

Jardines
de la
Agricultura

Av de Cervantes

C la Bodega

Córdoba
de Veraduz

C Alonso de Burgos

Jardines
Diego
de Rivas

C Concepción

Av de la República Argentina

Paseo de la Victoria

C Lope de Hoces

Puerta de
Almodóvar

Puerta de
Almodóvar

C de los Judíos

C Fernández

C de Cairuana

C Doctor Fleming

C Doctor Barraquer

C Doctor Marañón

C Doctor Barraquer

Av Conde de Vallellano

C San Basilio

**ESSENTIAL
INFORMATION**
Municipal Tourist Office 1 E5
Policía Nacional 2 D5
Regional Tourist Office 3 E5

EXPLORING CÓRDOBA
Alcázar de los Reyes
    Cristianos 4 E6
Casa Andalusí 5 D4
Cathedral 6 F5
Centro de Idomas Larcos 7 H2
Córdoba Vision 8 D5
Hammam Baños Árabes 9 F5
Mezquita 10 F5
Museo Arqueológico 11 F4
Museo de Bellas Artes .... (see 12)
Museo Diocesano .... (see 15)
Museo Julio Romero de
    Torres 12 G4
Museo Taurino 13 E4
Palacio de Viana 14 G1
Palacio Episcopal 15 E5
Patio de los Naranjos 16 F5
Posada del Potro 17 G4
Puente Romano 18 F5
Puerta del Perdón 19 E4
Sinagoga 20 D4

**GASTRONOMIC
HIGHLIGHTS** 🍴
Amaltea 21 F5
Bar Santos 22 F4
Bodega Campos 23 H4
Casa Pepe de la Judería 24 E4
El Astronauta 25 G3
Taberna Salinas 26 G3
Taberna San Miguel/El
    Pisto 27 F2
Taberna Sociedad de
    Plateros 28 G4

NIGHTLIFE 📺 📷
Bodega Guzmán 29 D4
Jazz Café 30 G3
Magister 31 E2
Tablao Cardenal 32 E5

ACCOMMODATION 🏠
Casa de los Azulejos 33 G3
Hostal el Reposo de
    Bagdad 34 E4
Hotel González 35 E5
Hotel Lola 36 E4
Hotel Mezquita 37 F4

TRANSPORT
Bus No 1 .... 38 D2
Bus No 3 to City Centre 39 B1
Bus No 3 to Train Station 40 E5
Bus Station 41 B1
Taxi Stand 42 F2

PARKING 🅿
Parking 43 F5
Parking 44 D5
Underground Car Park 45 B2

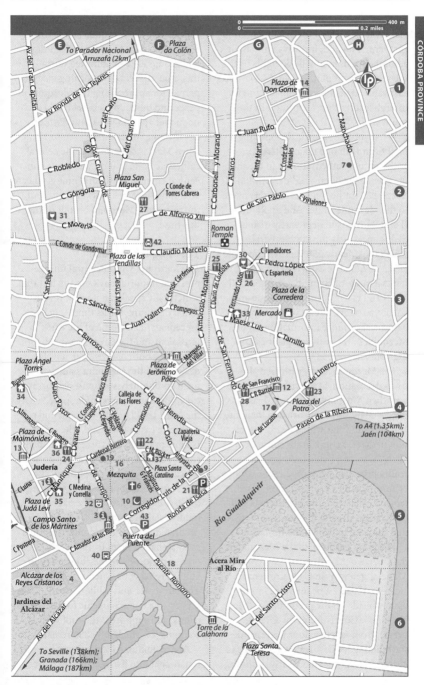

for Córdoba's expanding population. Al-Hakim II also added the existing mihrab (prayer niche) and, for extra light, built a number of domes with skylights over the area in front of it. Under Al-Mansur, eastward extensions were made and the mihrab lost its central position in the south wall.

What you see today is the building's final form with one major alteration – a 16th-century cathedral right in the middle (hence the often-used description of 'Mezquita-Cathedral'). Extensions made to the Mezquita under Abd ar-Rahman II and Al-Mansur were partly dismantled to make way for the cathedral, which took nearly 250 years to complete (1523–1766). The cathedral thus exhibits a range of changing architectural styles and tastes, from plateresque and late Renaissance to extravagant Spanish baroque. For more information on the Mezquita's architectural qualities and importance, see p333.

The Mezquita hints, with all its lustrous decoration, at a lavish and refined age when Muslims, Jews and Christians lived side by side and enriched their city and surroundings with a heady interaction of diverse and vibrant cultures. It's likely, however, that a less glamorous reality prevailed, with medieval Córdoba brimming with racial and class-based tension. That said, the Mezquita is still captivating, despite the hordes of tourists that threaten to drown the romance.

The main entrance to the Mezquita is the Puerta del Perdón, a 14th-century Mudéjar gateway on Calle Cardenal Herrero. There's a ticket office immediately inside on the pretty Patio de los Naranjos (Courtyard of the Orange Trees), from where a door leads inside the building itself. A leaflet given free to visitors contains a map clearly outlining the stages of the building's construction. Entrance to the Mezquita is free from 8.30am to 10am Monday to Saturday and groups are not admitted during this time, so weekday morning visits are perfect for appreciating the Mezquita in peace and quiet. Mass is held at 11am, noon and 1pm on weekdays. Entrance is also free on Sunday from 9am to 11am, when Mass is celebrated in the central cathedral. Note that on weekends you cannot enter the cathedral unless you are attending the Mass in its entirety, and the rest of the Mezquita is unlit during this time.

The Mosque-Cathedral

The Mezquita's architectural uniqueness and importance lies in the fact that, structurally speaking, it was a revolutionary building for its time. It defied precedents. The Dome of the Rock in Jerusalem and the Great Mosque in Damascus both had vertical, navelike designs, but the Mezquita's aim was to form an infinitely spacious, democratically horizontal and simple space, where the spirit could be free to roam and communicate easily with God. The original Islamic prayer space (usually the open yard of a desert home) was transformed into a 14,400-sq-m metaphor for the desert itself. Men prayed side by side on the *argamasa,* a floor made of compact, reddish slaked lime and sand. A flat roof, decorated with gold and multicoloured motifs, shaded them from the sun. The orange patio, where the ablution fountains gurgled with water, was the oasis. The terracotta-and-white-striped arches suggested a hallucinogenic forest of date palms, and supported the roof with 1293 columns (of which only 856 remain).

Abd ar-Rahman I's initial mosque was a square split into two rectangular halves – a covered prayer hall and an open ablutions courtyard. The prayer hall was divided into 11 'naves' by lines of two-tier arches striped in red brick and white stone. The columns used for the Mezquita were a mishmash of material collected from the Visigothic cathedral that had previously occupied the site, Córdoba's Roman buildings and places as far away as Constantinople. This, predictably, presented problems in keeping the ceiling height consistent and making it high enough to create a sense of openness. Inventive builders came up with the idea of using the tall columns as a base and planting the shorter ones on top in order to create the ceiling arches. Later enlargements of the mosque extended these lines of arches to cover an area of nearly 120 sq metres and create one of the biggest mosques in the world. The arcades are one of the much loved Islamic architectural motifs. Their simplicity and number give a sense of endlessness to the Mezquita.

Originally there were 19 doors, filling the interior of the mosque with light. Nowadays, only one door sheds its light into the dim interior, dampening the vibrant effect of the red-and-white voussoirs of the double arches. Christian additions to the building, such as the solid mass of the cathedral in the centre and the 50 or so chapels around the fringes, further enclose and impose on the airy space.

At the furthest point from the entrance door, on the southern wall of the mosque, the aisles draw you towards qibla (the direction of Mecca) and the mosque's greatest treasure, the mihrab built by Al-Hakim II.

Mihrab & Maksura
Like Abd ar-Rahman II a century earlier, Al-Hakim lengthened the naves of the prayer hall, creating a new mihrab at the south end of the central nave. The bay immediately in front of the mihrab and the bays to each side form the *maksura,* the area where the caliphs and their retinues would have prayed. Inside the mihrab a single block of white marble was sculpted into the shape of a scallop shell, a symbol of the Quran. This formed the dome that amplified the voice of the imam throughout the mosque.

The arches within and around the *maksura* are the mosque's most intricate and sophisticated, forming a forest of interwoven horseshoe shapes. These ingenious curves are subtly interwoven to form the strongest elements of the structure. But they were not only physically functional: their purpose was to seduce the eye of the worshipper with their lavish decorations, leading it up to the mihrab – to the focus of prayer and the symbolic doorway to heaven. Equally attractive are the sky-lit domes over the *maksura,* decorated with star-patterned stone vaulting. Each dome was held up by four interlocking pairs of parallel ribs, a highly advanced technique in 10th-century Europe.

The greatest glory of Al-Hakim II's extension was the portal of the mihrab itself – a crescent arch with a rectangular surround known as an *alfiz,* surmounted by a blind arcade. For the decoration of the portal, Al-Hakim asked the emperor of Byzantium, Nicephoras II Phocas, to send him a mosaicist capable of imitating the superb mosaics of the Great Mosque of Damascus, one of the great 8th-century Syrian Omayyad buildings. The Christian emperor sent the Muslim caliph not only a mosaicist but also a gift of 1600kg of gold mosaic cubes. These shimmering cubes, shaped into flower motifs and inscriptions from the Quran, decorated the whole *maksura.*

Patio de los Naranjos & Minaret

Outside the mosque, the leafy, walled courtyard and its fountain were the site of ritual ablutions before prayer. The crowning glory of the whole complex was the minaret, which at its peak towered 48m (only 22m of the minaret still survives). Now encased in its 16th-century shell, the original minaret would have looked something like the Giralda in Seville, which was practically a copy. Córdoba's minaret influenced all the minarets built thereafter throughout the western Islamic world.

The Cathedral

For three centuries following the Reconquista (Christian reconquest) in 1236, the Mezquita remained largely unaltered save for minor modifications such as the Mudéjar tiling added in the 1370s to the Mozarabic and Almo-

had Capilla Real (located nine bays north and one east of the mihrab, and now part of the cathedral). In the 16th century King Carlos I gave permission (against the wishes of Córdoba's city council) for the centre of the Mezquita to be ripped out to allow construction of the Capilla Mayor (the altar area in the cathedral) and *coro* (choir). However, the king was not enamoured with the results and famously regretted: 'You have built what you or others might have built anywhere, but you have destroyed something that was unique in the world.'

Subsequent additions included a rich 17th-century jasper and red-marble retable (ornamental screenlike structure behind the altar) in the Capilla Mayor, and fine mahogany stalls in the choir, which were carved in the 18th century by Pedro Duque Cornejo.

ACCOMMODATION

Córdoba province has some quirky small hotels, as well as more lush options and restored old country houses – read about them in our dedicated accommodation chapter (p378). Our top five picks in the area:

★ **Hotel Lola** (p391) Antiques and quirky details in Córdoba town.

★ **Casa de los Azulejos** (p391) Andalucía and Mexico converge in this elegant Córdoba hotel.

★ **Finca Buytrón** (p392) A gorgeous country house that's perfect for relaxing.

★ **Cortijo La Haza** (p392) A quarter-century old Andalusian farmhouse.

★ **Posada Real** (p392) A modest and pretty restored house in Priego de Córdoba.

❧ AROUND THE MEZQUITA //
EXPLORE VILLAS, CASTLES, BRIDGES AND TOWERS
Opposite the Mezquita and next door to the regional tourist office is the Palacio Episcopal (Bishops' Palace; Calle de Torrijos), now a conference centre but originally the old Hospital of San Sebastián. A lovely Isabelline-style villa with an internal patio, the palace stages exhibitions, often of regional pottery, to which admission is free if you have a Mezquita ticket. The palace also houses the Museo Diocesano (Diocesan Museum; ☎ 957 49 60 85; Calle de Torrijos; admission €3; ☉ 9.30am-3pm), which has a collection of religious art. The best of this art is some outstanding medieval woodcarving, including the 13th-century *Virgen de las Huertas*.

Continuing southwest from the Mezquita, down Calle Amador de los Ríos, will bring you to the massive fortified **Alcázar de los Reyes Cristianos** (Castle of the Christian Kings; ☎ 957 42 01 51; Campo Santo de los Mártires s/n; adult/child €4/2, Wed free; ⏱ 10am-2pm & 4.30-6.30pm Tue-Sat mid-Oct–Apr, 10am-2pm & 5.30-7.30pm Tue-Sat May, Jun & Sep–mid-Oct, 8.30am-2.30pm Tue-Sat Jul & Aug, 9.30am-2.30pm Sun & public holidays year-round). Built by Alfonso X in the 13th century on the remains of Roman and Arab predecessors, the castle began life as a palace, hosting both Fernando and Isabel. From 1490 to 1821 it became a home for the Inquisition, later being converted into a prison that only closed in 1951. Its large terraced gardens – full of fish ponds, fountains, orange trees, flowers and topiary – were added in the 15th century and are among the most beautiful in Andalucía.

Situated on the banks of the Río Guadalquivir, the castle overlooks a much restored Roman bridge, the **Puente Romano**. The bridge formed part of the old medieval walls that are reputed to have been some 22km in length.

🌿 JUDERÍA // MARVEL AT THE MAZE OF THE JEWISH QUARTER

Córdoba's Judería is a charming labyrinth of narrow streets and small squares, whitewashed buildings with flowers dripping from window boxes, and wrought-iron doorways that give glimpses of plant-filled patios. The Judería is one of Córdoba's main tourist attractions and despite a number of shops selling numerous tacky souvenirs, there are still quiet residential streets that offer a glimpse into the real life of the neighbourhood.

Spain had one of Europe's biggest Jewish communities, recorded from as early as the 2nd century AD. Persecuted by the Visigoths, they allied themselves with the Muslims following the Arab conquests.

By the 10th century they were established as some of the most dynamic members of society, holding posts as administrators, doctors, jurists, philosophers, poets and functionaries. The importance of the community is illustrated by the proximity of the Judería to the Mezquita and the city's centres of power. In fact, one of the greatest Jewish theologians, Maimónides, was from Córdoba. He summarised the teachings of Judaism and completed his magnum opus, the *Mishne Torah,* which systemises all of Jewish law, before fleeing persecution to Fès and later to Egypt.

Although somewhat diminished, what remains of the old Jewish quarter extends west and northwest from the Mezquita, almost to the beginning of Avenida del Gran Capitán. The most famous street in the area is known as **Calleja de las Flores** (Flower Alley) and gives a picture-postcard view of the Mezquita bell tower framed between the narrow alley walls.

Sinagoga

The medieval **Sinagoga** (Synagogue; Calle de los Judíos 20; non-EU/EU citizen €0.30/free; ⏱ 9.30am-2pm & 3.30-5.30pm Tue-Sat, 9.30am-1.30pm Sun & public holidays), built in 1315, is a beautiful little building, decorated with some extravagant stucco-work that includes Hebrew inscriptions and intricate Mudéjar star and plant patterns. There's a solitary menorah, probably where the ark (the cabinet where the Torah is held) used to be. It has a women's gallery upstairs.

Casa Andalusí & Museo Taurino

The **Casa Andalusí** (Calle de los Judíos 12; admission €2.50; ⏱ 10am-7pm) is a 12th-century house with a bit of an exaggerated, slightly tacky idea of Al-Andalus. It has a tinkling fountain in the patio and a variety of exhibits, mainly relating to

Córdoba's medieval Muslim culture, as well as a Roman mosaic in the cellar, and a shop selling North African items.

The **Museo Taurino** (Bullfighting Museum; ☎ 957 20 10 56; Plaza de Maimónides) was closed for refurbishments at the time of research. It celebrates, in a 16th-century Renaissance mansion, Córdoba's legendary matadors, with rooms dedicated to El Cordobés and Manolete.

❧ PATIOS CORDOBESES //
ENTER THE SECRET WORLD OF CORDOBAN PATIOS

As you're squeezing yourself down the mini-streets of the Judería, the green, airy patios will be stealing your attention at every point. The famed patios of Córdoba have provided shade during the searing heat of summer for centuries.

Weekends stretching from April to June see Córdoba's streets and alleyways covered in 'patio' signs, which means that you're invited to enter and view what are for the rest of the year closed to the outside world. A group of homeowners sign up to open their doors from 11am to 2pm on Fridays, Saturdays and Sundays. At this time of year the patios are at their prettiest, and many are entered in an annual competition, the **Concurso de Patios Cordobeses** (Competition of Cordoban Patios). A map of patios open for viewing is available from the tourist office, as well as a yearly timetable. Some of the best patios are on and around Calle San Basilio, about 400m southwest of the Mezquita. During the competition, the patios are generally open from 5pm to midnight Monday to Friday, and noon to midnight Saturday and Sunday. Admission is usually free but sometimes there's a container for donations.

The origin of these patios probably lies in the Ancient Greek megaron and the Roman atrium, but the tradition was continued by the Arabs with the addition of a central water fountain. The internal courtyard was an area for women to go about family life and household chores.

❧ PLAZA DEL POTRO // ADMIRE A GORGEOUS HISTORIC PLAZA AND ITS SURROUNDING MUSEUMS

Córdoba's famous Plaza del Potro (Square of the Colt) has in its centre a lovely 16th-century stone fountain topped by a rearing *potro* that gives the plaza its name. The plaza is home to an attractive old charity hospital that houses two of the city's most visited museums, the **Museo Julio Romero de Torres** (☎ 957 49 19 09; Plaza del Potro 1; adult/concession €4/2) and the **Museo de Bellas Artes** (☎ 957 35 55 50; Plaza del Potro 1; admission free). The square's heyday was in the 16th and 17th centuries, when it was the preferred gathering ground for traders, vagabonds and adventurers. On the plaza's western side is the legendary 1435 inn, **Posada del Potro** (☎ 957 48 50 18; Plaza del Potro 10; admission free; ☽ 10am-2pm & 5-8pm Mon-Fri Aug-May), described in *Don Quijote* as a 'den of thieves'. Cervantes once lived here for a short period, and was no doubt robbed and cheated several times by the rough lot hanging out on the square.

Just west of the Plaza del Potro on Plaza de Jerónimo Páez is the excellent **Museo Arqueológico** (Archaeological Museum; ☎ 957 47 40 11; Plaza de Jerónimo Páez 7; non-EU/EU citizen €1.50/free; ☽ 3-8pm Tue, 9am-8pm Wed-Sat, 9am-3pm Sun & public holidays), housed in a Renaissance mansion that was once the site of an original Roman villa. The museum has a wonderful collection of Iberian, Roman and Muslim artefacts, and provides real insight into pre-Islamic Córdoba.

❦ PLAZA DE LA CORREDERA // ENJOY A GRAND SQUARE AND A STUNNING PALACE

North of Plaza del Potro is the grand 17th-century Plaza de la Corredera, a square with an elaborate history of public entertainment and gory showbiz. This was the site of Córdoba's Roman amphitheatre, and the location for horse races, bullfights and Inquisition burnings. Nowadays the extensively restored square hosts tame rock concerts and other events (ask at the tourist office for details). A daily fruit market is held here, and on Saturday there's a lively flea market.

Some 500m north of Plaza de la Corredera is the stunning Renaissance **Palacio de Viana** (☎ 957 49 67 41; Plaza de Don Gome 2; whole house/patios only €6/3; ⏰ 9am-2pm Mon-Fri, 10am-1pm Sat Jun-Sep, 10am-1pm & 4-6pm Mon-Fri, 10am-1pm Sat Oct-May), which has 12 beautiful patios and a formal garden that are a real pleasure to visit in the spring. The palace was occupied by the Marqueses de Viana until a couple of decades ago. The charge covers a one-hour guided tour of the rooms (packed with art and antiques) and access to the patios and garden. It takes about half an hour to stroll around the garden and patios.

❦ HAMMAM BAÑOS ÁRABES // RELAX AND REVITALISE IN ANCIENT ARAB STYLE

When you've had enough of being active, try utter laziness at the newly renovated Arab baths, **Hammam Baños Árabes** (☎ 957 48 47 46; www.hammamspain.com/cordoba, in Spanish; Calle Corregidor Luis de la Cerda; bath/bath & massage €25/32; ⏰ 2hr sessions at 10am, noon, 2pm, 4pm, 6pm, 8pm & 10pm). In its glory days Córdoba had 60 of these wonderful baths where you could hop from hot pools to tepid and cold pools, sipping mint tea after being pleasantly pummelled and squeezed by the aromatherapy masseuse or masseur. You must wear a swimming costume here, but don't worry if you forget yours, as they rent them on the spot.

There's a lovely, cushion-strewn *tetería* (tearoom) upstairs where you can smoke a hookah, drink tea and eat Arabic sweets. Reservations for the baths and massages are required at least a day in advance.

❦ MEDINA AZAHARA // DISCOVER CÓRDOBA'S PLEASURE DOME AND POWERHOUSE

Legend has it that Abd ar-Rahman III built his palace-city, **Medina Azahara** (Madinat al-Zahra; ☎ 957 32 91 30; Carretera Palma del Río; non-EU/EU citizen €1.50/free; ⏰ 10am-8.30pm Tue-Sat May–mid-Sep, 10am-6.30pm Tue-Sat mid-Sep–Apr, 10am-2pm Sun year-round), for his favourite wife, Az-Zahra. Dismayed by her homesickness and yearning for the snowy mountains of Syria, ar-Rahman tuned into his poetic side; he surrounded his new city with almond and cherry trees, replacing snowflakes with fluffy white blossoms.

More realistically, it was probably the case that Abd ar-Rahman's rivalry with the Abbasid dynasty in Baghdad drove him to build an opulent royal complex outside Córdoba. Building started in AD 936 and chroniclers record some staggering construction statistics: 10,000 labourers set 6000 stone blocks a day, with outer walls extending to 1518m west to east and 745m north to south.

It is almost inconceivable to think that such a city, built over 40 years, was only to last a mere 30 years before the usurper Al-Mansur transferred the seat of government to a new palace complex of his own in 981. Then, between 1010 and 1013, the Azahara was wrecked by Berber soldiers.

During succeeding centuries its ruins were plundered repeatedly for building materials. Less than one-tenth of the site has been excavated to date.

Located at the foot of the Sierra Morena, the complex spills down over three terraces with the caliph's palace on the highest terrace overlooking what would have been the court and town. The visitors' route takes you down through the city's original northern gate to the **Dar al-Wuzara** (House of the Viziers) and then to the centrepiece of the site, the **Salón de Abd ar-Rahman III**. Inside, the royal reception hall has been much restored, and the exquisitely carved stuccowork, a riot of vegetal designs, has been painstakingly repaired to cover most of the wall's surface. It gives just a glimpse of the lavishness of the court, which was said to be decorated with gold and silver tiles, and arches of ivory and ebony that contrasted with walls of multicoloured marble. For special effect, a bowl at the centre of the hall was filled with mercury so that when it was rocked the reflected light flashed and bounced off the gleaming decoration.

To reach the site with your own vehicle, follow the signs down Avenida de Medina Azahara, which leads west out of Córdoba onto the A431. Medina Azahara is signposted 8km from the city centre and there is free parking at the site, although this gets very full. Try to visit before 11am to avoid the buses.

A taxi costs €28 for the return trip, including one hour to view the site, or you can take an organised bus tour with Córdoba Vision (see p198). The nearest you can get by public transport is the Cruce de Medina Azahara, the turn-off from the A431, from which it's an uninspiring 3km walk, slightly uphill, to the site. City bus No 1 will drop you at the Cruce de Medina Azahara – the bus departs from the northern end of Avenida de la República Argentina.

FESTIVALS & EVENTS

Spring and early summer are the chief festival times in Córdoba.

Semana Santa (Holy Week) Every evening during the week before Easter Sunday, up to 12 *pasos* (decorated platforms on which statues are carried in a religious procession) and their processions file through the city, passing along the *carrera oficial* (official trail) – Calle Claudio Marcelo, Plaza de las Tendillas, Calle José Cruz Conde – between about 8pm and midnight. The climax is the *madrugá* (dawn) of Good Friday, when six *pasos* pass between 4am and 6am.

Cruces de Mayo (Crosses of May) Flower crosses decorate squares and patios, which become a focus for wine and tapas stalls, music and merrymaking; first few days of May.

Feria de Mayo (May Fair) A massive town party with concerts, a big fairground in the El Arenal area southeast of the city centre, and the main bullfighting season in Los Califas ring on Gran Vía Parque; last week of May and the first days of June.

Festival Internacional de la Guitarra (International Guitar Festival; www.guitarracordoba .com) A two-week celebration of the guitar, with live performances of classical, flamenco, rock, blues and more; top names play in the Jardines del Alcázar at night; late June or early July.

GASTRONOMIC HIGHLIGHTS

Food is among Córdoba's greatest drawcards. Córdoba's culinary legacy is *salmorejo*, a delicious chilled soup of blended tomatoes, garlic, bread, lemon, vinegar and olive oil, sprinkled with crumbled hard-boiled egg and strips of *jamón* (ham). *Rabo de toro* (bull's tail stew) is another juicy favourite. Whatever you do, don't miss the wine from nearby Montilla and Moriles. Although similar to sherry, it prides itself on being naturally alcoholic. Like sherry, it comes in *fino* (dry), *amontillado* (moderately dry, and amber in colour) or *oloroso* (sweet and dark; see p373 for more details), and there's also the sweet Pedro Ximénez variety made from raisins.

☙ AMALTEA €€
☎ 957 49 19 68; Ronda de Isasa 10; mains €8-16; Ⓥ

This place specialises in organic food and wine, serving up excellent meat dishes and a great range of vegetarian fare such as a delicious green salad with avocado and walnuts, and Lebanese-style tabbouleh. A haven in a vegetarian desert.

☙ BAR SANTOS €
Calle Magistral González Francés 3; tortilla €2.50

The legendary Santos serves the best *tortilla de patata* (potato omelette) in town – and don't the *cordobeses* (Córdoba locals) know it. They rush here for a tapa of tortilla, and eat it with plastic forks on paper plates while gazing at the Mezquita. Don't miss it.

☙ BODEGA CAMPOS €€
☎ 957 49 75 00; Calle de Lineros 32; tapas €5, mains €13-21; Ⓨ closed Sun evening

One of Córdoba's most atmospheric and famous bodegas, walking in here is like getting lost in a different world. There are dozens of different rooms and patios, and each room is lined with oak barrels that have been signed by local and international celebrities (such as the Spanish Queen Sofia and UK prime minister Tony Blair). This bodega produces its own house Montilla, and the restaurant, frequented by swankily dressed *cordobeses*, serves up a delicious array of meals. For a cheaper but no less enjoyable evening, try the huge plates of tapas in the bar.

☙ CASA PEPE DE LA JUDERÍA €€
☎ 957 20 07 44; Calle Romero 1; mains €10-20

This place has a great rooftop terrace with views of the Mezquita, and a labyrinth of dining rooms that are always packed. Start off with a complimentary glass of Montilla on the patio before choosing any of the delicious house specials, such as *rabo de toro* or venison fillets.

☙ EL ASTRONAUTA €
☎ 957 49 11 23; Calle Diario de Córdoba 18; menú €9, mains €5-10

A relative Córdoba newbie and a fantastic little place where you can have a coffee and cake, or delicious lunch and dinner. The decor is modern and simple, the food traditional and the local clientele loyal. The little stage in the corner sometimes hosts concerts, readings and other cultural happenings.

☙ TABERNA SALINAS €
☎ 957 48 01 35; Calle Tundidores 3; tapas from €2, raciones from €8; Ⓨ closed Sun & Aug

A historic *taberna* that dates back to 1879, with a reputation so good the tables are always busy. Try the delicious aubergines with honey, potatoes with garlic, *flamenquín* (rolled pork and *jamón*) and *rabo de toro*.

☙ TABERNA SAN MIGUEL/ EL PISTO €
☎ 957 47 01 66; Plaza San Miguel 1; tapas €3, mediaraciones €5-10; Ⓨ closed Sun & Aug

Full of local characters and open since 1880, El Pisto (the barrel) is one of Córdoba's best *tabernas*, both in terms of atmosphere and food. Traditional tapas and *media-raciones* (half-serves of mealsized tapas dishes) are done perfectly, and inexpensive Moriles wine is ready in jugs on the bar.

☙ TABERNA SOCIEDAD DE PLATEROS €

☎ 957 47 00 42; Calle de San Francisco 6; tapas €3, raciones €8-10; ⌚ closed Sun

Run by the silversmiths' guild, this well-loved restaurant in a converted convent serves a selection of generous *raciones* (meal-sized servings of tapas) in its light, glass-roofed patio.

NIGHTLIFE

The magazines *¿Qué Hacer en Córdoba?* and *¡Welcome & Olé!*, issued free by tourist offices, have some 'what's on' information, as does the daily newspaper *Córdoba*. Flyers for live bands are posted outside music bars and at the Instalación Juvenil Córdoba, across the road from the municipal tourist office. Bands usually start around 10pm and there's rarely a cover charge.

☙ BODEGA GUZMÁN

Calle de los Judíos 7

Close to the Sinagoga, this atmospheric local favourite oozes alcohol from every nook. Check out the room dedicated to bullfighting and don't leave without trying some *amargoso* (bitter-tasting) Montilla from the barrel.

☙ JAZZ CAFÉ

☎ 957 47 19 28; Calle Espartería s/n; ⌚ 8am-late

Black-and-white tiled floors, a dark bar with glittering optics and pictures of jazz legends set the tone for this fabulous laid-back bar. It's a haven for late-morning coffee away from the tourist hordes and regularly puts on live jazz (Wednesdays) and jam sessions (Tuesdays).

☙ MAGISTER

Avenida del Gran Capitán 2

This place caters to the more mature drinker, playing soporific background music and brewing beer on the spot to assure patrons the alcohol won't run out. The beer comes in five tasty varieties: blonde *rubia* and *tostada*, the dark *caramelizada* and *morenita*, and the *especial*, which varies from season to season.

☙ TABLAO CARDENAL

☎ 957 48 33 20; www.tablaocardenal.com; Calle de Torrijos 10; show incl 1 drink €20; ⌚ 10.30pm-late Mon-Sat

This place vibrates with the intoxicating sound of tapping heels when its flamenco shows get going. Performances, which vary in quality, can be enjoyed on the open-air patio. Guitar players and singers also add to the vibe.

TRANSPORT

BUS // The **bus station** (☎ 957 40 40 40; Plaza de las Tres Culturas) is behind the train station. Each bus company has its own terminal. The biggest operator, **Alsina Graells** (www.alsina.es), runs services to Seville, Granada and Málaga. It also serves Carmona, Antequera and Almería. Bacoma runs to Baeza and Úbeda. Transportes Ureña serves Jaén, while **Secorbus** (www.socibus.es) operates buses to Madrid. **Empresa Carrera** (☎ 957 50 03 02) heads south, with several daily buses to Priego de Córdoba and Cabra, and a couple to Zuheros, Rute and Iznájar.

PARKING // Metered street parking around the Mezquita and along the riverside is demarcated by blue lines. Charges are €0.50 for 30 minutes or €1.50 for two hours, from 9am to 9pm. Overnight parking outside these hours is free. There is secure parking just off Avenida Doctor Fleming costing €1/6/12/45 for one hour/ overnight/12 hours/24 hours. There is an underground car park on Avenida de América that has similar prices. Charges for hotel parking are about €10 to €12.

TRAIN // Córdoba's modern **train station** (☎ 957 40 02 02; www.renfe.com; Avenida de América) is 1km northwest of Plaza de las Tendillas. For Seville, there are dozens of Andalucía Exprés regional trains, Alta Velocidad trains and AVEs. To Madrid, options include several daily AVEs and a night-time Estrecho. Several trains head to Málaga and Barcelona, and there is a service to Jaén. For Granada you need to change at Bobadilla.

TAXI // In the city centre, taxis congregate at the north-eastern corner of Plaza de las Tendillas. The fare from the train or bus station to the Mezquita is around €5.

SOUTH OF CÓRDOBA

· · · · · ·

The south of Córdoba province straddled the Islamic-Christian frontier from the 13th to the 15th centuries, so many towns and villages cluster around huge, fortified castles. The beautiful, mountainous southeast is known as La Subbética after the Sistema Subbético range that crosses this corner of the province. The mountains, canyons and wooded valleys of the 316-sq-km Parque Natural Sierras Subbéticas offer some enjoyable walks.

The southern boundary of the region is demarcated by the Embalse de Iznájar, a long, wriggling reservoir overlooked by the village of Iznájar. There are some good walks that can be done around the reservoir. The northern section of the park has a number of attractive settlements of which Zuheros and Priego de Córdoba are among the most appealing.

BAENA

pop 18,000
The name 'Baena' is synonymous with fine olive oil. This small market town, surrounded by endless serried ranks of olive trees, produces olive oil of such superb quality, it has been accredited with its own Denominación de Origen (DO; a designation that indicates the product's unique geographical origins,

production processes and quality) label. The periphery of the town is dotted with huge storage tanks and it is possible to visit the best oil-producing mill in the province for a guided tour.

The small **tourist office** (☎ 957 67 19 46; Calle Domingo de Henares s/n; ⊙ 9am-2pm & 5-8pm Tue-Fri, 10am-2pm Sat & Sun) has limited information but tries to be as helpful as possible. It stocks a range of leaflets on the town, and a useful map.

❧ NÚÑEZ DE PRADO // **SAMPLE OLIVE OIL MADE WITH LOVE**
The best reason for coming to Baena is to experience the best working olive-oil mill in Córdoba, **Núñez de Prado** (☎ 957 67 01 41; Avenida de Cervantes s/n; admission free; ⊙ 9am-2pm & 4-6pm Mon-Fri, 9am-1pm Sat), where Paco Núñez de Prado himself will give you a tour of the facilities. Overall, the family owns something like 90,000 olive trees and their organic methods of farming result in a very high quality product. Unlike some other producers, there are no hi-tech gimmicks here. Rather, olives are still painstakingly hand-picked to prevent bruising and high acidity and are then crushed in the ancient stone mills. The mill is famous for *flor de aceite,* the oil that seeps naturally from the ground-up olives. It takes approximately 11kg of olives to yield just 1L of oil. The mill shop sells the oil at bargain prices.

ZUHEROS & AROUND

pop 850 / elevation 625m
Rising above the low-lying *campiña* (countryside) south of the C0241, Zuheros sits in a dramatic location, crouching in the lee of a craggy mountain. It's approached via a steep road through a series of hairpin bends and provides a beautiful base for exploring the south of the province.

Turismo Zuheros (☎ 957 69 47 75; Carretera Zuheros-Baena s/n; ☉ 9am-2pm & 5-8pm) has a small office at the entrance to the village on the Baena road where you can find plenty of leaflets and information on walking and bike hire. The staff can also put you in contact with an English-speaking walking guide, **Clive Jarman** (☎ 957 69 47 96), who lives in Zuheros. There is a **park information point** (☎ 957 33 52 55), open occasionally in summer, a few hundred metres up the road towards the Cueva de los Murciélagos. There is a good car park at the heart of the village below the castle. **Empresa Carrera** (☎ 957 40 44 14) runs buses to/from Córdoba.

ZUHEROS TOWN // ENJOY FANTASTIC VIEWS FROM THIS RELAXED TOWN

Zuheros has a delightfully relaxed atmosphere. All around the western escarpment on which it perches are miradors (lookouts) with exhilarating views of the dramatic limestone crags that tower over the village and create such a powerful backdrop for Zuheros' castle. The ruined Islamic castle juts out on a pinnacle and has a satisfying patina of age and decay in its rough stonework. Zuheros is also renowned for its local cheeses and there is a wonderful organic-cheese factory, **Fábrica de Queso Biológico**, on the road entering the village. Here you can buy delicious varieties of local cheese – some cured with pepper or wood ash – complete hams, wines, olive oil and honey.

♥ CUEVA DE LOS MURCIÉLAGOS // DUCK FROM THE BATS IN THIS NEOLITHIC CAVE

Some 4km above the village is the **Cueva de los Murciélagos** (Cave of the Bats; ☎ 957 69 45 45; www.cuevadelosmurcielagos.com; adult/child €5/4; ☉ guided tours noon & 5.30pm Mon-Fri Apr-Sep, 12.30pm & 4.30pm Mon-Fri Oct-Mar, 11am, 12.30pm, 2pm & 5.30pm Sat & Sun year-round, extra tours Sat & Sun summer/winter 6.30/4pm), which was

∼ WORTH A TRIP ∼

Behind Zuheros village lies a dramatic rocky gorge, the **Cañon de Bailón**, through which there is a pleasant circular walk of just over 4km (taking about three to four hours).

To pick up the trail find the **Mirador de Bailón**, just below Zuheros on the village's southwestern side, where the approach road CO241 from the A316 Doña Mencía junction bends sharply. There is a small car park here and the gorge is right in front of the mirador (lookout). From the car park's entrance – with your back to the gorge – take the broad stony track heading up to the left. Follow the track as it winds uphill and then curves left along the slopes above the gorge. In about 500m the path descends and the valley opens out between rocky walls. The path crosses the stony riverbed to its opposite bank and, in about 1km, a wired-down stone causeway that recrosses the river appears ahead. A few metres before you reach this crossing, bear up left on what is at first a very faint path. It becomes much clearer as it zigzags past a big tree and a twisted rock pinnacle up on the right.

Keep climbing steadily and then, where the path levels off, keep left through trees to reach a superb **viewpoint**. Continue on an obvious path that passes a couple of Parque Natural noticeboards and takes you to the road leading up to the Cueva de los Murciélagos. Turn left and follow the road back down to Zuheros.

inhabited by Neanderthals more than 35,000 years ago. It is worth visiting for its Neolithic rock paintings that date back to 6000–3000 BC. Opening times in winter can be unreliable. The drive up to the cave is fantastic, as the road twists and turns through the looming mountains with spectacular views from a number of miradors. From one of these you actually get a weird vertiginous, aerial view of the town.

❦ PARQUE NATURAL SIERRAS SUBBÉTICAS // HIKE, BIRDWATCH AND ANIMAL-SPOT IN THIS BEAUTIFUL PARK

Exploring the Parque Natural Sierras Subbéticas, southwest of Zuheros, is made easier if you have a copy of the CNIG 1:50,000 map *Parque Natural Sierras Subbéticas*; it's best to get a copy before arriving in the area (see p406). The park's Centro de Visitantes Santa Rita (☎ 957 33 40 34; A340) is located, not very conveniently, 10km east of Cabra. This natural park has an abundance of springs and streams and is wonderful for hiking among oak, maple, wild olive and mastic trees. Birdwatchers will be able to spot eagles (golden and imperial), falcons and vultures and wildlife lovers might spot wild cats and boar, though the area prides itself on the presence of the rare cabrera shrew.

PRIEGO DE CÓRDOBA

pop 23,150 / elevation 650m

Priego de Córdoba is a sophisticated market town full of 18th-century mansions, extravagant baroque churches and fine civic buildings that will turn your head. Perched on an outcrop over the valley, the town looks like a big vanilla cake. It was one of the towns in the 18th century that was famous for its silk production and, like many of the small

neighbouring towns, it grew rich on the proceeds. The narrow lanes of the Barrio de La Villa (the old Arab quarter) all converge on the handsome Balcón de Aldarve with its elevated promenade and magnificent views over the Río Salado. Two of the province's highest peaks, 1570m La Tiñosa and 1476m Bermejo, rise to the southwest.

ESSENTIAL INFORMATION

TOURIST OFFICE // The helpful tourist office (☎ 957 70 06 25; Calle del Río 33; ☙ 10am-1.30pm & 5-7.30pm Tue-Sat, 10am-1pm Sun) is a short walk south of the central Plaza de la Constitución.

EXPLORING PRIEGO DE CÓRDOBA

❦ TOWN CENTRE // ADMIRE THE TOWN'S GOLDEN-HUED STONEWORK AND WHITEWASHED WALLS

The town's catalogue of elegant architecture has earned it a reputation as the capital of Cordoban baroque. The most notable church is the Parroquia de la Asunción (Calle Plaza de Abad Palomino) with its fantastic Sagrario chapel (sacristy) where a whirl of frothy white stuccowork surges upwards to a beautiful cupola. The sacristy (off the left-hand aisle) and the ornate *retablo* (retable) represent a high point in Andalusian baroque and are now considered national monuments. Similarly ornate are the Iglesia de San Francisco (Calle Buen Suceso) and Iglesia de la Aurora (Carrera de Álvarez), whose brotherhood takes to the streets of the town in a procession each Saturday at midnight. They play guitars and sing hymns in honour of La Aurora (Our Lady of the Dawn). All the churches normally open from 11am to 1pm.

The main area of interest for visitors to Priego lies 200m northeast of Plaza de la Constitución and is reached by following Calle Solana on through Plaza San Pedro. At a junction with Calle Doctor Pedrajas you can turn left to visit the well-preserved 16th-century slaughterhouse, the **Carnicerías Reales** (admission free; 10am-1pm & 5-7pm). It has an enclosed patio and a wonderful stone staircase; exhibitions of paintings are often held here. Turning right along Calle Doctor Pedrajas takes you to Plaza de Abad Palomino, where you can visit the Parroquia de la Asunción. On the square's northern side is Priego's **castillo**, an Islamic fortress built on original Roman foundations in the 9th century and later rebuilt in the 16th century. Privately owned, and closed to the public, the castle has been the subject of much archaeological investigation, which among other things has turned up dozens of stone cannonballs.

Beyond the castle lie the winding streets of the **Barrio de La Villa**, where potted geraniums transform the white-washed walls, especially in Calle Real and Plaza de San Antonio. Other pretty alleyways lead down from the heart of the barrio to the Paseo de Adarve, where there are fine views across the rolling countryside and mountains. On the southern edge of the barrio and ending in a superb **mirador** is the Paseo de Colombia, with fountains, flowerbeds and an elegant pergola.

At the opposite end of town, you will find Priego's extraordinary 19th-century fountain, **Fuente del Rey** (Fountain of the King; Calle del Río), with its large three-tiered basins continually filled with splashing water from 180 spouts. The fountain writhes with classical sculptures of Neptune and Amphitrite and when the level of the water rises to cover Neptune's

modesty, the townsfolk know that it will be a good harvest. Behind the Fuente del Rey is the late-16th-century **Fuente de la Virgen de la Salud**, less flamboyant, but further enhancing the square's delightful tranquillity. If you take the stairs to the left of the Fuente de la Virgen de la Salud you can walk to the **Ermita del Calvario** (Calvary Chapel) from where there are scenic views.

Also worth a visit is the **Museo Histórico Municipal** (☎ 957 54 09 47; Carrera de las Monjas 16; admission free; 10am-2pm Tue-Fri, 11am-2pm Sat & Sun), just west of Plaza de la Constitución. Here, imaginative displays exhibit artefacts dating from the Palaeolithic to medieval periods. The museum also organises archaeological tours in the area.

GASTRONOMIC HIGHLIGHTS

❤ EL ALJIBE €
☎ 957 70 18 56; Calle de Abad Palomino; raciones €4-9, menú €7

Next to the Castillo, El Aljibe has a nice terrace, and part of the downstairs area has a glass floor through which you can view some old Islamic baths. Try some cold soup – gazpacho or *ajo blanco* – both of which are served in tall glasses. A real refreshment on a summer's day.

❤ BALCÓN DEL ADARVE €€
☎ 957 54 70 75; Paseo de Colombia 36; mains €8-17

In a wonderful location overlooking the valley, this place is both a good tapas bar and an excellent restaurant. Specialities include *solomillo de ciervo al vino tinto con grosella* (venison in gooseberry and red-wine sauce) and *salmón en supremas a la naranja* (salmon in orange sauce).

TRANSPORT

BUS // Priego's bus station is about 1km west of Plaza de la Constitución on Calle Nuestra Señora de los Reme-

GETTING OUT OF TOWN

South of Priego de Córdoba, stranded on a dramatic promontory above a huge reservoir, is the isolated pueblo of **Iznájar**, which is dominated by its Islamic castle. Despite the poverty of the region, it is a place of outstanding natural beauty and tranquillity, where you can enjoy the beautiful scenery and indulge in a host of outdoor activities.

dios. Bus 1 from Plaza Andalucía takes you there. **Empresa Carrera** (☎ 957 40 44 14) runs buses from the station to Córdoba, Granada, Cabra and elsewhere. **PARKING //** There is parking just by the football and basketball pitches on Calle Cava north of Plaza de la Constitución. There is a small car park in Plaza Palenque along Carrera de las Monjas, the street that runs east from Plaza de la Constitución. The centre of Priego can become very busy with traffic.

MONTILLA

If you fancy getting closer to wine-making country and tasting some of that sweet wine, Montilla is the place for you. The **tourist information office** (☎ 957 65 24 62; www.turismomontilla.com; Calle Capitán Alonso de Vergas 3; ⏱ 10am-2pm Mon-Fri, 11am-2pm Sat & Sun Jul & Aug, 10am-2pm & 5-7pm Mon-Fri, 11am-2pm Sat & Sun Jun-Sep) has details of wines and bodegas.

The highlight of a visit here is a trip to the winery at **Bodegas Alvear** (☎ 957 66 40 14; www.alvear.es; Avenida María Auxiliadora 1; guided tour & tasting weekday/weekend €5/4; ⏱ shop 10am-2pm Mon-Sat), to sample some renowned Pedro Ximénez wine (see the boxed text, p218). Tours take place at 12.30pm Monday to Friday (it's recommended you book in advance), and there are weekend tours too, but you must call in advance to find out what time they're happening.

For food, Montilla's excellent **Las Camachas** (☎ 957 65 00 04; Avenida de Europa 3; mains €8-11) has won prizes for its delicious local specialities, served in the expansive, comfortable restaurant.

WEST OF CÓRDOBA

· · · · · ·

🌿 ALMODÓVAR DEL RÍO //
HIDE IN THE SHADE OF THIS MONUMENTAL CASTLE
Almodóvar's monumental and sinister-looking, eight-towered **castle** (☎ 957 63 51 16; admission €3, EU citizen free Wed afternoon; ⏱ 11am-2.30pm & 4-8pm, closes 7pm Oct-Mar) dominates the view from miles around. It was built in AD 740 but owes most of its present appearance to post-Reconquista rebuilding. Pedro I ('the Cruel') used it as a treasure store because the castle had never been taken by force. Its sense of impregnability is still potent within the massive walls. The castle has now been over-restored by its owner, the Marqués de la Motilla, and is full of some rather silly exhibits including limp, manacled mannequins. The towers – with names such as 'the Bells', 'the School' and 'the Tribute' – have various stories attached to them and there are information placards in Spanish and English.

If you're driving, the best way to the castle (avoiding the busy town centre) is to ignore the signs ahead for Centro Urbano at the junction as you enter town. Instead, go right and follow the A431 ring road, signed to Posadas and Palma del Río. There is parking below the castle, but you can also drive up the stony approach track (there is no official parking area but you can park). You can easily walk down into the old town centre from the castle.

THE SWEETEST OF WINES

Pedro Ximénez wine is a treat after dinner and its taste will linger on your tongue for hours. For miles and miles across the rolling *campiña* (countryside) its vines grow in soggy, rain-drenched soil under a glaring sun. Such conditions would destroy other vines, but not Pedro Ximénez (sometimes called Pe Equis in Spanish, or PX). This is a tough one, a Rambo of vines: it loves hardship and thrives on extreme weather. In fact it is exactly these conditions that give it the unusual flavours, ranging from a very thin, dry, almost olive taste through to a sweet, dark treacle.

Originally thought to be a type of Riesling, legend has it that the Ximénez grape was imported to the region in the 16th century by a German called Peter Seimens (the Spanish adapted it to Pedro Ximénez). Its intensely sweet wine is endlessly compared to sherry, much to the irritation of the vintners. The fundamental difference between the Jerez sherries and Montilla is the alcoholic potency – alcohol is added to Jerez wine, while Montilla grapes achieve their own high levels of alcohol (15% proof) and sweetness from the intense summer temperatures experienced by the grapes when they are laid out to dry. Left to darken in the sun, the grapes produce a thick, golden must when crushed. What results from this was traditionally racked off into huge terracotta *tinajas,* now steel vats, for ageing. Wine that is clean and well formed goes on to become the pale, strawlike *fino;* darker amber wines with nutty flavours create the *amontillado;* and full-bodied wines become the *oloroso.* The wines are then aged using a *solera* system, where younger vintages are added to older ones in order to 'educate' the young wine.

❦ HORNACHUELOS & PARQUE NATURAL SIERRA DE HORNACHUELOS // ENJOY SOME TRANQUILLITY AND EASY HIKING OPTIONS

The pleasant village of Hornachuelos is the ideal base for spending a couple of days enjoying the quiet charms of **Parque Natural Sierra de Hornachuelos**. The park is a 672-sq-km area of rolling hills in the Sierra Morena, northwest of Almodóvar del Río. The park is densely wooded with a mix of holm oak, cork oak and ash, and is pierced by a number of river valleys that are thick with willow trees. It is renowned for its eagles and other raptors, and harbours the second-largest colony of black vultures in Andalucía.

Hornachuelos stands above a small reservoir and on its banks is a delightful little picnic area. The **tourist office** (☎ 957 64 07 86; Carretera San Calixto; ☺ 8am-3pm Thu-Tue, 8am-3pm & 4-6pm Wed) is located in the sports complex on Carretera de San Calixto, the main road to the west of the centre. From Plaza de la Constitución, a lane called La Palmera, with a charming palm-tree pebble mosaic underfoot, leads up to the **Iglesia de Santa Maride de las Flores** and a **mirador** on Paseo Blas Infante.

Heading 1.5km northwest from Hornachuelos on the road to San Calixto will take you to the **Centro de Visitantes Huerta del Rey** (☎ 957 64 11 40; ☺ 10am-2pm & 4-7pm Mon-Fri, 10am-7pm Sat). This visitor centre features interesting displays on the area and its creatures, has information on visiting the Parque Natural Sierra de Hornachuelos and sells local produce. You can get information on any of the walking trails that fan out from the centre and you can book a guided walk, hire bikes or arrange horse-riding sessions here. There is a bar-restaurant situated just by the centre car park that serves mains from €5 to €12.

Just south of the road that leads into the village you'll find **Bar Casa Alejandro** (Avenida Guadalquivir 4; raciones €5-10). This bar is very popular with locals and the walls are heavy with hunting trophies.

Autocares Pérez Cubero (☎ 957 68 40 23) runs buses to/from Córdoba (€3.20, 50 minutes, four times daily Monday to Friday, one to two times daily on weekends).

NORTH OF CÓRDOBA

· · · · · ·

🌿 **LOS PEDROCHES & AROUND // TREAD AROUND CÓRDOBA'S LITTLE-EXPLORED MYSTERIOUS NORTH**

Exploring Córdoba's mysterious north you'll find wild landscapes, dark-green hills and tiny, hard-working pueblos (villages), untouched by the tourist mania of the south. The Sierra Morena rises sharply just north of Córdoba city then rolls back gently over most of the north of the province. The N432 runs northwest into Extremadura, but after 50km, detour onto the lengthy N502, which will take you to the far north along some incredible landscapes in the area of Los Pedroches. The area is known for being covered with holm oak, and during the era of Al-Andalus it was called 'the Land of Acorns'. Thanks to the acorns, this area, along with Jabugo in Huelva, is a source of quality *jamón ibérico de bellota* which comes from small black pigs who feast on the October harvest of acorns. The acorns give the meat its slightly sweet, nutty flavour. Salted and cured over a period of six to 12 months, the resulting dark-pink ham is usually

TOP FIVE

CASTLES IN CÓRDOBA

★ **Almodóvar del Río** (p217) – sinister and dramatic post-Reconquista structure

★ **Castillo de los Sotomayor** (above) – one of Andalucía's eeriest fortifications

★ **Belalcázar** (above) – unusual and little-seen

★ **Santa Eufemia** (above) – off-the-beaten track

★ **Castillo de Miramonte** (above) – a ruin with stunning views

served wafer thin with bread and Montilla. And, luckily for you, it can be sampled it in almost every village in this area.

If you enjoy off-the-beaten-track destinations, head to the castles at Belalcázar and Santa Eufemia. The 15th-century Castillo de los Sotomayor looms over remote Belalcázar, and is one of the spookiest fortifications in Andalucía. The castle is in private hands so you can't go inside, but it still provides a dramatic focus amid the low-lying hills. Santa Eufemia, 26km east of Belalcázar across empty countryside, is Andalucía's northernmost village. The Castillo de Miramonte, on a crag to the north above the village, is a tumbled ruin of Islamic origin, but the 360-degree views are stupendous. To reach the castle turn west off the N502 at Hostal La Paloma in the village, and after 1km turn right at the 'Camino Servicio RTVE' sign, from which it's a 1.5km drive uphill to the castle. The tourist office (☎ 957 15 82 29; Plaza Mayor 1; ⏰ 9am-2.30pm Mon-Fri) in the *ayuntamiento* also has a leaflet (in Spanish) detailing two walks, one up to the castle and the other to the nearby *ermita* (chapel).

JAÉN PROVINCE

3 PERFECT DAYS

♥ DAY 1 // IMMERSE YOURSELF IN ÚBEDA'S BAROQUE

Give yourself over to a day of admiring some of Spain's most stunning architecture – the baroque of Vandelvira (see boxed text, p238), Jaén province's grand architect. Delve into exploring Úbeda's countless aristocratic palaces, simple and elegant squares and small streets full of architectural surprises (p236). Eat well in one of the marvellous restaurants and then stock your larder with some quality olive oil (p238).

♥ DAY 2 // DEDICATE A DAY TO BAEZA

Baeza (p230) is a smaller bite than Úbeda, but it's just as delicious. It is a more concentrated baroque bonanza, with elegant palaces, a spacious town centre, steep streets of the old town and a fantastic cathedral. And, just in case you forget you're in *aceite de oliva* (olive oil) land, there is a constant foggy air that whiffs of nearby olive oil production.

♥ DAY 3 // HEAD OUT TO THE COUNTRY

Jaén province is Andalucía's top area for nature lovers. Choose from Cazorla's easy day walks around the town (p240) or more demanding treks (p242) to self-guided expeditions around the mountains by car (p244). Enjoy the views, or head for Parque Natural Sierra de Andújar (p230) for more demanding hikes. The region's flora and fauna, rugged mountain peaks and rich cultural heritage are bound to fascinate, and discovering small, isolated villages – by car or on foot – is hugely satisfying.

JAÉN

· · · · · ·

pop 116,000 / elevation 575m

Overshadowed by the beauty of nearby Úbeda and Baeza, Jaén is often passed over by visitors to the region. And it's not so difficult to understand why, given the industrial approach to the city. But this market town has its own bustle, hidden neighbourhoods, some excellent tapas bars and a grandiose cathedral, all of which make it a good day trip.

Jaén was made grand by its strategic importance during the Reconquista (Christian Reconquest). It was a bone of contention between the Muslims in Granada and the Castilians to the north until the ruling emir, Mohammed ibn Yusuf ibn Nasr, struck a deal with Castile's Fernando III in 1247, which meant ibn Nasr would pay tribute if the Christian monarch respected the borders of his shrinking kingdom. Thus Jaén became the thin end of the wedge, and the Muslims were eventually driven from Granada in 1492.

Centuries of decline set in after the Reconquista, with many *jiennenses* (locals of Jaén) emigrating to the Spanish colonies – hence the existence of other Jaéns in Peru and the Philippines. Jaén now has a largely impoverished populace, many of whom struggle to make ends meet.

ESSENTIAL INFORMATION

EMERGENCIES // Policía Municipal (Municipal Police; ☎ 953 21 91 05; Carrera de Jesús) Just behind the *ayuntamiento*. Policía Nacional (National Police; ☎ 953 26 18 50; Calle del Arquitecto Berges)

TOURIST OFFICE // Regional tourist office (☎ 953 19 04 55; otjaen@andalucia.org; Calle de la Maestra 13; ☷ 10am-7pm Mon-Fri Oct-Mar, 10am-

8pm Mon-Fri Apr-Sep, 10am-1pm Sat, Sun & public holidays year-round) Has helpful, multilingual staff and plenty of free information about the city and province.

ORIENTATION

Old Jaén, with its narrow, winding streets, huddles around the foot of the Cerro de Santa Catalina, the wooded, castle-crowned hill above the western side of the city. Jaén's monumental cathedral is near the southern end of the old city.

EXPLORING JAÉN

♥ **CATHEDRAL //** A MAGNIFICENT CATHEDRAL BY A MASTER ARCHITECT

They say one should be able to worship God from anywhere, and that proved to be particularly true in Jaén. The Christians worshipped in an old mosque for over 100 years following the Reconquista, and it wasn't until the 16th century that the ambitious plans for Jaén's huge cathedral (☎ 953 23 42 33; Plaza de Santa María; ☷ 8.30am-1pm & 4-7pm Mon-Sat Oct-Mar, 8.30am-1pm & 5-8pm Mon-Sat Apr-Sep, 9am-1pm & 5-7pm Sun & holidays year-round) were conceived and the master architect Andrés de Vandelvira (who was also responsible for many fabulous buildings in Úbeda and Baeza) was commissioned.

Its size and opulence still dominate and dwarf the entire city, and the cathedral is fantastically visible from the hilltop eyrie of Santa Catalina. The southwestern facade, set back on Plaza de Santa María, was not completed until the 18th century, and it owes more to the late baroque tradition than to the Renaissance, thanks to its host of statuary by Seville's Pedro Roldán. The overall Renaissance aesthetic is dominant, however, and is particularly evident in the overall size and solidity of the internal and

(Continued on page 227)

JAÉN PROVINCE

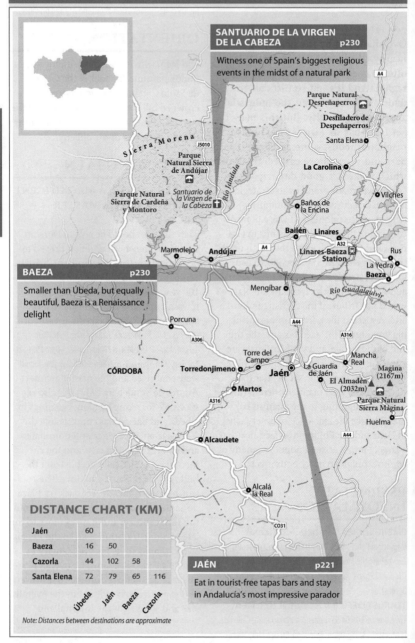

SANTUARIO DE LA VIRGEN DE LA CABEZA p230

Witness one of Spain's biggest religious events in the midst of a natural park

BAEZA p230

Smaller than Úbeda, but equally beautiful, Baeza is a Renaissance delight

JAÉN p221

Eat in tourist-free tapas bars and stay in Andalucía's most impressive parador

Sierra Morena

J5010

Parque Natural Sierra de Andújar

Parque Natural Despeñaperros

Desfiladero de Despeñaperros

Santa Elena

La Carolina

Vilches

Parque Natural Sierra de Cardeña y Montoro

Santuario de la Virgen de la Cabeza

Río Jándula

Baños de la Encina

Bailén

Linares

Rus

Marmolejo

Andújar

A4

Linares-Baeza Station

A32

La Yedra

Baeza

Mengíbar

Río Guadalquivir

Porcuna

A306

A44

A316

Torre del Campo

Mancha Real

CÓRDOBA

Torredonjimeno

Jaén

La Guardia de Jaén

Magina (2167m)

Martos

El Almadén (2032m)

A316

Parque Natural Sierra Mágina

Huelma

A44

Alcaudete

Alcalá la Real

CO31

DISTANCE CHART (KM)

	Úbeda	Jaén	Baeza	Cazorla
Jaén	60			
Baeza	16	50		
Cazorla	44	102	58	
Santa Elena	72	79	65	116

Note: Distances between destinations are approximate

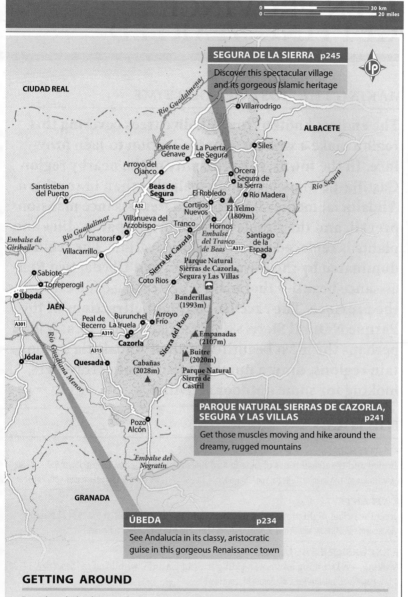

SEGURA DE LA SIERRA p245

Discover this spectacular village and its gorgeous Islamic heritage

CIUDAD REAL

ALBACETE

Río Guadalmena

Villarrodrigo

Puente de Génave   La Puerta de Segura
Arroyo del Ojanco
Siles

Santisteban del Puerto
Beas de Segura
El Robledo
Orcera
Segura de la Sierra
Río Madera
Río Segura

A32
Cortijos Nuevos
El Yelmo (1809m)

Villanueva del Arzobispo   Tranco
Hornos
Santiago de la Espada

Embalse de Giribaile
Río Guadalimar
Iznatoraf
Embalse del Tranco de Beas
A317

Villacarrillo

Sabiote
Torreperogil
Coto Ríos
Parque Natural Sierras de Cazorla, Segura y Las Villas

Úbeda
JAÉN
Banderillas (1993m)

A301
Peal de Becerro
Burunchel
La Iruela
Arroyo Frío

Jódar
A319
Cazorla
Empanadas (2107m)

A315
Buitre (2020m)

Quesada
Cabañas (2028m)
Parque Natural Sierra de Castril

Río Guadiana Menor

Pozo Alcón

PARQUE NATURAL SIERRAS DE CAZORLA, SEGURA Y LAS VILLAS p241

Get those muscles moving and hike around the dreamy, rugged mountains

Embalse del Negratín

GRANADA

ÚBEDA p234

See Andalucía in its classy, aristocratic guise in this gorgeous Renaissance town

0 ———— 30 km
0 ———— 20 miles

JAÉN PROVINCE

GETTING AROUND

Even though the distances between cities are quite short in Jaén province and can be done by public transport, having your own car will allow you to reach some of the more remote mountain areas, especially if you want to do some more challenging treks. The area around Parque Natural Sierras de Cazorla, Segura y Las Villas is perfect for driving – see the boxed text on p244.

JAÉN PROVINCE
GETTING STARTED

MAKING THE MOST OF YOUR TIME

The endless knotted rows of olive trees covering this region make a wonderful introduction to Jaén province. In the towns, the proximity of the nearby region Castilla-La Mancha is more palpable than in southern Andalucía; medieval castles and Renaissance mansions prevail, and the simple cheer of bright patios, tiles and plants is replaced by stern sophistication. The region is dominated by the towns of Baeza and Úbeda, two Renaissance beauties that make a perfect base for exploring the province. The excellent outdoor attractions of the Parque Natural Sierras de Cazorla, Segura y Las Villas, perhaps the most beautiful of all of Andalucía's mountain regions, draw a number of discerning travellers looking for some outdoor activities.

TOP TOURS

ARTIFICIS
Guided and theatrical tours of Úbeda and Baeza's monuments. (Map p235; ☎ 953 75 81 50; www.artificis.com, in Spanish; Calle Baja de El Salvador 14, Úbeda; ☼ tours 11am & 5pm year-round, 6pm Jun-Sep)

ATLANTE
Great theatrical night-time tours of Úbeda and Baeza. (Map p235; ☎ 953 79 34 22; Plaza del Ayuntamiento s/n, Úbeda; adult/child €6/free; ☼ tours 11am & 5pm year-round, 6pm Jun-Sep)

EXCURSIONES BUJARKAY
Walking, 4WD, biking and horse-riding trips in Cazorla, with local guides. (☎ 953 71 30 11; www.swin.net/usuarios/jcg; Calle Borosa 81, Coto Ríos)

TURISNAT
Trips to Cazorla include 4WDs with English-speaking guides. (☎ 953 72 13 51; www.turisnat .org, in Spanish; Paseo del Santo Cristo 17, Cazorla)

GETTING AWAY FROM IT ALL

There are no shortage of stunningly picturesque destinations in which to leave the crowds far behind.

★ **Go walking around Segura de la Sierra** Watch the landscape unfold before you from the castle of this beautiful village (p245)

★ **Discover isolated villages** Walk the 15km to the lovely, seldom-visited village of Río Madera (p245)

★ **Go on a driving tour** You can't be more solo than in your car with only the mountains and valleys of Sierra de Cazorla for company (p244)

ADVANCE PLANNING

Jaén province makes for pretty easy and spontaneous travel, but a little planning can be useful around busy times of the year or if you have your heart set on completing a particular mountain hike.

★ **Cazorla** (p239) Book your accommodation early during the Easter holidays, when Spaniards who love hiking descend upon the town

★ **Parque Natural Sierras de Cazorla, Segura y Las Villas** (p241) Plan your walks in advance and choose between hiking the south or north sides of the park

TOP RESTAURANTS

🌢 **TABERNA LA MANCHEGA**
Simple, delicious tapas in a 19th-century bar (p228)

🌢 **LA IMPRENTA**
Modern cuisine and stunning tapas in a converted print house (p237)

🌢 **RESTAURANTE ANTIQUE**
A modern twist on traditional recipes in elegant surroundings (p238)

🌢 **PARADOR CONDESTABLE DÁVALOS**
The top spot in Úbeda town with great local specialities (p238)

🌢 **MESÓN RESTAURANTE LA GÓNDOLA**
A jolly Jaén local with fantastic food (p234)

RESOURCES

★ **Ayuntamiento de Jaén** (www.aytojaen.es) The *ayuntamiento's* website; information in English, French, German and Spanish

★ **Diputación Provincial de Jaén** (www .promojaen.es) Lots of interesting information in English, French, German and Spanish

★ **Jaén Online** (www.jaenonline.com, in Spanish) Useful information

★ **Walking in Andalucía** (Guy Hunter-Watts) Great book that details walks between 5km and 15km in length

JAÉN PROVINCE

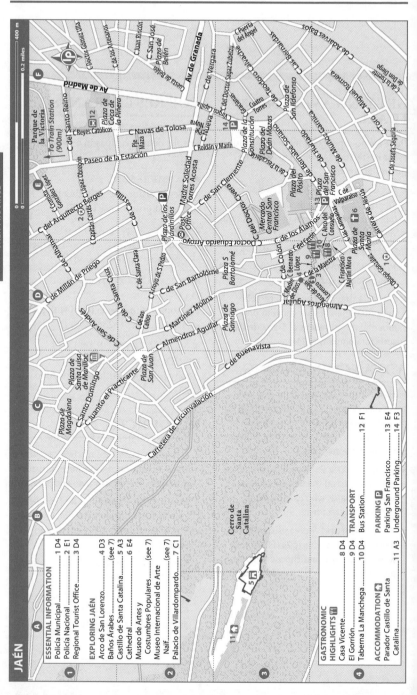

JAÉN

ESSENTIAL INFORMATION
Policía Municipal..................... 1 D4
Policía Nacional....................... 2 E1
Regional Tourist Office........... 3 D4

EXPLORING JAÉN
Arco de San Lorenzo................ 4 D3
Baños Árabes.......................(see 7)
Castillo de Santa Catalina....... 5 A3
Cathedral................................ 6 E4
Museo de Artes y
  Costumbres Populares.........(see 7)
Museo Internacional de Arte
  Naïf.....................................(see 7)
Palacio de Villardompardo...... 7 C1

GASTRONOMIC
HIGHLIGHTS
Casa Vicente........................... 8 D4
El Gorrión............................... 9 D4
Taberna La Manchega............ 10 D4

ACCOMMODATION
Parador Castillo de Santa
  Catalina.............................. 11 A3

TRANSPORT
Bus Station............................ 12 F1

PARKING
Parking San Francisco............ 13 E4
Underground Parking............. 14 F3

400 m
0.2 miles

(Continued from page 221)

external structures, with huge, rounded arches and clusters of Corinthian columns that lend it great visual strength.

The cult of the Reliquia del Santo Rostro de Cristo – the cloth with which St Veronica is believed to have wiped Christ's face on the road to Calvary – has its home behind the main altar, in the **Capilla del Santo Rostro**. On Friday at 11.30am and 5pm long queues of the faithful assemble to kiss the cloth.

❧ **NORTH OF THE CATHEDRAL //
DELVE INTO ANDALUCÍA'S MOST
INTRIGUING ARCHAEOLOGICAL
COLLECTION**
Northwest of the cathedral, a warren of steep, narrow alleyways disappear into the heart of the old Arab quarter. Calle Madre de Dios takes you through the **Arco de San Lorenzo**, then runs into Calle Almendros Aguilar, which heads up to the handsome Renaissance **Palacio de Villardompardo** (☎ 953 23 62 92; Plaza de Santa Luisa de Marillac; non-EU/EU citizen €1.50/free; ☒ 9am-8pm Tue-Fri, 9.30am-2.30pm Sat & Sun, closed public holidays & Mon). The *palacio* (palace) houses two museums and what are claimed to be the largest Arab baths in Spain open to visitors. There are pamphlets, in French and English, giving some information on the baths and the museums.

The complex is Jaén's most rewarding attraction and houses one of the most intriguing collections of artefacts and archaeological remains found under one roof in Andalucía. The signposted route around the palace leads you first over a glass walkway that reveals Roman ruins, into the bowels of the building and then into the **Baños Árabes** (Arab Baths). The 11th-century baths are in a remarkably good state of preservation, with the usual

ACCOMMODATION

Accommodation in Jaén province is moderately priced and often located in some fantastic palaces. You can also get beautiful rural hotels, close to the hiking options. Read all about the options in our dedicated accommodation chapter (p378). Below are some of the province's highlights:

★ **Hotel Palacete Santa Ana** (p393) A converted 16th-century nunnery in Baeza

★ **Hotel Puerta de la Luna** (p393) Ultimate luxury in Baeza

★ **Palacio de la Rambla** (p394) A stunning Renaissance palace in Úbeda

★ **Parador Condestable Dávalos** (p394) Divine decor and prime location

★ **Molino la Farraga** (p394) A tranquil old mill in Cazorla, with a paradisiacal, lush garden

horseshoe arches and star-shaped skylights lending them an intimate, relaxed atmosphere. After the Reconquista, the Christians, suspicious of what they considered to be a decadent and vice-inducing habit (that also nurtured the Muslim faith), converted the baths into a tannery. The baths then disappeared altogether during the 16th century when the Conde (Count) de Villardompardo built a palace over the site, and were only rediscovered in 1913.

Emerging from the baths, the route takes you through the palace's numerous salons, which are divided into different exhibits of the **Museo de Artes y Costumbres Populares** (Museum of Popular Art & Customs), a wonderfully comprehensive collection that demonstrates every aspect of the Andalusian home. The **Museo Internacional de Arte Naïf**

(International Museum of Naïve Art) has the work and art collection of the museum's founder, Manuel Moral, a native of Jaén province, complementing the folk exhibits of the Museo de Artes y Costumbres Populares.

🌱 **CASTILLO DE SANTA CATALINA //**
CLIMB UP AND EXPLORE THE
CITY'S SILENT GUARD
Watching the city from atop the cliff-girt Cerro de Santa Catalina is the former Islamic fortress **Castillo de Santa Catalina** (☎ 953 12 07 33; admission €3; ☺ 10am-2pm & 5-9pm Tue-Sun Apr-Sep, 10am-2pm & 3.30-7pm Tue-Sun Oct-Mar), where audiovisual gimmicks (in Spanish only) explain each point of interest of the keep, the chapel and the dungeon. Past the castle at the end of the ridge stands a large **cross**, from where there are magnificent views over the city and the olive groves beyond.

If you don't have a vehicle for the circuitous 4km drive up from the city centre, you can take a taxi (€6). You can also walk (about 40 minutes from the city centre) by heading uphill from the cathedral to join Calle de Buenavista. Go up the right-hand branch before crossing over onto the Carretera de Circunvalación; a short distance along to the right, take the path that heads off steeply uphill to the left.

FESTIVALS & EVENTS

Semana Santa (Holy Week) The week leading up to Easter Sunday is celebrated in a big way, with processions through the old city by members of 13 *cofradías* (brotherhoods).

Feria y Fiestas de San Lucas This is Jaén's biggest party, with concerts, funfairs, bullfights and general merrymaking in the eight days leading up to the saint's day on 18 October.

GASTRONOMIC HIGHLIGHTS

Some of Andalucía's quirkiest tapas bars are here, and the *jiennenses* cherish and preserve them.

ESSENTIAL OIL

In Jaén, the *aceituna* (olive) rules. The pungent smell of *aceite de oliva* (olive oil) perfumes memories of Jaén. Jaén's olive statistics are pretty staggering: over 40 million olive trees stud a third of the province – more than 4500 sq km. In an average year these trees produce 900,000 tonnes of olives, most of which are turned into some 200,000 tonnes of olive oil – meaning that Jaén provides about half of Andalucía's olive oil, one-third of Spain's and 10% of that used in the entire world.

The olives are harvested from late November to January. Despite some mechanisation, much is still done traditionally – by spreading nets beneath the trees, then beating the branches with sticks. The majority of Jaén's (and Andalucía's) olive groves are owned by a handful of large landowners. The dominance of this one crop in the province's economy means that unemployment in Jaén rises from 10% during the harvest to around 45% in summer. An olive picker earns about €30 a day.

Once harvested, olives are taken to oil mills to be mashed into a pulp that is then pressed and filtered. Oil that is considered good enough for immediate consumption is sold as *aceite de oliva virgen* (virgin olive oil), the finest grade, and the best of the best is *virgen extra*. *Aceite de oliva refinado* (refined olive oil) is made from oil that's not quite so good, and plain *aceite de oliva* is a blend of refined and virgin oils. Specialist shops in Jaén, Baeza and Úbeda sell quality oil.

♥ CASA VICENTE €€€

☎ 953 23 28 16; Calle Francisco Martín Mora; menú €32

Located in a restored mansion with a patio, Casa Vicente is one of the best restaurants in town. It has a great bar where you can take a tipple with tapas, or you can sit down in the patio or interior dining room (the best option in winter) to enjoy specialities such as the *cordero mozárabe* (lamb with honey and spices).

♥ EL GORRIÓN €

☎ 953 23 22 00; Calle Arco del Consuelo 7; tapas from €1.50

Lazy jazz plays on the stereo, old newspaper cuttings are glued to the walls, and paintings of bizarre landscapes hang lopsidedly next to oval oak barrels. It feels as though local punters have been propping up the bar for centuries (or at least since 1888, when it opened). The tapas are simple and traditional, and are best enjoyed with the sherry and wine on offer.

♥ TABERNA LA MANCHEGA €€

☎ 953 23 21 92; Calle Bernardo López 12; platos combinados €4-11; ☷ 10am-5pm & 8pm-1am Wed-Mon

This place has been in action since the 1880s and apart from eating great, simple tapas here, you can drink wine and watch local characters devour hot potatoes. La Manchega has entrances on both Calle Arco del Consuelo and Calle Bernardo López.

TRANSPORT

BUS // From the bus station (☎ 953 25 01 06; Plaza de Coca de la Piñera), **Alsina Graells** (www.alsa.es) runs buses to Granada, Baeza, Úbeda and Cazorla. The Ureña line travels up to Córdoba and Seville. Other buses head for Málaga and Almería.

CAR // Driving in Jaén can be mighty stressful due to the one-way road system and the weight of traffic. Jaén is 92km north of Granada taking the fast A44. This road continues on to Bailén, where it meets the Córdoba–

Madrid A4. To get to or from Córdoba, take the A306 via Porcuna.

PARKING // If you end up in the centre, there is underground parking at Plaza de la Constitución and at Parking San Francisco, off Calle de Bernabé Soriano, near the cathedral. Costs are €1 per hour or €15 for 24 hours.

TRAIN // Jaén's **train station** (☎ 953 27 02 02; www.renfe.com; Paseo de la Estación) is at the end of a branch line and there are only five departures most days. A train leaves at 8am for Córdoba and Seville. There are also trains to Madrid.

NORTH OF JAÉN

· · · · · ·

The A4 north out of Andalucía to Madrid passes through indifferent countryside to the north of Jaén until the hills of the Sierra Morena appear on the horizon. Ahead lies the Desfiladero de Despeñaperros (Pass of the Overthrow of the Dogs), so named because the Christian victors of the 1212 battle at nearby Las Navas de Tolosa are said to have tossed many of their Muslim enemies from the cliffs.

The full drama of the pass is not appreciated until the last minute, when the road from the south descends suddenly and swoops between rocky towers and wooded slopes to slice through tunnels and defiles.

PARQUE NATURAL DESPEÑAPERROS & SANTA ELENA

Road and rail have robbed the Desfiladero de Despeñaperros of much of its historic romance, but the splendid hill country to either side is one of Spain's most beautiful and remote areas. Clothed with dense woods of pine, holm oak

JAÉN PROVINCE

and cork trees from which protrude dramatic cliffs and pinnacles of fluted rock, the area around the pass is now a natural park, home to deer and wild boar, and maybe the occasional wolf and lynx. There are no local buses, so you need your own transport to get the most out of the area. The main visitor centre is the **Centro de Visitantes Puerta de Andalucía** (☎ 953 66 43 07; Carretera Santa Elena a Miranda del Rey; ☉ 10am-2pm & 4-8pm Apr-Sep, 10am-2pm & 3-7pm Oct-Mar) on the outskirts of Santa Elena, the small town just south of the pass. The centre has information and maps on walking routes in the area. You can also contact a park guide directly (☎ 610 28 25 31).

Santa Elena is an ideal base for exploring the park, and has shops, bars and cafes. Several buses from Jaén run on weekdays to La Carolina, from where **La**

Sepulvedana (☎ 953 66 03 35) runs about four or five buses to Santa Elena, weekdays only. It's best to check the current schedules.

EAST OF JAÉN

· · · · · ·

This part of the region is where most visitors spend their time, drawn in by the allure of Baeza and Úbeda and their Renaissance architecture, and the leafy hills and hiking trails of Cazorla.

BAEZA

pop 15,000 / elevation 790m

If the Jaén region is known for anything (apart from olives) it's the twin towns of Baeza (ba-*eh*-thah) and Úbeda, two shining examples of Renaissance beauty.

~ WORTH A TRIP ~

Thirty-one kilometres north of Andújar on the J-5010 is the 13th-century **Santuario de la Virgen de la Cabeza**. It is tucked away in the secluded **Parque Natural Sierra de Andújar**, and is home to one of Spain's biggest religious events, the Romería de la Virgen de la Cabeza. The original shrine was destroyed during the civil war, when it was seized by 200 pro-Franco troops. The shrine was only 'liberated' in May 1937 after eight months of determined Republican bombardment.

On the last Sunday in April nearly half a million people converge to witness a small statue of the Virgin Mary – known as La Morenita (The Little Brown One) – being carried around the Cerro del Cabezo for about four hours from around 11am. It's a festive, emotive occasion: children and items of clothing are passed over the crowd to priests who touch them to the Virgin's mantle.

The park is said to have the largest expanse of natural vegetation in the Sierra Morena. Full of evergreen and gall oaks, the park is home to plenty of bull-breeding ranches, a few wolves, lynx and boars, plus deer, mouflon and various birds of prey. Information is available from the **Centro de Visitantes** (Visitor Centre; ☎ 953 54 90 30), at Km12 on the road from Andújar to the Santuario de la Virgen de la Cabeza, and from Andújar's **tourist office** (☎ 953 50 49 59; Plaza de Santa María; ☉ 8am-2pm Tue-Sat Jul-Sep, 10am-2pm & 5-8pm Tue-Sat Oct-Jun).

Buses run daily from Jaén to Andújar (€4, four daily) and there are buses from Andújar to the sanctuary on Saturday and Sunday.

Smaller Baeza makes a good day trip from Úbeda, some 9km away. It has a richness of architecture that defies the notion that there is little of architectural interest in Andalucía apart from structures from the Islamic period. Here, a handful of wealthy, fractious families left a staggering catalogue of perfectly preserved Renaissance churches and civic buildings.

Baeza was one of the first Andalusian towns to fall to the Christians (in 1227), and little is left of its Muslim heritage after so many years of Castilian influence.

ESSENTIAL INFORMATION

TOURIST OFFICE // Tourist office (☎ 953 74 04 44; otbaeza@andalucia.org; Plaza del Pópulo; ◔ 9am-6pm Mon-Fri, 10am-1pm & 4-6pm Sat Oct-Mar, 9am-7pm Mon-Fri, 10am-1pm & 5-7pm Sat Apr-Sep, 10am-1pm Sun year-round) In a beautiful 16th-century courthouse on Plaza del Pópulo, just southwest of Paseo de la Constitución; has plenty of useful information.

ORIENTATION

The heart of town is Plaza de España, with the long, wide Paseo de la Constitución stretching to its southwest.

The bus station is about 700m northeast of Plaza de España on a street officially called Avenida Alcalde Puche Pardo, though it is more commonly known as Paseo Arco del Agua.

EXPLORING BAEZA

Baeza's sights cluster around the central Plaza de España and Paseo de la Constitución. You can take them all in during a leisurely day's stroll. The opening hours of some of the buildings are unpredictable, so check at the tourist office first.

❧ PASEO DE LA CONSTITUCIÓN & AROUND // ADMIRE SAND-COLOURED CHURCHES AND HUGE MANSION PALACES

The small Plaza de España is the centre of the town and merges with the sprawling, cafe-lined Paseo de la Constitución, once Baeza's marketplace and bullring. The lonely Torre de los Aliatares (Tower of the Aliatares; Plaza de España) is one of the few remnants of Muslim Bayyasa (as the town was called by the Muslims), having miraculously survived the destructive Isabel la Católica's 1476 order to demolish the town's fortifications. The order was meant to end the feud between the Benavide and Carvajal noble families.

On Plaza del Pópulo is the old entrance to the city, the Puerta de Jaén (Jaén Gate), connected to the huge Arco de Villalar (Villalar Arch). The arch was erected by Carlos I in 1526 to commemorate the crushing of a serious insurrection in Castilla that had threatened to overthrow his throne. It dominates Plaza del Pópulo, also called Plaza de los Leones after the Fuente de los Leones (Fountain of the Lions) at its centre. The fountain is made of carvings from the Iberian and Roman village of Cástulo and is topped by a statue reputed to represent Imilce, an Iberian princess and the wife of the notorious Carthaginian general Hannibal. On the southern side of the square is the lovely 16th-century Casa del Pópulo, formerly a courthouse and now Baeza's tourist office. It was built in the plateresque style, an early phase of Renaissance architecture noted for its decorative facades.

On the eastern side of the square stands the Antigua Carnicería (Old Butchery), a beautiful building that must rank as the one of the most elegant tanning sheds in the world.

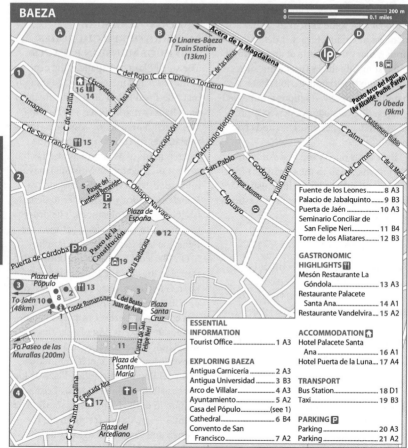

BAEZA

0 — 200 m
0 — 0.1 miles

ESSENTIAL INFORMATION
Tourist Office 1 A3

EXPLORING BAEZA
Antigua Carnicería 2 A3
Antigua Universidad 3 B3
Arco de Villalar...................... 4 A3
Ayuntamiento 5 A2
Casa del Pópulo...................(see 1)
Cathedral................................ 6 B4
Convento de San
Francisco................................ 7 A2
Fuente de los Leones............ 8 A3
Palacio de Jabalquinto......... 9 B3
Puerta de Jaén 10 A3
Seminario Conciliar de
San Felipe Neri.................. 11 B4
Torre de los Aliatares........... 12 B3

GASTRONOMIC HIGHLIGHTS
Mesón Restaurante La
Góndola............................... 13 A3
Restaurante Palacete
Santa Ana............................ 14 A1
Restaurante Vandelvira.... 15 A2

ACCOMMODATION
Hotel Palacete Santa
Ana 16 A1
Hotel Puerta de la Luna.... 17 A4

TRANSPORT
Bus Station............................ 18 D1
Taxi.. 19 B3

PARKING
Parking 20 A3
Parking 21 A2

Through the Puerta de Jaén and along to the Paseo de las Murallas, a path loops around the old city walls to a point near the cathedral. From here, Baeza's fantastic position on the escarpment can be easily appreciated.

♥ CATHEDRAL // A CASTILIAN BEAUTY AND A PATCHWORK OF STYLES

As was the case in much of Andalucía, the Reconquista destroyed the mosque and in its place built Baeza's **cathedral** (Plaza de Santa María; admission free, donations welcome; ⏰ 10.30am-1pm & 4-6pm Oct-Mar, 10.30am-1pm & 5-7pm Apr-Sep). This was the first step towards the town's transformation into a Castilian gem. The cathedral itself is an aesthetic hotchpotch, although the overall style is 16th-century Renaissance, clearly visible in the **main facade** on Plaza Santa María. The cathedral's oldest feature is the 13th-century Gothic-Mudéjar **Puerta de la Luna** (Moon Doorway) at its western end, which is topped by a 14th-century rose window.

The Cathedral is on Plaza de Santa María, the most typical of all the town's squares, this plaza was designed to be a focus of religious and civic life, and is surrounded by mansions and churches, such as the Seminario Conciliar de San Felipe Neri on the square's northern side, a seminary that now houses the Universidad Internacional de Andalucía.

❧ PLAZA SANTA CRUZ // VISIT A STUNNING PALACE AND ONCE-REVOLUTIONARY SCHOOL

Baeza's most extraordinary palace, the Palacio de Jabalquinto (Plaza Santa Cruz; admission free; ☽ 9am-2pm Mon-Fri), was probably built in the early 16th century for one of the Benavides clan. It has a spectacularly flamboyant facade typical of Isabelline Gothic style, and a patio with Renaissance marble columns, two-tiered arches and an elegant fountain. A fantastically carved baroque stairway ascends from one side.

Next door to the Jabalquinto is Baeza's Antigua Universidad (Old University; ☎ 953 74 01 54; Calle del Beato Juan de Ávila; admission free; ☽ 10am-1pm & 4-6pm Thu-Tue). It was founded in 1538 and became a fount of progressive ideas that generally conflicted with Baeza's conservative dominant families, often causing scuffles between the high-brows and the well-heeled. It closed in 1824, and since 1875 the building has housed an *instituto de bachillerato* (high school). The main patio, with its elegant Renaissance arches, is open to the public, as is the classroom of poet Antonio Machado (see p360), who taught French at the high school from 1912 to 1919.

❧ NORTH OF PASEO DE LA CONSTITUCIÓN // SEE THE DIFFERENCE BETWEEN THE ORIGINAL AND RESTORED

A block north of the Paseo de la Constitución is the ayuntamiento (☎ 953 74 01 54; Pasaje del Cardenal Benavides 9), with a marvellous plateresque facade. The four finely carved balcony portals on the upper storey are separated by the coats of arms of the town, Felipe II (in the middle) and the magistrate Juan de Borja, who had the place built. The building was originally a courthouse and prison (entered by the right- and left-hand doors respectively).

A short walk from the *ayuntamiento* is the ruined (and controversially restored, its quality deemed inferior to the original) Convento de San Francisco (Calle de San Francisco). One of Andrés de Vandelvira's masterpieces, it was conceived as the funerary chapel of the Benavides family. Devastated by an earthquake and sacked by French troops in the early 19th century, it is now partly restored and converted into a hotel, banquet hall and restaurant. At the eastern end, a striking arrangement of curved girders traces the outline of its dome over a space adorned with Renaissance carvings. The cloister, occupied by the Restaurante Vandelvira, is worth a look, too.

TOP FIVE

RENAISSANCE STRUCTURES

★ **Jaén Cathedral** (p221) – a dominant temple that dwarfs the province's capital

★ **Baeza Cathedral** (p232) – a 16th-century Castilian gem

★ **Palacio de Jabalquinto** (p233) – a mix of Gothic and Renaissance in Baeza's most stunning palace

★ **Capilla del Salvador del Mundo** (p236) – pure, unadulterated Renaissance architecture

★ **Hospital de Santiago** (p237) – the beginning of baroque

FESTIVALS & EVENTS

Semana Santa (Holy Week) A typically big, raucous celebration complete with devotional processions. Held in the week before Easter Sunday.

Feria Held in mid-August, this is a Castilian carnival procession of *gigantones* (papier-mâché giants), along with fireworks and a huge funfair.

GASTRONOMIC HIGHLIGHTS

Baeza is good if you want to eat in elegant restaurants. However, it's sadly rather short on good tapas bars. The tourist office can give you a small booklet (in Spanish only) detailing a tapas trail, but they may not be as great as in other towns.

❤ MESÓN RESTAURANTE LA GÓNDOLA €€

☎ 953 74 29 84; Portales Carbonería 13, Paseo de la Constitución; mains €10-17

A terrific local, atmospheric restaurant, helped along by the glowing, wood-burning grill behind the bar, cheerful service and good food. Try *patatas baezanas,* a vegetarian delight that mixes a huge helping of sautéed potatoes with mushrooms.

❤ RESTAURANTE PALACETE SANTA ANA €€€

☎ 953 74 16 57; Calle Escopeteros 12; menú/mains €17/25

This large restaurant and bar complex occupies several floors and serves up regional specialities that are usually complemented by the local olive oil. Reservations required.

❤ RESTAURANTE VANDELVIRA €€

☎ 953 74 81 72; Calle de San Francisco 14; mains €9-18; ⏱ closed Sun night & Mon

Inside the restored Convento de San Francisco, this is a classy, friendly res-

taurant. If you want to spoil yourself you might try the partridge pâté salad or the *solomillo al carbón* (chargrilled steak).

TRANSPORT

BUS // From the **bus station** (☎ 953 74 04 68; Paseo Arco del Agua), **Alsina Graells** (www.alsa.es) runs 11 daily buses to Jaén, 15 to Úbeda and five to Granada. There are also buses to Cazorla, Córdoba, Seville and Madrid.

PARKING // Parking in Baeza is fairly restricted, but there are parking spots around the Paseo de la Constitución and in Pasaje del Cardenal Benavides.

TRAIN // The nearest train station is **Linares-Baeza** (☎ 953 65 02 02), 13km northwest of town, where a few trains a day leave for Granada, Córdoba, Seville, Málaga, Cádiz, Almería, Madrid and Barcelona. Buses connect with most trains from Monday to Saturday.

TAXI // Taxis wait for fares in Paseo de la Constitución. A taxi to the train station costs €14.

ÚBEDA

pop 33,000 / elevation 760m

Úbeda (*oo*-be-dah) is a slightly different proposition to its little sister, Baeza. Aside from the splendour of its architecture, the town has good tapas bars and restaurants, crazy old junk shops, gorgeous antique shops and pottery outlets along the narrow streets.

Úbeda became a Castilian bulwark on the inexorable Christian march south. As Fernando III reclaimed and reconquered Muslim Andalucía, aristocratic families such as the Molinas, de la Cuevas and Cobos benefited and were rewarded with huge estates. Their ownership moulded the character of the province and still endures today.

ESSENTIAL INFORMATION

EMERGENCIES // **Policía Municipal** (☎ 953 75 00 23; Plaza de Andalucía) In the busy centre. **Policía Nacional** (☎ 953 75 03 55; Plaza Vázquez de Molina) Occupies the Antiguo Pósito.

JAÉN PROVINCE

JAÉN PROVINCE

ÚBEDA

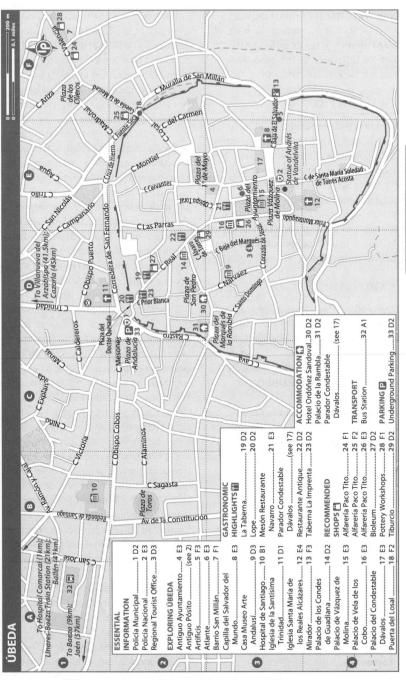

ESSENTIAL INFORMATION

Policía Municipal	1 D2
Policía Nacional	2 E3
Regional Tourist Office	3 D3

EXPLORING ÚBEDA

Antiguo Ayuntamiento	4 E3
Antiguo Pósito	(see 2)
Artificis	5 F3
Atlante	6 E3
Barrio San Millán	7 F1
Capilla del Salvador del Mundo	8 E3
Casa Museo Arte Andalusí	9 D3
Hospital de Santiago	10 B1
Iglesia de la Santísima Trinidad	11 D1
Iglesia Santa María de los Reales Alcázares	12 E4
Mirador	13 F3
Palacio de los Condes de Guadiana	14 D2
Palacio de Vázquez de Molina	15 D2
Palacio de Vela de los Cobo	16 E3
Palacio del Condestable Dávalos	17 E3
Puerta del Losal	18 F2

GASTRONOMIC HIGHLIGHTS

La Taberna	19 D2
Lope	20 D2
Mesón Restaurante Navarro	21 E3
Parador Condestable Dávalos	(see 17)
Restaurante Antique	22 D2
Taberna La Imprenta	23 D2

RECOMMENDED SHOPS

Alfarería Paco Tito	24 F1
Alfarería Paco Tito	25 F2
Alfarería Paco Tito	26 E3
Bioleum	27 E3
Pottery Workshops	28 F1
Tiburcio	29 D2

ACCOMMODATION

Hotel Ordóñez Sandoval	30 D2
Palacio de la Rambla	31 D2
Parador Condestable Dávalos	(see 17)

TRANSPORT

Bus Station	32 A1

PARKING

Underground Parking	33 D2

TOURIST OFFICE // Regional tourist office (☎ 953 75 08 97; otubeda@andalucia.org; Calle Baja del Marqués 4; ☺ 9am-2.45pm & 4-7pm Mon-Fri, 10am-2pm Sat) Located in the 18th-century Palacio Marqués de Contadero, in the old quarter.

ORIENTATION

Most of Úbeda's splendid buildings – the main reason for visiting the town – are in the southeast of the town, among the maze of narrow, winding streets and expansive squares that constitute the *casco antiguo* (old quarter). The bus station is about 600m away, in the drab new town to the west and north. Plaza de Andalucía marks the boundary between the two parts of town.

EXPLORING ÚBEDA

Nearly all of Úbeda's main sights are located within the *casco antiguo,* which can be thoroughly explored in a day or two.

❧ PLAZA VÁZQUEZ DE MOLINA // SEE THE LEGACY OF ÚBEDA'S ARISTOCRACY

Following the success of the Reconquista, Úbeda's aristocratic lions lost no time jockeying for power in the Castilian court. In the 16th century, Francisco de los Cobos y Molina secured the post of privy secretary to King Carlos I and was later succeeded by his nephew Juan Vázquez de Molina. Exposed to the cultural influences of the Italian Renaissance that were then seeping into Spain, and benefiting from the wealth and privilege of high office, the Molina family turned their attention to self-aggrandising civic projects in its home town. They commissioned what are now considered to be some of the purest examples of Renaissance architecture in Spain.

The purity of Renaissance lines is best expressed in the **Capilla del Salvador del Mundo** (☎ 953 75 81 50; adult/child €3/1, last hr free; ☺ 10am-2pm & 4.30-7pm), the first of many works executed in Úbeda by celebrated architect Andrés de Vandelvira (see boxed text, p238). A pre-eminent example of the plateresque style, the chapel's **main facade** is modelled on Diego de Siloé's Puerta del Perdón at Granada's cathedral. The classic portal is topped by a carving of the transfiguration of Christ, flanked by statues of St Peter and St Paul. The underside of the arch is an orgy of classical sculpture, executed by French sculptor Esteban Jamete, depicting the Greek gods – a Renaissance touch that would have been inconceivable a few decades earlier. Viewed at night, the whole facade leaps out in dynamic 3-D.

The church is still privately owned by the Seville-based ducal Medinaceli family, descendants of the Cobos (original owners), and one of Andalucía's major landowning families.

In fact, the whole beautifully proportioned plaza (180m long) was the Cobos family precinct. Next door to the *capilla* (chapel) stands the **Palacio del Condestable Dávalos**. Partly remodelled in the 17th century, the mansion is now Úbeda's luxurious parador. To the west the huge **Palacio de Vázquez de Molina** (☎ 953 75 04 40; ☺ 10am-2pm & 5-9pm), now Úbeda's *ayuntamiento,* was built by Vandelvira for Juan (Francisco's nephew and successor to the post of privy secretary), whose coat of arms surmounts the doorway.

Facing the Palacio de Vázquez de Molina is the site of Úbeda's old mosque, now the location of the **Iglesia Santa María de los Reales Alcázares**.

East of the square, 150m along Baja de El Salvador, a **mirador** (lookout) gives fine views across the olive fields, overshadowed by the snowcapped Cazorla mountains in the distance.

🌱 NORTH OF PLAZA DE VÁZQUEZ DE MOLINA // WANDER AROUND ELEGANT SQUARES AND GAZE AT GORGEOUS PALACES

A warren of winding streets north of Úbeda's main plaza gives way to a series of elegant squares. The first of these is the broad Plaza del Ayuntamiento, watched over from its northwestern corner by the Palacio de Vela de los Cobo (admission free). This palace can be visited by prior arrangement with the tourist office.

Another of the town's best mansions is the 17th-century Palacio de los Condes de Guadiana, three blocks up Calle Real (once Úbeda's main commercial street), with some elegant carving around the windows and balconies. For an insight into a typical *palacio* visit Casa Museo Arte Andalusí (☎ 619 07 61 32; Calle Narvaez 11; admission €1.50; ⏰ 11am-2pm & 5-8pm, closed Jan & Feb), which is full of period antiques.

Northeast of the Plaza del Ayuntamiento is the even bigger Plaza del 1° (Primer) de Mayo, originally the town's market square and bullring. It was also the site of Inquisition burnings, which local worthies used to watch from the gallery of the Antiguo Ayuntamiento (Old Town Hall) in the southwestern corner.

🌱 BARRIO SAN MILLÁN // DISCOVER ÚBEDA'S FASCINATING POTTERY NEIGHBOURHOOD

Heading through the impressive Puerta de Losal takes you down into the Barrio San Millán, Úbeda's famous potters' quarter, with pottery workshops located on Calle Valencia. Pop in and see what they do and how they do it, and if luggage allows, purchase a piece or two.

🌱 HOSPITAL DE SANTIAGO // SEE VANDELVIRA'S LAST MAGNIFICENT CELEBRATION OF BAROQUE STYLE

Alternatively, if you turn left at the Puerta de Losal and walk down Calle Fuente Seca and then Calle Cruz de Hierro to link up with Corredera de San Fernando, past the unusual baroque Iglesia de la Santísima Trinidad (Corredera de San Fernando), you will eventually reach Vandelvira's last architectural project, the Hospital de Santiago (☎ 953 75 08 42; Calle Obispo Cobos; admission free; ⏰ 8am-3pm & 4-10pm Mon-Fri, 11am-3pm & 6-10pm Sat & Sun). Completed in 1575, it has often been dubbed the Escorial of Andalucía – a reference to a famous old monastery outside Madrid, which was a precursor to the kind of baroque architecture employed by Vandelvira. It now acts as Úbeda's cultural centre, housing a library, municipal dance school and an exhibition hall.

FESTIVALS & EVENTS

Semana Santa (Holy Week) Solemn brotherhoods, devotional processions and lots of atmospheric drama in the week leading up to Easter Sunday.
Festival Internacional de Música y Danza Ciudad de Úbeda Varied music and dance performances throughout the month of May.
Fiesta de San Miguel Celebrates the capture of the town in 1233 by Fernando III, with firework shows, parades, concerts, a flamenco festival, a bullfighting season and more. It's held from 27 September to 4 October.

GASTRONOMIC HIGHLIGHTS

Úbeda has some good places to eat. Start by sampling the tapas, which you get free with your drinks, then try one of the excellent nouvelle-cuisine restaurants.

🌱 LA TABERNA €
☎ 953 79 24 70; Calle Real 7; mains €6-10
Children run around screaming, their parents clink glasses and scoff tapas, bar

JAÉN PROVINCE

MASTER BUILDER

Most of what you see in Úbeda, Baeza and Jaén is the work of one man: Andrés de Vandelvira. Born in 1509 in Alcaraz (in Castilla-La Mancha), 150km northeast of Úbeda, Vandelvira almost single-handedly brought the Renaissance to Jaén province. Influenced by the pioneering Renaissance architect Diego de Siloé, Vandelvira designed numerous marvellous buildings and, astonishingly, his work spanned all three main phases of Spanish Renaissance architecture: the ornamental early Renaissance phase known as plateresque, as seen in the Capilla del Salvador del Mundo (p236); the much purer line and classic proportions, which emerged in the later Palacio de Vázquez de Molina (p236); and the austere late Renaissance style called Herreresque, as shown in his last building, the Hospital de Santiago (p237). With all these achievements, Vandelvira's was certainly a life well spent.

people sweat and work like crazy – a typical Spanish evening scene in this popular tapas bar. Order a drink, get your tapa, and join in. It's good for breakfasts too.

☙ LOPE €

Calle Real 1; cake from €1.20; 🕑 9.30am-8pm Mon-Fri, 10am-6pm Sat & Sun

This old-school cafe and cake shop is perfect for breakfasts and cake fixes. Try its *yemas* (soft, crumbly biscuit cakes), *bollos* (sweet buns stuffed with cream) and other sweets with a good *café con leche* (coffee with milk).

☙ MESÓN RESTAURANTE NAVARRO €€

☎ 953 79 06 38; Plaza del Ayuntamiento 2; raciones €4-12

Always crammed, smoky and noisy, the Navarro is a cherished local favourite. Eat your tapas at the bar, or in summer sit out on the sunny plaza. Note that the sign just says 'Mesón Restaurante'.

☙ PARADOR CONDESTABLE DÁVALOS €€€

☎ 953 75 03 45; Plaza Vázquez de Molina; mains €12-17, menú €25

This deservedly popular restaurant serves up delicious, elegant dishes. While a tad pricier than most, this is definitely *the* place to eat in Úbeda and even in the low season the dining room buzzes happily well into the evening. Try the local specialities: *carruécano* (green peppers stuffed with partridge) or *cabrito guisado con piñones* (stewed kid with pine nuts).

☙ RESTAURANTE ANTIQUE €€€

☎ 953 75 76 18; www.restauranteantique.com, in Spanish; Calle Real 25; tapas from €6, mains €12-26

A fantastic new place in town that plays on twisting traditional recipes with modern, high-quality cuisine – try their plum gazpacho or grilled red tuna with a broadbean mash and fish-egg foam. The restaurant is elegant, with simple, stylish decor.

☙ TABERNA LA IMPRENTA €€

☎ 650 37 50 00; Plaza del Doctor Quesada 1; mains €10-13

This wonderful old print shop, done stylishly and frequented by Úbeda's posh noshers, provides delicious free tapas with your drinks. You can also sit down and eat baked asparagus, excellent meat dishes, and creamy cheesecakes.

RECOMMENDED SHOPS

The main high-street style shopping streets are Calle Mesones and Calle Obispo Cobos, between Plaza de Andalucía and the Hospital de Santiago, with everything from ubiquitous international chains to independent local shops.

☙ ALFARERÍA PACO TITO

Calle Valencia 22, Calle Fuente Seca 17 & Plaza del Ayuntamiento 12

This is the largest pottery workshop in Barrio San Millán, selling plates, cups and gorgeous large bowls decorated with typical local patterns.

☙ BIOLEUM

Calle Real 17; ☺ 10am-2pm & 5-9pm

A great little shop where you can taste quality olive oil before buying. It also stocks a number of items for purchase – alimentary and cosmetic – made from olive oil. Take-home bottles cost between €3.50 and €20.

☙ TIBURCIO

☎ 679 34 68 00; Calle Álvaro de Torres 4; ☺ 11am-3pm & 5-8pm Sat & Sun

Take your time in this junk shop and be rewarded with real treasures, such as old coffee tins, tiles and ancient pictures, as well as old pots and bowls.

GOING POTTY

The typical emerald green glaze on Úbeda's attractive pottery remains from Islamic times. The potters' quarter still retains three original kilns from this period (there are only six left in the whole of Spain).

Several workshops sell pottery in Barrio San Millán, northeast of the old town, and the potters are often willing to explain some of the ancient techniques they use. These include adding olive stones to the fire to intensify the heat, which results in a more brilliant glaze.

TRANSPORT

BUS // The **bus station** (☎ 953 75 21 57; Calle San José 6) is located to the northwest in the new part of town. **Alsina Graells** (www.alsina.es) runs 15 buses to Baeza, Jaén, Cazorla and Granada. Bacoma goes to Córdoba and Seville. Other buses head to Málaga and Madrid.

PARKING // There is a convenient underground car park in Plaza de Andalucía (one hour €1.20, 12 hours €10).

TRAIN // The nearest station is **Linares-Baeza** (☎ 953 65 02 02; www.renfe.es), 21km northwest of town, which you can reach on Linares-bound buses. Trains depart from here daily for Granada, Córdoba, Seville, Málaga, Cádiz, Almería, Madrid and Barcelona.

CAZORLA

pop 8000 / elevation 836m

Huffing and puffing up the steep streets of this modern rural town is perfect for those who want to continue huffing and puffing in the Parque Natural Sierras de Cazorla, Segura y Las Villas, which begins dramatically amid the cliffs of Peña de los Halcones (Falcon Crag), towering above the town. From here, you can see the passive landscape of the plains, and the rugged swathe of mountains and valleys that unfolds enticingly to the north and east.

Cazorla becomes crowded during Spanish holiday times and on weekends from spring to autumn.

ESSENTIAL INFORMATION

EMERGENCIES // **Policía Local** (☎ 953 72 01 81) In the *ayuntamiento,* just off Plaza de la Corredera. **TOURIST OFFICE //** **Municipal tourist office** (☎ 953 71 01 02; Paseo del Santo Cristo 17; ☺ 10am-1pm & 5.30-8pm) Found 200m north of Plaza de la Constitución. It provides useful information on the park and town.

ORIENTATION

The A319 from the west winds up into Cazorla and is known as Calle Hilario

Marco. This road ends at Plaza de la Constitución, the often frantically busy main square of the newer part of town. The second important square is Plaza de la Corredera, 150m south of Plaza de la Constitución. Plaza de Santa María, 300m further southeast and reached along even more narrow, winding streets, is the heart of the oldest part of town, and stands directly below the castle and crags.

EXPLORING CAZORLA

❦ PLAZA DE LA CORREDERA & AROUND // EXPLORE PALACIOS AND CASTLES AMID FANTASTIC MOUNTAIN PEAKS

Here, as in the rest of Jaén province, local history has been shaped by the rich landowning classes, and the town's *palacios* used to (or still) belong to a few wealthy families. The central square, Plaza de la Corredera, is the civic centre of the town, and the elegant ayuntamiento dominates the square with its landmark clock tower.

Canyonlike streets radiate south of the plaza to the Balcón de Zabaleta. This little mirador (lookout) is like a sudden window in a blank wall – it has stunning views over the town and up to the Castillo de la Yedra (Castle of the Ivy). The dramatic castle is of Roman origin, though it was largely built by the Muslims, then restored in the 15th century after the Reconquista. Much money has been spent on a modern restoration, and the castle now houses the Museo del Alto Guadalquivir (Museum of the Upper Guadalquivir; non-EU/EU citizen €1.50/free; ✆ 3-8pm Tue, 9am-8pm Wed-Sat, 9am-3pm Sun & public holidays), a mishmash of art and local artefacts.

The shortest way up to the castle is from the attractive Plaza de Santa María, starting along the street to the right of the ruined Iglesia de Santa María. The devastated – and now being restored – church was built by Vandelvira and was wrecked by Napoleonic troops in reprisal for Cazorla's tenacious resistance. It is now used for occasional open-air concerts.

FESTIVALS & EVENTS

La Caracolá The image of Cazorla's patron saint, San Isicio (a Christian apostle supposedly stoned to death at Cazorla in Roman times) gets carried from the Ermita de San Isicio to the Iglesia de San José on 14 May.

Fiesta de Cristo del Consuelo Fireworks and fairgrounds mark Cazorla's annual fiesta, celebrated between 17 and 21 September.

GASTRONOMIC HIGHLIGHTS

There are good bars on Cazorla's three main squares, where you can choose tapas and *raciones* (meal-sized tapas).

❦ BAR LAS VEGAS €
Plaza de la Corredera 17; raciones €6

The best of Cazorla's bars. You can try tasty prawn-and-capsicum *revuelto* (scrambled eggs), as well as the town's best breakfast *tostadas* (toasted bread with toppings).

❦ LA CUEVA DE JUAN PEDRO €€
Plaza de Santa María; raciones €9, menú €10-12

An ancient, wood-beamed place with dangling *jamones* and clumps of garlic and drying peppers. Taste the traditional Cazorla *conejo* (rabbit), *trucha* (trout), *rin-rán* (a mix of salted cod, potato and

FOOD TIP

In late summer or autumn, locals disappear into the woods after rain to gather large, delicious, edible mushrooms that they call *níscalos*. If these appear in your restaurant, be sure to get your share.

dried red peppers), *jabalí* (wild boar), *venado* (venison) and even mouflon. The *menú* includes rabbit in vinaigrette.

TRANSPORT

BUS // Alsina Graells (www.alsa.es) runs buses to/from Úbeda, Jaén and Granada. The main stop in Cazorla is Plaza de la Constitución; the tourist office has timetable information. A few buses run from Cazorla to Coto Ríos in the park. It makes stops at Arroyo Frío and Torre del Vinagre.

PARKING // There is a convenient car park in Plaza del Mercado, located below Plaza de la Constitución.

PARQUE NATURAL SIERRAS DE CAZORLA, SEGURA Y LAS VILLAS

One of the biggest drawcards in the whole of Jaén province is the lushly wooded, 2143-sq-km Parque Natural Sierras de Cazorla, Segura y Las Villas. It is the largest protected area in Spain, and its corrugated, craggy mountain ranges are memorably beautiful, as is the huge, snaking 20km reservoir in its midst. This is also the origin of the Río Guadalquivir, Andalucía's longest river, which

JAÉN PROVINCE

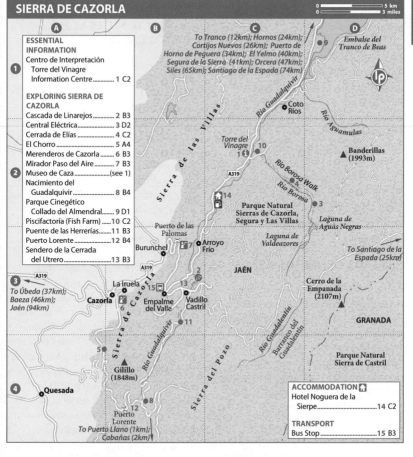

SIERRA DE CAZORLA

0 —— 5 km
0 —— 3 miles

ESSENTIAL INFORMATION
Centro de Interpretación Torre del Vinagre Information Centre............. 1 C2

EXPLORING SIERRA DE CAZORLA
Cascada de Linarejos............. 2 B3
Central Eléctrica...................... 3 D2
Cerrada de Elías 4 C2
El Chorro.................................. 5 A4
Merenderos de Cazorla 6 B3
Mirador Paso del Aire 7 B3
Museo de Caza...................(see 1)
Nacimiento del Guadalquivir............................ 8 B4
Parque Cinegético Collado del Almendral....... 9 D1
Piscifactoría (Fish Farm) 10 C2
Puente de las Herrerías........11 B3
Puerto Lorente.......................12 B4
Sendero de la Cerrada del Utrero............................13 B3

To Tranco (12km); Hornos (24km); Cortijos Nuevos (26km); Puerto de Horno de Peguera (34km); El Yelmo (40km); Segura de la Sierra (41km); Orcera (47km); Siles (65km); Santiago de la Espada (74km)

Embalse del Tranco de Beas

Coto Ríos

Río Guadalquivir

Río Aguamulas

Torre del Vinagre

Río Borosa Walk

Banderillas (1993m)

Sierra de las Villas

A319

Río Borosa

Parque Natural Sierras de Cazorla, Segura y Las Villas

Laguna de Aguas Negras

Puerto de las Palomas

Laguna de Valdeazores

To Santiago de la Espada (25km)

Burunchel

Arroyo Frío

JAÉN

A319

Sierra de Cazorla

La Iruela

Cazorla

Empalme del Valle

Vadillo Castril

Cerro de la Empanada (2107m)

To Úbeda (37km); Baeza (46km); Jaén (94km)

GRANADA

Río Guadalquivir

Río Guadalentín

Barranco del Guadalentín

Gilillo (1848m)

Sierra del Pozo

Parque Natural Sierra de Castril

Quesada

Puerto Lorente

To Puerto Llano (1km); Cabañas (2km)

ACCOMMODATION
Hotel Noguera de la Sierpe................................14 C2

TRANSPORT
Bus Stop...............................15 B3

rises between the Sierra de Cazorla and Sierra del Pozo in the south of the park and flows northwards into the reservoir, before heading west towards the Atlantic Ocean.

The best times to visit the park are in the shoulder seasons of spring and autumn, when the vegetation is at its most colourful and the temperatures are mild. In winter the park is often blanketed in snow. When walking, be sure to equip yourself properly, with enough water and appropriate clothes. Temperatures up in the hills are generally several degrees lower than down in the valleys, and the wind can be cutting at any time.

Exploring the park is a lot easier if you have a vehicle, but some bus services exist and there are plenty of places to stay inside the park. If you don't have a vehicle to get to the more remote regions, you do have the option of taking guided excursions to those areas.

The park is hugely popular with Spanish tourists and attracts an estimated 600,000 visitors a year – some 50,000 of those coming during Semana Santa. The other peak periods are July and August, and weekends from April to October.

ESSENTIAL INFORMATION

TOURIST OFFICE // The main park information centre, the **Centro de Interpretación Torre del Vinagre** (☎ 953 71 30 40; Carretera del Tranco Km51; ⊠ 11am-2pm & 5-8pm Apr-Sep, 11am-2pm & 4-7pm Oct-Mar), is at Torre del Vinagre. It has a rather dry display on the park's ecology. The centre also has the park's only easily accessible public toilets. There are seasonal tourist offices at Cortijos Nuevos, Hornos, Segura de la Sierra, Orcera, Siles and Santiago de la Espada.

PARK MAPS

The best maps of the region are Editorial Alpina's 1:40,000 *Sierra de Cazorla,* covering the southern third of the park and *Sierra de Segura,* covering the northern two-thirds. Quercus produces an excellent driving map (1:100,000), *Parque Natural de las Sierras de Cazorla, Segura y Las Villas,* showing all the park's points of interest. The *Sierra de Cazorla* map produced by El Olivo is available in English and is sold in the reception of Villa Turística in Cazorla.

EXPLORING PARQUE NATURAL SIERRAS DE CAZORLA, SEGURA Y LAS VILLAS

❧ THE SOUTH OF THE PARK //
THE MOST POPULAR AND EASILY ACCESSIBLE AREA
The park begins just a few hundred metres up the hill east of Cazorla town. The footpaths and dirt roads working their way between the pine forests, meadowlands, crags and valleys of the park's mountains offer plenty of scope for day walks or drives, with fine panoramas. The park's abrupt geography, rising to 2107m at the summit of the **Cerro de la Empanada**, and descending to 460m, makes for rapid and dramatic changes in landscape.

The A319, east from Cazorla, doesn't enter the park until Burunchel, 7km from Cazorla. From Burunchel it winds 5km up to the 1200m Puerto de las Palomas, with the breezy **Mirador Paso del Aire** a little further on. Five twisting kilometres downhill from here is Empalme del Valle, a junction where the A319 turns north towards the park's first major centre, **Arroyo Frío**. From here the road follows the north-flowing Río Guadalquivir.

An interesting detour from Empalme del Valle will take you to the river's source (Nacimento del Guadalquivir). From here you can continue a further 8km south to Cabañas, which at 2028m is one of the highest peaks in the park.

Further good walks in the south of the park are to be had in the Sierra del Pozo, which rises above the eastern side of the upper Guadalquivir Valley, and in the Barranco del Guadalentín, a deep river valley further east. The latter is particularly rich in wildlife, but you need your own vehicle, or a guide with one, to reach these areas.

Continuing along the A319 from Arroyo Frío, the road continues down the Guadalquivir Valley to Torre del Vinagre, where you will find the park's Centro de Interpretación Torre del Vinagre (Information Centre). Beyond Torre del Vinagre is Coto Ríos and the beginning of the Embalse del Tranco de Beas. The bus from Cazorla only goes this far and to explore the park further you will need your own transport.

🌱 THE NORTH OF THE PARK //
DISCOVER A GAME PARK AND
SUPERB PANORAMIC VIEWS
From Coto Ríos the road follows the western edge of the huge, wide reservoir, with tantalising glimpses of the water through the trees. Just 7km north of

DISCOVER THE PARK'S BEST LOVED WALK

The most popular walk in the Parque Natural Sierras de Cazorla, Segura y Las Villas follows the Río Borosa upstream. It goes through scenery that progresses from the pretty to the majestic, via a gorge and two tunnels (a torch is useful) to two beautiful mountain lakes – an ascent of 500m. This a 24km, seven-hour walk (return, not counting stops).

A road signed 'Central Eléctrica', east of the A319 opposite the Centro de Interpretación Torre del Vinagre, crosses the Guadalquivir after about 500m. Within 1km of the river, the road reaches a piscifactoría (fish farm), with parking areas close by. The marked start of the walk is on your right, shortly past the fish farm.

The first section is an unpaved road crisscrossing the tumbling, trout-rich river over bridges. After about 4km, where the road starts climbing to the left, take a path forking right. This takes you through a beautiful 1.5km section where the valley narrows to a gorge, Cerrada de Elías, and the path changes to a wooden walkway. You re-emerge on the dirt road and continue for 3km to the Central Eléctrica, a small hydroelectric station.

The path passes between the power station and the river, and crosses a footbridge, where a 'Nacimiento de Aguas Negras, Laguna de Valdeazores' sign directs you ahead. About 1.5km from the station, the path turns left and zigzags up into a tunnel cut into the cliff. This tunnel allows water to flow to the power station. A narrow path, separated from the watercourse by a fence, runs through the tunnel, which takes about five minutes to walk through. There's a short section in the open air before you enter a second tunnel, which takes about one minute to get through. You emerge just below the dam of Laguna de Aguas Negras, a picturesque little reservoir surrounded by hills and trees. Cross the dam to the other side of the lake then walk about 1km south to reach a similar-sized natural lake, the Laguna de Valdeazores.

You can do this walk as a day trip from Cazorla if you take the bus to Torre del Vinagre. Be sure to carry plenty of water with you.

Coto Ríos, on a spur of land between the A319 and the reservoir, you will find the **Parque Cinegético Collado del Almendral**, a large enclosed game park where ibex, mouflon and deer are kept. A 1km footpath leads from the parking area to three miradors where you might see animals – your chances are best at dawn and dusk. Fifteen kilometres further north, the A319 crosses the dam that holds back the reservoir near the small village of Tranco.

Twelve kilometres north of the dam at Tranco, the A319 runs into a T-junction from which the A317 winds 4km up to Hornos, a village atop a high rock out-crop with panoramic views. About 10km northeast of Hornos on the A317 is the **Puerto de Horno de Peguera** junction. One kilometre up the road to the north (towards Siles), a dirt road turns left at some ruined houses to the top of **El Yelmo** (1809m), one of the most distinctive mountains in the northern part of the park. It's 5km to the top – an ascent of 360m. At a fork after 1.75km, go right (the left fork goes down to El Robledo and Cortijos Nuevos). The climb affords superb long-distance views and gliding griffon vultures. The road is OK for cars, if narrow, but this is also a good walk (about six to seven hours round trip).

∼ WORTH A TRIP ∼

This 60km itinerary offers a great route to explore the **Sierra de Cazorla** (Map p241) by car, and is a good introduction to the parts of the park nearest to Cazorla town. Much of it is on unpaved roads, but it's all quite passable for ordinary cars. Allow two hours for the trip – without stops.

Head first to La Iruela and turn right along Carretera Virgen de la Cabeza soon after entering La Iruela. You reach the **Merenderos de Cazorla** mirador (lookout) after about 700m, with fine views over Cazorla. After another 4km you pass the Hotel de Montaña Riogazas; 7km further is **El Chorro**, a gorge that's good for watching Egyptian and griffon vultures.

Keep on the current track, ignoring another dirt road just beyond El Chorro that forks down to the right. The track you are on winds around over the **Puerto Lorente** (Lorente Pass) and, after 12km, down to a junction. Head northward, with the infant Guadalquivir river on your right – a beautiful trip down the wooded valley with the river bubbling to one side and rugged crags rising all around. It's 11km to the **Puente de las Herrerías**, a bridge over the Guadalquivir supposedly built in one night for Queen Isabel la Católica to cross during her campaigns against Granada. Here the road becomes paved, and 3km further on, past the large Complejo Puente de las Herrerías camping ground, you reach a T-junction. Go left and after 400m, opposite the turning to Vadillo Castril village, is the start of the **Sendero de la Cerrada del Utrero**, a beautiful 2km marked loop walk passing imposing cliffs, the **Cascada de Linarejos** (Linarejos Waterfall) and a small dam on the Guadalquivir – a great chance to get out and stretch your legs.

One kilometre further on from the turning to Vadillo Castril is the left-hand turn to the Parador El Adelantado hotel (which is 5km up a paved side road) and after another 2.5km you're at Empalme del Valle junction, from which it's 17km back to Cazorla.

♥ SEGURA DE LA SIERRA // VISIT THE PARK'S MOST SPECTACULAR VILLAGE

Easily the most beautiful village in the park, Segura de la Sierra sits perched on a 1000m-high hill crowned by an Islamic castle. It's 20km north of Hornos; turn east off the A317 4km after Cortijos Nuevos. Characterised largely by its Islamic heritage, the village actually dates way back to Phoenician times and ultimately became part of the Christian defensive front line when it was taken from the Muslims in 1214.

As you approach the upper, older part of the village, there's a tourist office (☎ 953 12 60 53; 🕑 10.30am-2pm & 6.30-8.30pm) beside the Puerta Nueva, an arch that was one of four gates of Islamic Saqura. The two main attractions, the castle and the Baño Moro (Muslim Bath), are normally left open all day every day, but check at the tourist office first (especially for the castle).

You can walk or drive up to the castle, which is at the top of the village. If you're walking, take the narrow Calle de las Ordenanzas del Común to the right after the Iglesia de Nuestra Señora del Collado, the parish church. After a few minutes you'll emerge alongside Segura's tiny bullring (which has seen famous fighters such as Enrique Ponce during the October festival), with the castle track heading up to the right. Wonderful views of the surrounding countryside unfurl all the way up, and if you climb the three-storey castle keep you get a bird's-eye view across to El Yelmo, about 5km to the south-southwest. You can drive most of the way up to the castle by heading past the parish church and around the perimeter of the village.

Segura's other attraction, the Baño Moro, is just off the central Plaza Mayor.

Built around 1150, probably for the local ruler Ibn ben Hamusk, it has three elegant rooms (for cold, temperate and hot baths), with horseshoe arches and barrel vaults studded with skylights. Nearby is the Puerta Catena, the best preserved of Segura's four Islamic gates; from here you can pick up the waymarked GR-147 footpath to the splendidly isolated village of Río Madera (a 15km downhill hike).

TRANSPORT

BUS // Carcesa (☎ 953 72 11 42) runs two buses daily (except Sunday) from Cazorla's Plaza de la Constitución to Empalme del Valle, Arroyo Frío, Torre del Vinagre and Coto Ríos. Pick up the latest timetable from the tourist office. No buses link the northern part of the park with the centre or south, and there are no buses to Segura de la Sierra. However, coming from Jaén, Baeza or Úbeda, you could get an Alsina Graells (www .alsina.es) bus to La Puerta de Segura (leaving Jaén daily at 9.30am and returning from La Puerta at 3pm).

CAR // If you're driving, approaches to the park include the A319 from Cazorla, roads into the north from Villanueva del Arzobispo and Puente de Génave on the A32, and the A317 to Santiago de la Espada from Puebla de Don Fadrique in northern Granada province. There are at least seven petrol stations in the park.

GRANADA PROVINCE

3 PERFECT DAYS

♣ DAY 1 // GRANADA'S ISLAMIC HERITAGE
Start your sightseeing early, with a morning visit to the Moorish palaces of the Alhambra (p254). For lunch, sample Spanish–Middle East fusion at Ruta del Azafrán (p266), then retire for a well-deserved siesta. In the late afternoon, head uphill again, this time to the winding streets of the Albayzín district (p260) and the fantastic sunset vistas at Mirador San Nicolás (p260), followed by tapas at El Ají (p265) and other bars on this plaza.

♣ DAY 2 // CITY PLEASURES
Pay your respects to Fernando and Isabel at their final resting place in Granada's Capilla Real (p259), then treat yourself to ice cream at Los Italianos (p265) and a bit of shoe shopping around Plaza Bib-Rambla (p259). Elbow up to the bar for a seafood lunch at Oliver (p266) or Los Diamantes (p265). After siesta, you might need just one more small ice cream… Later, it's off for tapas at iconic bars such as Bodegas Castañeda (p267). If you're still feeling lively, drop by Eshavira (p268) for a late-night flamenco session.

♣ DAY 3 // ALPUJARRAN IDYLL
In the mountains south of Granada, get into the slow groove of village life in Pitres (p278), then set out on foot for the villages just downhill, descending all the way to a centuries-old bridge over a rushing river. After your hike back up, you'll have an appetite for the delectable food at L'Atelier (p278). Crawl into bed and enjoy the silence, broken only by the occasional goat bell.

GRANADA

· · · · · ·

pop 258,000 / elevation 738m

Seville may have the *pasión* and Córdoba a medieval charm, but Granada has an edge. Most visitors dash straight to the alluring Alhambra, but if you stick around, you'll find Andalucía's hippest, most youthful city, with a 'free tapas' culture, innovative bars and tiny flamenco holes. Here the Islamic past feels recent, as Muslim North Africans make up some 10 percent of the population; there's even a modern mosque in the medieval district of the Albayzín. And though Granada looks alpine, with the white-capped Sierra Nevada peaks startlingly close, you could just as easily go swimming down on the coast for the day and be back in time to enjoy the city's *marcha* (nightlife).

But as lively as Granada is today, it's hardly what it was five centuries ago. The city came into its own late in Spain's Islamic era. As Córdoba and Seville fell to the Catholics in the mid-13th century, a minor potentate called Mohammed ibn Yusuf ibn Nasr established an independent state based in Granada. The town was soon flooded with Muslim refugees, and the Nasrid emirate became the last bastion of Al-Andalus. The Alhambra was developed as royal court, palace, fortress and miniature city, and the Nasrids ruled from this increasingly lavish complex for 250 years. During this time, Granada became one of the richest cities in Europe, with a population of more than 350,000. Under emirs Yusuf I (r 1333–54) and Mohammed V (r 1354–59 and 1362–91), traders did booming business, and artisans perfected such crafts as wood inlay.

As usual, though, decadent palace life bred a violent rivalry over succession. One faction supported the emir Abu al-Hasan and his Christian concubine, Zoraya, while the other backed Boabdil (Abu Abdullah), Abu al-Hasan's son by his wife Aixa – even though Boabdil was still just a child. In 1482 Boabdil started a civil war and, following Abu al-Hasan's death in 1485, won control of the city. With the emirate weakened by infighting, the Catholics pounced in 1491.

(Continued on page 253)

GRANADA PROVINCE (sidebar)

GRANADA PROVINCE ACCOMMODATION

The city of Granada has a great selection of places to sleep, at reasonable rates, and out in the rural areas, the prices drop even lower – with no loss in standards. Read all about the options in our dedicated accommodation chapter (p378). Here are some of the best choices:

★ A sanctuary in Granada's Albayzín neighbourhood, **Casa Morisca** (p395) conjures the Moorish past.

★ Live the high life at **Room Mate Shalma** (p395), a suitably cool hotel in Granada's coolest neighbourhood.

★ The best hotels in Las Alpujarras, such as **Las Chimeneas** (p397), work both as relaxing retreats and bases for active walking trips.

★ Sure, sleeping in a cave is a novelty. But it's also wonderfully cool and comfortable, especially at **Cuevas Mirador de Rolando** (p396).

GRANADA PROVINCE

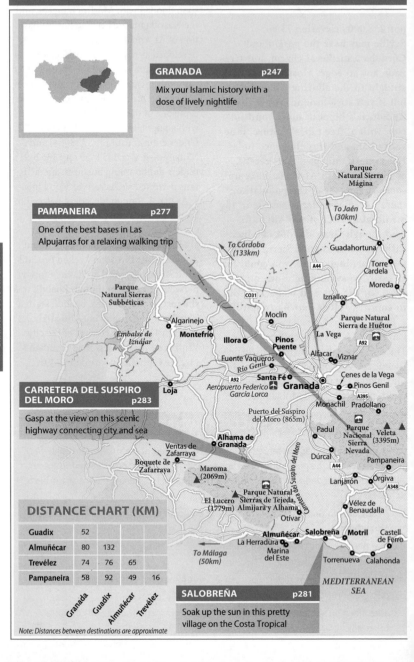

GRANADA p247

Mix your Islamic history with a dose of lively nightlife

PAMPANEIRA p277

One of the best bases in Las Alpujarras for a relaxing walking trip

CARRETERA DEL SUSPIRO DEL MORO p283

Gasp at the view on this scenic highway connecting city and sea

SALOBREÑA p281

Soak up the sun in this pretty village on the Costa Tropical

Parque Natural Sierra Mágina

To Jaén (30km)

Guadahortuna

Torre Cardela

Moreda

To Córdoba (133km)

A44

CO31

Iznalloz

Parque Natural Sierra de Huétor

Moclín

La Vega

A92

Parque Natural Sierras Subbéticas

Algarinejo

Embalse de Iznájar

Montefrío

Illora

Pinos Puente

Alfacar

Viznar

Fuente Vaqueros

Río Genil

Cenes de la Vega

Santa Fé

Granada

Pinos Genil

A92

Loja

Aeropuerto Federico García Lorca

A395

Monachil

Pradollano

Puerto del Suspiro del Moro (865m)

Padul

Parque Nacional Sierra Nevada

Veleta (3395m)

Alhama de Granada

Dúrcal

Pampaneira

Ventas de Zafarraya

A44

Lanjarón

Órgiva

Boquete de Zafarraya

Maroma (2069m)

A348

El Lucero (1779m)

Parque Natural Sierras de Tejeda, Almijara y Alhama

Vélez de Benaudalla

Otívar

DISTANCE CHART (KM)

	Granada	Guadix	Almuñécar	Trevélez
Guadix	52			
Almuñécar	80	132		
Trevélez	74	76	65	
Pampaneira	58	92	49	16

Note: Distances between destinations are approximate

Almuñécar

La Herradura

Marina del Este

Salobreña

Motril

Castell de Ferro

To Málaga (50km)

Torrenueva

Calahonda

MEDITERRANEAN SEA

GRANADA PROVINCE

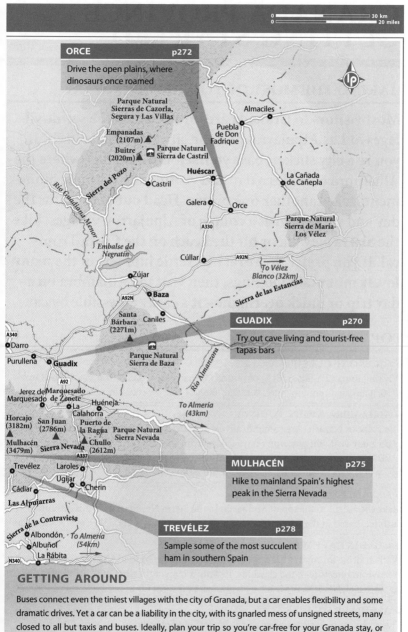

GRANADA PROVINCE

ORCE p272

Drive the open plains, where dinosaurs once roamed

GUADIX p270

Try out cave living and tourist-free tapas bars

MULHACÉN p275

Hike to mainland Spain's highest peak in the Sierra Nevada

TREVÉLEZ p278

Sample some of the most succulent ham in southern Spain

GETTING AROUND

Buses connect even the tiniest villages with the city of Granada, but a car enables flexibility and some dramatic drives. Yet a car can be a liability in the city, with its gnarled mess of unsigned streets, many closed to all but taxis and buses. Ideally, plan your trip so you're car-free for your Granada stay, or leave your car in an underground car park (p269) for the duration. Trains are of limited help – the only stops are in Granada and Guadix.

GRANADA PROVINCE
GETTING STARTED

MAKING THE MOST OF YOUR TIME

Most visitors to Granada are torn between the scenic villages of Las Alpujarras and the city of Granada itself. If you're a city slicker, base yourself in Granada – where the Alhambra occupies a day and visiting the Catholic monuments takes another one or two. Head out of town for the day and you can visit a couple of Alpujarran villages, hike the Sierra Nevada or hit the beach on the Costa Tropical. If you prefer the rural life, settle into one of the many lovely mountain lodgings, then visit the Alhambra on a day trip or quick overnight – it's easily accessible by car.

TOP TOURS

❦ CICERONE CULTURA Y OCIO
Walking tours (2½ hours, €12) of central Granada leave daily from Plaza Bib-Rambla, at 10.30am, or 11am in winter. (Map p261; ☎ 670 54 16 69; www.ciceronegranada.com)

❦ ALHAMBRA NIGHT TOUR
The Palacios Nazaríes are romantically lit in the evening. You won't get to see as much as on a day visit, but you won't have to deal with the same crowds either. (Map p255; ☎ 902 44 12 21; www.alhambra-patronato.es; adult/EU senior/Generalife only €12/6/6, disabled & child under 12yr free; ☽ 10-11.30pm Tue-Sat Mar-Oct, 8-9.30pm Fri & Sat Nov-Feb)

❦ NEVADENSIS
Make the ascent to the top of Mulhacén in the Sierra Nevadas, with this mountain outfitter, based in the Alpujarras village of Pampaneira. (☎ 958 76 31 27; www.nevadensis.com)

❦ GUADIX CAVE WALK
Walk or drive through the largest cosy cave neighbourhood in Guadix and admire the creative architecture in the clay hills. Pick up a map of the district at the tourist office. (☎ 958 66 26 65; Avenida Mariana Pineda; ☽ 9am-1.30pm & 4-6pm Mon-Fri)

❦ ALPUJARRA TOURS
These experts in Mairena offer a five-day self-guided walking trip across the mountains, with transport back to base in Mairena. Or choose from a menu of day hikes. (☎ 958 76 03 52; www.alpujarra-tours.com)

GETTING AWAY FROM IT ALL

Leave the crowds and go deep into wild Granada – or take a soothing urban retreat.

★ **Stroll in Sacromonte** Head for the hills of Granada's *gitano* (Roma) neighbourhood, with great views of the city (p263)

★ **Take a bath** Relax in the steamy confines of a modern hammam (p263)

★ **Walk in Las Alpujarras** Narrow footpaths connect the mountain villages, and you'll likely have them to yourself (p275)

★ **Carretera del Suspiro de Moro** Take this dramatic drive over the mountain pass where Boabdil wept when he left his surrendered city (p283)

ADVANCE PLANNING

★ **Semana Santa** Granada's Easter processions inspire awe. Book your hotel at least four months ahead; rates spike Wednesday to Sunday

★ **Alhambra** (☎ 902 88 80 01; www.alhambra -tickets.es) For a €1 fee, purchase tickets up to three months in advance and select your time slot. You can also buy tickets at La Caixa bank ATMs

★ **Bono Turístico** Avid sightseers will benefit from this discount card (€30), which you can purchase ahead of time (see the boxed text, p259)

★ **Dump your car** Turn in the hire car before you get to Granada, or stash it in an underground car park (p269)

★ **Walking shoes** You'll need them in hilly Granada as well as out in the mountains

TOP RESTAURANTS

🍽 **BODEGAS CASTAÑEDA**
Old-fashioned Granada tapas icon (p267)

- -

🍽 **AL SUR DE GRANADA**
Sample rural products in the city (p266)

- -

🍽 **LOS ITALIANOS**
Where *granadinos* get their *granizados* (slushy drinks) and gelato (p265)

- -

🍽 **CAFÉ FUTBOL**
Chocolate and *churros* in art nouveau style (p265)

- -

🍽 **MESÓN JOAQUÍN**
The best ham in the hills, and other tasty treats (p279)

- -

🍽 **RESTAURANTE ABEN HUMEYA**
Hearty mountain fare made with local ingredients (p280)

- -

🍽 **LA YERBABUENA**
Modern, unpretentious Andalusian food (p284)

- -

RESOURCES

★ **Turismo de Granada** (www.turismode granada.org) Provincial tourist office

★ **Tales of the Alhambra** Washington Irving's Moorish fairy tales

★ **Walk! The Alpujarras** (www.walking .demon.co.uk) Invaluable guide to trails

★ **South from Granada** Gerald Brenan's recollections of 1920s Alpujarras

★ **Ayuntamiento de Granada** (www .granada.org, in Spanish) Government website with good maps; click on 'La Ciudad'

GRANADA PROVINCE

GRANADA

To Hospital Clínico San
Cecilio (650m); FM (1.3km);
Bus Station (1.8km);
A4 Northbound (2km);
Jaén (99km)

To Train
Station (400m);
Fuente Vaqueros
(17km); Airport (17km)

To Monasterio de la Cartuja (600m);
Víznar (8km); Alfacar (8km)

To Guadix
(55km)

Jardines del
Triunfo

C Pagés

Placeta
Fátima

Plaza del
Triunfo ● 2

Cuesta de la Alhacaba

Plaza
Larga C Panderos
C de San Gregorio

14

Callejón de las Monjas

Plaza de
San Nicolás

Placeta de
San Miguel
Bajo

12

8

7

5

Cuesta Cabras

C de San Agustín

C de Santa Isabel la Real   Camino Nueva de San Nicolás

21

15

C Tiña

Cuesta del

22

10

19

See CENTRAL GRANADA Map (p261)

Albayzín

26

Carrera del Darro

16

Cathedral

Plaza Isabel
La Católica

Cuesta de Gomérez

Bosque
Alhambra

Callejón Niño del Royo

Plaza de la
Trinidad

Plaza Bib-
Rambla

Plaza
Real

Puerta
Real

Realejo

Campo
Príncipe

Plaza de
Gracia

Plaza de
Mariana
Pineda

To Huerta de
San Vicente (600m)

Paseo del Salón

27

Río Genil

Cuesta de
la Bomba

EXPLORING GRANADA

Aljibe San Miguel Baños Arabes	1 A4
Arco de Elvira	2 B2
Baños Árabes El Bañuelo	3 D3
Baños de Elvira	(see 25)
Colegiata del Salvador	4 D2
El Huerto de Juan Ranas	5 D2
Iglesia de San Juan de Díos	6 A2
Mezquita Mayor de Granada	7 D2
Mirador San Nicolás	8 D2
Monasterio de San Jerónimo	9 A2
Museo Arqueológico	10 D3
Museo Cuevas del Sacromonte	11 F1
Palacio de Dar-al-Horra	12 C2
Rastro (Flea Market)	13 B6

Parking Palacio
de Congresos

13

Palacio de
Congresos

To A44 Southbound (1.6km);
Motril (68km)

Paseo del Violón   C Poeta Manuel Góngora

To Monachil (8km);
Los Cahorros (13km)

GRANADA PROVINCE

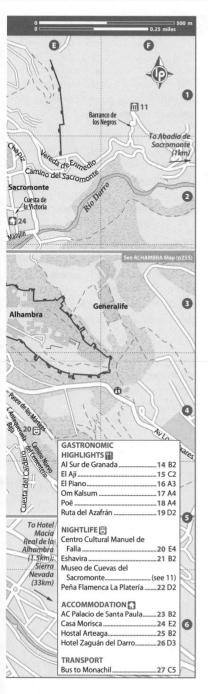

(Continued from page 247)

Queen Isabel in particular had been smitten by Granada – so fittingly named for the jewel-like pomegranate, she thought, its buildings clustered like seeds along the hillsides – and she wanted it for herself. After an eight-month siege, Boabdil agreed to surrender the city in return for the Alpujarras valleys, 30,000 gold coins and political and religious freedom for his subjects. Boabdil hiked out of town – letting out the proverbial 'Moor's last sigh' as he looked over his shoulder in regret – and on 2 January 1492, Isabel and Fernando entered the city ceremonially in Muslim dress, to set up court in the Alhambra.

Their promises didn't last. They soon divided the populace, relegating the Jews to the Realejo and containing the Muslims in the Albayzín. Subsequent rulers called for full-scale expulsion, first in 1570 and again in 1610, and Granada – once the Catholic Monarchs' prize jewel – became a backwater. In 1828 American writer Washington Irving visited the ruined palace and decided to move in. His fabulist *Tales of the Alhambra,* published in 1832, brought tourists from all over the world to marvel at the city's Islamic heritage; they helped give the city a little push into the modern age. Now Granada thrives on a culture that mixes Spanish, Moroccan, *gitano* and a bit of international traveller.

ESSENTIAL INFORMATION

EMERGENCIES // **Policía Nacional** (National Police; Map p261; ☎ 091; Plaza de los Campos) The most central police station. **Police hotline** (☎ 902 10 21 12) For reporting theft; various languages spoken. **Hospital Clínico San Cecilio** (Map pp252–3; ☎ 958 02 32 17; Avenida del Doctor Olóriz 16) Central hospital with good emergency facilities.

GRANADA PROVINCE

48 HOURS IN GRANADA

FREE STUFF

Granada isn't expensive, but you can offset the blockbuster of the Alhambra with visits to **Palacio de Dar-al-Horra** (p260), **Baños Árabes El Bañuelo** (p260), **La Madraza** and **Corral del Carbón** (p260). The view from **Mirador San Nicolás** (p260) doesn't cost a cent, nor does getting an eyeful of gold at the **Iglesia de San Juan de Díos** (p262).

SIESTA SECRETS

If you're feeling wide awake when the rest of city snoozes, you can stop by the **Museo Arqueológico** (p260) and of course the **Alhambra** (below), where it's a good strategy to visit the Generalife and Alcazaba first, then enter the Palacios Nazaríes near the end of the day. The tea shops on **Calle Calderería Nueva** can be a good afternoon haven, or if you're hungry, try **Reca** (p268) and **Om Kalsum** (p267), where the kitchens are open all day.

FURTHER AFIELD

With so much right in the centre, it's easy to forget that Granada is a big city. Invest in a bus pass or some good walking shoes and head for the **Monasterio de la Cartuja** (p262). Hike up into the hills to the **Abadía de Sacromonte** (p263). Savour cult octopus at **FM** (p265), and trek over to the Palacio de los Congresos for the weekly **Rastro flea market** (p264) on Sunday, if your schedule allows. The city will seem a lot bigger when you're done.

TOURIST OFFICES // Provincial tourist office (Map p261; ☎ 958 24 71 28; www.turismode granada.org; Plaza de Mariana Pineda 10; ☒ 9am-10pm Mon-Fri, 10am-7pm Sat) Regional tourist office Alhambra (Map p255; ☎ 958 54 40 02; Pabellón de Acceso, Avenida del Generalife; ☒ 8am-7.30pm Mon-Fri, 8am-2.30pm & 4-7.30pm Sat & Sun Mar-Oct, 8am-6pm Mon-Fri, 8am-2pm & 4-6pm Sat & Sun Nov-Feb, 9am-1pm holidays); Plaza Nueva (Map p261; ☎ 958 57 52 02; Calle Santa Ana 4; ☒ 9am-7.30pm Mon-Sat, 10am-3.30pm Sun & holidays)

ORIENTATION

Gran Vía de Colón is Granada's main boulevard, with the Albayzín rising northeast of it, and the cathedral and commercial areas immediately southwest of it. A few blocks to the east, Plaza Nueva sits between the Albayzín on one hillside and the Alhambra on the other; the Río Darro runs between them. Downhill off the southern side of the Alhambra is the Realejo district. The bus and train stations are both northwest of the centre but linked by buses.

EXPLORING GRANADA

Most major sights are an easy walk within the city centre, and there are buses (p269) for when the hills wear you out.

♥ ALHAMBRA // IMAGINE YOURSELF IN ISLAMIC-ERA SPLENDOUR

The sheer red walls of the **Alhambra** (Map p255; ☎ 902 44 12 21; www.alhambra-patronato.es; adult/EU senior/Generalife only €12/6/6, disabled & child under 12yr free; ☒ 8.30am-8pm Mar-Oct, 8.30am-6pm Nov-Feb, closed 25 Dec & 1 Jan) rise from woods of cypress and elm. Inside is one of the more splendid sights of Europe, a network of lavishly decorated palaces and irrigated gardens, a World Heritage Site and the subject of scores of legends and fantasies.

But at the height of summer, some 6000 visitors tramp through daily, making it difficult to pause to inspect a pretty detail, much less mentally transport yourself to the 14th century. Schedule a visit in quieter months, if possible; if not, then book in advance (see p251) for the very earliest or latest time slot.

The Alhambra takes its name from the Arabic *al-qala'a al-hamra* (the Red Castle). The first palace on the site was built by Samuel Ha-Nagid, the Jewish grand vizier of one of Granada's 11th-century Zirid sultans. In the 13th and 14th centuries, the Nasrid emirs turned the area into a fortress-palace complex, adjoined by a village of which only ruins remain. After the Reconquista (Christian reconquest), the Alhambra's mosque was replaced with a church, and the Convento de San Francisco (now the Parador de Granada) was built. Carlos I (also known as the Habsburg emperor Charles V), grandson of the Catholic Monarchs, had a wing of the palaces destroyed to make space for his huge Renaissance work, the Palacio de Carlos V. During the Napoleonic occupation, the Alhambra was used as a barracks and nearly blown up. What you see today has been heavily but respectfully restored.

Palacios Nazaríes

The central palace complex is the pinnacle of the Alhambra's design. Though the Nasrid Palaces were erected late in Spain's Islamic era, when the empire was already well in decline (and

GRANADA PROVINCE

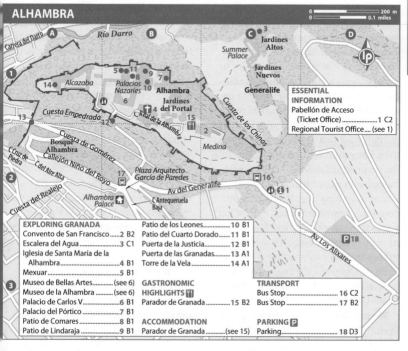

ALHAMBRA

ESSENTIAL INFORMATION
Pabellón de Acceso
(Ticket Office)..........................1 C2
Regional Tourist Office....(see 1)

EXPLORING GRANADA
Convento de San Francisco......2 B2
Escalera del Agua........................3 C1
Iglesia de Santa María de la
Alhambra.................................4 B1
Mexuar..5 B1
Museo de Bellas Artes..........(see 6)
Museo de la Alhambra...........(see 6)
Palacio de Carlos V.....................6 B1
Palacio del Pórtico......................7 B1
Patio de Comares.........................8 B1
Patio de Lindaraja.......................9 B1

Patio de los Leones....................10 B1
Patio del Cuarto Dorado.......11 B1
Puerta de la Justicia................12 B1
Puerta de las Granadas.........13 A1
Torre de la Vela.......................14 A1

GASTRONOMIC HIGHLIGHTS
Parador de Granada..............15 B2

ACCOMMODATION
Parador de Granada............(see 15)

TRANSPORT
Bus Stop................................16 C2
Bus Stop................................17 B2

PARKING
Parking...................................18 D3

architects had switched from stone to more expedient, cheaper brick), they make up one of the finest Islamic structures in Europe, a harmonious synthesis of space, light, shade, water and greenery that sought to conjure the gardens of paradise for the rulers who dwelt here. Expanses of tile, *muqarnas* (honeycomb) vaulting and wood trim survive, but most mesmerising is the intricate stucco work that adorns the walls. The Arabic inscription *Wa la ghaliba illa Allah* (There is no conqueror but God) covers nearly every surface in various calligraphy styles, transforming the words from ritual praise into geometric pattern. But virtually no documents confirm the functions of the palaces, built in two main phases – about the only certainty is that the niches in the walls held water pitchers. So the rooms are now largely a blank slate for visitors' imaginations.

Entrance is through the 14th-century **Mexuar**, perhaps an antechamber for those awaiting audiences with the emir. Two centuries later, it was converted to a chapel, with a prayer room at the far end. Look up here and elsewhere to appreciate the geometrically carved wood ceilings. From the Mexuar, you pass into the **Patio del Cuarto Dorado**. It appears to be a forecourt to the main palace, with the symmetrical doorways to the right, framed with glazed tiles and stucco, setting a cunning trap: the right-hand door leads nowhere but out, but the left passes through a dogleg hall (a common strategy in Islamic domestic architecture to keep interior rooms private) into the **Patio de Comares**, the centre of a palace built in the mid-14th century as Emir Yusuf I's private residence.

Rooms (likely used for lounging and sleeping) look onto the rectangular pool edged in myrtles, and traces of cobalt blue paint cling to the *muqarnas* vaults in the side niches on the north end. Originally, all the walls were lavishly coloured; with paint on the stucco-trimmed walls in the adjacent **Sala de la Barca**, the effect would have resembled flocked wallpaper. Yusuf I's visitors would have passed through this annex room to meet him in the **Salón de Comares**, where the marvellous domed marquetry ceiling uses more than 8000 cedar pieces to create its intricate star pattern representing the seven heavens.

Adjacent is the **Patio de los Leones** (Courtyard of the Lions), built in the second half of the 14th century under Muhammad V, at the political and artistic peak of Granada's emirate. But the centrepiece, a fountain that channelled water through the mouths of 12 marble lions, dates from the 11th century. The courtyard layout, using the proportions of the golden ratio, demonstrates the complexity of Islamic geometric design – the varied columns are placed in such a way that they are symmetrical on numerous axes. The porticoes jutting into the centre are uncommon – this is effectively the previous patio built inside-out, creating complex shadows by day and moonlit night. The stucco work, too, hits its apex here, with almost lacelike detail.

Walking counterclockwise around the patio, you first pass the **Sala de Abencerrajes**. The Abencerraje family supported the young Boabdil in a palace power struggle between him and his own father, the reigning sultan. Legend has it that the sultan had the traitors killed in this room, and the rusty stains in the fountain are the victims' indelible blood. But the multicoloured tiles on the walls and the great octagonal ceiling are far more eye-catching. In the **Sala de los Reyes**

(Hall of the Kings) at the east end of the patio, the painted leather ceilings depict 10 Nasrid emirs. The European style (the artists were probably Genoans) indicates the cross-cultural foment of the 14th century.

On the patio's north side, doors once covered the entrance to the **Sala de Dos Hermanas** (Hall of Two Sisters) – look for the holes on either side of the frame where they would have been anchored. The walls are adorned with local flora – pine cones and acorns – and the band of calligraphy at eye level, just above the tiles, is a poem praising Muhammad V for his victory in Algeciras of 1369, a rare triumph this late in the Islamic game. The dizzying ceiling is a fantastic *muqarnas* dome with some 5000 tiny cells. The carved wood screens in the upper level enabled women (and perhaps others involved in palace intrigue) to peer down from hallways above without being seen. At the far end, the tile-trimmed **Mirador de Lindaraja** was a lovely place for palace denizens to look onto the garden below. Traces of paint still cling to the window frames, and a few panels of coloured glass set in the wood ceiling cast a warm glow.

From the Sala de Dos Hermanas a passageway leads past the domed roofs of the baths on the level below and into rooms built for Carlos I in the 1520s and later used by Washington Irving. From here you descend to the pretty **Patio de Lindaraja**. In the southwest corner is the bathhouse – you can't enter, but you can peer in at the rooms lit by star-shaped skylights.

You emerge into an area of terraced gardens created in the early 20th century, and the reflecting pool in front of the small **Palacio del Pórtico** (Palace of the Portico), the oldest surviving palace in the Alhambra, from the time of Mohammed III (r 1302–09). You can leave the gardens by a gate facing the Palacio de Carlos V or continue along a path to the Generalife.

Alcazaba, Christian Buildings & Museums

The west end of the Alhambra grounds are the remnants of the **Alcazaba**, chiefly its ramparts and several towers. The **Torre de la Vela** (Watchtower), with a narrow staircase leading to the top terrace, is where the cross and banners of the Reconquista were raised in January 1492.

By the Palacios Nazaríes, the hulking **Palacio de Carlos V** clashes spectacularly with its surroundings. In a different setting its merits might be more readily appreciated – it is the only example in Spain of the Renaissance-era circle-in-a-square ground plan. Begun in 1527 by Pedro Machuca, a Toledo architect who studied under Michelangelo, it was financed, perversely, from taxes on Granada's *morisco* (converted Muslim) population but never finished because funds dried up after the *morisco* rebellion.

Inside, the **Museo de la Alhambra** (☎ 958 02 79 00; admission free; ☺ 9am-2.30pm Tue-Sat) has a collection of Alhambra artefacts, including the door from the Sala de Dos Hermanas, and the **Museo de Bellas Artes** (Fine Arts Museum; ☎ 958 22 14 49; non-EU/EU citizen €1.50/free; ☺ 9am-2pm Mon-Fri) displays paintings and sculptures from Granada's Christian history.

Further along, the 16th-century **Iglesia de Santa María de la Alhambra** sits on the site of the palace mosque, and at the crest of the hill the **Convento de San Francisco**, now the Parador de Granada hotel (p396), is where Isabel and Fernando were laid to rest while their tombs in the Capilla Real were being built.

ALHAMBRA PRACTICALITIES

Tickets are timed for either morning (from 8am) or afternoon (after 2pm) entry to the grounds, and, more important, for admission to the Palacios Nazaríes within a 30-minute period (you can stay as long as you like). Allow three hours or more to see the whole complex, and at least 10 minutes to walk from the Generalife to the Palacios Nazaríes. Guards allow absolutely no late entries; in high season, be in the queue at the palaces at the start of your time slot.

Same-day tickets sell out early, so it's more convenient to buy tickets up to three months ahead (p251). Pick up phone or internet orders at the yellow machines to the right of the ticket office, using the credit card with which you made the purchase. When full-access tickets are sold out, you can still buy a ticket to the **Generalife and gardens** (€6). The Palacios Nazaríes are open for **night visits** (☾ 10-11.30pm Tue-Sat Mar-Oct, 8-9.30pm Fri & Sat Nov-Feb), good for atmosphere rather than detail.

There is no explanatory signage in the complex; an average-quality audioguide is available for €4. No outside food is allowed, but there is a slightly pricey cafeteria at the **Parador de Granada** (p266), plus vending machines by the ticket office and the Alcazaba. Outside the complex, no restaurants are notable, but the bar at the **Alhambra Palace** hotel (☎ 958 22 14 68; Plaza Arquitecto García de Paredes 1; drinks €4-6) offers a smashing view.

Walk up one of three ways: Cuesta de Gomérez, through woods to the Puerta de la Justicia (enter here if you already have your ticket) or, further along, to the ticket office; Cuesta de los Chinos, to the east end of the complex; and up Cuesta de Realejo via the Alhambra Palace hotel.

Buses 30, 32 and (less directly) 34 run temporarily from near Plaza Isabel La Católica (permanently from near Plaza Nueva, set to resume sometime in 2010) from 7am to 11pm, stopping at the ticket office and in front of the Alhambra Palace. By car, follow 'Alhambra' signs from the highway to the **car park** (per hour/day €2.40/16.25), just uphill from the ticket office.

Generalife

From the Arabic *jinan al-'arif* (the overseer's gardens), the **Generalife** is a soothing arrangement of pathways, patios, pools, fountains, tall trees and, in season, flowers of every imaginable hue. To reach the complex you must pass through the Alhambra walls on the east side, then head back northwest. You approach through topiary gardens on the south end, which were once grazing land for the royal herds. At the north end is the emirs' **summer palace**, a whitewashed structure on the hillside facing the Alhambra. The courtyards here are particularly graceful; in the second courtyard, the trunk of a 700-year-old cypress tree suggests what delicate shade once graced the patio. Climb the steps outside the courtyard to the **Escalera del Agua**, a delightful bit of garden engineering where water flows along a shaded staircase.

♣ CATHOLIC LANDMARKS // BAROQUE GRANDEUR AND CREEPY CRYPTS

The buildings representing Granada's Catholic authority adjoin each other just off the Gran Vía. Commissioned by

Queen Isabel as the final resting place for her and husband Fernando, the **Capilla Real** (Royal Chapel; Map p261; ☎958 22 92 39; www.capillarealgranada.com; Calle Oficios; admission €3.50; ☺10.30am-1.30pm & 4-7.30pm Apr-Oct, 10.30am-1pm & 3.30-6.30pm Nov-Mar, from 11am Sun year-round, closed Good Friday) is such a vanity project that the exterior roof line is even emblazoned with the monarchs' initials. But the Gothic confection wasn't finished until 1521, several years after their deaths, so they were interred in the Alhambra's Convento de San Francisco. The monarchs lie in the chapel crypt in simple lead coffins, along with their daughter Juana and her husband, Felipe I (aka Phillip the Handsome), who died young, in 1506; Juana, dubbed La Loca, a likely schizophrenic, lived in confinement until 1555, and both their bodies were transferred to the crypt by their son, Carlos I. The smallest coffin is that of Miguel, Isabel and Fernando's grandchild who died at the age of two. Carlos I installed marble effigies of his parents and grandparents. The more delicate set is Isabel and Fernando; a Latin inscription lauds them as 'subjugators of Islam and extinguishers of obstinate heresy'.

The adjoining **museum** provides a neat slice of art history, with Isabel's personal collection of 15th-century paint-

ings that bridge the transition from flat, Byzantine-style iconography to the more lush work of the Renaissance, with a number of works by Flemish artists who came to work in Spain.

Around the corner, Granada's cavernous **cathedral** (Map p261; ☎958 22 29 59; admission €3.50; ☺10.45am-1.30pm & 4-8pm Mon-Sat, 4-8pm Sun, to 7pm daily Nov-Mar) was another Isabel commission, but construction began only after her death, and didn't finish until 1704. The result is a mishmash of styles: baroque outside, by the 17th-century master Alonso Cano, and Renaissance inside, where the Spanish pioneer in this style, Diego de Siloé, directed operations to construct huge piers, white as meringue, a black-and-white tile floor and the gilded and painted chapel. Even more odd, the roof vaults are distinctly Gothic.

🌱 **CENTRAL PLAZAS // GRAB A SEAT TO WATCH THE URBAN PARADE**
Built on the site of one of the old city gates, the large **Plaza Bib-Rambla** (Map p261) is jammed with cafes, flower stalls and ice-cream shops. Its proximity to major sights makes it a bit of a tourist haunt, but the chocolate and *churros* (€4) at **Cafetería Alhambra** (Map p261; Plaza Bib-Rambla 27)

GRANADA'S BONO TURÍSTICO

Valid for five days, the Bono Turístico Granada (€30) is a card that gives admission to the city's major sights, plus 10 rides on city buses, use of the sightseeing bus for a day and discounts on the Cicerone Cultura y Ocio walking tour (p250) and a city audioguide. When you add it all up, the savings are significant only if you visit virtually all of the sights.

You can buy the Bono at **this.is:granada** (Map p261), a red kiosk opposite Plaza Nueva, where the bus to the Albazyín stops. For a €2.50 surcharge, you can pre-order by phone from the **Bono information line** (☎902 10 00 95, English spoken) or on the internet (www.caja-granada.es, in Spanish), then pick it up at the **CajaGranada** (Map p261; Plaza Isabel La Católica 6; ☺8.30am-2.15pm Mon-Fri) bank. Buying in advance gives you the advantage of choosing your Alhambra entrance time, rather than being assigned one.

are excellent, as is the ice cream at Helad-ería Tiggiani (Map p261; Plaza Bib-Rambla 11) – you might need these restoratives after a bout of shoe shopping in the surrounding streets. Northwest out of Bib-Rambla, pedestrianised Calle Pescadería forms its own small plaza, edged with fish restaurants, and this connects almost directly with Plaza de la Romanilla, with several chic bars. Heading the other direction off Pescadería, you reach shady, quiet Plaza de la Trinidad, with good inexpensive bars in the surrounding streets.

❦ ISLAMIC TRACES // MOORISH RELICS HIDDEN AMID THE CATHOLIC CITY

Opposite the Capilla Real you'll see the trompe l'oeil painted baroque facade of the old Muslim university, La Madraza (Map p261; Calle Oficios). Inside is an octagonal domed prayer room with stucco lacework and pretty tiles. The building is part of the modern university; you can look inside whenever it's open. Southwest of here is the complex called the Alcaicería (Map p261), the Islamic-era exchange for silk produced in the Alpujarras. Now it has a decidedly faux souk feel; it's best experiences in the early morning light when it's peacefully quiet. Across Calle Reyes Católicos, you can't miss the elaborate horseshoe arch of the Corral del Carbón (Map p261; Calle Mariana Pineda), which began life as a 14th-century inn for merchants. It has since been used as an inn for coal dealers (hence its modern name, Coal Yard) and later a theatre. It is home to government offices and hosts occasional concerts.

❦ ALBAYZÍN // GET LOST IN GRANADA'S OLDEST QUARTER

In contrast to the studied, urbane serenity of the Alhambra, the Albayzín, the neighbourhood on the hill facing the Moorish palace, is a tangle of sloping streets, an organically evolved village within the city. Sheer walls on narrow lanes disguise *carmen* houses with gardens (from the Arabic *karm,* for vineyard), following models established by Muslim rulers before the 13th century. Other Islamic traces can be seen in gates, fountains, ramparts and more.

The best route through the maze is whichever one you take. That said, it's easiest to start along the Río Darro, from the Iglesia de Santa Ana (Map p261) off the northeast edge of Plaza Nueva, which incorporates a mosque's minaret in its bell tower (as do several churches in the Albayzín). Further along, peek into the 11th-century Islamic bathhouse, the Baños Árabes El Bañuelo (Map pp252-3; ☎ 958 02 78 00; Carrera del Darro 31; admission free; ☽ 9.30am-2pm Tue-Sat), which are far larger than they look from the outside. Nearby, the Museo Arqueológico (Archaeological Museum; Map pp252-3; ☎ 958 57 54 08; Carrera del Darro 43; non-EU/EU citizen €1.50/free; ☽ 2.30-8.30pm Tue, 9am-8.30pm Wed-Sat, 9am-2.30pm Sun), housed in a Renaissance mansion, displays ancient tools, mammoth molars and astrolabes.

From here, work your way uphill, through the various plazas, to the Colegiata del Salvador (Map pp252-3; ☎ 958 27 86 44; Plaza del Salvador; admission €0.75; ☽ 10am-1pm & 4-7.30pm Mon-Sat Apr-Oct, 10.30am-12.30pm & 4.30-6.30pm Mon-Sat Nov-Mar), a 16th-century church on the site of the Albayzín's former main mosque, the patio of which still survives at the church's western end. Further up the hill are the graffitied city walls and the Palacio de Dar-al-Horra (Map pp252-3; Callejón de las Monjas; admission free; ☽ 10am-2pm Tue & Thu), a mini-Alhambra that was home to Aixa, Boabdil's mother.

At sunset, join the scene at Mirador San Nicolás (Map pp252–3) for amazing

GRANADA PROVINCE

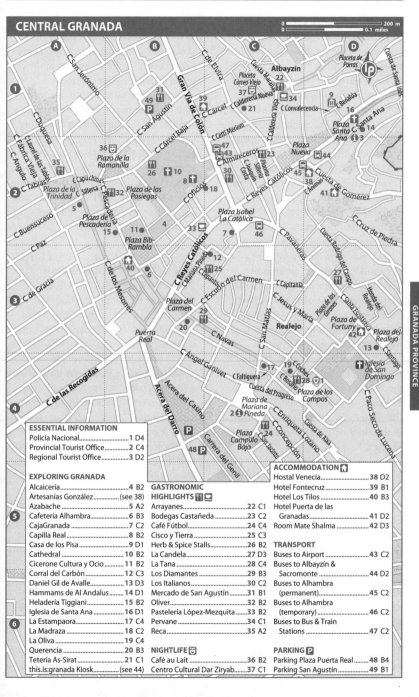

CENTRAL GRANADA

GRANADA PROVINCE

ESSENTIAL INFORMATION
Policía Nacional................................1 D4
Provincial Tourist Office..............2 C4
Regional Tourist Office................3 D2

EXPLORING GRANADA
Alcaicería...4 B2
Artesanías González..............(see 38)
Azabache..5 A2
Cafetería Alhambra.....................6 B3
CajaGranada...................................7 C2
Capilla Real......................................8 B2
Casa de los Pisa............................9 D1
Cathedral......................................10 B2
Cicerone Cultura y Ocio..........11 B2
Corral del Carbón......................12 C3
Daniel Gil de Avalle..................13 D3
Hammams de Al Andalus........14 D1
Heladería Tiggiani.....................15 B2
Iglesia de Santa Ana................16 D1
La Estampaora............................17 C4
La Madraza...................................18 C2
La Oliva..19 C4
Querencia......................................20 B3
Tetería As-Sirat...........................21 C1
this.is:granada Kiosk...........(see 44)

GASTRONOMIC
HIGHLIGHTS
Arrayanes......................................22 C1
Bodegas Castañeda..................23 C2
Café Fútbol....................................24 C4
Cisco y Tierra...............................25 C3
Herb & Spice Stalls....................26 B2
La Candela.....................................27 D3
La Tana...28 C4
Los Diamantes.............................29 B3
Los Italianos.................................30 C2
Mercado de San Agustín.........31 B1
Oliver..32 B2
Pastelería López-Mezquita.....33 B2
Pervane..34 C1
Reca...35 A2

NIGHTLIFE
Café au Lait...................................36 B2
Centro Cultural Dar Ziryab....37 C1

ACCOMMODATION
Hostal Venecia............................38 D2
Hotel Fontecruz..........................39 B1
Hotel Los Tilos............................40 B3
Hotel Puerta de las
   Granadas...................................41 D2
Room Mate Shalma....................42 D3

TRANSPORT
Buses to Airport..........................43 C2
Buses to Albayzín &
   Sacromonte.............................44 D2
Buses to Alhambra
   (permanent)............................45 C2
Buses to Alhambra
   (temporary).............................46 C2
Buses to Bus & Train
   Stations.....................................47 C2

PARKING
Parking Plaza Puerta Real........48 B4
Parking San Agustín..................49 B1

views of the Alhambra and the Sierra Nevada. (Don't let the vista distract you from your wallet, however; this is prime pickpocket territory.) Just next door, the Albayzín's first new mosque in 500 years, the **Mezquita Mayor de Granada** (Map pp252-3; ☎ 958 20 23 31; ⏱ 11am-2pm & 6-9.30pm), opened in 2003. The public can enter the gardens, but the mosque itself is open only to Muslims. **El Huerto de Juan Ranas** (Map pp252-3; ☎ 958 28 69 25; Calle de Atarazana 8), just below the mirador (lookout), has a beautiful terrace for a drink, though get there on the early side, as they shut the door to drinkers just at sunset.

Coming back down, pass through **Calle Calderería Nueva**, centre of the city's modern Muslim community. The touristy shops brim with hookahs, slippers and scarves, but the mellow teahouses, such as **Tetería As-Sirat** (Map p261; Calle Calderería Nueva 4; teas €3), are popular with nondrinking Muslim youth.

For a shortcut up the hill, take bus 31 or 32 from Plaza Nueva, looping around the Albayzín, stopping by the Mirador de San Nicolás and descending through the **Arco de Elvira**, an 11th-century gate in the old walls at the north of Calle de Elvira.

❦ CASA DE LOS PISA // AN ODD MUSEUM TELLS A SAINT'S RAGS-TO-RICHES STORY

Granada's most famous resident saint, San Juan Robles (San Juan de Díos), dedicated his life to healing the destitute and inspired a medical fraternity. He died in 1550, at the age of 55, in the **Casa de los Pisa** (Archivo Museo San Juan de Díos; Map p261; ☎ 958 22 21 44; Calle de la Convalencia 1; suggested donation €2.50, admission only by guided tour in Spanish; ⏱ 10am-1.30pm Mon-Sat). The mansion of the wealthy Pisa family, who took the saint off the streets when he fell ill, now

displays a treasure trove of liturgical art, as well as secular oddities such as boa skins and even a shrunken head. Tours take about 45 minutes, ending in the very room where the saint expired.

The humble saint's death in a mansion is odd enough; it's even stranger to see his final resting place, the stunningly gaudy **Iglesia de San Juan de Díos** (Map pp252-3; ☎ 958 27 57 00; Calle San Juan de Díos; admission free; 10am-1pm & 4-7pm Apr-Oct, 10am-1pm & 4-6pm Nov-Mar), not far from the Monasterio de San Jerónimo. The saint's remains are set deep in a niche surrounded by gold, gold and more gold.

❦ MAGNIFICENT MONASTERIES // GET AN EYEFUL OF SPANISH BAROQUE ARCHITECTURE

Two of the most stunning Catholic buildings in Granada are a little out of the centre. At the 16th-century **Monasterio de San Jerónimo** (Map pp252-3; ☎ 958 27 93 37; Calle Rector López Argüeta 9; admission €3.50; ⏱ 10am-2.30pm & 4-7.30pm Apr-Oct, 10am-2.30pm & 3-6.30pm Nov-Mar), where nuns still sing vespers, every surface of the church has been painted – the stained glass literally pales in comparison. Gonzalo Fernández de Córdoba, known as El Gran Capitán and the Catholic Monarchs' military man, is entombed here, at the foot of the steps, and figures of him and his wife stand on either side of the enormous gilt retable, which rises eight levels. Almond cookies, baked by the nuns, are for sale at the front desk, to stop your head from spinning.

To be boggled some more, head for the **Monasterio de la Cartuja** (off Map pp252-3; ☎ 958 16 19 32; Paseo de la Cartuja; admission €3.50; ⏱ 10am-1pm & 4-8pm Apr-Oct, 10am-1pm & 3.30-6pm Nov-Mar, 10am-noon Sun year-round). Built between the 16th and 18th centuries by the Carthusian monks themselves, the monastery church is trimmed in Mudéjar wedding-cake stucco (the same technique used at the Alhambra, repurposed for Catholic tastes) and brown-and-white marble from Lanjarón. That's nothing compared with the sacristy, lined with mirrors for the priests to check their robes, which would've been stored in the intricately inlaid cabinets, a high point of marquetry art. And *that* pales next to the weird sanctuary, dominated by a tabernacle carved from a single piece of red marble. Only one priest was permitted in this room, to handle the communion wafers; others could peer through the glass windows on the side. San Bruno, founder of the Carthusian order, can be seen everywhere, looking wan and contemplating a skull; a few of his bones are embedded in the gilt and mirrored altar.

From the centre, catch bus 8, C or U north from Gran Vía de Colón. On school days, get off at Paseo de la Cartuja I; on weekends, the bus stops directly in front of the monastery.

❦ SACROMONTE // HIKE UP TO EXPLORE GRANADA'S CAVE QUARTER

The primarily *gitano* (Roma) neighbourhood northeast of the Albayzín is renowned for its flamenco traditions, drawing tourists to nightclubs and aficionados to music schools. But it still feels like the fringes of the city, literally and figuratively, as the homes dug out of the hillside alternate between flashy and highly extemporaneous, despite some of them having been established since the 14th century. The area is good for an idle stroll, yielding great views (especially from an ad-hoc cafe on Vereda de Enmedio). For some insight into the area, the Museo Cuevas del Sacromonte (Map pp252-3; ☎ 958 21 51 20; www.sacromontegranada.com; Barranco de los Negros; admission €5; ☾ 10am-2pm & 5-9pm Tue-Sun Apr-Oct, 10am-2pm & 4-7pm Tue-Sun Nov-Mar) provides an excellent display of all the local folk arts. It's set in large herb gardens and hosts art exhibitions, as well as flamenco and films at 10pm on Wednesday and Friday from June to September.

The diligent can press on to the Abadía de Sacromonte (off Map pp252-3; ☎ 958 22 14 45; admission €3; ☾ 11am-1pm & 4-6pm Wed-Mon), at the very top of the hill, where you can squeeze into underground cave chapels.

Wander up from the Albayzín, or take bus 34 to the Venta El Gallo Flamenco School, 250m along the road from El Camborio cave disco, and follow the signs up Barranco de los Negros to the museum. For the abbey, take the bus two more stops, then walk up through the arch. (Several times a day, the bus goes all the way to the abbey.) If you're feeling like it's a long walk up, imagine what it's like in the fifth hour of a Semana Santa procession.

❦ HAMMAMS // WASH AWAY YOUR CARES IN NEO-ISLAMIC STYLE

Granada has three *baños árabes* (Arab-style baths), though none is historic – nor much like a Middle Eastern hammam. Here the emphasis is on lazy lounging in pools, rather than getting scrubbed clean. But the dim, tiled rooms are suitably sybaritic and a relaxing end to a long sightseeing day. All offer pool access in two-hour sessions, with the option of a 15-minute or 30-minute massage for a bit more; reservations are required. Swimwear is obligatory (you can rent it), a towel is provided and all sessions are mixed.

GRANADA PROVINCE

The best option is **Hammams de Al Andalus** (Map p261; ☎ 902 33 33 34; www.granada .hammamspain.com; Calle Santa Ana 16; bath/bath & massage €19/28), with three pools of different temperatures, plus a steam room and the option of a proper skin-scrubbing massage (*masaje kesse*, €35). In the same vein, but smaller, is **Baños de Elvira** (Map pp252-3; ☎ 958 20 26 53; www.banosdeelvira.com; Calle Arteaga 3; bath/bath & massage €18/25); the first and third Tuesday of the month are clothing optional. **Aljibe San Miguel Baños Árabes** (Map pp252-3; ☎ 958 52 28 67; www.aljibesanmiguel .es; Calle San Miguel Alta 41; bath/bath & massage €19/28) is the largest, with seven pools, but no steam room and no scrubbing.

❦ LOCAL PRODUCTS // TAKE HOME A MEMENTO FROM GRANADA

Granada's craft specialities include *taracea* (marquetry) – the best work has shell, silver or mother-of-pearl inlay, applied to boxes, tables, chess sets and more. **Artesanías González** (Map p261; ☎ 958 22 20 70; Cuesta de Gomérez 2) has exceptionally fine examples.

An equally big creative outlet is flamenco. Get a guitar for those flamenco classes from **Daniel Gil de Avalle** (Map p261; ☎ 958 22 16 10; Plaza del Realejo 15; ☺ closed Sat afternoon), where you can also see the construction process. Dress the part with an outfit from **Azabache** (Map p261; Calle de los Mesones 1). And even nondancers may appreciate the quirky, flamenco-inspired fashion at **Querencia** (Map p261; Plaza del Carmen).

For foodstuffs, check **La Oliva** (Map p261; Calle Rosario), for a large selection of olive oil and plenty of samples. For general souvenirs, **La Estampaora** (Map p261; Calle San Matías 8) produces distinctive, colourful posters, T-shirts and more. And you never know what you'll find at the **Rastro** (Map pp252-3; Palacio de Congresos), Granada's weekly flea market, every Sunday morning at the convention centre.

FESTIVALS & EVENTS

Semana Santa (Holy Week) The two most striking events in Granada's Easter Week are Los Gitanos

LORCA'S LEGACY

The great writer Federico García Lorca (see p361) was born just outside Granada and died here, shot in an open field by Nationalists at the beginning of the civil war. His summer house, **Huerta de San Vicente** (off Map pp252-3; ☎ 958 25 84 66; Calle Virgen Blanca; admission €3, Wed free, admission only by guided tour in Spanish; ☺ 10am-12.30pm & 4-6.30pm Tue-Sun Oct-Mar, 10am-12.30pm & 5-7.30pm Tue-Sun Apr-Jun, 10am-12.30pm Tue-Sun Jul-Aug) is a museum in a tidy park, a 15-minute walk from Puerta Real: head 700m down Calle de las Recogidas, turn right on Calle del Arabial, and the park entrance is ahead on the left.

In Lorca's birthplace, the village of Fuente Vaqueros, 17km west of Granada, the **Museo Casa Natal Federico García Lorca** (☎ 958 51 64 53; www.museogarcialorca.org; Calle Poeta Federico García Lorca 4; admission €1.80; ☺ guided visits hourly 10am-1pm & 5-7pm Tue-Sun Apr-Jun, 10am-2pm Tue-Sun Jul-Aug, 10am-1pm & 5-7pm Tue-Sun Sep, 10am-1pm & 4-6pm Tue-Sun Oct-Mar) displays photos, posters and costumes for the writer's plays. Buses (€1.50, 20 minutes) operated by **Ureña** (☎ 958 45 41 54) leave from Avenida de Andaluces in front of Granada train station roughly hourly between 9am and 8pm weekdays, and every two hours till 5pm on weekends. Lorca's remains – and thousands of others – lie in mass graves between Víznar and Alfacar, northeast of the city off the A92. It's now a memorial park.

(Wednesday), when the *fraternidad* toils to the Abadía de Sacromonte, lit by bonfires, and El Silencio (Thursday), when the streetlights are turned off for a silent, candlelit march.

Día de la Cruz (Day of the Cross) On 3 May, squares, patios and balconies are adorned with floral crosses, beginning three days of revelry.

Feria del Corpus Cristi (Corpus Christi Fair) The big annual fair, which starts 60 days after Easter Sunday, is a week of bullfights, dancing and street puppets; most of the action is at fairgrounds by the bus station.

Festival Internacional de Música y Danza (www.granadafestival.org) For three weeks in June and July, first-class classical and modern performance takes over the Alhambra and other historic sites.

GASTRONOMIC HIGHLIGHTS

Granada's a place where gastronomy stays down to earth. What it lacks in flashy *alta cocina* (haute cuisine) it makes up for in generous portions of Andalusian standards. Granada also has a wealth of places serving decent tapas and *raciones* (meal-sized tapas).

❤ CAFÉ FUTBOL €

Map p261; Plaza de Mariana Pineda 6; churros €2

There's sawdust on the floor and chandeliers above the long bar where white-shirted waiters attend to the morning rush with hot chocolate, delicate fingers of *churros* and dense but tasty *roscos* (doughnuts). (Pay at the separate cashier when you're done.) For a calmer, sit-down snack, choose tables in the high-ceilinged back room or out on the plaza.

❤ EL AJÍ €€

Map pp252-3; ☎ 958 29 29 30; Plaza San Miguel Bajo 9; mains €12-20

Up in the Albayzín, this chic but cosy neighbourhood restaurant is no bigger than a shoebox but serves from breakfast right through to the evening. Chatty staff at the tiny marble bar can point out some of the highlights of the creative menu (such as spicy grilled chicken). But even the simple items, like the tortilla, are done with special care. It's a good place to get out of the sun and rest up after a stroll around the area.

❤ FM €€

off Map pp252-3; ☎ 958 15 70 04; Carretera de Jaén 54; mains €12-16; ☒ closed Mon, Jul & Aug

A trek out from the centre (take bus 3 to Carretera de Jaén II), but arguably the best seafood in Granada and not a tourist in sight. This tiny, unassuming restaurant-bar trucks its fish in from Motril daily, and you can taste the difference. The signature dish is *pulpo seco*, slices of perfectly caramelised octopus in a crunchy salad.

❤ LOS DIAMANTES €€

Map p261; ☎ 958 22 70 70; Calle Navas 26; raciones €9-14

This bar-restaurant near Plaza del Carmen shows off the Andalusian penchant for frying, particularly in the marine realm. The plates are heaped with an amazing mix of *pescado frito* (fried fish) and succulent prawns. A little *caña* (small glass of beer) makes perfect company – as will all the other enthusiastic eaters who descend on the place at midday, so try to get in a little early.

❤ LOS ITALIANOS €

Map p261; Gran Vía de Colón 4; ice cream €1-4; ☒ 9am-1am

Stretched along a long zinc bar, a battalion of white-jacketed women stands ready to scoop up a *barquillo* (cone) or *terrana* (cup) of the ice cream of your choice. Our local informant swears by pistachio and raspberry, but the orange is equally divine. If the crowd at the front looks too daunting, try the back entrance in Calle Abenamar. Alas, this *helado* heaven is closed in winter.

☙ MERCADO DE SAN AGUSTÍN €
Map p261; Calle San Agustín; ☺ closed Sun
For fresh fruit and veg, and a general feast for the eyes, head for the large, covered market a block west of the cathedral. As a bonus, herb and spice stalls are set up along the Calle Cárcel Baja side of the cathedral, dealing medicinal and culinary herbs out of bulging sacks. (It goes without saying, though, that the stuff labelled 'saffron' is nothing of the sort.)

☙ OLIVER €€
Map p261; ☎ 958 26 22 00; Calle Pescadería 12; mains €12-18; ☺ closed Sun
The seafood bars on this square are a Granada institution, and Oliver is one of the best for food and unflappable service in the midst of the lunch rush. Sleek business types pack in alongside streetsweepers to devour *raciones* of garlicky fried treats at the mobbed bar, which can be ankle deep in crumpled napkins and shrimp shells come 4pm. The only place for any peace is the back dining room or the terrace tables, which fill up early.

☙ PARADOR DE GRANADA €€
Map p255; ☎ 958 22 14 40; Calle Real de la Alhambra; mains €19-22; ☺ 8am-11pm
On one side, the Parador de Granada is a hushed, swanky dinner experience, with a Moroccan-Spanish-French menu that also features local goat and venison. On the other, it's a stylish little canteen for sightseers, where even your *bocadillo de jamón* tastes special – and it ought to, considering its €12 price tag. Overall, a bit inflated, but a lovely treat for the location.

☙ PASTELERÍA LÓPEZ-MEZQUITA €
Map p261; ☎ 958 22 12 05; Calle Reyes Católicos 39; pastries €2-6; ☺ 9am-6.30pm Mon-Sat
This venerable pastry shop provides great on-the-go snacks – a flaky *empanadilla* filled with bacon and dates, for instance, or a piece of cinnamon-rich *pastela moruna,* a Moorish-style chicken pie. Take a number to order at the counter, or sit down and rest your feet in the back room.

☙ RUTA DEL AZAFRÁN €€
Map pp252-3; ☎ 958 22 68 82; www.rutadelazafran .es; Paseo del Padre Manjón 1; mains €13-20; ☺ 1-11pm Sun-Thu, 1pm-midnight Fri & Sat
One of the few high-concept restaurants in Granada, this sleek spot makes the connection between Spanish and Middle Eastern food, with inventive use of spice. But for every plate of veal with cardamom, there's also a traditional Spanish combo, such as broad beans with mushrooms and ham – and portions are typical too (that is, enormous). The terrace outside on the Río Darro is a great place for a snack, but inside you'll get better service.

Tapas
The city – in fact, the whole province – proudly carries on the tradition of free tapas, with each round of drinks earning you a slightly better bite. But these are seldom a bar's best, so you'll want to order a little something off the menu as well. Most bars are open for lunch too. Also try the bars around the Plaza de Toros, a 15-minute walk northwest from the Gran Vía, renowned for their food.

☙ AL SUR DE GRANADA €
Map pp252-3; ☎ 958 27 02 45; Calle de Elvira 150; ☺ closed Sun night
This delicatessen, dedicated to the best food and wine from around Granada

province, doubles as a bar. A downstairs room often hosts flamenco concerts, and there are wine tastings every Thursday at 7pm (€10). Get a sampler cheese platter, and try some of the various mountain liqueurs. If you want to visit the source, the friendly owners can even arrange lodging. Also a great place to pick up some local products to take home.

♣ BODEGAS CASTAÑEDA €
Map p261; Calle Almireceros

An institution among locals and tourists alike, this buzzing bar doles out hearty portions of food (try a hot or cold *tabla,* or platter; a half order, €6, is ample for two) and dispenses drinks from big casks mounted in the walls. The best choice is a lively, herbaceous *vermut* (vermouth) topped with soda. Don't confuse this place with Antigua Bodega Castañeda around the corner, which is not as tasty.

♣ CISCO Y TIERRA €
Map p261; Calle Lepanto 3

All the tapas here come from cans, or are preserved in some other way – but that's nowhere near as dismal as it sounds. Try the special cheese, a super-aged manchego with a caramel-like richness. The ceiling is decorated with policemen's hats, siphon bottles and other knick-knacks, while romantic tunes crackle from a vintage-look radio behind the bar.

♣ LA CANDELA €
Map p261; Calle Santa Escolástica 9

For a taste of hip Realejo, stop in at this golden-lit bar where the house speciality is the *montaditos,* slices of bread topped with all manner of meats, vegies and cheese. Pick one or two from the epic list to round out your tapa allotment. They're artfully (slowly) constructed one by one, but you can pass the time checking out concert posters and fellow drinkers' tattoos.

♣ LA TANA €
Map p261; ☎ 958 22 52 48; Calle Rosario

The wall of wine bottles at this Realejo bar can be a little intimidating, but you can always start with one of the featured 'wines of the month', or give the

GRANADA PROVINCE

TOP FIVE

INTERNATIONAL FLAVOURS

Granada's cosmopolitan population has some delicious global cuisine. It's a great place to give your palate a break from pork, should you need it.

* **Arrayanes** (Map p261; ☎ 958 22 84 01; Cuesta Marañas 4; mains €8-15; ⏲ from 8pm; Ⓥ) Rich tagines and delicate couscous, though portions run small, and there's no alcohol.

* **El Piano** (Map pp252-3; Calle Gran Capitán 7; ⏲ 11am-11pm; Ⓥ) Heavenly vegetarian deli where you can pick and mix from Indian, Middle Eastern and Asian treats.

* **Om Kalsum** (Map pp252-3; Calle Jardines 17; media-raciones €3; Ⓥ) A taste of North Africa beyond the Albayzín tourist corridor, this friendly tapas bar is open all day.

* **Pervane** (Map p261; Calle Calderería Nueva 24; teas €2-3; ⏲ 10am-late; Ⓥ) A tea cafe with delicious *batidos* (smoothies). Follow the stairs all the way up to a quiet attic room filled with plants.

* **Poë** (Map pp252-3; Calle Paz; media-raciones €3) Your choice of Brazilian tapas.

bartender a little idea what you like – a *suave* (smooth) red, or something more *fuerte* (strong). The tapas are generous and very meaty, and the place feels intimate and pleasantly old – but not old-fashioned.

❦ RECA €

Map p261; ☎ 636 89 11 89; Plaza de la Trinidad; raciones €8; ⊘ closed Tue

One of Granada's top tapas places, Reca is always packed with people hungering after its wonderfully presented, modernised versions of classics like couscous and *salmorejo* (a thicker version of gazpacho). It's one of the few bars in the area that serves food through the afternoon, without a break.

NIGHTLIFE

Granada buzzes with flamenco devotees, footloose travellers and grooving students. The latter congregate on the Calle de Elvira, while the Realejo draws a hipper crowd (Calle Navas is a good place to start), and the centre, near Plaza Nueva, has some excellent vintage bars. Cave clubs in Sacromonte are known for flamenco shows, but these are largely spectacles staged for tour groups. Given the scores of music students in town, there are usually far more enthusiastic shows to be seen in more casual venues. Start with these reliable spots (and Al Sur de Granada, p251), and look out for posters and leaflets.

❦ CAFÉ AU LAIT

Map p261; ☎ 958 20 20 47; Plaza de la Romanilla 10

This small French-run restaurant hosts some of the better organised flamenco shows in town, usually with local *gitano* musicians and student dancers, plus

an international crowd of aficionados. Shows (at 8pm and 9.30pm) are free, but you're expected to order some food (mains €8 to €12). Make reservations earlier in the day, as the place usually fills up.

❦ ESHAVIRA

Map pp252-3; ☎ 958 29 08 29; Postigo de la Cuna 2; ⊘ from 10pm

Just off Calle Azacayas, duck down the spooky alley, cross the small patio and battle with the hefty door to slip into one of the best jazz and flamenco haunts in the city, with local musicians coming down from Sacromonte to jam. But the party doesn't get rolling till at least 1am, and that's on weeknights. There's a good formal show (earlier) on Sunday nights, if you can't stick it out till the wee hours.

❦ PEÑA FLAMENCA LA PLATERÍA

Map pp252-3; ☎ 958 21 06 50; www.laplateria.org .es, in Spanish; Placeta de Toqueros 7

Buried in the Albayzín warren, Peña La Platería claims to be the oldest flamenco aficionados' club in Spain. It's a private affair, though, and not always open to nonmembers. Performances are usually Thursday and Saturday at 10.30pm – look presentable, and speak a little Spanish at the door, if you can.

OTHER VENUES

Centro Cultural Dar Ziryab (Map p261; ☎ 958 22 94 29; Calle Calderería Nueva 11) Middle Eastern music and dance.

Centro Cultural Manuel de Falla (Map p255; ☎ 958 22 00 22; Paseo de los Mártires) Weekly classical concerts.

Museo Cuevas del Sacromonte (Map pp252-3; ☎ 958 21 51 20; www.sacromontegranada.com; Barranco de los Negros) Summer flamenco program.

TRANSPORT

AIR // **Aeropuerto Federico García Lorca** (off Map pp252-3; ☎ 902 40 05 00) is 17km west of the city, near the A92. **Autocares J González** (☎ 958 49 01 64; www.autocaresjosegonzalez.com; €3) runs buses to Gran Vía de Colón opposite the cathedral. Departures from the airport are timed with each flight; from the centre, they leave nearly hourly between 5.20am and 8pm. A taxi costs about €20.

BUS // Granada's **bus station** (off Map pp252-3; Carretera de Jaén) is almost 3km northwest of the city centre; it has luggage lockers and an internet cafe. Take city bus 3 to the centre or a taxi for €6. **Alsina Graells/Alsa** (☎ 958 18 54 80; www.alsa.es) handles buses in the province and across the region, plus a night bus direct to Madrid's Barajas airport (€24.50, six hours).

LOCAL BUS // Individual tickets are €1.20, or pay €2 for a refillable pass card, then add at least €5, for rides as low as €0.80. Both can be bought with notes or coins from the bus driver. Most lines stop on Gran Vía de Colón; the tourist office dispenses maps and schedules.

CAR // Granada is at the junction of the A44 and the A92. The Alhambra has easy car access from the A395 spur.

PARKING // **Alhambra Parking** (Map p255; Avenida Los Alixares; per hr/day €2.40/16.25) **Parking San Agustín** (Map p261; Calle San Agustín; per hr/day €1.75/20) **Parking Plaza Puerta Real** (Map p261; Acera del Darro; per hr/day €1.45/17).

TAXI // Pick up at Plaza Nueva or call **Teleradio taxi** (☎ 958 28 06 54).

TRAIN // The **train station** (off Map pp252-3; ☎ 958 20 40 00; Avenida de Andaluces) is 1.5km northwest of the centre, off Avenida de la Constitución. For the centre, walk straight ahead to Avenida de la Constitución and turn right to pick up buses 1, 3, 5, 7 or 33 to Gran Vía de Colón; taxis cost about €4.50. Four trains run daily to/from Seville (€23, three hours) and Almería (€15, 2¼ hours) via Guadix. Three go to Ronda (€13, 2½ hours) and Algeciras (€19.50, four to 4½ hours). Two go to Córdoba (€33, 2½ hours). For Málaga (€14 to €23, 2½ hours) take an Algeciras train and change at Bobadilla (€9, 1½ hours). Three trains go to Linares-Baeza daily (€12 to €32, 2½ to three hours), and two each to Madrid (€64, 4¾ hours), Valencia (€48 to €69.50, 7½ to eight hours) and Barcelona (€58 to €125, 12 to 13 hours).

LA VEGA & EL ALTIPLANO

· · · · · ·

Surrounding Granada is a swathe of fertile land known as La Vega, planted with shimmering poplar groves, as well as food crops. Heading northeast, the A92 passes through the hilly Parque Natural Sierra de Huétor before entering an increasingly arid landscape, made all the more dramatic by the white peaks of the Sierra Nevadas looming to the south. Up close, the terrain around the town of Guadix is also fascinating, with the biggest concentration of cave houses in Spain, and perhaps in Europe.

Outside Guadix the A92 veers southeast towards Almería, crossing the

BUSES FROM GRANADA

Destination	Cost	Duration	Daily Frequency
Almería	€13.50	2¼-4hr	9
Baza	€8.50	1½-2hr	7-10
Córdoba	€12.50	2¾-4½hr	8
Guadix	€5	1hr	8-14
Málaga	€10	2hr	18
Mojácar	€18	4hr	3
Seville	€19.50	3-4hr	9

Marquesado de Zenete district below the northern flank of the Sierra Nevada, while the A92N heads northeast across the Altiplano, Granada's 'High Plain', which breaks out into mountains here and there and affords superb long-distance views all the way to northern Almería province.

GUADIX

pop 20,300

Guadix (gwah-*deeks*), 55km from Granada near the foothills of the Sierra Nevada, is famous for its cave dwellings – not prehistoric remnants, but the homes of at least 3000 present-day townsfolk, carved into the hills' heavy clay. Cave hotels (p396), which are wonderfully cool in summer and cosy in winter, let you try the lifestyle. The *accitanos* (from the town's Moorish name, Wadi Acci) also enjoy some excellent, tourist-free tapas bars. The **tourist office** (☎ 958 66 26 65; Avenida Mariana Pineda; ☺ 9am-1.30pm & 4-6pm Mon-Fri) is on the road leaving the town centre towards Granada.

EXPLORING GUADIX

**❧ BARRIADA DE LAS CUEVAS //
PEEK INSIDE A HOBBIT HOLE**
Up in the hills on the south side of town is Guadix's largest cave district, whitewashed dwellings nestled among rolling hills, with spindly chimneys, satellite dishes and full connections to the town's power and water lines. You can walk or drive a route past some rather splendid homes, as well as some more ramshackle ones. The excellent **Cueva Museo** (☎ 958 66 55 69; Plaza de Padre Poveda; admission €2.50; ☺ 10am-2pm & 4-6pm Mon-Fri, 10am-2pm Sat Sep-Apr, 10am-2pm & 5-7pm Mon-Fri, 10am-2pm Sat May-Aug) re-creates cave life of years past. For more insight, stop into the **Ermita**

Nueva**, across the plaza, and have a beer at **Mesón Virgen de Gracia** (Plaza Ermita Nueva), a family-friendly neighbourhood bar – that just happens to be in the cave neighbourhood (with your back to the museum, head to the right).

**❧ THE OLD CENTRE // STROLL
AMID RENAISSANCE LANDMARKS**
Most visitors make a beeline to the cave district, but the town's old centre has its own distinctive architecture, much of it rendered in warm sandstone. At the centre of Guadix is a fine **cathedral** (Calle Santa María del Buen Aire; admission €3; ☺ 10.30am-1pm & 2-7pm Mon-Sat, 9.30am-1pm Sun), built between the 16th and 18th centuries on the site of the town's former main mosque in a mix of Gothic, Renaissance and baroque styles. Nearby, the **Plaza de la Constitución** feels almost fortified, edged with porticos and gracefully worn brick steps. Just up the hill, look for the off-kilter tile Mudéjar tower of the 16th-century **Iglesia y Monasterio de Santiago** (Placeta de Santiago; ☺ hrs of service), with an elaborate plateresque facade by Diego Siloé. Just to the west, you'll find the 10th- and 11th-century Islamic castle, the **Alcazaba** (Calle Barradas 3; admission €1.20; ☺ 11am-2pm & 4-6.30pm Tue-Sat, 10am-2pm Sun), which gives views across town and into the main cave quarter, the Barriada de las Cuevas, some 700m south.

**❧ TAPAS TOUR // FREE SNACKS
AND FRIENDLY BARS**
No need for a sit-down meal in Guadix – you can feed yourself well, and meet the locals, at the exceptional bars around town. At every place, you'll pay less than €1.50 for a beer, and *raciones* cost about €5. Between Avenida Medina Olmos and the river, **La Bodeguilla** (Calle Doctor Pulido 4) is one of the best. Here, old men and

families sprawl around a red-tiled room with wine casks along the walls and eat delicious tapas as well as baked spuds, and raw *habas* (broad beans) when in season. From there, you can cross back over Medina Olmos to **Bodega Calatrava** (Calle La Tribuna) for some sherry and excellent bites like juicy fried prawns. **Mesón Granadul** (Calle de Encarnita Martínez Jabalera 6), west of the cathedral, doubles as a delicatessen, so many of its tapas comprise especially good ham, cheese or sausage. This is also a good spot for a proper lunch, at the small tables at the back.

TRANSPORT

BUS // Buses run to Granada (€5, one hour, seven to nine daily), Almería (€8, 1½ to 2¼ hours, three or four daily), Baza (€4, one hour, six to eight daily) and Mojácar (€13.50, three hours, two or three daily). The **bus station** (☎ 958 66 06 57; Calle Concepción Arenal) is off Avenida Medina Olmos, about 700m southeast of the centre.

TRAIN // There are four trains daily to either Granada (€7, one hour) or Almería (€8, 1¼ hours). The station is off the Murcia road, about 2km northeast of the town centre – walkable, but dusty and not scenic; a cab costs €4 to the centre, and about €8 to the cave district.

LA CALAHORRA

☙ CASTILLO DE LA CALAHORRA // ROAD-TRIP TO AN ABANDONED RENAISSANCE CASTLE

During the Reconquista, the flatlands between Guadix and the mountains fell under the command of Marqués Rodrigo de Mendoza, whose tempestuous life included a spell in Italy unsuccessfully wooing Lucrezia Borgia. About 20 km southeast of Guadix, his forbidding **Castillo de La Calahorra** (admission €3; ☺ 10am-12.30pm & 4-5.30pm Wed) looms on a hilltop, guarding the pass over the Sierra Nevada. Built between 1509 and 1512, the domed corner towers and blank walls enclose an elegant Renaissance courtyard with a staircase of Carrara marble. Guided tours (in Spanish) take about 30 minutes, and if you arrive while one is going on, you'll have to wait for the door to be opened. For guided tours outside of regular hours contact the caretaker Antonio Trivaldo (☺ 958 67 70 98) to make a time. To drive up to the castle, turn onto the dirt road opposite La Hospedería del Zenete in La Calahorra, and take the winding route uphill. Or park in the town plaza and walk up the stone footpath.

BAZA

The market town of Baza, 44km northeast of Guadix, dates back to Iberian times. It has an attractive historic centre and its own small cave-dwelling district, and while there's not enough sightseeing for a long stay, it's a good place to stop for a few hours to break up a day's drive. The **tourist office** (☎ 958 86 13 25; Plaza Mayor 2; ☺ 10am-2pm & 4-6.30pm, closed holidays) is on the plaza, south of the main road through town.

☙ HISTORIC CENTRE // A GRAND CHURCH AND A GRANDE DAME

The Plaza Mayor, several blocks south from the main road through town, is dominated by the 16th-century **Iglesia Concatedral de la Encarnación**, its stone facade weathered and worn. Inside, the pulpit drips with intricate carvings. Adjacent to the cathedral on the plaza, the town's good **Museo Municipal** (☎ 958 70 35 55; admission €1.20; ☺ 9.30am-1.30pm Tue, 9.30am-1.30pm & 5-6.30pm Wed-Fri, 11am-2pm Sat & Sun) has a collection of finds from nearby archaeological sites. The most remarkable item is a copy of the *Dama de Baza*, a person-sized Iberian goddess statue unearthed in 1971 (the original is in Madrid's Museo Arqueológico Nacional).

🌱 LA CURVA // LUNCH ON LAVISH SEAFOOD TREATS

Perched on a sharp curve on the main street through town, **La Curva** (☎ 958 70 00 02; Carretera de Granada; mains €12-18, menú €10) is hard to miss. It's a popular local option for a big meal. Dapper waiters in white shirts dole out local wines and platters of perfectly fresh clams, oysters and whole fish, some fried, some doused in vinegary *escabeche*. Note that much of the fish is priced per kilo.

TRANSPORT

BUS // The **bus station** (☎ 958 70 21 03; Calle Reyes Católicos) is 200m north of the Plaza Mayor. Between six and eight buses per day run to/from Guadix (€4, one hour) and Granada (€8.50, 1¾ hours), and three run to Vélez Rubio (€5, one hour) in the Almería province.

SIERRA NEVADA & LAS ALPUJARRAS

Granada's dramatic alpine backdrop is the Sierra Nevada range, which extends about 75km from west to east and into Almería province. Its wild snow-capped peaks include the highest point in mainland Spain, while the lower reaches of the range, known as Las Alpujarras (sometimes just La Alpujarra), are dotted with tiny scenic villages. From July to early September, the higher elevations offer wonderful multiday trekking and day hikes. Outside of this period, there's risk of serious inclement weather, but the lower Alpujarras are always welcoming, with most snow melting away by May.

The 862-sq-km Parque Nacional Sierra Nevada, Spain's largest national park, is

GRANADA PROVINCE

~ WORTH A TRIP ~

A dusty Altiplano village, **Orce** (Map pp248-9) is the centre of a debate about humanity's ancient history. The town and the surrounding rolling, empty plains, studded with crumbling farmhouses, makes an interesting, scenic detour on a drive between Granada and Almería's Los Vélez area (p308).

Near Orce in 1982, archaeologist Josep Gilbert found a fossilised bone fragment that he believed was from a *Homo erectus* skull, some 1.7 million years old – substantially older than any similar fragment yet found in Europe. Sceptics, however, have since said the fragment is more likely from a horse and not nearly so old. Regardless, Orce can still claim Spain's oldest evidence of human presence, in the form of stone tools that are 1.3 million years old. And further digging has unearthed bones of mammoths, sabre-tooth tigers and other beasts that met their end at the lake that once filled this basin.

The finds are on show in Orce's **Museo de Prehistoria y de Paleontología** (☎ 958 74 61 01; admission €1.50; 🕙 10am-2pm & 4-6pm Tue-Sun Oct-May, 10am-2pm & 5-9pm Tue-Sun Jun-Sep), in a castle just off the village's central square.

To reach Orce from the A92N, turn north 18km east of Baza onto the A330 towards Huéscar. After 23km, turn east along the GR9104 for Orce (6km away). Continuing east from Orce it's a further 30km to María, the first village in Los Vélez.

home to 2100 of Spain's 7000 plant species, among them unique types of crocus, narcissus, thistle, clover, poppy and gentian. Andalucía's largest ibex population (about 5000) is here, too, frolicking above 2800m. Surrounding the national park at lower altitudes is the Parque Natural Sierra Nevada, with a lesser degree of protection.

Along the southern edge of the protected area the Alpujarras is a 70km-long jumble of valleys along the southern flank of the Sierra Nevada. It is a beautiful, diverse and even slightly strange place. Heavenly in its landscape of arid slopes, deep crags and egg-white villages that look as if they were spilled onto the mountainside, the towns on the mountain's lower belts simmer with spiritual seekers, long-term travellers and rat-race dropouts, while the higher villages have a disorienting timelessness.

Even the most-visited Alpujarran towns are appealing, as the villages' Berber-style flat-roofed houses and the winding lanes between them look out on hillsides that have been carefully terraced and irrigated since the earliest Moorish times. With well-trod footpaths connecting each settlement, it's a delightful area to explore on foot.

ESSENTIAL INFORMATION

TOURIST INFORMATION // Capileira tourist office (Servicio de Interpretación de Altos Cumbres; ☎ 958 76 34 86, 671 56 44 06; picapileira@oapn.mma.es; ☙ 10am-2pm & 5-8pm) The main tourist office in Capileira. Mulhacén and Veleta tourist office (Hoya de la Mora; Map p274; ☎ 630 95 97 39; ☙ about 8.30am-2.30pm & 3.30-7.30pm in season) Information for Mulhacén and Veleta. Órgiva tourist office (☎ 958 78 44 84; 9am-2pm & 5-7pm Mon-Fri, 10am-2pm Sat). Pampaneira tourist office (Punto de Información Parque Nacional de

MAPS

The best maps for the Sierra Nevada and Las Alpujarras are Editorial Alpina's *Sierra Nevada, La Alpujarra* (1:40,000) and Editorial Penibética's *Sierra Nevada* (1:40,000). Both come with booklets describing walking, cycling and skiing routes. Available at the Centro de Visitantes El Dornajo, near the ski station, and at the tourist office in Pampaneira.

Sierra Nevada; ☎ 958 76 31 27; Plaza de la Libertad; ☙ 10am-3pm Sun & Mon year-round, 10am-2pm & 5-7pm Tue-Sat, 10am-2pm & 4-6pm mid-Oct–May). **Sierra Nevada tourist office** (Centro de Visitantes El Dornajo; ☎ 958 34 06 25; alhori@imfe.es; ☙ 9.30am-2.30pm & 6-8pm Apr-Sep, 10am-2pm & 4.30-7.30pm Oct-Mar) Information centre for the Sierra Nevada, about 10km before the ski station. Stocks maps and guides.

ORIENTATION

To reach the higher elevations of the Sierra Nevada, and the ski area, take the A395 from the eastern edge of Granada. The main road into Las Alpujarras from the west is the A348, which leaves the A44 34km south of Granada to pass through the relative lowlands. Just west of Órgiva, the A4132 turns off to the north to wind along the mountain slopes and pass through many of the higher villages; it merges with the A4130 and then rejoins the A348 a few kilometres north of Cádiar, via the A4127.

EXPLORING THE SIERRA NEVADA

❦ **LOS CAHORROS // A SCENIC HIKE MINUTES FROM GRANADA**
A short drive southeast of Granada, not far from the village of Monachil, the area known as Los Cahorros (off Map

GRANADA PROVINCE

GRANADA PROVINCE

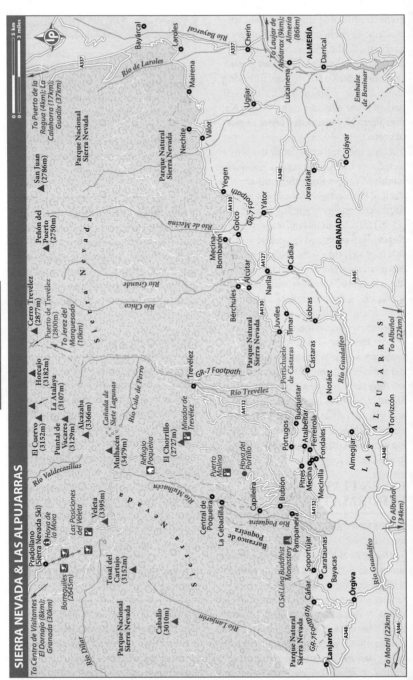

SIERRA NEVADA & LAS ALPUJARRAS

pp252-3) is good for short walks, with trails running through dramatic gorges alongside the Río Monachil. The most popular route – the Cahorros Altos, heading upstream – passes over a suspension bridge and alongside waterfalls. Look for the start of the 5km route just east of Monachil. You can also take a bus from Granada to Monachil (€3, 30 minutes), from Paseo del Salón in Granada (Map pp252–3); buses run nearly hourly from 8.10am to 11.10pm, except Saturday afternoon or Sunday.

☙ SIERRA NEVADA SKI // HIT THE SLOPES 30 MINUTES FROM THE CITY

The ski station **Sierra Nevada Ski** (☎ 902 70 80 90; www.sierranevadaski.com, in Spanish), at Pradollano, 33km from Granada on the A395, often has better snow conditions and weather than northern Spanish ski resorts, so it can get very crowded on weekends and holidays in season. A few of the 85 marked runs start almost at the top of 3395m-high Veleta. There are cross-country routes, too, and a dedicated snowboard area, plus a whole raft of other activities for non-skiers. In summer you can mountain-bike, ride horses and more.

In winter **Tocina** (☎ 958 46 50 22) operates three daily buses (four on the weekends) to the resort from Granada's bus station (€5/8 one-way/return, one hour). Outside the ski season there's just one daily bus (9am from Granada, 5pm from the ski station). A taxi from Granada costs about €50.

☙ MULHACÉN & VELETA // CLIMB TO DIZZYING HEIGHTS

The Sierra Nevada's two highest peaks are Mulhacén (3479m) and Veleta (3395m). Two of three known as Los Tresmiles, because they rise above 3000m, they're

on the western end of the range, close to Granada. From the ski station on the mountains' north flank, a road climbs up and over to Capileira (p278), the highest village in the Barranco de Poqueira in the Alpujarras on the south side, but it's closed to motor vehicles on the highest stretch. From late June to the end of October (depending on snow cover), the national park operates two shuttle buses to give walkers access to the upper reaches of the range – or just a scenic guided drive. One bus runs up from 3km above the ski station, starting at the national park information post at **Hoya de la Mora** (Map p274; ☎ 630 95 97 39; ⌚ about 8.30am-2.30pm & 3.30-7.30pm in season). The other leaves from the town of Capileira in Las Alpujarras. Tickets are €4.80 one-way or €8 return, and it doesn't hurt to call to reserve.

From the end of the bus route on the north side, it's about 4km up Veleta, an ascent of about 370m with 1½ hours' walking (plus stops); or 14km to the top of Mulhacén, with four to five hours' walking; or about 15km (five or six hours) all the way over to Mirador de Trevélez (avoiding the summits). From the Mirador de Trevélez (the end stop on the Capileira side), it's around three hours to the top of Mulhacén (6km, 800m ascent).

If you want to make it an overnight trip, you can bunk down for the night at the Refugio Poqueira (see p396).

EXPLORING LAS ALPUJARRAS

☙ WALKING TRAILS // WALK LIKE AN ALPUJARRAN ON NUMEROUS TRAILS

The alternating ridges and valleys of the Alpujarras are criss-crossed with a network of mule paths, irrigation ditches and hiking routes, for a near-infinite number of good walks between villages or into the wild. The best time for walking in Las Alpujarras is April to mid-June, and also mid-September to early November, when the temperatures are just right and the vegetation at its most colourful.

The villages in the beautiful Barranco de Poqueira (opposite) are the most popular starting point, but even there, you'll rarely pass another hiker on the trail. Colour-coded routes ranging from 4km to 23km (two to eight hours) run up and down the gorge, and you can also hike to Mulhacén (p275) from here. Get maps and advice at Capileira's **Servicio de Interpretación de Altos Cumbres** (☎ 958 76 34 86, 671 56 44 06; picapileira@oapn.mma.es; ☽ about 9am-2pm & 4.30-7.30pm), at the main street junction. Or you can make do with the Editorial Alpina map, which shows most of the trails in the gorge – the hardest part is getting out of Capileira (p278), where the trailheads are notoriously hard to find.

Of the long-distance footpaths that traverse Las Alpujarras, the **GR-7** (which runs all the way to Greece) follows the most scenic route; you could walk it from Lanjarón to Laroles in one week. From Bubión, you can follow it over the ridgeline to Pitres (p278), in the next valley, and catch a bus back in the late afternoon (4.30pm or 6pm).

For road-trippers looking to stretch their legs, Pampaneira's well-marked **La Atalaya** trail is a good option, with green-flagged posts leading down to the roaring river and up to a ruined building on the opposite hillside, about two hours round-trip.

♥ LANJARÓN // A HIGH-MOUNTAIN SPA TOWN – WITH A SIDE OF HAM

The closest of the Alpujarras villages to Granada, Lanjarón often bustles with

tourists. Second only to Trevélez in ham production, it's also packed with shops selling the stuff. And that bottled water you've been drinking? It's from here as well. The therapeutic waters have been harnessed at the large **Balneario de Lanjarón** (☎ 958 77 01 37; www.balneariodelanjaron .com, in Spanish; Avenida de la Constitución; 1hr bath €25), a spa on the west edge of town, just opposite the tourist office. If you'd rather snack than swim, wander down the main street to the middle of town, to **Arco de Noé** (Jamones Gustavo Rubio; Avenida de Andalucía 38), one of the better ham shops, where you can stock up on supplies or order a tasting tray and a swig of sherry out the back. A little further down the street are two bakeries, for completing your picnic purchases, if need be.

♥ ÓRGIVA // THE CROSSROADS OF THE ALPUJARRAS

The main town of the western Alpujarras, Órgiva is probably most well known as the home of Chris Stewart, British author of *Driving Over Lemons* and other entertaining books about his life here as a sheep farmer. It's a bit scruffier than neighbouring villages, but it's a convenient base. The **tourist office** (☎ 958 78 44 84; 9am-2pm & 5-7pm Mon-Fri, 10am-2pm Sat) is at the west end of town, just off the main road by the BP station. The landmark 16th-century twin-towered **church** stands beside Órgiva's central traffic lights, and the plaza in front is one of town's main gathering spots. The **Alsina Graells bus stop** (Avenida González Robles 67) is about 300m downhill along the main street.

The best of the bars on the plaza, **Mesón Casa Santiago** (Plaza García Moreno; mains €6-12) has a snug, traditional feel and does full meals too. If you need a break from ham, stop at all-female-owned **Café Libertad** (Calle Libertad 36; sandwiches €5-6;

ALPUJARRAS ITINERARIES

Although it's rarely more than 30 minutes' drive between villages, don't spread yourself too thin, or they'll all start to look alike. Better to settle in one or two spots and appreciate the quiet and local specialities.

* **One day** – Pick up fixings for a picnic at a ham shop in Lanjarón (opposite), then head to Yegen (p280) for a short hike. Have dinner in Válor (p280).
* **Two days** – Base yourself in Capileira (p278) or Pampaneira (below) for day hikes: one down to Pampaneira and back, and another over to Pitres, catching the bus back.
* **Four days** – Spend two nights in Mairena (p280), with day hikes or drives to neighbouring villages. Drive over the Puerto de la Ragua pass for a night in Guadix (p270), then loop back across to Granada the next morning.

9am-2.30pm Mon-Fri; Ⓥ), above the main plaza, just left and uphill from the town hall, for fruit shakes, sandwiches and organic wine.

♥ BARRANCO DE POQUEIRA // A DRAMATIC RAVINE, IDEAL FOR HIKING

When seen from the bottom of the Poqueira gorge, the three villages of Pampaneira, Bubión and Capileira, 14km to 20km northeast of Órgiva, look like splatters of white paint, Jackson Pollock–style, against the grey stone behind. They're the most beautiful villages of the Alpujarras, and the most visited – but don't let their popularity deter you. Even the scores of craft shops are tastefully done, and the villages are linked by hiking trails that are perfectly doable in a day. The best-stocked tourist office is in Pampaneira.

Pampaneira

The lowest village in the gorge has a lively plaza, and ham-curing operations lurking in its back streets. The **Punto de Información Parque Nacional de Sierra Nevada** (☎ 958 76 31 27; Plaza de la Libertad, Pampaneira; Ⓨ 10am-3pm Sun & Mon year-round, 10am-2pm & 5-7pm Tue-Sat, afternoons 4-6pm about

mid-Oct–Easter) is the area's best, with plenty of information about the region, plus maps and books for sale.

Opposite the village, 2km up the western side of the gorge, you can just make out the stupa of the small stone Buddhist monastery of **O.Sel.Ling** (☎ 958 34 31 34; www.oseling.com), established in 1982 by a Tibetan monk. It's open to visitors between 3.30pm and 6pm daily, and makes a good destination for a hike.

For dining, **Restaurante Casa Diego** (☎ 958 76 30 15; Plaza de la Libertad 3; mains €6-9), on the plaza opposite the 16th-century church, serves good *conejo a lo cortijero* (rabbit stewed with garlic) on its upstairs terrace.

Bubión

The highlight of Bubión is the **Casa Alpujarreña** (Calle Real; admission €1.80; Ⓨ 11am-2pm Wed-Sun, 11am-2pm & 5-7pm Fri, Sat & holidays), in the lower village beside the church. This folk museum set in a village house gives a glimpse of bygone Alpujarran life, both good and bad – a washboard is dedicated to the women of Bubión who have endured this 'cruel instrument'. For another glimpse of the past, visit the French-owned weaving workshop **Taller del Telar**

(Calle Santísima Trinidad; ⏰ 11am-2.30pm & 5-8.30pm), with ancient looms from Granada.

A good restaurant on the main road, **Teide** (☎ 958 76 30 84; Carretera de Sierra Nevada; menú €8.50; ⏰ 10am-10.30pm Wed-Mon) has a hearty *menú del día* and is frequented by a local clientele of characters stopping in for *jamón* and wine. **Estación 4** (☎ 958 76 31 16; Calle Estación 4; mains €7-11; ⏰ 5-11pm Tue-Fri, 1-11pm Sat; Ⓥ), a bit below the main road, is a more elegant affair, with a serene minimalist dining room and lighter takes on Spanish standards.

Capileira

Most everyone who comes to Poqueira's highest village soon sets out on a walk. Fortify yourself first at Capileira's village tavern, **Bar El Tilo** (☎ 958 76 31 81; Plaza Calvario; raciones €6-8), on a lovely whitewashed square with a terrace. *Raciones* such as *albóndigas* (meatballs) are enormous. When you return, try dinner at the bohemian **Casa Ibero** (☎ 958 76 32 56; Calle Parra 1; mains €10-14, menú €15; ⏰ 7-10.45pm Jul-Sep; Ⓥ), for a gastronomic fusion of Andalusian, Arabic and Indian.

If you do stick around town, don't miss the excellent leatherwork at **J Brown** (☎ 958 76 30 92; Calle Doctor Castilla), all handmade, at very reasonable prices.

❧ LA TAHÁ // PRETTY VILLAGES CLUSTERED WITHIN EASY WALKING DISTANCE

In the next valley east from Poqueira, life gets substantially more tourist-free. Still called by the Arabic term for the administrative districts into which the Islamic caliphate divided the Alpujarras, this region consists of the town of **Pitres** and a cluster of lovely small villages – **Mecina**, **Mecinilla**, **Fondales**, **Ferreirola** and **Atalbéitar** – in the valley just below. Day-trippers are few, and the expat residents have nearly blended in with the scenery. Ancient paths between these hamlets (marked with signposts labelled 'Sendero Local Pitres-Ferreirola') wend their way through lush woods and orchards, while the tinkle of running water provides the soundtrack. About 15 minutes' walk below Fondales, an old Moorish-era bridge spans the deep gorge of the Río Trevélez. Park at the top of the town and follow signs saying 'Camino de Órgiva' and 'Camino del Campuzano'.

For dining, vegetarians and anyone with a bent for local produce shouldn't miss **L'Atelier** (☎ 958 85 75 01; Calle Alberca 21, Mecina; mains €10-14; ⏰ lunch Sat & Sun, dinner Wed-Mon; Ⓥ), in Mecina, a snug, candlelit restaurant where the globetrotting meatless dishes (Burma curry, Moroccan soup) are exceptional. Call ahead to reserve; at lunch, there's a €10 set menu. For a sweet treat, you can visit the kitchens of **Chocolates Sierra Nevada** (☎ 625 93 88 22; Calle Paseo Marítimo 5, Pitres) – look (or sniff) for it on the main road west of Pitres. A tearoom in Ferreirola, **Fa-Ré** (⏰ 10am-4pm), provides a little refreshment for hikers; follow 'cafe' signs in the village.

And for tiles that are more than a tourist trinket, **Alizares Fatima** (☎ 958 76 61 07; Calle Paseo Marítimo 19, Pitres), on the edge of Pitres, does beautiful work.

❧ TREVÉLEZ // SAMPLE THE REGION'S BEST HAM

In a gash in the mountainside almost as impressive as the Poqueira gorge, Trevélez claims to be the highest village in Spain, located at 1476m; it's a starting point for routes into the high Sierra Nevada. It also produces some of Spain's best *jamón serrano*, with hams trucked in from far and wide for curing in the dry mountain air. Along the main road you're confronted by a welter of ham and souvenir shops, but the upper part is a lively, typically Alpujarran village, where you're just as likely to hear the clip-clop of a donkey as the buzz of a motorbike. A small information kiosk by the bus stop dispenses trail advice, snacks, gear and maps.

One of the town's better restaurants is **Mesón Joaquín** (☎ 958 85 85 60; Calle Puente; mains €9-14), just west of the main junction. White-coated *jamón* technicians slice up transparent sheets of the local product, and the trout comes from the wholesaler just behind. Ask about the day's special stew. Heading uphill, you pass **Jamones González** (☎ 958 85 86 32; Calle Nueva), with one of the town's best selections of meats and local foodstuffs. In the upper plaza, **Café Bar Los Rosales** (Plaza Rosales) offers an array of tapas surprisingly light on the ham – you might even get succulent garlic shrimp. Finally, **Restaurante La Fragua** (☎ 958 85 86 26; Barrio Alto; mains €8-13; Ⓥ) is at the very top of the village – a deterrent unless you're staying at the neighbouring hotel (p397) – but worth the hike up for partridge in walnut sauce, and the fig ice cream.

If you're staying in the middle or upper villages, you can drive up past the hard right turn to the *barrio medio*. There's a very small car park here, by Café Bar Rosales, but if it's full, you'll likely have to backtrack to the larger car park just by the turn.

❤ **EASTERN ALPUJARRAS // EVER MORE REMOTE MOUNTAIN SPOTS**
Seven kilometres south of Trevélez, the A4132 crosses the Portichuelo de Cástaras pass and turns east into a harsher, barer landscape, yet still with oases of greenery around the villages. Significantly fewer tourists make it this far from

---

TOP **FIVE**

ALPUJARRAN SPECIALITIES

In addition to the ubiquitous and incredibly hearty *plato alpujarreño* (a platter of eggs fried in olive oil, potatoes, pork sausage and mellow, oniony blood sausage, or *morcilla*), try these local culinary standards:

★ **Patatas a lo pobre** – potatoes pan-fried in olive oil with green peppers, onions and garlic

★ **Perdiz en escabeche** – partridge in a vinegary onion broth, an ages-old treatment brought by the Arabs

★ **Garbanzos** and **lentejas** – chickpeas and lentils, made into hearty stews, usually a daily special at restaurants

★ **Migas** – another crossover dish from Moorish times, often aptly translated as couscous, and usually studded with tasty bacon nubbins

★ **Vino de costa** – the local rosé, raw and bright, and very refreshing on a hot day

Granada, and those that do are often on long, solitary walking excursions. Many of the pleasures here are in eating: fresh, local products are the focus at the casual restaurants and inns.

Bérchules
In a green valley back in the hills, this village is a walkers' waypoint. **Hotel Los Bérchules** (☎ 958 85 25 30; mains €10-14), at the crossroads at the bottom of the village, has an excellent restaurant, with such local specialities as lamb with mint. **Cuatro Vientos** (☎ 958 76 90 39; Calle Carretera 4; Ⓨ closed Mon), the unassuming bar just down the hill, dishes out equally tasty meaty tapas.

Cádiar

Eight kilometres south of Bérchules, Cádiar is one of the bigger Alpujarras villages, down in the lowlands by the Río Guadalfeo. It hosts an all-purpose market on the 28th of each month, and the wonderful Alquería de Morayma (see p397) is a fine rural inn nearby.

Yegen

East of Bérchules, the 400-strong village of Yegen is best known as the home of writer Gerald Brenan, a peripheral Bloomsbury Group member whose *South from Granada* depicted life here in the 1920s. A plaque marks **Brenan's house**, just off the fountain plaza below the main road. Walkers can explore the dramatically eroded red landscape on the **Sendero Gerald Brenan**, a 1.9km loop (one hour) – look for a map of the route on the main plaza. On the eastern edge of the village, the excellent restaurant at **El Rincón de Yegen** (☎ 958 85 12 70; mains €14-20; ✆ closed Tue) offers treats such as pears in Contraviesa wine and hot chocolate.

On the road midway between Yegen and Mecina-Bombarón, there's a public swimming pool with amazing views of the valley; it's open July to September.

Válor

Válor, 5km northeast of Yegen, was the birthplace of Aben Humeya, a *morisco* (converted Muslim) who led a 1568 rebellion against Felipe II's repressive policies banning Arabic names, dress and even language. The two years of guerrilla war throughout the mountains ended only after Don Juan of Austria, Felipe's half-brother, was brought in to quash the insurrection and Aben Humeya was assassinated by his cousin Aben Aboo. To re-create the historical clash, Válor musters a large **Moros y Cristianos** (Moors & Christians) festival on 14 and 15 September, with colourfully costumed 'armies' battling it out.

The village is known for its olive oil, goats cheese and partridge, all of which you can sample at the notable **Restaurante Aben Humeya** (☎ 958 85 18 10; Calle Los Bolos; mains €7-12), downhill off the main road. Its menu features seasonal treats, such as local mushrooms, along with standards like rabbit in a garlic-almond sauce and delicate *croquetas* (croquettes). For dessert, there's the deadly rich *tocino del cielo* (egg-yolk custard), or soft cheese with honey, washed down with *vino rosado* from Albuñol.

Mairena

Up a very winding road just 6km from Válor, Mairena feels much further away, with fine views from its elevated position. The restaurant at **Las Chimeneas** (☎ 958 76 00 89; Calle Amargura 6; menú €20), a good guest house (p397), serves good dinners using largely organic produce from its own farm plot. Just east of Mairena is easy access to the Sierra Nevadas, via the A337 and the 2000m Puerto de la Ragua pass. The road then heads down to La Calahorra (p271).

TRANSPORT

BUS // **Alsina Graells/Alsa** (☎ Granada 958 18 54 80, Órgiva 958 78 50 02, Málaga 952 34 17 38, Almería 950 23 51 68) operates local buses. From Granada, they run on two routes: one twice daily on the low road through Cádiar and Válor; the other three times daily to the higher villages and ending in Trevélez or Bérchules; see the boxed text, opposite, for details. Return buses start before 6am and mid-afternoon. There is a Málaga–Órgiva bus (€10.10, 2¾ hours, one daily except Sunday), and a bus from Almería runs to Cádiar (€7.84, 3¼ hours, daily).

CAR // Narrow mountain roads call for exceptionally slow driving.

LAS ALPUJARRAS BUS SERVICE

Destination	Cost	Duration	Daily Frequency
Bérchules	€8.50	3hr	2
Bubión	€6	2¼hr	3
Cádiar	€7.50	3hr	2
Capileira	€6	2½hr	3
Lanjarón	€4	1hr	6-9
Pampaneira	€5.50	2hr	3
Pitres	€6	2¾hr	3
Órgiva	€4.50	1¾hr	6-9
Trevélez	€7	3¼hr	3
Válor	€9	3¾hr	2
Yegen	€8.50	3½hr	2

PARKING // Most villages have a municipal parking lot near the edge of town.

COSTA TROPICAL

• • • • • •

The coast of Granada may look typically Mediterranean, with barren hills and wiry pomegranate trees, but it's warm enough to grow tropical crops such as custard apples, avocados, mangoes and sugarcane; there's even a rum distiller in Motril. This stretch of the coast is not grossly overdeveloped, as in neighbouring Málaga, but it's not empty either. With frequent bus service, it makes an easy beach getaway from Granada.

SALOBREÑA

pop 12,000

Between the N340 and the sea, Salobreña's huddle of white houses rises on a crag, topped with an impressive Islamic castle. The dark-sand beach isn't breathtaking, but it is wide, and its distance from the centre of town (about 1km) has kept the place from getting overbuilt. It's a low-key place for most of the year but jumps in August. The **tourist office** (☎ 958 61 03 14; Plaza de Goya; ☺ 9am-3pm Mon-Thu & Sat, 9am-3pm & 4.30-6.30pm Fri) is on a small roundabout near the eastern exit from the N340.

EXPLORING SALOBREÑA

❧ THE OLD TOWN // HIKE UP FOR VIEWS AND HISTORY

At the top of the hill, the **Castillo Árabe** (Arab Castle; admission incl Museo Histórico €3; ☺ 10.30am-1.30pm & 5.30-8pm) dates from the 12th century, though the site was fortified as early as the 10th century. The castle was a summer residence for the Granada emirs, but a legend has it that Emir Muhammad IX had his three daughters, Zaida, Zoraida and Zorahaida, held captive here. Washington Irving relates the story in *Tales of the Alhambra*. The inner Alcazaba, a setting for cultural events, retains much of its Nasrid structure. You can walk along parts of the parapets and take in views over the surf and the sugarcane fields.

Just below the castle is the 16th-century Mudéjar **Iglesia de Nuestra**

Señora del Rosario, with an elegant tower and striking arched doorway. The **Museo Histórico** (Plaza del Ayuntamiento; admission incl Castillo Árabe €3; 10.30am-1.30pm & 5.30-8pm) is nearby, below the church, exhibiting some archaeological finds that date back 6000 years.

A zigzagging walkway leads from the beach to the castle, and a town bus runs to the church.

❦ AT THE BEACH // SPREAD OUT ON THE WIDE SANDS

About 1km from the centre of town along Avenida del Mediterráneo, Salobreña's long beach is divided by a rocky outcrop, El Peñón. Playa de la Charca, the eastern part, is grey sand; the western Playa de la Guardia is more pebbly. There are loads of restaurants, beachside *chiringuitos* (small open-air eateries) and bars, and a spot of nightlife, on and near the sand. **Restaurante El Peñón** (958 61 05 38; Paseo Marítimo; mains €6-12; closed Mon) is probably better for its position, almost on top of the waves, than for its average seafood – the setting is particularly dramatic at night. For fish, you're better off a few steps off the beach at **Cervecería El Tapeo** (Avenida del Mediterráneo; raciones €6-12), just inland on the main avenue, where a blackboard outside advertises the day's catch.

❦ HEARTY MEALS // MEATY MAINS IN SALOBREÑA'S BETTER RESTAURANTS

It's not all fish, fish and more fish at the beach: Salobreña has two very good restaurants that also look inland for inspiration. **La Bodega** (958 82 87 39; Plaza de Goya; menú €8, mains €17-24), right by the tourist office, conjures country life, with farm tools on the walls and hanging meats, and you can mix a bit of the sea (excellent clams) with a steak and a glug of sherry

from the barrel. **Mesón de la Villa** (958 61 24 14; Plaza Francisco Ramírez de Madrid; mains €11-16; closed Wed) is hidden away on a quiet plaza. Locals come here for standards like broad beans with ham served in a warm, candlelit room – ideal if you're in town before the full heat of summer arrives.

TRANSPORT

BUS // The bus stop is diagonally across the street from the tourist office, and the beach is 1km further on. **Alsina Graells/Alsa** (958 61 25 21; www .alsa.es) has at least 14 daily buses to Almuñécar (€1.50, 15 minutes), nine to Granada (€6, one hour), 11 to Nerja (€3.50, one hour) and five to Málaga (€7, 2¼ hours). There are also two buses daily to Almería (€9, three hours) and one at 4.45pm (except Sunday) to Órgiva (€2.80, one hour).

PARKING // Salobreña's steep streets make parking exceptionally difficult. Stick to the flatlands or consult with the tourist office about the locations of municipal car parks on the hill.

LOCAL BUS // A bus (€1) runs a circular route through town and up to the Castillo Árabe roughly every hour 9am to 1.35pm and 4pm to 6.45pm Monday to Friday, and 9am to 1.35pm Saturday.

ALMUÑÉCAR & LA HERRADURA

pop 26,200

Dedicated to beach fun, Almuñécar fares best when measured against the gaudy pleasure strips of Málaga. In comparison, Almuñécar is not too expensive, a little rough around the edges and very relaxed. Many of the tourists on its pebbly beaches are Spanish, and its old city centre is a scenic maze below a 16th-century castle. The next-door village of La Herradura handles some of the overflow, but maintains a more castaway feel as it caters to a younger crowd of windsurfers. The N340 runs across the northern part of both towns.

ESSENTIAL INFORMATION

TOURIST INFORMATION // Main tourist office (☎ 958 63 11 25; www.almunecar.info; Avenida Europa; ☼ 10am-2pm & 6-9pm Jul–mid-Sep, 10am-2pm & 5-8pm Apr-Jun & mid-Sep–Oct, 10am-2pm & 4.30-7pm approx Nov-Mar) A few blocks back from Playa de San Cristóbal on the east side, in a pink neo-Moorish mansion. Information kiosk (☎ 958 63 11 25; Avenida Fenicia; ☼ 10am-2pm & 5-8pm, 10am-2pm & 4-7pm approx Oct-Apr) Just north of the bus station near the N340 roundabout.

EXPLORING ALMUÑÉCAR & LA HERRADURA

❧ THE OLD CITY // **EXPLORE THE CITY'S ROMAN ROOTS**
At the top of a hill overlooking the sea, the Castillo de San Miguel (☎ 958 63 12 52; adult/child incl Museo Arqueológico €2/1.50; ☼ 10.30am-1.30pm & 6.30-9pm Jul–mid-Sep, 10.30am-1.30pm & 5-7.30pm Tue-Sat Apr-Jun & mid-Sep–Oct, 10.30am-1.30pm & 4-6.30pm Tue-Sat Nov-Mar, 10.30am-1.30pm Sun year-round) was built by the conquering Christians over Islamic and Roman fortifications. The sweaty, circuitous climb up to the entrance rewards with excellent views and an informative little museum. A few streets northeast, the Museo Arqueológico (☎ 958 63 12 52; Calle Málaga; ☼ 10.30am-1.30pm & 4-6.30pm Tue-Sat approx Oct-Apr, 10.30am-1.30pm & 5-7.30pm Tue-Sat approx Nov-Mar, 10.30am-1.30pm Sun year-round) is set in 1st-century underground galleries called the Cueva de Siete Palacios, built when the Romans called the port town Sexi. The museum displays finds from local Phoenician, Roman and Islamic sites plus a 3500-year-old Egyptian amphora.

❧ BEACH LIFE // **RIDE THE WAVES OR RELAX ON THE SAND**
Almuñécar's beachfront is divided by a rocky outcrop, the Peñón del Santo, with Playa de San Cristóbal – the best beach (grey sand and small pebbles) – stretch-

～ WORTH A TRIP ～

A spectacular alternative to the A44 from the coast to Granada is the **Carretera del Suspiro del Moro**. Straight through, the drive takes about two hours, but you can stop for a good walk en route. From the N340 in Almuñécar, turn northwest out of the main roundabout (McDonald's is off to the south side), where a small sign points towards Otívar.

In Otívar, note your car's odometer reading. The road ascends sharply here, with breathtaking panoramas. Where it finally levels off, after 13km, the landscape is barren limestone studded with pine trees. Just over 16km from Otívar, the trailhead for **Sendero Río Verde** starts on the left side of the road. This trail descends nearly 400m into the deep valley of the Río Verde, with a good chance of sighting ibex as you go. The full loop is 7.4km (about 3½ hours), but requires walking back to your car along the road, so when you reach the Fuente de las Cabrerizas, a water pump near the bottom of the gorge, you may prefer to turn around and head back the way you came.

Back on your way, and descending the other side of the mountain, 43.5km from Otívar you'll see a road signed 'Suspiro del Moro' heading to the left. Follow this, and in five minutes you emerge in front of the Suspiro del Moro tourist restaurant, a modern marker of the pass where, legend has it, the emir of Granada, Boabdil, looked back and let out a last regretful sigh as he left the city in 1492. Follow the 'Granada' signs to continue to the city, 12km further.

ing to its west, and **Playa Puerta del Mar** to the east, backed by a strip of cool cafes.

If you're craving a more remote beach, or more activity, consider heading 7km west to the small, horseshoe-shaped bay at **La Herradura**, where windsurfers and paragliders congregate. **Windsurf La Herradura** (☎ 958 64 01 43; www.windsurflaherradura .com; Paseo Andrés Segovia 34) is one good operator for these, as well as less extreme water sports, including kayaking. The *chiringuitos* here have a good reputation.

♥ GREEN SPACES // ENJOY THE SHADE IN ALMUÑÉCAR'S PARKS

Just behind the Peñón del Santo is a tropical bird aviary, **Parque Ornitológico Loro-Sexi** (☎ 958 63 02 80; adult/child €4/2; ☼ 11am-2pm & 5-7pm, 11am-2pm & 4-6pm approx Oct-Apr), full of squawking parrots. Beyond that spreads the **Parque Botánico El Majuelo** (admission free; ☼ 9am-10pm), a ramshackle park built around the remains of a Carthaginian and Roman fish-salting workshop, where the sauce called *garum* was produced and then shipped to kitchens across the empire. The park hosts the international **Jazz en la Costa** (www .jazzgranada.es) festival in mid-July.

GASTRONOMIC HIGHLIGHTS

Plaza Kelibia is a good start for tapas.

♥ LA ÚLTIMA OLA // ALMUÑÉCAR €€

☎ 958 63 00 18; Calle Puerta del Mar 4-6; mains €15-24

A solid option for a seafood lunch, on Almuñécar's eastern beach. Sit on the outside terrace or take refuge in the wood-panelled bar inside and enjoy carefully prepared seafood, simply grilled or in more elaborate dishes, such as monkfish with mushrooms and almonds. Even the basic grilled vegetables are tasty.

♥ LA YERBABUENA // ALMUÑÉCAR €€

☎ 958 63 00 18; Calle Puerta del Mar 4-6; mains €9-18 ☼ closed Tue

Pass through the front bar to the adjacent dining room with plush cushions, low candles and little pots of mint *(yerba buena)* on every table. The menu of Spanish standards reflects a similar attention to detail, with the best-quality ingredients employed in dishes such as grilled baby lamb and rich asparagus gratin with shrimp. Service is attentive and helpful with wine recommendations.

♥ EL CHAMBAO DE JOAQUÍN // LA HERRADURA €

☎ 958 64 00 44; Paseo Andrés Segovia; paella €8

Head to the far eastern end of the beach in La Herradura to find this laid-back restaurant with a beachside garden. Paella is dished out from an enormous pan at 2pm every day in summer (Saturday and Sunday only in the low season), and there's a whole range of other tasty things cooked over an open fire. When you're done, you can retire to a lounge chair to digest. Call ahead to reserve for Sunday.

TRANSPORT

BUS // The **Almuñécar bus station** (☎ 958 63 01 40; Avenida Juan Carlos I 1) is just south of the N340. At least six buses a day go to Almería (€10, two hours) and Málaga (€6.50, 1¾ hours), eight to Granada (€7.50, 1½ hours), 11 to La Herradura (€1, 10 minutes), and 13 to Nerja (€2.50, 30 minutes) and Salobreña (€1.50, 15 minutes). A bus goes to Órgiva (€4, 1¼ hours) at 4.30pm Monday to Saturday. **La Herradura's bus stop** is at the top of Calle Acera del Pilar, by the N340; services from here are slightly more limited.

CAR // On the N340, three intersections access the main town. One-way streets create a loop through town and the central beaches.

PARKING // Park wherever you can, or follow signs to an underground car park at the beach, or another near the market, on the northwest side.

ALMERÍA PROVINCE

3 PERFECT DAYS

🐾 DAY 1 // BEACH BUMMING

Stock up on picnic goods at the supermarket in the coastal town of San José (p302; or, for the more prepared, Lamarca gourmet shop before you head out from Almería, p296), then spend the day at the beaches southwest of town (p302). Pack light so you can hike over the rocks to the Calas del Barronal, the most private coves. Back in San José in the evening, enjoy a big meal of fresh seafood at Casa Miguel (p304).

🐾 DAY 2 // DRIVING THE COAST

Head up the coast road north of San José, stopping at the Mirador de la Amatista for stunning views and in the village of Rodalquilar (p303) to see the botanic gardens and the ruined gold mines. Refresh at nearby Playa del Playazo (p303) with an afternoon swim. Depending on your larger itinerary, head to Mojácar (p305) for dinner, or back to Almería for a tapas tour (p294).

🐾 DAY 3 // DESERT AND MOUNTAINS

Make a morning visit to one of the western movie sets among the dramatic canyons and rock formations of the Desierto de Tabernas (p297), then have lunch at olive-oil mill Los Albardinales (p298). In the afternoon head for the slightly cooler elevations of the Alpujarras for some leisurely wine-tasting, or a hike in the mountains above Laujar de Andarax (p300).

ALMERÍA PROVINCE

GETTING AROUND

Almería's mountain villages are linked by bus service, but travelling along the coast around Cabo de Gata is trickier, as the infrequent buses head only to Almería city, and not to neighbouring towns. To see the whole coast, a car is a must. Driving in the city is not difficult, though in the small historic core, many streets are pedestrian-only. On-street parking is scarce, but there are many underground lots. Trains connect only Almería to Granada and Guadix.

TABERNAS   p297

The surrounding desert is a popular setting for movie westerns

LAUJAR DE ANDARAX   p300

The capital of Almería's main winemaking region, just below the Sierra Nevada

ALMERÍA   p290

Visit the monumental Alcazaba in this unpretentious port city

Orce

GRANADA

To Baza (17km);
Guadix (60km)

A334

Parque
Natural Sierra
de Baza

To Guadix (29km);
Granada (82km)

A92

Doña María
Ocaña

Gérgal

Puerto de
la Ragua

Buitre
(2465m)

Abla

Parque Nacional
Sierra Nevada

Cinema Studios
Fort Bravo

Chullo
(2612m)

Western
Leone

Sierra Nevada

Ohanes

Parque Natural
Sierra Nevada

Los
Millares

A92

Laujar de
Andarax

Laroles

Canjáyar

A348   Santa Fe de
Mondújar

Gádor

Fondón

Ugíjar

Cherín

Las Alpujarras

Alhama de
Almería

Rioja

Morrón
(2236m)

Benahadux

Huércal de
Almería

To Cádiar (5km);
Órgiva (38km)

Sierra de Gádor

Almería

Sierra de la Contraviesa

Berja

Aguadulce

Dalías

Santa María
del Águila

El Ejido

Roquetas
de Mar

Adra

Balerma

To Almuñécar
(55km)

Almerimar

To Melilla
(148km)

To Nador
(160km)

ALMERÍA PROVINCE

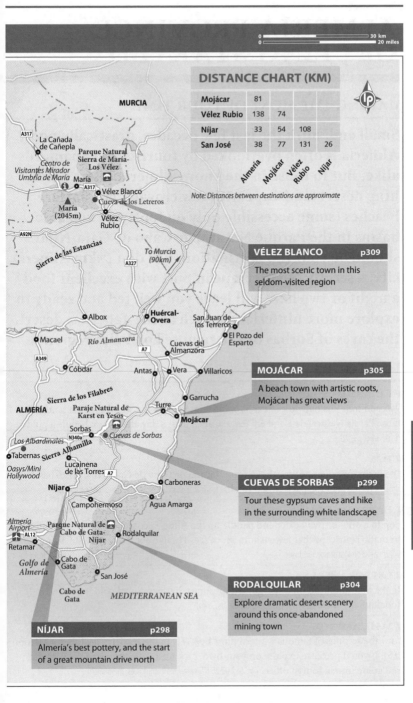

DISTANCE CHART (KM)

	Almería	Mojácar	Vélez Rubio	Níjar
Mojácar	81			
Vélez Rubio	138	74		
Níjar	33	54	108	
San José	38	77	131	26

Note: Distances between destinations are approximate

VÉLEZ BLANCO   p309

The most scenic town in this seldom-visited region

MOJÁCAR   p305

A beach town with artistic roots, Mojácar has great views

CUEVAS DE SORBAS   p299

Tour these gypsum caves and hike in the surrounding white landscape

RODALQUILAR   p304

Explore dramatic desert scenery around this once-abandoned mining town

NÍJAR   p298

Almería's best pottery, and the start of a great mountain drive north

ALMERÍA PROVINCE

ALMERÍA PROVINCE
GETTING STARTED

MAKING THE MOST OF YOUR TIME

Small and, until the last few decades, drastically poor, Almería is often overlooked by tourists and Spaniards alike. But to those in the know, Almería offers a stunning desert landscape with few crowds. The austere beaches (some accessible only on foot) and volcanic basins in the Parque Natural de Cabo de Gata-Níjar should be your top destination. But don't skip Almería city, a scruffy Mediterranean port with excellent food – a night or two here will leave you well fed and ready to explore more hinterlands, such as the Tabernas desert, the caves of Sorbas or the remote Los Vélez region.

TOP TOURS

❦ CUEVAS DE SORBAS
Descend into this network of caves, some 8km long, in the weird gypsum landscape of the Paraje Natural de Karst en Yesos. Call at least a day ahead to schedule a guided visit; see p298.

❦ J126
The main tour operator for the Parque Natural de Cabo de Gata-Níjar, J126 has 4WD access to parts of the park closed to others. (☎ 950 38 02 99; www.cabodegata-nijar.com)

❦ HAPPY KAYAK
Hop in a one- or two-seater and paddle up the Almería coast, getting a view of the dramatic landscape that few visitors get to see. Three-hour tours start at €38. (☎ 609 64 47 22; Paseo de Maritimo, San José)

❦ EXPLORA ESPAÑA
Rent a bike and head on a self-guided tour into the abandoned gold mines behind Rodalquilar. (☎ 678 78 46 39; www.exploraespana.com)

❦ MALCAMINO'S
Tour the settings of famous western films by 4WD in the Desierto de Tabernas (from €15). If you'd prefer to explore on your own, pick up a 'Landscapes of the Cinema' trail guide from a tourist office. (☎ 652 02 25 82; www.malcaminos.es, in Spanish)

GETTING AWAY FROM IT ALL

The whole province of Almería is already well off the usual route. But these spots will ensure peace, quiet and something a little out of the ordinary.

* **Refugios de la Guerra Civil** Go underground in Almería to tour the bomb shelters built in the 1930s (p294)

* **Cala de Enmedio** The 30-minute hike to this beach guarantees you'll have a peaceful swim (p303)

* **Rodalquilar** Everyone else goes to the beach; savvy travellers enjoy the desert valley just inland (p303)

* **Los Vélez** The faraway corner of a faraway province, this mountainous region's caves and castles see few visitors (p308)

ADVANCE PLANNING

Most of Almería's pleasures can be enjoyed on the fly, but a few details should be arranged ahead.

* **Summer accommodation** July and August are peak months on the Almería coast – make hotel arrangements as far in advance as possible (see p399)

* **Clisol** Contact this group at least a week ahead for a greenhouse tour (see p297)

* **Hiking logistics** Walking from beach to beach over several days is a pleasure; make hotel reservations, check bus schedules and assemble your gear

* **Sunscreen and water** Sounds obvious, but the desert sun can take its toll in less than an hour. Don't get caught unprepared

TOP EATING EXPERIENCES

❦ CASA PUGA
Tasty tiny plates, huge wine selection (p294)

❦ CASA JOAQUÍN
Exquisitely prepared seafood in an unpretentious setting (p295)

❦ TETERÍA ALMEDINA
Sample Moroccan sweets in Almería's old city (p296)

❦ LA TABERNA
Have a tiny fried quail egg on toast, among other tapas (p308)

❦ MESÓN EL MOLINO
Traditional Spanish food in a beautiful village (p310)

❦ TOMATE RAF
Look for this local tomato variety at better restaurants in winter and spring (see the boxed text, p305)

RESOURCES

* **Andalucia.com** (www.andalucia.com) Several pages dedicated to Almería

* **Turismo de Almería** (www.turismode almeria.org) Municipal tourist office

* **Los Vélez** (www.losvelezturismo.org) Local tourism board

* **Editorial Alpina** (www.editorialalpina.com) Best map of Cabo de Gata

* **800 Bullets** (Alex de la Iglesias) Sharp film about Almería's 'Wild West'

ALMERÍA PROVINCE

ALMERÍA

· · · · · ·

pop 181,000

Almería is something like the Marseilles of Spain, a rough-around-the-edges port with a large North African population. Its biggest buildings show a distinct 1960s flair, the palm trees along the boulevards are a bit dusty, and relics of an industrial past lie rusting in the salt air. But as the capital of a province that since the 1980s has been completely remade by industrial agriculture in the surrounding province, it has recently gained fresh momentum, and its streets have palpable energy.

The name Almería comes from the Arabic *al-mariyya* (the watchtower), in reference to the grand Alcazaba, the only remaining Islamic monument in town. (More metaphorical linguists prefer the similarity to *al-miraya*, the mirror, as the city reflects North Africa back to itself.) At the peak of the Andalusian caliphate, the streets thronged with merchants from Egypt, Syria, France and Italy, as this was the largest, richest port in Moorish Spain and the headquarters of the Umayyad fleet. Following the Reconquista (Christian reconquest), the city began a long, slow decline, exacerbated by the shifting of naval interests – and money – to the Atlantic ports and the Americas. A 1658 census revealed the city had only 500 inhabitants, thanks to a devastating earthquake and persistent attacks by Barbary pirates. Fortunes have only recently turned, with the booming, controversial *plasticultura* industry – the vast, white-plastic greenhouses that extend from the city limits.

ESSENTIAL INFORMATION

EMERGENCIES // Hospital Torrecárdenas (☎ 950 01 61 00; Avenida de Torrecárdenas) Main public hospital, 4km northeast of the centre. Policía Local (Local Police; ☎ 950 62 12 06; Calle Santos Zárate 11) North end of Avenida de Federico García Lorca. Policía Nacional (National Police; ☎ 950 62 30 40; Avenida del Mediterráneo 201) Northeast of the bus station. Red Cross (Cruz Roja; ☎ 950 22 22 22) For an ambulance.

TOURIST OFFICES // Municipal tourist office (☎ 950 28 07 48; Rambla de Belén, Avenida de Federico García Lorca; ⊙ 10am-1pm & 5.30-7.30pm Mon-Fri, 10am-noon Sat) Regional tourist office (☎ 950 27 43 55; Parque de Nicolás Salmerón; ⊙ 9am-7pm Mon-Fri, 10am-2pm Sat & Sun)

ORIENTATION

Old and new Almería lie either side of the Rambla de Belén, a pedestrian street down the centre of Avenida de Federico García Lorca, running towards the sea. East of the Rambla is the commercial district; to its west, the city centre and most sights. The old city's main artery, Paseo de Almería, leads diagonally north from Rambla de Belén to a busy intersection called Puerta de Purchena. The combined bus-train station is on the Carretera de Ronda, a few hundred metres east of the seaward end of Rambla de Belén.

EXPLORING ALMERÍA

Aside from the enormous Alcazaba, which can be explored in a couple of hours, Almería is not a monumental city, but there are plenty of interesting distractions in its meandering streets, particularly in its superlative tapas bars. Almería's beach is a good kilometre out of the centre and can be crowded in the

ACCOMMODATION

The best places to stay in Almería make the most of the stunning, spare scenery. Read all about the options in our dedicated accommodation chapter (p378). Here are some of the best choices:

★ Solar-powered **Cortijo El Saltador** (p398), in the seldom-visited Sierra de Alhamilla north of Níjar, is the ultimate mountain retreat: essential comforts, but no electronic connections.

★ In the basin of the Rodalquilar valley, **El Jardín de los Sueños** (p399) feels remote but is walking distance to the village, and a quick drive to the beach.

★ **Hotel Almirez** (p398) is the best kind of inexpensive Spanish roadside hotel – clean, spacious and open to the Alpujarras views just outside Laujar de Andarax.

summer. A better alternative is a day or two in the Parque Natural de Cabo de Gata-Níjar (p301), an easy trip from here.

♥ ALCAZABA & AROUND // ENJOY THE VIEW FROM ALMERÍA'S FORTRESS

A monstrous fortification rising from the cliffs, the **Alcazaba** (☎ 950 17 55 00; Calle Almanzor; non-EU/EU citizen €1.50/free; ⏰ 9am-8.30pm Tue-Sun Apr-Oct, to 6.30pm Tue-Sun Nov-Mar, closed 25 Dec & 1 Jan) was built in the 10th century by Abd ar-Rahman III, the greatest caliph of Al-Andalus. It lacks the intricate decoration of the Alhambra (p254), but it is nonetheless a compelling monument; allow a couple of hours to see everything. Past a grand horseshoe arch, the interior is divided into three compounds. The lowest area, the **Primer Recinto**, was the civic centre, with houses, baths and other necessities – now replaced by lush gardens and water channels, some using the antique system of hydraulics set up with the cisterns. From the battlements you can see the **Muralla de Jayrán**, a fortified wall built by the first ruler of Almería when it became an independent *taifa* (small kingdom) in the 11th century.

In the **Segundo Recinto** you'll find the ruins of the Muslim rulers' palace, built by Almotacín (r 1051–91), under whom medieval Almería reached its peak. A reflecting pool suggests a bit of the former elegance, but in fact, this was built in the early 20th century. Also within the compound is a chapel, the **Ermita de San Juan**, once a mosque and now used as a screening room. The highest part, the **Tercer Recinto**, is a fortress added by the Catholic Monarchs. Its keep is used as an exhibition space.

After visiting the Alcazaba, you can descend into the mazelike streets of the old medina – one good destination is Tetería Almedina (p296). If it's the weekend, seek out the market on **Plaza de Pavia**, a rowdy mix of produce, cheap shoes and *churros* (long thin doughnuts). To the north and west is the district called **La Chanca**, where the houses are dug into the Alcazaba hill and painted bright colours. The area has a somewhat sketchy reputation, but by day it's not threatening.

♥ THE CATHEDRAL & AROUND // A CATHOLIC MONUMENT AND ISLAMIC REMNANTS

Almería's fortresslike **cathedral** (Plaza de la Catedral; admission €2; ⏰ 10am-1.15pm & 4-5pm Mon-Fri, 10am-1.15pm Sat), built to withstand pirate raids, is shaded by tall palms and fronted by a peaceful square. The vast interior, trimmed in jasper, marble and carved walnut, is by guided tour only,

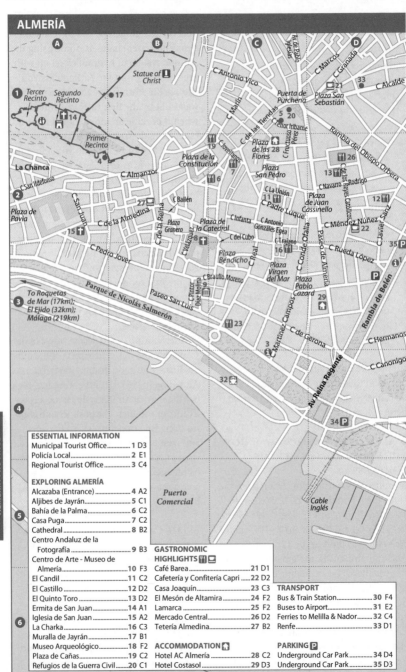

ALMERÍA

ESSENTIAL INFORMATION
Municipal Tourist Office 1 D3
Policía Local 2 E1
Regional Tourist Office 3 C4

EXPLORING ALMERÍA
Alcazaba (Entrance) 4 A2
Aljibes de Jayrán 5 C1
Bahía de la Palma 6 C2
Casa Puga 7 C2
Cathedral 8 B2
Centro Andaluz de la
  Fotografía 9 B3
Centro de Arte - Museo de
  Almería 10 F3
El Candil 11 C2
El Castillo 12 D2
El Quinto Toro 13 D2
Ermita de San Juan 14 A1
Iglesia de San Juan 15 A2
La Charca 16 C3
Muralla de Jayrán 17 B1
Museo Arqueológico 18 F2
Plaza de Cañas 19 C2
Refugios de la Guerra Civil 20 C1

**GASTRONOMIC
HIGHLIGHTS** 🍴 🍺
Café Barea 21 D1
Cafetería y Confitería Capri 22 D2
Casa Joaquín 23 C3
El Mesón de Altamira 24 F2
Lamarca 25 F2
Mercado Central 26 D2
Tetería Almedina 27 B2

ACCOMMODATION 🏠
Hotel AC Almería 28 C2
Hotel Costasol 29 D3

TRANSPORT
Bus & Train Station 30 F4
Buses to Airport 31 E2
Ferries to Melilla & Nador 32 C4
Renfe 33 D1

PARKING 🅿
Underground Car Park 34 D4
Underground Car Park 35 D3

Puerto
Comercial

Cable
Inglés

but its most notable feature is on the outside, on the eastern (Calle del Cubo) end of the building: the exuberant **Sol de Portocarrero**, a 16th-century relief of the sun that's now a city symbol.

Remains of Almería's Islamic past are evident in a couple of nearby landmarks. The **Iglesia de San Juan** (Calle San Juan; ☽ 6pm Apr-Oct, 7pm Nov-Mar), the city's old mosque, still has its 11th-century mihrab, marking the direction of Mecca. The old Arab souk, where livestock, fruits and vegetables were sold and no doubt lots of tea was drunk, is now the **Plaza de la Constitución** (also known as Plaza Vieja), a 17th-century arcaded square with the city's theatrical city hall on its northwest side.

❦ MUSEUMS // PEEK AT OLD BONES, AND OTHER DISTRACTIONS

Almería's modern **Museo Arqueológico** (☎ 950 17 55 10; Carretera de Ronda 91; non-EU/EU citizen €1.50/free; ☽ 2.30-8.30pm Tue, 9am-8.30pm Wed-Sat, 9am-2.30pm Sun) presents finds from Los Millares (p299) and other ancient settlements in the region, as well as Roman and Islamic traces. Even if potsherds and bone fragments normally make you yawn, don't skip this – it's a rare example of multimedia technology deployed to excellent effect, touched with a uniquely Spanish flair for the macabre.

Almería's other museums are less reliable – it all depends on what temporary exhibits are up. The **Centro de Arte – Museo de Almería** (☎ 950 26 96 80; Plaza de Barcelona; admission free; ☽ 6-9pm Mon, 11am-2pm & 6-9pm Tue-Sat, 11am-2pm Sun) puts up mostly contemporary work by Spanish artists. The **Centro Andaluz de la Fotografía** (☎ 950 18 63 60; Calle Pintor Díaz Molina 9; admission free; ☽ 11am-2pm & 5.30-9.30pm) may also have something interesting on.

ALMERÍA PROVINCE

RAILS TO NOWHERE

The big rusting railroad trestle that curves towards Almería's seafront is the **Cable Inglés**, a viaduct built by the British-run Alquife Mines and Railway Company in 1904. It's a small master-piece of industrial architecture, inspired in part by the Eiffel Tower and employing some 3800 tonnes of steel. Mineral ore from the mountains was brought here by train and loaded directly onto freight-ers waiting in the harbour. During the Franco years, the mines were tapped out, and the pier was last used in 1973.

♥ REFUGIOS DE LA GUERRA CIVIL // A HIDDEN WAR MONUMENT

During the civil war, Almería was the Republicans' last holdout province in Andalucía, and was repeatedly and mer-cilessly bombed. In one raid by German fighters, 40 civilians were killed. This prompted a group of engineers to design and build the **Refugios** (☎ 950 26 86 96; Plaza de Manuel Pérez García; admission €2; ☺ hourly tours 9.30am-1.30pm Tue-Thu & Sat, 9.30am-1.30pm, 5.30pm & 6pm Fri, 9.30am, 12.30pm & 1pm Sun), a 4.5km-long network of concrete shelters under the city, containing storerooms and an operating theatre. Visitors can see more than 1km of the tunnels, though tours are in Spanish only, and must be reserved ahead.

♥ TAPAS TOUR // STAND UP AND EAT WELL

Along with Granada, Almería maintains the tradition of free tapas. But it does its neighbour one better: here, all tapas are *al elegir*, meaning you choose what you want from a list. Portions are so gener-ous that you can easily make a meal over a few drinks, and most places are open

for lunch as well. Note that on week-nights many of these bars don't open till 8.30pm or 9pm, then shut by 11pm (Thursday nights roll on until midnight, weekends till 1am).

The undisputed tapas champ, **Casa Puga** (Calle Jovellanos 7; drink & tapa €1.90) should be your first stop for lunch or dinner, as its little bar fills up fast. Shelves of ancient wine bottles are the backdrop for a tiny cooking station that churns out small saucers of stews, griddled goodies such as mushrooms, and savoury *hueva de maru-ca* (smoked fish roe). Up the street is the more modern **Plaza de Cañas** (Calle Marín 20; drink & tapa €2.20), which presents tradi-tional combos such as *remojón* (salt cod, orange and potatoes) with style. At **Bahía de la Palma** (Calle Mariana; drink & tapa €2), it might be worth paying extra for a plate of *papas a la paja* (shoestring fries topped with crisp-fried ham and eggs) if you've already had a lot to drink. This place oc-casionally sees some live music, too.

Closer to Paseo de Almería, **La Charka** (Calle Trajano 8; drink & tapa €2.15) is at the centre of the densest concentration of tapas bars, most catering to a youngish crowd. It's raucous with the clatter of dishes and shouted orders for tapas such as fried eggs with chorizo, or stuffed baked potatoes. After this, lighten up at **El Candil** (Calle La Unión 7; drink & tapa €2.10; ☺ closed Sun; ⓥ), a chic black box of a bar that serves tapas, including aubergine gratin or goats cheese with quince paste, with a good selection of wines by the glass.

Near the market, **El Castillo** (Calle Javier Sanz 4; drink & tapa €2) is a very locals-only place with lots of hot tapas served in small dishes. And finally, **El Quinto Toro** (Calle de los Reyes Católicos; drink & tapa €2) rivals Casa Puga in charm, with the ob-ligatory bull's head over the bar. Treats include *pulpo in allioli* (octopus in blinding-white garlic mayo) and rich *albóndigas* (meatballs) in a wine sauce.

♥ FLAMENCO UNDERGROUND // LISTEN TO MUSIC IN CENTURIES-OLD CISTERNS

North of Plaza de las Flores, the **Aljibes de Jayrán** (☎ 950 27 30 39; Calle Tenor Iribarne; admission free; ⊗ 10am-2pm Mon-Fri) were built in the early 11th century to supply the city's water. They're well preserved and now regularly used as the meeting point for **Peña El Taranto** (☎ 950 23 50 57; www .eltaranto.net), the city's top club of flamenco aficionados. Live performances often happen on weekends, down in the cisterns themselves, a wonderfully intimate setting. Shows are open to the public, and admission ranges from free to €20. But if the weather is warm, it's worth dropping by even when there's not a show on, as there's a lively bar-cafe up on the roof.

FESTIVALS & EVENTS

Noche de San Juan Carousing and enormous bonfires on the beach, here and in every small town up the coast on 23 June.

Feria de Almería Ten days and nights of live music, bullfights, fairground rides, exhibitions and full-on partying in late August.

GASTRONOMIC HIGHLIGHTS

Needless to say, you can subsist very well on tapas alone (see Tapas Tour, opposite). But if you'd like a more leisurely meal, a big breakfast or a sweet treat, the following are great options.

♥ CAFÉ BAREA €

Calle Granada 2; tostadas €3-5; ⊗ 8am-11pm Mon-Fri, to midnight Sat & Sun

One asset of this bustling, old-fashioned cafeteria: a great terrace, by the pretty

Plaza San Sebastián, to watch the world go by. Another: all the standard menu items, particularly the tostadas, are fresher and tastier than at the pavement cafes on Paseo de Almería. There's a second one on the Rambla del Obispo Orbera in front of the market, but…no terrace.

♥ CAFETERÍA Y CONFITERÍA CAPRI €

Calle Méndez Núñez 14; pastries €2-5

Great for an afternoon pick-me-up. Wade past the overexcited kids at the sweets case to settle in at the back bar, where you can tuck into a range of delicious pastries – such as a *rosca de Alcalá,* a flaky round filled with a candied egg yolk – or enjoy a cool *granizado* (slushy drink) or a hot coffee with a slug of brandy.

♥ CASA JOAQUÍN €€

☎ 950 26 43 59; Calle Real 111; mains €14-21; ⊗ closed Sat evening, Sun & Sep

Reserve one of the few tables for lunch if you're really serious about your seafood. If you don't mind standing, you can jostle at the bar for platters of baby purple clams swimming in garlic, delicately fried pieces of monkfish liver and other briny treats. The bartenders seem to have a psychic sense for what you're curious about, and bring you a free plate of it. The setting is casual, but the crowd is well dressed and discerning.

♥ EL MESÓN DE ALTAMIRA €€

☎ 950 22 67 13; Calle Altamira 35; mains €11-17

This seafood restaurant east of Avenida Lorca is a no-frills affair. In the evening, the pavement is packed with rickety tables piled high with paper-thin slices of fried aubergine and platters of golden, crispy fried fish, surrounded by happy families. Go early to snag an outside table; the interior is not well ventilated.

❤ LAMARCA €€

☎ 950 08 66 25; Calle Doctor Gregorio Marañón 33; raciones €6-12; ⊙ 8am-midnight Mon-Sat, 10am-5pm Sun

If you can make it past the distracting array of gourmet goods up front, the back room of this food shop is the place to sample wine, sausages and cheeses from all over Spain, in single bites or in *raciones* (plates to share). It's handily located near the archaeology museum, for a post-sightseeing bite. There's music – flamenco, Cuban, jazz – Wednesday through to Saturday nights.

❤ MERCADO CENTRAL €

Circunvalación Ulpiano Díaz; ⊙ 8am-2pm Mon-Sat

Almería's central market is in a grand old building near the top of Paseo de Almería. Go early in the morning to see squid so fresh they're still changing colour, as well as a profusion of vegetables from the surrounding greenhouses, including some very odd-looking varieties of tomato. Produce is upstairs; seafood, meats and deli items are in the basement.

❤ TETERÍA ALMEDINA €

☎ 629 27 78 27; Calle Paz 2, off Calle de la Almedina; teas €2-3, mains €7-12; ⊙ 11am-11pm Tue-Sun, to midnight Jun-Aug; Ⓥ

This lovely little cafe in the old city serves a fascinating range of teas, delectable sweets and good couscous. It's run by a group dedicated to restoring and revitalising the old city, and functions as a sort of casual Islamic cultural centre. There's usually live music on Sundays, in addition to art shows and the like.

TRANSPORT

AIR // Almería's small **airport** (☎ 950 21 37 00; www.aena.es) is 10km east of the city. City bus 20 (€0.95, 30 minutes) runs to the centre, near Avenida de Federico García Lorca, on weekdays every 50 minutes from 7.33am to 10.33pm, and on Saturday and Sunday every 1½ hours between 7.25am and 10.25pm. A taxi costs about €20.

BOAT // For Morocco, **Acciona Trasmediterránea** (☎ 950 23 61 55, 902 45 46 45; www.trasmediterranea.es), **Ferrimaroc** (☎ 950 27 48 00; www.ferrimaroc.com) and **Comarit** (☎ 950 23 61 55; www.comarit.com, in Spanish) sail from the passenger port to Melilla and/or Nador (eight hours). Prices start at €47 for a one-way adult fare.

BUS // The combined bus-train station is just east of the centre; at the **information desk** (⊙ 6.45am-10.45pm), ask for the appropriate ticket window. **Alsina Graells/Alsa** (☎ 902 42 22 42; www.alsa.es) provides the main services across the region (see the boxed text, below). For other destinations in Almería province, see the respective Transport sections.

CAR // The A7/E15 runs a large ring around Almería; the easiest access to the centre is along the seafront, on the Carretera de Málaga from the west and the AL12

BUSES FROM ALMERÍA

Destination	Cost	Duration	Daily Frequency
Córdoba	€25	5hr	1
Guadix	€8	1¼-2hr	3
Granada	€12-13.50	2-4hr	11
Jaén	€17-21	4-5½hr	3
Madrid	€25	7½hr	5
Málaga	€16	3½-5hr	8
Murcia	€17.50	3hr	7
Seville	€32	9hr	2

(Autovía del Aeropuerto) from the east. Driving on the main avenues is not difficult.

PARKING // Street parking is scarce. Large underground car parks below the Rambla de Belén are €16 per day.

TAXI // Catch a taxi at ranks on Paseo de Almería, or call ☎ 950 22 61 61 or ☎ 950 25 11 11.

TRAIN // Trains go from the bus-train station, next door to the old (empty) train station, to/from Granada (€15, 2¼ hours, four daily), Seville (€36.50, 5½ hours, four daily) and Madrid (€42.50, 6¼ hours, two daily). Buy tickets at the station or the Renfe office (☎ 950 23 18 22; www.renfe.es; Calle Alcalde Muñoz 7; ☺ 9.30am-1.30pm & 5-10pm Mon-Fri, 10am-1pm Sat) near Puerta de Purchena.

AROUND ALMERÍA

· · · · · ·

❤ **RESTAURANTE ALEJANDRO // MAKE A SPECIAL TRIP FOR A SPECIAL DINNER**
The coast west of Almería is crowded with greenhouses and big resorts. A surprising outpost of taste is the elegant Restaurante Alejandro (☎ 950 32 24 08; www.restaurante alejandro.es, in Spanish; Avenida Antonio Machado 32, Roquetas de Mar; tasting menu €40-60, mains €18-22; ☺ lunch & dinner Wed-Sat, lunch Tue & Sun), in the resort town of Roquetas de Mar. The kitchen is creative and seasonal-minded, with an especially good touch for seafood. There's the obligatory foie gras, but also homestyle *migas*, a traditional dish similar to couscous, served with a delicious shrimp broth. It's all complemented by a thoughtful wine list. You can drive here from Almería in about 45 minutes.

❤ **GREENHOUSE TOURS // TAKE A PEEK UNDER THE PLASTIC**
If Almería's *plasticultura* piques your curiosity, take a tour behind the scenes with Clisol Agro (☎ 620 84 33 85; www.clisol.com; Paraje La Cumbre, El Ejido; tours €9). The tone is naturally a bit industry-happy and upbeat, but it's fascinating for anyone curious about food production. The company is based in El Ejido, the unofficial capital of the 'plastic sea'; contact it a week in advance to arrange an English-speaking guide.

NORTH OF ALMERÍA

· · · · · ·

❤ **DESIERTO DE TABERNAS // VISIT THE WILD WEST OF THE SILVER SCREEN**
Outside the city of Almería to the northeast is a stretch of desert so stark that it's still largely untouched by greenhouses. But that doesn't mean the land hasn't been prosperous. Clint Eastwood and Charles Bronson once walked these badlands, when they were used as locations for westerns such as *The Magnificent Seven* and *Once Upon a Time in the West*, as well as *Lawrence of Arabia*. More recently, Spanish director Alex de la Iglesia made the film *800 Bullets* here, in the shells of the movie sets that remain as tourist attractions. His film is a tribute to the leather-skinned Spanish cowboys who work here, staging shoot-outs and stunts on horseback, then scrambling around the back of the sets to serve paella to the customers.

Oasys/Mini Hollywood (☎ 950 36 52 36; adult/child €19/9; ☺ 10am-9pm Jun-Oct, to 7pm Sat & Sun Nov-May) is the best-known and most expensive, though what distinguishes it from the others is a not-very-inspiring zoo and a small water park. It's on the N340 just southwest of Tabernas. The more ramshackle (but more likeable) Cinema Studios Fort Bravo (☎ 950 06 60 14; www.fort-bravo.com; adult/child €12/6.50; ☺ 10am-10pm), just a little further down the N340, and **Western Leone** (☎ 950 16 54 05; admission €11; ⏱ 9.30am-sunset daily Apr-Sep, 9.30am-sunset Sat & Sun Oct-Mar), on the A92, both have forts, Western villages and saloons, and run horse treks.

♥ NÍJAR // A SCENIC VILLAGE SPECIALISING IN POTTERY

This small town in the foothills of the Sierra Alhamilla northeast of Almería is known for producing some of Andalucía's most attractive glazed pottery. The main street running uphill, Avenida Federico García Lorca, is lined with touristy shops, while the **Barrio Alfarero** (Potters' Quarter), just to the west, has some more specialised selections. These include **La Tienda de los Milagros** (Callejón del Artesanos), the workshop of a husband-wife team who make beautiful ceramics and quality *jarapa* rugs, woven from cloth scraps; it's just off Calle Real de las Eras, about midway down the hill, before the jarringly modern craft centre.

At the top of Avenida Lorca, the road bends and leads up into the heart of old Níjar, with **Plaza la Glorieta**, the church of **Santa María de la Anunciación** and, further still, the delightfully shady **Plaza del Mercado**, with a huge central plane tree. Hiking up even further, following signs, you eventually reach the **Atalaya**, a ruined tower above the village that takes in the whole valley below.

For sustenance, you can't do better than **La Untá** (☎ 950 36 11 09; Avenida Federico García Lorca 10; raciones €7-12), a bustling orange-walled bar-restaurant with a huge list of tapas and daily fish specials. Next door, **Cafetería Pastelería Virgen de Fátima** (Avenida Federico García Lorca 14; pastries €1-2) provides desserts such as lemon-peel-flecked doughnuts and refreshing lemon *granizados*.

From Almería, Níjar is served by two buses Monday to Saturday, and one on Sunday (€2.50, 45 minutes to 1¼ hours), but the schedule makes a day-trip impossible. By car, Níjar is 4km north of the A7, 31km northeast of Almería – you arrive at the very bottom of the village. There are parking bays all the way up Avenida Federico García Lorca.

♥ SORBAS // CLAMBER THROUGH CAVES OR HIKE ALONG A RIVER

Another prosperous pottery town, Sorbas lies about 34km by road from Níjar and can be reached by a scenic drive through the compact mountains of the Sierra de Alhamilla, passing the old mining town of **Lucainena de las Torres**.

Sorbas is decorated with pots of desert succulents hanging from the houses, some painted a rich red. Like Níjar, it has its own pottery district. But the town is perhaps more interesting for its position on the edge of a dramatic limestone

---

∼ WORTH A TRIP ∼

East of Tabernas, the terrain gets a little more lush – enough to support the olive groves maintained by organic oil producer **Los Albardinales** (☎ 950 61 17 07; N340, Tabernas; ⏱ 9am-7pm Fri-Wed), a little more than 2km out of town. Visitors can tour the facilities, to see how the oil is pressed and bottled, as well as sample the stuff – just a small taste, or in the form of lunch or dinner at the restaurant, which emphasises local artisanal food, including organic wines. A shop is stocked with the oil, as well as organic wines, soaps, vinegars and other local products.

gorge in the Paraje Natural de Karst en Yesos, where water erosion over millions of years has resulted in the stunning Cuevas de Sorbas (☎ 950 36 47 04; www .cuevasdesorbas.com; adult/child €12/8; ☺ guided tours 10am-8pm). The excellent guided tours (complete with pit helmets and lights) through the glittering gypsum caves need to be reserved at least one day ahead.

For more information on the area, stop at the Centro de Visitantes Los Yesares (☎ 950 36 45 63; Calle Terraplén; ☺ 11am-2pm & 4-7pm Tue-Sun Apr-Jun, 11am-2pm & 4.30-8pm Jul-Sep, 11am-2pm & 4-6pm Tue-Sun Oct-Mar), at the entrance to Sorbas. It has informative displays on the cave system and the odd flora and fauna that thrives there. You can also pick up a guide for the Sendero de Los Molinos del Río Aguas, a trail following a river through a gypsum-flecked canyon. It begins 5km along the A1102, past the entrance to the caves.

For food, the best options are Cafetería Caymar (Plaza de la Constitución; tapas €1.80) or the good-quality Restaurante el Rincón (☎ 950 36 41 52; Plaza de la Constitución; mains €10-16) next door. Both are on the central plaza.

Buses run from Almería to Sorbas (€4.50, one hour); there are four on weekdays, three on Saturday and two on Sunday. Returning, there are four daily Monday to Saturday, three on Sunday.

LAS ALPUJARRAS DE ALMERÍA

· · · · · ·

Less visited than their Granada counterpart, Las Alpujarras (as the lower reaches of the Sierra Nevadas are known) in Almería province are notably more arid. The landscape is at first relentlessly barren, with serrated ridges stretching to infinity. But it gradually becomes more vegetated, with lemon and orange orchards, as you approach Fondón. Many of the towns along the A348, the narrow highway winding along the Río Andarax, specialise in grape-growing. (For more details on the Alpujarras, see p275.)

ESSENTIAL INFORMATION

TOURIST OFFICE // For information on walking routes in the area and further up in the Sierra Nevadas, which rise from the north side of Las Alpujarras, visit the Centro de Visitantes Laujar de Andarax (☎ 950 51 35 48; ☺ 10am-2pm & 6-8pm Wed-Sun Apr-Sep, 10am-2pm Thu-Sun Oct-Mar), on the access road just west of Laujar de Andarax.

EXPLORING LAS ALPUJARRAS DE ALMERÍA

❤ LOS MILLARES // REMNANTS OF ANCIENT IBERIAN CULTURE
Just before ascending into the mountains, by the Río Andarax, is the archaeology site of Los Millares (☎ 608 90 34 04, 677 90 34 04; admission free; ☺ 10am-2pm Wed-Sun). As it's very spread out and completely unshaded, a visit is really recommended only for the enthusiast. The Copper Age culture that thrived here, from around 2700 BC to 1800 BC, built successive lines of defensive walls as the population expanded; outlines of these remain, as do ruined stone houses and some reconstructions of distinctive domed graves. The Museo Arqueológico (p293) in Almería presents the best finds from the area, such as pottery

with the distinctive goggle-eyes motif. Signs indicate the Los Millares turn-off from the A348, shortly before Alhama de Almería.

♥ LAUJAR DE ANDARAX // DRINK SOME WINE AND TAKE A HIKE

One of the larger towns in the Almería Alpujarras, Laujar de Andarax (population 1200) is where Boabdil, the last emir of Granada, settled briefly after losing Granada. It was also the headquarters of Aben Humeya, the first leader of the 1568–70 Morisco uprising. Today the town produces a great deal of Almería's wine. You'll spot the Bodega Valle de Laujar (🕑 8.30am-2pm & 3.30-7pm Mon-Sat) on the access road into town from the A348, where you can sample the local wines and *digestifs* and watch the bottling operations. The organic vineyard Cortijo El Cura (☎ 950 52 40 26; www.cortijoelcura.com; 🕑 8am-8pm May-Sep, 9am-6pm Oct-Apr), a small family operation, does some better wines, and enjoys a beautiful old farmhouse setting. Look for the signs pointing south off the A348, just west of Laujar.

Just east of the main plaza, a signposted road leads 1km north to El Nacimiento, a series of waterfalls in a deep valley, with a couple of restaurants nearby. On weekends, it's packed with families out for a barbecue. Continuing up the road less than 2km, you'll reach the start of Sendero del Aguadero, signed as PR-37, a good walk up through fragrant pines – the whole trail is 8km (3½ hours), but you can, of course, double back sooner. Look out for wild boar and the *abubilla,* a black-and-white bird with an elaborate orange crest.

In the town proper, there's a handsome three-tiered town hall and a 17th-century brick church, with a minaretlike tower. For eating, the shiny, mirror-lined Café Bar Rodriguez (Plaza Mayor de la Alpujarra) is the central tapas hang-out, on the main plaza; it sells wine at €2 per litre, should you want some for your hike. The restaurant at Hotel Almirez (☎ 950 51 35 14; mains €9-14) is good, though it caters largely to travellers.

The bus from Almería to Laujar (€5.50, two hours) leaves at 9am daily and returns at 3.50pm. From Laujar, to continue on to the Granada Alpujarras, take a bus to Berja (€2, 30 minutes to one hour, two on weekdays, one Saturday and Sunday), then another to Ugíjar or beyond.

∼ WORTH A TRIP ∼

Detour off the A348 onto the winding route up to Ohanes. The tiny village specialises in *vino rosado* (rosé wine), and while that's as good a reason to visit as any, it's really the drive here and down that's remarkable. On the 9km road, you wind up through stark red rock along the south-facing side of the valley. When you finally curve around the ridge to the more protected mountain face, the scenery changes completely, to green terrace fields and flourishing vineyards. To explore the village, park at the top and walk down. When leaving, continue along the top of town, then bear left (downhill) where the road splits. This route to the valley is shorter than the ascent, but slightly more nerve-racking, dwindling to one lane as it zigzags down through the fields. It comes out just west of Canjáyar.

COSTA DE ALMERÍA

· · · · · ·

PARQUE NATURAL DE CABO DE GATA-NÍJAR

Some of Spain's most flawless and least crowded beaches – some reachable only on foot – are strung between the rugged cliffs of the Parque Natural de Cabo de Gata-Níjar along the Almerian coast. The rugged terrain, formed by volcanic activity, is studded with agave plants and other desert succulents, and the stark landscapes are interrupted by only a few small settlements of whitewashed flat-roofed houses. The area is one of the highlights of not only Andalucía, but the whole of Spain.

With just 100mm of rain in an average year, Cabo de Gata is the driest place in Europe, yet more than 1000 varieties of animal and plant wildlife thrive in the arid, salty environment. It's also a bonanza of bizarre rock formations, and is part of the European Geoparks network. The largest town in the park is San José, a second home for many Almería city folk where you'll find all the usual necessities.

ESSENTIAL INFORMATION

TOURIST OFFICES // Centro de Visitantes Las Amoladeras (☎ 950 16 04 35; Km7 Carretera Cabo de Gata-Almería; ⏲ 10am-2pm & 6-9pm Jun-Sep, 10am-3pm Oct-May) Main park information centre, on the main road from Almería about 1.1km before (west of) the turn to Cabo de Gata. San José visitor centre (☎ 950 38 02 99; Avenida San José 27; ⏲ 10am-2pm & 5-8pm Jun-Sep, 10am-2pm Oct-May) On the left-hand side of main street, midway through town.

EXPLORING PARQUE NATURAL DE CABO DE GATA-NÍJAR

❦ **CABO DE GATA & AROUND // SPOT BIRDS IN THE SALT FLATS**
When people dreamily talk of Cabo de Gata, they're usually referring to the whole park, not the village itself. The coarse-sand beach gets crowded with Almería day-trippers, but is windswept and deserted outside of July and August. Southeast of the town, the **Salinas de Cabo de Gata**, some of the last functioning salt flats in Spain, draw flocks of flamingos starting in spring and peaking in autumn. An 11km trail loops around the flats, with bird hides placed strategically along the way.

At the far end of the lagoons, the collected salt is piled up in great heaps at the desolate village of La Almadraba de Monteleva where the semiruined Iglesia de las Salinas dominates the area for miles around.

❦ **FARO DE CABO DE GATA & AROUND // SEE THE SEA FROM A LIGHTHOUSE PROMONTORY**
At the southernmost point of the cape, the Faro de Cabo de Gata is a lighthouse overlooking the jagged volcanic reefs of the **Arrecife de las Sirenas** (Reef of the Mermaids), named for the monk seals that used to lounge here. The view into the water is fantastically clear.

You can get a different perspective on the lighthouse on a boat trip with El Cabo a Fondo (☎ 637 44 91 70; www.elcaboafondo.es; 1hr tour €20); it's a wonderful way to see the dramatic coastline. Boats leave from a kiosk in La Fabriquilla, a tiny settlement back west along the coast, near the salt flats; reserving ahead is essential.

Driving on past the lighthouse (bear left at El Faro restaurant), you pass several

ALMERÍA PROVINCE

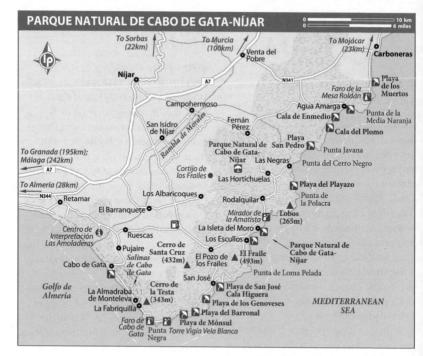

PARQUE NATURAL DE CABO DE GATA-NÍJAR

access trails to small, isolated beaches, an easy way to stretch your legs. After about 3km, at an 18th-century watchtower, the **Torre de Vigía Vela Blanca**, the coast road is blocked to cars; the track, popular with walkers and cyclists, runs on about 5km to San José.

♥ BEACHES // SCENIC SANDS, RARELY CROWDED

The beaches in the natural park fall into two categories: those accessible by car and those accessible only on foot. Very few have any natural shade, and only those in villages have any kind of services. Of those accessible by car, some of the most beautiful are near **San José**. The town has its own small sandy beach: the main street leads to the central Plaza Génova, and the beach is off to the left.

But most people come here to spend the day along the water southwest of

town. A dirt road runs behind several beaches; to reach it follow 'Playas' signs pointing southwest at the inland edge of San José . Along the road, the first you reach is **Playa de los Genoveses**, a 1km-long stretch where the Genoan navy landed in 1147 to aid in the attack on Almería. Getting there calls for a bit of a walk from the parking area. From the nude beach **Playa del Barronal**, further along (and not visible from the road), you can clamber over the rocks back up the coast to a series of small coves, the **Calas del Barronal**. Nearer the end of the road is **Playa de Mónsul** (you may recognise the rock overhang from *Indiana Jones and the Last Crusade*), busier than the others because the car park is close to the water, and the quieter **Cala de la Media Luna** and **Cala Carbón**. From about mid-July to mid-September, the beach road is closed to cars after about 10am – you must park in the lot by the traffic circle at the entrance to town, then take a bus, which stops at each beach parking lot.

Other good beaches accessible by car include the wide **Playa del Playazo**, the closest beach to Rodalquilar, between two headlands; **Los Escullos**, a blip on the map with a few houses and a couple of hotels nearby; and the grey-sand beach at the fishing village of **La Isleta del Moro**, which is quiet on weekdays. The latter two are convenient if you prefer less of a wilderness experience – there are restaurants and bars steps away.

For beaches accessible on foot, see Coast Walking, below.

❦ COAST WALKING // EXPLORE HIDDEN COVES ON FOOT

A network of roads and trails leads about 60km around the cape, from the town of Cabo de Gata up to **Agua Amarga**, a boho-chic beach getaway for the Madrid jet set. The full hike takes three leisurely days, and should be attempted only in spring or, better, autumn, when the sea is warm; the summer heat is deadly, and

there is no shade. You can embark on sections of the walk for a day or afternoon, visiting beaches that are otherwise inaccessible.

From San José northeast to Los Escullos, it's a 2½-hour mostly level walk, partially on old mining roads. North of Los Escullos, you can walk to quiet rocky coves; another 45 minutes brings you to La Isleta del Moro. Ask at the information centre in San José for directions to the trailhead.

Another good stretch is from Rodalquilar across the valley to Playa del Playazo, then up the coast along scenic cliff edges to the town of **Las Negras** (about two hours from Rodalquilar). It's another 1½ hours to the real prize: **Playa San Pedro**, an abandoned village that supports a small crew of hippie squatters. The beach has some of the finest sand on the coast, with clear water and medium waves. You can, of course, also drive to Las Negras (which has its own nice beach, though marred by ongoing construction), then make the hike to Playa San Pedro from there.

Cala del Plomo, accessible by road north of Playa San Pedro, is a somewhat uninviting grey-sand beach, but **Cala de Enmedio**, just up the coast, is prettier and very private. About five minutes' walk inland from the Cala del Plomo parking area, look for a trail leading off to the right. Follow this up and over a low ridge for 20 minutes, then bear right down a dry streambed to Cala de Enmedio.

❦ VALLE DE RODALQUILAR // CABO DE GATA'S DRAMATIC DESERT VALLEY

Northeast of La Isleta del Moro, the road climbs to the breathtaking viewpoint **Mirador de la Amatista**, before heading down into the basin of the

---

> ## TOP **FIVE**
>
> **BEACHES ON THE COSTA DE ALMERÍA**
>
> ★ **Playa San Pedro** (right) – a ruined hamlet beach and hippie hang-out
>
> ★ **Playa de los Genoveses** (opposite) – one kilometre of fine sand
>
> ★ **Playa del Playazo** (above) – a wide beach with calm water
>
> ★ **Calas del Barronal** (opposite) – walk to these small seductive coves
>
> ★ **Cala de Enmedio** (right) – tiny, and accessible only on foot

Rodalquilar valley, a vast caldera. It's here, among the time-worn lava, that the complexity of Cabo de Gata's flora is most evident, especially after the very brief spring rains, when delicate plants, some with a lifespan of only a few days, flourish.

The village of Rodalquilar, in the centre of the valley, was until very recently a ghost town, with just a few residents among the shells of a gold-mining industry abandoned in the 1970s. Now it's a rather chic getaway, with a cluster of whitewashed holiday homes and some bohemian-chic hang-outs. As for sights, there's the thorough and beautifully arranged Jardín Botánico El Albardinal (☎ 671 56 12 26; ⌚ 10am-2pm & 4-6pm Tue-Sun Oct-May, 10am-1pm & 6-9pm Tue-Sun Jun-Sep), as well as the ruined gold mines themselves, a fascinating bit of crumbling industrial wreckage in a barren red-rock landscape. You can follow a rugged road back up behind the main structures. At the entrance to the mines, La Casa de los Volcanes (☎ 950 38 97 42; ⌚ 11am-2pm Tue-Fri, 10am-2pm & 4-6.30pm Sat) has an interesting display on the area's geological history. The visitor centre (☎ 950 38 98 20; ⌚ 10am-2pm Fri-Sun Oct-Mar, 9am-2pm & 6-8pm Fri-Sun Apr-May, 9am-2pm & 6-8pm Jun-Sep) often has art exhibitions. Ask here for directions to El Cortijo de los Frailes, the true-life setting for the tragic revenge story related in Federico García Lorca's best-known play, Blood Wedding. The romantically ruined farmhouse is in the wilderness midway between Rodalquilar and Los Albaricoques, and can be a bit hard to find from the Rodalquilar side.

GASTRONOMIC HIGHLIGHTS

In San José, the fish restaurants along the marina (north end of the beach) stay open through the afternoon, if you're in need of an off-hours' lunch.

❦ CASA CAFÉ DE LA LOMA // LA ISLETA DEL MORO €€

☎ 950 38 98 31; www.degata.com/laloma; dishes €6-16; ⌚ 7pm-1am; Ⓥ

A Mediterranean heaven with terrific views of the sea and the village beach, this old cortijo (country property) runs a restaurant in July and August only. The creative menu of crêpes, salads and more is vegie-friendly, and there are jazz and flamenco concerts several times a week in the garden, by candlelight. Look for the turn off the main road just north of La Isleta del Moro.

❦ CASA MIGUEL // SAN JOSÉ €€

☎ 950 38 03 29; Avenida de San José 43-45; mains €18-22

The best restaurant in San José, understandably strong on seafood, has footpath seating and good service. Skip the pallid paella, however, in favour of the rich arroz negro (mixed seafood and rice, black from squid ink). Or pick and mix with the daily fish specials. The bar inside also does good tapas.

❦ COSTAMARGA // AGUA AMARGA €€

☎ 950 13 80 35; Playa de Aguamarga; mains €11-16

One of several restaurants along Agua Amarga's beach, this place does fish, of course, but it also has a big menu section devoted to seasonal vegetables, such as artichoke hearts with crunchy bits of ham. You can also augment your seafood with hearty (and inexpensive) mixed plates such as chatarra (schnitzel, French fries, egg and velvety aubergine paste, or pisto). From the fryer, chipirones (thimble-sized squid) and croquetas (croquettes) are recommended.

♥ LA GALLINETA // EL POZO DE LOS FRAILES €€

☎ 950 38 05 01; Pozo de los Frailes; mains €14-24; ⏱ 8pm-late Tue-Sun, closed mid-Jan–Feb

This small elegant restaurant 4km north of San José is where urbanites on weekend escapes come for inventive food with an international twist, served in a modern yet warm dining room. Some dishes veer into too-creative territory, but most use always-satisfying combos (veal in a sherry reduction, for instance). Daily specials are usually worth trying.

TRANSPORT

BUS // Alsina Graells/Alsa (☎ 902 42 22 42; www.alsa.es) connects Almería to El Cabo de Gata (€2.50, one hour, six daily) and Las Negras (€4.50, 1¼ hours, one daily Monday to Saturday). Autocares Bernardo (☎ 950 25 04 22; www.autocares bernardo.com) runs buses from Almería to San José (€3.50, 1¼ hours, three Monday to Saturday, two Sunday) and back (four Monday to Saturday, two Sunday). It also runs one bus to La Isleta del Moro (€4, 1¼ hours) on Mondays and Saturdays. Autocares Frahermar (☎ 950 29 02 12) in Almería runs to/from Agua Amarga (€5, 1¼ hours) once on Monday, Wednesday, Friday, Saturday and Sunday; service increases to daily in July and August. An alternative is to take a taxi from Agua Amarga to Carboneras (€20, 20 minutes), the next town north, where buses to Almería run four times on weekdays and once on weekends (€6, two hours). There is no bus service connecting towns within the park.

CAR // From Las Negras to Agua Amarga, you must head inland via Las Hortichuelas. From a turn east in Fernán Pérez, wind 10km northeast on a tarmac road to meet the AL-5106 at the Cortijo Los Malenos; turn right for Agua Amarga.

TAXI // Taxi de Gata (☎ 669 07 14 42; www.taxi degata.com) In Níjar. Taxi Ramón Ruíz López (☎ 950 13 00 08, 606 41 47 24) In Carboneras.

MOJÁCAR

pop 6200

There are two Mojácars: old Mojácar Pueblo, a multilevel wedding cake of white houses atop a steep hill, and new Mojácar Playa, a typical modern resort along a broad beach. As recently as the 1960s, the pueblo was decaying and almost abandoned. A savvy mayor lured artists and others with bargain property offers, which set a distinct bohemian tone that is still palpable, despite an overlay of more generic tourism. In the pueblo's winding streets, mellow bars,

ALMERÍA PROVINCE

TWO WAYS TO GROW A TOMATO

In Almería's unprotected flatlands, *invernaderos* (white greenhouses) sprawl like some extraterrestrial colony. The tomatoes produced here have brought wealth to a previously dirt-poor corner of Spain. But water quality has suffered due to pesticide runoff, and exploitation of immigrant labour has been a constant issue.

Meanwhile, mountain-dwellers lament the spoiled view over the valleys, and they stand by the complex system of *huertas* (terraces) and *acequias* (water channels) installed by the Arabs when they came to Spain, more than a millennium ago. No room for hypermodern agriculture here – the old way is the only way to eke a living out of the steep mountainsides.

But the real test is, how do the tomatoes taste? In summer, mountain-grown, sun-ripened tomatoes are delectable. But surprisingly, the *tomate RAF,* a greenish heirloom variety, does very well in the hothouses – and ripens in winter, through to April or May. It's the province's pride; look for it on Almería menus only.

galleries and little boutiques abound, and the views from Plaza Nueva, where kids play and painters work *en plein air,* often keep many visitors here longer than they intended.

ESSENTIAL INFORMATION

EMERGENCIES // Centro Médico (medical centre; ☎ 950 47 51 05; Parque Comercial, Mojácar Playa; ☼ 10am-1pm & 5.30-8pm) English and French spoken. Policía Local (☎ 950 47 20 00; Calle Glorieta, Mojácar Pueblo) Next to the pueblo tourist office.

TOURIST OFFICES // Mojácar Playa (☎ 950 47 23 51; Avenida del Mediterráneo; ☼ 9am-4pm Mon-Fri, 9.30am-2pm Sat) Kiosk opposite the Parque Comercial. Mojácar Pueblo (☎ 950 61 50 25; info@mojacar.es; Calle Glorieta; ☼ 10am-2pm & 5-7pm Mon-Fri, 10.30am-1.30pm Sat) Just north of Plaza Nueva.

ORIENTATION

To reach the pueblo from the *playa* (beach), turn inland at the roundabout by Parque Comercial, a large shopping centre. The road up is 2km; regular buses connect the two. In the pueblo, the main

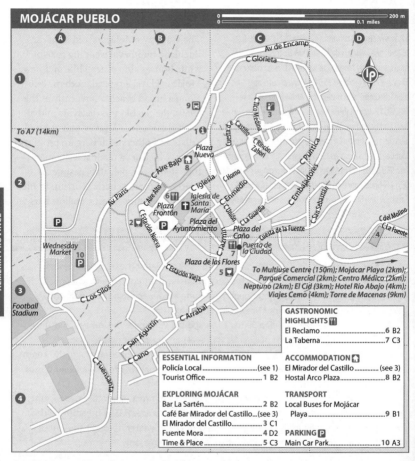

MOJÁCAR PUEBLO

GASTRONOMIC HIGHLIGHTS
El Reclamo 6 B2
La Taberna 7 C3

ESSENTIAL INFORMATION
Policía Local ....(see 1)
Tourist Office 1 B2

EXPLORING MOJÁCAR
Bar La Sartén.................................... 2 B2
Café Bar Mirador del Castillo...(see 3)
El Mirador del Castillo................... 3 C1
Fuente Mora 4 D2
Time & Place 5 C3

ACCOMMODATION
El Mirador del Castillo .... (see 3)
Hostal Arco Plaza........................... 8 B2

TRANSPORT
Local Buses for Mojácar
   Playa 9 B1

PARKING
Main Car Park................................. 10 A3

ALMERÍA PROVINCE

road goes one way only, looping around and back down.

EXPLORING MOJÁCAR

🌱 EL MIRADOR DEL CASTILLO // AN ART CENTRE WITH 360-DEGREE VIEWS

A by-product of Mojácar's revival as an arts colony, the bohemian retreat called **El Mirador del Castillo** (☎ 950 47 30 22; ☾ 11am-11pm or later) occupies the very top of the hill, a mirador (lookout) to end all miradors. From here, you can appreciate the area's weird geology – the sea is off to one side, while the inland vista is studded with volcanic cones just like the one Mojácar occupies. A cafe-bar here provides sustenance after the hike up, along with jazz on the stereo and plenty of space to relax over a coffee or tapa.

🌱 FUENTE MORA // A MONUMENT TO A MOORISH HERO

Near the foot of the village, the Fuente Mora (Moorish Fountain) is a village landmark. A plaque above it is inscribed with the words of the last Muslim governor, Alabez y Garcilaso, who retorted to the Catholic Monarchs' order to leave in 1488: 'I am as Spanish as you are… I have not taken up arms against the Christians… I believe it is only just we are treated as brothers, not as enemies.' But his statement ended with what could have been a subtle threat: 'Rather than be delivered as a coward, I will die as a Spaniard.' His plea actually worked, for a time, and as part of the deal, the Mojácar coat of arms incorporated the two-headed eagle of the Habsburg empire, of which Spain was then a part.

In the 16th century, aggressive campaigns resumed against the population of Andalucía (now mostly *moriscos*, converted Muslims, under threat of the Inquisitions), and in 1609, there was a final push, with refugees marched to port cities with only the belongings they could carry, and often without their young children, who were taken to Catholic orphanages. But no matter how thorough the Inquisition claimed to be, a certain percentage of the Muslim population remained, especially in this fringe of Spain. Polish photographer Kurt Hielscher visited Mojácar in the early 20th century, and his images document women dressed in black, with veils over their faces. At the entrance to the village, a sign read 'Mojácar, Kingdom of Granada', as though the last 400 years had never happened.

🌱 BEACHES // FIND YOUR SPOT IN THE SUN

Stretching some 7km, Mojácar Playa has enough sand for everyone. Distinct stretches of beach are known by different names, though in the central part, there's not much to distinguish the character of each patch of sand. Of the many *chiringuitos* (beach restaurants), **Neptuno** (☎ 616 00 53 87; Playa del Descargador; mains €12-16) is well regarded, especially for its wood-fire sardine feasts. It's just north of the intersection of Avenida del Mediterráneo (the beach road) and the road to the pueblo, which locals call the *cruce*. A landmark *chiringuito* is **El Cid** (☎ 950 47 20 63; Avenida del Mediterráneo; drinks €2-5), south of the *cruce*, which has been cultivating the good life since 1972. A few kilometres further south, the beaches start to become less crowded, and once you get to the fringes of town, there are a number of more secluded areas. Some of those beyond the **Torre de Macenas**, an 18th-century fortification right on the sand, are naturist beaches.

☕ BAR-HOPPING // GET COSY IN MOJÁCAR'S SNUG WATERING HOLES

In summer, Mojácar Pueblo has a hopping nightlife, with a number of friendly bars tucked into small houses. For tapas, many people start at La Taberna (below), and Café Bar Mirador del Castillo (see p307) often has some kind of live music or other performance. **Time & Place** (Plaza de las Flores) is good for conversation, with pillows on benches outside, Dylan on the stereo and a view of the old city gate. **Bar La Sartén** (Calle Estación Nueva) often keeps going later, with drinkers lingering in the candlelit corners under the heavy wood ceiling beams until the wee hours.

FESTIVALS & EVENTS

Swap Meet (⏰ 8.30am-1.30pm Sun) At the multi-use centre at the bottom of the village.

Moros y Cristianos Locals don costumes to re-enact the Christian conquest. Dances, processions and festivities are held on the weekend nearest 10 June.

Noche de San Juan Bonfires and strong drink, in equal measure, coinciding with the summer solstice on 23 June.

GASTRONOMIC HIGHLIGHTS

☕ EL RECLAMO €

☎ 950 47 28 81; Calle Alcalde Jacinto; mains €7-10
With a big TV and fluorescent lights, you're not coming to this bare-bones place for the atmosphere. But the honest home cooking that comes out of the kitchen – pork in rich tomato sauce and the like – more than makes up for it. It's often served by a man who seems genuinely smitten by his wife's cooking.

☕ LA TABERNA €

☎ 647 72 43 67; Plaza del Caño 1; tapas & platos combinados from €4; ⏰ closed mid-Dec–Feb; Ⓥ
Good tapas and tasty vegetarian bites get everyone cramming into this thriving lit-tle restaurant inside a warren of intimate rooms, full of chatter and belly-full diners. There's also an enormous house kebab that arrives on its own scaffolding. To get here, head downhill and pass through the old city gate – just on the right, you'll see the tiny tapas *plancha* (griddle) in action.

TRANSPORT

BUS // There is a bus stop at the foot of Mojácar Pueblo and another at the Parque Comercial in Mojácar Playa. **Enatcar/Alsa** (☎ 902 42 22 42; www.alsa.es) runs buses to/from Almería (€7, 1¾ hours, four on weekdays, two on weekends), Granada (€18, four hours, two daily), Madrid (€36, eight hours, two daily), Madrid Barajas (€36, 8½ hours, one daily at 8.55pm) and Málaga (€23, 7½ hours, one daily). For Almería and Granada, buy tickets on the bus; for Málaga and Madrid, you must buy online or book at a travel agency such as **Viajes Cemo** (☎ 950 47 28 35; Paseo del Mediterráneo, Mojácar Playa), 2km south of the Parque Comercial (Pueblo Indalo bus stop). Buses to Alicante, Valencia and Barcelona go from Vera, 16km north, which is served by several daily buses from Mojácar (€1.20, 50 minutes, nine daily). A local bus (€1) runs a circuit from Mojácar Pueblo down along the full length of the beach, roughly every half-hour from 9am to 11.30pm, April to September, till 7.30pm October to March.

CAR // Mojácar is 14km east of the A7 and 3.4km south of the A370.

PARKING // Follow the main road through town to reach two large parking lots on the far edge. Do not leave your car overnight on Tuesdays in the upper lot, as it's used for a market on Wednesday morning.

TAXI // Taxis wait in the Plaza Nueva, or call ☎ 950 47 81 84.

LOS VÉLEZ

• • • • • •

The beautiful, sparse landscape of the remote district of Los Vélez, in the northernmost part of Almería, lies 55km inland from Mojácar. In contrast with the rest of the province, parts of it are quite lush and forested, and its main settlements are the three small towns Vélez Rubio, Vélez Blanco and María, which nestle in the shadow of the stark Sierra de María range, part of a natural park. Cave paintings here are the source of the *indalo*, the prehistoric symbol that's seen everywhere in Almería.

Vélez Rubio is the largest town, with an enormous 18th-century baroque church, but the most attractive and interesting town is Vélez Blanco, with about 2000 people in a scramble of houses with red-tile roofs, overshadowed by a dramatic castle. At 1070m, it's often up above the clouds – you can watch the valley below fill with fog, and by afternoon the streets are wreathed in mist.

ESSENTIAL INFORMATION

TOURIST OFFICES // Centro de Visitantes Almacén del Trigo (☎ 950 41 53 54; Avenida del Marqués de Los Vélez, Vélez Blanco; ☺ 10am-2pm Tue, Thu & Sun, 10am-2pm & 4-6pm Fri & Sat) On the northern edge of Vélez Blanco. Centro de Visitantes Mirador Umbría de María (☎ 950 52 70 05; ☺ 10am-2pm Tue, Thu & Sun, 10am-2pm & 4-6pm Fri & Sat) Two kilometres west of María off the A317.

EXPLORING LOS VÉLEZ

❦ MUSEO ANTONIO MANUEL CAMPOY // A SURPRISING MUSEUM IN A CASTLE

On the drive up from the coast, in the foothills 6km north of Vera, you pass by Cuevas del Almanzora, a busy but generally unremarkable agricultural town. The handsome Castillo Marqués de Los Vélez lords over the town from a hilltop, housing a basic archaeology museum as well as the Museo Antonio Manuel Campoy (☎ 950 45 80 63; Plaza de la Libertad; admission free;

☺ 10am-1pm & 5-8pm Tue-Sat, 10am-1pm Sun). The latter exhibits a large and fascinating selection of paintings and sculpture, including works by Picasso and Miró, from the outstanding private collection of Campoy, a native of Cuevas who was one of Spain's greatest 20th-century art critics.

❦ CASTILLO DE VÉLEZ BLANCO // TOUR AN EERILY EMPTY FORTRESS

The 16th-century castle (☎ 607 41 50 55; adult/child €1/0.50; ☺ 10am-2pm & 6-8pm Wed-Sun May-Oct, 10am-2pm & 4-6pm Wed-Sat Nov-Apr) at the top of the village seems to spring naturally from its rocky pinnacle. It confronts the great sphinxlike butte dubbed La Muela (The Tooth) across the tiled roofs of the village, as if in a bizarre duel. From the outside, the structure is a pure feudal fortress, built in the early 16th century to establish Catholic control over this region filled with Muslim and *morisco* refugees. But the inside is pure Renaissance palace – or it was until 1904, when the marble details were picked off, save for one lone gargoyle, and sold as a lot by the impoverished owners. American millionaire George Blumenthal bought the entire marble patio and later donated it to the Metropolitan Museum of Art in New York, where it is on permanent display. There is an ongoing project to make a copy of the patio and reinstall it.

A stroll around Vélez Blanco before or after is rewarding, not least for its delightful maze of streets and its many attractive houses, which display a particularly stylish domestic architecture, with overhanging roof tiles and handsome wrought-iron balconies.

❦ CUEVA DE LOS LETREROS // THE SOURCE OF ALMERÍA'S GOOD-LUCK CHARM

Just south of Vélez Blanco, signs point to the Cueva de los Letreros (☎ 617 88

28 08; A317; admission free; ⊙ noon-6pm May-Oct,
to 4.30pm Nov-Apr), off the west side of the
road opposite the Pinar del Rey camping ground. Of several collections of
cave paintings in the area, this has the
most outstanding examples. The reddish
drawings were made sometime between
6000 BC and 3500 BC and depict what
appear to be interconnected people – a
sort of family tree, goes one theory. More
important is the now ubiquitous *indalo*,
a stick figure with arms connected by
an arc. It's seen all over the province,
on walls and pendants and government
letterhead, and there's enough evidence
of its use in earlier centuries (and mil-
lennia) that ethnologists surmise it may
be one of the longest continually used
symbols in human culture.

You can drive most of the way to the
cave, but first it's a good idea to stop at
the kiosk across the road from the turn-
off (in front of the camping ground)
and ask the caretaker if the metal fence
around the cave can be opened. If no
one's at the kiosk, it means the caretaker
is probably at the site. (Tours are also
available, for €12 for a group of six, but
in Spanish only.)

From the A317, it's 600m along the
signposted dirt track, then a right turn
on a steep uphill cement road. This turns
to dirt again and winds its way up to a
parking area. A set of stone stairs leads
to the cave – more like a rock overhang.
This is the area that's fenced in, but you
can see the drawings up above regardless.

❦ PARQUE NATURAL SIERRA DE MARÍA-LOS VÉLEZ // HIKE ALONE IN DRAMATIC MOUNTAINS

If you go walking in the arid mountains
of this natural park, a refuge for many
birds of prey, foxes and mountain goats,
you will almost certainly have the trails

to yourself. A visit in spring or autumn
is best, as shade can be hard to come
by on some trails. Vélez Blanco makes
a good base, as does the tiny upland
town of María, in a fine position against
the awesome backdrop of the Sierra de
María. The park visitor centres in either
town (p309) have information on walking trails.

Just west of María on the A317 is the
Jardín Botánico Umbría de la Virgen
(☎ 697 95 60 46; ⊙ 10am-2pm & 6-8pm Tue-Sun
May-Sep, 10am-4pm Tue-Sun Oct-Apr). Stop in
here if you're going hiking – the gardens highlight the unique flora in the
mountains.

About 6km west of María, the A317
heads north onto a high plateau towards the lonely village of La Cañada
de Cañepla, from where it continues, by
a superbly scenic road, into the Parque
Natural Sierras de Cazorla, Segura y Las
Villas (see p241).

❦ MESÓN EL MOLINO // RURAL GASTRONOMY AT ITS FINEST

Tucked away up a narrow lane near the
centre of Vélez Blanco is a superb restaurant, Mesón El Molino (☎ 950 41 50 70; Calle
Curtidores 1, Vélez Blanco; mains €17-22; ⊙ closed Thu
evening). It's the best kind of grand, old-
fashioned place, with a real emphasis on
the best quality products from all over
Spain, proudly displayed at the entrance:
aged beef, perfect tomatoes, obscure
cheeses and, of course, luscious hams.
The menu also includes game birds such
as partridge and duck. In warm weather
you can dine on the patio, where a
stream gurgles past.

TRANSPORT

BUS // Alsina Graells (☎ 968 29 16 12) runs
buses from Vélez Rubio to Granada (€12.50, 2¼ hours,

five daily), Guadix (€8.50, 1¾ hours, three daily) and
Murcia (€8, 1½-2¼ hours, five daily). For Almería (€13,
3½ hours), there's a bus every day but Sunday. Autobuses Giménez García (☎ 968 44 19 61)
connects María, Vélez Blanco and Vélez Rubio. The bus
stop in Vélez Rubio is on Avenida de Andalucía at the
junction by Hostal Zurich.

CAR // A bypass runs along the top of Vélez Blanco.
Coming from Vélez Rubio, the first turn into town takes
you to a stretch of road where you can park and continue
on foot. The second turn leads directly to the castle
(where there is parking). The third turn takes you into
the far side of the village, near the information office.

BACKGROUND

☙ HISTORY
Andalucía's story is one of history's grand epics, spanning the great civilisations of antiquity to the sophisticated centuries of Islamic Al-Andalus and beyond. (opposite)

☙ ANDALUSIAN ARCHITECTURE
Islam and Christianity may have battled over the soil of Andalucía for centuries, but the architectural landmarks they left behind are, quite simply, extraordinary. (p332)

☙ EXPLORING NATURAL ANDALUCÍA
Mountains of rare beauty and a coast of stunning variety – getting out among the wildlife and wilderness is a perfect reason to visit Andalucía. (p343)

☙ FLAMENCO & BEYOND
Andalucía's soundtrack is guaranteed to move your soul – this is where flamenco was born and where it's woven into the fabric of daily life. (p354)

☙ ANDALUSIAN ARTS (& BULLFIGHTING)
Andalusian culture is Spain in microcosm, from its literature, painting and cinema to that most controversial Spanish pastime – bullfighting. (p360)

☙ THE ANDALUSIAN KITCHEN
A fiercely defended outpost of Spain's glorious culinary traditions, Andalucía is where you get the essence of tastes that came to define a country. (p367)

HISTORY

· · · · · ·

Just a stone's throw from Africa and open to both the Mediterranean Sea and the
Atlantic Ocean, Andalucía's destiny has often been tied less to Spain and Europe than
to regions beyond. Indeed this pivotal location at the meeting point of continents and
oceans has frequently placed Andalucía at the forefront of Spanish and even European
history. It was through this frontier territory that Spain was introduced to defining
epochs of its history such as the Bronze Age, the Roman era, the Muslim era and the
American empire. Andalucía is one of history's great crossroads and its story is a fascinating parade of peoples, cultures, ideas and colourful characters – from Hadrian,
Al-Mansur and Boabdil to Pedro the Cruel, Isabel La Católica and Christopher
Columbus.

EARLY IMMIGRANTS

Many important early human advances originating in Africa and the eastern Mediterranean reached Andalucía first before spreading around the Iberian Peninsula.

Ancient stone tools found near Orce (p272) in Granada province reveal the presence of an early version of humanity, possibly *Homo erectus,* cohabiting with mammoths, rhinoceroses, sabre-tooth tigers, hippopotamuses, giant hyenas and elephants
about 1.3 million years ago. Anthropologists agree that humanity originated in Africa
but *Homo erectus* may have travelled to Spain via the eastern end of Europe.

By the start of the last glacial period about 100,000 BC, Andalucía, like much of the
rest of Europe, was home to Neanderthal humans. Neanderthals began their terminal
decline around 35,000 BC as a result of climate change and the arrival of Europe's
first *Homo sapiens* around this time, probably from North Africa. Neanderthals appear to have survived longer in Andalucía than anywhere else. Recent excavations at
Gorham's Cave in Gibraltar show that they were still hanging on there as late as 24,000
years ago.

The first *Homo sapiens* were hunter-gatherers. Like 21st-century tourists, they gravi-
tated to Andalucía's relatively warm climate, which permitted varied fauna and thick
forests to develop and made hunting and gathering somewhat easier. Between 20,000
and 16,000 years ago they left impressive rock paintings of some of the animals they
hunted in Andalusian caves such as the Cueva de Ardales (p184), the Cueva de la Pileta (p182) and the Cueva de Nerja (p192).

» C 35,000 BC	» 18,000–14,000 BC	» C 6000 BC
The first modern humans reach Spain from Africa, hunt mammoths, bison and rein- deer, displace Neanderthals and shelter in caves such as the Cueva de Nerja.	Palaeolithic hunter-gatherers paint quarry such as aurochs, stags, horses and fish in the Cueva de la Pileta (near Ronda), Cueva de Ardales and Cueva de Nerja.	The Neolithic period reaches eastern Spain, bringing revo- lutionary innovations such as the plough, crops, domes- ticated livestock, pottery, textiles and village life.

The Neolithic or New Stone Age reached eastern Spain from Egypt and Mesopotamia around 6000 BC, bringing the revolution of agriculture – the plough, crops, domesticated livestock – and with it pottery, textiles and villages.

The pace of change was reaching dizzy heights by now and it was only another 3500 years or so before the people of Los Millares (p299), near Almería in eastern Andalucía, learnt how to smelt and shape local copper deposits and became Spain's first metalworking culture – a big agricultural and military breakthrough. Around the same time, Spain's most impressive dolmens (megalithic tombs, constructed of large rocks covered in earth) were erected near Antequera, during the same era as the megalithic age in France, Britain and Ireland.

> 'Like 21st-century tourists, early European Homo sapiens gravitated to Andalucía's warm climate'

About 1900 BC the people of El Argar (Almería province) learned to make bronze, an alloy of copper and tin that is stronger than copper – ushering in the Bronze Age on the Iberian Peninsula.

TRADERS & INVADERS

Andalucía's rich resources and settled societies eventually attracted seafaring traders from more sophisticated societies around the Mediterranean. Traders were later replaced by invaders as imperialistic states emerged in the Mediterranean and sought not only to tap local wealth but also to exert military control. All these newcomers – Phoenicians, Greeks, Carthaginians, Romans and Visigoths – left their own indelible marks on Andalusian life and identity.

PHOENICIANS, GREEKS & TARTESSOS

By about 1000 BC, a flourishing culture rich in agriculture, animals and metals arose in western Andalucía. This attracted Phoenician traders, ranging far from their home in present-day Lebanon, who arrived to exchange perfumes, ivory, jewellery, oil, wine and textiles for Andalusian silver and bronze. The Phoenicians set up coastal trading settlements at places such as Almuñécar (which they called Ex or Sex), Cádiz (Gadir) and Huelva (Onuba), and museums in those cities preserve many Phoenician artefacts today. In the 7th century BC the Greeks arrived too, trading much the same goods as the Phoenicians.

BACKGROUND

» 2700–1800 BC	» C 1900 BC	» C 1000–800 BC
The people of Los Millares learn to smelt and shape local copper deposits, becoming Spain's first metalworking culture – a big agricultural and military breakthrough.	The people of El Argar learn to make bronze, an alloy of copper and tin that is stronger than copper. By 1200 BC bronze technology spreads throughout Andalucía.	Phoenicians bring perfume, ivory, jewellery, oil, wine and textiles to trade for Andalusian silver and bronze, establishing coastal colonies such as Gadir (Cádiz) and Onuba (Huelva).

DON'T MISS...

WHERE HISTORY WAS MADE

* **Alhambra, Granada** // The final flowering of Muslim Spain (p254)
* **Lugares Colombinos, Huelva Province** // Where Columbus dreamed, discussed, planned, prayed and set sail (p82)
* **Mezquita, Córdoba** // The great statement of early Hispanic Islam (p201)
* **Cádiz** // From Phoenician sarcophagi to Francis Drake and the 1812 constitution, it all happened here (p110)
* **Alcázar, Seville** // The palace of generations of Muslim and Christian rulers (p44)
* **Capilla Real, Granada** // The Catholic Monarchs' mausoleum and monument to themselves and their religion (p259)
* **Minas de Riotinto, Huelva Province** // Mines, trains and soccer; from Roman imperialism to British capitalism (p98)

The Phoenicians and Greeks brought with them the potter's wheel, writing and such quintessentially Andalusian plants and animals as the olive tree, the vine and the donkey.

The Phoenician- and Greek-influenced culture of western Andalucía in the 8th and 7th centuries BC, with Phoenician-type gods, is known as the Tartessos culture. The Tartessians developed advanced methods of working gold, but it was iron that replaced bronze as the most important metal. Tartessos was described centuries later by Greek, Roman and biblical writers as the source of fabulous riches. Whether it was a city, a state or just a region no one knows. Some argue that it was a trading settlement near modern Huelva; others believe it may lie beneath the marshes near the mouth of the Río Guadalquivir.

CARTHAGE & ROME

From the 6th century BC the Phoenicians and Greeks were pushed out of western Mediterranean trade by a former Phoenician colony in modern Tunisia – Carthage. Unhappily for the Carthaginians, the next new power to arise in the Mediterranean was Rome. After losing out to Rome in the First Punic War (264–241 BC), which was fought for control of Sicily, Carthage conquered southern Spain. The Second Punic

» C 700–600 BC	» 206 BC	» 100 BC TO 300 AD
Iron replaces bronze as the most important metal around the lower Guadalquivir valley. The Tartessos culture that develops here is mythologised as having fabulous wealth.	Roman legions under General Scipio Africanus defeat the army of Carthage at Ilipa, near Seville. Itálica, the first Roman town in Spain, is founded near the battlefield.	Andalucía becomes one of the wealthiest, most civilised areas of the Roman empire, with Corduba (Córdoba) its most important city.

War (218–201 BC) saw Carthaginian general Hannibal march his elephants on from here and over the Alps to threaten Rome, but also saw Rome open a second front by bringing legions to fight Carthage in Spain. Rome's victory at Ilipa, near modern Seville, in 206 BC, gave it control of the Iberian Peninsula. The first Roman town in Spain, Itálica (p63), was founded near the battlefield soon afterwards.

It's a curious thought that if Carthage had won the Second Punic War, the capital of western civilisation would have been, for a while at least, in Africa…but anyway, the Roman Empire went from strength to strength, and Andalucía quickly became one of its most civilised and wealthiest areas. Rome imported Andalusian wheat, vegetables, grapes, olives, copper, silver, lead, fish and *garum* (a spicy seasoning derived from fish, made in factories whose remains can be seen at Bolonia, p147, and Almuñécar, p283). Andalucía also gave Rome two emperors, Trajan and Hadrian, both from Itálica. Rome brought Spain aqueducts, temples, theatres, amphitheatres, baths, its main language (Spanish is basically colloquial Latin 2000 years on), a sizeable Jewish population (Jews spread throughout the Mediterranean part of the Roman Empire) and, in the 3rd century AD, Christianity.

THE VISIGOTHS

When the Huns erupted into Europe from Asia in the late 4th century AD, displaced Germanic peoples moved westwards across the crumbling Roman Empire, some overrunning the Iberian Peninsula. One Germanic group, the Visigoths, eventually made Iberia their own in the 6th century, with Toledo, in central Spain, as their capital.

The long-haired Visigoths, numbering about 200,000, had little culture of their own and their precarious rule over the relatively sophisticated Hispano-Romans was undermined by strife among their own nobility. But ties were strengthened in 587 when King Reccared converted to Roman Christianity from the Visigoths' Arian version (which denied that Christ was God). The Andalusian city of Seville was an important cultural centre, especially in the time of St Isidoro (AD 565–636), Spain's leading scholar of the period.

AL-ANDALUS: ISLAMIC RULE

Following the death of the prophet Mohammed in 632, Arabs carried Islam through the Middle East and North Africa. If you believe the myth, they were ushered onto the Iberian Peninsula by the sexual exploits of the last Visigothic king, Roderic. Chronicles relate how Roderic seduced young Florinda, the daughter of Julian, the Visigothic

» 3RD CENTURY AD	» 500–600 AD	» 711
Rome, having introduced Spain to aqueducts, temples, theatres, baths and amphitheatres, introduces Christianity.	Byzantium conquers Andalucía. The Visigoths, a Christian Germanic people now controlling the Iberian Peninsula, drive Byzantium out in 622.	Muslim forces from North Africa decimate the Visigothic army near the Río Guadalete. Within a few years, the Muslims overrun almost the whole Iberian Peninsula.

governor of Ceuta in North Africa; and how Julian sought revenge by approaching the Muslims with a plan to invade Spain. In reality, Roderic's rivals probably just sought support in the endless struggle for the Visigothic throne. In any case, by 700, with famine and disease in Toledo, strife among the aristocracy and chaos throughout the peninsula, Visigothic control was disintegrating.

In 711 Tariq ibn Ziyad, the Muslim governor of Tangier, landed at Gibraltar with around 10,000 men, mostly Berbers (indigenous North Africans). Roderic's army was decimated, probably near the Río Guadalete in Cádiz province, and he is thought to have drowned as he fled. Within a few years, the Muslims had taken over the whole Iberian Peninsula except for small areas in the Asturian mountains in the far north. The Muslims were to be the dominant force on the Iberian Peninsula for nearly four centuries and a potent force for a further four. Between wars and rebellions, the Islamic areas of the peninsula developed the most cultured society in medieval Europe. The name given to these Muslim territories was Al-Andalus, which lives on today in the modern name of what was always the Muslim heartland – Andalucía.

Al-Andalus' frontiers were constantly shifting as the Christians strove to regain territory in their stuttering 800-year Reconquista (reconquest), but up to the mid-11th century the small Christian states developing in northern Spain were too weak and quarrelsome to pose much of a threat to Al-Andalus, even though the Muslims had their internal conflicts too.

Islamic political power and culture centred first on Córdoba (756–1031), then Seville (c 1040–1248) and lastly Granada (1248–1492). In the main cities, the Muslims built beautiful palaces, mosques and gardens, established bustling *zocos* (markets) and public bathhouses (which most people attended about once a week), and opened universities.

> '*the Islamic areas of the Iberian Peninsula developed the most cultured society in medieval Europe*'

Although military campaigns against the northern Christians could be bloodthirsty affairs, the rulers of Al-Andalus allowed freedom of worship to Jews and Christians under their rule. Jews, on the whole, flourished, but Christians in Muslim territory (Mozarabs; *mozárabes* in Spanish) had to pay a special tax, so most either converted to Islam (to become known as *muladíes,* or *muwallads*) or left for the Christian north.

The Muslim ruling class was composed of various Arab groups prone to factional friction. Below them was a larger group of Berbers, who rebelled on numerous oc-

» 756–929	» 929–1031	» 11TH CENTURY
The Muslim emirate of Córdoba rules over most of the Iberian Peninsula. The name Al-Andalus is given to Muslim-controlled areas.	The caliphate of Córdoba: ruler Abd ar-Rahman III declares himself caliph in 929; Al-Andalus attains its greatest power; and Córdoba becomes Western Europe's biggest city.	The caliphate implodes in civil war and disintegrates into dozens of *taifas* (small kingdoms). Seville emerges as the strongest, returning peace and prosperity to the region.

casions. Before long, Muslim and local blood merged in Spain and many Spaniards today are partly descended from medieval Muslims.

THE CORDOBAN EMIRATE & CALIPHATE

Initially, Muslim Spain was a province of the emirate of North Africa. In 750 the Omayyad dynasty of caliphs in Damascus, supreme rulers of the Muslim world, was overthrown by a group of non-Arab revolutionaries, the Abbasids, who shifted the caliphate to Baghdad. One of the Omayyad family, Abd ar-Rahman, escaped the slaughter and somehow made his way to Morocco and then to Córdoba, where in 756 he set himself up as an independent ruler. Abd ar-Rahman I's Omayyad dynasty more or less unified Al-Andalus for 2½ centuries.

In 929 Abd ar-Rahman III (r 912–961) gave himself the title caliph (meaning deputy to Mohammed and therefore supreme leader of the Muslim world) to assert his authority in the face of the Fatimids, a growing Muslim power in North Africa. Thus Abd ar-Rahman III launched the caliphate of Córdoba, which at its peak encompassed three-quarters of the Iberian Peninsula and some of North Africa. Córdoba became the biggest, most dazzling and most cultured city in Western Europe. Its Mezquita (Mosque; p201) is one of the world's wonders of Islamic architecture. Astronomy, medicine, mathematics, philosophy, history and botany flourished, and Abd ar-Rahman III's court was frequented by Jewish, Arabian and Christian scholars.

Later in the 10th century, the fearsome Cordoban general Al-Mansur (or Almanzor) terrorised the Christian north with 50-odd *razzias* (forays) in 20 years. In 997 he destroyed the cathedral at Santiago de Compostela in northwestern Spain – home of the cult of Santiago Matamoros (St James the Moor-Slayer),

PATH OF KNOWLEDGE

It was through Al-Andalus that much of the learning of ancient Greece and Rome found its way to Christian Europe, where it was ultimately to exert a profound influence on the Renaissance. The Arabs, during their conquests in the eastern Mediterranean and Middle East, absorbed the philosophy of Aristotle, the maths of Euclid and Pythagoras, the astronomy of Ptolemy, and the medical ideas of Hippocrates and Galen, translating their writings into Arabic. There were three places around the medieval Mediterranean where the Islamic and Christian worlds met and where this knowledge could find its way northwards – one was the Crusader kingdoms of the Middle East, one was southern Italy, and the other was Al-Andalus.

» C 1090s	» 1140s	» 1160–73
A strict Muslim sect of Saharan nomads, the Almoravids, conquers Al-Andalus, rules it from Marrakesh as a colony and persecutes Jews and Christians.	The Almoravid control of Al-Andalus crumbles as revolt spreads across the territory, and the region again splits into *taifas*.	Another strict Muslim sect of Saharan nomads, the Almohads, conquers Al-Andalus. They make Seville the capital of their whole realm and revive arts and learning.

a key inspiration to Christian warriors. But after Al-Mansur's death, the caliphate disintegrated into dozens of *taifas* (small kingdoms), ruled by local potentates, who were often Berber generals.

THE ALMORAVIDS & ALMOHADS

In the 1040s Seville, in the wealthy lower Guadalquivir valley, emerged as the strongest *taifa* in Andalucía. By 1078 the writ of its Abbasid dynasty ran all the way from southern Portugal to Murcia, restoring a measure of peace and prosperity to Andalucía.

Meanwhile, the northern Christian states were starting to raise their game. When one of them, Castilla, captured Toledo in 1085, a scared Seville begged for help from the Almoravids, a strict Muslim sect of Saharan Berbers who had conquered Morocco. The Almoravids came, defeated Castilla's Alfonso VI, and ended up taking over Al-Andalus too, ruling it from Marrakesh as a colony and persecuting Jews and Christians. But the charms of Al-Andalus seemed to relax the Almoravids' austere grip: revolts spread across the territory from 1143 and within a few years it had again split into *taifas*.

In Morocco, the Almoravids were displaced by another strict Muslim Berber sect, the Almohads, who in turn invaded Al-Andalus, bringing it under full control by 1173. Al-Andalus was by now considerably reduced from its 10th-century heyday: the frontier now ran from south of Lisbon to north of Valencia. The Almohads made Seville capital of their whole realm and revived arts and learning in Al-Andalus. The great Cordoban Islamic philosopher Averroës (1126–98) exerted a major influence on medieval European thought with his commentaries on Aristotle, trying to reconcile science with religion.

In 1195, the Almohad ruler Yusuf Yakub al-Mansur thrashed Castilla's army at Alarcos, south of Toledo, but this only spurred the northern Christians to join forces against him. In 1212 the combined armies of Castilla, Aragón and Navarra routed a large Almohad force at Las Navas de Tolosa, north of Jaén. Then, with the Almohad state riven by a succession dispute after 1224, the Christian kingdoms of Castilla, Portugal, León and Aragón moved down the Iberian Peninsula. Castilla's Fernando III (El Santo, the Saint) moved into Andalucía, taking strategic Baeza in 1227, Córdoba in 1236, and Seville, after a two-year siege, in 1248.

THE NASRID EMIRATE OF GRANADA

The Granada emirate was a wedge of territory carved out of the disintegrating Almohad realm by Mohammed ibn Yusuf ibn Nasr, after whom it's known as the Nasrid

» 1212	» 1248	» 1249–1492
The combined Christian armies of Castilla, Aragón-Catalonia and Navarra rout a large Almohad force at Las Navas de Tolosa, signalling Al-Andalus' decline.	Castilla's Fernando III (El Santo, the Saint) takes Seville after a two-year siege, having already captured strategic Baeza in 1227 and Córdoba in 1236.	The emirate of Granada, ruled from the lavish Alhambra palace, sees the final flowering of medieval Muslim culture on the Iberian Peninsula.

BACKGROUND

emirate. Comprising primarily the modern provinces of Granada, Málaga and Almería, with a population of about 300,000, it held out for nearly 250 years as the last Muslim state on the Iberian Peninsula.

The Nasrids ruled from the lavish Alhambra palace (p254), which witnessed the final flowering of Islamic culture in Spain. The emirate reached its peak in the 14th century under Yusuf I and Mohammed V, creators of the greatest splendours of the Alhambra. Its final downfall was precipitated by two things. One was Emir Abu al-Hasan's refusal in 1476 to pay any further tribute to Castilla; the other was the unification in 1479 of Castilla and Aragón, Spain's biggest Christian states, through the marriage of their monarchs Isabel and Fernando (Isabella and Ferdinand). The Reyes Católicos (Catholic Monarchs), as the pair are known, launched the final crusade of the Reconquista, against Granada, in 1482.

> *'the lavish Alhambra palace witnessed the final flowering of Islamic culture in Spain'*

Harem jealousies and other feuds between Granada's rulers degenerated into a civil war that allowed the Christians to push across the emirate, devastating the countryside. They captured Málaga in 1487, and Granada itself, after an eight-month siege, on 2 January 1492.

The surrender terms were fairly generous to the last emir, Boabdil, who received the valleys of Las Alpujarras, south of Granada, as a personal fiefdom. He stayed only a year, however, before departing to Africa. The Muslims were promised respect for their religion, culture and property, but this didn't last long.

Pious Isabel and machiavellian Fernando succeeded in uniting Spain under one rule for the first time since the Visigothic days.

CHRISTIAN CONTROL

In areas that fell under Christian control in the 13th century, Muslims who stayed on (Mudéjars) initially faced no reprisals. But in 1264 the Mudéjars of Jerez de la Frontera rose up against new taxes and rules that required them to celebrate Christian feasts and live in ghettos. After a five-month siege they were expelled to Granada or North Africa, along with the Mudéjars of Seville, Córdoba and Arcos.

The new Christian rulers handed large tracts of land to nobility and knights who had played important roles in the Reconquista. These landowners turned much of their vast estates over to sheep, ruining former food-growing land, and by 1300, rural

» 1250–80	» 14TH CENTURY	» JANUARY 1492
Fernando III's son Alfonso X (El Sabio, the Learned) makes Seville one of his capitals and launches a cultural revival.	The Black Death and bad harvests ravage Christian areas of Andalucía. Discontent finds its scapegoat in the Jews, who suffer pogroms in the 1390s.	After a 10-year war Granada falls to the armies of Castilla and Aragón, which are now united through the marriage of their rulers Isabel and Fernando, the 'Catholic Monarchs'.

IN ISLAMIC FOOTSTEPS

The medieval Muslim era left a profound stamp on Andalucía. Great architectural monuments such as Granada's Alhambra and Córdoba's Mezquita are the stars of the Muslim heritage, but the characteristic tangled, narrow street layouts of many a town and village also date from the Muslim period – as do the Andalusian predilections for fountains, running water and decorative plants. The Muslims developed Spain's Hispano-Roman agricultural base by improving irrigation and introducing new fruits and crops, many of which are still widely grown, often on the very irrigated terracing systems created by the Muslims. The Spanish language still contains many common words of Arabic origin including the names of some of those new crops – *naranja* (orange), *azúcar* (sugar), *arroz* (rice).

Today the medieval Muslim imprint is stamped all over Andalucía. Here are a few highlight sites where the spirit of that age lingers strongest:

★ **Albayzín** (p260) Where Granada began, and where its Muslims lived on after Christian conquest

★ **Mezquita, Almonaster la Real** (p102) This lovely 10th-century mosque is like a miniature version of the Córdoba Mezquita

★ **Bobastro** (p184) Hilltop hideout of Omar ibn Hafsun, Andalucía's 9th-century 'Robin Hood'

★ **Giralda** (p40) The minaret of the Seville mosque is a masterpiece of Almohad building

★ **Las Alpujarras** (p275) The spirit of medieval Muslim Andalucía still hangs in the air here, in the Muslims' last refuge

★ **Medina Azahara** (p209) Abd ar-Rahman III's palace-city outside Córdoba

Christian Andalucía was almost empty. The nobility's preoccupation with wool and politics allowed Jews and foreigners, especially Genoese, to come to dominate Castilian commerce and finance.

Fernando III's son Alfonso X (El Sabio, the Learned; r 1252–84) made Seville one of Castilla's capitals and launched something of a cultural revival there, gathering scholars around him, particularly Jews, who could translate ancient texts into Castilian Spanish. But Alfonso was plagued by further uprisings and plots, even from within his own family. Rivalry within the royal family, and challenges from the nobility, plagued the Castilian monarchy right through till the late 15th century when the Catholic

» APRIL 1492	» LATE 1492	» 1500
Under the influence of Grand Inquisitor Tomás de Torquemada, Isabel and Fernando expel all Jews who refuse Christian baptism. Some 200,000 Jews leave.	Christopher Columbus, funded by Isabel and Fernando, sails from Palos de la Frontera and finds the Bahamas, opening up a whole new hemisphere of opportunity for Spain.	Persecution of Muslims in the former Granada emirate sparks rebellion. Afterwards, Muslims are compelled to adopt Christianity or leave. An estimated 300,000 undergo baptism.

BACKGROUND

Monarchs took things in hand. Feuding reached a bloody peak under Pedro I 'El Cruel' (1350–69), who is said to have eliminated a dozen relatives and friends to stay on the throne. Pedro was in fact on better terms with Mohammed V of Granada, who helped him build the sumptuous Palacio de Don Pedro in Seville's Alcázar (p44), than with most of his own family.

PERSECUTION OF THE JEWS

After the Black Death and several bad harvests in the 14th century, discontent found its scapegoat in the Jews, who were subjected to pogroms around the peninsula in the 1390s. As a result, some Jews converted to Christianity (they became known as *conversos*); others found refuge in Muslim Granada. In the 1480s the *conversos* became the main target of the Spanish Inquisition, founded by the Catholic Monarchs. Many *conversos* were accused of continuing to practise Judaism in secret. Of the estimated 12,000 deaths for which the Inquisition was responsible in its three centuries of existence, 2000 took place in the 1480s.

In 1492 Isabel and Fernando ordered the expulsion of every Jew who refused Christian baptism. Around 50,000 to 100,000 converted, but some 200,000, the first Sephardic Jews (Jews of Spanish origin), left for other Mediterranean destinations. A talented middle class was decimated.

MORISCO REVOLTS & EXPULSION

The task of converting the Muslims of Granada to Christianity was handed to Cardinal Cisneros, overseer of the Inquisition. He carried out forced mass baptisms, burnt Islamic books and banned the Arabic language. As Muslims found their land being expropriated too, a revolt in Las Alpujarras in 1500 spread right across the former Granada emirate, from Ronda to Almería. Afterwards, Muslims were ordered to convert to Christianity or leave. Most, an estimated 300,000, converted, becoming known as *moriscos* (converted Muslims), but they never assimilated to Christian culture. When the fanatically Catholic King Felipe II (Philip II; r 1556–98) forbade them in 1567 to use the Arabic language, Arabic names or *morisco* dress, a new revolt in Las Alpujarras spread across southern Andalucía and took two years to put down. The *moriscos* were then deported to western Andalucía and more northerly parts of Spain, before being expelled altogether from Spain by Felipe III between 1609 and 1614.

» C 1500–1600	» 1568–70	» 1609–14
The riches from Spain's American colonies turn Seville into the cosmopolitan hub of world trade and a focus of Spain's artistic Siglo de Oro (Golden Century).	Persecution of the *moriscos* (converted Muslims), including the banning of Arabic names and traditional *morisco* dress, leads to a two-year revolt centred on Las Alpujarras.	The *moriscos* (converted Muslims) are eventually expelled altogether from Spain by Felipe III.

SEVILLE & THE AMERICAS: BOOM & BUST

In April 1492 the Catholic Monarchs granted the Genoese sailor Christopher Columbus (Cristóbal Colón to Spaniards) funds for a voyage across the Atlantic in search of a new trade route to the Orient. Columbus instead found the Americas (see the boxed text, p81) and opened up a whole new hemisphere of opportunity for Spain, especially for the river port of Seville.

During the reign of Carlos I (Charles I; r 1516–56), the first of Spain's new Habsburg dynasty, the ruthless but brilliant conquerors Hernán Cortés and Francisco Pizarro subdued the Aztec and Inca empires respectively with small bands of adventurers, and other Spanish conquerors and colonists occupied vast tracts of the American mainland. The new colonies sent huge quantities of silver, gold and other treasure back to Spain, where the crown was entitled to one-fifth of the bullion (the *quinto real,* or royal fifth).

Seville became the hub of world trade, a cosmopolitan melting pot of money-seekers, and remained the major city in Spain until late in the 17th century, even though a small country town called Madrid was named the national capital in 1561. New European ideas and artistic movements reached Seville and made it a focus of Spain's artistic Siglo de Oro (Golden Century). The prosperity was shared to some extent by Cádiz, and less so by cities such as Jaén, Córdoba and Granada. New universities in Seville (1505), Granada (1531) and Baeza (1542) spread the humanist ideas of the Renaissance, which led to a questioning of Roman Catholic dogma by so-called *protestantes* in a few centres. These nascent flickers of Protestantism were soon snuffed out by the Inquisition.

> *'Seville remained the major city in Spain until late in the 17th century'*

In rural Andalucía a small number of big landowners continued to do little with large tracts of territory except run sheep on them. Most Andalusians owned no land or property.

Spain never developed any strategy for absorbing the American wealth, spending too much on European wars and opulent palaces, cathedrals and monasteries, while wasting any chance of becoming an early industrial power. Grain had to be imported while sheep and cattle roamed the countryside. The ensuing centuries of neglect and economic mismanagement would turn Andalucía into a backwater, a condition from which it only started to emerge in the 1960s.

» 17TH CENTURY	» 18TH CENTURY	» 1805
Silver shipments from the Americas shrink disastrously while Spain continues to spend heavily on European wars. Epidemics and bad harvests kill 300,000 Andalusians.	Spain recovers from the previous century's disasters. A new road is built from Madrid to Seville and Cádiz, and new settlers from the north boost Andalucía's population.	In the Napoleonic Wars, Spanish sea power ends when a combined Spanish-French navy is defeated by the British fleet, under Admiral Nelson, off Cabo de Trafalgar.

In the 17th century, silver shipments from the Americas shrank disastrously and epidemics and bad harvests killed some 300,000 Andalusians, including half of Seville in 1649. The lower Guadalquivir, Seville's lifeline to the Atlantic, became increasingly silted up and in 1717 control of commerce with the Americas was transferred to the seaport of Cádiz.

THE BOURBONS

Felipe V's (Philip V's) accession to the throne in 1701 marked the beginning of the Spanish Bourbon dynasty, still in place today. In the 18th century Spain made a limited recovery from the social and economic ravages of the previous century. The monarchy financed incipient industries, such as Seville's tobacco factory. A new road,

THE DUKES (AND DUCHESS) OF MEDINA SIDONIA

The Andalusian family that once owned more of Spain than any other traces its lineage back to the Reconquista hero Alonso Pérez de Guzmán, legendary for his heroism while defending Tarifa back in 1294. Guzmán and his descendants acquired vast landholdings in western Andalucía, and the title Duque de Medina Sidonia was conferred on Juan Alonso de Guzmán in 1445. By the early 16th century it was possible to travel right across the present-day provinces of Huelva, Sevilla and Cádiz without leaving Medina Sidonia land.

In 1588 the seventh Duque de Medina Sidonia, despite a tendency to seasickness and lack of naval experience, was appointed by Felipe II to command the Spanish Armada to invade England. Contrary to popular legend, the duke was neither incompetent nor a coward and the Armada's disastrous defeat is now put down chiefly to a flawed strategy ordered by the king. The 15th duke's wife María, Duchess of Alba, is reputed to have had a fling with the artist Goya and is often claimed to be the subject of Goya's scandalous nude portrait *La Maja Desnuda*.

But none of the dukes' lives matches the colour of that of the 21st of the line, Duchess Luisa Isabel Álvarez de Toledo, who died in 2008. Dubbed the 'Red Duchess', Doña Luisa was a committed republican who spent time in jail and exile during the Franco dictatorship, gave away most of the Medina Sidonia estates to agricultural cooperatives, and on her deathbed married her long-time companion and administrator of the huge historical archive at the family home in Sanlúcar de Barrameda (p124), Lilian Dahlmann, thus partially disinheriting her three children, with whom she had fallen out.

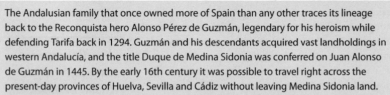

BACKGROUND

» 1810–12	» 19TH CENTURY	» 1873
With most of Spain under Napoleonic occupation, Cádiz withstands a two-year siege. The Cádiz parliament adopts a new constitution proclaiming sovereignty of the people.	Andalucía declines into one of Europe's most backward, socially polarised regions. Illiteracy, disease and hunger are rife.	During Spain's chaotic, short-lived First Republic, numerous cities and towns declare themselves independent states. Seville and nearby Utrera even declare war on each other.

the Carretera General de Andalucía, was built from Madrid to Seville and Cádiz. New land was opened up for wheat and barley, and trade through Cádiz (which was in its heyday) grew. New settlers from other parts of Spain boosted Andalucía's population to about 1.8 million by 1787.

NAPOLEONIC INVASION

When Louis XVI of France (a cousin of Spain's Carlos IV) was guillotined in 1793, Spain declared war on France. Two years later, Spain switched sides, pledging military support for France against Britain in return for French withdrawal from northern Spain.

In 1807, France (under Napoleon Bonaparte) and Spain agreed to divide Portugal, Britain's ally, between the two of them. French forces poured into Spain, supposedly on the way to Portugal, but by 1808 this had become a French occupation of Spain. In the ensuing Spanish War of Independence, or Peninsular War, the Spanish populace took up arms guerrilla-style and, with help from British and Portuguese forces led by the Duke of Wellington, drove the French out by 1813.

SOCIETY POLARISES

The 19th century was one of interminable rivalry in Spain between liberals, who wanted vaguely democratic reforms, and conservatives who liked the status quo. King Fernando VII (r 1814–33) persecuted opponents and even temporarily re-established the Inquisition. During his reign most of Spain's American colonies seized their independence – desperate news for Cádiz, which had been totally reliant on trade with them.

The Disentailments of 1836 and 1855, in which liberal governments auctioned off church and municipal lands to reduce the national debt, were a disaster for the peasants, who lost the use of municipal grazing lands. Despite having a quarter of Spain's 12 million population in 1877, Andalucía declined into one of Europe's most backward, socially polarised areas, little touched by the Industrial Revolution, which finally reached Madrid and northern Spain by the late 19th century. Andalucía's few successful industries, such as the Riotinto mines and the Jerez and Málaga wineries, owed much to British investment and management. At one social extreme were the few bourgeoisie and rich aristocratic landowners; at the other, a very large number of impoverished *jornaleros* – landless agricultural day labourers who were without work for a good half of the year. Illiteracy, disease and hunger were rife.

» 1891–1918	» 1923–30	» 1931–36
Impoverished Andalusian rural workers launch waves of anarchist strikes and revolts. The powerful anarchist union, the CNT, is founded in Seville in 1910.	An eccentric general from Jerez de la Frontera, Miguel Primo de Rivera, rules Spain in a moderate military dictatorship. He is dismissed by King Alfonso XIII in 1930.	The Second Republic: the king goes into exile and Spain is ruled first by the left, then the right, then the left again, with political violence spiralling.

In 1873 a liberal government proclaimed Spain a republic – a federal grouping of 17 states – but this 'First Republic' was totally unable to control its provinces and lasted only 11 months, with the army ultimately restoring the monarchy.

Andalusian peasants began to stage uprisings, always brutally quashed. The anarchist ideas of the Russian Mikhail Bakunin, who advocated strikes, sabotage and revolts as the path to spontaneous revolution and a free society governed by voluntary cooperation, gained a big following. The powerful anarchist union, the Confederación Nacional del Trabajo (CNT; National Labour Confederation), was founded in Seville in 1910. By 1919, it had 93,000 members in Andalucía.

> *'Andalucía declined into one of Europe's most backward areas, little touched by the Industrial Revolution'*

In 1923 an eccentric Andalusian general from Jerez de la Frontera, Miguel Primo de Rivera, launched a comparatively moderate military dictatorship for Spain, which won the cooperation of the big socialist union, the Unión General de Trabajadores (UGT; General Union of Workers), while the anarchists went underground. Primo was unseated in 1930 as a result of an economic downturn and discontent in the army.

THE SECOND REPUBLIC

When the republican movement scored sweeping victories in Spain's municipal elections in April 1931, King Alfonso XIII departed to exile in Italy. The ensuing Second Republic (1931–36) was an idealistic, tumultuous period that ended in civil war. Leftists and the poor welcomed the republican system; conservatives were alarmed. Elections in 1931 brought in a mixed government, including socialists, centrists and republicans, but anarchist disruption, an economic slump and disunity on the left all helped the right win new elections in 1933. The left, including the emerging communists, called increasingly for revolution and by 1934 violence was spiralling out of control.

In the February 1936 elections a left-wing coalition narrowly defeated the right-wing National Front. Society polarised into left and right and violence continued on both sides of the political divide. The anarchist CNT had over a million members and the peasants were on the verge of revolution.

But when the revolt came, on 17 July 1936, it came from the other end of the political spectrum. On that day the Spanish garrison at Melilla in North Africa revolted

BACKGROUND

» 17 JULY 1936	» 1936–37	» 1936–39
The Spanish garrison at Melilla (North Africa) revolts against the government, starting the Spanish Civil War. The plot is led by five 'Nationalist' generals, including Fransisco Franco.	Western Andalucía falls to the Nationalists, who also take Málaga, with Italian help, in February 1937. Massacres are carried out by both the Nationalists and Republicans.	Helped by Nazi Germany and fascist Italy, Franco leads the Nationalists to victory. Some 350,000 Spaniards are killed. Much of eastern Andalucía stays Republican throughout.

against the leftist government, followed the next day by some garrisons on the mainland. The leaders of the plot were five generals. The Spanish Civil War had begun.

THE CIVIL WAR

The civil war split communities, families and friends. Both sides committed atrocious massacres and reprisals, especially in the early weeks. The rebels, who called themselves Nationalists, shot or hanged tens of thousands of supporters of the Republic. Republicans did likewise to those they considered Nationalist sympathisers, including some 7000 priests, monks and nuns. Political affiliation often provided a convenient cover for settling old scores. Altogether, an estimated 350,000 Spaniards died in the war (some writers put the figure as high as 500,000).

In Republican-controlled areas, anarchists, communists or socialists ended up running many towns and cities. Social revolution followed. In Andalucía this tended to be anarchist-led, with private property abolished and churches and convents often burned and wrecked. Large estates were occupied by the peasants and around 100 agrarian communes were established. The Nationalist campaign, meanwhile, quickly took on overtones of a holy crusade against those they considered to be the enemies of God.

The basic battle lines were drawn very early. Cities whose garrisons backed the rebels (most did) and were strong enough to overcome any resistance fell immediately into Nationalist hands – as happened at Cádiz, Córdoba and Jerez. Seville was in Nationalist hands within three days and Granada within a few more. The Nationalists killed an estimated 4000 people in and around Granada after they took the city, including the great writer Federico García Lorca (see p361). There was slaughter in Republican-controlled areas, too. An estimated 2500 were murdered in a few months in anarchist-controlled Málaga. But the Nationalists executed thousands there in reprisals when they and their fascist Italian allies took the city in February 1937. Much of eastern Andalucía – Almería and Jaén provinces, eastern Granada province and northern Córdoba province – remained in Republican hands until the end of the war.

By late 1936 General Francisco Franco emerged as the undisputed Nationalist leader, calling himself Generalísimo (Supreme General). Before long, he also adopted the title *caudillo*, roughly equivalent to the German word führer. The scales of the war were tipped in the Nationalists' favour by weapons, planes and 92,000 troops from Nazi Germany and fascist Italy. The Republicans had some Soviet planes, tanks, artillery and advisers, and 25,000 or so French soldiers fought with them, along with a similar number of other foreigners in the International Brigades.

» 1939–75	» LATE 1940s	» 1950s & 1960s
The Franco dictatorship: Franco leads the army and the only political party. Strikes and divorce are banned, and church weddings become compulsory.	Spain suffers a UN-sponsored trade boycott, which helps to turn the late '40s into the *años de hambre* (years of hunger) – particularly hungry in poor areas such as Andalucía.	Some 1.5 million Andalusians leave to find work elsewhere in Spain or Europe. New mass tourism on Andalucía's Costa del Sol helps to stimulate an economic recovery.

The Republican government moved from besieged Madrid to Valencia in late 1936, then to Barcelona in autumn 1937. In 1938 Franco swept eastwards, isolating Barcelona, and the USSR withdrew from the war. The Nationalists took Barcelona in January 1939 and Madrid in March. Franco declared the war won on 1 April 1939.

FRANCO'S SPAIN

After the civil war, instead of reconciliation, more blood-letting ensued and the jails filled up with political prisoners. An estimated 100,000 Spaniards were killed, or died in prison, after the war. A few communists and Republicans continued their hopeless struggle in small guerrilla units in the Andalusian mountains and elsewhere until the 1950s – a little-known story that is only now starting to be properly told. David Baird's book *Between Two Fires* (2008) documents for the first time, in fascinating detail, the struggle between the 'Maquis' guerrillas and the Guardia Civil (Civil Guard) around the village of Frigiliana in the 1940s and '50s.

Spain stayed out of WWII, but was afterwards excluded from the UN until 1955 and suffered a UN-sponsored trade boycott that helped turn the late 1940s into the *años de hambre* (years of hunger) – particularly hungry in poor areas such as Andalucía where, at times, peasants subsisted on soup made from wild herbs.

Franco ruled absolutely. He was commander of the army and leader of the sole political party, the Movimiento Nacional (National Movement). Army garrisons were maintained outside every large city, strikes and divorce were banned and church weddings became compulsory.

> '*mass foreign tourism was launched on the Costa del Sol in the late 1950s*'

In Andalucía, some new industries were founded and mass foreign tourism was launched on the Costa del Sol in the late 1950s. But 1.5 million hungry people still left Andalucía in the 1950s and '60s to look for work in Madrid, northern Spain and other European countries. By the 1970s many Andalusian villages still lacked electricity, reliable water supplies and paved roads, and the education system was pathetically inadequate: today many Andalusians over 50, especially in rural areas, are still illiterate.

NEW DEMOCRACY

Franco's chosen successor, Alfonso XIII's grandson Prince Juan Carlos, took the throne, aged 37, two days after Franco's death in 1975. Much of the credit for Spain's

» 1975–78	» 1978	» 1982–96
Following Franco's death, King Juan Carlos I and prime minister Adolfo Suárez engineer a transition to democracy.	The 1978 constitution makes Spain a parliamentary monarchy with no official religion.	Sevillano Felipe González, of the left-of-centre Partido Socialista Obrero Español (PSOE), is elected and enjoys 14 years as prime minister.

BACKGROUND

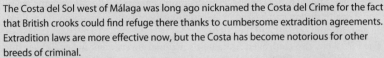

COSTA DEL CRIME

The Costa del Sol west of Málaga was long ago nicknamed the Costa del Crime for the fact that British crooks could find refuge there thanks to cumbersome extradition agreements. Extradition laws are more effective now, but the Costa has become notorious for other breeds of criminal.

One facet of the problem is corruption in town halls, especially over the granting of building permits during the tourism and construction boom, which has helped turn long stretches of Andalusian coast into ugly concrete jungles. Most notorious has been the town of Marbella, which became a byword not just for glitzy ostentation but also for overdevelopment, municipal corruption and international Mafia activity. In 2006 over 60 people were arrested in connection with a web of bribery and illegal building permits, including Marbella's mayor, deputy mayor and planning chief. Most of the resulting legal proceedings were still ongoing in mid-2009. For a while the threat of demolition hung over as many as 18,000 illegally built villas and apartments in Marbella, many of them owned by foreigners. But in November 2008 an amnesty was declared for most of these properties, under which they would be retrospectively legalised.

The culture of corruption has helped to provide an attractive climate for heavier crime. An estimated one-third of organised crime in Spain, including gangs from Russia, Colombia, Eastern Europe and Britain, is based in the Costa del Sol, where it is relatively easy to launder proceeds from drug dealing, murders, kidnappings, arms trafficking and prostitution into property. Law-abiding visitors will be oblivious to all this and tourists are not targeted by organised crime and have no need to fear for their safety.

ensuing transition to democracy goes to the king. The man he appointed prime minister, Adolfo Suárez, pushed through the Cortes (Spain's parliament) a proposal for a new, two-chamber parliamentary system. In 1977 political parties, trade unions and strikes were legalised and Suárez' centrist party won nearly half the seats in elections to the new Cortes.

Spain enjoyed a sudden social liberation after Franco. Contraceptives, homosexuality and divorce were legalised, adultery was decriminalised, and a vein of hedonism was unleashed that still looms large today.

In 1982 Spain made a final break with the Franco era by voting the left-of-centre Partido Socialista Obrero Español (PSOE; Spanish Socialist Worker Party) into power.

» 1980s	» 1982	» 1986
Ten years of consistent PSOE government policy helps to eradicate the worst of Andalusian poverty.	Under Spain's new regional autonomy system, Andalucía gets its own parliament, dominated ever since by PSOE.	Spain joins the EU (European Union) and enjoys a five-year economic boom.

The PSOE's leader, Felipe González, a young lawyer from Seville, was to be the country's prime minister for 14 years, and his party's young, educated leadership included several other Andalusians. The PSOE made improvements in education, launched a national health system and basked in an economic boom after Spain joined the European Community (now the EU) in 1986.

The PSOE has also controlled Andalucía's regional government in Seville ever since it was inaugurated in 1982, when limited autonomy was devolved to the 17 Spanish regions. Manuel Chaves, one of the strongmen of the PSOE, headed the Andalusian executive, known as the Junta de Andalucía, from 1990 right through to 2009, when he moved to Madrid as a minister in the national government. PSOE government eradicated the worst of Andalusian poverty in the 1980s and early 1990s with grants, community works schemes and a generous dole system. Education and health provision have steadily improved and the PSOE government has also given Andalucía Spain's biggest network of environmentally protected areas (see p345).

The PSOE lost power nationally in 1996 to the centre-right Partido Popular (PP; People's Party), led by former tax inspector José María Aznar, who presided over eight years of steady economic progress. The unemployment rate in Andalucía almost halved in the PP years, though it remained the highest in Spain, at 16%. Andalucía benefited from steady growth in tourism and industry, massive EU subsidies for agriculture (which still provides one job in eight), and a long construction boom.

THE 21ST CENTURY

As in other parts of Spain, economic progress attracted thousands of economic migrants, legal and illegal, to Andalucía in the early years of the 21st century. They came chiefly from Latin America, Morocco, sub-Saharan Africa and Eastern Europe. By 2008, Andalucía had a record 650,000 foreign residents (8% of the population) according to official figures, and the real number may have been much higher. Moroccans, Britons, Romanians and Argentines comprised almost half the foreigners, and they gathered chiefly in Málaga province, with its tourism and construction work, and Almería province, for agricultural work. Meanwhile hundreds, possibly thousands, of would-be immigrants continued to die each year trying to reach Andalusian beaches from Morocco in small boats unfit for the short but often rough crossing.

The PP was unseated by the PSOE in the 2004 national election, which took place three days after the Madrid train bombings of 11 March, in which 191 people were killed and 1800 injured. The attackers were a group of North Africans settled in Spain,

» 1992	» 1996–2004	» 2000–2006
Hundreds of thousands of people visit Expo '92 in Seville, and the superfast AVE Madrid–Seville rail link opens. Andalusian roads get a major upgrade, too.	Spain is governed by the right-of-centre PP. Andalusian unemployment nearly halves (to 16%) thanks to a construction boom, tourism and industrial growth, and EU subsidies.	Hundreds of thousands of northern and eastern Europeans, Africans and Latin Americans migrate to Andalucía. Some are sun-seekers, more are job-seekers.

who were inspired by, though without direct links to, Al-Qaeda. The PP's support for the 2003 US-led invasion of Iraq, and its decision to send 1300 Spanish troops to Iraq after the war, had made Spain a target for Islamic terrorism. The new PSOE government, led by José Luis Rodríguez Zapatero, pulled Spain's troops out of Iraq within two weeks of taking office.

Zapatero's government legalised gay marriages, made divorce easier, took religion out of the school curriculum, and declared an amnesty for illegal immigrants, while continuing to bask in steady economic growth. The PSOE won again in the national elections of March 2008, which took place, fortunately for it, just before the world recession really started to bite. In the following 12 months unemployment in Spain leapt to record levels (over 17%) and Andalucía, with its excessive dependence on construction, real estate and tourism, was one of the worst-affected regions. Construction and real estate had already been hit by the beginnings of an overdue crackdown on municipal corruption and illegal building. Come the credit crunch and international recession in 2008 and 2009, these sectors more or less ground to a halt. Things were made worse by a slump in value of the British pound against the euro, which removed a large group of potential buyers from the Andalusian property market. By spring 2009 Andalusian unemployment was running at 24% and despite a minor improvement in summer 2009, some forecasters still predicted the rate could reach 27% – 1.1 million people – by the end of 2009.

> *'By 2008, Andalucía had a record 650,000 foreign residents according to official figures'*

» 2004	» 2006	» 2008–09
The PSOE wins the Spanish national and Andalusian regional elections, days after the Madrid train bombings, by Islamic extremists, kill 191 people and injure 1800.	Over 50 officials in Marbella are arrested over bribery, corruption and illegal building permits. Most of the resulting legal proceedings were still ongoing in mid-2009.	Andalucía, heavily dependent on tourism and construction, is savaged by the credit crunch and world recession; unemployment jumps from 14% to 24% in a year.

ANDALUSIAN ARCHITECTURE

· · · · · · ·

The vast sweep of Andalucía's history is most stirringly on display through the architecture left by the ancient civilisations and the patchwork of peoples who called Andalucía home and moulded it in their own image. Roman sophistication, the soaring structures of Islamic Al-Andalus, extravagant Christian churches and gaudy 20th-century confections: such are the highpoints of Andalucía's architectural heritage, of its rulers' aspirations to leave their enduring mark on history. But the more prosaic reality of daily life for ordinary Andalusians is equally important in understanding the region's tumultuous history. Villages cling to impregnable hilltops much as they did in the days when invading armies swept across the landscape, and white clusters of houses huddle in valleys to escape Andalucía's blistering summer heat. More than anything else, however, it was the centuries-long struggle for control between Christians and Muslims that defines the region's architecture.

ISLAMIC ARCHITECTURE

It's difficult to overestimate the influence of Islamic rule on the aesthetics of modern Andalucía. Spain's eight Islamic centuries (AD 711–1492) bequeathed to the region, more than anywhere else on the continent, a strong whiff of the exotic with foreign architectural styles transplanted onto European soil.

Exquisite monuments on a breathtaking scale – Granada's Alhambra and Córdoba's Mezquita, for example, which stand like bookends to Islam's reign – were the means through which the Islamic rulers of Al-Andalus brought architectural sophistication to Europe and remain the most visible legacy of Andalucía's Islamic past. The effect can be overpowering from whichever perspective you view them, whether up close in the intricate detail or in the entirety of their staggering monumental grandeur as statements of power and the glory of Allah.

DON'T MISS...

ANDALUSIAN ARCHITECTURE

★ **Granada's Alhambra //** Peerless monument to Islamic Al-Andalus (p254)

★ **Córdoba's Mezquita //** Sublime grace, harmony and striped horseshoe arches (p201)

★ **Seville's Alcázar //** Gardens and Islamic architectural flourishes like a re-creation of paradise (p44)

★ **Renaissance architecture of Úbeda //** Spain's highpoint of 16th-century Christian architecture (p234)

★ **Seville's cathedral //** Gothic Christian architecture overlaid on the glories of Islam (p40)

★ **White villages of Las Alpujarras //** The quintessential *pueblos blancos* for which Andalucía is famous (p275)

But Islam's impact ripples through seemingly every corner of Andalucía's architecture. In villages across the region, and in the heart of cities such as Granada's Albayzín, intricate tangles of streets resemble nothing so much as a North African medina. Islam's roots in hot climates and relatively conservative social codes also brought to Andalucía a love of expansive greenery, magnificent gardens filled with scents and ornate fountains, and a sense of protecting private spaces from prying public eyes; an example of the latter is the beguiling interior tiled courtyard (see, for example, Patios Cordobeses, p208) that was brought to Andalucía by the Romans and perfected by Islam's architects.

> *'Granada's Alhambra and Córdoba's Mezquita stand like bookends to Islam's reign'*

THE OMAYYADS, THE MEZQUITA DE CÓRDOBA & BEYOND

The story of the marriage between Islam and architecture on Andalusian soil begins in the 8th century AD with the Omayyads. Islam, which was founded by the Prophet Mohammed in the Arabian city of Mecca in the 7th century AD, reached Spain in 711, at a time when the Damascus-based Omayyad dynasty of caliphs were the rulers of the Muslim world. In 750, the Omayyads of Damascus were overthrown by the revolutionary Abbasids, who shifted the seat of Islamic power east to Baghdad. One influential Omayyad, Abu'l-Mutarrif Abd ar-Rahman bin Muawiya, escaped and, aged only 20, he made for Morocco and then Spain. In 756 he set himself up as an independent emir, Abd ar-Rahman I, in Córdoba, launching a dynasty based in that city that lasted until 1009 and made Al-Andalus, at the western extremity of the Islamic world, the last outpost of Omayyad culture. But it was Abd ar-Rahman I's successor, Al Hakim II (r 961–76), who would leave the Omayyads' most enduring architectural mark in Andalucía.

❧ MEZQUITA OF CÓRDOBA // ANDALUCÍA'S HIGHPOINT OF OMAYYAD ARCHITECTURE (P201)

The oldest significant surviving Spanish Islamic building, the Mezquita de Córdoba is the epitome of Islamic architecture's grace and pleasing unity of form. This sense of harmony – perhaps the Mezquita's most enduring miracle – is all the more remarkable given the significant alterations carried out over the centuries, quite apart from the Christian cathedral that was plonked right in the middle in the 16th century.

THE HORSESHOE ARCH

A primary reason why Andalucía's Islamic architecture is considered unique is that the architects of Al-Andalus fused styles and techniques taken up from the Christian Visigoths, whom the Omayyads replaced as rulers of the Iberian Peninsula. Chief among these was what became the hallmark of Spanish Islamic architecture: the horseshoe arch. So called because it narrows at the bottom like a horseshoe, rather than being a simple semicircle, the horseshoe arch appears elsewhere in the Islamic world, but its Andalusian origins serve as a reminder that Islam's influence over Andalucía was never a one-way street.

BACKGROUND

The Mezquita was founded by Abd ar-Rahman I in AD 785. In its original form, the mosque was a square split into two rectangular halves: a covered prayer hall, and an open courtyard where the faithful performed their ritual ablutions before entering the prayer hall. This early structure drew on the essential elements of Omayyad architecture elsewhere. It maintained, for example, the 'basilical' plan of some early Islamic buildings by having a central 'nave' of arches, broader than the others, leading to the mihrab, the niche indicating the direction of Mecca (and thus of prayer) that is key to the layout of any mosque. But the Mezquita's prayer hall broke away from the verticality of earlier landmark Omayyad buildings, such as the Great Mosque of Damascus and the Dome of the Rock in Jerusalem. Instead it created a broad horizontal space that evoked the yards of desert homes that formed the original Islamic prayer spaces. It also conjured up visions of palm groves with mesmerising lines of two-tier, red-and-white-striped arches in the prayer hall.

As Córdoba grew into its role as the increasingly sophisticated capital of Al-Andalus, each emir was desperate to leave his personal stamp on Al-Andalus' landmark building. Later enlargements extended the lines of arches to cover an area of nearly 120 sq metres, making it one of the biggest of all mosques. These arcades afford ever-changing perspectives, vistas disappearing into infinity and interplays of light and rhythm that rank among the Mezquita's most mesmerising features.

For all its 8th-century origins, and the later extensions, the Mezquita's golden age was the 10th century. It was then, particularly during the 960s under the reign of Al-Hakim II, that the Mezquita came to be considered the highpoint of the splendid 10th-century 'caliphal' phase of Spanish Islamic architecture. Al-Hakim II created a magnificent new mihrab, decorated with superb Byzantine mosaics that imitate those of the Great Mosque of Damascus. In front of the mihrab Al-Hakim II added a new royal prayer enclosure, the *maksura*. The *maksura*'s multiple interwoven arches and lavishly decorated domes were much more intricate and technically advanced than anything previously seen in Europe. The *maksura* formed part of a second axis to the building, an aisle running along in front of the wall containing the mihrab – known as the qibla wall because it indicates the qibla, the direction of Mecca.

> '*the Mezquita of Córdoba is the epitome of Islamic architecture's grace and pleasing unity of form*'

ARCHITECTURE BOOKS

★ **Moorish Architecture in Andalusia, Marianne Barrucand & Achim Bednorz** Wonderfully illustrated with a learned but readable text

★ **Houses & Palaces of Andalucía, Patricia Espinosa De Los Monteros & Francesco Ventura** A coffee-table tome full of beautiful photography

★ **The Alhambra, Robert Irwin** Challenges the myths that have coalesced around this most famous of Spanish buildings and brings the place to life

★ **Art & Architecture: Andalusia, Brigitte Hintzen-Bohlen** A stunning overview of the subject, combining a comprehensive photographic record with informative text

This transverse axis creates the T-plan that features strongly in many mosques. In its 'final' 10th-century form the Mezquita's roof was supported by 1293 columns.

♣ MEDINA AZAHARA // THE PLEASURE DOME OF THE OMAYYADS (P209)

By the 10th century, local Iberian influences had seen Al-Andalus develop its own architectural flourishes yet to be seen elsewhere in the Muslim world. Nonetheless, its rulers, informed by political, cultural and trade emissaries between the two worlds, kept a careful eye on trends in the Middle East. Thus it was that, in AD 936, Abd ar-Rahman III built himself a new capital just west of Córdoba. Medina Azahara, named after his favourite wife, Az-Zahra, was planned as a royal residence, palace and seat of government, set away from the hubbub of the city in the same manner as the Abbasid royal city of Samarra, north of Baghdad. Its chief architect was Abd ar-Rahman III's son, Al-Hakim II, who later embellished the Córdoba Mezquita so superbly. In contrast to Middle Eastern palaces, whose typical reception hall was a domed *iwan* (hall opening to a forecourt), Medina Azahara's reception halls had a 'basilical' plan, each with three or more parallel naves – similar to mosque architecture. Although wrecked during the collapse of the Córdoba caliphate less than a century after it was built, its imposing horseshoe arches, exquisite stucco work and extensive gardens suggest that it was a large and lavish place.

♣ ALMONASTER LA REAL // TENTH-CENTURY OMAYYAD SPLENDOUR (P102)

Relatively few other buildings survive from the Omayyad era in Spain, but the little 10th-century *mezquita* in remote Almonaster la Real is one of Spain's loveliest Islamic buildings. Though later converted into a church, the mosque remains more or less intact. It's like a miniature version of the Córdoba Mezquita, with rows of arches forming five naves, the central one leading to a semicircular mihrab.

THE ALMORAVIDS & ALMOHADS

As the centuries wore on, power shifted as powerful North African dynasties turned their attention to the glittering prize of Al-Andalus. Some, such as the Almoravids – a Berber dynasty from Morocco from the late 11th to mid-12th centuries – yielded few notable buildings in Spain. But the second wave of Moroccan Berbers to conquer Al-Andalus, the Almohads, more than made up for the Almoravids' lack of architectural imagination.

Late in the 12th century, the Almohads made a priority of building huge Friday mosques in the main cities of their empire, with Seville especially benefiting from their attention. The design of the mosques was simple and purist, with large prayer halls conforming to the T-plan of the Córdoba Mezquita, but the Almohads introduced some important and beautiful decorative innovations. The bays where the naves meet the qibla wall were surmounted by cupolas or stucco *muqarnas* (stalactite or honeycomb vaulting composed of hundreds or thousands of tiny cells or niches), an architectural style with its origins in Iran or Syria. On walls, large brick panels with designs of interwoven lozenges were created. Tall, square, richly decorated minarets were another Almohad trademark.

♣ GREAT MOSQUE OF SEVILLE // THE GLORIOUS HISTORY OF ANDALUCÍA IN A SINGLE BUILDING (P40)

Seville's cathedral, the city's Great Mosque in Islamic times, is where Almohad architecture is most stunningly on show. The Giralda, the minaret of the Seville mosque,

BACKGROUND

ISLAMIC FORTRESSES

Mosques glorifying Allah and luxurious palaces for the emirs were all well and good. But with Christian forces eating away at the territory of Al-Andalus to the north, defence was also a primary preoccupation. With its borders constantly under threat and its subjects often rebellious, it's hardly surprising that Al-Andalus boasts more Islamic castles and forts than any comparably sized territory in the world.

Those built in the 10th-century caliphate period were fairly simple, with low, rectangular towers and no outer rings of walls, while the 11th-century Taifa period of internal strife saw many towns bolster their defences. In the 12th and early 13th centuries the Almohads rebuilt many city defences, such as those at Córdoba, Seville and Jerez de la Frontera, while the increasingly precarious situation of the Granada emirate in the 13th to 15th Nasrid centuries prompted the reinforcement of numerous fortresses. The finest examples of these periods include the following:

★ **Alcazaba, Almería** (p291) Caliphate period

★ **City Walls & Castillo de los Guzmán, Niebla** (p83) Taifa period

★ **Torre del Oro, Seville** (p47) Almohad period

★ **Alcazaba, Antequera** (p185) Nasrid period

★ **Castillo de Gibralfaro, Málaga** (p164) Nasrid period

★ **Alhambra, Granada** (p254) Nasrid period

is the masterpiece of surviving Almohad buildings in Spain, with its beautiful brick panels. The Seville mosque's prayer hall was demolished in the 15th century to make way for the city's cathedral, but its ablutions courtyard, Patio de los Naranjos, and its northern gate, the handsome Puerta del Perdón, survive.

❧ PATIO DEL YESO // ALMOHAD ARCHITECTURE AT ITS MOST INTRICATE (P44)

Many rooms and patios in Seville's Alcázar palace-fortress date from Almohad times, but only the Patio del Yeso has substantial Almohad remains. The most noticeable feature is superbly delicate trelliswork of multiple interlocking arches.

❧ ALCÁZAR // THE HARMONY OF ALMOHAD AUSTERITY (P127)

Another Almohad mosque, more palace-chapel than large congregational affair, stands inside the Alcázar at Jerez de la Frontera. This tall, austere brick building is based on an unusual octagonal plan inscribed within a square.

THE NASRIDS

With the armies of the Christian Reconquista continuing their seemingly inexorable march southwards, the last emirate of Islamic Al-Andalus, the Nasrid emirate of Granada (1249–1492), could have been forgiven for having its mind on nonarchitectural matters. But in a recurring theme that resonates down through Andalusian history, it was the architecture that emerged from this period that best captures the spirit of the age. The Alhambra is at once an expansive fortification that reflected uncertain times and an extraordinary palace of last-days opulence.

❦ THE ALHAMBRA // THE ISLAMIC WORLD'S MOST DECORATED FORTIFIED PALACE COMPLEX (P254)

Granada's magnificent palace-fortress, the Alhambra, is the only surviving large medieval Islamic palace complex in the world. It's a palace-city in the tradition of Medina Azahara but it's also a fortress, with 2km of walls, 23 towers and a fort-within-a-fort, the Alcazaba. Within the Alhambra's walls were seven separate palaces, mosques, garrisons, houses, offices, baths, a summer residence (the Generalife) and exquisite gardens.

BATHHOUSES

Public bathhouses – an echo of Roman baths that served as both public meeting places and an essential ingredient in civic hygiene before the advent of running water – were embraced with great enthusiasm in Al-Andalus.

In fact, so important were cleanliness and the public hammam (bathhouse) in Al-Andalus – Córdoba had 60 public baths – that the Muslims' Christian enemies believed bathhouses to be dens of wild orgies and came to view even simple washing with huge suspicion. To make their point, some Spanish monks took pride in wearing the same woollen habit uninterrupted for a whole year, and the phrase 'Olor de Santidad' (Odour of Sanctity) became a euphemism for the stench of the unwashed. After the Christian reconquest of Andalucía, the *moriscos* (Muslims who converted to Christianity) were expressly forbidden to take baths.

Nevertheless medieval Islamic bathhouses have survived in some Andalusian towns, although not all have been restored to full working order. Their layout generally comprises a changing room, cold room, temperate room and hot room, in succession, with the heat in the hot rooms being provided by underfloor systems called hypocausts. Beautiful original bathhouses that you can admire today, their rooms lined by arched galleries and lit by star-shaped skylights, include the following:

★ **Baño de Comares** (p256) Inside the Salón de Comares, Alhambra, Granada

★ **Baños Árabes El Bañuelo** (p260) Albayzín, Granada

★ **Baños Árabes** (p127) Alcázar, Jerez de la Frontera

★ **Baños Árabes** (p227) Palacio de Villardompardo, Jaén

★ **Baños Árabes** (p179) Ronda

★ **Baño Moro** (p245) Segura de la Sierra

★ **Hammam Baños Árabes** (p209) Córdoba

The baths in Córdoba have been restored so you can luxuriate in the hammam experience yourself. More modern, medieval-style bathhouses have also opened in Seville (see Baños Árabes, p53), Granada (see Hammams, p263), Jerez de la Frontera (see Hammam Andalusi, p128) and Málaga (see Baños Árabes, p168).

BACKGROUND

The Alhambra's designers were supremely gifted landscape architects, integrating nature and buildings through the use of pools, running water, meticulously clipped trees and bushes, windows framing vistas, carefully placed lookout points, interplays between light and shadow, and contrasts between heat and cool. The juxtaposition of fountains, pools and gardens with domed reception halls reached a degree of perfection suggestive of the paradise described in the Quran. In keeping with the Alhambra's partial role as a sybarite's delight, many of its defensive towers also functioned as miniature summer palaces.

A huge variety of densely ornamented arches adorns the Alhambra. The Nasrid architects refined existing decorative techniques to new peaks of delicacy, elegance and harmony. Their media included sculptured stucco, marble panels, carved and inlaid wood, epigraphy (with endlessly repeated inscriptions of 'There is no God but Allah') and colourful tiles. Plaited star patterns in tile mosaic have since covered walls the length and breadth of the Islamic world, and Nasrid Granada is the dominant artistic influence in the Maghrib (northwest Africa) even today.

Granada's splendour reached its peak under emirs Yusuf I (r 1333–54) and Mohammed V (r 1354–59 and 1362–91). Each was responsible for one of the Alhambra's two main palaces. Yusuf created the Palacio de Comares (Comares Palace), in which the brilliant marquetry ceiling of the Salón de Comares (Comares Hall), representing the seven levels of the Islamic heavens and capped by a cupola symbolising the throne of Allah, served as the model for Islamic-style ceilings in state rooms for centuries afterwards; the ceiling contains more than 8000 tiny wooden panels. Mohammed V takes credit for the Palacio de los Leones (Palace of the Lions), focused on the famed Patio de los Leones (Patio of the Lions), with its colonnaded gallery and pavilions and a central fountain channelling water through the mouths of 12 stone lions. This palace's Sala de Dos Hermanas (Hall of Two Sisters) features a fantastic *muqarnas* dome of 5000 tiny cells, recalling the constellations.

MUDÉJAR & MOZARABIC ARCHITECTURE

The days of Islam's rulers may have been numbered in Al-Andalus, but Islam's architectural legacy lived on, even in areas under Christian rule. Gifted Muslim artisans were frequently employed by Christian rulers and the term Mudéjar – from the Arabic *mudayan* (domesticated) – which was given to Muslims who stayed on in areas reconquered by the Christians, came to stick as an architectural label.

You'll find Mudéjar or part-Mudéjar churches and monasteries all over Andalucía (Mudéjar is often found side by side with the Christian Gothic style). One hallmark of Mudéjar style is geometric decorative designs in brick or stucco, often further embellished with tiles. Elaborately carved timber ceilings are also a mark of the Mudéjar hand. *Artesonado* is the word used to describe ceilings with interlaced beams leaving regular spaces for decorative insertions. True Mudéjar *artesonados* generally bear floral or simple geometric patterns.

The term Mozarabic, from *musta'rib* (Arabised), refers to Christians who lived, or had lived, in Muslim-controlled territories in the Iberian Peninsula. Mozarabic architecture was, unsurprisingly, much influenced by Islamic styles and includes, for instance, the horseshoe arch. The majority of Mozarabic architecture is found in

DON'T MISS...

ANDALUCÍA'S FORMAL GARDENS

Paradise, according to Islamic tradition, is a garden. It's an idea that architects took to heart in Al-Andalus, surrounding some of Andalucía's loveliest buildings with abundant greenery, colour, fragrances and the tinkle of water.

★ **Generalife gardens, Alhambra, Granada //** Landscaped gardens of near-perfect sophistication (p258)

★ **Alcázar gardens, Seville //** A classic Islamic palace pleasure garden (p46)

★ **Gardens of the Alcázar de los Reyes Cristianos, Córdoba //** Lush terrace with abundant water (p207)

★ **Parque de María Luisa, Seville //** Sprawling greenery in the heart of Seville (p47)

★ **Palacio de Viana gardens, Córdoba //** Formal gardens with an emphasis on symmetry (p209)

northern Spain: the only significant remaining Mozarabic structure in Andalucía is the rock-cut church at Bobastro (p184).

❧ PALACIO DE DON PEDRO // **THE FINEST MUDÉJAR MONUMENT IN ANDALUCÍA (P45)**

Andalucía's classic Mudéjar building is the exotic Palacio de Don Pedro, built in the 14th century inside the Alcázar of Seville for the Christian King Pedro I of Castile. Pedro's friend, Mohammed V, the Muslim emir of Granada, sent many of his best artisans to work on Pedro's palace, and, as a result, the Palacio de Don Pedro is effectively a Nasrid building, and one of the best of its kind. Nowhere is this more evident than in the beautiful Patio de las Doncellas at its heart, with its sunken garden surrounded by exquisite arches, tiling and plasterwork.

CHRISTIAN ARCHITECTURE

The churches and monasteries built by the Christian conquerors, and the palaces and mansions of their nobility, are a superb part of Andalucía's heritage. But there is, as always, a uniquely Andalusian twist: after the Christian reconquest of Andalucía (1227–1492), many Islamic buildings were simply repurposed for Christian ends. Many Andalusian churches occupy converted mosques (most famously at Córdoba), many church towers began life as minarets, and the zigzagging streets of many an old town – such as Granada's Albayzín district (p260) – originated in labyrinthine Islamic-era street plans.

ANDALUSIAN GOTHIC

Christian architecture reached northern and western Andalucía with the Reconquista during the 13th century. The prevailing architectural style throughout much of Christian Europe at the time was Gothic, with its distinctive pointed arches, ribbed ceilings, flying buttresses and fancy window tracery. Dozens of Gothic or part-Gothic churches, castles and mansions are dotted throughout Andalucía. Some of these buildings combine Gothic with Mudéjar style (see p338), others have mixed Gothic with later styles and ended up as a stylistic hotchpotch.

The final flourish of Spanish Gothic was Isabelline Gothic, from the time of Queen Isabel la Católica. Isabelline Gothic features sinuously curved arches and tracery, and facades with lacelike ornament and low-relief sculptures (including lots of heraldic shields).

THE CLEAN LINES OF THE RENAISSANCE

The Renaissance in architecture was an Italian-originated return to classical ideals of harmony and proportion, dominated by columns and shapes such as the square, circle and triangle. Many Andalusian Renaissance buildings feature elegant interior courtyards lined by two tiers of wide, rounded arcades. Whereas the Gothic period left its most striking mark upon public Christian architecture, the Renaissance period was an era in which the gentry built themselves gorgeous urban palaces with delightful patios surrounded by harmonious arched galleries.

Spanish Renaissance architecture had three phases. First came plateresque, taking its name from the Spanish for silversmith, *platero*, because it was primarily a decorative genre, with effects resembling those of silverware. Round-arched portals were framed by classical columns and stone sculpture. Next came a more purist style, while the last and plainest phase was Herreresque, after Juan de Herrera (1530–97), creator of the austere palace-monastery complex of El Escorial, near Madrid, and Seville's Archivo de Indias (p46).

All three phases of Renaissance architecture were spanned in Jaén province by the legendary master architect Andrés de Vandelvira (1509–75), who gave the town of Úbeda one of the finest ensembles of Renaissance buildings in Spain (see the boxed text, p238). Vandelvira was much influenced by Burgos-born Diego de Siloé (1495–1563), who was primarily responsible for the cathedrals of Granada (p258), Málaga (p163) and Guadix (p270).

DON'T MISS...

THE BEST OF GOTHIC ANDALUCÍA

★ **Cathedral, Seville** // Seville's five-naved cathedral, the biggest in Spain, is almost entirely Gothic (p40)

★ **Catedral de San Salvador, Jerez de la Frontera** // Gothic traces amid Mudéjar, baroque and neoclassical styles (p127)

★ **Cathedral, Málaga** // A Gothic structure with later Renaissance and baroque touches (p163)

★ **Capilla Real, Granada** // Isabel la Católica's own burial chapel is the supreme example of Isabelline Gothic of the late Gothic period (p258)

★ **Palacio de Jabalquinto, Baeza** // Another lovely Isabelline building (p233)

DON'T MISS...

THE BEST OF RENAISSANCE ANDALUCÍA

★ **Palacio de Carlos V, Granada** // Andalucía's ultimate expression of the purist Renaissance style inside Granada's Alhambra, designed by the Rome-trained Pedro Machuca (p257)

★ **Palacio de la Condesa de Lebrija, Seville** // A 16th-century mansion with a fine Renaissance-Mudéjar patio (p50)

★ **Casa de Pilatos, Seville** // Alcázar-like mansion of Seville's nobility (p50)

★ **Jaén Cathedral** // The Renaissance on the grandest possible scale (p221)

★ **Baeza Cathedral** // Sixteenth-century magnificence in Jaén's Renaissance heartland (p232)

★ **Palacio de Vázquez de Molina, Úbeda** // One of Úbeda's most beautiful Renaissance buildings (p236)

★ **Capilla del Salvador del Mundo** // A classic creation of Andrés de Vandelvira (p236)

★ **Castillo de La Calahorra** // A formidable castle in Marquesado de Zenete with an astonishing Renaissance courtyard (p271)

THE BAROQUE BACKLASH

The inevitable reaction to Renaissance sobriety came in the colours and dramatic sense of motion of baroque. This style really seemed to catch the Andalusian imagination, and this was one of the places where baroque blossomed most brilliantly, reaching its peak of elaboration in the 18th century.

Baroque style was at root classical, but it specialised in ornamental facades crammed with decoration, and interiors chock-full of ornate stucco sculpture and gilt paint. Retables – the large, sculptural altarpieces that adorn many Spanish churches to illustrate Christian stories and teachings – reached extremes of gilded extravagance. The most hyperbolic baroque work is termed *churrigueresco* after a Barcelona family of sculptors and architects named Churriguera.

Before full-blown baroque there was a kind of transitional stage, exemplified by more sober works such as Alonso Cano's 17th-century facade for Granada's cathedral.

Seville has probably more baroque churches per square kilometre than any city in the world. However, the church at Granada's Monasterio de La Cartuja (p262), by Francisco Hurtado Izquierdo (1669–1725), is one of the most lavish baroque creations in all Spain with its multicoloured marble, golden capitals and profuse sculpture. Hurtado's followers also adorned the small town of Priego de Córdoba (p215) with seven or eight baroque churches.

MODERN ANDALUSIAN ARCHITECTURE

In the 19th century, Andalucía acquired some neo-Gothic and neobaroque examples, but most prevalent were neo-Mudéjar and neo-Islamic, harking back to an age that was now catching the fancy of the Romantic movement. Mansions such as the Palacio de Orleans y Borbon (p125) in Sanlúcar de Barrameda, and public buildings ranging from train stations in Seville to markets in Málaga and Tarifa were constructed in colourful imitation of past Islamic architectural styles. For the 1929 Exposición Ibero-americana, fancy buildings in almost every past Andalusian style were concocted in Seville, chief among them the gaudy Plaza de España ensemble (p47) by local architect Aníbal González.

Since then, sad to say, Andalusian architects and builders have displayed an uncharacteristic lack of imagination. During the Franco dictatorship, drab Soviet-style blocks of workers' housing were erected in many cities, and Andalucía's decades-long tourism boom spawned, for the most part, architecture that ranges from the forgettable to the kind of concrete eyesores that you wish you could forget.

On a much smaller scale, but almost saving the day, Andalucía's architects and builders have demonstrated greater flair in restoring older edifices to serve as hotels, museums or other public buildings. Projects such as Málaga's Museo Picasso (p164) and Jaén's Palacio de Villardompardo (p227) are both 16th-century urban palaces turned into top-class modern museums. For more on Andalusian hotel conversions, see p96.

EXPLORING NATURAL ANDALUCÍA

· · · · · · ·

Beautiful wilderness areas and a whole raft of activities that enable you to get up close and personal with nature could just be Andalucía's greatest gift to the traveller. This section is about taking you on a tour of Andalucía's natural world – its natural spaces, its protected areas and its wildlife – then giving you ideas for how best to explore it.

ANDALUCÍA'S NATURAL SPACES

Andalucía has mountains in abundance, from the relatively low hills of the geographically distinct Sierra Morena to the dizzying heights of the Sierra Nevada. The Sierra Morena, which rarely surpasses 1000m, rolls across the north of Andalucía like the last outpost of rugged southern Spain before it yields to the sweeping flatlands and empty horizons of central Spain's high *meseta* (plateau). It's more beautiful than dramatic, divided between evergreen oak woodlands, scrub, rough grazing pasture and scattered old stone villages.

Closer to the coast, the Cordillera Bética was pushed up by pressure of the African tectonic plate on the Iberian subplate 15 to 20 million years ago. This band of jagged mountains widens out from its beginnings in southwest Andalucía to a breadth of 125km or so in the east. The 75km-long Sierra Nevada southeast of Granada, with a series of 3000m-plus peaks, including Mulhacén (3479m), the highest mountain on mainland Spain, forms a subchain of the Cordillera Bética. It then continues east from Andalucía across Spain's Murcia and Valencia regions, before re-emerging from the Mediterranean as the Balearic Islands of Ibiza and Mallorca. Much of it is composed of limestone, yielding some wonderful karstic rock formations.

'Beautiful wilderness areas and a whole raft of activities that enable you to get up close and personal with nature'

Apart from the coastal plain, which varies in width from 50km in the far west to virtually nothing in parts of Granada and Almería provinces, the fertile valley of the

---

DON'T MISS...

EXPLORING NATURAL ANDALUCÍA

* ★ **Flamingos //** Vast flocks like an echo of Africa
* ★ **Whales & dolphins //** A superhighway of marine mammals in the Strait of Gibraltar
* ★ **Barbary apes //** Europe's only wild primates on Gibraltar's rock
* ★ **Hiking the high country //** Trails over the roof of Andalucía, far from the madding crowd
* ★ **Horse riding //** Beach and mountain foothills astride Andalucía's famous horses

BACKGROUND

660km-long Río Guadalquivir is Andalucía's other major geographical landmark. Andalucía's longest river, the Guadalquivir rises in the Cazorla mountains of Jaén province, flows westward through Córdoba and Seville and enters the Atlantic at Sanlúcar de Barrameda. Before entering the ocean the river splits into a marshy delta known as Las Marismas del Guadalquivir, which includes the Parque Nacional de Doñana.

ANDALUCÍA'S ENVIRONMENTAL SCORECARD

Andalucía's regional government, the Junta de Andalucía, has much to be proud of in its record of environmental protection. Not only has it set aside significantly more of its territory (20%) as protected areas than any other Spanish region, it has also set a target of generating 15% of its electricity from renewable sources by 2015. But these impressive achievements pale in comparison to the challenges that lie ahead.

The UN reported in 2005 that the Sahara Desert could jump the Mediterranean, and that within 50 years 90% of Spanish territory bordering the Mediterranean – including a significant proportion of Andalucía – could be desert. Droughts are already a regular feature of Andalusian life and rainfall in southeastern Spain decreased by 23% during the last 100 years. Rising temperatures also mean that some bird species no longer bother migrating to Africa, while Spain's Centre for Scientific Research has begun talking of the 'tropicalisation of the Mediterranean', with 20% of the Mediterranean's fish species having migrated from the Red Sea in recent years. A Spanish government report in 2006 warned that the average Spanish beach will shrink by 15m by 2050 as a direct result of rising sea levels.

Not all of these problems are of Andalucía's making: Spain produces 53% more greenhouse gas emissions than it did when it signed the Kyoto Protocol in 1990 and, during the same period, carbon dioxide emissions caused by motor vehicles in Spain have increased by 80%. But some of the problems can be attributed largely to Andalucía. The coastal building boom that has been so important to Andalucía's economy has placed intolerable pressure upon already scarce water resources. The encouragement of golf tourism – in excess of 700,000 people visit Andalucía annually primarily to play golf – is also a factor: Andalucía's almost 100 golf courses use more water than a city of one million people. Vital wildernesses such as the Parque Nacional de Doñana and Parque Natural de Cabo de Gata-Níjar are also under constant pressure from mainly tourism-related schemes.

When it comes to Andalucía's beaches, the results are mixed. In 2009, 44 of them proudly flew the blue flag of the Foundation for Environmental Education, an international body that annually awards the flags to beaches that satisfy certain criteria of water quality, safety and services; however, this figure is down from 62 in 2005. A full list can be found at Blue Flag (www.blueflag.org). At the same time, 46 Andalusian beaches (up from 34) were given *banderas negras* (black flags) by the Spanish environmental group Ecologistas en Acción (www.ecologistasenaccion.org, in Spanish), mainly for pollution by raw sewage entering the sea or for counter-ecological coastal building developments.

PARKS & PROTECTED AREAS

Andalucía has the biggest environmental protection program in Spain, having set aside more than 90 protected areas covering some 17,000 sq km. This amounts to 20% of Andalusian territory and more than 60% of the total protected area in Spain.

In a model for other areas of Spain, the regional government, the Junta de Andalucía, has done far more than simply set aside officially protected areas. Vastly improved facilities (including visitor centres, information points, detailed maps, marked footpaths, rural accommodation and active-tourism companies) actively encourage locals and visitors alike to get out and explore the Andalusian outdoors.

Parques nacionales (national parks) are areas of exceptional importance for their fauna, flora, geomorphology or landscape, and whose conservation is considered to be in the national interest. These are the most strictly controlled protected areas and may include reserve areas closed to the public, or restricted areas that can only be visited with permission. Spain has just 14 *parques nacionales,* and only two of them – Doñana and Sierra Nevada – are in Andalucía.

Parques naturales (natural parks), of which there are 24 in Andalucía, account for most of its protected territory and include nearly all of its most spectacular country. They are intended to protect cultural heritage as well as nature, and to promote economic development that's compatible with conservation. Many of them include roads, networks of walking trails, villages and even small towns, with accommodation often available within the park. Like national parks, they may include areas that can only be visited with permission.

> '*Andalucía has the biggest environmental protection program in Spain*'

Other types of protected areas in Andalucía include *parajes naturales* (natural areas; there are 31 of these) and *reservas naturales* (nature reserves; numbering 29). These are generally smaller, little-inhabited areas, with much the same goals as natural parks. There are also 37 *monumentos naturales* (natural monuments), protecting specific features such as waterfalls, forests or dunes.

WILDLIFE

Andalucía is a haven for wildlife that no longer exists elsewhere, and wildlife enthusiasts, if you know where to look, are unlikely to return home disappointed. Before you set out, a terrific source of up-to-date information on Andalusian fauna and flora is the English-language Iberianature (www.iberianature.com).

SIGNATURE MAMMALS

Many large mammal species that once roamed across Western Europe are now confined to small, isolated populations surrounded by an ever-expanding sea of humanity. That they survive at all in Andalucía is thanks to the region's varied, often untamed terrain, but even here they remain at serious risk.

Andalucía's most celebrated mammal, and one of its most endangered, is the Iberian lynx (see the boxed text, p347). It's near-on impossible to see in the wild.

The same can be said for the estimated 60 to 80 wolves *(lobos)* that survive in the Sierra Morena, mostly in Jaén province's Parque Natural Sierra de Andújar. Cut off from the rest of Europe's wolves – around 1500 survive in northern Spain – the wolf was, in 1986, declared in danger of extinction in Andalucía. In an effort to protect it from hunters and farmers, farmers are now awarded compensation if their animals are attacked by wolves. The wolf population has nonetheless sunk to levels that are probably fatally low.

Hunting throughout the 20th century is a primary reason why lynx and wolf populations have declined so alarmingly. In order to satisfy rural Andalusians' passion for hunting, and to provide an alternative prey to endangered species, the Andalusian government has introduced the mouflon *(muflón)*, a wild sheep that's relatively plentiful, especially in the Parque Natural Sierras de Cazorla, Segura y Las Villas.

In no apparent danger of extinction, and one of the region's most easily viewed mammals, is the ibex *(cabra montés)*, a stocky wild mountain goat whose males have distinctive long horns. Around 15,000 ibex live in Andalucía, with the largest populations found in the Sierra Nevada, Parque Natural Sierras de Cazorla, Segura y Las Villas, Sierras de Tejeda y Almijara and Sierra de las Nieves. The ibex spends its summer hopping with amazing agility around high-altitude precipices; it descends to lower elevations in winter.

One of Spain's most unusual wildlife-watching experiences is the sight of Barbary apes, the only wild primates in Europe, clambering Gibraltar's heights. For more information, see Upper Rock, p150.

Just as the sight of Barbary apes can seem like an apparition of Africa on European soil, whales *(ballenas)* and dolphins *(delfines)* are more often associated in the popular mind with the open waters of the Atlantic than the Mediterranean. Even so, the Bahía de Algeciras and Strait of Gibraltar harbour plenty of common, striped and bottlenose dolphins, as well as some pilot, killer and even sperm whales – see p153 and p143 for more information.

More common, less iconic mammals abound. Although some are nocturnal, those you may come across once you leave behind well-trodden trails include: wild boar *(jabalí)*, red deer *(ciervo)*, roe deer *(corzo)*, fallow deer *(gamo)*, genet *(gineta)*, Egyptian mongoose *(meloncillo)*, red squirrel *(ardilla)*, badger *(tejón)* and otter *(nutria)*.

A BIRDWATCHER'S PARADISE

If Andalucía is something of a last refuge for large mammal species, it serves a similar purpose for several highly endangered raptor species. When it comes to migratory bird species, however, Andalucía is a veritable superhighway.

For many in the birdwatching fraternity, raptors (birds of prey) are the soul birds of the avian world and Andalucía has 13 resident species as well as a handful of summer visitors from Africa. Glowering in the almost-sinister manner of its kind, Europe's biggest bird, the rare and endangered black vulture *(buitre negro)* has established a stronghold in the Sierra Morena, with around 230 pairs scattered from Huelva's Sierra Pelada to Jaén's Sierra de Andújar. As probably the world's biggest population, the black vulture's survival here is critical to the viability of the species.

MISSING LYNX?

The Iberian (or pardel) lynx (*lince ibérico* to Spaniards, *Lynx pardina* to scientists) is the most endangered cat species in the world. The species once ranged across southern Europe (the Hispanic Legions of the Roman Empire wore breastplates adorned with the Iberian lynx) and a century ago there were still 100,000 Iberian lynx left in the wild. Now there are fewer than 200 confined to an area smaller than a medium-sized European city.

So plentiful was the lynx until 1966 that the Spanish government classed them as 'vermin', encouraging hunters to declare open season on the lynx. By 1973, the species was officially protected. But this has, until recently, done little to slow the lynx's precipitous decline, prompting fears that it would soon be the first cat species to become extinct since the sabre-toothed tiger 10,000 years ago. Until 2007, when the Spanish government confirmed the presence of 15 Iberian lynx in the Montes de Toledo region of Castilla La Mancha, the only proven breeding populations were in two areas of Andalucía: one is the eastern Sierra Morena, with perhaps 100 adult lynx; the other is the Parque Nacional de Doñana with around 30 adult lynx.

A falling rabbit population, caused by disease and hunting, has played a significant role in the lynx's demise, but human beings are the primary offenders. Of all lynx deaths since 2000, almost 80% were caused directly by humans through: a loss of habitat due to new farmland, roads, dams and pine or eucalyptus plantations; illegal traps and snares set for other animals (especially foxes and wolves); and road accidents (33 lynx were run over in the area around the Parque Nacional de Doñana from 1995 to 2006).

But there are tentative signs that the lynx may have turned the corner. An in-captivity breeding program was set up at El Acebuche in Parque Nacional de Doñana (p84) in 1992 and it has proved an extraordinary success: 18 lynx were born in the first four months of 2009 alone. Live film of lynxes in the breeding program is displayed on a screen at the Parque Nacional de Doñana's El Acebuche visitor centre (p85), though the breeding centre itself is closed to the public. There are also breeding centres elsewhere in Andalucía, including at Jerez de la Frontera's zoo and in the Sierra de Andújar, Jaén province. There are plans to begin reintroducing lynx into the wild in 2010.

For information, check out the **Programa de Conservación Ex-Situ** (www.lynxexsitu .es, in Spanish), the official website of El Acebuche Breeding Centre, **SOS Lynx** (www .soslynx.org), **El Lince Ibérico** (www.ellinceiberico.com) or the Iberian lynx section of the **Iberianature** (www.iberianature.com/material/iberianlynx.htm) website. For a local insight into the lynx, see the boxed text, p87.

Also emblematic and extremely rare is the Spanish imperial eagle (*águila imperial ibérica*), found in no other country. Its total numbers have increased from about 50 pairs in the 1960s to some 200 pairs today, helped by an active government protection plan operative since 2001. About 50 pairs are in Andalucía – mostly in the Sierra Morena, with about eight pairs in the Doñana area. Poisoned bait put out by farmers or hunters is the imperial's greatest enemy.

The bearded vulture or lammergeier (*quebrantahuesos*), with its majestic 2m-plus wingspan, disappeared from Andalucía – its last refuge in Spain except the Pyrenees – in 1986. But all, it seems, is not lost. A breeding centre has been established in the

Parque Natural Sierras de Cazorla, Segura y Las Villas and, as a first step, three young bearded vultures were released into the wild in 2006.

Other large birds of prey in Andalucía include the golden eagle *(águila real)*, the griffon vulture *(buitre leonado)* and the Egyptian vulture *(alimoche)*, all found in mountain regions.

If Andalucía's raptors lend gravitas to birdwatching here, the waterbirds that visit Andalucía add a scale rarely seen in Europe. Andalucía is a haven for waterbirds, mainly thanks to extensive wetlands along the Atlantic coast, such as those at the mouths of the Guadalquivir and Odiel rivers. Hundreds of thousands of migratory birds, including an estimated 80% of Western Europe's wild ducks, winter in the Doñana wetlands at the mouth of the Guadalquivir, and many more call in during spring and autumn migrations.

> 'When it comes to migratory bird species…Andalucía is a veritable superhighway'

Laguna de Fuente de Piedra (p187), near Antequera, sees as many as 20,000 greater flamingo *(flamenco)* pairs rearing chicks in spring and summer. This beautiful pink bird can also be seen in several other places, including Cabo de Gata, Doñana and the Paraje Natural Marismas del Odiel (p75); the latter has extensive wetlands that serve as a haven for other waterbirds. For advice on the best birdwatching sites in Huelva province, see p79.

The large, ungainly white stork *(cigüeña blanca)*, actually black and white, nests from spring to summer on electricity pylons, trees and towers (sometimes right in the middle of towns) across western Andalucía; the Dehesa de Abajo (see the boxed text, p52) is home to a large woodland colony of white storks. A few pairs of the much rarer black stork *(cigüeña negra)*, which is actually all black, also nest in western Andalucía, typically on cliff ledges. In spring both types of stork migrate north from Africa across the Strait of Gibraltar (see p148).

For more information on Andalucía's bird life, check out the website of SEO/BirdLife (Spanish Ornithological Society; www.seo.org, in Spanish).

GETTING ACTIVE IN ANDALUCÍA

Andalucía's varied terrain and long coastline have always drawn action-lovers and thrill-seekers with a high-adrenaline mix of activities. Some of these are covered in the sections that follow. But the region's most rewarding activities, such as walking, cycling and horse riding, are often those that take you out into the wilderness at a more leisurely pace – quieter thrills, perhaps, but ones that better allow you to fully appreciate Andalucía's natural wonders. Other activities not covered here – such as climbing, canyoning, paragliding, canoeing and kayaking – are covered throughout the destination chapters.

WALKING

The thousands of kilometres of paths and tracks traversing Andalucía's verdant valleys and rugged hills provide marvellous walking of any length or difficulty you like. In some areas you can string together day walks into a trek of several days, sleeping along the way in a variety of hotels, *hostales* (budget hotels), camping grounds or occasionally mountain refuges or wild camping areas. For about half the year the climate is ideal, and in most areas the best months for walking are May, June, September and October. Although walking in Andalucía is increasingly popular among both Spaniards and foreigners, you'll rarely encounter anything that resembles a crowd on any walk.

Trail marking is erratic: some routes are well signed with route numbers, on others just the odd dab of red paint might tell you you're heading in the right direction, while on yet others you're left entirely to your own devices.

The two main categories of marked walking routes in Spain (even so, not always well marked) are *senderos de gran recorrido* (GRs, long-distance footpaths) and *senderos de pequeño recorrido* (PRs, shorter routes of a few hours or one or two days). The GR-7 long-distance path runs the length of Spain from Andorra in the north to Tarifa in the south, part of the European E-4 route from Greece to Andalucía. It enters Andalucía near Almaciles in northeast Granada province, then divides at Puebla de Don Fadrique, with one branch heading through Jaén and Córdoba provinces and the other through Las Alpujarras southeast of Granada before the two rejoin near Antequera in Málaga province. Signposting of this path throughout Andalucía is still in progress. There are also plenty of paths that are neither GRs nor PRs.

Further information on walks is given in this book's regional chapters. Tourist offices and visitors centres often have plenty of information on routes and conditions. The best in-depth walking guides to regions of Andalucía in English (and probably any language) are those published by Discovery Walking Guides (www.walking.demon.co.uk) on Las Alpujarras, the Sierra de Aracena and La Axarquía. The first two are accompanied by excellent maps, which you can buy separately if you wish. Further walking guides to specific areas are often available locally. For information on maps, see p406.

HORSE RIDING

The horse has been part of rural Andalusian life since time immemorial and Andalucía is the home of the elegant and internationally esteemed Spanish thoroughbred horse, also known as the Cartujano or Andalusian. Excellent riding tracks criss-cross the region's marvellous landscapes, and an ever-growing number of *picaderos* (stables) are ready to take you on a guided ride for any duration, or give you classes. Many of the mounts are Andalusians or Andalusian-Arab crosses – medium-sized, intelligent, good in traffic, and usually easy to handle and sure-footed.

Typical prices for a ride or lesson are €25 to €30 for one hour, €60 to €70 for a half day and around €100 for a full day. Most stables cater for all levels of experience, from lessons for beginners or children to trail rides for more competent riders. The ideal months to ride in Andalucía are May, June, September and October.

The provinces of Sevilla and Cádiz have perhaps the highest horse populations and concentrations of stables, but there are riding opportunities throughout the region. Andalucía te Quiere (www.andalucia.org) has a directory of over 100 stables and other equestrian establishments.

Among the many highlights of riding experiences in Andalucía are trail rides around Ronda (p180) and the Sierra Nevada (see Sierra Nevada Ski, p275), and beach and dune riding just out of Tarifa on Cádiz' Costa de la Luz (p145). Recommended stables are listed throughout this book's destination chapters.

BACKGROUND

ANDALUCÍA'S BEST HIKING AREAS

LA AXARQUÍA
In La Axarquía (p188), in the east of Málaga province, you can choose from gentle valley strolls close to the villages or climbs to summits with majestic views.

LAS ALPUJARRAS
One of the most picturesque corners of Andalucía, Las Alpujarras (p275) is a 70km-long jumble of valleys along the south flank of the Sierra Nevada. Arid hillsides split by deep ravines alternate with oasislike white villages surrounded by vegetable gardens, orchards, rapid streams and woodlands. Ancient paths wind up and down through constantly changing scenery between labyrinthine, Berber-style villages.

PARQUE NATURAL DE CABO DE GATA-NÍJAR
The combination of a dry, desert climate with volcanic cliffs plunging into azure Mediterranean waters produces a landscape of stark grandeur around the Cabo de Gata promontory (p301), southeast of Almería. By combining paths, dirt roads and occasional sections of paved road, you can walk right around the 60km coast in three or four days.

PARQUE NATURAL SIERRAS DE CAZORLA, SEGURA Y LAS VILLAS
The Parque Natural Sierras de Cazorla, Segura y Las Villas (p241) is Spain's largest protected area (2143 sq km), a crinkled, pinnacled region of several memorably beautiful mountain ranges divided by high plains and deep river valleys.

PARQUE NATURAL SIERRA DE ARACENA Y PICOS DE AROCHE
This verdant, sometimes lush, sometimes severe region (p101) is dotted with timeless stone villages and strung with an extensive network of well-maintained trails.

PARQUE NATURAL SIERRA DE GRAZALEMA
The hills of the Parque Natural Sierra de Grazalema (p139) in Cádiz province encompass pastoral river valleys, dense Mediterranean woodlands, rocky summits and precipitous gorges. Some of the best walks are within a reserve area for which permits or guides are required.

PARQUE NATURAL SIERRA DE LAS NIEVES
Southeast of Ronda, the Sierra de las Nieves (p183) includes the highest peak in western Andalucía, Torrecilla (1919m), climbable in a day from Ronda.

PARQUE NATURAL SIERRA NORTE
The rolling Sierra Morena country (p72) in the north of Sevilla province presents ever-changing panoramas of green valleys, woodlands, rivers and atmospheric old villages. The spring wildflowers are spectacular here.

SIERRA NEVADA
The Sierra Nevada (p272) is Andalucía's ultimate walking experience. During July, August and early September (the best months for walking up here) a national park bus service gives walkers access to the upper reaches of the range. It's feasible to cap mainland Spain's highest peak, Mulhacén (3479m), or the second-highest peak, Veleta (3395m), in a day trip. There are also many other possible routes.

BACKGROUND

All horse-lovers should put Jerez de la Frontera high on their itinerary. The town stages several exciting annual equine events – especially its Feria del Caballo (Horse Fair) in May – and its famous Real Escuela Andaluza del Arte Ecuestre (Royal Andalusian School of Equestrian Art; p130) and the nearby Yeguada de la Cartuja – Hierro del Bocado (p133) breeding centre are fascinating to visit.

WINDSURFING & KITESURFING

Tarifa, on the Strait of Gibraltar, is one of *the* top spots in Europe for windsurfing (see p145), thanks to the strong breezes blowing through the strait almost year-round. The long, sandy beaches are an added attraction and there's a hip international scene to go with the boards and waves. Rental of a board, sail and wetsuit costs around €35 per hour or €75 per day, with a six-hour beginner's course at around €120.

Some pretty good winds blow further up the Atlantic coast as well, including at Los Caños de Meca and Isla Cristina.

Kitesurfing is also possible at Tarifa and Punta Umbría. A six-hour beginner's course should cost about €120.

DIVING & SNORKELLING

Andalucía's coasts don't provide the universally spectacular sights of tropical waters but there's still some interesting diving here and plenty of dive schools and shops in the coastal resorts to help you enjoy it. Most establishments offer courses under the aegis of international diving organisations such as **PADI** (www.padi.com) or **NAUI** (www.nauiww.org), as well as dives for qualified divers and 'baptism' dives. A single dive with full equipment costs around €50. Introductory courses for up to three hours run from about €75.

The strong currents off Tarifa are probably best left for experienced divers. Gibraltar has some rewarding wreck-diving, while the coast of Granada province, especially La Herradura, has some good dive sites. Cabo de Gata in Almería province is also good, with sea floors of seagrass, sand and rocks, often with caves, crevices or passages.

Snorkelling is best along the rockier parts of the Mediterranean coast – between Nerja and Adra, and from Cabo de Gata to Mojácar.

SKIING & SNOWBOARDING

Andalucía's only ski station, the very popular Estación de Esquí Sierra Nevada (Sierra Nevada Ski Station; p275), is the most southerly ski resort in Europe; its runs and facilities are of championship quality. The season usually runs from December to April, and gets pretty crowded (with a thriving nightlife) on weekends for most of that period and around the Christmas–New Year and Día de Andalucía (28 February) holidays.

The resort has over 70 marked downhill runs of varied difficulty, totalling over 80km, plus cross-country routes and a dedicated snowboarding area. Some runs start almost at the top of Veleta (3395m), the Sierra Nevada's second-highest peak.

A day pass plus equipment rental costs between €50 and €65, depending on when you go. Six hours of group classes at ski school are €65.

The best deals for accommodation are ski packages, bookable through the station's website or phone number; they start at around €150 for two days and two nights with lift passes and half-board.

BACKGROUND

ANDALUCÍA'S TOP PARKS & PROTECTED AREAS

❦ **PARQUE NACIONAL DE DOÑANA** // **BEST TIME: ANY (P84)** **MILLIONS OF BIRDS** and the Iberian lynx give the park its fame (Doñana is one of the endangered cat's last footholds). Its habitat range is astonishing – wetlands, dunes, beaches and woodlands at the mouth of the Guadalquivir – and supports deer and wild boar, and is best explored by 4WD.

❦ **PARQUE NATURAL DE DOÑANA** // **BEST TIME: ANY (P84)** **MORE ACCESSIBLE** than the Parque Nacional de Doñana, for which it provides a buffer zone, this *parque natural* contains similar habitats and wildlife to its more restricted neighbour. Apart from wildlife-watching, its appeal lies in the range of 4WD trips, horse riding and walking possibilities.

❦ **PARQUE NACIONAL SIERRA NEVADA** // **BEST TIME: JUL–EARLY SEP (P272)** **SPECTACULAR HIGH-MOUNTAIN WILDERNESS** dominates here. Its high peaks often snowcapped even as the rest of Andalucía bakes in the sweltering heat, this *parque nacional* is best explored on foot. Along its many trails you'll find ibex (around 5000 inhabit the park) and high-altitude plants you won't find elsewhere.

❦ **PARQUE NATURAL SIERRA NEVADA** // **BEST TIME: DEPENDS ON ACTIVITY (P273)** **TIMELESS VILLAGES** of a quintessentially Andalusian hue are the main attraction of this park on the Sierra Nevada's lower slopes. More accessible than its national park neighbour, its activities range from hiking and horse riding, to mountain biking, skiing and climbing.

❦ **PARQUE NATURAL DE CABO DE GATA-NÍJAR** // **BEST TIME: ANY (P301)** **FLAMINGO COLONIES, VOLCANIC** cliffs and sandy beaches make for a combination unlike in any other protected area in Andalucía. One of the region's driest corners, the park showcases semidesert and promises a range of activities, including swimming, birdwatching, walking, horse riding, diving and snorkelling.

❦ **PARQUE NATURAL LOS ALCORNOCALES** // **BEST TIME: APR–OCT (P147)** **CORK-OAK FORESTS** *(alcornoque)*, some of the most extensive examples of this distinctive southern Spanish phenomenon, carpet the rolling hill country of this park in Cádiz province, north of Algeciras. It's one of Andalucía's lesser-known protected areas, ensuring that its extensive hiking trails rarely get overwhelmed.

BACKGROUND

❧ PARQUE NATURAL SIERRA DE GRAZALEMA // BEST TIME: OCT–JUN (P139)
IBEX, GRIFFON VULTURES and other species occupy this beautiful, damp, hilly region that is notable for its vast sweeps of Mediterranean woodlands and stands of Spanish firs. Archetypal white Andalusian villages serve as gateways to fantastic hiking trails, but you can also climb, canyon, paraglide and go caving to your heart's content.

❧ PARQUE NATURAL SIERRA DE LAS NIEVES // BEST TIME: APR–JUN AND SEP–NOV (P183)
SPECTACULAR VISTAS and deep valleys characterise this mountain region buried deep in the interior of Málaga province. With two iconic examples of Andalusian flora (stands of Spanish firs) and fauna (ibex) and other species, the park is an ideal choice for those looking to hike through the Andalusian wilds.

❧ PARQUE NATURAL SIERRA NORTE // BEST TIME: MAR–OCT (P72)
SPRING WILDFLOWERS carpet the rolling Sierra Morena country of this northern Andalusian park, but its appeal extends further, to ancient villages and expansive panoramas. There's no better way to explore this remote country than hiking or horse riding from village to village.

❧ PARQUE NATURAL SIERRAS DE CAZORLA, SEGURA Y LAS VILLAS // BEST TIME: SPRING AND AUTUMN (P241)
ABUNDANT, EASILY VISIBLE WILDLIFE, craggy mountains, deep valleys and thick forests – it's difficult to overestimate the charms of this beautiful park, Spain's largest (2143 sq km). Red and fallow deer, wild boar, mouflon and ibex provide the wildlife interest. Hike or explore on horseback or by 4WD.

❧ PARAJE NATURAL TORCAL DE ANTEQUERA // BEST TIME: MAR–NOV (P187)
STRIKING LIMESTONE FORMATIONS are what most visitors remember about this mountainous natural area close to Antequera in Málaga province. It contains some of the strangest landforms in Andalucía and has a handful of walking trails. Not surprisingly given the terrain, it also draws climbers from across Europe.

❧ RESERVA NATURAL LAGUNA DE FUENTE DE PIEDRA // BEST TIME: FEB–AUG (P187)
OVER 20,000 FLAMINGO pairs inhabit this shallow lake, Andalucía's largest, from January or February to August. It's an extraordinary wildlife experience of epic, almost African proportions and a hugely significant site: the lake is one of the flamingo's most important European breeding grounds (the other's in France).

BACKGROUND

FLAMENCO & BEYOND

· · · · · · ·

Flamenco, Andalucía's soul-stirring gift to the world of music, provides the ever-present soundtrack to Andalusian life. The passion of the genre is accessible to anyone who has heard its melancholy strains in the background in a crowded Andalusian bar or during a spine-tingling live performance. At the same time, flamenco can seem like an impenetrable world of knowledgeable yet taciturn initiates. Where these two worlds converge is in that rare yet famous, almost mystical flamenco moment known as *duende,* when a flamenco performer sparks an audience response that draws every-one – first-time listeners and flamenco veterans alike – into their passion and onto the edge of their seats, oblivious to all else.

FLAMENCO'S ANDALUSIAN ROOTS

Flamenco's origins have been lost to time. Some have suggested that flamenco de-rives from Byzantine chants used in Visigothic churches. But most musical historians speculate that it probably dates back to a fusion of songs brought to Spain by the *gi-tanos* (Roma people) with music and verses from North Africa crossing into medieval Muslim Andalucía. Flamenco as we now know it first took recognisable form in the late 18th and early 19th centuries among *gitanos* in the lower Guadalquivir valley in western Andalucía.

Early flamenco was *cante jondo* (deep song), an anguished form of expression for a people on the margins of society. Flamenco has come a long way in the two centuries since, but, true to its roots, the Seville–Jerez de la Frontera–Cádiz axis is still flamen-co's heartland and *jondura* (depth) remains the essence of flamenco. The power that such traditions still hold over modern performers was illustrated by flamenco legend Paco de Lucía, who told Spain's *El País* newspaper in May 2009 that 'flamenco's roots are so powerful that they do not allow us to fool around with it – the result has to sound like An-dalucía, its people and its traditions'.

FLAMENCO LEGENDS

In the early years of the 20th century, flamenco's reputation for quality and popular appeal seemed unassailable, thanks largely to the great singers of this period such as Seville's La Niña de los Peines (1890–1969), and Manuel Torre from Jerez (1878–1933). The latter's singing, legend has it, could drive people

> ### DON'T MISS...
>
> **FLAMENCO**
>
> ★ **Seville //** Flamenco at its most accessible (p60)
>
> ★ **Barrio de Santiago, Jerez de la Frontera //** Fine festivals and flamenco venues in the genre's spiritual home (p129)
>
> ★ **Barrio de Santa María, Cádiz //** Gritty barrio (p111)
>
> ★ **Festival Internacional de la Guitarra, Córdoba //** Prestigious festival drawing the best flamenco guitarists (p210)
>
> ★ **Jueves Flamenco, Arcos de la Frontera //** Small-town feel with big-name flamenco stars (p136)

BACKGROUND

FLAMENCO – THE ESSENTIAL ELEMENTS

A flamenco singer is known as a *cantaor* (male) or *cantaora* (female); a dancer is a *bailaor/a*. Most songs and dances are performed to a blood-rush of guitar from the *tocaor/a*. Percussion is provided by tapping feet, clapping hands and sometimes castanets. Flamenco songs come in many different styles, from the anguished *soleá* and the despairing *siguiriya* to the livelier *alegría* or the upbeat *bulería*. The traditional flamenco costume – shawl, fan and long, frilly *bata de cola* (tail gown) for women, flat Cordoban hats and tight black trousers for men – dates from Andalusian fashions in the late 19th century.

The *sevillana*, a popular dance with high, twirling arm movements, is not, for purists at least, flamenco at all. Consisting of four parts, each coming to an abrupt halt, the *sevillana* is probably an Andalusian version of a Castilian dance, the *seguidilla*.

to rip their shirts open and upturn tables – true *duende*. The fast, dynamic, unfeminine dancing and wild lifestyle of Carmen Amaya (1913–63), from Barcelona, made her *the* flamenco dance legend of all time. For good measure, her long-time partner Sabicas was the father of the modern solo flamenco guitar.

By the mid-20th century, however, flamenco was in a sorry state. With the repression of the Franco dictatorship at its peak, the genre was dominated by the lightweight flamenco of the *tablaos* – touristy shows emphasising the sexy and the jolly. In all but the clandestine flamenco bars in dark Andalusian corners, flamenco-light was in danger of taking over the real thing.

It was not until the 1970s that *flamenco puro* returned to centre stage and entered what many consider to have been a new golden age. That it did so owed much to singers such as Terremoto and La Paquera from Jerez. But more than anyone else, it was the extraordinary coming together of Paco de Lucía (b 1947), from Algeciras, and El Camarón de la Isla (1950–92), from San Fernando near Cádiz, that sparked flamenco's revival. Starting in 1968, flamenco's most exciting partnership recorded nine classic albums and they remain the standard by which all other flamenco artists are measured.

El Camarón was the leading light of contemporary *cante jondo* and it's impossible to overstate his influence over the art; his introduction of electric bass into his songs, for example, paved the way for a generation of artists to take flamenco in hitherto unimagined directions. His collaboration with the master guitarist Paco de Lucía may have been one of world music's most prestigious double acts, but, in his later years, El Camarón also teamed up with Tomatito, one of Paco de Lucía's protégés, and the results were similarly ground-breaking. The story of El Camarón's life (his real name was the far less evocative José Monje Cruz) has been made into an excellent movie (*Camarón*, 2005), directed by Jaime Chávarri. El Camarón's incredible vocal range and his wayward lifestyle made him a legend well before his tragically early death in 1992 at the age of 42. An estimated 100,000 people attended his funeral.

Paco de Lucía is the doyen of flamenco guitarists with a virtuosity few can match. He is also almost single-handedly responsible for transforming the guitar, formerly the junior partner of the flamenco trinity, into an instrument of solo expression far beyond traditional limits. Such is his skill that de Lucía can sound like two or three people playing together and, for many in the flamenco world, he is the personification of *duende*. The double album *Paco de Lucía Antología* is a great introduction to his work. He vowed that his 2004 world tour would be his last tour, but he still performs.

Another artist who has reached the level of cult figure is Enrique Morente (b 1942), referred to by one Madrid paper as 'the last bohemian' and another driving force behind flamenco's 1970s revival. While careful not to alienate flamenco purists, Morente, through his numerous collaborations across genres, helped lay the foundations for *nuevo flamenco* (new flamenco) and fusion.

Also belonging to the pantheon of late-20th-century flamenco stars is the Jaén-born Carmen Linares (b 1951), one of Andalucía's most venerable *cantaoras*. Although existing somewhat in Paco de Lucía's shadows, other guitar maestros include members of the Montoya family (some of whom are better known by the sobriquet of Los Habichuela), especially Juan (b 1933) and Pepe (b 1944).

FLAMENCO TODAY

Flamenco is as popular as it has ever been and probably more innovative. While established singers such as Enrique Morente, José Menese and Carmen Linares remain at the top of the profession, new generations continue to broaden flamenco's audience. Among the most popular is José Mercé from Jerez, whose exciting albums *Del Amanecer* (Of the Dawn; 1999), *Aire* (Air; 2000) and *Lío* (Entanglement; 2002) were all big sellers. El Barrio, a 21st-century urban poet from Cádiz, Estrella Morente from Granada (Enrique's daughter), Arcángel from Huelva and La Tana from Seville have also carved out big followings.

> *'Flamenco is as popular as it has ever been and probably more innovative'*

Flamenco dance has reached its most adventurous horizons in the person of Joaquín Cortés, born in Córdoba in 1969. Cortés fuses flamenco with contemporary dance, ballet and jazz, to music at rock-concert amplification. He tours frequently both in Spain and all over the world with spectacular solo or ensemble shows. Antonio Canales (b 1962), from Seville, is more of a flamenco purist and has a devoted following as a result.

On the guitar, keep an ear open for Manolo Sanlúcar from Cádiz, Tomatito from Almería (who used to accompany El Camarón de la Isla), and Vicente Amigo from Córdoba and Moraíto Chico from Jerez who accompany today's top singers or perform solo.

ROOTS OF THE GUITAR

The 9th-century Córdoba court musician Ziryab added a fifth string to the four-string Arab lute, producing an instrument that was widespread in Spain for centuries. Around the 1790s a sixth string was added, probably by a Cádiz guitar maker called Pagés. In the 1870s Antonio de Torres of Almería brought the guitar its modern shape by enlarging its two bulges and placing the bridge centrally over the lower one to give the instrument its acoustic power.

BACKGROUND

FARRUQUITO: FALLEN STAR?

Andalucía's most exciting young dance talent is Farruquito from Seville (b 1983), but he is also one of the most controversial. Born into one of Andalucía's most distinguished flamenco families – his father was the singer Juan Fernandez Flores 'El Moreno', his grandfather the late legendary flamenco dancer Farruco – Farruquito was once ranked among the world's '50 Most Beautiful People' by US *People* magazine. The flamenco world was, it seemed, his oyster.

That all changed in 2003 when Farruquito left the scene of a hit-and-run accident in Seville, leaving a 35-year-old man dead. After initially claiming that his 15-year-old brother was driving at the time, Farruquito confessed and was arrested six months later, then released on bail. Following a series of trials, some of which were interrupted so that Farruquito could travel around Europe to perform, he was finally sentenced in 2006 to two years in prison for manslaughter and for failing to render assistance to the victim. Imprisoned in early 2007, Farruquito soon left prison on 'conditional release' and continues to perform.

NUEVO FLAMENCO & FUSION

In the 1970s musicians began mixing flamenco with jazz, rock, blues, rap and other genres. The purists loathe these changes – in the proud *gitano* world, innovation has often met with abrasive scorn – but this *nuevo flamenco* greatly broadened flamenco's appeal. The seminal recording was a 1977 flamenco-folk-rock album, *Veneno* (Poison), by the group of the same name centred on Kiko Veneno (see Other Music, p358) and Raimundo Amador, both from Seville. Amador and his brother Rafael then formed Pata Negra, which produced four fine flamenco-jazz-blues albums culminating in *Blues de la Frontera* (1986); others have labelled their music 'gypsy rock'. Amador, a self-taught pianist, is now a solo artist. The piano is not a classic instrument of flamenco but Amador makes it work.

The group Ketama, whose key members are all from Granada's Montoya flamenco family, mixes flamenco with African, Cuban, Brazilian and other rhythms. Wide-ranging in their search for complementary sounds and rhythms, Ketama's *Songhai* (1987) and *Songhai II* (1995) – collaborations with Malian *kora* (harp) player Toumani Diabaté – are among the group's best albums.

A more traditional flamenco performer, Juan Peña Lebrijano, better known as El Lebrijano, has created some equally appealing combinations with classical Moroccan music. Diego el Cigala, one of modern flamenco's finest voices, relaunched his career with an exceptional collaboration with Cuban virtuoso pianist Bebo Valdés (*Lagrimas Negras;* Black Tears; 2004).

The latest generation includes artists such as Cádiz's Niña Pastori, who arrived in the late 1990s singing jazz- and Latin-influenced flamenco. Her albums, such as *Entre dos Puertos* (Between Two Ports; 1997), *María* (2002) and *Joyas Prestadas* (Borrowed Jewels; 2006), are great listening. The Málaga group Chambao combines flamenco with electronic beats on *Flamenco Chill* (2002), *Endorfinas en la Mente* (Endorphins in the Mind; 2004), *Pokito a Poko* (Little by Little; 2005) and *Con Otro Aire* (With Another Air; 2007).

SEEING FLAMENCO

Flamenco is easiest to catch in the summer when many fiestas include flamenco performances (see the boxed text, opposite). The rest of the year there are intermittent big-name performances in theatres, occasional seasons of concerts, and regular flamenco nights at some bars and clubs for the price of your drinks. Flamenco fans also band together in clubs called *peñas,* which stage performance nights – most will welcome interested visitors and the atmosphere here can be very intimate. Seville (see the boxed text, p60), Jerez de la Frontera (p129), Almería (p295), Cádiz (see Traditional Barrios, p111) and Granada (p268) are flamenco hotbeds, but you'll often be able to find something in Málaga, Córdoba and elsewhere.

Tablaos are regular shows put on for largely undiscriminating tourist audiences, usually with high prices. Tourist offices may steer you towards these unless asked otherwise.

OTHER MUSIC

Few Andalusian performers of any genre are completely untouched by the flamenco tradition. One of the most interesting characters is singer-songwriter Kiko Veneno (www.kikoveneno.net), who has spent most of his life around Seville and Cádiz. Though also a practitioner of flamenco fusion, he's more in a rock-R&B camp now, mixing rock, blues, African and flamenco rhythms with lyrics that range from humorous snatches of everyday life to Lorca poems. His compilations *Puro Veneno* (Pure Poison; 1997) and *Un Ratito de Gloria* (A Moment of Glory; 2001) are excellent introductions to his music.

Recent interest in excavating medieval Andalusian musical forms has produced some stunning results. Begoña Olavide has resurrected the harplike *salterio* and her *Mudejar* (1994) and *Salterio* (2000) albums are quiet masterpieces that blend 13th- and 14th-century Andalusian and North African sounds. The partly Andalusian Radio Tarifa, who first appeared in the early 1990s with a mesmerising mix of flamenco, Andalusian folk, North African and other medieval rhythms, mines similar territory and emerges with a more flamenco sound. Its albums include *Rumba Argelina* (Algerian Rumba; 1993), *Cruzando El Rio* (Crossing the River; 2001) and *Fiebre* (Fever; 2003).

Flamenco has even brought its influence to bear upon the region's classical music. Arguably the finest Spanish composer of all, Manuel de Falla was born in

FLAMENCO ON THE WEB

A few dedicated flamenco websites provide lists of upcoming live performances:

Centro Andaluz de Flamenco (www
.centroandaluzdeflamenco.es) The website of the Andalusian Centre for Flamenco based in Jerez de la Frontera.

De Flamenco (www.deflamenco.com) A terrific resource for forthcoming events.

EsFlamenco (www.esflamenco.com) Mostly a shop selling flamenco products, its 'News' tab lists some upcoming performances with a handful in Andalucía.

Flama – La Guía de Flamenco (www.guia flama.com, in Spanish) The best source of upcoming live concerts with a focus on Andalucía.

Flamenco World (www.flamenco-world.com) Another online shop with 'News', 'Features' and 'Festivals' links offering concert and festival updates.

MUSIC FESTIVALS OF ANDALUCÍA

Festival de Jerez (www.festivaldejerez.es) Two-week flamenco bash in Jerez de la Frontera in late February/early March (see p129).

Festival Internacional de Música y Danza Ciudad de Úbeda (www.festivaldeubeda.com) Mainly classical music performed in Úbeda's beautiful historic buildings in May and early June (see p237).

Potaje Gitano (www.potajegitano.com) Big Saturday-night flamenco fest held in June in Utrera, Sevilla province.

Festival Internacional de la Guitarra (www.guitarracordoba.com) Two-week celebration of the guitar in late June and early July in Córdoba (see p210).

Festival Internacional de Música y Danza (www.granadafestival.org) A 2½-week international festival of mainly classical music and dance held in Granada in late June to early July (see p264).

Caracolá Lebrijana Another big Saturday-night flamenco festival held in Lebrija, Sevilla province, in June/July.

Noches en los Jardines del Real Alcázar (www.actidea.com) Eclectic concert season in Seville's beautiful Alcázar gardens, held in July and August.

Bienal de Flamenco Month-long Seville megafest held in September in even-numbered years featuring just about every big star of the flamenco world (see p55).

Festival Internacional de Jazz Jazz festival held in November in several Andalusian cities including Almería, Granada, Jaén and Málaga.

Fiesta Mayor de Verdiales Celebration of folk music unique to the Málaga area on 28 December (see p169).

Cádiz in 1876. He grew up in Andalucía before heading off to Madrid and Paris, then returned to live in Granada until the end of the civil war, when he left for Argentina. De Falla's three major works, all intended as ballet scores, have deep Andalusian roots: *Noches en los Jardines de España* (Nights in the Gardens of Spain) evokes the Muslim past and the sounds and sensations of a hot Andalusian night, while *El Amor Brujo* (Love, the Magician) and *El Sombrero de Tres Picos* (The Three-Cornered Hat) are rooted in flamenco. Andrés Segovia from Jaén province was one of the major classical guitarists of the 20th century, and Málaga's Carlos Álvarez ranks among the top baritones of the opera world today.

In the realm of *canción española* (Spanish song), a melodic, romantic genre most popular with an older generation, the undoubted rising star is Pasión Vega from Málaga, whose beguiling voice may draw you in even if you don't normally go for this kind of thing. Vega incorporates influences including flamenco, pop, blues, Portuguese fado, jazz and bossa nova. Her two 2005 albums, *Flaca de Amor* (Weak with Love) and the live *Pasión Vega en el Maestranza,* are both well worth hearing.

ANDALUSIAN ARTS (& BULLFIGHTING)

· · · · · · ·

Federico García Lorca, Pablo Picasso, Diego Velázquez, Antonio Banderas… Andalucía has produced some of Spain's most important cultural figures down through the centuries. Yes, with the exception of Lorca, most made their names only after leaving Andalucía, but their Andalusian origins serve as reminders of Andalucía's rich and creative artistic heritage, both as a producer of outstanding talent, and as a character in its own right. And then there's bullfighting. Call it an art (as many Andalusians do), or call it barbaric – either way, it's a quintessentially Andalusian pastime that leaves no one indifferent.

LITERATURE

Despite two Nobel literature laureates, and with the exception of the iconic Federico García Lorca, name recognition of Andalusian writers for a non-Spanish readership is fairly low; few works have been translated into other languages. Even so, as a reflection of Andalusian life, the story of the region's literature is well worth telling.

Spain's literary Siglo de Oro (Golden Century), from the mid-16th to the mid-17th centuries, offered up the Andalusian playwrights Juan de la Cueva and Lope de Rueda, part of the circle that gathered in Seville around Christopher Columbus' great-grandson Álvaro Colón, and Córdoba's Luis de Góngora (1561–1627). Considered by many the greatest of all Spanish poets, Góngora's metaphorical, descriptive verses, some celebrating the more idyllic aspects of the Guadalquivir valley, were conceived as a source of sensuous pleasure.

Although no Andalusian, Miguel de Cervantes (1547–1616) spent 10 troubled years here, collecting unpaid taxes and procuring oil and wheat for the Spanish navy, as well as several lawsuits, spells in jail and even excommunications – no doubt grist to the mill for one of the inventors of the novel. His *Don Quijote* appeared in 1605. Some of Cervantes' short *Novelas Ejemplares* (Exemplary Novels) chronicle turbulent 16th-century Seville.

Things fell quiet until the late 19th century when the Generation of '98, a loose grouping of Spanish intellectuals who shared a deep disturbance about national decline, came to the fore. Antonio Machado (1875–1939), the group's

---

DON'T MISS...

ANDALUSIAN ARTS (& BULLFIGHTING)

★ **Museo Picasso //** Málaga pays homage to Andalucía's most famous artistic export (p164)

★ **Spaghetti Western film sets //** Almería remembers the days when Clint Eastwood and his gang came to town (p297)

★ **Corridas Goyescas //** Spain's most picturesque bullfights, like a Goya etching coming to life (see the boxed text, p178)

★ **Federico García Lorca //** Andalucía's most talented and tragic literary figure of the 20th century (opposite)

BACKGROUND

leading poet, was born in Seville and later spent some years as a teacher in Baeza. Juan Ramón Jiménez (1881–1958), the 1956 Nobel literature laureate from Moguer near Huelva, touchingly and amusingly brought to life his home town in *Platero y Yo* (Platero and I), a prose poem that retells his childhood wanderings with his donkey and confidant, Platero.

Three decades later, the loose-knit Generation of '27, whose nationwide luminaries included Salvador Dalí and film-maker Luis Buñuel, also counted the poets Rafael Alberti (from El Puerto de Santa María) and Vicente Aleixandre (the 1977 Nobel literature laureate from Seville) among their number. But the outstanding literary figure was Federico García Lorca, from Granada.

> *'Andalucía has produced some of Spain's most important cultural figures down through the centuries'*

FEDERICO GARCÍA LORCA

For many the most important Spanish writer since Cervantes, Federico García Lorca (1898–1936) was a poet, playwright, musician, artist, theatre director and much more. Though charming and popular, he felt alienated – by his homosexuality, his leftish outlook and, probably, his talent itself – from his home town of Granada (which he called 'a wasteland populated by the worst bourgeoisie in Spain') and from Spanish society at large. Lorca identified with Andalucía's marginalised *gitanos* and empathised with women stifled by conventional mores. He longed for spontaneity and vivacity and eulogised both Granada's Islamic past and what he considered the 'authentic' Andalucía (to be found in Málaga, Córdoba, Cádiz – anywhere except Granada).

Lorca first won major popularity with *El Romancero Gitano* (Gypsy Ballads), a colourful 1928 collection of verses on *gitano* themes, full of startling metaphors and with the simplicity of flamenco song. Between 1933 and 1936 he wrote the three tragic plays for which he is best known: *Bodas de Sangre* (Blood Wedding), *Yerma* (Barren) and *La Casa de Bernarda Alba* (The House of Bernarda Alba) – brooding, dark but dramatic works dealing with themes of entrapment and liberation, passion and repression. Lorca was executed by the Nationalists early in the civil war, but his passionate, free, genial and troubled spirit lives on in the many productions of his plays and other creative work he still inspires.

Travellers can visit Lorca's summer home in Granada, Huerta de San Vicente, and his birthplace outside the city; for more information, see the boxed text, p264. For those who want to follow the Lorca trail to the bitter end, the place he was killed is now a memorial park. Ian Gibson's *Federico García Lorca* (1990) is an excellent biography of Andalucía's most celebrated writer. Gibson also penned *The Assassination of Federico García Lorca* (1979), revealing the murky story of Lorca's murder near Granada during the civil war.

CONTEMPORARY ANDALUSIAN LITERATURE

Antonio Muñoz Molina (born in Úbeda, Jaén province, in 1956) is one of Spain's leading contemporary novelists. One of his best novels, *El Jinete Polaco* (The Polish Jockey;

THE ROMANCE OF ANDALUCÍA

Andalucía may join the ranks of Tuscany and Provence in 'The-First-Year-of-My-New-Life-in-an-Old-Farmhouse-on-the-Continent' genre – think Chris Stewart's *Driving Over Lemons* (1999) and Miranda Innes' *Getting to Mañana* (2003). But these are merely the latest instalment in a distinguished literary tradition in which Andalucía – home to fiesta, flamenco, bullfighting and dark-haired, dark-eyed people – is one of the main characters. The result is a romantic image of Andalucía that will probably never die.

One of the first Romantic writings set in Andalucía (Seville, in this case) was Lord Byron's *Don Juan*, although Byron was not the first to write about this legendary character – Don Juan first appeared in a play by renowned 17th-century Spanish playwright Tirso de Molina. Byron visited Andalucía in 1809 and wrote the mock-epic poetic masterpiece in the early 1820s. In 1826 France's Viscount Chateaubriand published an influential melancholic novella, *Les Aventures du Dernier Abencerage* (The Adventures of the Last Abencerraj), in which a Muslim prince returns to Granada after the Christian reconquest. The Alhambra was then established as the quintessential symbol of exotic Andalucía by *Les Orientales* (1829) by Victor Hugo (who didn't visit Granada), and *Tales of the Alhambra* (1832) by the American Washington Irving (who lived there for a few months). *Carmen,* a violent novella of *gitano* love and revenge, written in the 1840s by Frenchman Prosper Mérimée, forever added subtropical sensuality to the Andalusian mystique.

Composers, too, felt the pull of Andalusian images. The Don Juan story inspired an operatic version, *Don Giovanni,* by Mozart in the 18th century. Then Georges Bizet's 1875 opera *Carmen* finally fixed the stereotype of Andalusian women as full of fire, guile and flashing beauty.

Alexandre Dumas came close to summing up the prevailing image of Andalucía when he characterised Andalucía as a 'gay, lovely land with castanets in her hand and a garland on her brow'.

1991), is set in 'Mágina', a fictionalised Úbeda, in the mid-20th century. *Sefarad* (Sepharad; 2003) weaves 17 separate stories into a multilayered exploration of themes raised by the expulsion of Spain's Jews in the 15th century, the Soviet gulag and the Nazi holocaust.

Antonio Soler (b 1956) from Málaga is building a reputation as a perceptive drawer of character and atmosphere, and a weaver of intriguing plots. His *El Camino de los Ingleses* (The Way of the English; 2004), tracking a group of friends' summer of transition from adolescence to adulthood, has been filmed by Antonio Banderas.

Finally, the highly popular playwright, poet and novelist Antonio Gala (b 1930), from Córdoba, sets much of his work in the past, which he uses to illuminate the present. *La Pasión Turca* (Turkish Passion; 1993) is his best-known novel.

PAINTING & SCULPTURE

Andalucía produced two of Spain's greatest ever artists – Pablo Picasso and Diego Velázquez – although both made their name after leaving Andalucía.

Perhaps the greatest artist of Spain's 17th-century Siglo de Oro, Diego Velázquez (1599–1660) left Seville in his 20s to become a court painter in Madrid. Velázquez' friend Alonso Cano (1601–77), a gifted painter, sculptor and architect, did some of his best work at Granada and Málaga cathedrals. Mystical Francisco de Zurbarán (1598–1664) lived most of his life in and around Seville. His clear, spiritual paintings of saints, churchmen and monastic life often utilise strong chiaroscuro, as did two Italy-based contemporaries, Caravaggio and José de Ribera.

Bartolomé Esteban Murillo (1617–82) and his friend Juan de Valdés Leal (1622–94), both Seville-born, led the way to full-blown baroque art. With its large, colourful, accessible images, the baroque movement took deep root in Andalucía. Murillo's soft-focus children and religious scenes emphasising the optimism of biblical stories made him highly popular in a time of economic decline. Valdés Leal's greatest works hang alongside several Murillos in Seville's Hospital de la Caridad (p49).

Sevillano sculptor Juan Martínez Montañés (1568–1649) carved such dramatic and lifelike wooden images that contemporaries called him 'El Dios de la Madera' (The God of Wood). You'll find his carvings in many Andalusian churches, and many of the statues still carried in Seville's Semana Santa (Holy Week) processions are his work.

Francisco de Goya (1746–1828), from Aragón in northern Spain, immortalised Andalusian bullfights at Ronda, and tradition has it that he painted his famous *La Maja Vestida* and *La Maja Desnuda* – near-identical portraits of one woman, clothed and unclothed – at a royal hunting lodge in what is now the Parque Nacional de Doñana. A few Goyas are on view in Andalucía including in Seville's cathedral (p40) and Cádiz's Oratorio de la Santa Cueva (see the boxed text, p116).

Maverick genius Pablo Picasso (1881–1973) was born in Málaga, but moved to northern Spain when he was nine. Since 2003 the city of his birth has had a fine Picasso museum (p164), with a large collection of his works donated by his family.

Granada-born abstract expressionist José Guerrero (1914–91) followed Picasso's footsteps out of Andalucía, finding fame in New York in the 1950s. Seville-born Luis Gordillo (b 1934) spent time in Paris, Madrid and elsewhere, becoming Spain's leading exponent of pop art. Later he veered towards postmodern abstraction.

BULLFIGHTING

An epic drama of blood and sand or a cruel blood 'sport' that has no place in modern Europe? This most enduring and controversial of Spanish traditions is all this and more, at once compelling theatre and an ancient ritual that sees 40,000 bulls killed in around 17,000 bullfights every year in Spain. Perhaps it was best summed up by Ernest Hemingway – a bullfighting aficionado – who described it as 'a wonderful nightmare'.

It was probably the Romans who staged Spain's first bullfights. *La lidia,* as the modern art of bullfighting on foot is known, took off in an organised fashion in the 18th century. The Romero family from Ronda, in Málaga province, established most of the basics of bullfighting on foot, and Andalucía has been one of its hotbeds ever since. Previously, bullfighting had been done on horseback, as a kind of cavalry-training-cum-sport for the gentry.

ANDALUCÍA ON THE SILVER SCREEN

Andalucía's most famous cinematic export is undoubtedly Antonio Banderas. Born in Málaga in 1960, the dashing and talented Banderas made his name in the films of Pedro Almodóvar (including *Women on the Verge of a Nervous Breakdown* and *Tie Me Up! Tie Me Down!*). His move to Hollywood, and marriage to Melanie Griffiths, transformed him into an international star, with hits such as *Philadelphia, The Mask of Zorro* and *House of the Spirits*. He has since turned his hand to directing, including *Crazy in Alabama* (1999) and the Spanish-language *El Camino de los Ingleses* (The Way of the English; 2006); this tale of transition from adolescence to adulthood has a largely Andalusian cast and is set in and around Málaga. He remains devoted to his home city, where he has set up a drama school. Perhaps following in his footsteps is Paz Vega (*Spanglish;* 2004), from Seville, voted best new actress at the Cannes Film Festival in 2001.

One of the most successful Andalusian productions of recent years was Pablo Carbonell's comic *Atún y Chocolate* (Tuna and Chocolate; 2004), filmed in the fishing town of Barbate in Cádiz province, with a plot revolving around weddings, tuna fishing and hashish smuggling. Andalusian director Benito Zambrano, from Lebrija (Sevilla province), has won acclaim with *Solas* (Alone; 1999) and *Habana Blues* (Havana Blues; 2005), while the underside of Andalusian society is vividly portrayed in sevillano Alberto Rodríguez' 2005 realist film *7 Vírgenes* (7 Virgins); it follows a teenager living 48 hours of intense freedom on leave from a juvenile reform centre.

Non-Andalusian productions with Andalusian themes have included Fernando Colomo's charming *Al Sur de Granada* (South from Granada; 2003), a version of English writer Gerald Brenan's life in an Andalusian village in the 1920s. In a bizarre twist, Seville's Casa de Pilatos (p50) and Plaza de España (p47) stood in for Cairo, Jerusalem and Damascus in *Lawrence of Arabia*. The Tabernas desert and Almería's Cabo de Gata also provided the backdrop for such classics as *Cleopatra, Doctor Zhivago* and *Indiana Jones and the Last Crusade*.

But Andalucía's greatest claim to cinematic fame could be spaghetti Westerns. The Clint Eastwood trilogy of *A Fistful of Dollars, For a Few Dollars More* and *The Good, the Bad and the Ugly*, directed by Italian Sergio Leone (hence the 'spaghetti' label), were the most celebrated of over 150 films made in 10 years around Tabernas, Almería. Three Wild West town sets remain today (see Desierto de Tabernas, p297). For a hilarious look at these film sets, check out Alex de la Iglesia's *800 Bullets*.

Andalucía stages several film festivals every year, the most important being Málaga's **Festival de Cine Español** (www.festivaldemalaga.com, in Spanish) in late April/early May.

The bullfight *(corrida de toros)* is so ingrained in Andalusian culture that the question of whether it's cruel just doesn't frame itself to many people. Plenty of people are uninterested in the activity, but relatively few actively oppose it. For its aficionados, bullfighting is a pageant with a long history and many rules, and they defend it against charges of cruelty by saying that fighting bulls have been bred for conflict and that before the fateful day they are treated like kings. In the eyes of such supporters, the *corrida* is also about many other things – bravery, skill, performance and a direct confrontation with death.

For its opponents, bullfighting is intolerably cruel, akin to bear-baiting, and a blight on Spain's conscience in these supposedly more enlightened times. The anti-bull-fighting lobby is bigger and more influential in parts of northern Spain, especially Catalonia. Spanish anti-bull-fighting organisations include the Barcelona-based **Asociación para la Defensa de los Derechos del Animal** (ADDA; Association for the Defence of Animal Rights; www.addaong .org) and the Madrid-based **Equanimal** (www.equanimal.org, in Spanish). International organisations such as the **World Society for the Protection of Animals** (www.wspa.org.uk) and the **League Against Cruel Sports** (www.leagueagainstcruelsports.org) also campaign against bullfighting. For information about creative protests against bullfighting, visit www.runningofthenudes.com.

> *'Perhaps it was best summed up by Ernest Hemingway… who described it as "a wonderful nightmare"'*

THE FIGHT

Bullfights usually begin at about 6pm and, as a rule, three different matadors will fight two bulls each. Each fight takes about 15 minutes.

After entering the arena, the bull is first moved about by junior bullfighters known as *peones,* wielding great capes. The colourfully attired matador (killer) then puts in an initial appearance and makes *faenas* (moves) with the bull, such as pivoting before its horns. The more closely and calmly the matador works with the bull, the greater the crowd's appreciation. The matador leaves the stage to the *banderilleros,* who attempt to goad the bull into action by plunging a pair of banderillas (short prods with harpoon-style ends) into his withers. Next, the horseback picadors take over, to shove a lance into the withers, greatly weakening the bull. The matador then returns for the final session. When the bull seems tired out and unlikely to give a lot more, the matador chooses the moment for the kill. Facing the animal head-on, the matador aims to sink a sword cleanly into its neck for an instant kill – the *estocada.*

A skilful, daring performance followed by a clean kill will have the crowd on its feet waving handkerchiefs in appeal to the fight president to award the matador an ear of the animal.

WHEN & WHERE

The main bullfighting season in Andalucía runs from Easter Sunday to October, with most *corridas* held as part of a city or town fiesta. A few bullrings (eg Seville's) have regular fights right through the season.

The big bang that launches Andalucía's bullfighting year is Seville's Feria de Abril (April Fair; p55), with fights almost daily during the week of the fair and the week before. It's Seville, too, where the year ends with a *corrida* on 12 October, Spain's National Day. Other major fight seasons on the Andalusian bullfight calendar include the following:

Feria de Nuestra Señora de la Salud Held in Córdoba, a big bullfighting stronghold, in late May/early June.

Feria del Corpus Cristi In Granada in May or June (see p264).

BACKGROUND

Bullfight Season in El Puerto de Santa María Held on most Sundays June to August.

Fiestas Colombinas In Huelva, 29 July to 3 August (see p80).

Feria de Málaga Nine-day fair in Málaga in mid-August (see p168).

Feria de la Virgen del Mar In Almería in the last week of August.

Corridas Goyescas Held in Ronda in early September (see the boxed text, p178), with select matadors fighting in costumes such as those shown in bullfight engravings by Francisco de Goya.

Otherwise, for the latest information on the next bullfight near you, biographies of *toreros* (bullfighters) and more, check out www.portaltaurino.com.

If you plan on attending a bullfight, try to make it one featuring a top *torero*. José Tomás is well on the way to being a bullfighting legend in his own lifetime. Other names to look for include Enrique Ponce, Julián 'El Juli' López, David 'El Fandi' Fandila, Rivera Ordóñez, Manual Díaz 'El Cordobés' and Jesulín de Ubrique.

If, on the other hand, you're happy to take someone else's word for it, Edward Lewine's *Death and the Sun* (2005) follows matador Rivera Ordóñez and his supporting team through a whole season.

THE ANDALUSIAN KITCHEN

· · · · · · ·

The rest of Spain may have embraced the avant-garde world of experimental nouvelle cuisine and world-famous celebrity chefs, but Andalucía is where you'll find Spanish food in all its traditional glory. A bastion of the Spanish culinary tradition, the Andalusian kitchen is one that prides cultured simplicity above all else. As Andalusians see it, they have been blessed with the best ingredients that land and sea can offer, and to interfere with these through unnecessary tinkering is akin to culinary sacrilege. Furthermore, Andalusians make another claim designed to strengthen their role as the guardians of authentic Spanish cooking: it was they, Andalusians argue, who invented tapas.

Passions for the staples of Spanish cooking – the finest olive oil, lightly fried seafood, refreshingly chilled soups and *jamón* – run deep here. Add a few creative dishes to the menu if you wish, and we may even try them, Andalusians seem to say. But every restaurant owner in Andalucía knows that such meals must pass an exacting test: diners must be able to recognise the flavours and quality cooked up for them by their *abuelas* (grandmothers).

In Andalucía, eating is a social event and considered to be one of life's great pleasures. As such, it's best enjoyed in the company of friends and like-minded food connoisseurs. That can mean crowding together in a bar where you have to shout to make yourself heard or, especially in summer, spending hours over a meal and conversation at a restaurant overlooking the sea. If you eat in a hurry and miss out on this experience, you'll have missed one of the essential pillars of Andalusian life. If you plan to allocate hours of each day for the purpose of eating, you're halfway towards becoming an Andalusian.

> '*Andalucía is where you'll find Spanish food in all its traditional glory*'

Two final words of warning. First, the *menú del día* (daily set menu at lunchtime, usually Monday to Friday) may be economical, but it usually doesn't include the most exciting dishes on the menu; for those you'll need to order à la carte. And the Spanish eating timetable is at its most extreme in Andalucía, so it's a good idea to reset your stomach clock unless you want to be left starving when all the bars close for the afternoon.

TAPAS

In Andalucía, tapas are more than a way of eating – they're a way of life. *Tapeando* (going out for tapas) is a favourite Andalusian pastime and while it may serve as the prelude to lunch, it's often the main event in the evening when Andalusians drag out their evening meal through a combination of tapas and drink. It's a great way to sample a range of tastes.

There are many stories concerning the origins of tapas. One holds that in the 13th century, doctors to King Alfonso X advised him to accompany his small sips of wine between meals with small morsels of food. So enamoured was the monarch with the idea that he passed a law requiring all bars in Castile to follow suit. Another version attributes tapas to bar owners who placed a saucer with a piece of bread on top of a sherry glass either to deter flies or prevent the punter from eating on an empty stomach and getting too tipsy. As for the name, tapa (which means lid) is said to have attained widespread usage in the early 20th century when King Alfonso XIII stopped at a beachside bar in Cádiz province. When a strong gust of wind blew sand in the king's direction, a quick-witted waiter rushed to place a slice of *jamón* atop the king's glass of sherry. The king so much enjoyed the idea (and the *jamón*) that, wind or no wind, he ordered another and the name stuck.

These days there are no limits on what can constitute a tapa, ranging from little nibbles such as olives or cheese, to far more elaborate combinations. The best tapas are those that draw on the eating obsessions or even culinary peculiarities of a particular region, drawing you into flavours that hint at the cultural and historical story of wherever you find yourself. In Huelva, it would be a culinary crime to order anything but the local *jamón ibérico,* while in Granada, North African tagine tapas reflect the city's days as the historical capital of Islamic Al-Andalus. In Cádiz province, the real luxury is seafood tapas, whether marinated, fried or fresh; Cádiz, El Puerto de Santa María and Sanlúcar de Barrameda have some of the best seafood in Andalucía, from Atlantic *conchas finas* (Venus shell, the biggest of the clams) to *cangrejos* (tiny crabs, cooked whole) or *búsanos* (sea snails or whelks). A dish that makes a grown Andalusian weep with joy is *langostinos a la plancha,* grilled, sweet, juicy king prawns sprinkled with flakes of sea salt.

DON'T MISS...

THE ANDALUSIAN KITCHEN

- ★ **Jamón ibérico de bellota** // Wafer-thin slices of Spain's most sought-after ham, from Jabugo

- ★ **Gazpacho andaluz** // Cold soup on a hot day – Andalucía's gift to summer

- ★ **Pescaito frito (fried fish)** // If it came from the sea, it has surely been lightly fried, especially along the Cádiz coast

- ★ **Langostinos de Sanlúcar de Barrameda** // Andalucía's most famous prawns

- ★ **Extra virgin olive oil** // Appreciate its full, lingering flavour in seemingly every dish

- ★ **Sherry** // Sip it slow at the source of the world's most famous brands

- ★ **Manzanilla** // Sanlúcar de Barrameda's sharp white wine that's Spain's biggest seller

Bars sometimes display a range of tapas on the counter – if they do, you can either take a small plate and help yourself or point to the morsel you want. If you do this, it's customary to keep track of what you eat (by holding on to the toothpicks for example) and then tell the bar person when it comes time to pay. Otherwise, most places have a menu or a blackboard listing what's available and you order your choices in tapa, *media-ración* (half ration) or full *ración* size. It's easiest of all in Granada, Jaén and Almería, where the age-old tradition of free tapas with a drink still persists. The citizens of those regions are proud and indeed feel superior for their generosity over places such as Seville and Cádiz or Córdoba where you have to pay for each tapa.

FRUITS OF THE SEA

More than simply a much-loved staple of the local cuisine, seafood is a way of life all along the Andalusian coast. It is a relationship forged in the days when Andalucía was one of Spain's poorest regions, when fishing was the mainstay of the economy and generations of Andalusians took to the sea in fishing fleets that almost literally kept the region afloat. Fishing is now the preserve of big business and the smaller fishing fleets are something of an endangered species, surviving most often in nostalgic reminiscences in waterfront bars. But the spirit of that age lives on and the region's daily catch – from both the Mediterranean and Atlantic – is eagerly awaited by restaurant chefs, hungry patrons and *abuelas* alike. The variety is simply staggering.

Andalusians eat fish in a variety of ways, but they are, above all, famous for their *pescaíto frito* (fried fish). A particular speciality of Cádiz, El Puerto de Santa María and the Costa de la Luz (although you'll also find it in Granada), fried fish Andalusian-style is an art form with more subtlety than first appears. Just about anything that emerges from the sea is rolled in chickpea and wheat flour, shaken this way and that to remove the surplus, then deep-fried ever so briefly in olive oil, just long enough to form a light, golden crust that seals the essential goodness of the fish or other seafood within. There are few products of the sea that don't get the deep-fry treatment, but the more common ones include *chipirones* or *chopitos* (baby squid), *cazón en adobo* (dogfish or shark that feed on shellfish producing a strong, almost sweet flavour) and *tortilla de camarones,* a delicious, crispy frittata embedded with tiny shrimps.

Other choices you'll encounter again and again include: *boquerones* (anchovies), served either fried or marinated in garlic, olive oil and vinegar; *sardinas a la plancha* (grilled sardines); *gambas* (prawns) and *langostinos* (king prawns) served grilled, fried or cold with a bowl of fresh mayonnaise, with the most sought-after coming from Sanlúcar de Barrameda; *chanquetes* (similar to whitebait and served deep-fried), a speciality of Málaga; *ostras* (oysters); *pez espada* (swordfish); and *salmonetes* (red mullet). Stocks of *atún* (tuna) are rapidly depleting, but remain a favourite along the Costa de la Luz, especially in Barbate and Zahara de los Atunes. And if you're really keen to delve deep into local cuisine, you really must try *mojama,* tuna that's been salted and dried until it shrivels into a hard texture; it's eaten with almonds and best enjoyed with a cold glass of manzanilla from Sanlúcar de Barrameda.

FRUITS OF THE LAND

Coastal Andalucía is not alone in its devotion to the local produce. Andalusians from the interior make the grand (but by no means unfounded) claim to anyone who will listen that the olive and *jamón*, those mainstays of the Spanish table, produced here are the finest in all of Spain.

We'll get to those in a moment, but *jamón* is not the only meat that Andalusians get excited about. Throughout the bullfighting season (roughly May to September), bars and restaurants proudly announce '*hay rabo de toro*', which roughly translates as, 'yes, we have bull's tail'. If you don't think about where it came from, it really is rather tasty.

Andalusians also love their cheeses and although most are imported from elsewhere in Spain, there are exceptions. Typical Andalusian cheeses include Grazalema, from

BACKGROUND

the mountains of Cádiz, made from ewes' milk and similar to Manchego; Málaga, a goats cheese preserved in olive oil; and Cádiz, a strong, fresh goats cheese made in the countryside around Cádiz.

The region also produces what are arguably the finest fruits and vegetables in Spain due to its generous climate. That's not to say that vegetables dominate most restaurant menus across this most carnivorous of regions – they're there, but usually in the background – but this fantastic produce is eaten in season and generally bought fresh and in open-air morning markets. Almería province, east of Málaga, is Europe's winter garden, with miles of plastic-covered hothouses of intensively grown vegetables.

JAMÓN

There is no more taste-bud-teasing prospect than a few wafer-thin, succulent slices of *jamón*. Nearly every bar and restaurant in Andalucía has at least one *jamón* on the go at any one time, strapped into a cradlelike frame called a *jamónera*. More often, they have several hams, the skin and hooves still attached, hanging from the walls or ceiling.

Spanish *jamón* is, unlike Italian prosciutto, a bold, deep red, well marbled with buttery fat. At its best, it smells like meat, the forest and the field. Like wines and olive oil, Spanish *jamón* is subject to a strict series of classifications. *Jamón serrano,* which accounts for around 90% of cured ham in Spain, refers to *jamón* made from white-coated pigs introduced to Spain in the 1950s. Once salted and semidried by the cold, dry winds of the Spanish sierra, most now go through a similar process of around a year's curing and drying in a climate-controlled shed.

Jamón ibérico, also called *pata negra* (black leg), is more expensive and comes from a black-coated pig indigenous to the Iberian peninsula and a descendant of the wild boar. Gastronomically, its star appeal is its ability to infiltrate fat into the muscle tissue, thus producing an especially well-marbled meat. Considered to be the best *jamón* of all is the *jamón ibérico* of Jabugo, in Andalucía's Huelva province, which comes from pigs free-ranging in the Sierra Morena oak forests. The best Jabugo hams are graded from one to five *jotas* (Js), and *cinco jotas* (JJJJJ) hams come from pigs that have never eaten anything but acorns *(bellotas)*.

If the pig gains at least 50% of its body weight during the acorn-eating season,

BACKGROUND

it can be classified as *jamón ibérico de bellota,* the most sought-after designation for *jamón.*

Other much sought-after products from the pig include: *morcilla,* a blood sausage with rice or onions, best eaten lightly grilled; chorizo, a spicy pork sausage with paprika; and *lomo,* another cured pork sausage.

OLIVE OIL

Spain is the world's largest olive-oil producer and Andalucía's olive statistics are impressive: there are over 100 million olive trees in Andalucía; a remarkable 20% of the world's olive oil originates in Jaén province, which produces more olive oil than Greece; and Jaén's more-than-4500 sq km of olive trees are, it is sometimes claimed, the world's largest human-made forest. The seemingly endless olive groves of Córdoba, Jaén and Sevilla were originally planted by the Romans, but the production of *az-zait* (juice of the olive), from which the modern generic word for olive oil, *aceite,* is derived, was further developed by the Muslims. Both olives and olive oil continue to be a staple of the Andalusian kitchen.

Olive oil production is almost as complicated as that of wine, with a range of designations designed to indicate quality. The best olive oils are those classified as 'virgin' (which must meet 40 criteria for quality and purity) and 'extra virgin' (the best olive oil whose acidity levels can be no higher than 1%). Some extra virgin oils, such as Núñez de Prado (see p213), have nearly zero acidity; the olive-oil mills can be visited. Accredited olive-oil-producing regions receive Denominación de Origen (DO; a designation that indicates the unique geographic origins, production processes and quality of the product). Those in Andalucía include: Baena and Priego de Córdoba in Córdoba, and Sierra de Segura and Sierra Mágina in Jaén.

> '*a remarkable 20% of the world's olive oil originates in Jaén province*'

The most common type of olive is the full-flavoured and (sometimes) vaguely spicy *picual,* which dominates the olive groves of Jaén province and accounts for 50% of all Spanish olive production. It takes its name from its pointed *pico* (tip) and is considered ideal for olive oil due to its high proportion of vegetable fat, natural antioxidants and polyphenol; the latter ensures that the oil keeps well and maintains its essential qualities at a high cooking temperature. Another important type of olive is the *hojiblanca,* which is grown predominantly around Málaga and Sevilla provinces. Its oil, which keeps for less time and should be stored in a cool dark place, is said to have a taste and aroma reminiscent of fruits, grasses and nuts. For more on olive oil production, see the boxed text, p228.

COLD SOUPS

One of the most important influences over Andalusian chefs has always been the region's climate, and the perfect antidote to Andalucía's baking summers is *gazpacho andaluz* (Andalusian gazpacho). This cold soup appears in many manifestations, but its base is almost always a blended mix of tomatoes, peppers, cucumber, garlic, bread

NOUVELLE CUISINE IN ANDALUCÍA

Andalucía's culinary tastes may be more traditional than those of northern Spain, but Spanish nouvelle cuisine, whereby chefs take traditional cuisine, blow it apart and put it back together in weird and wonderful ways, has nonetheless left its mark on the region. Some of our favourite restaurants where you can sample the new wave in contemporary Spanish cooking include the following:

★ **Restaurante Tragabuches** (p181) Daniel García has earned a Michelin star for his *cocina creative* in Ronda

★ **La Moraga** (p170) Daniel García has taken his innovative tapas to Málaga

★ **Café de París** (p169) The home kitchen of Michelin-starred José Carlos García; in Málaga

★ **El Aljibe** (p117) Cádiz' answer to the celebrity chefs of the north; Pablo Grosso makes cooking a work of art

crumbs, oil and (sherry) vinegar. Aside from climate, history played a significant role in its popularity here: it's a legacy of the New World, when Columbus brought back tomatoes and peppers from his travels. The basis for gazpacho developed in Andalucía among the *jornaleros,* agricultural day labourers, who were given rations of oil and (often-stale) bread, which they soaked in water to form the basis of a soup, adding the oil, garlic and whatever fresh vegetables were at hand. All of the ingredients were pounded using a mortar and pestle and a refreshing and nourishing dish was made that would conquer the world. It is sometimes served in a jug with ice cubes, with side dishes of chopped raw vegetables such as cucumber and onion.

> *'the perfect antidote to Andalucía's baking summers is gazpacho andaluz (Andalusian gazpacho)'*

A thicker version of gazpacho is *salmorejo cordobés,* a cold tomato-based soup from Córdoba where soaked bread is essential; it's served with bits of *jamón* and crumbled egg. *Ajo blanco* is a white gazpacho, a North African legacy, made with almonds, garlic and grapes instead of tomatoes.

One final thing: yes, these soups are supposed to be cold. For that reason, you may not find it on offer in the cooler winter months when its refreshing temperature simply wouldn't make sense. And *please* don't make the mistake of one traveller in Seville who returned his gazpacho asking for it to be heated.

DRINKS

WINE

Vino production in Andalucía was introduced by the Phoenicians, possibly as early as 1100 BC. The Montilla-Morales DO in southern Córdoba province produces a wine that is similar to sherry but, unlike sherry, is not fortified by the addition of brandy – the *fino* variety is the most acclaimed. For more on Montilla wines, see the boxed text, p218. Andalucía's other DO is in Málaga province: sweet, velvety Málaga Dulce pleased palates from Virgil to the ladies of Victorian England, until the vines were blighted around the beginning of the 20th century. Today the Málaga DO area is Andalucía's smallest. You can sample Málaga wine straight from the barrel in some of the city's numerous bars.

Almost every village throughout Andalucía has its own basic wine, known simply as *mosto*. Eight areas in the region produce distinctive, good, non-DO wines that can be sampled locally: Aljarafe and Los Palacios (Sevilla province); Bailén, Lopera and Torreperogil (Jaén province); Costa Albondón (Granada province); Laujar de Andarax (Almería province); and Villaviciosa (Córdoba province).

Wine not only accompanies meals but is also a popular bar drink – and it's cheap: a bottle costing €5 in a supermarket or €12 in a restaurant will be a decent wine. *Vino de mesa* (table wine) may cost less than €1.50 a litre in shops. You can order wine by the *copa* (glass) in bars and restaurants: the *vino de la casa* (house wine) may come from a barrel for about €1.

SHERRY

Sherry, Andalucía's celebrated fortified wine, is produced in the towns of Jerez de la Frontera, El Puerto de Santa María and Sanlúcar de Barrameda, which make up the 'sherry triangle' of Cádiz province (see p119). A combination of climate, chalky soils that soak up the sun but retain moisture, and a special maturing process called the *solera* process (see the boxed text, p120) produces these unique wines.

The main distinction in sherry is between *fino* (dry and straw-coloured) and *oloroso* (sweet and dark, with a strong bouquet). An *amontillado* is an amber, moderately dry *fino* with a nutty flavour and a higher alcohol content. An *oloroso* combined with a sweet wine results in a cream sherry. A manzanilla – officially not sherry – is a chamomile-coloured, unfortified *fino* produced in Sanlúcar de Barrameda; its delicate flavour is reckoned to come from sea breezes wafting into the bodegas (wineries).

BEER

The most common ways to order a *cerveza* (beer) is to ask for a *caña* (a small draught beer; 250mL), or a *tubo* (a larger draught beer; about 300mL), which come in a straight glass. If you just ask for a *cerveza* you may get bottled beer, which tends to be more expensive. A small bottle (250mL) is called a *botellín* or a *quinto;* a bigger one (330mL) is a *tercio*. San Miguel, Cruzcampo and Victoria are all decent Andalusian beers.

COFFEE

In Andalucía the coffee is good and strong. A *café con leche* is half-milk, half-coffee (something like cafe latte), a *cortado* is espresso with a dribble of milk (like an Italian macchiato), and *solo* is a straight, black espresso. Ask for a *grande* or *doble* if you want a large cup (*pequeño* for small), *en vaso* if you want it in a glass and *sombra* or *manchado* if you want lots of milk.

BACKGROUND

HOT CHOCOLATE (& CHURROS!)

Spaniards brought chocolate back from Mexico in the mid-16th century and adopted it enthusiastically. OK, so it's not the world's healthiest, but there are few sweeter pleasures in life than a breakfast of fresh *churros* (coils of deep-fried doughnuts) dunked into thick, creamy *chocolate hecho* (hot chocolate) that you could stand your spoon up in. *Churros* are a Spanish institution and every town and village in Andalucía has a *churros* stand.

FOOD & DRINK GLOSSARY

· · · · · · ·

THE BASICS

arroz a·*ros* rice

bocadillo bo·ka·*dee*·yo filled roll

bollo *bo*·yo small soft roll; also *mollete*

gazpacho gas·*pa*·cho chilled soup of blended tomatoes, peppers, cucumber, garlic, breadcrumbs, oil and vinegar

huevo *we*·vo egg

huevos revueltos *we*·vos re·*vwel*·tos scrambled eggs

media ración *me*·dya ra·*syon* half a *ración*

menú del día me·*noo* del *dee*·a daily set lunch menu, usually Monday to Friday

mesa *me*·sa table

mollete mo·*ye*·te small soft roll; also *bollo*

montadito mon·ta·*dee*·to open sandwich

paella pa·e·ya rice dish with shellfish, chicken and vegetables

pan pan bread

plato combinado *pla*·to kom·bee·*na*·do 'combined plate'; seafood, omelette, meat with trimmings

queso *ke*·so cheese

ración ra·*syon* meal-sized serving of tapas

rosquilla ros·*kee*·ya toasted roll

tapas *ta*·pas light snacks, usually eaten with drinks

tortilla tor·*tee*·ya omelette

tostada tos·*ta*·da toasted bread often served with a variety of toppings such as tomatoes and olive oil

CARNE (MEAT)

cabra *ka*·bra goat

cabrito ka·*bree*·to kid; also *choto*

carne de monte *kar*·ne de *mon*·te 'meat of the mountain'; local game

carne de vaca *kar*·ne de *va*·ka beef

caza *ka*·sa game

charcutería char·koo·te·*ree*·a cured meat

chorizo cho·*ree*·so spicy pork sausage

choto *cho*·to kid; also *cabrito*

codorniz ko·dor·*nees* quail

conejo ko·*ne*·kho rabbit

cordero kor·*de*·ro lamb

hígado ee·ga·do liver

jamón kha·*mon* ham

jamón ibérico kha·*mon* ee·be·*ree*·ko ham from the black Iberian breed of pig

jamón ibérico de bellota kha·*mon* ee·*be*·*ree*·ko de be·*jo*·ta ham from Iberian pigs fed on acorns

jamón serrano kha·*mon* se·*ra*·no mountain-cured ham

jamón York kha·*mon* york uncured ham

liebre *lye*·bre hare

pato *pa*·to duck

pavo *pa*·vo turkey

pollo *po*·yo chicken

riñón/riñones ree·*nyon*/ ree·*nyo*·nes kidney/kidneys

solomillo so·lo·*mee*·yo sirloin; quality fillet of beef or pork

ternera ter·*ne*·ra veal

FRUTAS & VERDURAS (FRUIT & VEGETABLES)

aceituna a·say·*too*·na olive

aguacate a·gwa·*ka*·te avocado

ajo *a*·kho garlic

alcachofa al·ka·*cho*·fa artichoke

apio *a*·pyo celery

berenjena be·ren·*khe*·na aubergine/eggplant

calabacín ka·la·ba·*seen* courgette/zucchini

calabaza ka·la·*ba*·sa pumpkin

cebolla se·*bo*·ya onion

cereza se·*re*·sa cherry

frambuesa fram·*bwe*·sa raspberry

fresa *fre*·sa strawberry

lima *lee*·ma lime

limón lee·*mon* lemon

manzana man·*sa*·na apple

manzanilla man·sa·*nee*·ya camomile

melocotón me·lo·ko·*ton* peach
naranja na·*ran*·kha orange
piña *pee*·nya pineapple
plátano *pla*·ta·no banana
sandía san·*dee*·a watermelon
uva *oo*·va grape

PESCADOS & MARISCOS (FISH & SEAFOOD)

almeja al·*me*·kha clam
anchoa an·*cho*·a anchovy; also *boquerón*
atún a·*toon* tuna
bacalao ba·ka·*low* cod
bogavante bo·ga·*van*·te lobster; also *langosta*
boquerón bo·ke·*ron* anchovy; also *anchoa*
caballa ka·*ba*·ya mackerel
cangrejo kan·*gre*·kho crab
chipirón/chipirones chee·pee·*ron*/ chee·pee·*ro*·nes baby squid; also *chopito*
chopito cho·*pee*·to baby squid; also *chipirón*
gamba *gam*·ba prawn
langosta lan·*gos*·ta lobster; also *bogavante*
langostino lan·gos·*tee*·no king prawn
mejillón/mejillones me·khee·*yon*/me·khee·*yo*·nes mussel/mussels
merluza mer·*loo*·sa hake
ostra *os*·tra oyster
sardine sar·*dee*·na sardine
trucha *troo*·cha trout

TORTAS & POSTRES (CAKES & DESSERTS)

arroz con leche a·ros kon *le*·che rice pudding
churro *choo*·ro long thin doughnut with sugar
flan flan crème caramel
helado e·*la*·do ice cream
pastel pas·*tel* pastry or cake
torta *tor*·ta pie or tart
turrón too·*ron* nougat

TÉCNICAS (COOKING TECHNIQUES)

a la brasa a la *bra*·sa grilled or barbecued
a la parrilla a la pa·*ree*·ya grilled or barbecued

a la plancha a la *plan*·cha grilled on a hotplate
ahumado/a a·oo·*ma*·do/a smoked
al carbon al kar·*bon* chargrilled
asado/a a·*sa*·do/a roast
cocido/a ko·*see*·do/a cooked or boiled; *cocido* also means 'hotpot/stew'
crudo/a *croo*·do/a raw
frito/a *free*·to/a fried
guiso *gee*·so stew
rebozado/a re·bo·*sa*·do/a battered and fried
relleno/a re·*je*·no/a stuffed
salado/a sa·*la*·do/a salted, salty
seco/a *se*·ko/a dry, dried

NONALCOHOLIC DRINKS

agua de grifo *a*·gwa de *gree*·fo tap water
agua mineral *a*·gwa mee·ne·*ral* bottled water
agua potable *a*·gwa po·*ta*·ble drinking water
café con leche ka·*fe* kon *le*·che 50% coffee, 50% hot milk
café cortado ka·*fe* kor·*ta*·do short black with a dash of milk
café solo ka·*fe* so·lo short black
chocolate hecho cho·ko·*la*·te *he*·cho hot chocolate
con gas kon gas fizzy (bottled water)
refresco re·*fres*·ko soft drink
sin gas seen gas still (bottled water)
té te tea
zumo *soo*·mo fruit juice

CERVEZA (BEER)

botellín bo·te·*yin* bottled beer (250mL); also *quinto*
caña *ka*·nya draught beer (250mL) served in a small, wide glass
quinto *keen*·to bottled beer (250mL); also *botellín*
tercio *ter*·syo bottled beer (330mL)
tubo *too*·bo draught beer (300mL) served in a straight glass

VINO (WINE)

vino blanco *vee*·no *blan*·ko white wine
vino de la casa *vee*·no de la *ka*·sa house wine
vino de la mesa *vee*·no de la *me*·sa table wine

vino rosado *vee*·no ro·*sa*·do rosé wine
vino tinto *vee*·no *teen*·to red wine

OTHER ALCOHOLIC DRINKS

aguardiente a·gwar·*dyen*·te grape-based spirit
(similar to grappa)
anis a·*nees* aniseed liqueur
coñac *ko*·nyak brandy
sangria san·*gree*·a wine and fruit punch

ACCOMMODATION

FINDING ACCOMMODATION

Where you sleep in Andalucía is as much a part of the experience as the region's many outstanding sights, restaurants and cultural attractions. Hotel conversions – of palaces, mansions, former townhouses and just about any historically significant building – are a speciality of the region. The midrange and top-end categories include many places whose charming design or architecture (from ancient palaces to hip, minimalist boutique hotels), or their spectacular location, add greatly to their attractions, but there are also some outstanding, usually more intimate choices in the budget category. The greatest range of places are usually in larger cities, especially in Seville, Córdoba and Granada, but you'll find gems dotted across the region, sometimes even in the smallest villages.

While most places go by the name of hotel, you'll also see a range of other places, ranging from *pensión* and *hostal* (a cross between a hostel and a small guest house) in the budget category to *posada* or *hospedería* (both of which lit-erally mean an inn) for more upmarket conversions.

Remember that most hotels in Spain will only keep your booking until 6pm on your planned day of arrival – if you plan on arriving later, ring ahead to confirm that you still want the room. If you arrive before 2pm, your room may not be ready, but most places will allow you to leave your bags. Checkout time is nearly always noon.

PRICES & BOOKING

Prices for accommodation quoted in this book are intended as a guide only.

BOOK YOUR STAY ONLINE

For more accommodation reviews and recommendations by Lonely Planet authors, check out the online booking service at www.lonelyplanet.com/hotels. You'll find the true, insider low-down on the best places to stay. Reviews are thorough and independent. Best of all, you can book online.

PRICE GUIDE

The following is a guide to the pricing system used in this chapter. Unless stated otherwise, prices stated are for a double room with private bathroom.

€	up to €65
€€	€65 to €120
€€€	€120-plus

Accommodation rates fluctuate wildly depending on the season – *temporada alta* (high season), *temporada media* (shoulder season) and *temporada baja* (low season). Prices along the coast soar along with the temperatures in summer, but can drop by up to 50% during the winter months, while prices are at their highest anywhere whenever a festival or other major event occurs.

On the coast, July and August is the typical high season; inland, it's more likely to be May, June and September, when temperatures are more pleasant. Major events such as Semana Santa (Easter) can see prices spiral upwards as availability travels in the reverse direction. If you plan to stay in a town during such a period, ensure that you make reservations weeks, if not months, in advance. Accommodation prices given in this book are high-season prices unless stated otherwise – so you can expect some pleasant surprises at other times. See p10 for more information on the timing of festivals; see also the Festivals and Events section for towns in the regional chapters of this book.

SEVILLA PROVINCE

SEVILLE

The attractive Barrio de Santa Cruz, which is close to the cathedral and Alcázar, has many places to stay in all price brackets. So do El Arenal (west of Santa Cruz towards the river) and El Centro (the true city centre north of Santa Cruz).

Room rates reflect each establishment's high season – typically (but not strictly) from about March to June and again in September and October – and most rates don't include breakfast. Prices go down by at least 20% per room in low season. On the other hand, just about every room in Seville costs extra during Semana Santa and the Feria de Abril. The typical increase is between 30% and 60% over normal high-season rates, but a few places even double their prices. Some hotels extend this *temporada extra* (extra-high season) for a whole month from the start of Semana Santa to the end of the *feria*. It's vital to book ahead for rooms in Seville at almost any time of the year; during the *temporada extra* you'd better make your reservation several months in advance!

BARRIO DE SANTA CRUZ, ALCÁZAR & CATHEDRAL

♥ HOTEL AMADEUS €€

Map p42; ☎ 954 50 14 43; www.hotelamadeussevilla .com; Calle Farnesio 6; s/d €82/92; ℗ ⊠ ⊜
An entrepreneurial musician family has converted its 18th-century mansion into a unique hotel and named each of the 14 elegant, fabulously designed rooms after a different composer. If you want to practise piano or violin, there are instruments on the premises and a couple of soundproof rehearsal rooms. Avoid the ground-floor rooms which are a bit disappointing, and had an insect problem when we last stayed.

♥ HOTEL DOÑA MANUELA €€

Map p42; ☎ 954 54 64 00; www.hoteldmanuela.com; Paseo Catalina de Ribera 2; s/d €69/104; ⊠ ⊜

The spacious rooms here don't have a huge amount of character; it's essentially a business hotel with some extra flourishes, such as ornate, flower-bedecked bedheads and seemingly almost-genuine Roman statues. However, that doesn't detract from the fact that it's superb value, professionally run and brilliantly located opposite the Jardines de Murillo (and near a car park and main road making it perfect for drivers). Those weighed down under mountains of baggage will appreciate the hotel lift.

♥ HOTEL PUERTA DE SEVILLA €€

Map p42; ☎ 954 98 72 70; www.hotelpuertadesevilla .com; Calle Puerta de la Carne 2; s/d €69/95; ℗ ✷ ⚡

This superfriendly – and super-positioned – hotel is a great mix of the chintz and the stylish. There's an indoor water feature in the lobby lined with superb Seville tile work. The rooms are all flower-pattern textiles, wrought-iron beds and pastel wallpaper. It also features an unbeatable people-watching rooftop terrace.

♥ PENSIÓN DOÑA TRINIDAD €

Map p42; ☎ 954 54 19 06; www.donatrinidad.com; Calle Archeros 7; s/d from €30/55

A recently renovated *pensión* (guest house) run by an elderly, but young-at-heart couple who love to chitter-chatter (show us a Spaniard who doesn't?) with anyone in range. They've managed to put together one of the best cheapies in Seville. The shiny rooms surround a plant-filled, traditionally tiled courtyard.

♥ UN PATIO EN SANTA CRUZ €€

Map p42; ☎ 954 53 94 13; www.patiosantacruz.com; Calle Doncellas 15; s/d €58/68; ✷ ⚡

Feeling more like an art gallery than a hotel, with starched white walls coated in loud works of art, and strange sculptures

and preserved plants. The rooms are immensely comfortable, staff are friendly and there's a cool rooftop terrace with mosaic Moroccan tables. It's easily one of the hippest and best-value hotels in town.

EL ARENAL & TRIANA

♥ HOTEL PUERTA DE TRIANA €€

Map p48; ☎ 954 21 54 04; www.confortelhoteles.com; Calle Reyes Católicos 5; s/d €71/85; ✷ ⚡

The exterior of this hotel is all old-fashioned Andalusian style, but what you see isn't what you get and the interior – with small, minimalist and fully colour-coordinated, tech-crammed rooms – has been fully revamped to feel more like a cool, cutting-edge Tokyo hotel.

EL CENTRO

♥ HOTEL ALMÍNAR €€€

Map p51; ☎ 954 29 39 13; www.hotelalminar.com; Calle Álvarez Quintero 52; s/d €95/125; ✷ ⚡

Disguised inside a dusky yellow town house is this slick and stylish hotel. The blinding white rooms are bright and airy and full of technology, and the bathrooms have glass sinks and giant showers. All up it feels a bit like one of those swish New York apartments you see on glamorous TV shows. It's currently leading the crop as the most popular hotel in Seville.

♥ PATIO AL SUR €€

Map p51; ☎ 954 22 10 35; www.patioalsur.es; Calle Fernán Caballero 7; s/d €58/68; ✷ ⚡

This spanking new hotel is a pleasing clash of crazy-coloured paintings, a riot of plant life, and ancient inscriptions carved into stone. The rooms are simple but feel very exclusive and arty. The bright pink bougainvilleas surrounding the entrance seem to be in competition to try to out pink the pink building that contains the hotel.

ACCOMMODATION

ALAMEDA DE HÉRCULES, MACARENA & ISLA DE LA CARTUJA

☙ HOSTAL DOÑA FELI €

Map p54; ☎ 954 90 10 48; www.hostaldfeli.com; Calle Jesús del Gran Poder 130; s/d €35/45; ⊠

If you're looking for somewhere smart and with real Spanish character close to the nightlife of the Alameda then you can't do much better than this spotless, well-run *pensión* with rooms piled around a plant-crammed courtyard. Some of the rooms have baths as well as showers.

☙ HOTEL SACRISTÍA SANTA ANA €€

Map p54; ☎ 954 91 57 22, www.hotelsacristia.com; Alameda de Hércules 22; d from €79; ⊠ ☎

This newly opened and utterly delightful hotel is the best deal in Seville. The setting on the Alameda is great for the neighbouring bars and restaurants and the hotel itself is a heavenly place with a small fountain surrounded by bonsai trees greeting you in the central courtyard. Away from this spin old-fashioned rooms with big arty bedheads, circular baths and cascading showers. Service is equally excellent.

☙ PATIO DE LA CARTUJA €€

Map p54; ☎ 954 90 02 00; www.patiodelacartuja.com; Calle Lumbreras 8-10; s/d €80/112; Ⓟ ⊠

Perfect for those wanting to self-cater, this is an apartment hotel in a former *corral* – a three-storey patio community, filled with pink flowers and yellow canaries, that was once the typical form of *sevillano* lower-middle-class housing. Each of the 30 cosy apartments has a double bedroom, kitchen and sitting room with double sofa bed.

AROUND SEVILLE

At the places listed for Carmona, expect to pay up to 50% more during Semana Santa and Seville's Feria de Abril, and less in the low season (which includes July).

☙ CASA DE CARMONA // CARMONA €€€

Map p66; ☎ 954 14 41 51; www.casadecarmona.com; Plaza de Lasso 1; r incl breakfast from €160; Ⓟ ⊠ ☎ ⊠

This beautiful 16th-century palace once belonged to an aristocratic family and it feels as if they still live here: the rooms are furnished in an antique country-manor style, the wooden beds are laid with soft white-lace pillows, the bathrooms have old-fashioned taps and stand-alone baths. There isn't a lifeless room in the building.

☙ HOSPEDERÍA MARQUES DE LAS TORRES // CARMONA €

Map p66; ☎ 954 19 62 48; www.hospederiamarques delastorres.com; Calle Fermin Molpeceres 2; dm €23, s/d from €40/58; ☎ ⊠

A bizarre combination of dorm beds and hotel rooms in a converted *palacio*

ONLINE RESOURCES

Parador (www.parador.es) The best resource for Andalucía's converted castles, palaces and other distinguished buildings converted into hotels.

Rustic Blue (www.rusticblue.com) Good for holiday villas, especially for longer stays.

Turismo en Cazorla (www.turismoencazorla.com, in Spanish) Extensive listings for the Cazorla region.

Top Rural (www.toprural.com) At last count had some1281 listings of rural homes and hotels in Andalucía.

Rusticae (www.rusticae.es, in Spanish) Specialises in small hotels with charm.

Andalucía Te Quiere (www.andalucia.com) Andalucía's tourist office portal with good accommodation listings.

Acento Rural (www.acentorural.com) Another good site for generally classy rural accommodation.

ACCOMMODATION

(palace), with a fabulous turquoise pool that's a colour explosion between the surrounding terracotta walls. The dorms sleep two or four per cabin, with shared bathrooms. The cabins look a bit like train compartments and are separated by a fixed screen which doesn't go all the way up to the ceiling.

☙ POSADA SAN FERNANDO // CARMONA €€

Map p66; ☎ 954 14 14 08; www.posadasanfernando .com; Plaza de San Fernando 6; s/d €55/65; ☒ ☎

This is a fantastic-value new hotel situated on the liveliest square in the old town. All rooms differ from one another – some have romantic free-standing baths, others gushing showers built into the old stone walls. Where the rooms are all alike is in the copious amount of modern art gracing the walls, the flat-screen TVs and the old-fashioned geraniums on the tiny balconies.

☙ HOSTAL ESMERALDA // OSUNA €

☎ 955 82 10 73; www.hostal-esmeralda.com; Calle Tesorero 7; s/d €27/51; ☒ ☎

The faultless, family-run Esmeralda is about 200m south of Plaza Mayor. Rooms, with bath/shower combos, are sparkling and modelled along business-class lines. There's a cheerful downstairs bar and a pleasant covered patio. The owners are very traveller savvy and full of useful advice.

☙ LA CASONA DE CALDERÓN // OSUNA €€

☎ 954 81 50 37; www.casonacalderon.com; Plaza de Cervantes 16; s/d with breakfast €80/100; ☒ ☎

This beautiful little boutique hotel is inside an old palace with rose-red walls and antiques displayed in glass cabinets with explanatory labels so it all feels more like a museum than a hotel. The

rooms are colourful and have big, stone-walled walk-in showers. There's a sunny plaza with benches outside.

☙ HOSPEDERÍA DE LA CARTUJA // CAZALLA DE LA SIERRA €€

☎ 954 88 45 16; www.cartujadecazalla.com; s/d incl breakfast from €50/80; ℗ ☒ ☎

About that 'dream project' of yours – the one involving the old building on the continent that you renovate and live in happily ever after. Thirty-two years ago someone embarked on just such a project – only they took the 14th-century Cartuja de Cazalla monastery and converted it into quite a hotel. The cheaper rooms are nothing special, but the ones in former monks' cells simply smother you in history. Country-flavoured evening meals (residents only) cost €25.

☙ LAS NAVEZUELAS // CAZALLA DE LA SIERRA €

☎ 954 88 47 64; www.lasnavezuelas.com; s/d incl breakfast €51/62, 4-person cottage from €83; ☒ closed early Jan–late Feb; ℗ ☎

Everybody dreams of living in an old farmhouse in the southern sun and this 16th-century *cortijo* (country property) is exactly what that dream looks like. From the dusty, olive-tree-lined track that leads to it, to the vines clambering up your balcony this place is simply perfect. You could stay here for weeks lounging in the pool and exploring the sunburnt hills and never feel less than contented. It's signposted 2km south of Cazalla on the Seville road.

☙ PALACIO DE SAN BENITO // CAZALLA DE LA SIERRA €€€

☎ 954 88 33 36; www.palaciodesanbenito.es; Paseo El Moro; r with breakfast from €130; ℗ ☒ ☎ ☎

This luxurious hotel is completely overwhelming. It occupies what was once a

15th-century hermitage and pilgrims' hostel and still contains a Mudéjar church. The nine rooms are dripping in old-fashioned character and crammed with more antiques than many museums. There's a library that is dazzlingly ornate and then there's the pool, which is so extraordinary we actually had to enquire as to whether it was a pool or just a garden feature! Look online for occasional 40% discounts.

HUELVA PROVINCE

HUELVA

Huelva has a very limited range of accommodation and a lot of it caters for the business crowd.

♥ HOTEL FAMILIA CONDES €€

Map p80; ☎ 959 28 24 00; www.hotelfamiliacondes .com, in Spanish; Alameda Sundheim 14; s/d incl breakfast €55/67; ⓟ ⊠ 🛜

Alright, so it's located in a big tower block and lacks soul, but this laid-back business-class hotel is hard to beat in the value stakes. It's also very efficiently run, and the hotel's bright-orange rooms have plenty of space and gleaming bathrooms.

AROUND HUELVA

♥ HOTEL DOÑANA BLUES // MATALASCAÑAS €€

☎ 959 44 98 17; www.donanablues.com; Sector I, Parcela 129; s/d €84/120; ⊠ 🛜 🖾

With its sunny appearance and courtyard full of flowers the Doñana Blues won't give you the blues at all. Each room sports different art and furnishings but all have a terrace or balcony and there's a cool, blue pool. Seeing as it's the only place in town with any real character you'll need to book ahead. Rates come down about 30% outside of the high seasons.

♥ HOTEL EL PARAÍSO PLAYA // ISLA CRISTINA €€€

☎ 959 33 02 35; www.hotelparaisoplaya.com; Avenida de la Playa; s/d €65/129; ⓟ ⊠ 🛜 🖾

This friendly and attractively remodelled two-storey hotel, with restaurant and bar, is just a stone's throw from Playa Central. Prices here represent the best deal in town – especially outside peak season when prices drop substantially. The highlight is the pool, which is perfect for those without sea salt running through their veins.

♥ HOTEL PLAZA ESCRIBANO // MOGUER €

☎ 959 37 30 63; www.hotelplazaescribano.com; Plaza Escribano 5; s/d €40/55; ⊠ ⓟ 🛜

This new hotel is almost as good a reason for visiting Moguer as any of the town's tourist sights. The large rooms are painted in pastel shades and splashed in colour from the bright bedspreads. There's a small library for guest use, a sunny courtyard and lots of young and bright tile work.

EAST OF HUELVA

Accommodation during the Romería is often booked at least a year in advance, at sky-high prices, so be sure to book – or be prepared to sleep in the back of your car!

♥ EL CORTIJO DE LOS MIMBRALES // EL ROCÍO €€€

☎ 959 42 22 37; www.cortijomimbrales.com; Carretera A483 Km30; r with breakfast from €165; ⓟ ⊠ 🛜 🖾

This magnificent hotel is an Arabian fantasy brought to life in sunny Spain. The sublime rooms are virtual museums – just check out those doors – with real antique Moroccan masterpieces. The perfume of flowers wafts on the breeze and everywhere are little Moorish fountains and tile-lined streams that lead, after much meandering, to a stunning pool. Want to live like a princess? This is the place to do it.

❦ HOTEL LA MALVASÍA // EL ROCÍO €€

☎ 959 44 38 70; www.lamalvasiahotel.com; Calle Sanlúcar 38; s/d incl breakfast €75/105; Ⓟ ⊠ ⊚ �ⓓ
Overlooking the marshes, this idyllic hotel is located inside a truly magisterial building. The rooms are crushed with character including wobbly tiled floors, old B&W photos of the town and iron bedheads in floral designs. Try to snag one of the top-floor rooms from where you'll have a bird's-eye view of the birds.

❦ HOTEL TORUÑO // EL ROCÍO €€

☎ 959 44 23 23; www.toruno.es, in Spanish; Plaza Acebuchal 22; s/d incl breakfast €57/81; Ⓟ ⊠ ⊚
At this elegant 18th-century villa overlooking the *marismas* (wetlands), you can lie in bed in the morning looking out the big windows and watch the flamingos run through their morning beauty routine. Inside the hotel the ornithological theme continues with tile murals of the local bird life plastered on the walls. The rooms are spacious and supremely comfortable.

NORTH OF HUELVA

❦ LA CASA NOBLE // ARACENA €€€

Map p99; ☎ 959 12 77 78; www.lacasanoble.net; Calle Campito 35; s/d incl breakfast from €165/185; ⊠ ⊚
Merely describing this as a boutique hotel does it an enormous disservice. It's actually a divine palace to luxury and is filled with antiques, over-the-top tile work and beds so thick and bouncy they look like something from *The Princess and the Pea*. The dining room just has to be seen to be believed!

❦ MOLINO DEL BOMBO // ARACENA €

Map p99; ☎ 959 12 84 78; www.molinodelbombo .com, in Spanish; Calle Ancha 4; s/d €30/60; ⊠ ⊚
This welcoming hotel, with a tastefully rustic yet very comfortable style, stands near the top of the town. With attractive indoor and outdoor sitting areas and good bright rooms making use of little frescoes and exposed stone and brick work as design features, it's a great find. The only possible downside is that the walls are a bit thin.

❦ POSADA DEL CASTAÑO // CASTAÑO DEL ROBLEDO €

☎ 959 46 55 02; www.posadadelcastano.com; Calle José Sánchez Calvo 33; s/d with breakfast €40/50
This character-filled converted old village house, with its bendy roof beams that smell of the forest, has walkers foremost in mind and the young British owners (experienced travellers and hikers) are full of information and tips. They offer self-guided walking and horse-riding holidays (see website).

❦ HOTEL LA CRUZ // ALMONASTER LA REAL €

☎ 959 14 31 35; Plaza del Llano 8; s/d €26.30/33;
There might be fancier places to stay in the sierra but none come with the genuine time-warp feel of this place. The rooms are bare-bones basic indeed and the bathrooms rather cramped, but the elderly couple who run it will make sure you have a pleasant stay.

❦ MOLINO RÍO ALÁJAR // ALÁJAR €€€

☎ 959 50 12 82; www.molinorioalajar.com; Finca Cabezo del Molino s/n; d cottage for weekend from €225
Beautifully located beside a stream at the bottom of a hidden valley, the modern stone cottages here are made, success-

fully, to look like old farmhouses and are surrounded by big gardens with tennis courts and a pool. Kids will love all the farm animals. Two-night minimum.

CÁDIZ PROVINCE

CÁDIZ

☙ HOTEL ARGANTONIO €€

☎ 956 21 16 40; www.hotelargantonio.com, in Spanish; Calle Argantonio 3; s incl breakfast €58-86, d €80-107, ste €150-190; ⧯ ▣

This is our favourite hotel in Cádiz thanks to a sense of discreet charm and tasteful Mudéjar decor in the public areas. In some rooms the Mudéjar effect is understated, in others it's more obvious, but the sense of style is universal.

THE SHERRY TRIANGLE

☙ CASA NO 6 // EL PUERTO DE SANTA MARÍA €€

☎ 956 87 70 84; www.casano6.com; Calle San Bartolomé 14; s/d/q/apt incl breakfast €60/70/130/140; ℗

This place harks back to the understated elegance of 19th-century Andalucía, with its cool but light-filled pillared courtyard and individually styled rooms with wooden beams, high ceilings and comfy beds. Anna and Penny, the Spanish-English owners, are welcoming hosts and the buffet breakfast is another highlight.

☙ EL BAOBAB HOSTEL // EL PUERTO DE SANTA MARÍA €

☎ 956 54 21 23; www.casabaobab.es; Calle Pagador 37; s/d/tr incl breakfast from €20/40/60; ⧯ ▣ ♿

Just across from the Plaza de Toros in a converted 19th-century building, this small, six-room hostel is the best budget choice in El Puerto with a homely friendly feel. The interior renovations are tastefully done and the shared bathrooms are spotless.

☙ HOTEL DUQUES DE MEDINACELI // EL PUERTO DE SANTA MARÍA €€€

☎ 956 86 07 77; www.hotelesjale.com; Plaza de los Jazmines 2; s/d €179/218; ℗ ⧯ ▣ ▨

This is El Puerto's premier address. Converted from an 18th-century mansion (it's the former home of the Terry Irish sherry family), this place overflows with antiques and extravagant architectural signposts to the past, not to mention expansive manicured gardens. The 28 gorgeous rooms are equipped with every comfort, including four-poster beds in some.

☙ HOSPEDERÍA DUQUES DE MEDINA SIDONIA // SANLÚCAR DE BARRAMEDA €€

☎ 956 36 01 61; www.ruralduquesmedinasidonia.com; Plaza Condes de Niebla 1; d incl breakfast €70-120; ℗ ⧯

Baronial top-end luxury and town views dominate this aristocratic palace in the upper part of the old town. Old-world Spain unfolds before your eyes: the place has 800 years of history and is brimming with swish furnishings and decorations.

☙ HOTEL POSADA DEL PALACIO // SANLÚCAR DE BARRAMEDA €€

☎ 956 36 48 40; www.posadadepalacio.com; Calle Caballeros 11; s €72-125, d €88-157; ℗ ⧯

Plant-filled patios, gracious historical charm and 18th-century luxury add up to one of the best places to stay in this part of Andalucía. There's antique furniture, but it's rarely overdone and never weighs heavily on the surrounds thanks to the high ceilings and abundance of light.

☙ HOTEL CASA GRANDE // JEREZ DE LA FRONTERA €€

☎ 956 34 50 70; www.casagrande.com.es; Plaza de las Angustias 3; s & d €85-105, ste €115-125; ℗ ⧯ ▣ ♿

This brilliant hotel occupies a carefully restored 1920s mansion. Rooms are spread over three floors and set around a patio, or beside the roof terrace, which has views of Jerez's roof line. All is overseen by the congenial Monika Schroeder, a mine of information about Jerez.

❤ HOTEL CHANCILLERIA // JEREZ DE LA FRONTERA €€

☎ 956 30 10 38; www.hotelchancilleria.com; Calle Chancilleria 21; s €70-90, d €90-130; 🔀 🖵

Opened in January 2008, this stunning renovation of two 17th-century homes is a discreet temple to good taste. There are many highlights: African art, an original 17th-century wall, a lovely garden, stylish and spacious rooms, a delightful roof terrace and one of Jerez's best restaurants, Sabores.

ARCOS & THE SIERRA DE GRAZALEMA

❤ CASA CAMPANA // ARCOS DE LA FRONTERA €

☎ 956 70 47 87; www.casacampana.com; Calle Núñez de Prado 4; d/apt €50/65; 🔀 🖵

In the heart of old Arcos, and run by the superfriendly Emma and Jim who are extremely knowledgeable about the local area, Casa Campana has two simple doubles and a massive apartment that's filled with character. The quiet roof terrace is a fine place to relax with good rooftop views and a real sense of privacy.

❤ LA CASA GRANDE // ARCOS DE LA FRONTERA €€

☎ 956 70 39 30; www.lacasagrande.net; Calle Maldonado 10; s €59-84, d €70-110, ste €91-140; 🕲 closed 7 Jan-6 Feb; 🔀

A gorgeous, rambling, cliffside mansion that dates back to 1729, La Casa Grande once belonged to the great flamenco dancer Antonio Ruiz Soler. With each of the seven rooms done in different but always tasteful styles, it feels more like a

home-cum-artists' retreat than a hotel. Great breakfasts, a good library, terrific rooftop terrace, massage and yoga round out an outstanding package.

❤ PARADOR CASA DEL CORREGIDOR // ARCOS DE LA FRONTERA €€€

☎ 956 70 05 00; www.parador.es, in Spanish; Plaza del Cabildo; d €155; 🔀 🖵

This rebuilt 16th-century magistrate's residence combines typical parador luxury with another magnificent cliffside setting. Eight of the 24 rooms have balconies with sweeping cliff-top views. Otherwise, most of the rest of the rooms look out onto the pretty Plaza del Cabildo.

❤ LA MEJORANA // GRAZALEMA €

☎ 956 13 23 27, 649 61 32 72; www.lamejorana .net; Calle Santa Clara 6; d incl breakfast per day/week €52/312; 🕲

A lovely house towards the upper end of Grazalema village, hospitable La Mejorana has lovely rooms, some with beautiful wrought-iron bedsteads, plus a large lounge and kitchen, all in fetching country styles – and a leafy garden that even manages to fit in a pool.

COSTA DE LA LUZ & THE SOUTHEAST

❤ HOTEL LA CASA DEL CALIFA // VEJER DE LA FRONTERA €€

☎ 956 44 77 30; www.lacasadelcalifa.com; Plaza de España 16; s €56-82, d €64-122, ste €123-170; 🔀

This fantastic place fronting Plaza de España rambles over several floors of what were previously five houses. Twisting corridors and little staircases lead to peaceful, comfortable rooms, each with individual proportions and decor, though an Islamic theme and whitewashed walls predominate.

❤ HOTEL V // VEJER DE LA FRONTERA €€€

☎ 956 45 17 57; www.hotelv-vejer.com; Calle Rosario 11-13; d €215-315; ▨ ▣

From top to bottom, this place is something special. Opened in early 2008 after a painstaking three-year restoration of a 17th-century Vejer house, Hotel V is the last word in style and luxury. The spacious rooms are simply gorgeous with designer fittings, while the two roof terraces (one with a jacuzzi and lounge chairs in a foot pool) have Jerez's best views. There's also a small ayurvedic massage centre in the evocative Islamic-era cisterns, reached via a 6m spiral glass staircase.

❤ CASAS KAREN // LOS CAÑOS DE MECA €€

☎ 956 43 70 67, last-min bookings 649 78 08 34; www.casaskaren.com; Camino del Monte 6; q €90-155, 2-person traditional hut per night €45-130, 2-person traditional hut per week €515; ℗

This eccentric, laid-back gem is owned by warm, vibrant Karen Abrahams, who settled here around 20 years ago. Her large, pretty, mimosa-covered plot has numerous eclectic buildings, all with kitchen, bathroom, lounge and outdoor sitting areas: they range from a converted farmhouse to exotic, thatched *chozas* (traditional huts) built of local materials. Decor is casual Andalusian-Moroccan with a sensitive use of colour.

❤ HOSTAL AFRICA // TARIFA €€

☎ 956 68 02 20; hostal_africa@hotmail.com; Calle María Antonia Toledo 12; s/d €50/65, with shared bathroom €35/50

This revamped 19th-century house close to the Puerta de Jerez is one of the best *hostales* along the coast. The owners are hospitable and the rooms sparkle with bright and attractive colours and plenty

of space. There's a lovely, expansive roof terrace with an exotic cabana and views of Africa.

❤ LA ESTRELLA DE TARIFA // TARIFA €

☎ 956 68 19 85; www.laestrelladetarifa.com; Calle San Rosendo 2; d €47-75; ▣

One of the newest places in Tarifa's old town, the Star of Tarifa is a great combination of price and quality. The rooms are decked out with strategically placed Islamic decoration and arched window alcoves in soft Moroccan blue in some rooms. It tends more towards intimate than luxurious and is on one of the old town's quieter streets.

❤ MISIANA // TARIFA €€€

☎ 956 62 70 83; www.misiana.com; Calle Sancho IV El Bravo; s/d/ste incl breakfast €115/135/250; ▣

Don't be put off by the bland exterior: this is one of the funkiest places in Tarifa. The rooms – all spacious and filled with light – are designer modern with each floor following a different colour scheme. The gorgeous 5th-floor suite has its own private lift, a massive terrace and stunning views. Prices drop considerably outside the summer months.

❤ POSADA LA SACRISTÍA // TARIFA €€

☎ 956 68 17 59; www.lasacristia.net; Calle San Donato 8; d incl breakfast €115-135

Tarifa's most elegant boutique accommodation is in a beautifully renovated 17th-century town house. Attention to detail is impeccable with 10 stylish rooms, tasteful colour schemes, large comfortable beds and rooms on several levels around a central courtyard. Best of all, it maintains the same prices year-round. Its restaurant is similarly excellent.

☙ POSADA VAGAMUNDOS // TARIFA €€

☎ 956 68 13 13; www.posadavagamundos.com; Calle San Francisco 18; s incl breakfast €50-105, d incl breakfast €65-105; 🖳

On a lovely narrow street in Tarifa's old town, Posada Vagamundos has attractive rooms with wooden beams and some have mosaic-tiled floors, with hints of the building's 16th-century origins alongside furniture and decorations from Morocco, Indonesia and Mexico.

MÁLAGA PROVINCE

MÁLAGA

There are some new options on the Málaga accommodation scene but little of interest in the lower price range. Most top-end places usually have offers of some sort; many also have considerably cheaper weekend rates.

☙ AC MÁLAGA PALACIO €€€

Map p165; ☎ 952 21 51 85; www.ac-hotels.com; Calle Cortina del Muelle 1; d €140-400; 🅿 🗱 🖳

This 15-storey, sleek hotel has sensational views over the busy seafront. Smart, modern design and excellent facilities also make it the best of Málaga's luxury options. It has a rooftop pool and fully fitted-out gym.

☙ EL RIAD ANDALUZ €€

Map p162 ☎ 952 21 36 40; www.elriadandaluz.com; Calle Hinestrosa 24; s/d €55/70; 🗱

A characterful, slightly exotic place to stay in Málaga. This French-run guest house, near the Teatro Cervantes, has eight rooms set around the kind of atmospheric patio that's known as a *riad* in Morocco. The decoration is Moroccan but each room is different, including colourful tiled bathrooms. Breakfast is available.

☙ HOSTAL LARIOS €

Map p165; ☎ 952 22 54 90; www.hostallarios.com; Calle Marqués de Larios 9; s/d €50/60, with shared bathroom €41/51; 🗱

This central *hostal* outclasses all others in the lower price range. The 12 rooms are newly fitted out and sport cheerful apricot and blue paintwork. Only four rooms have private bathroom, and these rooms have windows onto the main street.

☙ HOTEL CORTIJO LA REINA €€€

☎ 951 01 40 00; www.hotelcortijolareina.com; Carretera Málaga-Colmenar; s/d €116/150; 🅿 🗱 🖳 ♿

This Andalusian-style *cortijo* is 30 minutes' drive north of Málaga. At 800m it enjoys beautiful views over the valleys, and rooms are sumptuously decorated with four-poster beds and lots of swishy fabrics. A great base for exploring the Parque Natural Montes de Málaga.

☙ PARADOR MÁLAGA GIBRALFARO €€€

Map p162; ☎ 952 22 19 02; www.parador.es, in Spanish; Castillo de Gibralfaro; s/d from €130/170; 🅿 🗱 🖳

With an unbeatable location perched on the pine-forested Gibralfaro, Málaga's stone-built Parador is a real winner. Most rooms have spectacular views from their terraces, and you can dine at the excellent terrace restaurant even if you are not a guest at the hotel.

COSTA DEL SOL

☙ CASA EL ESCUDO DE MIJAS // MIJAS €€

☎ 952 59 11 00; www.el-escudo.com; Calle Trocha de los Pescadores 7; s/d €70/80

A tidy midrange option with pretty colour washes, wrought-iron furnishings and tiled bathrooms.

❤ TRH MIJAS/HOTEL MIJAS // MIJAS €€€

☎ 952 48 58 00; www.trhhoteles.com; Plaza de la Constitución; s/d €102/125; P ⚡ ⚑

This sumptuous, Andalusian-style hotel has excellent facilities including horse riding, tennis and hydromassage.

THE INTERIOR

Ronda has some of the best character-filled and top-value accommodation in Málaga province. Accommodation can be tight, even on weekends outside of the summer high season. In the first half of May and from July to September, you definitely need to book ahead. Antequera hotel prices are refreshingly moderate.

❤ ALAVERA DE LOS BAÑOS // RONDA €€

Map p176; ☎ 952 87 91 43; www.andalucia.com /alavera; Hoyo San Miguel s/n; s/d incl breakfast €70/95; ⚡ ⚑

Taking its cue from the Arab baths next door, the Alavera de los Baños continues the Hispano-Islamic theme throughout, with oriental decor and tasty North African–inspired cuisine (much of it excellent vegetarian food). Ask for a room on the terrace, as they open out onto a small, lush garden.

❤ ENFRENTE ARTE // RONDA €€

Map p176; ☎ 952 87 90 88; www.enfrentearte.com; Calle Real 40; r incl breakfast & drinks €75-90; ⚡ ⚐ ⚑

On an old cobblestoned street, Belgian-owned EnFrente offers a huge range of facilities and funky modern/oriental decor. It has a bar, pool, sauna, recreation room, flowery patio with black bamboo, film room and fantastic views out to the Sierra de las Nieves. What's more, the room price includes all drinks, to which you help yourself, and a sumptuous buffet breakfast, overseen by two cooks.

❤ HOTEL MONTELIRIO // RONDA €€€

Map p176; ☎ 952 87 38 55; www.hotelmontelirio.com; Calle Tenorio 8; s/d €100/150; ⚡ ⚑

Hugging El Tajo gorge, the new Montelirio has magical views. The converted *palacio* has been sensitively refurbished, with sumptuous suites. The lounge retains its gorgeous Mudéjar ceiling and opens out onto a terrace complete with plunge pool. There is also a fantastic restaurant.

❤ HOTEL POLO // RONDA €€

Map p176; ☎ 952 87 24 47; www.hotelpolo.net; Calle Mariano Soubirón 8; s/d incl breakfast €74/110; P ⚡ ⚐

This is a charming hotel in a graceful 19th-century building. Inside all is light and airy, with elegant, high-ceilinged rooms, many with balconied French windows, and attractively furnished communal areas, such as the colonial-style lounge. The parking is a bonus.

❤ HOTEL SAN GABRIEL // RONDA €€

Map p176; ☎ 952 19 03 92; www.hotelsangabriel.com; Calle José M Holgado 19; s/d €66/82; ⚡

This charming hotel is filled with antiques and photographs that offer insight into Ronda's history – bullfighting, celebrities and all. Ferns hang down the huge mahogany staircase, there is a billiard room, a cosy living room stacked with books and a super cinema with 10 velvet-covered seats rescued from Ronda's theatre.

❤ JARDÍN DE LA MURALLA // RONDA €€

Map p176; ☎ 952 87 27 64; www.jardindelmuralla .com; Calle Espiritu Santo 13; s/d incl breakfast €80/91; ⚡ ⚐ ⚑

This newish Ronda hotel has stepped gardens which merge into the country-side yet it is only five minutes' walk from the centre and is in a zone chock-full of historic buildings. Such is Ronda! Decor is elegant, olde-worlde with fancy mirrors and vases of fresh flowers.

♥ HOTEL COSO VIEJO // ANTEQUERA €€

☎ 952 70 50 45; Calle Encarnación 9; www.hotelcoso viejo.es; s/d incl breakfast €62/78; Ⓟ ⓧ

A converted 17th-century neoclassical palace right in the heart of Antequera, opposite Plaza Coso Viejo where the superb town museum is found. The comfortable and stylish rooms are set around a handsome patio with a fountain and there's a cafeteria and restaurant.

♥ LA POSADA DEL TORCAL // ANTEQUERA €€€

☎ 952 03 11 77; www.laposadadeltorcal.com; Villanueva de la Concepción; r €155; Ⓟ ⓧ ⓡ ⓖ

Outside Antequera, close to El Torcal, this fantastic hilltop *cortijo* is surrounded by wonderful panoramic views. It offers luxurious rooms and facilities including tennis courts, riding treks and a pool with a view.

♥ PARADOR DE ANTEQUERA // ANTEQUERA €€

☎ 952 84 02 61; www.parador.es, in Spanish; Paseo García del Olmo s/n; s/d €100/120; Ⓟ ⓧ ⓡ

The Parador is in a quiet area of parkland north of the bullring and near the bus station. It's comfortably furnished and set in pleasant gardens with wonderful views, especially at sunset.

♥ MOLINO DEL REY // SIERRA DE LAS NIEVES €€€€

☎ 952 48 00 09; www.molinodelrey.com; Valle de Jorox, Alozaina; 1-week course per person from €700; Ⓟ ⓡ

To tap into the new wave of spiritual tourism in beautiful surroundings, check into this extraordinary converted mill. London's popular Triyoga centre brings its groups for hatha and ashtanga yoga courses. The mill overlooks the sierra and features a yoga room, meditation caves and a vegetarian restaurant.

EAST OF MÁLAGA

Nerja has a huge range of accommodation, but for the summer period rooms

---

RONDA'S RURAL HOTELS

The beautiful countryside surrounding Ronda has attracted a large number of enterprising individuals who have converted traditional houses into gorgeous rural accommodation. If you have your own car it is most certainly worth staying in one of these *cortijos* (country properties) that often offer a host of extras such as guided walks and both traditional fare and haute cuisine. For information on rural accommodation, try Ronda's municipal tourist office, the regional website www.serraniaronda.org, or www.rusticblue.com.

First up, the *Condé Nast Traveller* favourite, **Hotel Fuente de la Higuera** (☎ 952 11 43 55; www.hotellafuente.com; Partido de los Frontones, Ronda; d/luxury ste €148/211; Ⓟ ⓧ ⓡ ⓖ), a chic colonial villa, with a contemporary interior, that overlooks vast olive groves.

For sheer indulgence, cosmopolitan atmosphere and out-of-this-world views, opt for **El Nobo** (☎ 952 15 13 03; www.elnobo.co.uk; Apartado 46, Gaucín; d from €120; Ⓟ ⓧ ⓡ) or **Hotel Casablanca** (☎ 952 15 10 19; fax 952 15 14 05; Calle Llana 12, Gaucín; r incl breakfast €140-200; ⓨ closed Nov-Mar; Ⓟ ⓧ ⓡ).

A truly gourmet indulgence can be found at the welcoming and convivial **La Almuña Cottage** (☎ 952 15 12 00; www.i-escape.com; Apartado 20, Gaucín; d €91, cottage for 4 per week €710; Ⓟ ⓧ ⓡ), which serves up local, homegrown produce (dinner €44).

in the better hotels tend to be booked at least two months in advance.

❧ EL MOLINO DE LOS ABUELOS // COMARES €

☎ 952 50 93 09; d incl breakfast from €55

Located on the main plaza beside the lookout, this converted olive mill has four double rooms and two apartments. All the rooms are filled with antiques and have gorgeous carved-wood beds. The apartments are perfect honeymoon material, with open fires and views across the valley. The restaurant terrace has fantastic views and good food.

❧ HOTEL CARABEO // NERJA €€

Map p192; ☎ 952 52 54 44; www.hotelcarabeo .com; Calle Carabeo 34; d/ste incl breakfast €85/180; P ⊠ ▯ ▣

Full of stylish antiques, this small, family-run, seafront hotel is set above manicured terraced gardens. There's also a good restaurant and the pool is on a terrace overlooking the sea.

CÓRDOBA PROVINCE

CÓRDOBA

The town centre has plenty of charming midrange and top-end options, many with simple, elegant style and spacious rooms, others laden with antiques and history. This is also heaven for a traveller on a budget. There are more *hostales* (budget hotels) and *pensiones* (guest houses) around the Mezquita area than you can shake a pillow at. Booking ahead during the main festivals is essential.

❧ CASA DE LOS AZULEJOS €€€

☎ 957 47 00 00; www.casadelosazulejos.com/marco .htm; Calle Fernando Colón 5; s/d €107/130; ⊠ ▯ ☞

Mexican and Andalusian styles meet in this gorgeously stylish hotel, where the patio is all banana trees, fluffy ferns and tall palm plants, bathed in sunlight. The colonial-style rooms have tall antique doors, massive beds, walls in lilac and sky blues, and wi-fi. The floors are covered in the beautiful old *azulejos* (tiles) that give the place its name.

❧ HOSTAL EL REPOSO DE BAGDAD €

☎ 957 20 28 54; http://hostalelreposodebagdad.com; Calle Fernández Ruano 11; s/d €40/60

Hidden away in a tiny street in the Judería, this place is excellent for anyone wanting a characterful place to stay at bargain prices. The house is over 200 years old, and the en suite rooms are simple with crisp, white linen. The (dark) ground-floor rooms have lovely Andalusian tiling.

❧ HOTEL GONZÁLEZ €€

☎ 957 47 98 19; hotelgonzalez@wanadoo.es; Calle Manriquez 3; d €66; ⊠

Located in a building that was once home to the son of Córdoba's favourite artist, Julio Romero de Torres, this hotel has rich baroque decor with plenty of gold flourishes, and numerous paintings. There are 16 large, lavishly decorated rooms and the hotel's restaurant serves meals on the pretty flower-filled patio. The friendly proprietors speak fluent English.

❧ HOTEL LOLA €€

☎ 957 20 03 05; www.hotelconencantolola.com; Calle Romero 3; d incl breakfast €120; ⊠

Individualism and quirky style are the prime ingredients here. Each room, named after an Arab princess, is decorated with large antique beds and covetable items that you just wish you could purchase as keepsakes and take home. What's more, you can eat your breakfast on the roof terrace overlooking the Mezquita bell tower.

❦ HOTEL MEZQUITA €€

☎ 957 47 55 85; www.hotelmezquita.com; Plaza Santa Catalina 1; s/d €52/101; ❄

One of the best value-for-money places in town, the Hotel Mezquita is right opposite the Mezquita itself. The 16th-century mansion has large, elegant rooms, marble floors, tall doors and small balconies; some rooms have views of the great mosque.

❦ PARADOR NACIONAL ARRUZAFA €€€

☎ 957 27 59 00; www.parador.es, in Spanish; Avenida de la Arruzafa s/n; d €180; Ⓟ ❄ ⚓ ♿

This parador is 3km north of the city centre, which probably means it's a tad more convenient if you've got your own car. But it's fabulously situated on the site of Abd ar-Rahman I's summer palace and is a modern affair set amid lush green gardens where Europe's first palm trees were planted.

SOUTH OF CÓRDOBA

There is only a small selection of accommodation in Priego de Córdoba but places are seldom full.

❦ HOTEL ZUHAYRA // ZUHEROS €

☎ 957 69 46 93; www.zercahoteles.com; Calle Mirador 10; s/d €46/59; ❄ ⚓

This hotel is an excellent base for exploring the Zuheros area. The friendly proprietor, Juan Ábalos (who speaks English), can also provide a great deal of information on walking routes and guided walks. Guests get free use of the village pool and can also take part in cheese-making and painting workshops.

❦ POSADA REAL // PRIEGO DE CÓRDOBA €

☎ 957 54 19 10; www.laposadareal.com; Calle Real 14; d incl breakfast €48; Ⓟ ❄ ⚓

Juan López Calvo and his family have lovingly restored this wonderful old house, and decorated the four rooms (each with a balcony) and one apartment with wrought-iron beds and antiques. In the summer, breakfast is served on the quaint patio.

❦ FINCA BUYTRÓN // MONTILLA €

☎ 957 65 01 52, 649 57 75 20; www.fincabuytron.com; d €55; ❄ ⚓

If you want to stay the night in Montilla, your best choice is out of town in the charming farmhouse with a welcome swimming pool. Advance booking is necessary, as sometimes the house gets rented out completely – you may also find it empty in the low season, so calling in advance is highly advisable in any case.

❦ CORTIJO LA HAZA // IZNÁJAR €€

☎ 957 33 40 51; www.cortijolahaza.com; Adelantado 119; s/d €65/80

Outside the village of Iznájar, this is a 250-year-old Andalusian farmhouse, furnished in typical fashion with wrought-iron beds and rustic furniture, with lovely views from its terraces. There are five lovely rooms, and booking in advance is advisable. Check the website for comprehensive directions (and a map) giving details of how to reach it.

JAÉN PROVINCE

JAÉN

❦ PARADOR CASTILLO DE SANTA CATALINA €€

Map p226; ☎ 953 23 00 00; www.parador.es, in Spanish; d €120; Ⓟ ❄ ⚓

If you want character, this is the only place worth checking into. Part of the Castillo de Santa Catalina complex, the hotel has an incomparable setting, theatrical vaulted halls and huge fireplaces. Rooms are incredibly comfortable, with four-poster beds, Islamic tiled details and all the mod cons.

EAST OF JAÉN

Úbeda's midrange and top-end hotels have comfort and character, with many housed in old palaces. Hotel parking usually costs around €10 per day. As well as the accommodation in Cazorla, more accommodation can be found in or around the nearby village of La Iruela, which is 1km out of Cazorla in the direction of the Parque Natural de las Sierras de Cazorla, Segura y Las Villas. The park has plenty of accommodation but few places in the budget range, except for camping grounds, of which there are at least 10 (you can get details of these from the Cazorla tourist office). During peak visitor periods it's worth booking ahead. For excellent coverage of nearly all the hotels and camping grounds in the park visit www.turismoencazorla.com (in Spanish).

❤ HOTEL HACIENDA LA LAGUNA // BAEZA €€

☎ 953 76 51 42; www.ehlaguna.com/hotel, in Spanish; Puente del Obispo s/n; s/d €53/79; Ⓟ ⊠ ▣ ▣

If you love olive oil, stay in this enormous hacienda (10 minutes' drive from Baeza), where there's a museum of olive oil – the Museo de la Cultura del Olivo – and 18 stylishly furnished rooms. The excellent in-house restaurant, La Campana, is worth visiting even if you are not staying at the hotel. The ranch also has a stable that organises horse riding.

❤ HOTEL PALACETE SANTA ANA // BAEZA €

Map p232; ☎ /fax 953 74 16 57; www.palacetesantana .com; Calle Santa Ana Vieja 9; s/d €45/65; ⊠

This 16th-century converted nunnery is a stylish hotel that prides itself on its art and archaeology collection. The rooms are beautifully decorated with wide beds and luxurious furnishings, and the bathrooms have baths *and* showers. The nearby restaurant of the same name is under the same management.

❤ HOTEL PUERTA DE LA LUNA // BAEZA €€€

Map p232; ☎ 953 74 70 19; www.hotelpuertadelaluna .com, in Spanish; Calle Canónigo Melgares Raya s/n; d €70-175; Ⓟ ⊠ ▣

This is no doubt where the Benavides or Carvajals would stay if they were to visit Baeza and didn't already own half the town. Luxurious from start to finish, this mansion hotel has plenty of character to boot. There are manicured hedges on the cobbled Mudéjar patio (where you can have breakfast), beautifully furnished salons with welcoming fireplaces, bedrooms full of antiques, and lush damask sheets. There is also a lovely restaurant, modern bar, Turkish bath, spa, gym and library.

❤ HOTEL ORDÓÑEZ SANDOVAL // ÚBEDA €€

Map p235; ☎ 953 79 51 87; Calle Antonio Medina 1; s/d €80/90; Ⓟ

The family home of Amalia Perez Ordóñez, this 19th-century *palacio* has three vast bedrooms with somewhat stern antique furnishings and an atmosphere that verges on monastic. There is a verdant central patio, too. Amalia is a gracious and helpful hostess and takes pride in her home.

❦ PALACIO DE LA RAMBLA // ÚBEDA €€

Map p235; ☎ 953 75 01 96; www.palaciodelarambla
.com; Plaza del Marqués de la Rambla 1; d/ste incl breakfast €96/120; ⊙ closed 13 Jul–6 Aug

Úbeda's loveliest converted palace has
eight gorgeous rooms in the home of the
Marquesa de la Rambla. It's not an over-
statement to call this one of Andalucía's
most stunning places to stay. The ivy-
clad patio is wonderfully romantic and
entry is restricted to guests only. Each
room is clad in precious antiques and has
its own salon, so that you feel like you're
staying with aristocrat friends rather
than in a hotel. Breakfast can be served
in your room.

❦ PARADOR CONDESTABLE DÁVALOS // ÚBEDA €€€

Map p235; ☎ 953 75 03 45; www.parador.es, in Spanish; Plaza Vázquez de Molina; s/d €110/125; Ⓟ ❄

As paradors always get the town's best
location and building, Úbeda has surrendered its prime spot, looking out
over the wonderful Plaza Vázquez de
Molina, and has housed the hotel inside
an historic monument: the Palacio del
Deán Ortega. It has, of course, been
comfortably modernised and is appro-
priately luxurious. It also has the best
restaurant in town.

❦ MOLINO LA FARRAGA // CAZORLA €€

☎ 953 72 12 49; www.molinolafarraga.com; Calle
Camino de la Hoz s/n; s/d €50/70; ▣

Just up the valley from the Plaza de Santa
María is the tranquil old mill of La Farraga, nestling in a bucolic idyll of forested
slopes criss-crossed by rivers. Inside, the
decor is understated comfort, with lots
of dark mahogany colours, and the wild,
lush garden is heavenly.

❦ HOTEL NOGUERA DE LA SIERPE // PARQUE NATURAL DE LAS SIERRAS DE CAZORLA, SEGURA Y LAS VILLAS €€

Map p241; ☎ 953 71 30 21; Carretera del Tranco
Km44.5; s/d €60/90, 4-person chalet €120; Ⓟ ❄ ▣

A paradise for hunting aficionados, run
by an equally fanatical proprietor who
has decorated the place with stuffed animals and suitably proud photos of his exploits. The hotel is housed in a converted
cortijo and overlooks a picturesque lake.
You can arrange riding sessions at the
hotel's stables.

GRANADA PROVINCE

GRANADA

Central Granada – the level ground from
the Realejo across to Plaza de la Trinidad –
is very compact, so hotel location doesn't
matter much. The prettiest lodgings are
the Albayzín courtyard houses, though
these call for some hill-walking, and many
aren't accessible by taxi. The handful of
hotels up by the Alhambra are scenic, but
a hassle for extended sightseeing. Rates
are highest in spring and fall, spiking over
Easter. Parking, where offered, costs €15 to
€20 per day, and is usually at a municipal
parking lot, not on the hotel grounds.

CENTRAL GRANADA

❦ HOSTAL VENECIA €

Map p261; ☎ 958 22 39 87; Cuesta de Gomérez 2; d
€42, with shared bathroom €34

The house-proud hosts here are as sweet
as the flower-and-picture-filled turquoise
corridors. The nine rooms overflow with
character, and each is different: some
have private bathrooms, while others
share facilities, and many have small balconies. There's ample heat as well as piles
of blankets in the winter, and ceiling fans
keep rooms cool in the summer months.

♥ HOTEL FONTECRUZ €€€

Map p261; ☎ 958 21 78 10; www.fontecruz.com; Gran Vía de Colón 20; d/ste €120/370; ✖ ▢ ☗
Opened in 2009, the Fontecruz features large rooms that mix sleek and sumptuous, with black-and-white carpeting, dark-wood antique-look writing desks and lovely beds. All have at least one shallow balcony. Windows are double-glazed, but rooms overlooking the side street instead of the Gran Vía are noticeably quieter. A rooftop bar yields great views.

♥ HOTEL LOS TILOS €€

Map p261; ☎ 958 26 67 12; www.hotellostilos.com; Plaza Bib-Rambla 4; s/d €55/80; ✖
The spacious rooms, clean and renovated in 2008, overlook Plaza Bib-Rambla, and there are double-glazed windows to shut out the hubbub at night. There's a small but panoramic roof terrace if you don't get your own Alhambra view from your room. Lonely Planet readers can show their guides to receive free breakfast.

♥ HOTEL PUERTA DE LAS GRANADAS €€

Map p261; ☎ 958 21 62 30; www.hotelpuertade lasgranadas.com; Cuesta de Gomérez 14; d €104, superior r €114-170; ✖ ▢ ☗
This small hotel has a prime location just off the Plaza Nueva and halfway up the hill to the Alhambra. The red-and-dark-wood rooms overlook either a back garden (quiet) or the street (a little larger). Two top-floor rooms have grand views. Extra perks include a lift – rare in a hotel this size – and extremely helpful staff.

♥ ROOM MATE SHALMA €€

Map p261; ☎ 958 21 68 58; www.room-matehotels .com; Plaza de Fortuny 6; s/d incl breakfast €60/75; ✖ ☗
Live the stylish Realejo life at this cool hotel with 19 rooms that balance style with reasonable rates (wi-fi is free, as is breakfast). You'll either love or hate the eye-popping purple-and-red colour scheme. If you hate it, check out the chain's other two properties in town, with different distinctive styles but the same good value.

ALBAYZÍN

♥ AC PALACIO DE SANTA PAULA €€€

Map pp252-3; ☎ 902 29 22 93; www.ac-hotels.com; Gran Vía de Colón; r from €170; ℗ ✖ ▢
The most luxurious hotel in the centre, this five-star operation occupies a former 16th-century convent, some 14th-century houses with patios and wooden balconies, and a 19th-century aristocratic house, all with a contemporary overlay. The rooms sport every top-end luxury you might desire, and the hotel also has a fitness centre, sauna and Turkish bath.

♥ CASA MORISCA €€

Map pp252-3; ☎ 958 22 11 00; www.hotelcasa morisca.com; Cuesta de la Victoria 9; d interior €118, exterior €148; ✖ ▢ ☗
This late-15th-century mansion perfectly captures the spirit of the Albayzín. A heavy wooden door shuts out city noise, and rooms are soothing, with lofty ceilings, fluffy white beds and flat-weave rugs over brick floors. The least expensive ones look only onto the central patio with its fountain – cosily authentic, but potentially claustrophobic for some. The hotel is accessible by taxi.

♥ HOSTAL ARTEAGA €

Map pp252-3; ☎ 958 20 88 41; www.hostalarteaga .com; Calle Arteaga 3; s/d/t €40/49/60; ✖ ▢
A charming bargain option just off the Gran Vía de Colón. The rooms are spruced up with lavender walls, striped bedspreads and chequered blue bathroom tiles, for a tidy, modern feel. Stay

three nights, and you get a free session at the adjacent Baños de Elvira spa.

❤ HOTEL ZAGUÁN DEL DARRO €€

Map pp252-3; ☎ 958 21 57 30; www.hotelzaguan .com; Carrera del Darro 23; s/d €55/65; 🔲 🖥
This place offers excellent value for the Albayzín. The 16th-century house has been tastefully restored, with sparing use of antiques. Its 13 rooms are all different; some look out over the Río Darro. There's a good bar-restaurant below, and the main street in front means easy taxi access – but also a bit of evening noise.

ALHAMBRA

❤ HOTEL MACÍA REAL DE LA ALHAMBRA €€

off Map pp252-3; ☎ 958 21 66 93; www.maciahoteles .com; Mirador del Genil 2; d €70; 🅿 🔲 🖥 🛜 🖥 🚹
Great if you're dropping into Granada just to see the Alhambra – this good-value hotel on the edge of the city is an easy 10-minute drive to the monument, and a city bus goes right by too. Rooms are chic, in shades of grey, and there are steam baths (extra charge) downstairs.

❤ PARADOR DE GRANADA €€€

Map p255; ☎ 958 22 14 40; www.parador.es, in Span- ish; Calle Real de la Alhambra; s/d €249/311; 🅿 🔲 🛜
It'd be remiss not to mention this hotel, the most luxurious of Spain's paradors. But it's hard to justify the high price. Yet if you're looking for romance and history (it's in a converted 15th-century convent in the Alhambra grounds) and money is no object…then book well ahead.

LA VEGA & EL ALTIPLANO

❤ CUEVAS MIRADOR DE ROLANDO // GUADIX €

☎ 958 06 60 29, 670 79 91 38; www.cuevasde rolando.es; Rambla de Baza; d incl breakfast €40, 4-person apt €70; 🅿 🖥

A Spanish-German couple offer the genuine Guadix cave experience: families can spread out in fully stocked two-bedroom apartments, and there's a smaller room ideal for couples on shorter stays. All have terraces with stunning views of the mountains. (The hotel is not in the main cave district but northeast along the road to the A92.)

SIERRA NEVADA & LAS ALPUJARRAS

It's advisable to book ahead during Se-mana Santa (Holy Week), from July to September, and in spring and autumn for hotels that cater to walkers.

❤ REFUGIO POQUEIRA // MULHACÉN €

☎ 958 34 33 49; per person €15; 🕙 year-round
This modern, 87-bunk refuge has a res-taurant (breakfast €5, dinner €14) and hot showers, a just reward after a day of trekking the Sierra Nevada. You get here by walking 4km from the Mirador de Trevélez (about one hour), or following the Río Mulhacén for 2.3km down from the road beneath the western side of Mulhacén, then veering 750m southeast along a path to the refuge. Phone ahead, if possible.

❤ CASA RURAL JAZMÍN // ÓRGIVA €

☎ 958 78 47 95; www.casaruraljazmin.com; Calle Ladera de la Ermita; r €48-65; 🔲 🖥
A sanctuary in the upper town, Casa Jazmín is a French-run house with four rooms, each decorated in a different style (Asian and Alpujarran rooms are smaller; French and African, larger). There's a communal terrace and a pool set in a dense garden. On a cul-de-sac, it has space for parking, once you make it up the windy street.

☙ HOSTAL RUTA DEL MULHACÉN // **PAMPANEIRA €**

☎ 958 76 30 10; www.rutadelmulhacen.com; Avenida Alpujarra 6; s/d €36/45

Coming into Pampaneira, look for the tall white building covered with pots of geraniums. Most of the cosy rooms at this *hostal* have balconies, and a few, at the back of the building, have their own large terraces with views down the valley. Parking is available in a town lot just below.

☙ SIERRA Y MAR // **FERREIROLA €**

☎ 958 76 61 71; www.sierraymar.com; Calle Albaicín; s/d incl breakfast €42/62; Ⓟ ⌨

This complex of several small houses, run by a Danish-Italian couple, has been seeing guests since 1985. The rustic rooms have writing desks positioned just so for staring idly out the window at the mountain view – though you could also do this from your terrace, or the wild, grassy garden. Stays of more than one night are preferred.

☙ HOTEL LA FRAGUA // **TREVÉLEZ €**

☎ 958 85 86 26; www.hotellafragua.com; Calle San Antonio 4; d €45

The rooms at La Fragua are typical mountain-village style: pine-furnished, simple and clean. Some have balconies, and there's a large roof deck. Early-rising walking groups can be noisy, though. The hotel is at the top of town, a 200m walk (signposted) from the highest plaza. A second property nearby (doubles for €55) has a pool and great views.

☙ HOTEL LOS BÉRCHULES // **BÉRCHULES €**

☎ 958 85 25 30; www.hotelberchules.com; s/d €35/45; Ⓟ ⌨ ⬛

By the main road at the bottom of Bérchules, this modern hotel has good rooms (all with bathtub); singles are a bit small, but doubles all have balconies. The helpful English-speaking hosts can help set up all manner of activities, and there's a big pool, a good restaurant and a cosy lounge stocked with books on Spain.

☙ ALQUERÍA DE MORAYMA // **CÁDIAR €**

☎ 958 34 32 21; www.alqueriamorayma.com; d €61, 4-person apt €91; Ⓟ ⬛

One of the better places to stay in Las Alpujarras, with a bit of a New Age bent but still distinctly Spanish. It's an old farmstead lovingly renovated and expanded to provide 20 comfortable rooms and apartments. The restaurant serves very good food with locally made ingredients, and there's fine walking along the nearby river.

☙ LAS CHIMENEAS // **MAIRENA €€**

☎ 958 76 03 52; www.alpujarra-tours.com; Calle Amargura 6; d incl breakfast €70; ⬛ ▢ ⬛

An institution among walkers, this village house is run by a British couple who are extremely well informed about local history, ecology and tradition. They can arrange hikes, painting excursions, cooking classes and more. They also have fine taste: the expansive rooms have an antique yet uncluttered style, and the restaurant is quite good.

COSTA TROPICAL

Rates spike about €10 higher during August.

☙ HOSTAL SAN JUAN // **SALOBREÑA €**

☎ 958 61 17 29; www.hostalsanjuan.com; Calle Jardines 1; s/d €36/45, 3-person apt €54; ⬛ ▢ ⌨ ⬛

A lovely tiled and plant-filled patio-lounge welcomes you at this sparkly *hostal* on a quiet street about 400m from the tourist office. The rooms have wrought-iron bedsteads and red-and-white bathroom tiling, and many can accommodate families, as can two apartments with kitchenettes. A large roof terrace takes in the sunset.

❦ HOTEL AL NAJARRA // ALMUÑÉCAR €

☎ 958 63 08 73; www.hotelnajarra.com; Calle Guadix 12; d/t €58/81; 🅿 🖳 📶 🖳 ♿ 🅿

This modern hotel isn't bursting with character, but it represents excellent value in Almuñécar, where many properties are a bit tired. The large rooms all open onto terraces or balconies overlooking a back garden and pool (filled only in the summer). It's a couple of blocks' walk from the beach.

ALMERÍA PROVINCE

ALMERÍA

❦ HOTEL AC ALMERÍA €€

Map pp292-3; ☎ 950 23 49 99; www.ac-hotels.com; Plaza de las Flores 5; s/d €81/90; 🅿 🗶 🖳 📶 🖳

All edgy minimalist grey, the AC's interior is a sharp contrast to the crumbling baroque style in the plaza outside – an excellent location for a tapas crawl and minimal late-night traffic noise. This is a solid, well-maintained business-class hotel, with very comfortable beds, and helpful black-clad staff. Rates drop on the weekends.

❦ HOTEL COSTASOL €

Map pp292-3; ☎ 950 23 40 11; www.hotelcostasol .com; Paseo de Almería 58; d €54; 🅿 🗶 🖳 🖳 📶

This sensible hotel (renovated in 2009) has a few hip details, such as round red rugs and jaunty wall lamps, but the real perks are firm beds, spotless floors, vast bathrooms and some tiny balconies (with a sea view, way down the boul-

evard). Parking (€10) is in a city lot, half a block away.

NORTH OF ALMERÍA

❦ CORTIJO EL SALTADOR // LUCAINENA DE LAS TORRES €

☎ 676 43 71 28; www.elsaltador.com; Rambla Honda; s/d €40/60; 🅿

Beautiful and remote, this farmhouse enjoys almost complete silence, except for the chatter of birds. Rooms are whitewashed and spare (no TV), and guests have the run of the main house with a huge kitchen. Excellent dinners are an option, as are yoga classes, massage and other activities. Walking trails head off in all directions – including to an armchair on a mountain top, the only spot nearby with mobile-phone reception.

❦ HOSTAL MONTELÉS // SORBAS €

☎ 950 36 46 35; www.hostalmonteles.com; Calle Calvo Sotelo 4; d €60; 🖳 🖳 ♿

A great base for exploring the terrain around Sorbas, this old house has beautiful tiled floors, high ceilings and grand staircases. The 12 rooms are furnished in a simple, modern style, and guests have access to a kitchen, lounge and back garden with a whirlpool tub. A friendly cat makes the place extra homey.

LAS ALPUJARRAS DE ALMERÍA

❦ HOTEL ALMIREZ // LAUJAR DE ANDARAX €

☎ 950 51 35 14; www.hotelalmirez.es, in Spanish; s/d €36/47; 🅿 🗶 🖳 📶

Where else but the Alpujarras does a budget room come with a free bottle of wine? The vino is best enjoyed on your terrace, taking in the mountain view. Rooms have gleaming tile floors and groovy striped bedspreads, and the restaurant downstairs is tasty. It's on the road leading into the west edge of town.

COSTA DE ALMERÍA

✤ HOSTAL ALOHA // SAN JOSÉ €

☎ 950 38 04 61; www.hostalaloha.com; Calle Cala Higuera; d €55; 🞬 🖭

White walls, firm beds and gleaming bathrooms make this an appealing budget hotel to start with. Throw in the enormous pool on the back terrace, and it's one of the best deals in San José. It's a few blocks back from the beach; to reach it, turn left off the main street at the tourist office.

✤ MC SAN JOSE // SAN JOSÉ €€€

☎ 950 61 11 11; www.hotelesmcsanjose.com; Carretera El Faro; d incl breakfast €139; 🞬 🖳 🛜 🖭

The MC is the best of both hotel worlds: chic boutique design, with just 32 rooms and plenty of stylish details, but with the kind of hospitality that only comes from a local family. Open all year-round.

✤ EL JARDÍN DE LOS SUEÑOS // RODALQUILAR €€

☎ 950 38 98 43, 669 18 41 18; www.eljardindelos suenos.es; d/ste incl breakfast €90/110; 🅿 🞬 🖭

Just off the highway opposite Rodalquilar, this expanded old farmhouse is surrounded by lush gardens and fruit trees – some contribute to the tasty breakfasts. Bright colours, abstract art and the occasional chandelier distinguish the rooms. Suites – with terraces onto the desert valley and tubs with skylights – are worth the extra.

✤ EL MIRADOR DEL CASTILLO // MOJÁCAR €€

Map p306; ☎ 950 47 30 22; www.elcastillomojacar .com; El Mirador del Castillo; d €80, with shared bath €60; 🖭

Up at the tip-top of Mojácar's hill, this laid-back *hostal* is part of a larger art

centre and retreat, with a cafe-bar as well. The atmosphere is resolutely bohemian, but even with some peeling paint, it manages to stay just the right side of characterful, with richly coloured walls and art books on the bedside tables.

✤ HOSTAL ARCO PLAZA // MOJÁCAR €

Map p306; ☎ 950 47 27 77; fax 950 47 27 17; Calle Aire Bajo 1; s/d €40/60; 🞬

In the centre of the village, this *hostal* has spacious bathrooms, sky-blue rooms with wrought-iron beds, white sheets, and great views of the plaza and the valley below. The management is friendly and efficient. Some rooms open onto the plaza, which can be noisy in the evening, but it's silent after midnight.

✤ HOTEL RÍO ABAJO // MOJÁCAR €

☎ 950 47 89 28; www.rioabajomojacar.com; Calle Río Abajo; d €60; 🅿 🖭

Nestling amid trees in a residential cul-de-sac on the edge of the Lagunas del Río Aguas, this has to be the most tranquil hotel on Mojácar Playa. Nineteen blue-and-white cottages are dotted among lush gardens, with direct access to the broad, sandy beach. It's a fantastic place for kids.

LOS VÉLEZ

✤ HOTEL VELAD AL-ABYADH // VÉLEZ BLANCO €€

☎ 950 41 51 09; www.hotelvelad.com; Calle Balsa Parra 28; s/d incl breakfast €45/70; 🅿 🞬

A mock hunting lodge with almost medieval rooms and incredible views over the valley, the hotel is at the entrance to Vélez Blanco from Vélez Rubio. Rustic artefacts and exposed brickwork give the place an intimate atmosphere. The hotel also has a good restaurant.

DIRECTORY

BUSINESS HOURS

Banks generally open from 8.30am to 2pm Monday to Friday and 9am to 1pm Saturday. Post offices open from 8.30am to 8.30pm Monday to Friday and 9am to 1.30pm Saturday. There are, of course, some local and seasonal variations.

Restaurants and tapas bars typically open from around 1pm to around 4pm, and in the evening from 8pm or 8.30pm to around midnight. Reviews of bars and restaurants throughout this book don't list opening hours unless they differ significantly from those listed here. Many are closed one day a week (often Monday). Some bars open for breakfast and stay open throughout the day, while some close up as early as 11pm during the week. Gibraltar follows the same opening hours as the rest of Andalucía.

Most shops and nongovernment offices (such as travel agencies, airline offices and tour companies) open from 9am or 10am to 1.30pm or 2pm and 5pm to 8pm or 9pm, Monday to Saturday, though some skip the Saturday evening session.

Large supermarkets, department stores and *centros comerciales* (large, purpose-built shopping centres) normally stay open all day, from 9am to 9pm, Monday to Saturday.

Night-time bars generally open in the early evening, but get kicking from between 11pm and midnight to between 2am and 4am – the later in the week, the later they stay open.

CHILDREN

Travelling with children in Andalucía is easy. You can get just about everything you need, and Andalusians are generally very warm towards children. Any child whose hair is less than jet black will get called *rubia* (blonde) if she's a girl, *rubio* if he's a boy. Children accompanied by adults are welcome at all kinds of accommodation, and in virtually every cafe, bar and restaurant. In theory, those that allow smoking shouldn't allow children, although this is rarely enforced other than by parents themselves. Andalusian children stay up late and at fiestas it's commonplace to see even tiny ones toddling the streets at 2am or 3am. Visiting kids like this idea too, but can't always cope with it quite so readily.

Cots are usually available in hotels and high chairs in restaurants are increasingly common but by no means universal. Safety seats should always be available for hire cars, but are rarely found in taxis.

Some top-end hotels may be able to help arrange childcare. Nappy-changing facilities are rare and breastfeeding in public is unusual, though discreet breastfeeding is no problem.

Beaches are an obvious child-friendly attraction and you'll find playgrounds are plentiful. Special attractions, such as water parks and aquariums, are spread over the region but abound in Málaga province and especially along the Costa del Sol. Another feature of Andalucía that excites many young 'uns is being able to see wildlife such as dolphins, apes, deer, vultures and wild boar. To find out more, see p345.

There are a range of outdoor activities that will appeal to kids, including snorkelling (p351) and horse riding (p349), and some windsurfing spots (p351) offer instruction for kids. Even some quite small Andalusian towns have municipal swimming pools – ideal in summer.

Children benefit from reduced-cost or free entry at many sights and museums. Those under four years of age travel free on Spanish trains and those aged four to 11 normally pay 60% of the adult fare. Lonely Planet's *Travel with Children* has lots of practical advice and firsthand stories from many Lonely Planet authors and others.

CUSTOMS REGULATIONS

Duty-free allowances for entering Spain from outside the EU include 2L of wine, 1L of spirits and 200 cigarettes or 50 cigars. Limits on imports and exports of duty-paid goods between other EU countries and Spain include 110L of

PRACTICALITIES

* ⋆ UK and some other European newspapers are sold at kiosks wherever large numbers of expats and tourists are found.

* ⋆ The centre-left *El País* (www.elpais.es) is Spain's biggest-selling newspaper. Every sizeable Andalusian city has at least one daily paper of its own.

* ⋆ Spain uses the metric system for weights and measures.

* ⋆ Electric current in Spain is 220V, 50Hz, as in the rest of Continental Europe. Plugs have two round pins.

* ⋆ For radio stations *El País* publishes province-by-province wavelength guides in its *Cartelera* (What's On) section. Among the several stations of Radio Nacional de España (RNE), RNE3 plays a variety of pop and rock, RNE2 is classical.

* ⋆ Spain has between six and eight free-to-air channels including the state-run TVE1 and TVE2, and a couple of local channels. International satellite channels crop up on some hotel TVs.

* ⋆ DVDs bought in Spain are region two and may not be compatible with players in North America (region one), Australia (region four) and elsewhere.

beer, 90L of wine, 10L of spirits, 800 cigarettes and 200 cigars.

DANGERS & ANNOYANCES

Andalucía is generally a pretty safe place. The main thing you have to be wary of is petty theft (which may not seem so petty if your passport, money and camera go missing).

Most of the safety precautions are simple common sense, but you'd be surprised at how casual some travellers are with their belongings. To safeguard your money, keep a limited amount as cash on hand, and the bulk in more easily replaceable forms such as on plastic cards or as travellers cheques. If your accommodation has a safe, use it. Most risk of theft occurs in tourist resorts and big cities, and when you first arrive in a city and may be unaware of danger signs. Don't draw attention to your money or valuables by waving cameras or large notes around or having a wallet bulging in your pocket. Keep hold of your baggage and watch out for people who touch you or seem to be getting needlessly close at bus or train stations, on crowded streets, or in any situation. When using ATMs be wary of anyone who offers to help you, even if your card is stuck in the machine. Don't leave anything that even looks valuable visible in a parked car.

If you want to make an insurance claim for anything stolen or lost, you'll need to report it to the police and get a copy of the report. For help replacing a lost or stolen passport, contact your embassy or consulate.

DISCOUNTS

Student, teacher and youth cards can get you worthwhile discounts on airfares and other travel, as well as reduced prices at some museums, sights and entertainment venues.

The International Student Identity Card (ISIC), for full-time students, and the International Teacher Identity Card (ITIC), for full-time teachers and academics, are issued by colleges and student associations in the country where you're studying. The ISIC gives access to discounted air and train fares, 50% off national museums in Spain and up to 20% off trips with the Alsa bus company.

Anyone under 26 can get a Euro<26 card (Carnet Joven in Spain), which is available in Europe to people of any nationality, or an International Youth Travel Card (IYTC or GO25 card), available worldwide. These give similar discounts to the ISIC and are issued by many of the same organisations. Benefits for Euro<26 cardholders in Andalucía include 20% or 25% off many train fares, 20% off the cost of some car hire and bus fares with the Socibus company, 10% to 15% off the cost of some accommodation, and discounts at a few museums and tourist attractions.

For more information, including places you can obtain the cards, see www.istc.org and www.euro26.org.

A seniors' card, usually for people over 65, generally enables you to obtain similar discounts to those obtained by student-card holders, although some museums will only recognise seniors' cards issued in EU countries.

FOOD & DRINK

Prices for Gastronomic Highlights listings in this book are the average price you can expect to pay for a two-course meal with a drink. Reviews are presented in alphabetical order, and price categories are broken up into budget (under

€10), midrange (€10 to €25) and top end (more than €25), as indicated by €, €€ and €€€.

For opening hours see p400, and an overview of Andalusian cuisine can be found on p367.

WHERE TO EAT & DRINK

Like elsewhere in Spain, bars are places to eat and socialise as much as they are for drinking, but they do come in many guises. These include: bodegas (traditional wine bars), *cervecerías* (beer bars), *tascas* (bars specialising in tapas), *tabernas* (taverns) and even *pubs* (pubs). In many of them you'll be able to eat tapas at the bar but there will usually be a *comedor* (dining room) too, for a sit-down meal. You'll often save 10% to 20% by eating at the bar rather than at a table.

Restaurantes (restaurants) are usually more formal places, where you sit down to eat. A *mesón* is a simple restaurant attached to a bar with homestyle cooking. A *venta* is (or once was) a roadside inn – the food can be delicious and inexpensive. A *marisquería* is a seafood restaurant, while a *chiringuito* is a small open-air bar or kiosk, usually fronting onto the beach.

VEGETARIANS & VEGANS

Throughout Andalucía fruit and vegetables are delicious and fresh, and eaten in season, but unfortunately there are only a handful of avowedly vegetarian restaurants. A word of warning: 'vegetable' dishes may contain more than just vegetables (eg beans with bits of ham). Vegetarians will find that salads in most restaurants are a good bet, as are gazpacho (chilled tomato soup) and *ajo blanco* (a white gazpacho, made from a blend of almonds garlic and grapes). Another reliable dish is *pisto* (ratatouille), especially good when eaten with bread dipped into the sauce; or try *espárragos trigueros* (thin wild asparagus), either grilled or in *revueltos* (scrambled eggs cooked with slices of fried garlic). Tapas without meat include *pimientos asados* (roasted red peppers), *alcachofas* (artichokes), *garbanzos con espinacas* (chickpeas with spinach) and, of course, *queso* (cheese). A plate of Andalusian *aceitunas* (olives) is another staple of the region's tapas.

GAY & LESBIAN TRAVELLERS

Andalucía's liveliest gay scenes are in Málaga, Torremolinos, Seville and Granada, but there are gay- and lesbian-friendly bars or clubs in all major cities.

Websites such as www.gayinspain .com, www.guiagay.com (in Spanish) and www.cogailes.org have helpful listings of gay and gay-friendly accommodation, bars, clubs, beaches, cruising areas, health clubs and associations. Gayinspain and Cogailes have message boards too. Cogailes is the site of the Coordinadora Gai-Lesbiana, a gay and lesbian organisation based in Barcelona that operates a free national information telephone line in English, Spanish and Catalan on ☎ 900 60 16 01, from 6pm to 10pm daily. Other links to gay associations in Andalucía appear on www .orgullogay.org.

The **Asociación Andaluza de Lesbianas y Gais** (Calle Lavadero de las Tablas 15, Granada) runs the **Teléfono Andaluz de Información Homosexual** (☎ 958 20 06 02).

Even though gay marriage was legalised in Spain in 2005, some hotel receptionists still have difficulty understanding that two people of the same sex might want to share a double bed. One traveller suggested that, for the sake of efficiency, it can be a good idea for one of the pair to do the checking in before the other appears.

HEALTH

For emergency treatment, go straight to the *urgencias* (casualty) section of the nearest hospital, or call ☎ 061 for an ambulance.

Good health care is readily available and *farmacias* (pharmacies) offer valuable advice and sell over-the-counter medication. In Spain, a system of *farmacias de guardia* (duty pharmacies) operates so that each district has one open all the time. When a pharmacy is closed, it posts the name of the nearest open one on the door.

Tap water is generally safe to drink in Spain, but the city of Málaga is one place where many people prefer to play it safe by drinking bottled water. Do not drink water from rivers or lakes as it may contain harmful bacteria.

HOLIDAYS

Everywhere in Spain has 14 official holidays a year – some are holidays nationwide, some only in one village. The list of holidays in each place may change from year to year. If a holiday date falls on a weekend, sometimes the holiday is moved to the Monday or replaced with another at a different time. If a holiday falls on the second day following a weekend, many Spaniards take the intervening day off too, a practice known as making a *puente* (bridge).

The two main periods when Spaniards go on holiday are Semana Santa (Holy Week, leading up to Easter Sunday) and the six weeks from mid-July to the end of August. At these times accommodation in resorts can be scarce and transport heavily booked.

There are usually nine official national holidays:

Año Nuevo (New Year's Day) 1 January
Viernes Santo (Good Friday) 2 April 2010, 22 April 2011
Fiesta del Trabajo (Labour Day) 1 May
La Asunción (Feast of the Assumption) 15 August
Fiesta Nacional de España (National Day) 12 October
Todos los Santos (All Saints' Day) 1 November
Día de la Constitución (Constitution Day) 6 December
La Inmaculada Concepción (Feast of the Immaculate Conception) 8 December
Navidad (Christmas) 25 December

In addition, regional governments normally set three holidays, and local councils a further two. The three regional holidays in Andalucía are usually these:

Epifanía (Epiphany) or **Día de los Reyes Magos** (Three Kings' Day) 6 January
Día de Andalucía (Andalucía Day) 28 February
Jueves Santo (Holy Thursday) Easter

The following are often selected as local holidays by town halls:

Corpus Christi Around two months after Easter
Día de San Juan Bautista (Feast of St John the Baptist, King Juan Carlos II's saint's day) 24 June
Día de Santiago Apóstol (Feast of St James the Apostle, Spain's patron saint) 25 July

INSURANCE

MEDICAL INSURANCE

If you're an EU citizen, the free EHIC (European Health Insurance Card) covers you for most medical care in Spain, including maternity care and care for chronic illnesses such as diabetes (though not for emergency repatriation). However, you will normally have to pay for medicine bought from pharmacies, even if prescribed, and perhaps for some tests and procedures. The EHIC does not cover private medical consultations and treatment in Spain; this includes nearly all dentists, and some of the better clinics and surgeries. In the UK, you can apply for an EHIC online at www.ehic.org .uk/Internet/home.do, by telephone on ☎ 0845 606 2030, or by filling out a form available at post offices. Non-EU citizens should find out if there is a reciprocal arrangement for free medical care between their country and Spain.

TRAVEL INSURANCE

A travel-insurance policy to cover theft, loss and medical problems is a good idea. Travel agents will be able to make recommendations. Check the small print: some policies specifically exclude 'dangerous activities', which can include scuba diving, motorcycling, even trekking. Strongly consider a policy that covers you for the worst possible scenario, such as an accident requiring an ambulance or emergency flight home. Find out in advance if your insurance plan will make payments to doctors or hospitals directly, rather than you having to pay on the spot and claim later. The former option is generally preferable, as it doesn't leave you out of pocket. If you have to claim later, make sure you keep all documentation.

Buy travel insurance as early as possible. If you buy it in the week before you leave home, you may find, for example, that you are not covered for delays to your trip caused by strikes.

Paying for your airline ticket with a credit card often provides limited travel accident insurance, and you may be able to reclaim payment if the operator doesn't deliver.

For information on motor insurance, see p419.

INTERNET ACCESS

There are plenty of internet cafes throughout Andalucía, typically charging around €1.50 per hour. Some are equipped with CD burners, webcams, headphones and so on. But some of the smaller places may not have card readers, so bring your own or the camera-to-USB cable if you plan on burning photos to CD along the way.

For those travelling with a laptop or hand-held computer, a growing number of hotels in Andalucía provide wi-fi access (although often only in the lobby), or in-room cable connections; accommodation with any kind of internet access for guests receives a 🖳 icon in this book and accommodation with wi-fi availability is shown with a 🛜 icon. Many tourist offices also offer free wi-fi access.

LEGAL MATTERS

Spain has three main types of police. The **Policía Nacional** (National Police; ☎ 091) covers cities and bigger towns, sometimes forming special squads dealing with drugs, terrorism and the like. A further contingent is to be found shuffling paper in bunkerlike police stations called *comisarías*. The **Policía Local** (Local Police; ☎ 092), also known as Policía Municipal, are controlled by city and town halls and deal mainly with minor matters such as parking, traffic and bylaws. They wear blue-and-white uniforms. The responsibilities of the green-uniformed **Guardia Civil** (Civil Guard; ☎ 062) include roads, the countryside, villages and international borders.

If you need to go to the police (for example, if you're the victim of petty theft), any of them will do, but you're best bet is to approach the Policía Nacional or Policía Local.

Spain's once-liberal drug laws were severely tightened in 1992. The only legal drug is cannabis, and then only for personal use – which means very small amounts. Public consumption of any drug is illegal. It would be very unwise to smoke cannabis in hotel rooms or guest houses. Travellers entering Spain from Morocco, especially with a vehicle, should be prepared for intensive drug searches.

Spain's drink-driving laws are relatively strict – the blood-alcohol limit is 0.05%, or 0.01% for new drivers.

Under the Spanish constitution, anyone who is arrested must be informed immediately, in a manner understandable to them, of their rights and the grounds for the arrest. Arrested people are entitled to the assistance of a lawyer (and, where required, an interpreter) during police inquiries or judicial investigations. For many foreign nationalities, including British citizens, the police are also obliged to inform an arrested person's consulate immediately. Arrested people may not be compelled to make a statement. Within 72 hours of arrest, the person must be brought before a judge or released. Further useful information on Spanish legal procedures and lawyers is published on the website of the UK embassy in Madrid (www.ukinspain.com) under the 'Help for British Nationals' section.

MAPS

Michelin's 1:400,000 *Andalucía* (No 578) is excellent for overall planning and touring, with an edition published each year. It's widely available in and outside Andalucía – look for it at petrol stations and bookshops.

Maps provided by tourist offices are often adequate for finding your way

around cities and towns. For something more comprehensive, most cities are covered by one of the Spanish series such as Telstar, Escudo de Oro, Alpina or Everest, all with street indexes; they're available in bookshops. Be sure to check the publication dates.

Local availability of maps is patchy, so it's a good idea to try to obtain them in advance. **Stanfords** (☎ 020-7836 1321; www .stanfords.co.uk; 12-14 Long Acre, London WC2E 9LP, UK) has a good range of Spain maps and you can order them online. LTC in Seville (Map p42; ☎ 954 42 59 64; Avenida Menéndez Pelayo; ☽ Sun-Fri) is the best map shop in Andalucía, selling most Junta maps as well as SGE and CNIG maps.

WALKING MAPS

If you're going to do any walking in Andalucía you should arm yourself with the best possible maps, especially as trail-markings can be patchy.

Spain's **Centro Nacional de Información Geográfica** (CNIG; www.cnig.es, in Spanish), the publishing arm of the Instituto Geográfico Nacional (IGN), produced a useful *Mapa Guía* series of national and natural parks, mostly at 1:50,000 or 1:100,000, in the 1990s. The CNIG also covers about three-quarters of Andalucía in its 1:25,000 *Mapa Topográfico Nacional* maps, most of which are up to date. Both the CNIG and the Servicio Geográfico del Ejército (SGE; Army Geographic Service) publish 1:50,000 series: the SGE's, called *Serie L,* tends to be more up to date (most of its Andalucía maps have been revised since the mid-1990s). CNIG maps may be labelled CNIG, IGN or both.

The CNIG website lists where you can buy CNIG maps (click on 'Información y Venta') or you can buy online. There are sales offices in Andalucía's eight provincial capitals, including the following:

Granada (☎ 958 90 93 20; Avenida Divina Pastora 7 & 9)

Málaga (☎ 952 21 20 18; Calle Ramos Carrión 48)

Seville (☎ 955 56 93 20; Avenida San Francisco Javier 9, edificio Sevilla 2, 8th fl, módulo 7)

Good commercially published series, all usually accompanied by guide booklets, come from **Editorial Alpina** (www.editorial alpina.com, in Spanish), **Editorial Penibética** (www.penibetica.com, in Spanish) and Britain's **Discovery Walking Guides** (www.walking .demon.co.uk).

The Junta de Andalucía, Andalucía's regional government, also publishes a range of Andalucía maps, including a *Mapa Guía* series of natural and national parks. These have been published recently and are widely available, although perhaps better for vehicle touring than for walking, with a scale of 1:75,000. The covers are predominantly green, as opposed to the CNIG *mapas guías* that are mainly red or pink. Other Junta maps include 1:10,000 and 1:20,000 maps covering the whole of Andalucía – there are good maps but sales outlets for them are few.

MONEY

Spain's currency is the euro (€). The only exception to this in the places covered in this book is Gibraltar, where the currency is the Gibraltar pound. See the boxed text, p151, for more information.

You can get by very well in Andalucía with a credit or debit card enabling you to make purchases directly and to withdraw cash euros from *cajeros automáticos* (ATMs), which are plentiful and easy to find. Make sure the ATM you're using takes international cards – the logos of accepted cards are usually posted alongside.

Cash and travellers cheques can also be exchanged at virtually any bank or exchange office. Banks are plentiful and tend to offer the best rates. Exchange offices – usually indicated by the word *cambio* (exchange) – exist mainly in tourist resorts. Generally they offer longer opening hours and quicker service than banks, but worse exchange rates. Widely accepted brands of travellers cheques include Thomas Cook, Visa and American Express (Amex) and all have efficient replacement policies.

In some places the more money you change, the better the exchange rate you'll get. Check commissions first, and confirm that posted exchange rates are up to date. A typical commission is 2% to 3%, with a minimum of €4 or €5. Places that advertise 'no commission' usually offer poor exchange rates. In Spain you usually can't use travellers cheques like money to make purchases.

Spanish value-added tax (VAT) is called IVA (*ee*-ba; *impuesto sobre el valor añadido*). On accommodation and restaurant prices, it's 7% and is usually (but not always) included in the prices that you'll be quoted. On retail goods and car hire, IVA is 16%. As a rule, prices given in this book include IVA. To ask 'Is IVA included?', say '*¿Está incluido el IVA?*'

Visitors resident outside the EU are entitled to a refund of the 16% IVA on any purchases costing more than €90.15 from any shop if they are taking them out of the EU within three months. Ask the shop to give you an invoice showing the price and IVA paid for each item and the name and address of the vendor and purchaser. Then you will need to present both the invoice and goods to the customs booth for IVA refunds at the airport, port or border from which you leave the EU. The officer will stamp the invoice and you hand it in at a bank in the airport or port for the reimbursement.

CREDIT & DEBIT CARDS

Not every establishment accepts payment by card, but most do. You should be able to make payments by card in midrange and top-end accommodation and restaurants, and larger shops, but you cannot depend on it elsewhere. When you pay by card, you will be asked for ID such as your passport. Don't forget to memorise your PIN numbers as you may have to key these in as you pay, and do keep a note of phone numbers to call for reporting a lost or stolen card.

Visitors from outside the euro zone will get most value for their pound, dollar or whatever by making purchases by credit card or debit card; ATM withdrawals provide second-best value. Obtaining euros by exchanging cash or travellers cheques generally gives less value for your money, after you take into account commissions, handling fees, and exchange-rate differentials.

American Express (Amex) cards are much less widely accepted than Visa and MasterCard.

TIPPING

Spanish law requires menu prices to include the service charge, and tipping is a matter of personal choice – most people leave some small change if they're satisfied, and 5% is usually plenty. Porters will generally be happy with €2. Taxi drivers don't have to be tipped but a little rounding up won't go amiss.

POST

Postage stamps are sold at *estancos* (tobacconist shops with 'Tabacos' in yellow letters on a maroon background), as well as at *oficinas de correos* (post offices; www.correos.es). It's quite safe to post mail in the yellow street *buzones* (postboxes) as well as at post offices. Mail to or from other Western European countries normally arrives within a week; to or from North America within 10 days; and to or from Australia and New Zealand within two weeks.

TELEPHONE

Andalucía is fairly well provided with blue payphones, which (as long as they are in working order) are easy to use for both international and domestic calls. They accept coins and/or *tarjetas telefónicas* (phonecards) issued by the national phone company Telefónica. Phonecards come in €6 and €12 denominations and are sold at post offices and *estancos*. Payphone calls are generally 10% to 20% cheaper from 8pm to 8am Monday to Friday, and all day Saturday and Sunday. Coin payphones inside bars and cafes – often green – are normally a little more expensive than street payphones.

Many small grocery stores also sell private company phonecards (with pin numbers) which can be used from payphones and private phones for much cheaper than the usual rate.

Many towns also have cheap-rate call offices known as *locutorios,* where you can make international calls for low rates (eg around €0.20 a minute to the USA or €0.30 a minute to Australia), although calls within Spain are generally at similar rates to street payphones. Cheapest of all are internet phone calls, available at some *locutorios* and internet cafes, or on your laptop via sites such as www.skype.com.

MOBILE PHONES

If you're going to make lots of calls within Spain, it's worth considering buying a Spanish SIM card. Shops on every main street and in every shopping centre sell phones at bargain prices and Orange (www.orange.es), Movistar (www.movistar.es) and Vodafone (www.vodafone.es) are widespread and reputable brands.

If you're considering taking a mobile from your home country to Spain, you should find out from your mobile network provider whether your phone is enabled for international roaming, and what the costs of calls, text and voicemail are likely to be. Don't forget to take a Continental adaptor for your charger plug.

Spanish mobile phones operate on the GSM 900/1800 or 3G 2100 systems.

For more information visit Ofcom (www.ofcom.org.uk; go to 'Advice for Consumers') or GSM World (www.gsmworld.com), who both provide coverage maps, lists of roaming partners and links to phone companies' websites.

USEFUL NUMBERS & CODES

Spain has no telephone area codes. Every phone number has nine digits and for any call within Spain you just dial all those nine digits. The first digit of all Spanish fixed-phone numbers is ☎9. Numbers beginning with ☎6 are mobile phones. Phone numbers in Gibraltar have eight digits; for more information on phone calls to Gibraltar see p151.

Calls to Spanish numbers starting with ☎900 are free. Numbers starting with ☎901 to ☎906 are pay-per-minute numbers and charges vary; a common one is ☎902, for which you pay about €0.35 for three minutes from a payphone. For a rundown on these numbers, visit www.andalucia.com /travel/telephone/numbers.htm.

Some useful numbers include:
International Access Code ☎00
Country Code ☎34
Local Operator ☎1009

English-speaking International Operator ☎1008 (Europe) or ☎1005 (rest of world)
Local Directory Enquiries ☎11822 (€0.22 plus €0.01 per second)
International Directory Enquiries ☎11825 (€1 plus €0.75 per minute)

TIME

All mainland Spain is on GMT/UTC plus one hour during winter, and GMT/UTC plus two hours during the country's daylight-saving period, which runs from the last Sunday in March to the last Sunday in October. Most other Western European countries have the same time as Spain year-round, the major exceptions being Britain, Ireland and Portugal. Add one hour to these three countries' times to get Spanish time.

Spanish time is normally USA eastern time plus six hours, and USA Pacific time plus nine hours. In the Australian winter subtract eight hours from Sydney time to get Spanish time; in the Australian summer subtract 10 hours. The difference is nine hours for a few weeks in March.

Morocco is on GMT/UTC year-round, so is two hours behind Spain during Spanish daylight-saving time, and one hour behind at other times of the year.

TOILETS

Public toilets are almost nonexistent; many (but not all) tourist offices are an exception. It's OK to wander into many bars and cafes to use the toilet, although you're usually expected to order something while there. It's worth carrying some toilet paper with you as many toilets lack it.

TOURIST INFORMATION

All cities and many smaller towns and even villages in Andalucía have at least one *oficina de turismo* (tourist office). Staff are generally knowledgeable and increasingly well versed in foreign languages and can help with everything from town maps and guided tours to opening hours for major sights and, sometimes, bus timetables. Offices are usually well stocked with printed material. Opening hours vary widely.

Tourist offices in Andalucía may be operated by the local town hall, by local district organisations, by the government of whichever province you're in, or by the regional government, the Junta de Andalucía. There may also be more than one tourist office in larger cities: in general, regional tourist offices offer information both on the city and wider region, while municipal tourist offices deal just with the city and immediate surrounds. The Junta de Andalucía's environmental department, the Consejería de Medio Ambiente, also has visitor centres located in many of the environmentally protected areas (*parques naturales* and so on).

Many tourist offices have Bluetooth information points which allow you to download town maps, guided tours and events listings directly to your mobile phone.

You'll find details of useful tourist offices in the Essential Information sections of destination chapters throughout this book.

TRAVELLERS WITH DISABILITIES

Wheelchair accessibility in Andalucía is improving as new buildings (including hotels) meet regulations requiring them to have wheelchair access. Many midrange and top-end hotels are now adapting rooms and creating better access for wheelchair users; accessibility is poorer at some budget accommodation options. In this book we indicate with a wheelchair icon (♿) where a sight or accommodation option is particularly well set up for wheelchair users.

If you call a taxi and ask for a 'eurotaxi', you should be sent one adapted for wheelchair users.

International organisations that can offer (sometimes including Andalucía-specific) advice include the following:

Access-able Travel Source (☎ 303-232 2979; www.access-able.com; PO Box 1796, Wheatridge, CO, USA)

Accessible Travel & Leisure (☎ 0145 272 9739; www.accessibletravel.co.uk) Claims to be the biggest UK travel agent dealing with travel for the disabled. The company encourages the disabled to travel independently.

Holiday Care (☎ 0845 124 9971; www.holiday care.org.uk; The Hawkins Suite, Enham Place, Enham Alamein, Andover SP11 6JS, UK)

Mobility International USA (☎ 541-343 1284; www.miusa.org; 132 East Broadway, Suite 343, Eugene, Oregon 97401, USA)

Royal Association for Disability & Rehabilitation (RADAR; ☎ 020-7250 3222; www .radar.org.uk; 12 City Forum, 250 City Rd, London, EC1V 8AF, UK) Publishes a useful guide called *Holidays & Travel Abroad: A Guide for Disabled People.*

Society for Accessible Travel and Hospitality (☎ 212-447 7284; www.sath.org; 347 5th Ave, Suite 610, New York, NY 10016, USA)

VISAS

Citizens of EU countries, Switzerland, Norway, Iceland and Liechtenstein need only carry their passport or national identity document in order to enter Spain. Citizens of many other countries, including Australia, Canada, Japan, New Zealand, Singapore and the USA, do not need a visa for visits of up to 90 days but must carry their passport.

Citizens of other countries should consult a Spanish consulate well in advance of travel if you think you need a visa. The standard tourist visa issued when necessary is the Schengen visa, which is valid not only for Spain but also for all the 24 other countries that are party to the Schengen agreement. You normally have to apply for the visa in person at a consulate in your country of residence.

Remember that Gibraltar is not part of Schengen and if you do not have permission to enter the UK, you may not enter Gibraltar. See the boxed text, p151, for more information.

WOMEN TRAVELLERS

Women travellers in Spain will rarely experience harassment, although women travellers should be ready to ignore any stares, catcalls and comments from time to time. Although far from universal, men under about 40, who have grown up in the post-Franco era, are less prone to gender stereotyping than their older counterparts whose thinking and behaviour towards women is still directed by machismo.

Skimpy clothes are the norm in many coastal resorts, but people tend to dress more modestly elsewhere. As in France and Italy, many Spanish women like to get really dressed up. You can feel rather conspicuous on a Sunday when they take to the plazas and promenades for the afternoon *paseo* (walk) and you're in your casual gear. In general, consider avoiding plunging necklines, short skirts and bare shoulders to spare yourself unwanted attention.

Although most places you'll visit are safe, you still need to exercise common sense about where you go solo. Think twice about going alone to isolated stretches of beach or country, or down empty city streets at night. A lone woman, for example, would be better to forget wandering around the uninhabited parts of Granada's Sacromonte area. It's highly inadvisable for a woman to hitchhike alone, and not a great idea even for two women together. Remember the word for help *(socorro)* in case you need to use it. Some women travellers have also reported feeling more comfortable at the front of public transport.

Each province's national police headquarters has a special Servicio de Atención a la Mujer (SAM; literally Service of Attention to Women). The national **Comisión para la Investigación de Malos Tratos a Mujeres** (Commission for Investigation into Abuse of Women; ☎ emergency 900 10 00 09; www.malostratos.org, in Spanish; ☺ 9am-9pm) maintains an emergency line for victims of physical abuse anywhere in Spain. In Andalucía the **Instituto Andaluz de la Mujer** (☎ 900 20 09 99; ☺ 24hr) also offers help.

TRANSPORT

ARRIVAL & DEPARTURE

AIR

Getting to Andalucía by air from the rest of Europe couldn't be easier. Dozens of regular and charter airlines fly into the region's five airports from elsewhere in Europe, especially the UK, and a couple also fly from the UK to Gibraltar. Andalucía's busiest airport, Málaga, also has flights from Morocco. The region is also well-connected by domestic flights to other Spanish cities. From outside Europe, you'll need to change planes en route, usually at Madrid or Barcelona or in another European country.

High season generally runs from mid-June to mid-September, although flights can also be fully booked (and prices higher) during Semana Santa (Holy Week).

AIRPORTS

Málaga airport (AGP; ☎ 952 04 88 38) is the main international airport in Andalucía and Spain's fourth busiest with almost 60 airlines connecting the city to cit-

ies around Spain, Europe and further afield.

Seville (SVQ; ☎ 954 44 90 00), **Granada** (GRX; ☎ 958 24 52 07), **Jerez de la Frontera** (XRY; ☎ 956 15 00 00) and **Almería** (LEI; ☎ 950 21 37 00) also have connections to other Spanish and European cities, although apart from flights outbound from Seville, the choices are far more limited. To see which airlines fly into the airport you're hoping to start your journey in, visit www.aena.es, choose the airport from the pull-down menu on the left, then

TICKET WEBSITES

- **Atrapalo** (www.atrapalo.com, in Spanish)
- **Cheap Flights** (www.cheapflights.com)
- **Ebookers.com** (www.ebookers.com)
- **Expedia** (www.expedia.com)
- **Kayak** (www.kayak.com)
- **Last Minute** (www.lastminute.com)
- **Orbitz** (www.orbitz.com)
- **Opodo** (www.opodo.com)
- **Rumbo** (www.rumbo.es, in Spanish)
- **Travelocity** (www.travelocity.com)

click on 'Airlines' for a full list. The Aena website also has detailed information on facilities at each airport.

Gibraltar (GIB; ☎ 20073026) also receives a small number of flights direct from the UK.

BUS

Andalucía is well connected by bus with the rest of Spain. Although there are direct bus services from many European countries, it rarely works out cheaper than flying and takes a whole lot longer.

Places from where taking a bus may work out more economical include Lisbon and Morocco. There are regular daily services to Seville from Lisbon (seven hours) with **Alsa** (www.alsa.es) and **Anibal** (www.anibal.net), while **Eurolines** (www.eurolines.com), a grouping of 32 bus companies from different countries, and Alsa run several weekly buses between Moroccan cities such as Casablanca, Marrakesh and Fès, and Andalusian destinations such as Seville, Marbella, Málaga, Granada, Jerez de la Frontera and Almería, via the Algeciras–Tangier ferries. The Málaga–Marrakesh trip, for example, takes 19 to 20 hours.

Buses run to most Andalusian cities and medium-sized towns from else-

where in Spain, with the largest selection leaving from Madrid's **Estación Sur de Autobuses** (☎ 91 468 42 00; Calle Méndez Álvaro; metro Méndez Álvaro). The trip from Madrid to Seville, Granada or Málaga, for example, takes around six hours. There are also services down the Mediterranean coast from Barcelona, Valencia and Alicante to Almería, Granada, Jaén, Córdoba, Seville, Málaga and the Costa del Sol. The main bus companies serving Andalucía from other parts of Spain are **Alsa** (☎ 902 42 22 42; www.alsa.es), **Dainco** (☎ 902 42 22 42; www.dainco.es), **Damas** (☎ 959 25 69 00; www.damas-sa.es) and **Secorbus/Socibus** (☎ 902 22 92 92; www.socibus.es, in Spanish).

BORDER CROSSINGS

If you're coming from Morocco, journey times are increased by a couple of hours by border formalities, which are notoriously strict at the ferry departure and arrivals terminals.

CAR & MOTORCYCLE

Drivers can reach Andalucía from just about anywhere in Spain in a single day on the country's good-quality highways. The main routes run down the centre of the country from Madrid and along the Mediterranean coast from Barcelona. Popular vehicle ferries run from the UK to Bilbao and Santander in northern Spain, from which you can drive to Andalucía via Madrid. Ferry routes also connect Andalucía with Tangier and Nador in Morocco and with Ceuta and Melilla, the Spanish enclaves on the Moroccan coast.

The main highway from Madrid to Andalucía is the A4/AP4 to Córdoba, Seville and Cádiz. For Jaén, Granada, Almería or Málaga, turn off at Bailén. In the east, the AP7/A7 leads all the way down the Mediterranean side of Spain

CLIMATE CHANGE & TRAVEL

Climate change is a serious threat to the ecosystems that humans rely upon, and air travel is the fastest-growing contributor to the problem. Lonely Planet regards travel, overall, as a global benefit, but believes we all have a responsibility to limit our personal impact on global warming.

FLYING & CLIMATE CHANGE

Pretty much every form of motor travel generates CO_2 (the main cause of human-induced climate change) but planes are far and away the worst offenders, not just because of the sheer distances they allow us to travel, but because they release greenhouse gases high into the atmosphere. The statistics are frightening: two people taking a return flight between Europe and the US will contribute as much to climate change as an average household's gas and electricity consumption over a whole year.

CARBON OFFSET SCHEMES

Climatecare.org and other websites use 'carbon calculators' that allow jetsetters to offset the greenhouse gases they are responsible for with contributions to energy-saving projects and other climate-friendly initiatives in the developing world – including projects in India, Honduras, Kazakhstan and Uganda.

Lonely Planet, together with Rough Guides and other concerned partners in the travel industry, supports the carbon offset scheme run by climatecare.org. Lonely Planet offsets all of its staff and author travel.

For more information check out our website: lonelyplanet.com.

from La Jonquera on the French border as far as Algeciras, except for a couple of stretches in Andalucía where the old, unmodernised N340 remains.

If you just want to drive once you get to Andalucía, it usually works out cheaper (and quicker) to fly and hire a car there. In the UK, further information on driving in Europe is available from the **RAC** (☎ 0870 572 2722; www.rac.co.uk) or the **AA** (☎ 0800 085 2840 European breakdown cover enquiries; www.theaa.com).

For information on the paperwork needed for taking a vehicle to Spain and general information on driving in Spain, see p417.

BORDER CROSSINGS

If you're crossing with your car on the ferry from Morocco, vehicle checks range from perfunctory to (more often) rigorous and there are usually long queues at customs on the both sides of the Strait of Gibraltar.

TRAIN

The fastest way to get into Andalucía by train is on the AVE (Alta Velocidad Española) services from Madrid operated by Spain's national railway company **Renfe** (Red Nacional de los Ferrocarriles Españoles; Spanish National Railways; ☎ 902 24 02 02; www.renfe .es). Travelling at speeds of 280km/h, they connect Madrid to Córdoba (one-way from €57.30, 1¾ hours), Seville (from €69.80, around 2½ hours) and Málaga (from €73.60, three hours) in not much more time that in takes to travel by plane; work is underway to extend the Madrid–Seville service to Cádiz. From most other parts of Spain you can reach

Andalucía by train in one day, usually with a connection in Madrid.

Most long-distance trains have *preferente* (1st-class) and *turista* (2nd-class) carriages. They go under various names indicating standards of comfort and time of travel. An InterCity is a straightforward, limited-stop, daytime train on the Madrid–Córdoba–Málaga route. More comfortable (and more expensive) daytime trains may be called Altaria, Arco, Talgo, Talgo 200 or AVE. Overnight trains are classed as Estrella (with seats, couchettes and sleeping compartments) or the more comfortable Trenhotel. Both types offer seats, couchettes, and single or double compartments with and without shower.

Whichever train you take, it's best to buy your ticket in advance as trains can get fully booked, especially in July and August. You can do so in English by telephone and over the internet. Phone-booked tickets must be collected and paid for at a Renfe ticket office within 72 hours of booking and more than 24 hours before the train's departure from its starting point. Internet tickets can be paid for online. For the first online purchase with any individual credit card, tickets must be picked up at a Renfe ticket office at least one hour before the train's departure from its starting point; for further purchases, tickets can also be printed online.

Return fares on long-distance trains are 20% less than two one-way fares. Children aged under four years travel free; those from four to 11 (to 12 on some trains) get 40% off the cost of seats and couchettes. The Euro<26 card (see p402) gives 20% or 25% off long-distance and regional train fares.

If you're coming from elsewhere in Europe and can afford to take at least

a day to arrive, there are rail routes to Andalucía, always involving a change of train in Madrid or Barcelona. Direct trains run from Paris Gare d'Austerlitz to Madrid Chamartín (13½ hours). From Chamartín take the cross-town *cercanía* train service (10 minutes) to Atocha station for onward connections to Andalusian cities. More information is available from SNCF (French National Railways; ☎ 36 35 in France; www.sncf.com).

From London, the simplest and quickest route to Andalucía (about 24 hours) involves Eurostar (☎ 0870 518 6186; www.eurostar.com), the Channel Tunnel service from Waterloo to Paris, a change in Paris from the Gare du Nord to the Gare d'Austerlitz, an overnight sleeper-only train to Madrid's Chamartín station, and a change there to Atocha station for a fast train to Andalucía; it's generally cheaper (though less environmentally friendly) to fly. For information and bookings on rail travel from Britain, contact Rail Europe (☎ 0870 837 1371; www.raileurope.co.uk) or Eurostar.

No railway crosses from Portugal into Andalucía, but trains run along the Algarve to Vila Real de Santo António, where there's a ferry across the Río Guadiana to Ayamonte in Andalucía. To travel all the way by train from Lisbon (11 hours) to any Andalusian city you need to transfer in Madrid (and change from Chamartín to Atocha station there). Contact Renfe or Caminhos de Ferro Portugueses (Portuguese Railways; ☎ 808 208 208 in Portugal; www.cp.pt) for more information.

Direct trains run at least three times a week to Barcelona from cities in Switzerland and northern Italy, and daily from Montpellier in southern France. You can transfer to an Andalucía-bound train at Barcelona.

TRANSPORT

SEA

You can sail to Andalucía from the Moroccan ports of Tangier and Nador, as well as Ceuta or Melilla (Spanish enclaves on the Moroccan coast) and Ghazaouet (Algeria). The routes are: Melilla–Almería, Nador–Almería, Ghazaouet–Almería, Melilla–Málaga, Oran–Almería, Tangier–Gibraltar, Tangier–Algeciras, Ceuta–Algeciras and Tangier–Tarifa. All routes usually take vehicles as well as passengers and the most frequent sailings are to/from Algeciras. Usually, at least 10 sailings a day ply the routes between Algeciras and Tangier (1¼ to 2½ hours) and 16 between Algeciras and Ceuta (45 minutes). Extra services are added at busy times, especially during the peak summer period (mid-June to mid-September) when hundreds of thousands of Moroccan workers return home from Europe for holidays.

The main ferry companies are Acciona/Trasmediterránea (www.trasmediterranea.es), EuroFerrys (www.euroferrys.com), FRS (www.frs.es) and Balèria (www.baleria.com). There's little price difference between the rival lines. If you're taking a car, book well ahead for July, August or Easter travel, and expect long queues and customs formalities.

For further details see the Transport sections for Almería (p296), Gibraltar (p154), Málaga (p172) and Tarifa (p147).

If you're coming from the UK, P&O Ferries (www.poferries.com) operates a service twice-weekly from Portsmouth to Bilbao (29 to 34 hours), while Brittany Ferries (www.brittanyferries.com) operates a twice-weekly car ferry from Plymouth or Portsmouth to Santander (19 to 23 hours, March to November). From Bilbao and Santander, there are long-distance road, bus and rail connections to Andalucía.

GETTING AROUND

Andalucía has excellent road and bus networks, although having your own vehicle enables you to make the most of your time as bus services to smaller villages rarely operate more than once a day and there are often no services on weekends. Train services are similarly excellent, although they're not much use for getting around Cádiz province, or between Huelva province and anywhere but Seville.

BICYCLE

Andalucía is good biking territory, with wonderful scenery and varied terrain. While some mountain roads (such as those through the Sierra de Grazalema or Sierra Nevada) are best left to professional cyclists in training, there aren't too many corners of Andalucía that keen and reasonably fit cyclists can't reach. Plenty of lightly trafficked country roads, mostly in decent condition, enable riders to avoid the busy main highways. Road biking here is as safe as anywhere in Europe provided you make allowances for some drivers' love of speed. Day rides and touring by bike are particularly enjoyable in spring and autumn, avoiding weather extremes.

If you get tired of pedalling, it's often possible to take your bike on a bus (you'll usually just be asked to remove the front wheel). You can take bikes on overnight sleeper trains (not long-distance daytime trains), and on most regional and suburban trains; check at the train station before buying tickets for any special conditions you'll need to comply with.

Bicycles are quite widely available for hire in main cities, coastal resorts and inland towns and villages that attract tourism. They're often *bicis todo terreno* (mountain bikes). Prices range from €10 to €20 a day.

Bike lanes on main roads are rare, but cyclists are permitted to ride in groups up to two abreast. Helmets are obligatory outside built-up areas.

BOAT

The quickest and most enjoyable way to get between Cádiz and El Puerto de Santa María is by catamaran. See p119 for details.

BUS

Buses in Andalucía are mostly modern, comfortable and inexpensive, and run almost everywhere – including along some unlikely mountain roads – to connect remote villages with their nearest towns. The bigger cities are linked to each other by frequent daily services. On the less busy routes services may be reduced (or occasionally nonexistent) on Saturday and Sunday.

Larger towns and cities usually have one main *estación de autobuses* (bus station) where all out-of-town buses stop.

In smaller places, buses tend to operate from a particular street or square, which may be unmarked. Ask around; locals generally know where to go.

During Semana Santa (Holy Week) and July and August it's advisable to buy most bus tickets a day in advance. On a few routes, a return ticket is cheaper than two singles. Travellers aged under 26 should ask about discounts on intercity routes.

Buses on main intercity routes average around 70km/h, for a cost of around €1.20 per 14km. For detail on services, see this book's city and town sections.

All Andalucía's airports are linked to city centres by bus (and, in Málaga's case, also by train). Gibraltar airport is within walking distance of downtown Gibraltar and of the bus station in La Línea de la Concepción, Spain.

CAR & MOTORCYCLE

Andalucía's excellent road network and inexpensive rental cars make driving an attractive and practical way of getting around.

TRANSPORT

MAIN BUS COMPANIES

Company	Website	Telephone	Main destinations
Alsa	www.alsa.es	☎ 902 42 22 42	Almería, Córdoba, Granada, Jaén, Málaga, Seville
Casal	www.autocarescasal.com	☎ 954 99 92 90	Aracena, Carmona, Seville
Comes	www.tgcomes.es	☎ 902 19 92 08	Algeciras, Cádiz, Granada, Jerez, Málaga, Ronda, Seville
Damas	www.damas-sa.es	☎ 959 25 69 00	Ayamonte, Huelva, Seville
Linesur	www.linesur.com	☎ 956 34 10 63	Algeciras, Écija, Jerez, Osuna, Seville
Los Amarillos	www.losamarillos.es	☎ 902 21 03 17	Cádiz, Jerez, Málaga, Ronda, Seville
Portillo	www.ctsa-portillo.com	☎ 902 14 31 44	Algeciras, Costa del Sol, Málaga, Ronda
Transportes Ureña	-	☎ 957 40 45 58	Córdoba, Jaén, Seville

DISTANCE CHART (KM)

Note: Distances between destinations are approximate

	Almería	Antequera	Arcos de la Frontera	Cádiz	Córdoba	Gibraltar	Granada	Huelva	Jaén	Málaga	Marbella	Ronda	Seville	Tarifa
Antequera	247													
Arcos de la Frontera	435	148												
Cádiz	463	203	63											
Córdoba	316	136	280	261										
Gibraltar	339	180	112	124	294									
Granada	162	96	244	296	160	255								
Huelva	505	259	213	214	241	289	346							
Jaén	220	136	284	330	108	335	93	347						
Málaga	207	49	199	240	165	134	125	301	203					
Marbella	264	106	188	185	222	76	182	281	262	52				
Ronda	322	90	81	147	163	94	180	221	224	118	170			
Seville	410	162	118	126	143	201	252	95	246	209	191	132		
Tarifa	350	223	155	101	307	43	299	317	380	177	119	137	244	
Úbeda	224	193	340	403	144	386	145	376	56	254	306	280	284	436

TRANSPORT

BRINGING YOUR OWN VEHICLE

Bringing a vehicle of your own to Andalucía makes the most sense if you plan to stay for more than a couple of weeks. Petrol (around €1 per litre in Spain) is widely available. In the event of breakdowns, every small town and many villages will have a garage with mechanics on-site.

If the car is from the UK or Ireland, remember to adjust the headlights for driving in mainland Europe (motor accessory shops sell stick-on strips which deflect the beams in the required direction).

DRIVING LICENCE & DOCUMENTATION

All EU countries' licences (pink or pink-and-green) are accepted in Spain. Note, however, that the old-style UK green licence is rarely accepted. Licences from other countries are supposed to be accompanied by an International Driving Permit, but in practice your national li-

cence will suffice for renting cars or dealing with traffic police. The International Driving Permit, valid for 12 months, is available from automobile clubs in your country.

When driving a private vehicle in Europe, proof of ownership (a Vehicle Registration Document for UK-registered vehicles), driving licence, roadworthiness certificate (MOT), and either an insurance certificate or a Green Card (see Insurance, opposite) should always be carried. Also ask your insurer for a European Accident Statement form, which can greatly simplify matters in the event of an accident.

HIRE

If you plan to hire a car in Andalucía, it's a good idea to organise it before you leave. As a rule, local firms at Málaga airport or on the Costa del Sol offer the cheapest deals. You can normally get a four-door air-con economy-class car from local agencies for around €150 a week in August or €120 a week in January. Many local firms offer internet booking and you simply go to their desk in or just outside the airport on arrival. In general, rentals away from the holiday *costas* (coasts) are more expensive.

Well-established local firms with branches at Andalusian airports and/or major rail stations (such as Málaga and Seville) include the following:

Centauro (☎ 902 10 41 03; www.centauro.net)

Crown Car Hire (☎ 952 17 64 86; www.crown carhire.com)

Helle Hollis (☎ 952 24 55 44, in UK 0871 222 7245; www.hellehollis.com)

Holiday Car Hire (☎ 952 24 26 85; www .holidaycarhire.com)

Niza Cars (☎ 952 23 61 79; www.nizacars.es)

Pepecar.com (☎ 807 41 42 43; www.pepecar.com)

Major international rental companies are also present at many of the same arrival points and give assuredly high standards of service:

Avis (☎ 902 13 55 31; www.avis.com)

Europcar (☎ 913 43 45 12; www.europcar.com)

Hertz (☎ 917 49 90 69; www.hertz.es)

National/Atesa (☎ 902 10 01 01; www.atesa.es)

To rent a car you need to be aged at least 21 (23 with some companies) and to have held a driving licence for a minimum of one year (sometimes two years). Under-25s have to pay extra charges with many firms.

It's much easier, and often obligatory, to pay for your rental with a credit card.

As always, check the detail of exactly what you are paying for. Some companies will throw in extras such as child seats and the listing of additional drivers for free; others will charge for them. See the following section for some tips on rental-car insurance.

INSURANCE

Third-party motor insurance is a minimum requirement throughout Europe. If you live in the EU, your existing motor insurance will probably provide automatic third-party cover throughout the EU if you're travelling in your own vehicle. But check with your insurer about whether you will also be covered for medical or hospital expenses or accidental damage to your vehicle. You might have to pay an extra premium if you want the same protection abroad as you have at home. A European breakdown assistance policy such as the AA's or RAC's European Breakdown Cover, or the policies offered by Eurotunnel and many cross-Channel ferry companies, is also a good investment, providing services such as roadside assistance, towing, emergency repairs and 24-hour telephone assistance in English.

The Green Card is an internationally recognised document showing that you have the minimum insurance cover required by law in the country visited. It is provided free by insurers. If you're carrying an insurance certificate that gives the minimum legal cover, a Green Card is not essential, but it has the advantage of being easily recognised by foreign police and authorities.

If you're renting a vehicle in Andalucía, the routine insurance provided may not go beyond basic third-party requirements. For cover against theft or damage to the vehicle, or injury or death to driver or passengers, you may need to request extra coverage. Always read the fine print and don't be afraid to ask.

PARKING

Street parking space can be hard to find in larger cities during working hours (about 9am to 2pm Monday to Saturday and 5pm to 8pm Monday to Friday). You'll often have to use underground or multistorey car parks, which are common enough in cities, and well enough signposted, but not cheap (typically around €1 per hour or €10 to €15 for 24 hours); they are, however, generally more secure than the street. City hotels with their own parking usually charge for the right to use it, at similar or slightly cheaper rates to underground car parks.

Blue lines along the side of the street usually mean you must pay at a nearby meter to park during working hours (typically around €0.50 to €1 an hour). Yellow lines mean no parking. A sign with a red line through a blue backdrop also indicates that parking is prohibited. It's not sensible to park in prohibited zones, even if other drivers have (you risk your car being towed and paying at least €60 to have it released).

ROAD RULES

As elsewhere in continental Europe, drive on the right and overtake on the left (although the latter is just as often honoured in the breach!). The minimum driving age is 18 years. Rear seat belts, if fitted, must be worn and children under three must sit in child safety seats. The blood-alcohol limit is 0.05% (0.01% for drivers with a licence less than two years old) and breath-testing is carried out on occasion.

The police can – and do – carry out spot checks on drivers so it pays to have all your papers in order. Nonresident foreigners may be fined on the spot for traffic offences. You can appeal in writing (in any language) to the Jefatura Provincial de Tráfico (Provincial Traffic Headquarters) and if your appeal is upheld, you'll get your money back, but don't hold your breath for a favourable

result. Contact details for each province's traffic headquarters are given on the website of the **Dirección General de Tráfico** (www.dgt.es, in Spanish). Click on 'Trámites y Multas', then 'Direcciones y Teléfonos', then 'Jefaturas', then select the province you're in.

The speed limit is 50km/h in built-up areas, between 80km/h and 100km/h outside built-up areas, and 120km/h on *autopistas* (toll highways) and *autovías*.

In Spain it's compulsory to carry two warning triangles (to be placed 100m in front of and 100m behind your vehicle if you have to stop on the carriageway), and a reflective jacket, which must be donned if you get out of your vehicle on the carriageway or hard shoulder outside built-up areas.

It's illegal to use hand-held mobile phones while driving.

TAXI

Taxis are plentiful in larger places and even most villages have a taxi or two. Fares are reasonable – a typical 2km to 3km ride should cost about €3.50 to €4.50, with airport runs costing a bit extra. Intercity runs are around €0.60 per kilometre. You don't have to tip taxi drivers, but rounding up the change is always appreciated.

TRAIN

Renfe (☎ 902 24 02 02; www.renfe.es), Spain's national railway company, has an extensive and efficient rail system in Andalucía linking most of the main cities and many smaller places. Trains are at least as convenient, quick and inexpensive as buses on many routes. Remember, however, that the only services from Huelva go via Seville, while to get elsewhere in Andalucía by train from Cádiz, El Puerto de Santa María or Jerez de la Frontera, you'll need to go via Seville or Utrera.

Some of the long-distance routes linking Andalucía with other parts of Spain (see p414) are good for journeys within Andalucía as well. These include Córdoba–Málaga, Córdoba–Seville–Cádiz, and Córdoba–Ronda–Algeciras. Generally more frequent services between Andalusian destinations are provided by the cheaper (but slower), one-class *regional* and *cercanía* trains. *Regionales,* some of which are known as Andalucía Exprés, run between Andalusian cities, stopping at many towns en route. *Cercanías* are commuter trains that link Seville, Málaga and Cádiz with their suburbs and nearby towns.

Good or reasonable train services, with at least three direct trains running each way daily (often more), run on the following routes: Algeciras–Ronda–Bobadilla–Antequera–Granada, Málaga–Torremolinos–Fuengirola, Córdoba–Málaga, Seville–Jerez de la Frontera–El Puerto de Santa María–Cádiz, Seville–Antequera–Granada–Guadix–Almería Seville–Córdoba, Seville–Huelva and Seville–Bobadilla–Málaga.

Services on other routes tend to be infrequent and they often involve changing trains at the small junction station of Bobadilla in central Andalucía, where lines from Seville, Córdoba, Granada, Málaga and Algeciras all meet. It's also possible, if time-consuming to get to Jaén, the Sierra Norte of Sevilla province and the Sierra de Aracena by train.

Regional trains average around 75km/h, for a cost of around €1 per 15km. Return fares on many routes operated by Renfe (but not its *cercanía* services) are 20% less than two one-way fares. For more information on the possibilities, see this book's city and town sections.

TRANSPORT

LANGUAGE

Spanish, or Castilian *(castellano)* as it's often and more precisely called, is spoken throughout Andalucía. English isn't as widely spoken as many travellers might expect, though you're likely to find people who speak some English in the main cities and tourist areas. Generally, however, you'll be much better received if you make some attempt to communicate in Spanish.

For a more comprehensive guide to Spanish than we're able to offer in this book, pick up a copy of Lonely Planet's handy pocket-sized *Spanish Phrasebook*.

ANDALUSIAN PRONUNCIATION

Andalusians don't pronounce Spanish in quite the same way as do speakers from other parts of Spain, or as it is taught to foreigners, eg the lisped 's' found in standard Castilian is absent. Local accents vary, too, but whether you choose to use standard Castilian pronunciation or stick to the Andalusian pronunciation, you're sure to get your message across. The pronunciation guides included with the words and phrases below reflect the local Andalusian pronunciation.

VOWELS

a   as in 'father'
e   as in 'met'
i   as in 'marine'
o   as in 'or' (with no 'r' sound)
u   as in 'rule'; not pronounced after q and in the letter combinations **gue** and **gui**, unless it's marked with a diaeresis (eg *argüir*), in which case it's pronounced as English 'w'

CONSONANTS

While the consonants **ch**, **ll** and **ñ** are generally considered distinct letters, **ch** and **ll** are now often listed alphabetically under **c** and **l** respectively. The letter **ñ** is still treated as a separate letter and comes after **n** in dictionaries.

c   as 'k' before **a**, **o** and **u**; as 's' when followed by **e** or **i** (not the lisped 'th' of standard Castilian)
ch   as in 'choose'

d   as in 'dog' when initial or preceded by l or n; elsewhere as the 'th' in 'then', and sometimes not pronounced at all – thus *partido* (divided) is pronounced par·*tee*·o

g   as in 'go' before a, o and u; before e or i it's a harsh, breathy sound, similar to the 'ch' in Scottish *loch* (kh in our guides to pronunciation)

h   always silent (ie not pronounced)

j   as the 'ch' in the Scottish *loch* (kh in our guides to pronunciation)

ll   similar to the 'y' in 'yellow' but often closer to a 'j' in Andalucía

ñ   as the 'ni' in 'onion'

s   often not pronounced at all, especially when it occurs within a word; thus *pescados* (fish) can be pronounced pe·*ka*·o in Andalucía

x   as the 'x' in 'taxi' when between two vowels; as the 's' in 'sound' before a consonant

z   pronounced as 's' (not 'th' as in standard Castilian); z is often silent when at the end of a word

WORD STRESS

Stress is indicated by italics in the pronunciation guides included with all the words and phrases in this language guide. In general, words ending in vowels or the letters n or s have stress on the next-to-last syllable, while those with other endings have stress on the last syllable. Thus *vaca* (cow) and *caballos* (horses) both carry stress on the next-to-last syllable, while *ciudad* (city) and *infeliz* (unhappy) are both stressed on the last syllable.

Written accents indicate a stressed syllable, and will almost always appear in words that don't follow the rules above, eg *sótano* (basement), *porción* (portion).

GRAMMAR

In Spanish, nouns are either masculine or feminine. There are rules to help determine gender, although there are of course some exceptions. Feminine nouns generally end with -a or with the groups -ción, -sión or -dad. Other endings typically signify a masculine noun. Endings for adjectives also change to agree with the gender of the noun they modify (masculine/feminine -o/-a). Where both masculine and feminine forms are included in this language guide, they are separated by a slash, with the masculine form first, eg *perdido/a* (m/f).

If a noun or adjective ends in a vowel, the plural is formed by adding s to the end. If it ends in a consonant, the plural is formed by adding es to the end.

ACCOMMODATION

I'm looking for ...	*Estoy buscando ...*	e·*stoy* boos·*kan*·do ...
Where is ...?	*¿Dónde hay ...?*	*don*·de ai ...
a guest house	*una pensión/ un residencial/ un hospedaje*	*oo*·na pen·*syon/* oon re·see·den·*syal/* oon os·pe·*da*·khe
a hotel	*un hotel*	oon o·*tel*
a youth hostel	*un albergue juvenil*	oon al·*ber*·ge khoo·ve·*neel*
I'd like a ... room.	*Quisiera una habitación ...*	kee·*sye*·ra *oo*·na a·bee·ta·*syon* ...
double	*doble*	*do*·ble
single	*individual*	een·dee·vee·*dwal*
twin	*con dos camas*	kon dos *ka*·mas

Does it include breakfast?

¿Incluye el desayuno? een·*kloo*·ye el de·sa·*yoo*·no

May I see the room?

¿Puedo ver la habitación? pwe·do ver la a·bee·ta·*syon*

I don't like it.

No me gusta. no me *goos*·ta

It's fine. I'll take it.
OK. La alquilo.　　o·*kay* la al·*kee*·lo

I'm leaving now.
Me voy ahora.　　me *voy* a·o·ra

How much is it	¿Cuánto cuesta	kwan·to kwes·ta
per ...?	por ...?	por ...
night	noche	no·che
person	persona	per·so·na
week	semana	se·ma·na
full board	pensión	pen·syon
	completa	kom·ple·ta
too expensive	demasiado caro	de·ma·sya·do ka·ro
cheaper	más económico	mas e·ko·no·mee·ko
discount	descuento	des·kwen·to
private/shared	baño privado/	ba·nyo pree·va·do/
bathroom	compartido	kom·par·tee·do

CONVERSATION & ESSENTIALS

When talking to people familiar to you or younger than you, it's fine to use the informal form of 'you', *tú*, rather than the polite form, *Usted*. The polite form is always given in this guide; where options are given, the form is indicated by the abbreviations 'pol' and 'inf'.

Hello.	Hola.	o·la
Good morning.	Buenos días.	bwe·nos dee·as
Good afternoon.	Buenas tardes.	bwe·nas tar·des
Good evening/ night.	Buenas noches.	bwe·nas no·ches
Goodbye.	Adiós.	a·dyos
See you later	Hasta luego.	as·ta lwe·go
Yes.	Sí.	see
No.	No.	no
Please.	Por favor.	por fa·vor
Thank you.	Gracias.	gra·syas
Many thanks.	Muchas gracias.	moo·chas gra·syas
You're welcome.	De nada.	de na·da
Sorry.	Lo siento.	lo see·en·to
(when apologising)		

MAKING A RESERVATION

To ...	A ...
From ...	De ...
Date	Fecha
I'd like to book ...	Quisiera reservar ... (see 'Accommodation' for bed and room options)
in the name of ...	en nombre de ...
for the nights of ...	para las noches del ...
credit card (...)	(...) tarjeta de crédito
number	número de
expiry date	fecha de vencimiento de la
Please confirm ...	Puede confirmar ...
availability	la disponibilidad
price	el precio

Pardon me.	Perdón./	per·don/
	Discúlpeme.	dees·kool·pe·me

(before requesting information, for example)

Excuse me.	Permiso.	per·mee·so

(when asking permission to pass, for example)

How are things?
¿Qué tal?　　ke tal

What's your name?
¿Cómo se llama Usted? (pol)　ko·mo se ya·ma oo·ste
¿Cómo te llamas? (inf)　ko·mo te ya·mas

My name is ...
Me llamo ...　　me ya·mo ...

It's a pleasure to meet you.
Mucho gusto.　　moo·cho goos·to

Do you live here?
¿Vive/Vives aquí? (pol/inf)　vee·ve/vee·ves a·kee

Where are you from?
¿De dónde　　de don·de
es/eres? (pol/inf)　es/e·res

I'm from ...
Soy de ...　　soy de ...

Where are you staying?
¿Dónde está alojado? (pol)　don·de es·ta a·lo·kha·do
¿Dónde estás alojado? (inf)　don·de es·tas a·lo·kha·do

How long are you here for?
¿Cuánto tiempo se va a　kwan·to tyem·po se va a
quedar?　　ke·dar

May I take a photo?
¿Puedo hacer una foto?　pwe·do a·ser oo·na fo·to

SIGNS

Abierto	Open
Cerrado	Closed
Comisaría	Police Station
Entrada	Entrance
Información	Information
Prohibido	Prohibited
Prohibido Fumar	No Smoking
Salida	Exit
Servicios/Aseos	Toilets
Hombres	Men
Mujeres	Women

DIRECTIONS

How do I get to …?

¿Cómo puedo llegar a …?   ko·mo pwe·do ye·gar a …

Is it far?

¿Está lejos?   es·ta le·khos

Go straight ahead.

Siga/Vaya derecho.   see·ga/va·ya de·re·cho

Turn left.

Doble a la izquierda.   do·ble a la ees·kyer·da

Turn right.

Doble a la derecha.   do·ble a la de·re·cha

I'm lost.

Estoy perdido/a. (m/f)   es·toy per·dee·do/a

Can you show me (on the map)?

¿Me lo podría indicar   me lo po·dree·a een·dee·kar

(en el mapa)?   (en el ma·pa)

here	*aquí*	a·kee
there	*allí*	a·yee
traffic lights	*semáforos*	se·ma·fo·ros
north	*norte*	nor·te
south	*sur*	soor
east	*este*	es·te
west	*oeste*	o·es·te

EATING OUT

I'd like …, please.

Quisiera …, por favor.   kee·sye·ra … por fa·vor

I'm vegetarian.

Soy vegetariano/a. (m/f)   soy ve·khe·ta·rya·no/a

I'm allergic | *Soy alérgico/a* | soy a·ler·khee·ko/a
to … | *a … (m/f)* | a …
  dairy produce | *los productos* | los pro·dook·tos
  | *lácteos* | lak·te·os
  nuts | *las nueces* | las nwe·ses
  seafood | *los mariscos* | los ma·rees·kos

Please bring us the bill.

Por favor nos trae   por fa·vor nos tra·e

la cuenta …   la kwen·ta

That was delicious!

¡Estaba buenísimo!   es·ta·ba bwe·nee·see·mo

HEALTH

I'm sick.

Estoy enfermo/a.   es·toy en·fer·mo/a

Where's the hospital?

¿Dónde está el hospital?   don·de es·ta el os·pee·tal

I'm pregnant.

Estoy embarazada.   es·toy em·ba·ra·sa·da

I need a doctor (who speaks English).

Necesito un médico   ne·se·see·to oon me·dee·ko

(que habla inglés).   (ke a·bla een·gles)

I'm …	*Soy …*	soy …
asthmatic	*asmático/a*	as·ma·tee·ko/a
diabetic	*diabético/a*	dya·be·tee·ko/a
epileptic	*epiléptico/a*	e·pee·lep·tee·ko/a

I'm allergic | *Soy alérgico/a* | soy a·ler·khee·ko/a
to … | *a …* | a …
  antibiotics | *los antibióticos* | los an·tee·byo·tee·kos
  penicillin | *la penicilina* | la pe·nee·see·lee·na

I have …	*Tengo …*	ten·go …
diarrhoea	*diarrea*	dya·re·a
a fever	*fiebre*	fee·eb·ray
a headache	*un dolor de*	oon do·lor de
	cabeza	ka·be·sa
nausea	*náusea*	now·se·a

LANGUAGE DIFFICULTIES

Do you speak (English)?

¿Habla/Hablas   a·bla/a·blas

(inglés)? (pol/inf)   (een·gles)

I (don't) understand.

Yo (no) entiendo.   yo (no) en·*tyen*·do

How do you say ...?

¿Cómo se dice ...?   *ko*·mo se *dee*·se ...

What does ... mean?

¿Qué quiere decir ...?   ke *kye*·re de·*seer* ...

Could you	¿Puede ..., por	*pwe*·de ... por
please ...?	favor?	fa·*vor*
repeat that	repetirlo	re·pe·*teer*·lo
speak more	hablar más	a·*blar* mas
slowly	despacio	des·*pa*·syo
write it down	escribirlo	es·kree·*beer*·lo

NUMBERS

1	uno	*oo*·no
2	dos	dos
3	tres	tres
4	cuatro	*kwa*·tro
5	cinco	*seen*·ko
6	seis	says
7	siete	*sye*·te
8	ocho	*o*·cho
9	nueve	*nwe*·ve
10	diez	dyes
11	once	*on*·se
12	doce	*do*·se
13	trece	*tre*·se
14	catorce	ka·*tor*·se
15	quince	*keen*·se
16	dieciséis	dye·see·*says*
17	diecisiete	dye·see·*sye*·te
18	dieciocho	dye·see·*o*·cho
19	diecinueve	dye·see·*nwe*·ve
20	veinte	*vayn*·te
21	veintiuno	vayn·tee·*oo*·no
22	veintidós	vayn·tee·*dohs*
30	treinta	*trayn*·ta
31	treinta y uno	*trayn*·ta ee *oo*·no
32	treinta y dos	*trayn*·ta ee dos
40	cuarenta	kwa·*ren*·ta
50	cincuenta	seen·*kwen*·ta
60	sesenta	se·*sen*·ta
70	setenta	se·*ten*·ta
80	ochenta	o·*chen*·ta

EMERGENCIES

Help!	¡Socorro!	so·*ko*·ro
Fire!	¡Incendio!	een·*sen*·dyo
Go away!	¡Vete!/¡Fuera!	*ve*·te/*fwe*·ra

Call ...!	¡Llame a ...!	*ya*·me a ...
an ambulance	una	*oo*·na
	ambulancia	am·boo·*lan*·sya
a doctor	un médico	oon *me*·dee·ko
the police	la policía	la po·lee·*see*·a

It's an emergency.

Es una emergencia.   es *oo*·na e·mer·*khen*·sya

Could you help me, please?

¿Me puede ayudar,   me *pwe*·de a·yoo·*dar*
por favor?   por fa·*vor*

I'm lost.

Estoy perdido/a.   es·*toy* per·*dee*·do/a

Where are the toilets?

¿Dónde están los baños?   *don*·de es·*tan* los *ba*·nyos

90	noventa	no·*ven*·ta
100	cien	syen
101	ciento uno	*syen*·to *oo*·no
200	doscientos	do·*syen*·tos
1000	mil	meel
5000	cinco mil	*seen*·ko meel

SHOPPING & SERVICES

I'd like to buy ...

Quisiera comprar ...   kee·*sye*·ra kom·*prar* ...

I'm just looking.

Sólo estoy mirando.   *so*·lo es·*toy* mee·*ran*·do

May I look at it?

¿Puedo mirar(lo/la)? (m/f)   *pwe*·do mee·*rar*·(lo/la)

How much is it?

¿Cuánto cuesta?   *kwan*·to *kwes*·ta

That's too expensive for me.

Es demasiado caro   es de·ma·*sya*·do *ka*·ro
para mí.   *pa*·ra mee

Could you lower the price?

¿Podría bajar un poco   po·*dree*·a ba·*khar* oon *po*·ko
el precio?   el *pre*·syo

I don't like it.

No me gusta.   no me *goos*·ta

LANGUAGE

ROAD SIGNS

Acceso	Entrance
Aparcamiento	Parking
Ceda el Paso	Give Way
Despacio	Slow
Desvío	Detour
Dirección Única	One-way
Frene	Slow Down
No Adelantar	No Overtaking
Peaje	Toll
Peligro	Danger
Prohibido Aparcar/ No Estacionar	No Parking
Prohibido el Paso	No Entry
Vía de Accesso	Exit Freeway

I'll take it.

Lo llevo.   lo ye·vo

I'm looking for the ...	Estoy buscando ...	es·toy boos·kan·do ...
ATM	el cajero automático	el ka·khe·ro ow·to·ma·tee·ko
bank	el banco	el ban·ko
bookstore	la librería	la lee·bre·ree·a
chemist/ pharmacy	la farmacia	la far·ma·sya
embassy	la embajada	la em·ba·kha·da
laundry	la lavandería	la la·van·de·ree·a
market	el mercado	el mer·ka·do
post office	los correos	los ko·re·os
supermarket	el supermercado	el soo·per·mer·ka·do
tourist office	la oficina de turismo	la o·fee·see·na de too·rees·mo

Do you accept ...?	¿Aceptan ...?	a·sep·tan ...
credit cards	tarjetas de crédito	tar·khe·tas de kre·dee·to
travellers cheques	cheques de viajero	che·kes de vya·khe·ro

less	menos	me·nos
more	más	mas
large	grande	gran·de
small	pequeño/a	pe·ke·nyo/a

What time does it open/close?

¿A qué hora abre/cierra?   a ke o·ra a·bre/sye·ra

I want to change some money/travellers cheques.

Quiero cambiar dinero/   kye·ro kam·byar dee·ne·ro/
cheques de viajero.   che·kes de vya·khe·ro

What is the exchange rate?

¿Cuál es el tipo de   kwal es el tee·po de
cambio?   kam·byo

I want to call ...

Quiero llamar a ...   kye·ro ya·mar a ...

airmail	correo aéreo	ko·re·o a·e·re·o
letter	carta	kar·ta
registered mail	correo certificado	ko·re·o ser·tee·fee·ka·do
stamps	sellos	se·yos

TIME & DATES

What time is it?

¿Qué hora es?   ke o·ra es

It's one o'clock.

Es la una.   es la oo·na

It's seven o'clock.

Son las siete.   son las sye·te

midnight	medianoche	me·dya·no·che
noon	mediodía	me·dyo·dee·a
half past two	dos y media	dos ee me·dya
now	ahora	a·o·ra
today	hoy	oy
tonight	esta noche	es·ta no·che
tomorrow	mañana	ma·nya·na
yesterday	ayer	a·yer

Monday	lunes	loo·nes
Tuesday	martes	mar·tes
Wednesday	miércoles	myer·ko·les
Thursday	jueves	khwe·ves
Friday	viernes	vyer·nes
Saturday	sábado	sa·ba·do
Sunday	domingo	do·meen·go

LANGUAGE

January	enero	e·ne·ro
February	febrero	fe·bre·ro
March	marzo	mar·so
April	abril	a·breel
May	mayo	ma·yo
June	junio	khoo·nyo
July	julio	khoo·lyo
August	agosto	a·gos·to
September	septiembre	sep·tyem·bre
October	octubre	ok·too·bre
November	noviembre	no·vyem·bre
December	diciembre	dee·syem·bre

TRANSPORT

PUBLIC TRANSPORT

What time does	¿A qué hora	a ke o·ra
… leave/arrive?	sale/llega …?	sa·le/ye·ga …
the bus	el autobús	el ow·to·boos
the plane	el avión	el a·vyon
the ship	el barco	el bar·ko
the train	el tren	el tren

The … is delayed.
El … está retrasado.   el … es·ta re·tra·sa·do
I'd like a ticket to …
Quiero un billete a …   kye·ro oon bee·ye·te a …

the bus station	la estación de autobuses	la es·ta·syon de ow·to·boo·ses
the bus stop	la parada de autobuses	la pa·ra·da de ow·to·boo·ses
the left luggage room	la consigna	la kon·seeg·na
taxi	taxi	tak·see
the ticket office	la taquilla	la ta·kee·ya
the train station	la estación de tren	la es·ta·syon de tren

a … ticket	un billete de …	oon bee·ye·te de …
one-way	ida	ee·da
return	ida y vuelta	ee·da ee vwel·ta
1st class	primera clase	pree·me·ra kla·se
2nd class	segunda clase	se·goon·da kla·se
student	estudiante	es·too·dyan·te

Is this taxi free?
¿Está libre este taxi?   e·sta lee·bre es·te tak·see

What's the fare to …?
¿Cuánto cuesta hasta …?   kwan·to kwes·ta a·sta …
Please put the meter on.
Por favor, ponga el   por fa·vor pon·ga el
taxímetro.   tak·see·me·tro

PRIVATE TRANSPORT

(How long) Can I park here?
¿(Por cuánto tiempo)   (por kwan·to tyem·po)
Puedo aparcar aquí?   pwe·do a·par·kar a·kee
Where do I pay?
¿Dónde se paga?   don·de se pa·ga

I'd like to	Quisiera	kee·sye·ra
hire a/an …	alquilar …	al·kee·lar …
4WD	un todoterreno	oon to·do·te·re·no
car	un coche	oon ko·che
motorbike	una moto	oo·na mo·to
bicycle	una bicicleta	oo·na bee·see·kle·ta

Is this the road to …?
¿Se va a … por   se va a … por
esta carretera?   es·ta ka·re·te·ra
Where's a petrol station?
¿Dónde hay una   don·de ai oo·na
gasolinera?   ga·so·lee·ne·ra
Please fill it up.
Lleno, por favor.   ye·no por fa·vor
I'd like (20) litres.
Quiero (veinte) litros.   kye·ro (vayn·te) lee·tros

diesel	diesel	dee·sel
petrol/gas	gasolina	ga·so·lee·na

I need a mechanic.
Necesito un   ne·se·see·to oon
mecánico.   me·ka·nee·ko
The car has broken down (in …).
El coche se ha averiado   el ko·che se a a·ve·rya·do
(en …).   (en …)
The motorbike won't start.
No arranca la moto.   no a·ran·ka la mo·to
I have a flat tyre.
Tengo un pinchazo.   ten·go oon peen·cha·so

I've run out of petrol.

Me he quedado sin   me e ke·*da*·do seen
gasolina.   ga·so·*lee*·na

I've had an accident.

He tenido un accidente.   e te·*nee*·do oon ak·see·*den*·te

Do you mind if I breastfeed here?

¿Le molesta que dé   le mo·*les*·ta ke de
de pecho aquí?   de *pe*·cho a·*kee*

Are children allowed?

¿Se admiten niños?   se ad·*mee*·ten *nee*·nyos

TRAVEL WITH CHILDREN

I need ...

Necesito ...   ne·se·*see*·to ...

Do you have ...?

¿Hay ...?   ai ...

a car baby seat	*un asiento de seguridad para bebés*	oon a·*syen*·to de se·goo·ree·*da* pa·ra be·*bes*
a child-minding service	*un servicio de cuidado de niños*	oon ser·*vee*·syo de kwee·*da*·do de *nee*·nyos
a children's menu	*un menú infantil*	oon me·*noo* een·fan·*teel*
(disposable) diapers/nappies	*pañales (de usar y tirar)*	pa·*nya*·les (de oo·*sar* ee tee·*rar*)
an (English-speaking) babysitter	*un canguro (de habla inglesa)*	oon kan·*goo*·ro (de *a*·bla een·*gle*·sa)
infant formula (milk powder)	*leche en polvo*	*le*·che en *pol*·vo
a highchair	*una trona*	*oo*·na *tro*·na
a potty	*un orinal de niños*	oon o·*ree*·nal de *nee*·nyos
a stroller	*un cochecito*	oon ko·che·*see*·to

LANGUAGE

Also available from Lonely Planet:
Spanish phrasebook

GLOSSARY

For terms for food, drinks and other culinary vocabulary, see p375. For additional terms and information regarding the Spanish language, see the Language chapter on p422.

alameda – *paseo* lined (or originally lined) with *álamo* (poplar) trees

alcázar – Islamic-era fortress

artesonado – ceiling with interlaced beams leaving regular spaces for decorative insertions

autopista – toll highway

autovía – toll-free dual carriageway

AVE – Alta Velocidad Española; the high-speed train between Madrid and Seville

ayuntamiento – city or town hall

azulejo – tile

bahía – bay

bailaor/a – flamenco dancer

bandolero – bandit

barrio – district or quarter (of a town or city)

biblioteca – library

bici todo terreno (BTT) – mountain bike

bodega – winery, wine bar or wine cellar

buceo – scuba diving

bulería – upbeat type of flamenco song

buzón – postbox

cabalgata – cavalcade

cajero automático – automated teller machine (ATM)

calle – street

callejón – lane

cama individual – single bed

cama matrimonial – double bed

cambio – currency exchange

campiña – countryside (usually flat or rolling cultivated countryside)

camping – camping ground

campo – countryside, field

cantaor/a – flamenco singer

cante jondo – 'deep song', the essence of flamenco

capilla – chapel

capilla mayor – chapel containing the high altar of a church

carnaval – carnival; a pre-Lent period of fancy-dress parades and merrymaking

carretera – road, highway

carril de cicloturismo – road adapted for cycle touring

carta – menu

casa de huéspedes – guest house

casa rural – a village house or farmhouse with rooms to let

casco – literally 'helmet'; used to refer to the old part of a city *(casco antiguo)*

castellano – Castilian; the language also called Spanish

castillo – castle

caza – hunting

centro comercial – shopping centre

cercanía – suburban train

cerro – hill

cervecería – beer bar

chiringuito – small, often makeshift bar or eatery, usually in the open air

choza – traditional thatch hut

Churrigueresque – ornate style of baroque architecture named after the brothers Alberto and José Churriguera

cofradía – see *hermandad*

colegiata – collegiate church, a combined church and college

comedor – dining room

comisaría – station of the Policía Nacional (National Police)

consigna – left-luggage office or lockers

converso – Jew who converted to Christianity in medieval Spain

copla – flamenco song

cordillera – mountain chain

coro – choir (part of a church, usually in the middle)

corrida de toros – bullfight

cortes – parliament

cortijo – country property

costa – coast

coto – area where hunting rights are reserved for a specific group of people

cruce – cross

cuenta – bill (check)

cuesta – sloping land, road or street

custodia – monstrance (receptacle for the consecrated Host)

dehesa – woodland pastures with evergreen oaks

Denominación de Origen (DO) – a designation that indicates the unique geographical origins, production processes and quality of wines, olive oil and other products

duende – the spirit or magic possessed by great flamenco performers

duque – duke

duquesa – duchess

embalse – reservoir

ermita – hermitage or chapel

escalada – climbing

estación de autobuses – bus station

estación de esquí – ski station or resort

estación de ferrocarril – train station

estación marítima – passenger port

estanco – tobacconist

estrella – literally 'star'; also class of overnight train with seats, couchettes and sleeping compartments

farmacia – pharmacy

faro – lighthouse

feria – fair; can refer to trade fairs as well as to city, town or village fairs

ferrocarril – railway

fiesta – festival, public holiday or party

finca – country property, farm

flamenco – means flamingo and Flemish as well as flamenco music and dance

frontera – frontier

fuente – fountain, spring

gitano – the Spanish word for Roma people

Guardia Civil – Civil Guard; police responsible for roads, the countryside, villages and international borders. They wear green uniforms. See also *Policía Local, Policía Nacional*.

hammam – Arabic-style bathhouse

hermandad – brotherhood (which may include women), in particular one that takes part in religious processions; also *cofradía*

hospedaje – guest house

hostal – simple guest house or small place offering budget hotel-like accommodation

infanta – daughter of a monarch but not first in line to the throne

infante – son of a monarch but not first in line to the throne

instalación juvenil – youth hostel or youth camp

IVA – *impuesto sobre el valor añadido;* the Spanish equivalent of VAT (value-added tax)

jardín – garden
judería – Jewish barrio in medieval Spain
Junta de Andalucía – executive government of Andalucía

latifundia – huge estate
lavandería – laundry
levante – easterly wind
librería – bookshop
lidia – the modern art of bullfighting on foot
lista de correos – poste restante
lucio – pond or pool in the Doñana *marismas* (wetlands)

madrugada/madrugá – the 'early hours', from around 3am to dawn; a pretty lively time in some Spanish cities.
marismas – wetlands, marshes
marisquería – seafood eatery
marqués – marquis
medina – Arabic word for town or inner city
mercadillo – flea market
mercado – market
mezquita – mosque
mihrab – prayer niche in a mosque indicating the direction of Mecca
mirador – lookout point
morisco – Muslim converted to Christianity in medieval Spain
moro – 'Moor' or Muslim (usually in a medieval context)
movida – the late-night bar and club scene that emerged in Spanish cities and towns after Franco's death; a *zona de movida* or *zona de marcha* is an area of a town where people gather to drink and have a good time
mozárabe – Mozarab; Christian living under Islamic rule in medieval Spain
Mudéjar – Muslim living under Christian rule in medieval Spain; also refers to their decorative style of architecture
muelle – wharf, pier
muladí – Muwallad; Christian who converted to Islam, in medieval Spain

nazareno – penitent taking part in Semana Santa processions
nieve – snow
nuevo – new

oficina de correos – post office
oficina de turismo – tourist office
olivo – olive tree

palacio – palace
palo – literally 'stick'; also refers to the categories of flamenco song
panadería – bakery
papelería – stationery shop
parador – one of the Paradores Nacionales, a state-owned chain of luxurious hotels, often in historic buildings
paraje natural – natural area
parque nacional – national park
parque natural – natural park
paseo – avenue or parklike strip; walk or stroll
paso – literally 'step'; also the platform an image is carried on in a religious procession
peña – a club; usually for supporters of a football club or flamenco enthusiasts *(peña flamenca)*, but sometimes a dining club
pensión – guest house
pescadería – fish shop
picadero – riding stable
pícaro – dice trickster and card sharp, rogue, low-life scoundrel
pinsapar – forest of *pinsapo*
pinsapo – Spanish fir
piscina – swimming pool
plateresque – early phase of Renaissance architecture noted for its decorative facades
playa – beach
plaza de toros – bullring
Policía Local – Local Police; also known as Policía Municipal. Controlled by city and town halls, they deal mainly with minor matters such as parking, traffic and bylaws. They wear blue-and-white uniforms. See also *Guardia Civil, Policía Nacional.*
Policía Municipal – Municipal Police; see *Policía Local*

GLOSSARY

Policía Nacional – National Police; responsible for cities and bigger towns, some of them forming special squads dealing with drugs, terrorism and the like.

poniente – westerly wind

pozo – well

preferente – 1st-class carriage on a long-distance train

provincia – province; Spain is divided into 50 of them

pueblo – village, town

puente – bridge

puerta – gate, door

puerto – port, mountain pass

puerto deportivo – marina

puerto pesquero – fishing port

punta – point

rambla – stream

Reconquista – the Christian reconquest of the Iberian Peninsula from the Muslims (8th to 15th centuries)

refugio – shelter or refuge, especially a mountain refuge with basic accommodation for hikers

regional – train running between Andalusian cities

reja – grille; especially a wrought-iron one over a window or dividing a chapel from the rest of a church

Renfe – Red Nacional de los Ferrocarriles Españoles; Spain's national rail network

reserva – reservation, or reserve (eg nature reserve)

reserva nacional de caza – national hunting reserve

reserva natural – nature reserve

retablo – retable (altarpiece)

ría – estuary

río – river

romería – festive pilgrimage or procession

ronda – ring road

s/n – *sin numero* (without number); sometimes seen in addresses

sacristía – sacristy, the part of a church in which vestments, sacred objects and other valuables are kept

salina – salt lagoon

Semana Santa – Holy Week; the week leading up to Easter Sunday

sendero – path or track

sevillana – a popular Andalusian dance

sierra – mountain range

Siglo de Oro – Spain's cultural 'Golden Century', beginning in the 16th century and ending in the 17th century

taberna – tavern

tablao – flamenco show

taifa – one of the small kingdoms into which the Muslim-ruled parts of Spain were divided during parts of the 11th and 12th centuries

taquilla – ticket window

taracea – marquetry

tarjeta de crédito – credit card

tarjeta telefónica – phonecard

teléfono móvil – mobile telephone

temporada alta – high season

temporada baja – low season

temporada extra – extra-high season

temporada media – shoulder season

terraza – terrace; often means an area with outdoor tables at a bar, cafe or restaurant

tetería – Middle Eastern–style teahouse with low seats around low tables

tienda – shop, tent

tocaor/a – flamenco guitarist

torre – tower

trenhotel – sleek, expensive, sleeping-car-only train

turismo – means both tourism and saloon car; *el turismo* can also mean the tourist office

turista – 2nd-class carriage on a long-distance train

valle – valley

VO – *versión original;* foreign-language film

VOS – *versión original subtitulada;* foreign-language film subtitled in Spanish

zoco – large market in Muslim cities

zona de protección – protected area

zona restringida – restricted area

BEHIND THE SCENES

THIS BOOK

This 6th edition of *Andalucía* stands on the shoulders of the previous five editions: the first two editions were written by John Noble and Susan Forsyth, who were joined by Des Hannigan and Heather Dickson on the 3rd edition. The 4th edition was written by John, Susan, Heather and Paula Hardy, and the 5th by John, Susan and Vesna Maric. This edition was researched, restructured and written by Anthony Ham, Stuart Butler, Vesna Maric and Zora O'Neill, with assistance from John Noble. It was commissioned in Lonely Planet's London office, and produced by the following:

Commissioning Editor Lucy Monie
Coordinating Editor Martine Power
Coordinating Cartographer Anthony Phelan
Coordinating Layout Designer Wibowo Rusli
Managing Editor Annelies Mertens
Managing Cartographers Corey Hutchison, Alison Lyall, Herman So
Managing Layout Designer Laura Jane
Assisting Editors Andrew Bain, Michelle Bennett, Monique Choy
Assisting Cartographer Ross Macaw
Cover Research Katy Murenu, lonelyplanetimages.com
Internal Image Research Sabrina Dalbesio, lonelyplanetimages.com
Language Content Robyn Loughnane

THE LONELY PLANET STORY

Fresh from an epic journey across Europe, Asia and Australia in 1972, Tony and Maureen Wheeler sat at their kitchen table stapling together notes. The first Lonely Planet guidebook, *Across Asia on the Cheap,* was born.

Travellers snapped up the guides. Inspired by their success, the Wheelers began publishing books to Southeast Asia, India and beyond. Demand was prodigious, and the Wheelers expanded the business rapidly to keep up. Over the years, Lonely Planet extended its coverage to every country and into the virtual world via lonelyplanet.com and the Thorn Tree message board.

As Lonely Planet became a globally loved brand, Tony and Maureen received several offers for the company. But it wasn't until 2007 that they found a partner whom they trusted to remain true to the company's principles of travelling widely, treading lightly and giving sustainably. In October of that year, BBC Worldwide acquired a 75% share in the company, pledging to uphold Lonely Planet's commitment to independent travel, trustworthy advice and editorial independence.

Today, Lonely Planet has offices in Melbourne, London and Oakland, with over 500 staff members and 300 authors. Tony and Maureen are still actively involved with Lonely Planet. They're travelling more often than ever, and they're devoting their spare time to charitable projects. And the company is still driven by the philosophy of *Across Asia on the Cheap*: 'All you've got to do is decide to go and the hardest part is over. So go!'

SEND US YOUR FEEDBACK

We love to hear from travellers – your comments keep us on our toes and help make our books better. Our well-travelled team reads every word on what you loved or loathed about this book. Although we cannot reply individually to postal submissions, we always guarantee that your feedback goes straight to the appropriate authors, in time for the next edition. Each person who sends us information is thanked in the next edition – and the most useful submissions are rewarded with a free book.

To send us your updates – and find out about Lonely Planet events, newsletters and travel news – visit our award-winning website: **lonelyplanet.com/contact**.

Note: We may edit, reproduce and incorporate your comments in Lonely Planet products such as guidebooks, websites and digital products, so let us know if you don't want your comments reproduced or your name acknowledged. For a copy of our privacy policy visit lonelyplanet.com/privacy.

Project Manager Rachel Imeson

Thanks to Mark Adams, Imogen Bannister, Lucy Birchley, Yvonne Bischofberger, Sally Darmody, Janine Eberle, Owen Eszeki, Mark Germanchis, Michelle Glynn, Imogen Hall, Paula Hardy, Lauren Hunt, Nic Lehman, John Mazzocchi, Wayne Murphy, Darren O'Connell, Trent Paton, Julie Sheridan, Glenn van der Knijff

THANKS

ANTHONY HAM

A heartfelt *muchísimas gracias* to Alberto and Marina for providing such a homely El Puerto de Santa María base. Thanks also to Karen Abrahams, Eline Janssens, and everyone at the Centro Andaluz de Flamenco, FIRMM and tourist offices across the region. Thanks to my editor, Lucy Monie, my coauthors Stuart, Zora and Vesna, and Paula Hardy and Lauren Hunt for making my job so easy. And to Marina and Carlota: *sois mi vida, como siempre, para siempre*. My work on this book is dedicated to Susan, who died before research for this edition began, and to John Noble: together they made this book their own over so many editions.

STUART BUTLER

I'm indebted to a number of people for their help with my chapters on Seville and Huelva. Firstly, thank you to Gonzelo Dorado for making Doñana as fascinating as ever. In Seville thank you to Javier Vivó for the food and interviews, July Seban for showing me around the city, the two sisters at Kiwi Juice Bar for restaurant advice and keeping me hydrated and Laura for culinary tips. Thank you also to Anne and Bill for letting us stay when we were in the border region and finally, and as always, *gracias* to Heather for everything.

VESNA MARIC

Big thank yous to everyone in Málaga, especially Minja and Constancio, Marta and Blanca. *Gracias* to Susana, Alicia, Lucas and Pau. Huge *gracias* to the Melguizo family: Carlos, Marta, Marina and Blanca. Thanks to Pablo and Martin. Biggest thanks to R, as always. Thanks to my editor, Lucy Monie, coordinating author Anthony Ham, and the rest of the authors on this book. Finally, I'd like to honour the memory of Susan Forsyth.

ZORA O'NEILL

Many thanks to Adriana Valencia, for great leads in Granada; Heather Coburn-Flores, for a lovely home base; La Familia Chay (Maya, Freya, Heidi and Dan) for ice-cream consulting and more; Claudia Scholler and Alexis Timon for being guides to Almería; and especially to Peter Moskos and Beverly McFarland, for keeping me company and giving me a reason to order more food.

OUR READERS

Many thanks to the travellers who used the last edition and wrote to us with helpful hints, useful advice and interesting anecdotes:

Christian Byhahn, Fabio Calderoni, Jan Cornelis, Silvia Covelli, Dirk Depril, Julie Doherty, David Durell, Nic Geerts, Frank Gelok, Sheila Gemmell, M Heathcote, Maggy Heintz, Laura Herrod, Shu Fen Ho, Clare Joyner, Malcolm Kent, Simon King, Kim Leers, Niall Manning, Connie Menting, Richard Monteith, Peter Morfoot, Nicolas Notis, Steve Perlmuttr, Jeremy Pollack, Greg Powell, Hugo Prodano, Julie Ramsden, Jan Reund, Caroline Rose, Elin Satersdal, Henrik Schoppe, Richard Sctoo, Chris Shepherd, Istvan Szucs, Cherry Thanker, Kate Turner, Bram Van Boven, Rick Vedder, Nicola Wake, Isabel Wichmann, Mark Wilcox, Danielle Wolbers, Daphine Wong, Andrew Yale

ACKNOWLEDGMENTS

All images are the copyright of the photographers unless otherwise indicated. Many of the images in this guide are available for licensing from Lonely Planet Images: lonelyplanetimages.com.

INDEX

A

accommodation 9, 378-99
    Almería province 291, 398-9
    Cádiz province 118, 385-8
    Córdoba province 206,
        391-2
    Granada province 247,
        394-8
    Huelva province 103, 383-5
    internet resources 381
    Jaén province 227, 392-4
    Málaga province 167,
        388-91
    price guide 8, 378-9
    rural hotels 390
    Seville & Sevilla province
        40, 379-83
    terminology 378
activities 20-3, 348-51, *see also*
    individual activities
air travel 412-13
    internet resources 413
Alameda de Hércules (Seville)
    52, **54**
Alcaicería 260
Alcazaba (Almería) 291
Alcazaba (Antequera) 185
Alcazaba (Granada) 257
Alcazaba (Málaga) 166
Alcázar (Jerez de la Frontera)
    127, 336
Alcázar (Seville) 44-6, 92
Alhambra 254-8, 337-9, **4-5,**
    90-1
Almería 290-7, **292-3**
    accommodation 291, 398-9
    attractions 290-5
    festivals & events 295
    food 295-6
    history 290
    internet resources 289
    planning 288-9
    tourist information 290
    tours 288
    transport 296-7
Almería province 285-311,
    286-7, 24
Almodóvar del Río 217

000 MAP PAGES
000 PHOTOGRAPH PAGES

Almonaster La Real 102, 335
Almuñécar 282-4
Antequera 184-7
apes, Barbary 151, 346
Arab baths, *see* bathhouses
Aracena 99-101, **99**
archaeological sites
    Baelo Claudia 147, 92-3
    Los Millares 299-300
    Medina Azahara 209-10,
        335, **93**
    Ronda la Vieja 182
architecture 13, 332-42
    baroque 341
    books 334
    gothic 339-40
    Islamic 321, 332-9
    modern 341-2
    Renaissance 340, 341
Archivo de Indias 46
Arcos de la Frontera 133-7,
    135
Ardales 182-4
area codes 409, *see also inside*
    front cover
art galleries, *see also* museums
    Centro Andaluz de Arte
        Contemporáneo 53
    Centro Andaluz de la
        Fotografía 293
    Centro de Arte
        Contemporáneo 167
    Fundación NMAC 142
arts 13, 116, 360-3, *see also*
    literature, music, painting,
    sculpture
Atalbéitar 278
ATMs 407
Ayamonte 84

B

Baelo Claudia 147, 92-3
Baena 213
Baeza 230-4, **232**
Banderas, Antonio 364
Barbary apes 151, 346
baroque architecture 215
Barranco de Poqueira 277-8
Barrio de La Villa 216
Barrio de Santa Cruz (Seville)
    46-7, **42**

bathhouses 263, 337
    Aire de Sevilla (Seville) 53
    Aljibe San Miguel Baños
        Árabes (Granada) 264
    Balneario de Lanjarón
        (Lanjarón) 276
    Baño Moro (Segura de la
        Sierra) 245
    Baños Árabes (Málaga) 168
    Baños Árabes (Ronda) 179
    Baños Árabes El Bañuelo
        (Granada) 260
    Baños de Elvira (Granada)
        264
    Hammam Andalusi (Jerez
        de la Frontera) 128-9
    Hammam Baños Árabes
        (Córdoba) 209
    Hammams de Al Andalus
        (Granada) 264
bathrooms 409
Baza 271-81
beaches 22
    Almuñécar 282-4
    Cabo de Gata 302-3, **6,**
        20, 95
    Cabo de Trafalgar 142
    Costa de la Luz (Cádiz
        province) 140-7, **20**
    Costa de la Luz (Huelva
        province) 82-4
    Isla Cristina 83
    itinerary 33
    La Herradura 282-4
    Málaga 167-8
    Matalascañas 83
    Mojácar 307
    Parque Natural de Cabo
        de Gata-Níjar 302-3, **6,**
        20, 95
    Playa Burriana 191
    Playa Calahonda 191
    Playa Chica 145
    Playa de Cantarriján 192
    Playa de la Caleta 116
    Playa de la Cortadura 116
    Playa de la Malagueta 168
    Playa de la Muralla 122
    Playa de la Puntilla 122
    Playa de la Victoria 116
    Playa de los Genoveses 302

Playa de los Lances 145
Playa de Mónsul 302
Playa de Pedregalejo 168
Playa de Santa Catalina 122
Playa de Valdelagrana 122-3
Playa del Barronal 302
Playa del Cañuelo 192
Playa del Palo 168
Playa del Playazo 303
Playa el Salón 191
Playa Fuenterrabía 122
Salobreña 281-2
San José 302
beer 373
Bérchules 279
bicycle travel, see cycling
birds 148, 346-8
birdwatching 22
    Dehesa de Abajo 52
    Huelva province 79
    La Cañada de los Pájaros 52
    Laguna de Fuente de Piedra
        187-8
    Parque Nacional de Doñana
        84, 85
    Parque Natural Sierras
        Subbéticas 215
boat travel
    to/from Andalucía 416
    within Andalucía 417
Bobastro 184
bodegas, see also wineries
    Bodegas Alvear 217
    El Puerto de Santa María
        120, 122
    Jerez de la Frontera 130
    Sanlúcar de Barrameda 126
books 12, see also literature
    architecture 334
    bullfighting 366
    culture 362
    food 18, 370
    Franco's Spain 328
Bubión 277-8
bullfighters 178
bullfighting 14, 49, 178, 363-6
    books 366
    festivals 365-6
bullrings
    Plaza de Toros (El Puerto
        de Santa María) 122
    Plaza de Toros (Málaga)
        168
    Plaza de Toros (Mijas) 174
    Plaza de Toros (Ronda)
        179, 13
    Plaza de Toros de la Real
        Maestranza (Seville) 49

bus travel
    to/from Andalucía 413
    within Andalucía 417
bushwalking, see walking
business hours 400, see also
    inside front cover

C

Cabo de Gata 301-5, **302**, 6,
    20, 95
Cabo de Trafalgar 142
Cádiar 280-1
Cádiz 110-19, **112-13**, 7, 12
    accommodation 118, 385-8
    attractions 111, 114-16
    courses 116
    food 116-18
    history 111
    internet resources 109
    nightlife 118-19
    planning 108-9
    tourist information 110
    tours 108, 111
    transport 119
Cádiz province 105-48, **106-7**, 8
Capileira 278
Carmona 63-9, **66**
    walking tour 67-8, **67**
Carretera del Suspiro del Moro
    283
car travel 413-14, 417-20
    drink driving laws 406
    driving licences 418
    hire 418-19
    insurance 419
    maps 406
    parking 419-20
    road distance chart **418**
    road rules 420
    to/from Andalucía 413-14
    within Andalucía 417-20
Casa del Obispo 114
Casa Natal de Picasso 164
Castaño del Robledo 102
castles & forts 15, 336
    Alcazaba (Almería) 291
    Alcazaba (Antequera) 185
    Alcazaba (Granada) 257
    Alcazaba (Guadix) 270
    Alcazaba (Málaga) 166
    Alcázar (Jerez de la
        Frontera) 127, 336
    Alcázar (Seville) 44-6, **92**
    Alcázar de los Reyes
        Cristianos 207
    Almodóvar del Río Castle
        217
    Bobastro 184

Castillo Árabe 281
Castillo de Gibralfaro 164-6
Castillo de La Calahorra 271
Castillo de la Yedra 240
Castillo de los Guzmán 83
Castillo de los Sotomayor
    219
Castillo de Miramonte 219
Castillo de San Miguel 283
Castillo de Santa Catalina
    228
Castillo de Santiago 125
Castillo de Vélez Blanco 309
Castillo San Marcos 122
Iznájar 217
Moorish Castle (Gibraltar)
    153
Priego de Córdoba Castillo
    216
Zuheros Castle 214
cathedrals, see churches &
    cathedrals
caves
    Barriada de las Cuevas 270
    Cueva de Ardales 184
    Cueva de la Pileta 182
    Cueva de los Letreros
        309-10
    Cueva de los Murciélagos
        214-15
    Cueva de Nerja 192
    Cuevas de Sorbas 299
    Gruta de las Maravillas 100
    St Michael's Cave 151
Cazalla de la Sierra 71-2
Cazorla 239-41
cell phones 408-9
cemeteries
    Necrópolis Romana 68
    Trafalgar Cemetery 153
children, travel with 24, 62,
    174, 400-1
churches & cathedrals 206, see
    also mosques
    Abadía de Sacromonte 263
    Almería Cathedral 291-3
    Baeza Cathedral 232-3
    Basílica de La Macarena 52
    Basílica Menor de Santa
        María de la Asunción 134
    Cádiz Cathedral 114
    Capilla del Salvador del
        Mundo 236
    Capilla Real 259
    Castillo de Guzmán 143
    Catedral de San Salvador
        127
    Colegiata del Salvador 260

churches & cathedrals
continued
  Colegiata de Santa María de la Asunción 69
  Colegiata de Santa María la Mayor 185
  Granada Cathedral 259
  Guadix Cathedral 270
  Iglesia Concatedral de la Encarnación 271
  Iglesia de la Aurora 215
  Iglesia de la Encarnación 189
  Iglesia de la Santísima Trinidad 237
  Iglesia de las Salinas 301
  Iglesia de Nuestra Señora de la O 125
  Iglesia de Nuestra Señora del Rosario 281-2
  Iglesia de San Francisco 215
  Iglesia de San Juan 293
  Iglesia de San Juan de Díos 262
  Iglesia de San Luis 53
  Iglesia de San Mateo 143
  Iglesia de San Miguel 127
  Iglesia de San Pedro 134
  Iglesia de Santa Ana 260
  Iglesia de Santa María de la Alhambra 257
  Iglesia de Santa María La Mayor 178
  Iglesia de Santa Maride de las Flores 218
  Iglesia del Carmen 186
  Iglesia del Divino Salvador 141
  Iglesia Mozárabe (Bobastro) 184
  Iglesia y Monasterio de Santiago 270
  Jaén Cathedral 221, 227
  Málaga Cathedral 163-4
  Parroquia de la Asunción 215
  Seville Cathedral & Giralda 40-3
cinema, *see* film
Cinema Studios Fort Bravo 297-8
climate 8
coffee 373
Columbus, Christopher 81, 323
  Lugares Colombinos 82

000 MAP PAGES
000 PHOTOGRAPH PAGES

Comares 189
Cómpeta 189-90
convents, *see also* monasteries
  Convento de la Encarnación 134
  Convento de San Francisco 233, 257
Córdoba 200-13, **202-3**
  accommodation 206, 391-2
  attractions 201, 204-10
  courses 198
  festivals & events 210
  food 210-12
  history 200-1
  nightlife 212
  planning 198-9
  tourist information 201
  tours 198
  transport 212-13
Córdoba province 195-219, **196-7**
Costa de la Luz (Cádiz province) 140-7, **20**
Costa de la Luz (Huelva province) 82-4
Costa del Sol 329
costs 8, 408, *see also inside front cover*
courses
  flamenco 55
  food 18
  language 53, 55, 116
credit cards 408
culture 12-15, 360-6
customs regulations 401-2
cycling 416-17
  El Chorro 184

D

dangers 402
Dehesa de Abajo 52
disabilities, travellers with 410
diving 351
Dolmen del Romeral 186
Dolmen de Menga 186
Dolmen de Viera 186
dolphin watching 153
Dorado, Gonzelo (interview) 87
drinks 372-4, 376-7, 402-3, *see also* bodegas, sherry, wine
driving, *see* car travel
driving licences 418
driving tour Sierra de Grazalema 137-9, **138**
drug laws 406
DVD systems 401

E

eagles, Spanish imperial 347
Écija 70-1
El Arenal (Seville) 47, **48**
El Burgo 183
El Camarón de la Isla 355
El Chorro 182-4, **21**
El Lucero 190
El Mirador del Castillo 307
El Puerto de Santa María 119-24, **121**
El Rocío 88, 97
electricity 401
email services, *see* internet access
emergencies, *see also inside front cover*
  health 404
  police 405
environmental issues 23, 344, 414
events, *see* festivals & events
exchange rates 407, *see also inside front cover*

F

Farruquito 357
Ferreirola 278
festivals & events 10-11
  Almería 295
  Bienal de Flamenco 55
  Campeonato del Mundo de Motociclismo de Jerez (World Motorcycle Championship) 131
  Carnaval (Cádiz) 111
  Carreras de Caballos 126
  Concurso de Patios Cordobeses 208
  Córdoba 210
  Corpus Christi (Seville) 55
  El Puerto de Santa María 123
  Feria de Abril (Seville) 55
  Feria de la Manzanilla 126
  Feria de la Virgen de la Luz 145
  Feria de Málaga 168-9
  Feria de Primavera 123
  Feria de San Miguel 136
  Feria del Caballo 131
  Festival Cueva de Nerja 192
  Festividad Virgen del Carmen 123
  Fiestas Colombinas 80
  Fiestas de Otoño 131
  Fiestas del Vino Fino 123
  Granada 264-5

Huelva 80
Jaén 228
Jerez de la Frontera 131
Málaga 169
music festivals 359
Noche de San Juan 191-2
Reggae Festival 145
Romería del Rocío 88, 97, 126
Ronda 180
Sanlúcar de Barrameda 126
Semana Santa (Arcos de la Frontera) 134
Semana Santa (Seville) 55, 56
Seville 55
Tarifa 145
film 14, 364
    festivals 364
    sets 297-8, **24**
flamenco 12, 14, 60, 354-9, **12**
    courses 55
    internet resources 358
    museums 50, 52, 114
Fondales 278
food 16-19, 367-77, 402-3, **16**, **17**, *see also individual locations*
    Alpujarran specialities 279
    books 18, 370
    cooking courses 18
    customs 367
    gazpacho 371-2, **17**
    ham 18, 370-1, **16**
    internet resources 370
    itinerary 33
    language 375-7
    nouvelle cuisine 372
    olive oil 371
    seafood 369
    tapas 16, 367-8
    vegetarian travellers 403
forts, *see* castles & forts
fountains
    Fuente de la Virgen de la Salud 216
    Fuente del Rey 216
    Fuente Mora 307
Franco, General Francisco 327-8
Frigiliana 190-1

G

galleries, *see* art galleries
gardens 339, *see also* national parks, nature reserves, parks & protected areas
    Alameda Botanical Gardens 153

Alcázar de los Reyes Cristianos 207
Alcázar gardens 46
Generalife 258, **90-1**
Jardín Andalusí 134
Jardín Botánico El Albardinal 304
Jardín Botánico La Concepción 168
Jardín Botánico Umbría de la Virgen 310
Palacio de Viana gardens 209
Parque de María Luisa 47
gastronomy, *see* food
gay travellers 403-4
gazpacho 371-2
Generalife 258, **90-1**
Gibraltar 148-55, **150**, **152**, **23**
    attractions 149-53
    food 153-4
    history 148
    holidays 154
    money 151
    sovereignty 149
    tourist information 149
    transport 154-5
    visas 151
Goya, Francisco de 363
Granada 247-69, **252-3**, **255**, **261**
    accommodation 247, 394-8
    Alhambra 254-8, 337-9, **4-5**, **90-1**
    attractions 254-64
    Bono Turístico 259
    festivals & events 264-5
    food 265-8
    history 247, 253
    nightlife 268
    planning 250-1
    Sacromonte 263
    tourist information 253-4
    tours 250
    transport 269
Granada province 246-84, **248-9**
Guadix 270-1, **14**
guitars 356

H

ham 18, 370-1, **16**
hammams, *see* bathhouses
health 404
hiking, *see* walking
history 313-31
    Al-Andalus 316-20
    books (Franco's Spain) 328

Christian reconquest 320-2
democratic era 328-30
discovery of the Americas 323-4
early traders & invaders 314-16
Islamic rule 316-20
Renaissance 15
Spain under Franco 328
Spanish Civil War 327-8
the 21st Century 330-1
holidays 154, 404
Hornachuelos 218
horse riding 349-51
    Ronda 180
    Tarifa 145
horses 130-1
    equestrian school 130
    festivals 131
    stud farms 133
Hospital de Santiago 237
hostels, *see* accommodation
hot chocolate 374
hotels, *see* accommodation
houses, *see* palaces & mansions
Huelva 74-81, **80**
    accommodation 103, 383-5
    attractions 75, 80
    festivals & events 80
    food 80-1
    history 35
    planning 78-9
    tourist information 75
    transport 81
Huelva province 74-104, **76-7**

I

Iberian lynx 84-5, 87, 345-6, 347, **21**
ibex 346
insurance 404-5, 419
internet access 405
internet resources 9
    accommodation 378, 381
    air tickets 413
    Almería province 289
    Cádiz province 109
    Córdoba province 199
    environment 22
    flamenco 358
    food 370
    gay travellers 403
    Granada province 251
    Jaén province 225
    lesbian travellers 403
    Málaga province 161
    Sevilla province 39
    travelling with children 24

INDEX

Isla de la Cartuja (Seville) **54**
Islamic architecture 321, 332-9
Itálica 63
itineraries 30-3, 52, 72, 83,
    183, 184
    Almería 285
    Cádiz 105, 115
    Carmona 67-8, **67**
    Cazorla 244
    Córdoba 195
    Granada 246, 254
    Huelva 74
    Jaén 220
    Las Alpujarras 277
    Málaga 156, 163
    Seville 34, 41
    Sierra de Grazalema 137-9,
    138
Iznájar 217

J

Jaén 221-9, **226**
    accommodation 227, 392-4
    attractions 221, 227-8
    festivals & events 228
    food 228-9
    history 221
    internet resources 225
    planning 224-5
    tourist information 221
    tours 224
    transport 229
Jaén province 220-45, **222-3**
jamón 18, 370-1, **16**
Jerez de la Frontera 126-33,
    128-9, **15**, **18**
Judería (Córdoba) 207-8
Judería (Vejer de la Frontera)
    141

K

kitesurfing 145, 351, **22**

L

La Axarquía 188-91
La Calahorra 271
La Cañada de los Pájaros 52
La Capitana 72
La Cartuja Monastery 133
La Herradura 282-4
La Rábida 82
La Tahá 278
Laguna de Fuente de Piedra
    187-8

language 375-7, 422-9, see also
    inside front cover
    courses 53, 55, 116
Lanjarón 276
Las Alpujarras 272-81, **274**, **5**
Las Alpujarras de Almería
    299-300
Laujar de Andarax 300
legal matters 405-6
lesbian travellers 403-4
Linares, Carmen 356
literature 360-2, see also books
Lorca, Federico García 264,
    361
Los Albardinales 298
Los Millares 299-300
Los Pedroches 219
Los Vélez 308-11
Lugares Colombinos 82
lynx 84-5, 87, 345-6, 347, **21**

M

Macarena (Seville) **54**
Mairena 280
Málaga 157-73, **162**, **165**
    accommodation 167, 388-91
    attractions 157-69
    courses 160
    festivals & events 169
    food 169-71
    nightlife 171
    planning 160-1
    shopping 171-2
    tourist information 157
    tours 160
    transport 172-3
Málaga province 156-94,
    158-9
mansions, see palaces &
    mansions
maps 242, 273, 406-7
markets, see also shopping
    Cádiz 280
    El Jueves Market (Seville) 53
    El Postigo (Seville) 61
    Farmers Market (La
        Axarquía) 188
    Flea Market (Granada) 264
    Flea Market (Málaga) 172
    Flea Market (Nerja) 191
    Mercado Atarazanas
        (Málaga) 167
    Mercado Central (Almería)
        296
    Mercado Central (Cádiz)
        115
    Mercado de la Encarnación
        (Seville) 55

Mercado de San Agustín
    (Granada) 266
Mercado del Arenal (Seville)
    55
Nerja 191
Pet Market (Seville) 62
Plaza de la Corredera
    (Córdoba) 209
Plaza de Pavia (Almería)
    291
Marte Project 98
measures 401, see also inside
    front cover
Mecina 278
Mecinilla 278
Medina Azahara 209-10, 335,
    93
metric conversions, see inside
    front cover
Mezquita de Córdoba 201,
    204-6, 333-5, **4**, **91**
Mijas 173-5
Minas de Riotinto 98-9
Mirador San Nicolás 260
mobile phones 408-9
Moguer 82
Mojácar 305-8, **306**
Molina, Antonio Muñoz 361
monasteries, see also convents
    Conjunto Monumental de la
        Cartuja 53
    La Cartuja de Cazalla 71
    La Cartuja Monastery 133
    Monasterio de la Cartuja
        262
    Monasterio de la
        Encarnación 69
    Monasterio de la Rábida 82
    Monasterio de San Jerónimo
        262
    Monasterio de Santa Clara
        82
money 402, 407-8, see also
    inside front cover
Montilla 217
Morente, Enrique 356
mosques, see also churches &
    cathedrals
    Almonaster la Real 102
    Great Mosque of Seville
        335-6
    Mezquita de Córdoba 201,
        204-6, 333-5, **4**, **91**
    Mezquita Mayor de
        Granada 262
motorcycle travel 413-14,
    417-20
    driving licences 418

insurance 419
maps 406
parking 419-20
road distance chart **418**
road rules 420
to/from Andalucía 413-14
within Andalucía 417-20
movies, *see* film
Murillo, Bartolomé Esteban 363
museums, *see also* art galleries
   Capilla Real Museum 259
   Casa de los Pisa 262
   Casa del Obispo 114
   Casa Museo Arte Andalusí 237
   Casa Museo de Mijas 175
   Casa Museo Martín Alonso Pinzón 82
   Centro de Arte – Museo de Almería 293
   Gibraltar Museum 153
   Málaga Cathedral Museum 163-4
   Military Heritage Centre (Gibraltar) 152
   Museo Antonio Manuel Campoy 309
   Museo Arqueológico (Almería) 293
   Museo Arqueológico (Almuñécar) 283
   Museo Arqueológico (Córdoba) 208
   Museo Arqueológico (Granada) 260
   Museo Arqueológico (Seville) 47
   Museo Catedralicio (Cádiz) 114
   Museo Conventual de las Descalzas 185
   Museo de Ardales 183-4
   Museo de Artes y Costumbres Populares 227-8
   Museo de Bellas Artes (Córdoba) 208
   Museo de Bellas Artes (Granada) 257
   Museo de Bellas Artes (Seville) 50
   Museo de Cádiz 115-16
   Museo de la Alhambra 257
   Museo de las Cortes de Cádiz 116
   Museo de Málaga 167
   Museo de Prehistoria y de Paleontología 272

   Museo de Vinos y Toros (Cádiz) 116
   Museo del Alto Guadalquivir 240
   Museo del Baile Flamenco 50, 52
   Museo del Bandolero 178
   Museo del Mundo Marítimo 83
   Museo Diocesano 206
   Museo Histórico (Almuñécar) 282
   Museo Histórico Municipal (Priego de Córdoba) 216
   Museo Internacional de Arte Naïf 227-8
   Museo Julio Romero de Torres 208
   Museo Minero (Minas de Riotinto) 98
   Museo Municipal (Antequera) 185
   Museo Municipal (Baza) 271
   Museo Picasso 164
   Museo Provincial (Huelva) 75
   Museo Taurino (Córdoba) 208
   Museo Taurino (Ronda) 179
   Plaza de Toros (Málaga) 168
   Seville Maritime Museum 47
music 14, 354-9, *see also* flamenco
   festivals 359

national parks 343-5, 352-3, *see also* parks & protected areas, nature reserves, gardens
nature reserves, *see also* parks & protected areas, national parks, gardens
   Dehesa de Abajo 52
   La Cañada de los Pájaros 52
Necrópolis Romana 68
Nerja 191-4, **192**
newspapers 401
Niebla 83
Níjar 298

Oasys/Mini Hollywood 297
Ohanes 300
olive oil 228, 298, 371
opening hours 400, *see also inside front cover*

Orce 272
Órgiva 276-7
Osuna 69-70

Paco de Lucía 354-5
painting 362-3
palaces & mansions
   Alhambra 254-8, 337-9, **4-5, 90-1**
   Casa Andalusí 207
   Casa de los Pisa 262
   Casa de Pilatos 50
   Casa del Mayorazgo 141
   Casa del Rey Moro 179
   Medina Azahara 209-10, 335, **93**
   Palacio de Carlos V 257
   Palacio de Dar-al-Horra 260
   Palacio de Don Pedro 339
   Palacio de Jabalquinto 233
   Palacio de la Aduana 167
   Palacio de la Condesa de Lebrija 50
   Palacio de los Cepeda 69
   Palacio de los Condes de Guadiana 237
   Palacio de los Duques de Medina Sidonia 125
   Palacio de Mondragón 177
   Palacio de Orleans y Borbon 125
   Palacio de Puente Hermoso 69
   Palacio de Vázquez de Molina 236
   Palacio de Vela de los Cobo 237
   Palacio de Viana 209
   Palacio de Villardompardo 227
   Palacio del Condestable Dávalos 236
   Palacio del Marqués de La Gomera 69
   Palacio del Marqués de Salvatierra 179
   Palacio del Pórtico 257
   Palacio Episcopal 164, 206
   Palacio Mayorazgo 134
   Palacios Nazaríes 255-8
   Palacio Villavicencio 127
   Patios Cordobeses 208
   Posada del Potro 208
Palos de la Frontera 82
Pampaneira 277
parking 419-20
   Seville 36, 61

parks & protected areas 20, 352-3, *see also* gardens, national parks, nature reserves
Paraje Natural Marismas del Odiel 75, 80
Paraje Natural Torcal de Antequera 187
Parque Nacional de Doñana 84-8, 125, **21**
Parque Nacional Sierra Nevada 272-3, 275, **274**, **94-5**
Parque Natural de Cabo de Gata-Níjar 301-5, **302**, **6**, **20**, **95**
Parque Natural de Despeñaperros 229-30
Parque Natural los Alcornocales 147
Parque Natural Sierra de Andújar 230
Parque Natural Sierra de Aracena 101-4, **102**
Parque Natural Sierra de Grazalema 139-40, **94**
Parque Natural Sierra de Hornachuelos 218
Parque Natural Sierra de las Nieves 183
Parque Natural Sierra de María-Los Vélez 310
Parque Natural Sierra Norte 72-3
Parque Natural Sierras de Cazorla, Segura y Las Villas 241-5
Parque Natural Sierras Subbéticas 215
Upper Rock Nature Reserve 151
Parque Nacional de Doñana 84-8, 125, **21**
Parque Natural de Cabo de Gata-Níjar 301-5, **302**, **6**, **20**, **95**
Parque Natural los Alcornocales 147
Parque Natural Sierra de Aracena 101-4, **102**
Parque Natural Sierra de Grazalema 139-40, **94**
Parque Natural Sierra de las Nieves 183

Parque Natural Sierra Norte 72-3
Parque Natural Sierras de Cazorla, Segura y Las Villas, *see also* Sierra de Cazorla 241-5
Patios Cordobeses 208
Pedro Ximénez wine 218
phonecards 408
Picasso, Pablo 166, 363
Casa Natal de Picasso 164
Museo Picasso 164
planning 402, *see also* itineraries
Almería province 288-9
Cádiz province 108-9
Córdoba province 198-9
Gibraltar 108-9
Granada province 250-1
Jaén province 224-5
Málaga province 160-1
public holidays 404
Seville 38-9
playas, *see* beaches
plazas
Plaza Bib-Rambla 259-60
Plaza de España 141, 179
Plaza de la Corredera 209
Plaza de Topete 115
Plaza del Cabildo 134
Plaza del Potro 208
Plaza Vázquez de Molina 236
postal services 408
pottery 239, 298
Priego de Córdoba 215-17
pueblos blancos 32, **19**

R

radio 401
Refugios de la Guerra Civil 294
road distance chart **418**
Rock of Gibraltar 150-3, **23**
Rodalquilar 304
Ronda 175-82, **176**, **6-7**, **8**, **13**, **89**
accommodation 389-90
attractions 177-80
festivals & events 180
food 180-1
history 175-7
nightlife 181
rural hotels 390
tourist information 177
transport 181-2

S

safety 402, 411
Salobreña 281-4

Sanlúcar de Barrameda 124-6
Santa Elena 229-30
Santiponce 63
sculpture 362-3
Segura de la Sierra 245
Serranía de Ronda 182
Sevilla province 34-73, **64-5**
Carmona 63-9, **66**, **67**
Cazalla de la Sierra 71-2
Écija 70-1
Itálica 63
Osuna 69-70
Parque Natural Sierra Norte 72-3
Santiponce 63
Seville 34-62, **36-7**, **42**, **48**, **51**, **54**, **7**
accommodation 40, 379-83
attractions 40-55
children, travel with 62
festivals & events 55
food 55-9
history 35
internet resources 39
nightlife 59-60
planning 38-9
Semana Santa 56, **8**, **10**, **12**
shopping 60-1
tourist information 35, 40
tours 38, 44
transport 61-2
sherry 19, 373, **18**
bodegas 120, 122
production 120
shopping, *see also* markets
Málaga 171-2
Seville 60-1
Úbeda 238-9
Sierra de Aracena 101-4, **102**
Sierra de Cazorla 241-5, **241**, **19**
Sierra de Grazalema 138-40, **138**, **94**
driving tour 137-9, **138**
Sierra Nevada 272-5, 275, **274**, **94-5**
Siloé, Diego de 340
Sinagoga (Córdoba) 207
skiing 275, 351
snorkelling 351
snowboarding 351
Spanish language 375-7, 422-9, *see also inside front cover*
courses 53, 55, 116
Soler, Antonio 362
Sorbas 298-9

T

Tabernas 297-8
tapas 16, 367-8
    Almería 294-5
    Arcos de la Frontera 134-6
    Carmona 68
    Granada 266-8
    Guadix 270-1
    Málaga 172
    Ronda 180, 181
Tarifa 142-7, **144**, **9**, **22**
    accommodation 387-8
    attractions 143-5
    festivals & events 145
    food 145-6
    nightlife 146-7
taxis 420
telephone services 408
theatres
    Teatro Alameda (Seville) 52
    Teatro Romano (Cádiz) 114
theft 402
time 409
tipping 408
toilets 409
Torrecilla 183
tourist information 409-10
tours
    Almería 288
    Arcos de la Frontera 136
    Cádiz 108, 111
    Córdoba 198
    Granada 250
    Huelva 78
    Jaén 224
    Málaga 160
    Parque Nacional de Doñana 86
    Seville 38, 44
towers
    Torre de Guzmán El Bueno 143
    Torre de los Aliatares 231
    Torre de Poniente 114-15
    Torre del Oro 47
    Torre Tavira 115
train travel
    to/from Andalucía 414-15
    within Andalucía 420-1
transport 412-21, *see also*
    individual locations
travel to/from Andalucía 412-16
travel within Andalucía 416-21
trekking, *see* walking
Trevélez 278-9
Triana (Seville) 47-9, **48**
TV 401

U

Úbeda 234-9, **235**, **7**

V

vacations 154, 404
Valle de Rodalquilar 303-4
Válor 280, **5**
Vandelvira, Andrés de 238, 340
vegetarian travellers 403
Vejer Coast 142
Vejer de la Frontera 140-2
Velázquez, Diego 362
Vélez Málaga 188
Veneno, Kiko 358
visas 410-11

W

walking 21, 348-50
    Aracena 100
    Barranco de Poqueira 277-8
    Cañón de Bailón (Zuheros) 214
    Carmona walking tour 67-8, **67**
    El Chorro 184, **21**
    La Axarquía 190
    Las Alpujarras 272-81
    Málaga 173
    maps 242, 273, 406-7
    Mulhacén 275
    Parque Nacional de Doñana 86-7
    Parque Natural de Cabo de Gata-Níjar 303, **5**, **20**, **95**
    Parque Natural los Alcornocales 147
    Parque Natural Sierra de Aracena y Picos de Aroche 101
    Parque Natural Sierra de Hornachuelos 218
    Parque Natural Sierra de las Nieves 183
    Parque Natural Sierra de María-Los Vélez 310
    Parque Natural Sierras de Cazorla, Segura y Las Villas 241-5
    Parque Natural Sierras Subbéticas 215
    Sendero de las Laderas 71
    Sendero de Los Molinos del Río Aguas (Sorbas) 299
    Sendero del Aguadero 300
    Sendero del Arroyo de las Cañas 73

Sendero Los Castañares 73
Serranía de Ronda 182
Sierra de Aracena 102-4
Sierra Nevada 272-3, 275, **274**, **94-5**
Veleta 275
walking tour
    Carmona 67-8, **67**
weather 8
websites, *see* internet resources
weights 401, *see also inside front cover*
Western Leone 298
whale watching 143-5
white villages 32, **19**
wildlife 20, 84-5, 345-8
    itineraries 32
    Parque Nacional de Doñana 97
    Parque Natural Sierras de Cazorla, Segura y Las Villas 244
    Parque Natural Sierras Subbéticas 215
windsurfing 145, 351
wine 218, 372-4
wineries 217, 300, *see also* bodegas
wolves 346
women travellers 411

Y

Yegen 280

Z

Zuheros 213-15

MAP LEGEND

Note Not all symbols displayed below appear in this guide.

ROUTES

Tollway	Tunnel
Freeway	Pedestrian Mall
Primary Road	Steps
Secondary Road	Walking Track
Tertiary Road	Walking Path
Lane	Walking Tour
Unsealed Road	Walking Tour Detour
Under Construction	Pedestrian Overpass

TRANSPORT

Ferry Route & Terminal	Train Line & Station
Metro Line & Station	Underground Rail Line
Monorail & Stop	Tram Line & Stop
Bus Route & Stop	Cable Car, Funicular

AREA FEATURES

Airport	Land
Beach	Mall, Plaza
Building	Market
Campus	Park
Cemetery, Christian	Sportsground
Cemetery, Other	Urban

HYDROGRAPHY

River, Creek	
Canal	
Water	
Swamp	
Lake (Dry)	

BOUNDARIES

International	
State, Provincial	
Suburb	
City Wall	
Cliff	

SYMBOLS IN THE KEY

Essential Information
- Tourist Office
- Police Station

Exploring
- Beach
- Buddhist
- Castle, Fort
- Christian
- Diving, Snorkelling
- Garden
- Hindu
- Islamic
- Jewish
- Monument
- Museum, Gallery
- Place of Interest
- Snow Skiing
- Swimming Pool
- Ruin
- Tomb
- Winery, Vineyard
- Zoo, Bird Sanctuary

Gastronomic Highlights
- Eating
- Cafe

Nightlife
- Drinking
- Entertainment

Recommended Shops
- Shopping

Accommodation
- Sleeping
- Camping

Transport
- Airport, Airfield
- Cycling, Bicycle Path
- Border Crossing
- Bus Station
- Ferry
- General Transport
- Train Station
- Taxi Rank

Parking
- Parking

OTHER MAP SYMBOLS

Information
- Bank, ATM
- Embassy, Consulate
- Hospital, Medical
- Internet Facilities
- Post Office
- Telephone

Geographic
- Cave
- Lighthouse
- Lookout
- Mountain, Volcano
- National Park
- Picnic Area

LONELY PLANET OFFICES

AUSTRALIA
Head Office
Locked Bag 1, Footscray, Victoria 3011
☎ 03 8379 8000, fax 03 8379 8111
talk2us@lonelyplanet.com.au

USA
150 Linden St, Oakland, CA 94607
☎ 510 250 6400, toll free 800 275 8555
fax 510 893 8572
info@lonelyplanet.com

UK
2nd fl, 186 City Road, London EC1V 2NT
☎ 020 7106 2100, fax 020 7106 2101
go@lonelyplanet.co.uk

Published by Lonely Planet Publications Pty Ltd
ABN 36 005 607 983
© Lonely Planet 2010
© photographers as indicated 2010
Cover photograph Casares, Málaga province,
Jose Fuste Raga/Photolibrary. Internal title page
photograph Puente Nuevo stone bridge, Ronda,
Diana Mayfield/Lonely Planet Images. Many of the
images in this guide are available for licensing from
Lonely Planet Images: lonelyplanetimages.com.

Mixed Sources
Product group from well-managed
forests and other controlled sources
www.fsc.org Cert no. SGS-COC-005002
© 1996 Forest Stewardship Council